SOCIAL JUSTICE
and
SOCIAL
WORK

SOCIAL JUSTICE and SOCIAL WORK

Rediscovering a Core Value of the Profession

Michael J. Austin, Editor

University of California - Berkeley

Los Angeles | London | New Delhi
Singapore | Washington DC

Los Angeles | London | New Delhi
Singapore | Washington DC

FOR INFORMATION:

SAGE Publications, Inc.
2455 Teller Road
Thousand Oaks, California 91320
E-mail: order@sagepub.com

SAGE Publications Ltd.
1 Oliver's Yard
55 City Road
London, EC1Y 1SP
United Kingdom

SAGE Publications India Pvt. Ltd.
B 1/I 1 Mohan Cooperative Industrial Area
Mathura Road, New Delhi 110 044
India

SAGE Publications Asia-Pacific Pte. Ltd.
3 Church Street
#10-04 Samsung Hub
Singapore 049483

Acquisitions Editor: Kassie Graves
Editorial Assistant: Elizabeth Luizzi
Production Editor: Stephanie Palermini
Copy Editor: Patrice Sutton
Typesetter: Hurix Systems Pvt. Ltd.
Proofreader: Barbara Johnson
Indexer: Jennifer Pairan
Cover Designer: Anupama Krishnan
Marketing Manager: Erica DeLuca
Permissions Editor: Karen Ehrmann
Cover Illustration: Lisa Krieshok Illustration and Design

Copyright © 2014 by SAGE Publications, Inc.

Printed in the United States of America

Library of Congress Cataloging-in-Publication Data

Social justice and social work : rediscovering a core value of the profession / edited by Michael J. Austin, University of California, Berkeley.

pages cm

Includes bibliographical references and index.

ISBN 978-1-4522-7420-1 (pbk. : alk. paper)

1. Social justice. 2. Social service. I. Austin, Michael J.

HM671.S6233 2013

303.3'72—dc23

2012045607

This book is printed on acid-free paper.

SUSTAINABLE FORESTRY INITIATIVE

Certified Chain of Custody
Promoting Sustainable Forestry
www.sfiprogram.org
SFI-01268

SFI label applies to text stock

13 14 15 16 17 10 9 8 7 6 5 4 3 2 1

CONTENTS

Inside Human Service Organizations

ABOUT THE EDITOR

Michael J. Austin, PhD, is the Milton and Florence Krenz Mack Distinguished Professor of Nonprofit Management and director of the Mack Center on Nonprofit and Public Sector Management in the Human Services at the School of Social Welfare, University of California, Berkeley. He is the former dean of the University of Pennsylvania, School of Social Work, and teaches graduate students in the area of nonprofit management, community planning, and the social environmental dimensions of human behavior and the social environment. He received his doctorate in organizational research related to nonprofit human service organizations from the University of Pittsburgh, School of Social Work (1970). He holds two master's degrees, one in community organizing and social service administration from the University of California, Berkeley (1966), and the other in public health administration from the University of Pittsburgh (1969). He has taught at Florida State University (1970–1976), the University of Washington (1976–1985), the University of Pennsylvania (1985–1992), and the University of California, Berkeley (1992–present).

Since 1992, he has served as staff director of the Bay Area Social Services Consortium (BASSC) that is a collaborative composed of 11 county social service directors, five deans and/or directors of social work programs, and two foundation executives. Its primary activities include an applied research program, an executive development program, and a policy analysis–implementation program. The research program has completed 25 studies since 1995 related to child welfare and social services. The executive development program has graduated 400 participants in its first 18 years of operations, and the policy implementation program has produced eight reports over the past 4 years. The most recent BASSC research reports relate to evidence for child welfare practice (*Evidence for Child Welfare Practice,* Routledge, 2010). Since 2006, he has served as the staff director of the Bay Area Network of Nonprofit Human Service Agencies (BANNHSA) and recently published a Mack Center research report on pioneering nonprofit human service organizations (*Organizational Histories of Nonprofit Human Service Organizations,* Routledge, 2013). His work on management practice includes (with K. Hopkins) *Supervision as Collaboration in the Human Services: Building a Learning Culture* (Sage Publications, 2004) and (with R. Brody and T. Packard) *Managing the Challenges in Human Service Organizations: A Casebook* (Sage Publications, 2009).

His publications reflect a long-standing interest in the management of nonprofit and public sector organizations. He is the author or coauthor of 19 books, over 100 articles, and numerous reports. He serves on the editorial boards of seven journals and is the associate editor of *Administration in Social Work.*

LIST OF CONTRIBUTORS

Sarah Accomazzo
MSW, doctoral student
School of Social Welfare
University of California, Berkeley

Michael J. Austin
PhD, Mack Professor
School of Social Welfare
University of California, Berkeley

Christina Branom
MSW, doctoral student
School of Social Welfare
University of California, Berkeley

Brian Cahill
MSW, former executive director of Catholic Charities
Catholic Youth Organization, San Francisco, California

Mary E. A. Caplan
MSW, doctoral student
School of Social Welfare
University of California, Berkeley

Charity Samantha Fitzgerald
MSW, doctoral student
School of Social Welfare
University of California, Berkeley

Jaclyn Grant
MSW, research assistant
School of Social Welfare
University of California, Berkeley

Anupama Jacob
MSc, doctoral student
School of Social Welfare
University of California, Berkeley

Leah A. Jacobs
MA, MSW, doctoral student
School of Social Welfare
University of California, Berkeley

Bryn King
MSW, doctoral student
School of Social Welfare
University of California, Berkeley

Hyun Soo Kwon
MBA, MSW, doctoral student
School of Social Welfare
University of California, Berkeley

Amanda Lehning
PhD, postdoctoral fellow
School of Social Work
University of Michigan

Kelly LeRoux
PhD, assistant professor
University of Illinois, Chicago

Megan Moore
PhD, assistant professor
University of Washington

Jennifer Price Wolf
MPH, MSW, PhD
Alcohol Research Group
Oakland, California

Katherine E. Ray
MSW, research assistant
School of Social Work
University of California, Berkeley

Beth Glover Reed
PhD, professor
School of Social Work
University of Michigan

Juliene Schrick
MSW, psychiatric social worker
Department of Psychiatry
University of California, San Francisco

Jasmin Serim
MSW, research assistant
School of Social Welfare

Siroj Sirojudin
MSW, doctoral student
School of Social Welfare
University of California, Berkeley

Richard J. Smith
MFA, MSW, PhD, assistant professor
Wayne State University, Detroit, Michigan

Jenny Ventura
MSW, research assistant
School of Social Welfare
University of California, Berkeley

Kelly Whitaker
MPA, doctoral student
School of Social Welfare
University of California, Berkeley

Elizabeth White
MSW, MPP, research assistant
School of Social Welfare
School of Public Policy
University of California, Berkeley

Wendy Wiegmann
MSW, doctoral student
School of Social Welfare
University of California, Berkeley

Rhonda Y. Williams
PhD, associate professor
Case Western Reserve University,
Cleveland, Ohio

FOREWORD

This morning, I met with the mother of a murder victim. We spent nearly an hour talking about the tragic, sudden end to her son's life nearly 20 years ago, her dashed dreams as a parent, her feelings about the man who shot her son to death, and her fragile mental health ever since the murder. This was one of the most poignant conversations I have had in my social work career. And it forced me to think hard about what I believe about justice.

This was no ordinary social worker–client conversation. Since 1992, I have served as a member of my state's parole board. My seat on the board, as defined by state statute, requires that one member have expertise in social work and the field of corrections. It has been my privilege to bring my social work perspective to this daunting task, including my beliefs about both justice and social justice. These concepts—justice and *social* justice—are remarkably relevant to my work. As the essays in this rich collection amply demonstrate, social workers need a keen understanding of what it means to be just and, as well, promote social justice.

Let's take a closer look at these terms and their implications. As this anthology's authors observe, the terms *justice* and *social justice* lend themselves to multiple meanings and purposes. In a narrow legal sense, justice is what we seek in the criminal justice system and in the resolution of civil disputes. In principle, for example, police officers, prosecuting and defense attorneys, juries, judges, and parole board members serve justice by treating suspects, defendants, and inmates fairly. Those involved in administering criminal justice act justly when they weigh all evidence as neutrally as possible and do not knowingly discriminate. In this sense, justice is fairness.

Justice as fairness applies in many other social work domains as well, of course. Clinical social workers who serve people struggling with addictions, mental illness, chronic disease, and aging often find that they do not have enough staffers to help all those in need and, thus, must make decisions about the fairest way to allocate limited resources. Practitioners' decisions about whether to serve people based on first come, first served or degree of need or affirmative action criteria raise important justice and fairness issues.

Social workers who serve as community advocates and organizers also encounter justice-as-fairness issues. They may face difficult judgments about whether it is just to participate in acts of civil disobedience to protest discrimination against same-sex couples or undocumented immigrants.

But viewing justice only as issues of fairness seems too narrow. Indeed, social justice connotes justice issues that extend beyond one-on-one relationships and individual concerns. Justice issues with a "social" element involve the commonweal—the public good. As this anthology's essays make clear, social work has a long-standing commitment to the public good. The profession's earliest scholars and practitioners articulated their unique understanding of social work's preoccupation with social justice. When Jane Addams founded Hull House in Chicago in 1889, she understood the vital importance of social justice and reform to address the needs of that city's most vulnerable citizens. When

Julia Lathrop began serving as the first director of the U.S. Children's Bureau in 1912, she understood how important it was for social workers to address broad social justice issues affecting children. When Octavia Hill dedicated herself to urban and housing reform in London in the late 19th century, helped found the Charity Organization Society in England, and in 1905 joined the Royal Commission on the Poor Laws, she served as a role model for social workers who devoted their lives to social justice. When Sophonisba Breckinridge developed the Chicago School of Civics and Philanthropy in 1903, she became a lodestar among social work's earliest practitioners concerned about social justice.

Since these early days, social workers' pursuit of social justice has traveled a complicated path. Social workers' earliest concern about social justice focused especially on the problem of increasing poverty and inequity in the distribution of wealth. For many years, social workers addressed the nagging problems of inadequate housing, health care, and income, particularly the impact of persistent unfairness in the allocation of social and economic resources and wealth. During some periods, however, social workers as a group have focused more narrowly on mental health and behavioral challenges posed by individual clients and families, many of which are the by-products of daunting discrimination, oppression, exploitation, and other manifestations of unfairness in society. Throughout social work's history, focus on justice issues—both narrow and broad—has ebbed and flowed.

Social work's enduring and admirable preoccupation with issues of social justice is particularly evident in codes of ethics adopted throughout the world. For example, the International Federation of Social Workers' publication *Ethics in Social Work— Statement of Principles* features several principles pertaining directly to issues of social justice, particularly related to confronting negative discrimination, recognizing diversity, distributing resources equitably, and challenging unjust policies and practices. The British Association of Social Workers' *Code of Ethics* includes multiple references to social justice issues, especially related to the fair and equitable distribution of resources, fair access to public services and benefits, equal treatment and protection under the law, and nondiscrimination. The Canadian Association of Social Workers' *Code of Ethics* emphasizes social workers' duty to promote "social fairness" and "equitable" distribution of resources.

Several of this volume's authors highlight, in particular, language in the National Association of Social Workers' (NASW's) *Code of Ethics* pertaining to social justice. They acknowledge the prominence of social justice content in this code and its influence on the profession. And, these authors note, quite fairly, that the code's multiple statements concerning social justice are relatively abstract and do not provide explicit, detailed guidance for the ways in which social workers should pursue social justice.

I was privileged to have chaired the national task force that introduced, for the first time, these ambitious social justice principles in the NASW *Code of Ethics*. I clearly recall sitting in the spacious conference room at the NASW headquarters in Washington, D.C., in 1994, staring out the room's large window at the majestic U.S. Capitol located a handful of blocks away and suggesting to the task force members that it was time to include bold social justice language in the new code, language that would highlight the very issues that are so often debated in the Capitol building down the street. The group quickly agreed, and we spent months reviewing relevant literature, discussing social work history and the profession's core values, and crafting with great care the precious words that ultimately found their way into today's ethics code that concern social work's mission and several core principles related to social justice, nondiscrimination, and fairness in the allocation of social and economic resources. We agreed that our aim should be to identify key social justice concepts and construct inspirational statements. We also agreed that a code of ethics should not be a practice manual; rather, social work educators and practitioners should draw on the code's broad conceptual guidance and develop practical frameworks and protocols designed to pursue social justice. In fact, the essays in this volume exemplify this very notion.

Of course, social workers did not invent the concept of social justice. Rich discussions of justice have ancient historical and philosophical origins. Plato's *Republic* begins with the question, "What is justice?" In his *Politics,* Aristotle highlights the importance of nonarbitrary, consistent treatment of people according to morally relevant attributes. In the 17th century, the English philosopher John Locke explored fairness and social justice issues in his *Second Treatise of Civil Government,* and Karl Marx stirred considerable debate about distributive justice in his 19th century classic, the *Communist Manifesto.*

Contemporary moral philosophers have done much to sustain focus on issues of social justice, with compelling implications for social work. For example, since its publication in 1971, John Rawls's *A Theory of Justice* has shaped countless discussions of fairness in modern society, as has Robert Nozick's 1974 publication, *Anarchy, State, and Utopia.*

Several hours after I met with the mother of the murdered victim, I presided at the inmate's parole board hearing. As I sat in the prison hearing room, I asked the inmate about his early trauma-filled life, struggle with drug addiction that led to the murder, insights, and impressive efforts at recovery, and future plans. During and immediately after the hearing, I thought long and hard about justice and social justice. I struggled to understand what justice-as-fairness means when balancing the interests of a deeply traumatized victim and the man who committed her son's murder (an offender who now demonstrates impressive insight and for nearly two decades has worked very hard to address the demons in his life).

And I thought about the meaning of *social* justice. As I deliberated, there was little doubt in my mind that the inmate's chronic challenges stem in large part from broader issues of poverty, abuse, discrimination, and social inequities that greatly increased the chances that he would struggle in life. Social injustice does not excuse heinous conduct, of course, but I am convinced that social workers' efforts to address social justice in the broad sense, in addition to our earnest focus on clients' personal struggles, enhance our ability to prevent this world's darkest challenges related to poverty, violence, mental illness, addiction, and so on.

Social work's principal virtue is its understanding of the complex relationship between private troubles and public issues. The public issues that most concern social workers are permeated with matters of social justice that demand attention. As Jane Addams wrote in her 1910 autobiography *Twenty Years at Hull House,* "In the unceasing ebb and flow of justice and oppression we must all dig channels as best we may, that at the propitious moment somewhat of the swelling tide may be conducted to the barren places of life."

Frederic G. Reamer
Professor
School of Social Work
Rhode Island College

PREFACE

This book reflects a process of self-reflection that spans six decades. The roots of my interests in social justice can be traced to a young boy's discovery that he is the son of immigrant parents who fled Nazi Germany in the late 1930s. The injustice of this genocide took years to understand. New forms of indignation arose in my expanding consciousness as I watched one of my high school teachers in Berkeley, California, get summoned to appear before the House Un-American Activities Committee that traveled around the country looking for Communists in the 1950s. Simultaneously, my involvement in social action activities through my Jewish youth group helped to draw clearer lines in my mind between moral outrage and the democratic freedoms to speak and act upon one's convictions.

As I entered the university in the early 1960s, I became increasingly interested in understanding the seeds of the civil rights movement and the words and convictions of Reverend Martin Luther King. My rabbi, Sydney Akselrad, marched with him in Selma, Alabama, thereby creating another personal connection with the struggles for social justice. As a first year master of social work (MSW) student in 1964, I decided to focus my social policy paper on the newly enacted 1964 national Civil Rights Act as a way to learn more about the array of injustices that this law sought to address. My second year fieldwork experience in a community action agency (created by President Kennedy's War on Poverty legislation) sensitized me to the implications of one of its key concepts, namely, "maximum feasible participation of the poor." This service goal also evolved to include the hiring of people of color into paraprofessional staff positions in human service organizations, a topic that led to my doctoral dissertation on professionals and paraprofessionals in community action agencies.

As a master's student at the University of California, Berkeley, I frequently heard the claim that social justice was a core value of the social work profession. When I asked about literature on this core value, I was directed to the works on Jane Addams and her social justice activities at Hull House in Chicago. Despite dutifully reading about her work and being impressed by the issues of immigration, acculturation, and advocacy, the historical and theoretical roots of social justice still evaded me.

Some time later, as a faculty member at the University of California, Berkeley, a student approached me with a social justice question that she was formulating as chairperson of our graduate student association. Her concern focused on the desire to mount a campaign in support of a unisex bathroom in our school building. Given the complexity of such a change project, I encouraged her to consider an alternative campaign such as honoring the Martin Luther King Jr. holiday in January that received little attention in the School of Social Welfare. I urged her to think about some type of student-sponsored social justice event that would honor Dr. King's contribution to the civil rights movement, respond to student interest in social justice, and identify future content for inclusion in the MSW curriculum. Her efforts along with other students led to an annual day-long Social Justice Symposium where community social activists lead student-designed workshops. The students recently celebrated their sixth successful symposium based on raising their own funds, designing and evaluating the program, and completing their first comprehensive report to the faculty regarding the need to incorporate more social justice content into the curriculum.

My earlier interests in social justice were reignited as I watched the 2009 inauguration of our first African American president whose earlier experiences with discrimination and community organizing gave him a profound understanding of social justice. Based on this significant development in national politics, I sent an e-mail to the doctoral students in our program at the University of California, Berkeley, to inquire about their interest in a group independent study on the role of the humanities in understanding social justice. Eight students responded, and their work is reflected in the first section of this book. While I had originally assumed that this group effort would be a one-time event, the students encouraged me to keep going. A second group of doctoral students was recruited to focus on the social sciences, and a third group of master's and doctoral students responded to a call for examples of social injustice. Their work can be seen in sections two and three. And finally, several faculty members and master's students help to frame the practice and educational implications drawn from the various concepts reflected in the social sciences and humanities.

Acknowledgments

Without the contributions of a very talented group of graduate students at the University of California, Berkeley, this book would not have been possible. I am inspired by the depth of their interest and commitment to find ways to address social injustice along with a deep interest in exploring the sources of moral indignation and social empathy. I am also grateful to several of my academic colleagues for contributing chapters to this volume. The multi-year project that led to the completion of this book benefited greatly from the valuable administrative assistance of Leanna Lok, the editorial assistance of Susan Austin (aka my wife), and the talented publications staff at SAGE Publications. A special note of appreciation goes to one of our leading scholars on social work ethics, Professor Frederic Reamer, for his contribution of the Foreword.

This book is dedicated to all those embarked on the life-long journey to understand social justice and to address social injustice wherever they find it, at home or abroad.

Michael J. Austin, PhD
Mack Professor
School of Social Welfare
University of California, Berkeley

1

SEARCHING FOR THE MEANING OF SOCIAL JUSTICE

MICHAEL J. AUSTIN, CHRISTINA BRANOM, AND BRYN KING

The meaning of social justice is not self-evident

(Gil, 1998)

Stepping around a homeless person lying on the sidewalk in front of a downtown restaurant could be enough to ruin the evening if you allow your mind to wander. The flood of questions can overwhelm those of us who care about the needs of others:

How is it that in one of the richest countries in the world, we can't find acceptable ways to help those in greatest need?

What is the story behind this homeless person, this son or daughter, spouse or parent? Is this person suffering from some form of mental illness?

Are we deluding ourselves as social workers to think that the challenges of caring for the homeless are unique in comparison to other helping professionals in hospitals, jails, or mental health clinics?

Why has homelessness and poverty become such a political football with liberals arguing for collective responsibility to help the vulnerable in our society and the conservatives arguing that we are individually responsible for our own needs?

What are the sources of my personal sense of moral indignation? Was it the influence of my parents or a family member? Was it the impact of my religious upbringing? When did I first become aware of the reality that others in our society were suffering from poverty, discrimination, oppression, and social injustice?

Why do I feel guilty about the privilege of social class when so many homeless people of color suffer from discrimination based on the color of their skin?

Why do I feel so outraged by this situation and helpless at the same time? Why do I feel so agitated upon entering the restaurant when someone outside sleeping on the sidewalk may have so little to eat?

These are a few of the questions that flood our minds as we confront a homeless person on a downtown street and provide a wake-up call to think about one's personal connection with social justice and injustice. These personal reflections can also help us explore more existential social justice issues that social work practitioners are called upon to face. The following questions provide a context for this book and are adapted from Gil (1998):

- To what extent does the search for meaning in one's life include engaging in the struggles for social justice?
- How does one's religious faith or secular beliefs (humanistic values and ethics) inform one's social justice commitments to the survival and development of all people?
- How does the blending of the scholarly logic (historical and philosophical) associated with *understanding* social justice combine with one's personal commitment to *promote* social justice?
- If we are all part of "the problem" (both agent and recipient of exploitation and oppression), how do we become part of "the solution" by promoting social justice?
- To what extent does the transformation of consciousness related to human relations, personal behavior, lifestyles, and professional practices call for self-transformation?
- How does one's newly acquired understandings of social justice inform efforts to make the transition from focusing on the symptoms of social injustice to identifying and addressing the underlying causes of injustice related to exploitation and oppression?

All of these questions call for an increased understanding of social justice as well as the implications of social injustice.

The goal of this volume is to identify the variety of ways that social justice is viewed in the humanities and social sciences in order to develop frameworks that can inform social work practice. Social justice is a core value of the social work profession and calls for an understanding of its intellectual foundations within the context of multiple definitions and perspectives. The definitional complexity can be seen in the following examples of efforts to define social justice: Social justice can refer to a system of belief (liberal and conservative), a substitute for the term *social injustice* (oppression,

discrimination, exploitation, etc.), a form of advocacy or intervention (doing social justice work), a value of a profession (*Code of Ethics of the National Association of Social Workers* [NASW], 2009), and/or an organization (social justice nonprofit).

ONGOING CHALLENGES FACING THE PROFESSION

The definitional complexity of social justice can be seen in the approaches of social work scholars to social work education and practice. For example, Longres and Scanlon (2001) look for social justice in the research curriculum, Hong and Hodge (2009) analyze the social justice content of course syllabi, Carroll and Minkler (2000) locate Paulo Freire's message in social work practice, Reisch (2011) notes the historical and policy dimensions of social justice, and Morris (2002) alerts social workers to the human capabilities perspective of the economist Amartya Sen and political philosopher Martha Nussbaum.

Gil (1998) in his pioneering book, *Confronting Injustice and Oppression: Concepts and Strategies for Social Workers*, frames the tension between the role of social work as social control (representing the interests of the taxpayers as reflected in social policy) and social reform (representing the interests of the oppressed, marginalized, and poor as reflected in advocacy). He uses five concepts to describe how the members of the profession vacillate between and among the following dimensions of practice: (a) amelioration, (b) control, (c) adaptation, (d) reform, and (e) structural transformation (pp. 68–69).

Amelioration refers to the individual and collective support of people in need. Alleviating the suffering of those in society with low status involves the provision of assistance to meet essential needs (e.g., food, clothing, shelter) in the form of services (e.g., meals, homeless shelters, medical care) without focusing on the causes of poverty, disability, immigration, homophobia, race, gender, or age. *Control* refers to the provision of minimal public assistance (e.g., welfare for the poor, supplementary security income for the disabled, and health insurance for the poor and near poor). In the marketplace, control is reflected in laws regulating public assistance (e.g., work-related behaviors reflected in the 1996 federal legislation called Temporary Assistance to Needy Families, or TANF) and worker–employer relations. *Adaptation* involves a more humane version of control that is often provided by nonprofit charities that tend to focus on addressing personal vulnerabilities (often related to poverty) and the related social interventions needed to process, maintain, and/or change people.

The last two concepts are *reform* and *transformation*. While control and adaptation tend to conform to societal expectations, reform seeks to reduce injustice and oppression without necessarily confronting existing institutions, frequently promoted by the "enlightened" privileged classes in response to "social unrest caused by long-standing injustice and oppression" (e.g., New Deal in the 1930s, urban riots in the 1960s, and welfare reform in the 1990s). Social reform is often a core value that an advocacy organization can use to document social conditions or a human service organization can include in its service provision *and* advocacy (Kaseman & Austin, 2005; Kimberlin, 2010).

Structural transformation, while connected to reform, seeks to address the systemic roots of social injustice and oppression rather than simply reduce their intensity. It is based on the development of a critical consciousness on the eradication of social injustices by not "masking the symptoms." The consciousness is rooted in the moral dimensions of social justice that, most frequently, are reflected in the humanities noted in the next section. As Gil (1998) observes, "Though social workers abhor social injustice, they generally do not challenge the systemic sources. Practice is typically considered politically neutral and thus separated from the philosophical rejection of injustice and oppression" (p. 85). To address this dilemma, Gil (1998) calls for exploring everyday encounters with social injustice and oppression by (a) initiating political discourse that challenges the status quo, (b) promoting both reflection and consciousness raising that is critical for deviating from system-reinforcing behaviors, and (c) using challenging questions about the consequences for client well-being and quality of life. As Gil (1998) cautions, successful discourse is based on a readiness to engage as well as sensitivities to the thought, feelings, and circumstances of those

engaged in the dialogue (e.g., discussing flaws in the research on rape victims in a room that includes people who have been raped calls for this type of sensitivity). The process of challenging assumptions, values, and practices can generate significant discomfort and reluctance to engage in discussions about social injustice and oppression. According to Gil (1998), the use of discourse can also reduce the individual sense of alienation when social workers experience the daily contradictions between their agency experience rooted in supporting immediate short-term goals rather than long-range visions of fundamental social change (e.g., "We get paid to serve clients, not change the world."). As Gil (1998) notes, the goal of activists is to make the connections between seemingly disparate issues in order to identify common ground in the dominant social order (e.g., poverty and crime, gang violence and unemployment, toxic waste sites and health issues, etc.). In addition, the process includes amplifying client voice, organizing to promote clients' right to vote, and democratizing the governance structures of our agencies. Gil (1998) concludes that the meaning of social justice is not self-evident and that social injustice "coercively establishes and maintains inequalities, discrimination, and dehumanizing, developmentally-inhibiting conditions of living . . . (because) equality is not a continuum but a zero point on the continuum of inequality . . . (where) there can be varying degrees of oppression and injustice but there are not varying degrees of equality—it exists only in the absence of oppression and injustice" (p. 15).

Gil (1998) calls upon social workers to make the transition from the emotional and intuitive concerns about injustice and oppression experienced by clients to the process of acquiring a historical and theoretical understanding of social justice and social injustice. The goal of this book is to facilitate this transition.

Moral Indignation and Social Empathy

Moral indignation (or outrage) often emerges from the perceived gap between what is happening and what should be happening. It involves our assumptions about how people should be treated and what we mean by "doing the right thing" (fairness). As Folger (2001) notes, the perceptions of injustice can be viewed as the product of "evolved moral intuitions that can be automatically elicited when people witness or learn about harm-doing" (p. 4). The field of moral psychology provides us with an understanding of the role of intuition in the process of experiencing moral indignation associated with promoting social justice. Haidt (2001) defines moral intuition as "the sudden appearance of conscious-ness of a moral judgment, including an affective valence (good–bad, like–dislike), without any con-scious awareness of having gone through the steps of searching, weighing evidence or inferring a con-clusion" (p. 818). In essence, immediate reactions in the form of moral indignation emerge without identifying the reasons for the feelings of injustice. The heart responds, while the head attempts to understand (e.g., "It is just not right that the richest country in the world has homeless people sleeping on the streets!").

Once the head catches up with the heart over the occurrence of a moral violation, moral anger sets in. As O'Reilly and Aquino (2011) note, "Moral anger consists of a set of discrete emotional reactions that are related because they can lead people to think negatively about the perpetrators of injustice and want to see them punished" (p. 531). The greater the degree of perceived harm, the more likely it will be for people to judge the injustice and respond (Bradfield & Aquino, 1999).

So what does it take to respond to a situation that seems unjust? The evolving research on social empathy provides part of the answer, given that the social work profession is situated between the marginalized and those with power in our society. A central tenet of social work practice is the capac-ity to empathize with clients and the dilemmas they face. As Segal (2011) notes, "Social empathy is the ability to understand people by perceiving or expe-riencing their life situations and . . . gaining insight into structural inequalities and disparities" (p. 266). According to Gerdes and Segal (2009), the social work framework for empathy includes (a) mirroring another person's emotions, or affective responses; (b) cognitively processing the meaning and con-text of the mirrored emotions using self–other awareness, perspective taking, and emotional regu-lation; and (c) conscious decision making or action taking based on the collected information (p. 116). In essence, social empathy reflects the connection between the capacity for individual empathy and the capacity to acquire a substantial understanding of inequalities and disparities. One way of acquiring this understanding is to learn about the connection between social problems (homelessness) and public policies designed to address them. This is one exam-ple of the importance of studying social policies as a way to inform social work practice. Another way to acquire social empathy, according to Segal (2007) is to "1) gain exposure by visiting places and people who are different from you, 2) strive to understand those differences, and 3) put yourself into the life of the person of different socio-economic class, gender, ability, age, sexual identify, race or national origin" (pp. 333–337).

The psychology of moral indignation and the social psychology of social empathy provide an important context for understanding of social jus-tice. The intersection between these two domains also provides fertile ground for further research; namely, what is the relationship between indi-vidual empathy and social responsibility? What is the connection between social empathy and social policies and programs? How does one's individual background inform the level of moral indignation and social empathy? How do moral indignation and social empathy contribute to promoting social justice? How well do social workers understand the connection between their religious backgrounds and social empathy? Is there a way to measure the varying levels of social justice and social injustice? How does the profession cope with both liberal and conservative views of social justice? These ques-tions not only promote self-reflection but also lead to the search for definitions of both social justice and social injustice.

DEFINING SOCIAL JUSTICE

We all have our own working definition of social jus-tice. While some refer to equal opportunity or access to resources, others refer to equity dimensions of social policies. For example, to what extent is economic justice as might be reflected in a living wage policy or the growing inequality between the rich and the poor reflected in the occupy Wall Street movement an issue of equality or equity? Others view social justice in the context of action as in a social movement or doing social justice advocacy work that involves speaking truth to power. And still others view social justice through the lens of empowering the marginalized by searching for ways to amplify client voices. The umbrella of social justice can also be used to call for the rights of everyone to live in safe environments that promote the well-being as well as the worth and dignity of all.

While scholars in social work and in other fields have sought to define social justice, Banerjee (2011) captures the definitional struggle in social work as follows:

> Social work scholars commonly suggest that social justice means arranging social, economic, and political institutions in such a way that all people, especially poor, vulnerable, oppressed, and marginalized people, are able to meet their basic and developmental needs including democratic participation in decision-making processes. This requires equal political and civil freedoms, fair equality of opportunity in socioeconomic-political spheres, as well as special consideration for access to material and nonmaterial resources, services, and opportunities for differently able people. (p. 209)

The challenge for students and practitioners can be seen in this definition and the multiple questions it raises: (a) How are institutions best arranged to promote social justice, and who is in charge of interorganizational collaboration?; (b) who defines the process of meeting "basic and developmental needs," and how are they measured?; (c) what does it mean for the poor to be democratically included in decision-making processes?; (d) who defines and guarantees "equal" political and civil freedoms?; (e) what does "fair equality of opportunity" mean in our society; and (f) what does "special consideration" mean when it comes to accessing resources for people with different abilities? These questions illustrate the complexities facing social work scholars and social scientists when it comes to defining social justice.

Another approach to defining social justice is reflected in the work of Garcia and Van Soest (2006) as follows:

- Utilitarian perspective on social justice: Social justice is derived by "weighing relative benefits and harms and determining what maximizes the greatest good for the greatest number of people" (p. 13).
- Libertarian perspective on social justice: Social justice is derived from the distribution of resources based on a natural or social lottery and noninterference with the natural order of things where people hold certain rights by entitlement (p. 14).
- Egalitarian perspective on social justice: Social justice is based on avoiding extreme inequalities in order to create a just society where the redistribution of resources is a moral obligation to address the most needy (p. 15).
- Racial contract perspective on social justice: Social justice is based on a social contract that privileges Whites over non-Whites based on race and produces an unjust society where non-Whites are excluded from the distribution of resources (p. 17).
- Human rights perspective on social justice: Social justice is based on meeting basic human needs related to the equitable sharing of material resources in terms of universal and basic entitlements without discrimination and regardless of race, gender, or class and rooted in promoting human capabilities (p. 18).

Each of these social justice perspectives provides a different rationale for action. For example, Reisch (2002, 2011) notes that social justice is used to reflect the interests of a wide spectrum of political beliefs, from conservatives who base their social justice views on libertarian and utilitarian perspectives (balancing individual rights and responsibilities or balancing property rights with human rights) to liberals who base their views of social justice on groups related to egalitarian, racial, and/or human rights perspectives (distribution of benefits and burdens, existence of opportunities and conditions, and/or social cooperation and trust).

MORAL DIMENSIONS OF SOCIAL JUSTICE

Since the moral aspects of social justice are part of the core value of social work, it is important to explore the historical and philosophical foundations of the value. Discussions of morality and fairness can be found most explicitly in the humanities, including the disciplines of philosophy, literature, history, law, and religion. The concepts related to morality found in these disciplines can contribute to an understanding of moral indignation and social empathy. For example, each of the major religions includes concepts related to both reflection and action.

In order to make the transition from moral indignation to social empathy, the disciplines of the social sciences help address the question, How can we explain the existence of social injustice in order to do social justice work? The social science disciplines of anthropology, economics, political science, psychology, and sociology provide the concepts (e.g., privilege, oppression, discrimination, etc.) and tools of inquiry (e.g., qualitative and quantitative methods) that can help with the promotion of social justice. Research findings related to social injustice can mobilize groups and organizations as well as lead to changes in public policies (e.g., *Brown v. Board of Education*, [1954] and policies to address the issue of separate but unequal school systems for African American children).

With an understanding of the concepts related to social justice located in the disciplines of the humanities and social sciences, it is possible to return to a key aspect of the definitional challenge; namely, how does a comprehensive understanding of social justice inform one's understanding of social injustice? For many in the social work profession, the existence of social injustice is what attracted them to this profession of action. The theme of social injustice often provides the foundation for discussions about diversity and cultural competence where the topics of discrimination, oppression, privilege, social class, racism, sexism, homophobia, and ageism reside. In this book, several illustrative examples of social injustice are provided as they occur inside the human service organizations (child welfare services, aging service, mental health services) and outside the human service organizations (predatory lending, children of incarcerated parents, intimate partner violence, and discrimination against the lesbian, gay, bisexual, transgender [LGBT] community). Unfortunately, there are many examples of social injustice in both the developed and developing world, and mapping them all would require a multivolume effort.

TEXTBOOKS AS KNOWLEDGE TRANSFER

One approach to capturing the knowledge base of social justice and injustice is to review current textbooks to see how the issues are defined and illustrated. In social work education, this means searching for social justice content in the primary curriculum domains of social work practice and social policy. The other domains that could be searched include textbooks on research methods, biopsychosocial theories of human behavior and the social environment, and diversity. For the purpose of this volume, only repeatedly revised social policy textbooks were selected along with currently revised social work practice textbooks (with a few recently published textbooks also included). The reviews of these textbooks provided an important context for understanding the challenges and struggles related to incorporating social justice into the education of future practitioners.

Social Justice Themes in Social Work Practice Textbooks

In light of the challenges associated with defining and teaching social justice within the context of social work practice, an array of social work practice textbooks (17 revised and 4 relatively recent as noted in Figure 1.1) were reviewed in order to see the extent to which they incorporated themes of social justice and related issues (e.g., oppression, injustice, and empowerment). Based on the review, the textbooks were clustered according to the level of attention to social justice issues (e.g., little or no attention, some attention, and considerable attention to social justice).

As might be expected, the three specialized practices related to neurobiology (Applegate & Shapiro, 2005), clinical assessment and diagnosis (Corcoran & Walsh, 2010), and evidence-based practice (Roberts & Yeager, 2006) included little or no attention to social justice. While there are nine textbooks that give some attention to social justice concepts, they do not describe tangible strategies for integrating social justice into social work practice (Briggs & Corcoran, 2001; Canda & Furman, 2010;

Revised Textbooks

Brueggemann, W. G. (2006). *The practice of macro social work* (3rd ed.). Belmont, CA: Wadsworth/Thomson Learning.

Canda, E. R., & Furman, L. D. (2010). *Spiritual diversity in social work practice: The heart of helping* (2nd ed.). New York, NY: Oxford University Press.

Coady, N., & Lehman, P. (Eds.). (2008). *Theoretical perspectives for direct social work practice: A generalist-eclectic approach* (2nd ed.). New York, NY: Springer.

Corcoran, J., & Walsh, J. (2010). *Clinical assessment and diagnosis in social work practice* (2nd ed.). New York, NY: Oxford University Press.

Dolgoff, R., Loewenberg, F. M., & Harrington, D. (2009). *Ethical decisions for social work practice* (8th ed.). Belmont, CA: Thomson Brooks/Cole.

Gambrill, E. (2006). *Social work practice: A critical thinker's guide* (2nd ed.). New York, NY: Oxford University Press.

Goldstein, E. G. (1995). *Ego psychology and social work practice* (2nd ed.). New York, NY: Free Press.

Hepworth, D. H., Rooney, R. H., Rooney, G. D., Strom-Gottfried, K., & Larsen, J. A. (2010). *Direct social work practice: Theory and skills* (8th ed.). Belmont, CA: Brooks/Cole, Cengage Learning.

Johnson, L. C., & Yanca, S. J. (2010). *Social work practice: A generalist approach* (10th ed.). Boston, MA: Allyn & Bacon.

Lum, D. (2004). *Social work practice and people of color: A process-stage approach* (5th ed.). Belmont, CA: Thomson Brooks/Cole.

Miley, K. K., O'Melia, M., & DuBois, B. (2011). *Generalist social work practice: An empowering approach* (6th ed.). Boston, MA: Allyn & Bacon.

Netting, F. E., Kettner, P. M., & McMurtry, S. L. (2008). *Social work macro practice* (4th ed.). Boston, MA: Pearson.

Saleebey, D. (Ed.). (2009). *The strengths perspective in social work practice* (5th ed.). Boston, MA: Pearson.

Sheafor, B. W., & Horejsi, C. R. (2008). *Techniques and guidelines for social work practice* (8th ed.). Boston, MA: Pearson.

Turner, F. J. (Ed.). (1996). *Social work treatment* (4th ed.). New York, NY: Free Press.

Walsh, J. (2010). *Theories for direct social work practice* (2nd ed.). Belmont, CA: Wadsworth Cengage Learning.

Webb, N. B. (2003). *Social work practice with children* (2nd ed.). New York, NY: Guilford Press.

Relatively Recent Textbooks

Applegate, J. S., & Shapiro, J. R. (2005). *Neurobiology for clinical social work practice.* New York, NY: W. W. Norton.

Briggs, H. E., & Corcoran, K. (2001). **Social work practice: Treating common client problems**. Chicago, IL: Lyceum.

Roberts, A. R., & Yeager, K. R. (Eds.). (2006). **Foundations of evidence-based social work practice.** New York, NY: Oxford University Press.

Sue, D. W. (2006). **Multicultural social work practice.** Hoboken, NJ: Wiley & Sons.

Figure 1.1   Social Work Practice Textbooks

Coady & Lehman, 2008; Dolgoff, Loewenberg, & Harrington, 2009; Gambrill, 2006; Goldstein, 1995; Lum, 2004; Turner, 1996; Webb, 2011).

Textbooks With Considerable Attention to Social Justice

The textbooks in this category not only provide descriptions of social justice but also illustrate the ways in which it can be incorporated into social work practice, particularly generalist and macro practice.

Using an ecosystems-strengths perspective, Johnson and Yanca (2010) view social justice as the equal opportunity to receive the political, economic, and social benefits of participating in society. At the micro-practice level, individuals are empowered to address their own situations that include the use of case advocacy for resources or services that are being denied. At the macro-practice level, the authors clearly call for resistance to injustice through the use of community needs assessments, program planning, advocacy, and community organizing.

One of the most frequently revised textbooks by Hepworth, Rooney, Rooney, Strom-Gottfried, and Larsen (2010) define social justice as promoting equality and rights, especially among disadvantaged populations, as well as increasing the ability of vulnerable or oppressed people to control their own lives. Most of the textbook focuses on social work with individuals and small groups with one chapter dedicated to macro practice related to advocacy and social action. In a similar way, Sheafor and Horejsi (2008) feature the definition of social justice as fairness and moral rightness designed to support the basic human rights of all people in order to create a more just society where social workers apply their knowledge of social conditions to advocating for social change.

With seven out of their 16 chapters explicitly addressing social justice, Miley, O'Melia, and DuBois (2011) address both direct and indirect practice with a specific emphasis on building strengths and empowering clients where social justice is defined as the fair distribution of resources, equal access to opportunities, and freedom from discrimination. Throughout the textbook, emphasis is placed on recognizing the consequences of injustices and eliminating them wherever possible.

Building on the strengths perspective in social work practice, Saleebey (2009) defines social justice as the equitable and just distribution of the social goods that people depend on for survival, growth, development, and safety. Saleebey takes the view that social justice can be achieved at both the micro and macro levels by (a) recognizing the skills and capacities of all persons, (b) eliminating the power differential between professional helpers and their clients, (c) drawing on the strengths of communities to overcome disparities and oppression, (d) respecting all cultures and experiences, and (e) specifically calling on social workers to advocate for social justice. In a similar way, Walsh (2010) defines social justice as the empowerment of oppressed and vulnerable clients and the pursuit of social change. Walsh devotes a section in each chapter to relevance of social justice to the practice of social work by describing the different ways that theory is used in the pursuit of social change.

Taking a more macro-practice approach to social justice, Brueggemann (2006) notes that social workers have historically pursued social justice and describes methods for achieving social justice in practice. By describing social thinking as a change-oriented approach that brings people together to challenge injustices, Brueggemann argues that social workers should assist with social movements that challenge unequal power structures in pursuit of a just economic and political system. With a similar emphasis on macro practice, Netting, Kettner, and McMurtry (2008) not only define social justice and illustrate numerous examples of injustice, but also provide concrete strategies for incorporating social justice into practice. Social justice is defined in the text as the fair distribution of both tangible and intangible resources and benefits. With the use of historical and contemporary examples of movements and policies that have supported the poor and oppressed, the text describes how workers can mobilize key individuals, networks, and systems to promote positive social change. The textbook also offers guidance for balancing social justice principles with other ethical principles in social work, including autonomy and beneficence.

Based on a multicultural perspective, Sue (2006) calls for new approaches to social work practice that alter the traditional Eurocentric focus of social work and its potential for oppressive and discriminatory practices with persons of color. Defining social justice as "equal access and opportunity for all groups" (p. 21), Sue contends that individual interventions may be inappropriate for addressing problems related to unjust policies and practices and therefore encourages social workers to alter institutional processes of socialization that perpetuate prejudice, discrimination, and inequality, using the methods of multicultural organizational development.

In summary, this review examined the ways in which social justice is treated in social work practice textbooks in order to identify the ways in which social justice is being presented to the next generation of social workers. The key social justice concepts found in this review include (a) the promotion of human rights, (b) client empowerment, (c) challenges to oppression and discrimination, (d) equal or fair distribution of resources, and (e) multicultural competence. While many of the micro-social work practice textbooks show an uneven focus on the role of social justice in practice, most of the generalist or macro-practice textbooks display a clearer focus on social justice.

Considering the centrality of social justice among the core values of the social work profession, it is clear that a more comprehensive working definition of social justice would inform the development of micro- and macro-practice models, strategies, and skills that address injustices in social work practice textbooks. The challenge is to find ways to integrate social justice principles into social work practice at both the micro and macro levels.

Social Justice Themes in Social Welfare Policy Textbooks

In spite of ongoing calls for integrating social justice into social work education and practice, there has been a demonstrable lack of clarity regarding a consistent definition of this value and the question of the appropriate arena within the curriculum of social work education remains. To explore the role of social justice in the social policy domain of social work education, a textbook analysis was conducted to determine how schools of social work understand and educate students about social justice by focusing on the most frequently used introductory social policy textbooks used in required social policy courses. These textbooks represent one aspect of the common experience of MSW social work students but did not include advocacy textbooks because most students are not required to take advocacy courses. A search of the major academic publishers was completed and seven textbooks were selected on the basis of the number of revised editions (at least three) as one measure of curriculum decision making.

As noted in Figure 1.2, the textbooks were categorized based on their stated purpose and content, namely, histories of social welfare (Day, 2003; Trattner, 1999), policy analysis skills (Gilbert & Terrell, 2010; Popple & Leighninger, 2004), history and policy analysis (DiNitto & Cummins, 2005), or a combination of history, policy analysis, and advocacy (Jansson, 2009; Karger & Stoesz, 2006). In some textbooks social justice is defined while in others it is only mentioned. Some textbooks devote considerable attention to explicating various forms of discrimination or oppression, others much less. Overall, there is little consensus regarding the definitions of social justice or relevant content.

i. Histories of social welfare

Day, P. J. (2003). *A new history of social welfare* (4th ed.). Boston, MA: Allyn & Bacon.

Trattner, W. I. (1999). *From poor law to welfare state: A history of social welfare in America* (6th ed.). New York, NY: Free Press. (Original work published 1974)

ii. Social policy analysis skills

Gilbert, N., & Terrell, P. (2010). *Dimensions of social welfare policy* (7th ed.). Boston, MA: Allyn & Bacon.

Popple, P. R., & Leighninger, L. (2004). *The policy-based profession: An introduction to social welfare policy analysis for social workers* (3rd ed.). Boston, MA: Pearson/Allyn & Bacon.

iii. History and policy analysis skills

DiNitto, D. M., & Cummins, L. K. (2005). *Social welfare: Politics and public policy* (6th ed.). Boston, MA: Pearson/Allyn & Bacon.

iv. Combination of history, policy analysis skills, and advocacy

Jansson, B. (2009). *The reluctant welfare state: Engaging history to advance social work practice in contemporary society* (6th ed.). South Melbourne, Victoria, Australia: Brooks/Cole.

Karger, H. J., & Stoesz, D. (2006). *American social welfare policy: A pluralist approach* (5th ed.). Boston, MA: Pearson/Allyn & Bacon.

Figure 1.2   Social Policy Textbooks

Histories of Social Welfare

The two history of social welfare textbooks cover similar historical ground, yet neither devote significant attention to the definition or role of social justice. Interestingly, in spite of the fact that both authors are operating from diverging political and social perspectives, both texts cover the Judeo-Christian roots of social justice, rarely addressed in other textbooks.

Trattner's history, originally published in 1974 and now in its sixth edition, provides an interpretive and comprehensive history of social welfare in America from colonization to the present as a background to understanding the modern welfare state. Organized in chronological order up to the latter half of the Clinton presidency, he describes the values that formed the foundation for social welfare systems and locates the concept of justice and the duty to give to those in need in ancient Jewish doctrine and in 19th-century Christian doctrine underlying the charity movement. Social justice reappears and receives the most attention in the chapter on the settlement house movement, its relationship to religious feeling and its role in labor reform, even though it is not specifically defined. Overall, Trattner's text meets its stated objective and provides a comprehensive narrative on the development and current (as of the late 1990s) state of social welfare in the United States, but it does not identify the specific elements of a social justice perspective in examining this history.

In contrast, the textbook by Day (2003), now in its sixth edition, is a history of social welfare from the perspective of what she terms the "subjects/victims/recipients/clients" and seeks to "redress in part the loss of history for women, nonwhite people, and other groups oppressed by social institutions" (p. ix). She argues that social welfare, since its inception in the United States, has struggled in its dual quests to provide social treatment and engage in social control, which has ultimately led to social work's participation in maintaining structures of inequality. The text seeks to ask questions about the *why* of social welfare and how it has evolved through the dynamic interaction between the major social institutions of polity (the exercise of power in a society), religion, and economy. It begins by discussing American social values, issues of poverty and class, and institutional discrimination and follows this discussion by defining the institution of social welfare. Day locates social justice within the principles of Judeo-Christian charity that contribute to an array of American social values. While Judaic teachings on society's obligation to help those in need constitute the foundation of contemporary social altruism, Day maintains that if these values "still underlaid social welfare . . . no one would be without enough food, clothing, or shelter. Every child would be assured of equal opportunity . . . and society would take responsibility for the disadvantaged." (Day, 2003, p. 5)

Policy Analysis Textbooks

Both policy analysis textbooks in this section seek to provide students with the capacity to evaluate policy. While the focus on oppression and discrimination is relatively limited, critical analysis skills are described to help students analyze those issues in more meaningful ways.

The textbook by Gilbert and Terrell (2010), now in its seventh edition, specifies two major goals, namely, making choices about social welfare policy based on complex and sometimes contradictory empirical evidence and social values and examining the basic dimensions of choice designed to provide a method of analyzing and understanding social policy. The authors explicitly avoid arguing their own point of view, offering prescriptions, or promoting social justice as an ethical value for readers to adopt. In fact, the authors maintain that on some level, social justice has been achieved in developed market economies where the "mass of ordinary citizens enjoy middle-class standards of living" (Gilbert & Terrell, 2010, p. 29).

In their first chapter, Gilbert and Terrell offer a definition of social justice in terms of "advancing an allocation of resources that reduces inequalities in society, whether they take the form of income differences or excessive disparities in education, health, or housing" (Gilbert & Terrell, 2010, p. 19). To determine the intent of social policies, the authors examine the extent to which a given policy achieves distributive justice by identifying three core values: namely, equality, equity, and adequacy in the distribution of resources to the poor and needy. *Equality* refers to a numerical quantification of equal treatment or an equal share for everyone. *Equity* implies a proportional fairness in which "people's deservedness should be based on their contributions to society, modified only by special considerations for those whose inability to contribute is clearly not of their own making" (Gilbert & Terrell, 2010, p. 74). *Adequacy* is less concerned with whether benefits are equal or equitable and more concerned with the provision of a decent standard of physical and spiritual well-being. Using these values as one method for assessing the intent of policy, students are encouraged to develop their own critical perspective on social welfare policy.

The social policy textbook by Popple and Leighninger (2004), now in its third edition, also seeks to provide critical policy analysis skills related to every aspect of social work, including the agency's rules and regulations, the resources available to clients, and the welfare of the larger community. Understanding how they are developed, as well as how people and populations are affected by such policies, can facilitate the effective use, implementation, and ability to challenge policies and programs in the interest of its clients.

While there is little mention of social justice in this textbook, the authors do discuss the social values related to the definitions of social problems. For example, in describing the value of equality, they note that Americans "express strong support for the idea of equality as a philosophical principle, but our society is characterized by a high degree of inequality. . . . When most Americans speak of equality, they mean equality of opportunity, not of outcome" (Popple & Leighninger, 2004, p. 95). Although there is limited attention to oppression and injustice, the authors establish important links between social issues (e.g., poverty, racism, and sexism) and the formation and maintenance of policies such as TANF and family preservation.

History and Policy Analysis

DiNitto and Cummins (2005), in the sixth edition of their social policy textbook, view social welfare policy as a continuing political struggle over the nature of poverty, inequality, and other social problems in terms of the different ways of defining, measuring, and resolving them through the development and maintenance of programs and services. Since

they do not regard the development of social welfare policy as a rational process (despite the elements of rationality within it), they argue that the advocates for the disenfranchised need to understand the politics of policy making in order to have any impact on the critical decisions that affect the poor and disenfranchised.

In describing the political process, DiNitto and Cummins make two references to social justice, namely, distributive justice as liberal value (with only limited discussion) and the need for "a theory of justice" where fairness is defined, especially for those who are most vulnerable to social problems. The authors clearly identify class and the unequal distribution of wealth as root causes of social and political conflict and the role of government in settling conflicts by developing, enacting, maintaining, and enforcing policy. The political conceptualization of policy decision making forms the backdrop for describing the history of social welfare and the policies and programs that address social problems without providing the rationales or methods for seeking social justice.

History, Policy Analysis, and Advocacy

Unlike the previous texts, the textbooks in this category are more prescriptive about the meaning, operationalization, and active engagement of social justice. They are comprehensive texts that cover the history, values, analysis, and advocacy needed to link social policy with social work practice.

In their fifth edition, Karger and Stoesz (2006) make the case that conservative ideology and political power have undermined public support for centralized welfare and social insurance. They cite privatization, devolution, and faith-based programs as conservative themes that are driving mainstream ideology regarding social services. The crux of the pluralist approach is that social welfare services will continue to devolve from a federally driven system of entitlements and services to an increasingly complex, localized, and privatized social service model. The authors propose that the textbook can serve as a catalyst in the reemergence of social work as an influential force in social policy, particularly through the efforts of the nonprofit sector.

The authors also note that the traditional liberal views government as the only institution capable of promoting the public good and social justice for those disenfranchised by racism, sexism, and poverty. They define social justice in terms of "equity and fairness in all areas of social, political, and economic life, as well as the provision of basic necessities to all without regard to their participation in the market; an objective of liberals and progressives" (Karger & Stoesz, 2006, p. 498). They also maintain that discrimination and poverty "are inextricably linked in the fabric of American social welfare" (Karger & Stoesz, 2006, p. 59) and tend to be typical arenas for social justice values.

In contrast, Jansson (2009), in his sixth edition, seeks to expand the skills of policy advocates by emphasizing social welfare history and its impact on ethical reasoning, analytic skills, and policy identities. Emphasis is placed on the ethical value of social justice by focusing on the oppression of 13 different vulnerable populations (e.g., women, African Americans, "First" or Native Americans, Latinos, Asian Americans, immigrants, the LGBT population, the aging population, children, people with physical or mental disabilities, and people with criminal records). In each chapter, Jansson notes that the American welfare state is inherently reluctant and social welfare advocates have the task of making it increasingly humane.

Jansson defines social justice as "the right of members of vulnerable populations *not* to experience flagrant inequalities in civil rights, life conditions, and access to opportunities" (2009, p. 30). Jansson discusses utilizing ethical reasoning to delineate between right and wrong in social welfare policy analysis and formulates a special ethical case for social justice when assessing specific social policies in order to identify violations of social justice in civil rights, life conditions, or access to opportunities (e.g., disparities in income, housing, and educational opportunities). His perspective on the American welfare state and social justice is explicit as he seeks to bridge the gap between policy and practice by calling for increased advocacy skills in the service of clients and social justice.

In summary, the textbooks reviewed covered key themes related to social justice in the context of poverty and class inequality, discrimination, and social change. The textbooks provided different explanations of the etiology of poverty. While some textbook authors sought to clearly define and explore the causes and types of discrimination, others merely acknowledged its role in contributing to poverty, accessing opportunity, and/or appearing in social policies. While most textbooks included a wide range of populations (e.g., vulnerable or discriminated against or oppressed), others focused primarily on race and gender. In terms of social change, all of the textbook authors addressed the need to integrate knowledge of social policy into social work practice as a way of understanding how different issues affect clients, though few actually specified an array of methods for policy advocacy or social reform methods.

Most of the textbook authors reviewed or addressed aspects of the NASW's *Code of Ethics* related to social justice (e.g., social change, vulnerable and oppressed populations, poverty, discrimination, and other forms of injustice). However, when it comes to defining social justice or engaging in dialogue about how it is achieved, less attention is given to this aspect of social policy development and implementation. Three of the seven textbooks in this review actually contained definitions of social justice, and most of the authors acknowledged that social justice refers to a liberal value that seeks to remedy the effects of social and economic inequality.

HUMANITIES AND SOCIAL JUSTICE

Based on the review of existing social work practice and social policy textbooks, it seemed important to step back and take a broader view of social justice by evaluating the contributions of disciplines outside the profession of social work in order to inform future practice and policy development. In this book, the exploration of social justice begins with the humanities and the themes of morality. Chapter 2 ("The Influence of Western Philosophy on Definitions of Social Justice") focuses on the discipline of philosophy and the evolution of the concepts of justice in Western philosophy, from an emphasis on self-interest and the process of leading a virtuous life to a view of justice as supporting essential human capabilities. In Chapter 3 ("Legal Theories of Social Justice"), the author explores the relationship between social justice and legal perspectives by applying competing theories of social justice to a legal case that involves the equitable distribution of wealth related to public school financing.

In Chapter 4 ("Literary Theories and Social Justice"), social justice theories that inform literary criticism are featured (e.g., Marxism, feminism, postcolonialism, and queer theory). The goal is to identify how language shapes lived experiences (e.g., marginalizes and empowers as well as informs and influences social and political action). Chapter 5 ("Historical Perspectives on Social Justice") features the history of the term *social justice* and the evolution of ideas (e.g., the founding and professionalization period of the 1880s to the 1940s, the modern period of the new social history from the 1940s to the 1970s, and the postmodernism and socioculturalism period of the 1980s to the present).

By focusing on the moral dimensions of social justice, the author of Chapter 6 ("Social Justice and Religion") features the seven major themes of Catholic social teaching, the four major Islamic perspectives of social justice (tribal, modernists, revivalists, and neo-modernists), and the Judaic perspective of social justice related to the three core principles, namely, acts of loving kindness (*chesed/ gimilut chasidim*), repairing the world (*tikkun olam*), and righteousness or acts of righteousness (*tzedek/ tzedakah*).

The section on the humanities concludes with a synthesis in Chapter 7 ("Social Justice From a Humanities Perspective: A Synthesis to Inform Practice") where the concepts of social justice are displayed as part of a continuum from theory to application by drawing upon the previous chapters and identifying the implications for action related to debating philosophical and legal tensions, making moral commitments found in religious doctrine, and promoting catalytic action of righteous indignation to address social injustices.

SOCIAL SCIENCES AND SOCIAL JUSTICE

The next section features the contributions of the social sciences to our understanding of social justice. Chapter 8 ("Social Psychological Perspectives on Morality and Social Justice") captures the efforts of social psychologists in the field of moral psychology to promote understanding of the development of morality and how it contributes to notions of fairness and justice. Chapter 9 ("Social Justice and Anthropology: From Observation to Activism") addresses the contributions of activist anthropology to our understanding of social justice in terms of the philosophical concepts of cultural relativism and universalism as well as subjectivity and objectivity.

Chapter 10 ("Perspectives of Social Justice in Sociology") features the role of sociology in explicating major social problems that inform the social justice issues of discrimination, oppression, and inequality as well as calling for the need to combine rigorous science with community empowerment and emancipation. As a way of featuring the role of political science in expanding our understanding of social justice, two approaches were used, namely, the rights of children and the rights of parents. Chapter 11 ("Social Justice and the Politics of Children's Rights") focuses on the UN Convention on the Rights of the Child by emphasizing social rules and relationships (rather than distributive justice related to the possession of material goods and social positions), concepts of human rights (economic, political, and social), and concepts of equality (inclusion and participation in the major institutions and the opportunity to actively exercise one's rights). In contrast, Chapter 12 ("Social Justice in Political Thought: Examining the Rights of Parents") is focused on political science theory that addresses the balance between the state and the family, with a particular emphasis on issues of social justice and the rights of parents as reflected in court cases.

Chapter 13 ("Economic Theories of Social Justice") addresses the economic theories of social justice that are informed by the three principles of equality of opportunity to engage in productive work and own property and other assets, the right of every individual to be rewarded in proportion to his or her contribution, and the removal of barriers (such as monopolies or exploitation of certain groups of individuals) to establishing a fair economic order for all members of society.

In addition to the core social science disciplines, it is also important to capture the emerging interdisciplinary interest in social justice. Chapter 14 ("Theories of Organizational Justice: Interdisciplinary Social Science Perspectives") explores the three interdisciplinary theories of organizational justice, namely, distributive justice, procedural justice, and interactional justice (interpersonal and informational justice) along with reference to the concepts of equity, stratification, and wage disparity in relationship to perceptions of trust and fairness in the context of organizational culture and norms.

This section on the social science dimensions of social justice concludes with two chapters; namely a synthesis in Chapter 15 ("Interdisciplinary Social Science Perspectives: Key Concepts to Inform Practice") and Chapter 16 (Social Justice for Active Citizenship) which is a case example related to both the social sciences and the humanities. Chapter 15 captures four major social science themes namely, conceptualizations of justice and injustice, the role of perspective in the production of knowledge, the role of institutionalized power and government intervention, and factors that inhibit or motivate action for social change. These themes are used to construct a conceptual framework to inform practice. In contrast, Chapter 16 features a case example university-wide approach to social justice education by describing the experiences of including social justice in the development of the university's strategic plan that led to the establishment of a social justice institute with the capacity to influence future faculty hiring processes and new course development.

EXAMPLES OF SOCIAL INJUSTICE

Looking at the humanities and social sciences provides a context for exploring illustrations of social injustice, inside and outside human service organizations. Given the magnitude of injustice in our country and around the world, the next group of chapters provides a diverse, but limited, set of examples.

In focusing on social injustice outside human service organizations, Chapter 17's ("Predatory Lending") author addresses the breadth and depth of predatory lending where people without financial resources and poor or no credit often turn to predatory lenders who can be coercive, manipulative, usurious, and sometimes abusive. In addition to definitions, practices, and prevalence in the United States, this chapter describes two types of subprime services, namely, payday lending and subprime mortgage lending.

Chapter 18 ("The Injustices of Intimate Partner Violence") focuses on another form of social injustice, namely, intimate partner violence as a form of gender oppression. This form of violence occurs in the broad context of sexism and multiple intersecting oppressions that often include negative outcomes (e.g., psychological, physical, financial, reproductive, and, in some cases, death), especially for women with disabilities, immigrant women, and lesbians. Chapter 19 ("Social Injustices Experienced by Children of Incarcerated Parents") explores one of the most hidden forms of social injustice, namely, the impact of parental incarceration on children at each juncture of their parent's incarceration process (from arrest to community reentry), by describing a unique set of rights for children and youth. In Chapter 20, the last chapter on social injustices that occur primarily outside of human service organizations ("The Social Injustices Experienced by the Lesbian, Gay, Bisexual, and Transgender Community"), the emphasis is on the rights often denied to members of the gay, lesbian, bisexual, and transgender community (e.g., via hate crimes and violence, antihomosexual conduct laws, antidiscrimination protection, partnership recognition, queer youth in unsafe families and schools, family violence and homelessness, unsafe schools, and prevalence of suicide) with special attention to the unique experiences of LGBT people of color and transgender members of the community.

The next set of chapters describes social injustices inside human service organizations. Like the injustices hidden in the community, these injustices rarely receive the attention of human service agency staff members. Chapter 21 ("Procedural Injustices in Child Welfare") identifies some of the procedural injustices inside public child welfare programs by describing the pathway of a child welfare case. The pathway includes the investigatory phase related to assessing the allegations of child abuse or neglect and whether or not children are safe in their homes, the adjudication and disposition hearings phase, the ongoing or continuing family maintenance and/or reunification phase, and the permanency planning or adoption phase for providing long-term care services exclusively to the child.

Chapter 22 ("Elder Mistreatment: A Social Justice Perspective") is an exploration of the range of social injustice experienced by the mistreatment of elders by focusing on definitions, prevalence estimates, interventions, and the conditions that contribute to the vulnerability of older adults (e.g., ageist beliefs and attitudes, race, ethnicity and gender, the risk of social isolation, and physical and cognitive impairments).

The final chapter (23) on social injustices inside human service organizations ("Social Justice and the Injustices Experienced by People With Mental Health Disabilities") addresses public mental health services by highlighting the legal cases, defining the rights of people who live with a mental health disability and illustrating how discrimination is experienced in the areas of employment, housing, medical care, and criminal justice.

IMPLICATIONS FOR PRACTICE

How can theory inform practice? How can we incorporate the social justice concepts of procedural justice, praxis, and human capabilities into practice? The answers to these questions are explored in the chapters that compose the concluding section of the book. For translating an understanding of social justice into action, the author of Chapter 24 ("Client Voice and Expertise in Promoting Social Justice") focuses on the need for more attention to collecting, documenting, analyzing, and addressing issues raised by service users who make up the client populations of human service organizations. Moving from a client to an organizational focus, Chapter 25 ("Social Justice and the Role of Nonprofit Human Service Organizations in Amplifying Client Voice") features the role of nonprofit human service organizations as mediating civic intermediaries that link citizen-clients to governing systems and political processes in order to amplify client voices through advocacy organizations and community organizing groups that promote social change at both the micro and macro levels of social work practice.

The next chapter provides a case example (much like Chapter 16) related to preparing students for future practice and citizenship. Chapter 26 ("Educating Social Work Students About Social Justice Practice") on social justice theory, evaluation, learning, and change is a comprehensive case study of how faculty and students address the themes of privilege, oppression, discrimination, and social justice within the master's curriculum in the social work education programs at the University of Michigan School of Social Work.

The two concluding chapters pull together key threads identified and woven throughout the book. Chapter 27 ("Incorporating Social Justice Principles Into Social Work Practice") links the core social justice values of the social work profession with the human capabilities perspectives emerging out of the humanities and social science disciplines. It builds upon the themes of humanistic social work, restorative justice, and the four social justice principles found in the NASW's *Code of Ethics* in order to construct a social justice checklist that can be used by social workers in any field of practice. The checklist can be used in combination with the documentation of the client engagement and assessment process (compiling intake information and engaging in service planning and referral).

The second concluding chapter (28), "Finding the Courage of One's Convictions: Reflections on a Lifetime of Social Work Practice," captures the role of a social worker engaged in a lifetime of social justice practice. It represents one form of role modeling that can inspire future generations of practitioners who seek to move from the distressing nature of moral indignation to the activist approach to demonstrating social empathy.

A WORK IN PROGRESS

This volume is being written during a period of profound change. The trauma associated with the Great Recession (2007–2009), the greatest economic upheaval since the Great Depression of the 1930s, has raised new questions about inequality in our society. Fifty years ago, Harrington in *The Other America: Poverty in the United States* (1962) raised our society's consciousness about the existence and persistence of poverty. In a similar way, there is an emerging consciousness today about the existence and persistence of inequality between the richest 1% and the remaining 99%. Persistent unemployment and underemployment has placed many American families in serious economic jeopardy, again raising questions about economic justice.

The attention being given to inequality in connection with the occupy Wall Street movement reminds us of how we have faced the issues of profound inequalities earlier in our history in connection with the Great Depression. For example, by reflecting back nearly seventy years ago, we can see in the 1944 State of the Union speech by President Franklin D. Roosevelt a call for a second Bill of Rights in the form of an economic bill of rights (Roosevelt, 1944):

- "The right to a useful and remunerative job in the industries, or shops, or farms or mines of the Nation;
- The right to earn enough to provide adequate food and clothing and recreation;
- The right of every farmer to raise and sell his products at a return which will give him and his family a decent living;
- The right of every businessman, larger and small, to trade in an atmosphere of freedom from unfair competition and domination by monopolies at home and abroad;
- The right of every family to a decent home;
- The right to adequate medical care and the opportunity to achieve and enjoy good health;
- The right to adequate protection from economic fears of old age, sickness, accident, and unemployment;
- The right to a good education."

While some forms of exploitation and oppression have become more visible in our society since these words were uttered (discrimination, poverty, homelessness, etc.), other forms have become less visible (economic inequalities, class privilege, homophobia, sexism, and racism). It is hoped that the dialogue stimulated by this book provides future generations with the historical and philosophical tools to promote social justice and confront social injustices at home and abroad.

Both practitioners and students need a safe space to explore their views and understanding of social justice as well as social injustice. As a core value of the profession, social justice needs to be discussed and redefined by each generation as part of a values clarification process. One way to promote such a dialogue would be to reflect on the following sayings inscribed on the recently completed memorial honoring Reverend Martin Luther King Jr. in Washington, D.C. The authors contributing to this volume hope that the following sayings provide some "trail markers" for exploring the various concepts described in this volume (sayings as cited in King, 2004).

- "Injustice anywhere is a threat to justice everywhere. We are caught in an inescapable network of mutuality, tied in a single garment of destiny. Whatever affects one directly, affects all indirectly" (from the 1963 "Letter from Birmingham Jail," p. 13).
- "Darkness cannot drive out darkness, only light can do that. Hate cannot drive out hate, only love can do that" (from the 1963 *Strength to Love*, p. 17).
- "I believe that the unarmed truth and unconditional love will have the final word in reality. This is why right, temporarily defeated, is stronger than evil triumphant. . . . I have the audacity to believe that peoples everywhere can have three meals a day for their bodies, education and culture for their minds, and dignity, equality, and freedom for their spirits" (Nobel Prize Acceptance Speech, 1964, Oslo, Norway, p. 21).
- "Make a career of humanity. Commit yourself to the noble struggle for equal rights. You will make a better person of yourself, a greater nation of your country, and a finer world to live in" (1959 March for Integrated Schools, District of Columbia, p. 19).
- "If we are to have peace on earth, our loyalties must become ecumenical rather than sectional. Our loyalties must transcend our race, our tribe, our class, and our nation; and this means we must develop a world perspective" (Christmas Sermon, 1967, Ebenezer Baptist Church, Atlanta, Georgia, p. 8).
- "Every nation must now develop an overriding loyalty to mankind as a whole in order to preserve the best in their individual societies." (April 1967, Riverside Church in New York City, p. 31).
- "We must come to see that the end we seek is a society at peace with itself, a society that can live with its conscience" (1965 March from Selma to Montgomery, Alabama, p. 26).

REFERENCES

Banerjee, M. M. (2011). Social work scholar's representation of Rawls: A critique. *Journal of Social Work Education, 47*(2), 189–211.

Bradfield, M., & Aquino, K. (1999). The effects of blame attributions and offender likableness on forgiveness and revenge in the workplace. *Journal of Management, 25,* 607–631.

Carroll, J., & Minkler, M. (2000). Freire's message for social workers: Looking back, looking ahead. *Journal of Community Practice, 8*(1), 21–36.

Folger, R. (2001). Fairness and deonance. In S. W. Gilliland, D. D. Steiner, & D. P. Skarlicki (Eds.), *Research in social issues in management* (pp. 3–31). Charlotte, NC: Information Age.

Garcia, B., & Van Soest, D. (2006). *Social work practice for social justice: Cultural competence in action.* Alexandria, VA: Council on Social Work Education.

Gerdes, K. E., & Segal, E. A. (2009). A social work model of empathy. *Advances in Social Work, 10*(2), 114–127.

Gil, D. G. (1998). *Confronting injustice and oppression: Concepts and strategies for social workers.* New York, NY: Columbia University Press.

Haidt, J. (2001). The emotional dog and its rational tail: A social intuitionist approach to moral judgment. *Psychological Review, 108,* 814–834.

Harrington, M. (1962). *The other America: Poverty in the United States.* New York, NY: Simon & Schuster.

Hong, P. Y. P., & Hodge, D. R. (2009). Understanding social justice in social work: A content analysis of course syllabi. *Families in Society: The Journal of Contemporary Social Services, 90*(2), 212–219.

Kaseman, M., & Austin, M. J. (2005). Building a faith-based human service agency: A view from the inside. *Journal of Religion and Spirituality in Social Work, 24*(3), 69–91.

Kimberlin, S. (2010). Advocacy by nonprofits: Roles and practices of core advocacy organizations and direct service agencies. *Journal of Policy Practice, 9*(3/4), 164–182.

King, M. L. (2004). *Quotations of Martin Luther King, Jr.* Bedford, MA: Applewood Books.

Longres, J. F., & Scanlon, E. (2001). Social justice and the research curriculum. *Journal of Social Work Education, 37*(3), 447–463.

Morris, P. M. (2002). The capabilities perspective: A framework for social justice. *Families in Society: The Journal of Contemporary Social Services, 83*(4), 365–373.

National Association of Social Workers (NASW). (2009). *Code of ethics of the National Association of Social Workers.* Washington, DC: National Association of Social Workers.

O'Reilly, J., & Aquino, K. (2011). A model of third parties' morally motivated responses to mistreatment in organizations. *Academy of Management Review, 36*(3), 526–563.

Reisch, M. (2002). Defining social justice in a socially unjust world. *Families in Society: The Journal of Contemporary Social Services, 83*(4), 343–354.

Reisch, M. (2011). Defining social justice in a socially unjust world. In J. Birkenmaier, A. Cruce, E. Burkemper, J. Curly, R. J. Wilson, & J. J. Stretch (Eds.), *Educating for social justice: Transformative experiential learning* (pp. 11–28). Chicago, IL: Lyceum Books.

Roosevelt, F. D. (1944). "State of the Union Message to Congress," January 11, 1944. (1999–2012). G. Peters & J. T. Woolley (Compilers), *The American Presidency Project.* Retrieved from http://www.presidency.ucsb.edu/ws/?pid=16518

Segal, E. A. (2011). Social empathy: A model built on empathy, contextual understanding, and social responsibility that promotes social justice. *Journal of Social Service Research, 37*(3), 266–277.

Segal, E. A. (2007). Social empathy: A tool to address the contradictions of working but still poor. *Families in Society: The Journal of Contemporary Social Services, 88,* 333–337.

PART I

THE HUMANITIES PERSPECTIVES

The Moral Imperative—Shouldn't We Do Something?

2

THE INFLUENCE OF WESTERN PHILOSOPHY ON DEFINITIONS OF SOCIAL JUSTICE

RICHARD J. SMITH

INTRODUCTION

The discussions about social justice in philosophy begin with the definition of justice and then pose several questions. How is justice related to being human? Do we determine what is just using agreed upon rational principles? Or do we see what decision brings out the best outcome and replicate that decision? Since social justice is related to how one views conflict between the self and the social environment, the definition of community is important. This analysis begins with an examination of how philosophical debates among Western philosophers inform the *Code of Ethics of the National Association of Social Workers (NASW)* published by the NASW (2009) in the United States. The discussion of the social justice dimensions of the code is followed by highlights of the arguments of key Western philosophers. It explains how debates about social justice have been framed in contemporary philosophy, especially the fields of ethics and political philosophy. The analysis concludes with implications for applying philosophical concepts to the social justice dimensions of the social work profession.

SOCIAL JUSTICE AND THE SOCIAL WORK CODE OF ETHICS

Social work as a profession has evolved with respect to ethics and social justice as captured by Reamer (1998) in his four stages of social work history. The first stage is the morality period that was concerned with teaching the poor and immigrants proper morals and good conduct to bring harmony to the community. The next stage, called the values period, captures the profession as it came of age in the 1940s and 1950s when social work scholars seriously delved into the question of social work as a values-based profession. By the 1970s and 1980s, the third stage emerged, what Reamer calls "ethical theory and decision making" where applied ethics were integrated into social work training programs. It is during this period that Wakefield (1988a,

1988b) argues that clinical social work, unlike psychotherapy, sought to promote social justice. He says this because he does not believe that mental health or physical health is a matter of justice. This claim will be repudiated by subsequent thinkers. The fourth stage, the maturation and risk management phase, is a reaction to increasing litigation and the culmination of the struggle for licensure. It is in this phase the NASW updated the current revision of the *Code of Ethics*. Its main motivation, according to Reamer, is to resolve ambiguities that lead to risk in practice. In particular, he highlights client confidentiality, reporting duties, dual relationships, conflict between labor and management, and increasing electronic communication. For the first time, the code articulated the following core values of social work: (a) service, (b) social justice, (c) dignity and worth of the person, (d) importance of human relationships, (e) integrity, and (f) competence.

What does the NASW *Code of Ethics* (2009) mean by "social justice"? The term *social justice* is used six times in the code. The phrase is not well defined, but it co-occurs with other words that suggest a definition. It is used three times each with the words *community*, *change,* and *oppression*. Social justice is also found twice next to the words *equity* and *opportunity*. In the first instance, *social justice* is used as follows: "Social workers promote social justice and social change with and on behalf of clients" (Preamble section). In the second instance in the preamble, it is simply presented as a core value of social work, done both with and on behalf of clients. Note the logical conjunction *and*. This suggests that the promotion of social change requires the participation of clients. It is not simply done in the interests of the social worker or social work but with and on behalf of "individuals, families, groups, organizations, and communities." Accordingly, the locus of justice in the code is embedded in the relations of different levels of society.

In the third instance, *social justice* is defined not only in terms of the level of social justice for the client but also in terms of the position of the client in a social structure. Specifically, the code says, "Social workers are sensitive to cultural and ethnic diversity and strive to end discrimination, oppression, poverty, and other forms of social injustice" (NASW, 2009, Preamble section, para. 2). In this sentence, a value on changing social structure and social stratification is made clear. If we assume that social injustice is the opposite of social justice, we can conclude that discrimination, oppression, and poverty are also instances where social justice does not occur and that their elimination leads to justice. While *discrimination* can simply mean distinguishing between differences in quality or kind, in this instance, it is reasonable to conclude that the code is referring to discrimination in the context of human rights and civil rights violations. While discrimination generally refers to an act by an individual upon one or many individuals of the same class, *oppression* is the act of the state or a class of people privileged by institutions upon a class of people who structurally do not have equivalent privileges. There may be a continuum of oppression from mass violence and incarceration at one end to vestigial oppression left over from the legacy of slavery, differences in family wealth, and any genetic inheritance.

The code's key definition of social justice also ties oppression with ethnic diversity. The code does not appear to unpack debates in the literature about some of the potential conflicts between gender equity and the right of ethnic minorities to retain practices that are not egalitarian. Another aspect of this use of *social justice* is the call for social workers "to ensure access to needed information, services, and resources; equality of opportunity; and meaningful participation in decision making for all people" (NASW, 2009, Value: Social Justice section). This fascinating sentence reflects both the avenues for pursuing social justice and the dimensions of social service practice. In essence, this sentence of the code is a recommendation for three ways to promote social justice: (a) "provide access to information, services, and resources"; (b) "promote equality of opportunity"; and (c) "meaningful participation in decision making for all people" (Value: Social Justice section).

The fourth discussion of social justice in the code regards the profession's commitment to a broader society (section 6.01). For social workers, promoting values can be done through education, organizing, and building relationships. What does it mean to promote social welfare "institutions" (e.g., prisons, psychiatric hospitals, orphanages, schools), and how do these promote social justice? It seems clear that social workers should support social welfare institutions if and only if they are socially just. If not, then the institutions should be reformed or closed.

Next, the fifth reference to social justice is under the section on social and political action. Social workers are told they "should advocate for changes in policy and legislation to improve social conditions in order to meet basic human needs and promote social justice" (NASW, 2009, section 6.04[a]). It is important to note that the code does not say "must" but rather says "should." In the same section, the code sounds multiculturalist: "Social workers should promote conditions that encourage respect for cultural and social diversity within the United States and globally" (6.04[c]). The social worker seeks to "expand choice and opportunity for all people" (6.04[b]) but in particular the oppressed and vulnerable. At this point, the code gives us some clarity on the meaning of social justice for the profession. Because some people are less equal than others, they need "special regard" for their needs.

A holistic reading of the code is required to clear up ambiguities about social justice. The discussion about the value of the dignity and worth of the human being helps provide clarity in that it says, "Social workers are cognizant of their dual responsibility to clients and to the broader society" (NASW, 2009, Value: Dignity and Worth of the Person section). Clearly, social workers serve two masters: the state and the client. Thus, social justice is not simply about representing a client's interests to the community and state but also representing the interests of the state and community to the client. Since there is emphasis on serving the vulnerable, we can conclude that more is required with and on behalf of the oppressed. Many of the ambiguities in the Code reflect change over time and are addressed in the literature (Reamer, 2006).

HISTORICAL DEFINITIONS OF JUSTICE IN PHILOSOPHY

Given the ambiguous presentation of social justice in the NASW *Code of Ethics*, it is useful to review the evolution of concepts of justice in Western philosophy. There are other philosophical traditions that explore the meaning of social justice, and they are noted elsewhere in this volume.

Early Definitions of Justice: Virtue

For the early Greeks, it was assumed that people would pursue their own self-interests, and this principle was called *eudaemonistic*. It was argued that a rational person would have aligned self-interest with those of the Gods or society. The "good" and the "virtuous" were synonymous. This means that philosophical debates about justice also depended on what one considered to be the nature of being human.

The philosopher Socrates discusses the meaning of the word *justice* in the *Euthyphro* (Plato, 1954). He asks, "Is the good good because the God says it is good or do the Gods only do what is good because they are Gods?" Since *Euthyphro* is a dialogue and Socrates poses only questions, it is subject to multiple interpretations as to what Socrates meant to say about justice. One approach is to assess the justifications of a particular law. For example, do we follow the law because an authority (e.g., God or the state) says that it is good to do, or is it good to do so on its merits?

The philosopher Plato, in *The Republic,* argues that the pursuit of justice is intrinsically good. He likens it to an athlete who trains to win a marathon. The exercises may bring temporary pain but lasting benefit and happiness when the labors are done and the race is won. Social justice, in a Platonic sense, assumes that what is good for society is also good for the rational self. In this Platonic conception of the self, the mind is like a charioteer. He rides two wild horses: body and spirit. It would be irrational to let them run free. After all, you would not get anywhere. Subsequent thinkers will question this line of thinking based on introspection and the self as an analogy to the state.

Justice as Supporting Essential Human Capabilities

The philosopher Aristotle (Plato's student) saw justice not only as focused on self-interest but also as a branch of politics. For Aristotle, justice is about virtue and the intrinsic desire to do right. He says:

"Just acts occur between people who participate in things good in themselves and can have too much or too little of them; for some beings (e.g., presumably the gods) cannot have too much of them, and to others, those who are incurably bad, not even the smallest share in them is beneficial but all such goods are harmful, while to others they are beneficial up to a point; therefore justice is essentially something Human" (Aristotle, 350 BCE). Living the good life is simple, but there are many ways to go wrong for those who are "incurably bad." Aristotle's contribution to ethics is to situate it in the definition of what is human (Nussbaum, 1992; Sen, 1982). A human has a set of essential properties, and if one is deprived of one of these, it is a violation of social justice. Nussbaum's detailed list of the essential properties of being human includes the following: life, health, experience of pain and pleasure, five senses, love, reflection on the good, enjoyment of family and friends, living with nature, play, and a unique life in a context.

Justice as an Agreed Upon Social Contract

Post-Enlightenment thinkers take justice out of the self and into relationships with others. Justice is a function of the idealized social contract between gentlemen who agree to give up some freedoms in exchange for social order. Social justice is conformity to the social contract because it is argued that without the state, we humans would descend into the state of nature, which according to the philosopher Hobbes (1968) is "brutish nasty and short." For the philosopher Locke (2004), nature is abundant, and by mixing one's labor with the fruits of nature, value is added, and property is created. This mixing of labor transforms nature into property and justifies its protection by the state. In essence, a gentleman's social contract is to obey society's laws in exchange for a good life. The philosopher Hume (2004) makes the point that in a utopia where everyone had their needs met, the concept of justice would not exist because there would be no need to protect property rights if everyone had more than they needed. While Hume and Locke focus initially on a justice concerning property rights and the distribution of social and economic resources, Scanlon in recent times has developed a theory of contractualism that argues

that an act is unethical if it violates agreed upon, reasonable standards that no one would reject (Ashford & Mulgan, 2007). Similarly, contemporary debates about sexual harassment, racial discrimination, and access to health care for the poor and disabled expand the social justice concept of social contract from property and redistribution to respect for cultural values.

Justice as a Universal Ethical Maxim

In response to the conception of the social contract based on agreements, the continental rationalists used thought experiment and reason as a foundation for identifying different kinds of ethics. For example, the philosopher Kant (2008) developed the categorical imperative: A good ethical maxim is one that a reasonable person would wish to be universal; essentially, a rational person can judge an ethical act to be "just" and want it to apply in all circumstances. This position is sometimes referred to as deontology (Nagel, 1987, 2005; Nozick, 2006; Sen, 1982). Scanlon's contractualism is also consistent with this approach to ethics, because it depends on reasonable standards that no one would reject. Those who take universalist positions on ethics often find themselves at odds with the next group, the consequentialists.

Justice as Consequences and Outcomes

In a world where people have reasonable disagreements about universal principles, some argue that it is better to observe the outcome of an ethical principle and add up or aggregate this outcome to determine if the principle was a good idea. This conversation about justice takes us back to the British philosopher Bentham (2002) and his student Mill (2009) who reject Kant's ethics of kinds in favor of an ethics of outcomes. Instead of a rational test for each maxim, one should identify the acts that bring the most happiness and then maximize the expected utility for all. This approach assumes that outcomes add up over a population. and the sum of these is more important than the ethics of any individual action. However, Bentham and Mill are careful to warn readers not to confuse utility with selfish gratification. In essence, the pursuit of happiness is not at the expense of others. Many of the deontological thinkers reject the utilitarian and other consequentialists because they believe if an act is wrong, the outcome does not change the wrongness of the act. It also should not matter how many people benefit from an unjust act.

CONTEMPORARY DEBATES IN SOCIAL JUSTICE

Ideal Distributive Justice
Versus Protecting Freedoms

Is it more important to be free or equal? Throughout the 20th century, there has been considerable debate about the role of the market and the role of the state. The most pervasive discussion of social justice can be found in the controversy between a liberal (who believes in redistribution of wealth to promote equality) and the libertarian (who believes that the right to property that is justly acquired and any transfers should be voluntary). The liberal is an egalitarian who wants to see that a philosophy of equality is reflected in the distribution of wealth with the state ensuring that equality occurs even if this means taxing one to pay another. Philosopher John Rawls is often placed in the center of this debate because in "justice as fairness" (Rawls, 1958), he develops a rationale for redistributive social justice.

For Rawls, there are three components to a just society: (a) Everyone should have a floor of basic human rights, (b) any other rights or privileges should be a function of a person's position in society (e.g., a judge or legislator has special rights and immunities because the office she holds is unrelated to birth or other unearned characteristics), and (c) any change in the rights of one person would be for the benefit of the least well-off person. The argument for this type of fairness and equity is made in his thought experiment involving a "veil of ignorance." Imagine a set of heads of households blinded to their position in society. They are given a choice to live in a society with no guarantee of equality or one with such a guarantee and differentiation based on one's status obtained by merit. Since the heads of household do not know what status in society they will inhabit, the rational heads would choose to be in one that guaranteed fairness

so that the family would not end up at the bottom of the income distribution.

Those who hold a libertarian perspective on social justice (Nozick, 2006), on the other hand, disagree with the role of redistribution by the state since relationships in society are based on voluntary contracts. So any contract voluntarily held by two persons or a group of persons under justice is just. If one agrees to give money to another person, then that can be just. But it is not just for the state to use its powers to forcibly take property and redistribute it to another person if that property were justly obtained. The libertarian perspective is easy to operationalize, since it simply involves using a minimum amount of government's regulatory and redistributive functions. However, this perspective does not directly address historical redress for oppression or what to do in the case where people have property that they themselves received under justice but the person to whom it was given did not receive the property under a "just" situation. These situations are taken up by philosophers in the next section.

Meeting Minimum Human Needs, Equal Opportunity, and Maximum Social Benefit

How do we humans reconcile the conception of justice as a set of rights that may not be violated as opposed to a set of principles that we think will ensure the best outcome for the most number of people? Barry (2005) expands upon Rawls's first criterion for a just society, namely, that everyone should have an equal floor of basic rights. In *Why Social Justice Matters*, Barry sets the tone for his work by quoting Pinter: It matters "if to be a socialist is to be a person determined to do everything in his or her power to alleviate these unforgivably degraded lives, and socialism can never be dead because these aspirations never die" (p. 1). The main purpose of this book is to justify three elements of the Social Democratic platform: (a) support for trade unions and public ownership of utilities, (b) redistribution of wealth through taxation and transfer, and (c) equal availability of high quality education and health care. He argues that the concept of equal opportunity is the best way to think about meeting basic human needs.

Those in the libertarian and utilitarian tradition, namely, Dworkin, Gauthier, and Cohen, all have different takes on where and how to divide resources in a just society (Clayton & Williams, 2004). For Dworkin, it is about taking into account risky behavior, initial wealth, and genetic inheritance in a just society. With regard to risky behavior, the state should reward entrepreneurs but not people who refuse to wear seat belts. Inheritance, both in property and DNA, needs to be taken into consideration in order to have a fair society. Gauthier, on the other hand, argues that people do not seek justice as individuals but through voluntary associations of people with similar interests. Cohen rejects redistribution of income as the primary concern of justice and is more concerned about a society that promotes equal opportunity for advantage and leisure. Cohen would argue that redistributive taxation prevents people from generating wealth that could in turn be used to help the disadvantaged. Indeed, the tax loss made others unhappy, so this act is potentially unjust.

It may be possible to find a middle ground between those who espouse a rights-based framework and those interested in outcomes. Rawls and Daniels (1979) propose that ethics involves a "wide reflective equilibrium" where people make ethical choices in collaboration with others. Ethical frameworks are seen as evolving from collaborative processes designed to reach conclusions. This pluralist conception allows for people from different backgrounds to make similar ethical conclusions but for different reasons.

Daniels (1981, 2006) uses this idea in work on health care disparities. He argues that in order to achieve justice in health care, one must work for social justice because health care disparities often arise from the relative risks associated with certain occupations, workplaces, distressed communities, and other social structures. He believes that health should be defined as absence of disease and normal functioning. If this is a clear goal, then it would be possible to have a tiered system of care that focuses on the prevention and treatment needed to bring people into healthy, capable functioning and other tiers for elective procedures. Public policy should address geographic disparities by preventing brain drain from low-income countries and within the area

targeting regional incentives for health care providers. He warns of the dangers of aggregation. For example, he notes how many countries have decided to improve their child mortality figures by focusing on those who are easy to treat. This leaves out the poorest of the poor and the sickest of the sick and in his opinion does not further justice.

Members Only or Justice for All?

In the previous section, readers saw the tension between justice for all and nearly giving people what they deserve. David Miller (1999) describes the scope of social justice and the challenge of the nation-state by arguing that national identities create common bonds that lead to claims of justice. In essence, people should get what they deserve through the supportive actions of the welfare state, and those with unjust behavior should be punished. Social justice should guide people's behavior in order to preserve equality, protect basic rights, and prevent exploitation. In other words, Miller sees justice as situated in the role of the state, citizenship, and rights. Bosniak (2000) characterizes the debate about justice for all as taking place between the "liberal nationalist" or "statist" described by Nagel and the "moral universalist" or "cosmopolitan" position described by Nussbaum and Sen. The liberal nationalist, sometimes referred to as the "civic nationalist," sees citizenship as the justification for conferring certain rights, in particular the rights of the welfare state. The moral universalist, such as Nussbaum, declares herself a "citizen of the world" and argues for a rights-based regime of international development that is without regard to citizenship. For example, the moral universalist would reject claims that the "right to work" should be limited by citizenship. This debate is central to the phenomenon of welfare retrenchment, where developed countries that experience high immigration have been electing governments that cut benefits to immigrants.

Gender Equity Versus Social Equity

After seeing how the nation-state is both a facilitator and barrier to promoting social justice, the discussion turns to the complicated role of gender. Is justice for men only? Okin (1994, 1999) criticizes Rawls when he identified the person in the original position as the head of household and implicitly men. She asks what would happen if a person imagines that in the original position no one knew what his or her gender was? How would that change the structure of society in which people make choices? She goes on to argue that much of the inequality in the household is learned at a very young age. She contrasts this with the position of the multiculturalist who argues that minority groups have a right to a culture and that to deny people the right to culture is to impose one's values on another and therefore unjust. Furthermore, according to Okin, the multiculturalist argues that to be denied the exercise of one's own culture can be damaging to one's self-esteem. Okin argues that the extinction of some cultures (e.g., polygamy, honor killings, courtship by rape, and female genital mutilation) would make the women much better off. Okin further notes that arguments about group culture ignore the intergroup differences and any divisions that exist between public and private spheres.

How do we build on Rawls ideas to ensure gender equity? Munoz-Dardé (1998) takes on Okin's argument but suggests that feminists like Okin are unfair to both Rawls and his intellectual predecessors. She argues that it is not so much that Rawls devotes so little attention to the family but rather that he should give it even less attention. For Munoz-Dardé, the original position would work quite well to address the issue of gender equity if a person (a) had an individualistic conception of the veil of ignorance where she did not know her gender as Okin requires and (b) the person assumes that no individual is particularly attached to his or her descendants. Her argument for the latter is based on an optimistic vision of a society where people are concerned for other people not just their own family. She also endorses the idea that the family is just a brute, natural fact. Humans cannot conceive of a world without a family, however, different forms of family exist. Furthermore, we can identify some forms that are more just than others. These issues of inequality in the home have critical application for justifying a child protection system, eliminating family violence, and universalizing access to education. Both Okin and Munoz-Dardé

note the potential conflict between culture and women's right to education and the implications for living in an egalitarian society. To discuss this implication further, this review of contemporary debates concludes with a return to Nussbaum's Aristotelian conception of social justice.

Cultural Preservation
Versus Developing Capabilities

The multicultural and relativist ideas of the global postcolonial period (beginning after WWII) of the late 1960s reflect a radical doctrine of noninterference by former colonial powers in developing countries and the empowerment of indigenous people. For example, even providing vaccines and hospitals were seen as oppressive because they could destroy ancient cultural practices that compensated for high infant mortality. However, developmentalists like Nussbaum (1992) and Sen (1982) disagree with some of these basic tenets of relativism and argue in favor of a universal definition of what is human and the right to develop human capabilities.

In *Sex and Social Justice*, Nussbaum (1999) outlines five elements of her feminist perspective: (a) internationalist by situating women in a global context, (b) humanist that believes that all persons have equal worth, (c) liberal in that feudalism is rejected, (d) a recognition of how the social shapes our desires and preferences, and (e) the intrinsic value of women's sympathy. She advocates for ensuring human capabilities in international development. Nussbaum and Sen note that a socially just society constructs policies to maximize the capabilities of its people. In this sense, they are welfare universalists where membership should not matter in the context of justice. Neither should gender (man, woman, and child are human). This view captures the equal opportunity of Barry but in a global context. To complement Rawls, the mere income redistribution would not be enough if the deliberate efforts to develop the human ability to use broadly defined assets were not present. Furthermore, the just society needs to have strong institutions to guarantee the development of these human capacities.

However, Habermas (2005) expresses skepticism that it is even possible to prevent the globalization of traditional societies in a postmodern world. A modern, liberal egalitarian society simultaneously wants to protect freedom of cultural expression and freedom of self-expression. Since these two values clash and create certain problems for the state, it leaves traditional institutions, such as the Catholic Church, as an important force for global human development and social justice.

DISCUSSION AND CONCLUSION

In conclusion, balancing the competing values of the individual and the community are not easily reconciled. Does the NASW *Code of Ethics* promote social justice in the sense of a libertarian view of equal opportunity or a social democratic view to ensure basic human needs? While it promotes basic human needs by calling for an end to poverty (i.e., the deprivation of human need), it also seeks to balance the rights of the client with his obligations to the community. The code is also an exhortation to promote institutions with a set of values compatible with a vision of welfare and development. In a similar way, the use

of evidence-based practices sounds like a form of outcome-oriented consequentialism but seems based more on universalist intuitions about individuals than any attempt to aggregate what is best in society.

In Figure 2.1, the contemporary debates on social justice have been arranged along two axes. The first column contains those that see ethics as universal, rational, and necessary. The second column contains ethics that are goal and outcome oriented. Moving onto the first row are those concerned with the ethics of individual or small group actions. The state is a necessary evil that provides only a basic floor of rights and opportunities through institutions. The bottom row includes those more concerned with ethics in the aggregate. Rights and ethics come from the state, family, or culture, and members need to take reciprocal obligation to each other to guarantee these rights. Social justice as a concept hovers in the center as an ambiguous concept among radically different alternatives. As in many maps, these are not to scale, and there are many overlaps. For example, feminist philosophers may occupy different sections. For example, Nussbaum and Okin are developmentalists, but Munoz-Dardé is more of a contractionalist.

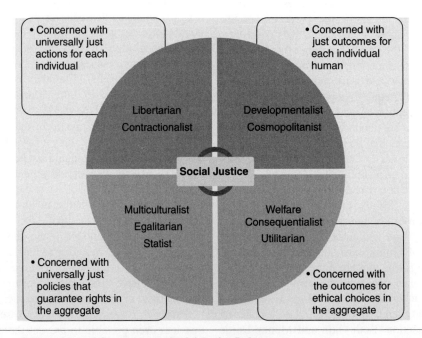

Figure 2.1   Concept Map of Contemporary Social Justice Debates

Multiculturalists are not exactly egalitarian, except to say they believe that cultural groups, but not necessarily members within the culture, have equal rights. Nussbaum arguably thinks that they are irrational, but I place them in the rationalist column because the multiculturalists are concerned with cultural preservation and not with considerations of members' well-being. Sen and Nussbaum, as cosmopolitan developmentalists, would object to my saying that they are not concerned with aggregate rights. After all, they think globally. However, I place them with libertarians and contractionalists because they begin with the definition of what it means to be human—a human individual.

How does this bring us back to virtue and the human soul? Using Plato's vision of a tripartite soul symbolized as a charioteer riding three beasts (the mind, the spirit, and the body), the NASW code for social workers serves as a vehicle to become part of the mind in its efforts to navigate between the self and the global society. Second, the social worker becomes part of the spirit that raises consciousness from daily human interaction with the most vulnerable in society. And finally, the social worker serves the body in relationship to the continuing needs for physical resources that range from food stamps to an earned income tax credit. A community of social justice, like any support group, provides social support and organization to rebuild ineffective institutions. Social workers in the 21st century cannot afford to be too introspective. The essence of the profession is social, and the whole concept of the self and human consciousness has acknowledged the social component of the self. Social justice then is always a negotiation of interests in order to make decisions about equity that increases fairness for a greater number of people.

REFERENCES

Aristotle. (350 BCE). Nicomachean ethics (W. D. Ross, Trans.). *The Internet classics archive.* Retrieved August 29, 2009, from http://classics.mit.edu/Aristotle/nicomachaen.html

Ashford, E., & Mulgan, T. (2007). Contractualism. Retrieved December 15, 2009, from http://plato.stanford.edu/entries/contractualism/

Barry, B. (2005). *Why social justice matters.* Cambridge, MA: Polity.

Bentham, J. (2002). Of the principle of utility. In *Introduction to the principles of morals and legislation.* Retrieved from http://www.laits.utexas.edu/poltheory/bentham/ipml/ipml.c01.html

Bosniak, L. S. (2000). Citizenship denationalized. *Indiana Journal of Global Law Studies, 7,* 447–509. Retrieved from http://papers.ssrn.com/sol3/papers.cfm?abstract_id=232082

Clayton, M., & Williams, A. (2004). Social justice. Oxford, UK: Wiley-Blackwell.

Daniels, N. (1979). Wide reflective equilibrium and theory acceptance in ethics. *Journal of Philosophy, 76*(5), 256–282.

Daniels, N. (1981). Health-care needs and distributive justice. *Philosophy and Public Affairs, 10*(2), 146–179.

Daniels, N. (2006). Equity and population health: Toward a broader bioethics agenda. *Hastings Center Report, 36*(4), 22–35.

Habermas, J. (2005). Equal treatment of cultures and the limits of postmodern liberalism (J. Flynn, Trans.). *Journal of Political Philosophy, 13*(1), 1–28.

Hobbes, T. (1968). *Leviathan.* Oxford, UK: Penguin Books.

Hume, D. (2004). Of justice. In M. Clayton & A. Williams (Eds.), *Social justice* (pp. 21–31). Oxford, UK: Wiley-Blackwell.

Kant, I. (2008). The moral law. In L. P. Pojman & L. Vaughn (Eds.), *Philosophy: The quest for truth* (7th ed.). New York, NY: Oxford University Press.

Locke, J. (2004). Of property. In M. Clayton & A. Williams (Eds.), *Social justice* (pp. 32–46). Oxford, UK: Wiley-Blackwell.

Mill, J. S. (2009). *Utilitarianism.* Retrieved August 31, 2009, from http://ebooks.adelaide.edu.au/m/mill/john_stuart/m645u/index.html

Miller, D. (1999). *Principles of social justice.* Cambridge, MA: Harvard University Press.

Munoz-Dardé, V. (1998). Rawls, justice in the family and justice of the family. *Philosophical Quarterly, 48*(192), 335–352.

Nagel, T. (1987). Moral conflict and political legitimacy. *Philosophy and Public Affairs, 16*(3), 215–240.

Nagel, T. (2005). The problem of global justice. *Philosophy & Public Affairs, 33*(2), 113–147.

National Association of Social Workers (NASW). (2009). *Code of ethics of the National Association of Social Workers.* Retrieved August 31, 2009, from http://www.socialworkers.org/pubs/code/default.asp

Nozick, R. (2006). Distributive justice. *Contemporary political philosophy: An anthology.*

Nussbaum, M. C. (1992). Human functioning and social justice: In defense of Aristotelian essentialism. *Political Theory*, *20*(2), 202–246.

Nussbaum, M. C. (1999). *Sex and social justice*. New York, NY: Oxford University Press.

Okin, S. M. (1994). Political liberalism, justice, and gender. *Ethics*, *105*(1), 23–43.

Okin, S. M. (1999). Is multiculturalism bad for women? *Boston Review*. Retrieved August 25, 2009, from http://www.bostonreview.net/BR22.5/okin.html

Plato. (1954). *Last days of Socrates*. Oxford, UK: Penguin Books.

Rawls, J. (1958). Justice as fairness. *Philosophical Review*, *67*(2), 164–194. doi:10.2307/2182612

Reamer, F. G. (1998). The evolution of social work ethics. *Social Work*, *43*(6), 488–500.

Reamer, F. G. (2006). *Social work values and ethics*. New York, NY: Columbia University Press.

Sen, A. (1982). Rights and agency. *Philosophy and Public Affairs*, *11*(1), 3–39.

Wakefield, J. C. (1988a). Psychotherapy, distributive justice, and social work: Part 1: Distributive justice as a conceptual framework for social work. *Social Service Review*, *62*(2), 187–210.

Wakefield, J. C. (1988b). Psychotherapy, distributive justice, and social work: Part 2: Psychotherapy and the pursuit of justice. *Social Service Review*, *62*(3), 353–382.

3

LEGAL THEORIES OF SOCIAL JUSTICE

JENNIFER PRICE WOLF

INTRODUCTION

The profession of social work is committed to the idea of social justice. The social work code of ethics encourages social workers to "promote social justice" (National Association of Social Workers [NASW], 2009) while social work schools are mandated to include social justice content in the curricula (Longres & Scanlon, 2001). Despite these dictums, social work professors at a major university were "at a loss" when asked to define the term for a study on the infusion of social justice in research courses (Longres & Scanlon, 2001, p. 453). As the study notes, "It was clear that most had not spent time reading and thinking about the concept" (p. 453). Social work faculty and students might accept that social justice is a positive goal without thinking closely about the concept, as it is usually attached to political messages that emphasize equal human rights and the fight against oppression (Sadurski, 1985). The lack of critical engagement by advocates of social justice was criticized by Hayek, who argued that they "do not know themselves what they mean by it and just use it as an assertion that a claim is justified without giving a reason for it," making the term "entirely empty and meaningless" (Hayek, 1976, p. xi). If social work academics have not spent time understanding theories of social justice, how can we expect their social work students

to promote social justice with a clear understanding of what it is?

Since there is no uniform conception of social justice or uniform sense of what is just, it is important to investigate competing theories of social justice. As we associate the law with justice, legal theories provide a rich source of ideas for examining social justice. Governments use the law to allocate resources in society, a process that can have clear winners and losers depending on how the laws are drafted (Dworkin, 2000). The force of the law is a powerful way of maintaining social control (Posner, 1997), just as it can be an effective tool for radical social change. Social workers are often involved with the legal system, acting as advocates for both victims and the accused. Social workers also actively lobby legislatures to enact laws or policy changes. As a result, it is important for social workers to understand what lawyers and judges mean when they discuss conceptions of justice.

Clear definitions are required to fully understand the legal theories of social justice. While some legal terms are familiar to many audiences, others often have a more specific meaning than their use in common conversation. *Black's Law Dictionary* (2009) defines justice as, "The fair and proper administration of laws" (Garner, 2009, p. 942). *Fairly* does not necessarily mean equally, only that individuals are treated rightly under the circumstances. There can be several fair outcomes to every decision, as fairness is a subjective concept and likely varies among judges. *Distributive justice* is concerned with how goods are distributed in society (Lamont and Favor, 2008); it acknowledges that access to goods and benefits in society is determined through governmental and societal policies. Distributive justice is concerned with whether these goods and benefits are distributed fairly; what defines *fair* is a contentious issue.

Similarly, contentious is the definition of *social justice*, as Sadurski writes, "A person formulating statements about justice rarely stands at a distance from his pronouncements to be able to say 'it is just, yet I do not like it'" (Sadurski, 1985, p. 11). *Social* implies a focus on society, thus, social justice is what is just for social groups versus an individual (Capeheart & Milovanovic, 2007). To Rawls, social justice is "a standard whereby the distributive aspects of the basic structure of society are to be assessed" (Rawls, 1972, p. 9). Sadurski argues similarly that "legal justice is about conforming to the rules *whatever they may be* (original emphasis), [whereas] social justice is about the distributive qualities of those rules" (Sadurski, 1985, p. 36). This paper builds upon the conception of social justice as a way to the "just" distribution of goods, services, and societal opportunities in order to examine theories from a variety of traditions.

Legal theories often borrow from other disciplines (e.g., philosophy, economics, and political science) and therefore reflect an interdisciplinary perspective. In addition, the role of legal theory in everyday adjudication is controversial. Theories are usually not cited in legal rulings because the law is a precedent-based system. Judges decide cases based on previous rulings, with lawyers trying to persuade judges to decide in their favor because precedent mandates such an outcome. This has led some scholars to challenge the validity of moral theories and theorists themselves, arguing that they are not "seers, prophets, saints, or even rebels" (Posner, 1998, p. 1687). Others have defended the role of theory in the law, noting that laws are embedded in a philosophical context. Dworkin argues, "You cannot think about the correct answer to questions of law unless you have thought through . . . a vast overarching theoretical system of complex principles"

(Dworkin, 1997, p. 354). This analysis takes a similar position, arguing that theories of social justice are not only influential in cases where the law is unclear and judges have to interpret untested statutes but also crucial to how laws are conceptualized, written, and enacted.

This analysis is designed as an introduction to several prominent legal theories of social justice. It focuses on relatively contemporary theories of the American and Anglo-American legal traditions. The analysis also examines issues of distributive justice instead of retributive justice (which examines whether punishments are fair). Although one could make the case that retributive justice is an element of social justice, especially in the case of individuals who are unfairly targeted by the law because of their social status, this analysis emphasizes the distributive elements of social justice.

This analysis begins with an examination of the theory of justice as fairness that focuses on universal rights and minimal inequalities. It then discusses the theory of complex equality, which argues for locally administered justice and resource distribution. The discussion continues with two theories that seek to bridge some of the differences between equalitarian and market-based theories, also known as "third way" theories that address equality of resources and asset-based equalitarianism (Dworkin, 2000, p. 7). The review of theories concludes with the wealth maximizing theory of justice and critical legal studies. A legal case, *Serrano v. Priest* (1971) related to equitable wealth distribution and public schools, is used to illustrate the application of the theories to the legal issues. The analysis concludes with a discussion of how these legal theories of social justice inform practice.

LEGAL THEORIES OF SOCIAL JUSTICE

Justice as fairness theory

Some theories of social justice are based upon the concept of equality, with theorists arguing that the more evenly that social resources and rights are divided, the more just the result. Most of these theories do not call for an absolutely equal division of social goods (Lamont & Favor, 2008). Instead these theories have adapted the idea of egalitarianism by prioritizing which resources should be evenly distributed and allowing for some inequalities. The justice as fairness theory, developed by John Rawls (Rawls, 2001), includes two main principles:

> First: Each person has the same indefeasible claim to a fully adequate scheme of equal basic liberties, which scheme is compatible with the same scheme of liberties for all; and

> Second: Social and economic inequalities are to satisfy two conditions: (a) they are to be attached to positions and offices open to all under conditions of fair equality of opportunity; and (b), they are to be to the greatest benefit of the least advantaged members of society. (p. 43)

In contrast to strict egalitarianism, justice as fairness focuses on actual versus comparative wealth (e.g., how well the least privileged members of society are doing rather than how well they are doing in comparison to the most privileged members of society). Inequalities can exist as long as there is a basic foundation of rights and goods for all citizens, although this foundation becomes more difficult to maintain as inequalities widen. The sanctioned inequalities are not designed to create a more advantaged social class; they only come from certain roles or offices that are accessible by all and designed to serve the disadvantaged.

The foremost element of the justice as fairness theory is that all people have access to a basic array of rights. Rawls (1972) uses a hypothetical exercise, called the veil of ignorance, to explore these rights. For example, imagine if members of a society were blindfolded and were not sure whether or not they had special rights or privileges. These members would then be asked to decide which rights should be available to all. Rawls argues that most people would choose a generous basic platform of rights in order to ensure themselves the most comfortable existence. He contends that the veil of ignorance is necessary to determine which rights and goods should be part of the basic platform, as without the veil, "cumulative social, historical, and natural tendencies" would give some individuals or groups an advantage (Rawls, 1985, n.p.). The veil of ignorance also assumes that individuals are "rational and mutually disinterested" (Rawls, 1972, p. 13). Rawls

argues that this self-interest will benefit society by enhancing the bundle of universal goods.

Is there an example of the justice as fairness theory in American government? The idea that all citizens should have fundamental rights is illustrated in the Bill of Rights in the Constitution of the United States, which sets aside 10 articles to protect individual rights, including the right to freedom of speech, religion, due process, and protection against unreasonable searches and seizures (United States of America, 1789). While the Bills of Rights might appear to be similar in concept to the first principle of the justice as fairness theory, it falls short of Rawls's ideals. When it first became part of the Constitution (1791), these rights were not extended to slaves, Native Americans, and women in theory or practice. In addition, the Bill of Rights was written by mostly highly advantaged men who were aware of their status (Zinn, 2003). As a result, proponents of the justice as fairness theory would likely argue the Bill of Rights is not as generous as it would be under the veil of ignorance. The Bill of Rights also does not address the theory's second principle, which demands that inequalities are allowed only for better serving the disadvantaged. Although some have argued that the justice as fairness theory is U.S.-centric (Posner, 1998), the Bills of Rights does not meet the principle requirements of fairness and would not be considered just.

As the ideas of the justice as fairness theory have gained attention, they have been met with substantial critique. Some have argued that the theory does not take into account the inherent disadvantages of some people (e.g., disabled) that would not be advantaged by the basic platform of rights (Lamont & Favor, 2008). They contend that the theory needs to correct for these natural disadvantages in order to truly provide a minimum standard of liberty. Others have taken issue with Rawls's portrayal of individuals under the veil of ignorance as primarily self-interested (Walzer, 1983). Those who believe it is our moral duty to place the needs of others above ourselves will find his ideas lacking a spirit of altruism and compassion. An additional critique is that no one set of basic rights and goods could be agreed upon in all contexts and across all time periods. Walzer (1983) argues that the veil of ignorance is "conceived in terms so abstract" that it loses all meaning (p. 8) and fails to consider cultural differences in lived experience and symbolic meaning that would make ultimate consensus impossible.

Other critics have questioned whether justice as fairness adequately addresses the role of personal responsibility in wealth acquisition and distribution (Posner, 1998). What about the role of ability? Some individuals have more ability and ambition than others. If they are able to accrue additional resources, should these be taken away from them in the name of equality? The political philosopher Robert Nozick (1974) argues that "no moral balancing act can take place among us; there is no moral outweighing of one of our lives by others so as to lead to a greater overall *social* good. There is no justified sacrifice of some of us for others" (p. 33). Nozick feels that the rights of individuals are paramount, and that the principles of justice as fairness require unwarranted interference in individuals' lives and actions. Like Walzer, Nozick also criticizes the theory's concept of social goods. He argues that social goods have a context and provenance and are not sitting in an empty room waiting to be distributed. In order for the state to distribute them, they need to be unjustly taken away from those who produced them. Dworkin (2000) shares similar concerns about the justice as fairness theory. He argues that while a large majority of the population might have abundant resources and rights, if a small group is disadvantaged, the theory would argue that the society is unjust. The theory also fails to consider why the small group is disadvantaged. If they have fewer resources because they are unwilling to work, Dworkin suggests that it is immoral to redefine society so that they will be wealthier. Dworkin argues that there is a fundamental contradiction in the justice as fairness theory, as it argues that "equality is in principle a matter of individual right" yet defines justice through group position (2000, p. 114).

These critiques notwithstanding, the justice as fairness theory is one of the most well-known political philosophies of the last 50 years. Advocates argue that the theory balances the oft-competing principles of equality and liberty by ensuring that all citizens are granted a basic platform of rights and resources, and, limiting inequalities to those that work specifically for the disadvantaged. The fact remains, however, that the theory is highly abstract.

As the veil of ignorance is a hypothetical exercise, it is unclear how the basic platform of rights could be determined in a real-life situation. Although Rawls has provided some ideas (Rawls, 2001), they have not been realized.

Theory of Complex Equality

The theory of complex equality differs from the hypothetical scenarios of the justice as fairness theory. In his book *Spheres of Justice* (1983), Walzer introduces and argues for many coexisting and locally understood concepts of justice. The theory makes no argument for one particular type of justice as superior to another. Instead, he asserts that a society is "just" when "its substantitive life is lived in a certain way—that is, in a way faithful to the shared understandings of the members" (p. 313). As long as the members of society agree with the social framework, there is social justice. He does argue that each society must have methods for resolving disputes if disagreement arises, especially if a minority is under the tyranny of a majority. These methods should allow for free expression and the redistribution of resources. The theorist also argues for localized inequalities as a way to prevent the tyranny of the majority. Walzer writes,

> Complex equality means that no citizen's standing in one sphere or with regard to one social good can be undercut by his standing in some other sphere, with regard to some other good. Thus, citizen X may be chosen over citizen Y for political office, and then the two of them will be unequal in the sphere of politics. But they will not be unequal generally so long as X's office gives him no advantage over Y in any other sphere—superior medical care, access to better schools for his children, entrepreneurial opportunities, and so on. (Walzer, 1983, p. 19)

From this perspective, complex equality allows for many inequalities, as long as those inequalities do not result in permanent structural differences. The separation of spheres seeks to ensure that an advantage in one sphere does not result in an advantage in another.

Another element of the theory of complex equality focuses on the distribution of social goods. Walzer notes that most philosophers of justice have assumed that there is only one way to distribute goods, namely, a rational and impartially chosen system. He suggests that, instead of devising hypothetical systems, we should turn our attention to the one that already exists, a social system where individuals are part of groups based upon culture, identity, and status. These cultural groups, in turn, imbue social goods with specific meaning. Since goods have different meanings for different people, distribution schemes cannot be completely egalitarian. Consider the case of hats (Walzer, 1983). Hats might seem like a practical basic good, especially in very cold and very sunny climates, but not all societies have hats. In others, headwear is laden with symbolic meaning, as the covering or uncovering of the head can demonstrate religious devotion, a gesture of respect or of disrespect. As a result, different societies would call for different hat distributions. Those with a strictly practical need for hats would likely be satisfied with one a piece, while those who use them to convey social meaning would likely require more. Consequently, simple equality would inadequately represent the unique needs of local societies.

The theory of complex equality argues for a pluralistic, common sense approach to justice. It stresses the individuality of communities, as well as the importance of cultural difference. Critics have argued, however, that the relativism of the theory is morally unacceptable (Mapel, 1989). Can all societies be considered just as long as their members agree? Some have argued that the theory of complex equality is "dangerous" as it does not "firmly establish individual rights *against* the community" (Mapel, 1989, p. 129). Without defined rights, individuals who have different needs from the rest of their community will have no recourse to ensure that their requirements are met. Walzer's goal of stepping away from hypothetical scenarios may also have worked too well, as the theory of complex equality has been criticized as too specific to local environments and lacks the moral compass needed in a theory of social justice. Other problematic issues also remain such as how the separation of spheres should be enforced and whether there can be too much advantage in one particular sphere. Unfortunately, Walzer's theory cannot definitively answer these questions, as it ultimately argues for context-specific remedies to justice dilemmas. By arguing that "it depends," the theory of complex equality remains as equally abstract as the justice as fairness theory.

Equality of Resources Theory

The equality of resources theory, like the justice as fairness theory, attempts to provide a universal concept of social justice. This does not mean that it defines an ideal distribution of resources, but rather, the theory "probably . . . accepts . . . a variety of distributions" (Dworkin, 2000, p. 108). Instead, the theory discusses the qualities of what a fair distribution would look like as well as how the distribution could hypothetically be determined. In constructing the equality of resources theory, the legal philosopher Ronald Dworkin offers two principles:

> The first is the *principle of equal importance*: it is important, from an objective point of view, that human lives be successful rather than wasted, and this is equally important, from that objective point of view, for each human life. The second is the *principle of special responsibility*: though we must all recognize the equal objective importance of the success of a human life, one person has a special and final responsibility for that success—the person whose life it is. (Dworkin, 2000, p. 5)

As in the justice as fairness theory, every human is equally important to all others. Thus, the theory advocates for equal access to all resources and opportunities. Inequalities are allowed in this scheme, but it is only when they are the result of differences in action and effort. Dworkin argues that his theory is consequently more "ambition-sensitive" than the justice as fairness theory because a person's life is dependent upon her or his own desire for success. In addition, the theory is "endowment insensitive" because any inequalities are due to ambition and not to inheritance or undeserving social position. Yet how would resources be distributed? What about differences between people that are not under their control such as differences in genetic makeup or innate ability? To address these concerns, Dworkin introduces the ideas of the hypothetical auction and insurance market.

The role of the hypothetical auction is to fairly distribute resources throughout society. It would begin in a society where talents and wealth are equal and all have access to an open auction of social resources. Dworkin argues that those participating would determine the value of resources, and since all had the same access, there would be no envy of other people's winnings. Success or failure would then depend on each individual's goals and ambitions. The hypothetical auction is based on the principle that inequalities are a result of personal ambition. The real world, however, contains many more inequalities, including ability. To correct this situation, Dworkin discusses a hypothetical insurance market. In this market, individuals would not know how much income their skills would earn in the workforce. For example, someone with a unique talent for calculations would not know whether or not this skill was lucrative. Each individual would then be offered an insurance policy to cover "against failing to have the skills that will produce whatever income they name" (Dworkin, 2000, p. 42). The theory argues that the amount that a person would have paid in premiums to insure against not having the skills to earn his or her desired income can be taxed and redistributed. He argues that this will ensure the eradication of differences based on ability and luck, leaving only inequalities resulting from differing work ethics.

Dworkin argues that the equality of resources theory is a bridge between strict equalitarian and market-based theories of justice. The theory emphasizes both equality and inequality: equality through equal access to opportunities and inequality due to personal effort, or "deserved" qualities. It calls for some redistribution, but it is also argued that people should be allowed to build a greater stake for themselves if they desire. With all the attention paid to the ambitious, however, it is easy to forget about others such as the lazy. In the equality of resources theory, the lazy are not guaranteed a basic platform of rights and goods as is the case in the justice as fairness theory. Instead they freely choose whether to take advantage of open access to opportunities and resources. Dworkin argues that it is the job of government to make citizens aware of "the choices they have made" (2000, p. 6). Consequently, the equality of resources theory does not advocate redistributing resources to individuals who have not pursued opportunities and resources.

Even though Dworkin has criticized the justice as fairness theory by arguing that hypothetical contracts are, by definition, hypothetical (Dworkin, 1999) his own theory has been criticized for having little utility for understanding real social environments (Mapel, 1989). Conversely, others have suggested that while the theory claims to include a universal metric of social justice, it is exclusively based on Anglo-American society (Posner, 1998). Given these critiques, it remains to be seen whether Dworkin's theoretical bridge between egalitarians and market libertarians can carry much weight.

Asset-Based Egalitarianism

Like the equality of resources theory, asset-based egalitarianism theories call for both limited wealth redistribution and individual responsibility. Unlike the equality of resources theory, asset-based egalitarians have specific plans for how wealth should be redistributed (Paine, 1797). One recent example of asset-based egalitarianism is the stakeholder society proposal that has been introduced by the legal scholars Ackerman and Alstott (1999). This proposal builds upon Ackerman's (1980) earlier abstract theoretical work by presenting a specific plan for wealth redistribution in the United States. The stakeholder society theorists propose that every citizen should be given a substantial grant (they propose $80,000) when they reach adulthood. Individuals would then be free to use this money however they wished (to fund education, business proposals, or leisure). Whether or not individuals maintained the wealth would be dependent on their own actions. Ackerman and Alstott (1999) argue that every recipient of the fund would become an active "stakeholder" in society. Nobody would be highly disadvantaged due to the circumstances in which they were raised, and everyone would have an initial opportunity to succeed. The fund would be paid for initially by taxes on the very wealthy then by a tax on the estates of those who received the "stake." Ackerman and Alstott contend that this redistribution of resources would lessen inequalities in society without stifling individuals with unique goals or talents.

The stakeholder proposal is meant to redress some of the limitations of other contemporary theories of social justice. The authors argue that the justice as fairness theory does not address the fundamental discord between individual liberty and social justice. They are particularly concerned about the second principle of the theory, namely, that all those with special privileges must work exclusively for the disadvantaged. How can we say that all of someone's efforts must benefit someone else? For the stakeholder society proposal, this is an unacceptable infringement of individual liberty, because "property is so important to the free development of individual personality that everybody ought to have some" (Ackerman and Alstott, 1999, p. 191). At the same time, Ackerman and Alstott note that market-driven theories cannot be defended morally, as some individuals will never have enough wealth to truly compete due to circumstances beyond their control. Consequently, their solution is a hybrid approach that aims to put in effect a practical plan for social justice.

While the stakeholder society proposal is not abstract, it does raise some questions. For example, what about those who squander their stake? The proposal argues that this will be unusual and decrease with time, as people begin to see the benefit of investing their stake in education or business. Ackerman and Alstott also contend that even if people remain in poverty, the fact that they had a chance to increase their wealth makes their poverty more morally acceptable than if they had never had the opportunity. It seems possible, however, that those who come from highly disadvantaged backgrounds would be more likely to miss the opportunity to become a stakeholder because of their limited access to social capital resources that could guide them on how to maximize their stake. Finally, what of those who lose their stake due to bad luck? The authors suggest minimal welfare state involvement as a backup in these situations, but the nature of this involvement is unclear. While Ackerman and Alstott's proposal has not been realized, there are several social policies based on asset-based egalitarianism (e.g., Individual Development Accounts [Sherraden, 1991] and the United Kingdom's Child Trust Fund [Child trust funds, 2009]).

Wealth Maximization Theory

Although all of the theories described so far are based on some measure of state-engineered equality, the wealth maximization theory is a market-driven theory that argues for the distribution of wealth without government involvement. Hayek (1976) argued that the most important role of government is *not* to provide goods but to provide circumstances where each person will have the opportunity to meet their own private desires. As each individual has their own particular interests, governments cannot fulfill every need. Instead, states should provide a free market and leave individuals unencumbered by excessive laws, regulations, and redistributions. Hayek acknowledged that some people will always fail but contends that failure teaches individuals what to do differently and is a necessary learning process. Hayek believed that social justice does not require special attention to the particular needs of minority groups. He wrote, "In many instances the satisfaction of collective interests of certain groups may be decidedly contrary to the general interests of society" (p. 6). The wealth maximization theory uses these ideas to value individual liberty over social equality.

The ideas of wealth maximization have been expanded in legal scholarship. The jurist and legal scholar Posner (1997) argues that social policies meant to address income inequalities create less incentive for business and result in economic stagnation. Posner contends, "poverty and inequality may be negatively correlated" (p. 350). In order to promote social justice, a society should provide a free market with business-friendly policies that maximize wealth. The wealth maximization theorists are less concerned with *who* has the wealth in society than by *the amount* of wealth created. Posner argues that there is more political stability in countries with a higher median income than a higher average income. Consequently, wealth, rather than social equality, is the deciding factor in political stability. Posner suggests that more egalitarian societies also have more envy, as people envy those that they can relate to (e.g., the social position of a neighbor with a slightly nicer house seems more achievable than that of a billionaire with a fleet of private jets). He argues that increased envy is one example of how those in more egalitarian societies are not necessarily happier than those in less egalitarian societies.

Many scholars have felt that the wealth maximization theory provides an unsatisfying view of social justice (Dworkin, 2000; Walzer, 1983). They ask, what about those who do not have the ability to succeed in the free market due to no fault of their own? Posner (1997) unapologetically argues that people are naturally divided into different earning classes based on attributes of character and intelligence. Some people are consequently destined to earn less than others, although promotion of free enterprise and protection of property rights would result in higher average incomes and more opportunities for all. While some critics have argued that the wealth maximization theory is immoral, Posner (1998) argues that there is no real universal moral code. Similar to the theory of complex equality, Posner contends that morality is local. Moreover, he asserts that moral theories are of little use to lawyers and judges, and most legal decisions are not based on overarching moral theory. He suggests that even legal cases that are upheld by reformers as triumphs of social justice (e.g., *Brown v. Board of Education,* 1954, which ended racial segregation of public schools in the South) are based more on practical analysis of prior rulings than moral beliefs.

The wealth maximization theory is markedly different from the other theories described in this review because it argues that only a free market and unobtrusive government are necessary for social justice to exist. To critics that argue that the wealth maximization theory does not provide for equality, its proponents would answer, so what? Equality is not the goal; wealth maximization is the goal of able individuals. However, can a society that does not provide welfare support for its members survive? Even Posner (1997) has admitted that without any redistributive policies (e.g., progressive taxes), extreme social inequality might cause political instability. The idea of a purely market-driven meritocracy also appears to be a myth, as wealth and privileges in capitalist societies are passed from generation to generation. The wealth maximization theory, unlike the stakeholder society proposal, does not attempt to correct for inborn privilege and leaves the fate of

children up to that of their parents rather than their own skills and abilities.

Critical Legal Studies

Critical legal studies emerged in the early 1970s as a critique of legal practice, adjudication, and scholarship "concerned with the relationship of legal scholarship and practice to the struggle to create a more humane, equalitarian, and democratic society" (Kennedy & Klare, 1984, p. 461). Kennedy and Gabel (1984) argue against formulating a theory of critical legal studies because (a) philosophical theories try to essentialize experience, losing meaning in the process, and (b) critical legal scholars cannot follow the rules of legal academia because this would imply acceptance of the framework that they hope to transform.

If not truly a theory, how might critical legal studies be helpful in understanding legal theories of social justice? The critical legal studies movement argues that "just" legal practice consists of doing things that "evoke successful moments of struggle" (Kennedy & Gabel, 1984, p. 3). For example, critical analysis is used to question the legitimacy of social institutions and rethink government structures. The critical legal studies movement might suggest that (a) all the theories in this review are a product of their historical context and representative of the system they critique, and (b) these theories are consequently not universal moral theories but rather products of their time and an oppressive legal system (Kennedy & Gabel, 1984). Although the critical legal studies lens is useful in understanding how theories evolve and relate to the political status quo, the lack of a specific direction and purpose to promote social justice makes it difficult to support. If social justice is not defined, there is a danger it will not be rigorously analyzed. While the critical legal studies movement provides ways to deconstruct other theories, its own goals remain atheoretical and open to multiple interpretations.

From Theory to Practice and Back Again

Most of the theories discussed in this review call for the redistribution of wealth and resources in society. Except for the wealth maximization theory, they all argue for some level of social equality. How might these theories be applied to a legal case involving resource distribution? A California Supreme Court case, *Serrano v. Priest* (1971), demonstrates how the use of different legal theories could lead jurists to reach different rulings.

In 1971, education financing in California varied widely by school district. While the state granted each school district basic aid, districts received additional funding through locally determined property taxes. As a result, districts in which residents voted for higher property taxes or had a wealthier population could allocate more money for local schools. In districts where property values were lower, more students were living in poverty and low-income households. Citing the disparity between school resources, a class action suit composed of public school children and their parents from Los Angeles County was filed against the state's Office of the Superintendent of Instruction. The plaintiffs alleged that education was a federally mandated right that guaranteed all students equal access to quality education. The state countered that it should be up to local districts to fund local services and that by providing basic aid they were ensuring that minimum standards were met.

The theories discussed in this review would suggest several different interpretations of *Serrano v. Priest*. The justice as fairness theory would likely side with the plaintiffs, the lawyers arguing that the California educational system did not meet the standards of social justice. Although each district received basic aid, this level was determined to be unacceptable to the plaintiffs in the case. If most citizens did not consider the level of aid generous, it presumably would not be as much as would have been determined under the veil of ignorance. As a result, the first principle of the justice as fairness theory would not apply. In addition, the inequalities in this case were not for the express purpose of serving the disadvantaged, invalidating the second principle of the theory.

The application of other theories would likely lead to similar conclusions. Although the equality of resources theory does not outlaw inequities, it argues that they should result from personal ambition, not individual endowment. As the quality of the schools was determined by the wealth of the parents, the children did not have equal access to opportunities, suggesting that the local funding policy was unjust. Critical legal studies would also probably find for the plaintiffs, as the movement aims to fight structural systems that oppress the disadvantaged. Since the differences in school funding led to fewer school resources for poorer students, these differences could be seen as a way of preventing them from fair competition in society. This could lead to the transmission of poverty from generation to generation, a reality that is antithetical to the critical legal studies movement.

Although the theories related to justice as fairness, equality of resources, and critical legal studies would likely find for the plaintiffs in *Serrano v. Priest*, the wealth maximization theory would lead jurists to side with the defense because the differences in school funding would not be seen as socially unjust. The theory argues that individual liberty is paramount; namely, the freedom of wealthy individuals paying increased property taxes to improve their local schools should be protected above any social desire to make public schools equitable.

It is less clear how the theories related to complex equality and asset-based equality would apply to this case. The theory of complex equality emphasizes the need for respecting local morality and rules, supporting the freedom of each district to determine its own financing structure. At the same time, the theory argues that each person has equal worth and that inequalities in one sphere should not have an effect on inequalities in another sphere. Having a substandard primary and secondary education can affect many factors in life, including the ability to obtain admission to college or obtain higher paying employment. As this sphere cannot be separated from others, the differences in school funding would likely not meet the standards of the theory of complex equality. Asset-based egalitarians might argue that the "stake" each person would receive later in life would help to equalize initial inequalities. However, the stake will be of less use to those who had inadequate public school education because

(a) these individuals would be less likely to be accepted at colleges where they could increase their earning potential and (b) they would likely have less information about financial planning to aid the management of their stake. Despite these concerns, the theorists argue that over time, communities will learn how to best utilize stakes to be utilized later in life and that stakes will eventually ensure adequate social justice. Consequently, some asset-based egalitarians might find for the defendant.

Despite the critique that moral theory has little to do with everyday adjudication (Posner, 1998), the analysis of the *Serrano v. Priest* case demonstrates how these theoretical ideas can be applied to real-world situations. The example also illustrates both the commonalities and differences between the theories. Although each theory reflects a unique vision of social justice, the application of theories related to justice as fairness, equality of resources, critical legal studies, and complex equality could lead to a ruling for the plaintiff. This illustrates their common emphasis on social equality, especially when

inequalities are out of the control of an individual (as is the case with children). At the same time, the wealth maximization and asset-based egalitarian theories could lead to a ruling for the defense. Although these theories are quite different, in this case, they might argue that school funding should be left up to local districts. This case example demonstrates how the facts can be supported by theories that reflect different underlying values. *Serrano v. Priest* was decided in favor the plaintiffs, a controversial ruling that eventually led to California's Proposition 13 where a taxpayer revolt lead to capped property taxes and limited the usage of local property taxes for school funding (Stubblebine & Kennard, 1981).

CONCLUSION

Theory is often criticized for its lack of relevance for understanding lived experiences (Posner, 1998). Whether hypothetical, pluralistic, or descriptive, all theories try to explain something in our world.

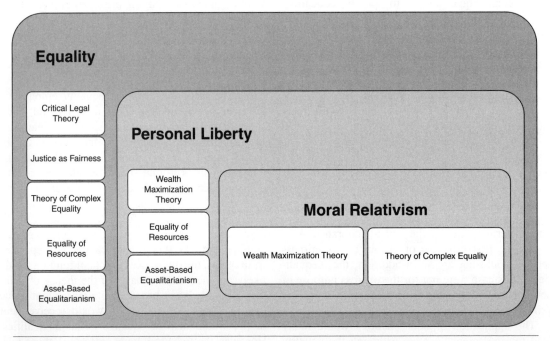

Figure 3.1   Conceptual Map

NOTE: Map links equality, personal liberty, and moral relativism to legal theories of social justice.

Theories challenge us to look more closely at some of the core values that underlie our perspectives. In order to effectively promote social justice, it needs to be defined in a way that informs practice. A theory of social justice can be a roadmap that gives substance to our policies and direction to our practice.

The legal theories described in this paper illustrate the difficulties in constructing a simple theory of social justice. Figure 3.1 provides a conceptual map of the similarities among the theories. The theories related to equality reflect some aspect of equal resource distribution or opportunity in society (the justice as fairness, critical legal studies, complex equality, equality of resources, and asset-based equalitarian theories). The theories related to personal liberty support individual rights either in addition to or above equal rights (the equality of resources, asset-based equalitarian, and wealth maximization theories). Finally, the theories that emphasize moral relativism in understanding social justice include wealth maximization and complex equality.

All of these theories reflect questions about the meaning of fairness, equality, and morality as well as how to best balance individual and social rights. A comprehensive theory of social justice needs to address these issues while remaining relevant for practice experience and policy advocacy. Should individuals be allowed to determine their own wealth and resources in society, even when handicapped by luck or lack of ability? Or does a moral society require equality of resources, either at one point in time or continuously? Social work students and faculty need to further debate whether the needs and desires of particular social groups can trump those of individuals, and in what circumstances.

REFERENCES

Ackerman, B. A. (1980). *Social justice in the liberal state.* New Haven, CT: Yale University Press.

Ackerman, B. A., & Alstott, A. (1999). *The stakeholder society.* New Haven, CT: Yale University Press.

Capeheart, L., & Milovanovic, D. (2007). *Social justice: Theories issues and movements.* New Brunswick, NJ: Rutgers University Press.

Child trust funds. (2009). Retrieved from https://gov.uk/child-trust-funds/overview

Dworkin, R. (1997). In praise of theory: Order of the Coif Lecture. *Arizona State Law Journal, 29*(2), 353–371.

Dworkin, R. (1999). Hypothetical contracts and rights. In J. P. Sterba (Ed.), *Justice: Alternative political perspectives* (pp. 126–136). Belmont, CA: Wadsworth.

Dworkin, R. (2000). *Sovereign virtue: The theory and practice of equality.* Cambridge, MA: Harvard University Press.

Garner, B. A. (Ed.). (2009). *Black's law dictionary* (9th ed.). St. Paul, MN: West.

Hayek, F. A. (1976). *Law, legislation and liberty: The mirage of social justice* (Vol. 2). Chicago, IL: University of Chicago Press.

Kennedy, D., & Gabel, P. (1984). Roll over Beethoven. *Stanford Law Review, 37*(1), 1–55.

Kennedy, D., & Klare, K. E. (1984). A bibliography of critical legal studies. *Yale Law Journal, 94*(2), 461–490.

Lamont, J., & Favor, C. (2008). Distributive justice. *The Stanford encyclopedia of philosophy.* Retrieved from http://plato.stanford.edu/archives/fall2008/entries/justice-distributive/

Longres, J. F., & Scanlon, E. (2001). Social justice and the research curriculum. *Journal of Social Work Education, 37*(3), 447–463.

Mapel, D. (1989). *Social justice reconsidered: The problem of appropriate precision in a theory of justice.* Chicago, IL: University of Illinois Press.

National Association of Social Workers (NASW). (2009). *Code of ethics of the National Association of Social Workers.* Retrieved from http://www.socialworkers.org/pubs/code/default.asp

Nozick, R. (1974). *Anarchy, state and utopia.* New York, NY: Basic Books.

Paine, T. (1797). *Agrarian justice.* Baltimore, MD: George Keatinge's.

Posner, R. A. (1997). Equality, wealth, and political stability. *Journal of Law, Economics & Organization, 13*(2), 344–365.

Posner, R. A. (1998). The problematics of moral and legal theory. *Harvard Law Review, 111*(7), 1637–1717.

Rawls, J. (1972). *A theory of justice.* Oxford, UK: Clarendon Press.

Rawls, J. (1985, Summer). Justice as fairness: Political not metaphysical. *Philosophy and Public Affairs, 14*(3), 223–251.

Rawls, J. (2001). *Justice as fairness: A restatement* (2nd ed.). Cambridge, MA: Harvard University Press.

Sadurski, W. (1985). *Giving desert its due: Social justice and legal theory.* Boston, MA: D. Reidel.

Sherraden, M. (1991). *Assets and the poor: A new American welfare policy*. Armonk, NY: M.E. Sharpe.

Stubblebine, W. M. C., & Kennard, D. N. (1981). California school finance: The 1970s decade. *Public Choice, 36*(3), 391–412.

Walzer, M. (1983). *Spheres of justice: A defense of pluralism and equality*. New York, NY: Basic Books.

Zinn, H. (2003). *A people's history of the United States: 1492–Present* (New ed.). New York, NY: HarperCollins.

U.S. Constitution. (1789). *Bill of rights*. U.S. National Archives and Record Administration. Retrieved from http://www.archives.gov/exhibits/charters/bill_of_rights.html

4

Literary Theories and Social Justice

Charity Samantha Fitzgerald

In the wake of the publication of *The Jungle* by Upton Sinclair, President Theodore Roosevelt created a special commission to investigate the claims of unsanitary conditions in Chicago's meatpacking district (Mookerjee, 1988). Using methods borrowed from muckraking journalism, Sinclair described the poor quality of meat sold that was not fit for human consumption (Mookerjee, 1988). The president's commission substantiated many claims made in the novel about the suboptimal meat quality, and as a result, he signed the Federal Food and Drugs Act, which created an overseeing body that later evolved into the Food and Drug Administration. Though few writers can claim to have written a book that incited federal action, Sinclair was disappointed in the novel's impact because it was not the impact he had intended (Mookerjee, 1988). His primary objective was to write a novel that exposed the ills of wage labor (Mookerjee, 1988, p. vii). Instead, the American public latched on to a secondary theme in the novel: the poor meat quality. Regardless of the unintended outcome, indubitably Sinclair was an author who used literature as a means to pursue social justice (Mookerjee, 1988). Through his works, he advocated for social change, and on at least one count, his efforts were successful.

Sinclair is not alone in his pursuit of social justice through literature. Other notable social justice-oriented works of American literature include Harriet Beecher Stowe's *Uncle Tom's Cabin*, John Steinbeck's *Of Mice and Men*, and Richard Wright's *Native Son*, among others. This paper builds on these literary works' commitment to social justice by inviting readers to examine these texts and others not explicitly geared toward advocacy through various lenses that provide insights into human existence. The paper identifies systematic approaches taken by literary scholars to discuss and to pursue social justice through exploring just about any text. Through literary theories, academics methodically approach literature to effect social change in order to create communities, societies, and a global village that are characterized as just. The paper later revisits *The Jungle* in its exploration of Marxism to examine the novel from a social justice perspective that extends beyond the legislation it evoked.

Merriam-Webster Online tidily defines literature as "writings in prose or verse; especially writings having excellence of form or expression and expressing ideas of permanent or universal interest" (n.d.). Literary theories, on the other hand, defy a simple definition. Spikes (2003) defines literary theories as inquiries into *how*, as opposed to *what*, texts mean. Questions that literary theories address, according to Spikes, include the following: (a) How do readers decipher the meanings of a text, (b) is there a distinction between the text's meaning and the author's intention, (c) what constitutes a valid interpretation of a text, (d) how do the personal narratives of readers and authors affect their relationships to the text, and (e) how do cultural and historical contexts shape a text? Thus, literary theories look beyond the aesthetic value of a text to focus on its historical context. Literary theories attempt to expose the values that underpin a text and to acknowledge the role literature plays as part of an ideological apparatus (Wolfreys, 1999).

Literary theories provide lenses through which to read texts. Examples of these lenses include psychoanalysis, Marxism, feminism, post-structuralism, postmodernism, postcolonialism, queer theory, historicism, and ethnic and cultural studies. Literary theories import ideas from other disciplines to bring new questions to bear on texts and to create spaces for fresh voices that differ from those "implicitly understood (Christian, humanist, Western, male European) in the conventional institutional approaches to literary study" (Wolfreys, 1999, pp. xi-xii). Implicit in literary theories is the notion that reality is neither fixed nor singular. Rather, literary theories recognize the diverse historical, cultural, and material contexts that can give rise to a plethora of meanings. Additionally, literary theories are mindful of differences. They do not seek to elevate one meaning above all others. Literary theories attempt to shatter what was thought to be a homogeneous, authoritative voice into alternative, dissenting voices (Wolfreys, 1999). Literary theories empower readers by withholding wholesale acceptance of what is being offered as the "right" interpretation of the text (Wolfreys, 1999). Instead, readers are invited to approach the text from multiple perspectives that evoke different interpretations.

Literary theories are also action driven with political agendas (Jackson, 1994). They attempt to drive literature from the ivy towers of academia into lived social contexts. Literary theories recognize literature as both a product and a shaper of social processes; literature both reflects and reproduces values and ideologies (Wolfreys, 1999). Literature can contribute to marginalization and silencing; it can also contribute to empowerment and liberation. Literary theories attempt to bring to light literature's marginalizing capacities and to harness its liberating capacities (Wolfreys, 1999).

Recent dissenters have seen the incorporation of literary theories into English departments as evidence that they have become de-radicalized and co-opted by the selfsame ideological apparatus that they attempt to expose. That is, some have argued that literary theories reproduce conventional criticism and dominant discourses (Wolfreys, 1999). West attempts to find a middle road between proponents and detractors of literary theories and to remind his audience that the goal of literary theories is improving the human condition. As West notes, "To be against theory *per se* is to be against inquiry into heuristic posits regarding the institutional and individual causes of alterable forms of human misery and human suffering, just as uncritical allegiance to grand theories can blind one from seeing and examining kinds of human oppression" (1991, p. 36). West argues that the goal of the academic should be to create the conditions that help individuals participate in democratic and free societies. He urges the academic to challenge the status quo by using analysis to expose structures of domination so as to promote the rights of the vulnerable. He argues that it is necessary to employ multiple theories in such a way as to create political action that promotes human rights and fulfills human needs. For him, this political action begins at a grassroots level. West's argument highlights how literary theories connect to the definitions of social justice.

In *Social Justice* (1976), Miller outlines parameters of the construct. He defines social justice as the means to obtain welfare and not the welfare itself. He argues that to develop a theory of social justice, there must be an institutional arrangement that impacts individuals' lives in an observable manner, and there must be a way to change the institutional arrangement in order to create opportunities congruent with obtaining welfare. Miller identifies the state as the primary vehicle for moving toward social justice. As previously discussed, West argues that intellectuals should apply literary theories to engage in political action and to expose discourses that oppress persons. Thus, the goals of literary theories related to political action and commitment to banish oppression mirrors Miller's focus on the state as a site of social justice-oriented action.

It is proposed in this paper that literary theories provide an untapped resource for understanding social justice. The first four sections are focused on specific bodies of literary theory: Marxism, feminism, postcolonialism, and queer theory. These four groups do not cover all groups of literary theories but rather serve as a sampling. Within these groupings, there is significant heterogeneity, and among these groupings, there is significant overlap. The discussion of each body of theory is followed with applications of theory to literary works. From the identification of common themes among the groups of theories discussed, the concluding section posits a social work theory of language.

MARXISM

Marxism, though often used in the realm of literature in a way unintended by Marx, laid the foundation for many literary theories. By introducing the idea of a different social order and the possibility of achieving that social order, it opened up possibilities for different kinds of discourse (Milne, 1996), such as feminism and postcolonialism. The political goals of Marxism are often transposed in literature from a theory of political economy to theory of oppression related to one's subjectivity. Literary theorists who adhere to a Marxist framework are sometimes at odds with each other. Marxism, thus, serves as a reference point for several related lines of academic inquiry, which share a few common foundations (Eagleton, 1996).

Marxism calls into question a fundamental contradiction of the capitalist economic system when a few get rich to the detriment of many. In other words, capitalism liberates "human potential while enslaving the world to a logic of capital divorced from human interests" (Milne, 1996, p. 16). Marxism embodies three basic tenets: a materialist critique of history, a deconstruction of capitalism, and a call for social revolution (Jackson, 1994). The first, the materialist critique of history, sees history as a narrative chain of different economic orders. An economic order consists of those who extract labor

and those who give labor. In each economic order, material conditions will eventually change so as to make the existing economic order untenable. As a result, a revolution can lead to the establishment of a new economic order. It is in reference to this point that Marx and Engels (1848/2004) wrote, "The history of all hitherto existing society is the history of class struggles" (chapter 1). The second tenet of Marxism, a deconstruction of capitalism, draws attention to the fact that workers are paid less than the worth of their labor. In this manner, capitalists are able to shore up money and resources for future financial investments. This system is inherently unstable and relies on the social and the political orders to sustain the unjust economic arrangement (Rivkin & Ryan, 1998). And the third tenet, the call for social revolution, is based on Marx's argument that one cannot change the world by changing a conception of it; rather, one changes the world by doing. As Marx and Engels (1848/2004) noted, "Workers of the world, unite. You have nothing to lose but your chains" (chapter 4).

The question now becomes how this theory of political economy can be incorporated into a literary theory. The answer lies in the social order. According to Marx, the economic system determines the social and the political orders (i.e., the superstructure). Literature is staunchly lodged within the social order (Haselett, 1999) by using language as a social convention. Thus, a Marxist reading situates texts in their respective historical contexts in order to identify the sociopolitical circumstances that shape language (Rivkin & Ryan, 1998). In fact, Marxist literary theorists have argued that there is no such category as literature but rather that each text is a political discourse (Jackson, 1994).

In essence, the Marxist perspective focuses on exposing the contradictions of capitalism. Both the production and the consumption of literature can be perceived as a way of subjugating the working class. Thus, argue some, it will rarely betray the interests of the dominant class (Rivkin & Ryan, 1998). Literature, according to this line of inquiry, serves to perpetuate the ideological interests of the ruling class, and it can do so because the dominant class controls the material means of production (i.e., printing presses and means of distribution). The task of a Marxist literary theorist entails close readings of the text as reflections of the capitalist order and exposure of the ways in which the text embodies the contradictions of capitalism in order to abolish false consciousness, or the truths accepted about the social order as self-evident or organic. Thus, in contrast to political economic Marxism, literary Marxism focuses on changing subjectivity and consciousness of its readership as a means of promoting social justice (Jackson, 1994). It aims to foment political engagement and social action to challenge the status quo, which were the intended goals of *The Jungle*.

Literary Illustration

The introductory paragraph of this essay referenced the legislation brought about by the publication of Upton Sinclair's *The Jungle*. A Marxist reading of the text sheds light on other ways in which the novel promotes social justice. The first step to read the text through a Marxist lens is to acknowledge its historical context. The novel was published at a time of enormous immigration influx to industrial centers, such as Pittsburgh and Chicago (Mookerjee, 1988). Immigrants came to the United States in pursuit of the American dream, and what they found was a nightmare of endless toil and exploitation. Sinclair empathized with the workers, which he likened to slave laborers, and thus set out to use the novel as propaganda. Sinclair believed that all art was propaganda, whether acknowledged or not (Mookerjee, 1988). The propagandist intentions of his novel were not only to expose the sordid working conditions but also to pin blame for these conditions on greedy, unscrupulous capitalists (Mookerjee, 1988). Sinclair aimed to change the consciousness of the workers and to provide them with a vision for a different political economic order (i.e., socialism). To do so, he wrote in a manner that challenged the elitist aesthetic. His intended audience was literate and semiliterate working people, and the language used in the novel avoids symbolism and verbosity (Mookerjee, 1988). Rather than using language to distance himself from working masses and to align himself with the upper classes, he used the novel to critique the selfishness of the dominant class. In sum, a Marxist approach to *The Jungle* reveals a social justice-oriented potency that

surpasses food quality-assurance legislation. The subversive potential of Marxism opened the door for feminism, postcolonialism, and queer theory to emerge.

FEMINISM

Proponents of feminist literary theories are reticent to define their perspective because any definition sets boundaries of inclusion and exclusion and oversimplifies what is complex (Rooney, 2006). Contemporary feminists are cognizant of feminism's checkered past in which the concerns of White, middle-class women were assumed to be the concerns of all women to the exclusion of women of color, women from varying social classes, women from different nations, women from rural areas, and women of various sexual orientations (Rooney, 2006). By trying to include those previously excluded, feminism remains an ever-expanding, alliance-forming collection of perspectives. It borrows from and contributes to such disparate fields as psychoanalysis, cultural studies, post-structuralism, and postcolonialism (Gilbert & Gubar, 1999). It is not a singular and uniform ideology (Morris, 1993); indeed, at times, the diversity of thought under the umbrella of feminism may even be contradicting (Rooney, 2006). Its malleability is both a boon and a deterrent to its efficacy (Robbins, 1999). In spite of the dispute over its definition, one assertion is agreed upon by most: Feminism has reshaped scholarship and discourse in powerful ways (Rooney, 2006).

In spite of the challenges of defining feminist literary theories, Robbins (1999) sketches underlying components of a literary theory that can be considered feminist. First, Robbins argues that a feminist literary theory assumes a relationship between words and the world; namely, words reflect the social order, words reproduce the social order, and words can remake the social order. Second, a feminist literary theory characterizes the relationship between words and the social order as political, namely, the power to coerce and to subvert. Third, a feminist literary theory acknowledges that social structures oppress women by propagating oppression based on internalized patriarchal values, such as those found in the home and the church, as well as in people (including women themselves). Feminist literary theories attempt to unravel unjust structures in terms of recognizing the capacity of literature both to oppress and to liberate.

Similar to the hesitancy to define feminist literary theories, feminists are also hesitant to define the evolution of ideas as it may not be sufficiently inclusive or balanced. Nevertheless, there are some broad trends that can be identified. A major milestone was the publication of Simone de Beauvoir's *The Second Sex* after World War II. Women are not born, she asserted famously, but rather "become" women. De Beauvoir projected a worldview in which women were often portrayed as the "Other" and men as the normative center (Gubar, 2007). De Beauvoir put her finger on the historical specificity of gender given that it is not a self-evident state. Overlaying de Beauvoir's thoughts onto literature, the first feminist literary theorists examined portrayals of women by male authors (Robbins, 1999). Male writers often presented two types of women: a Madonna and a whore, neither of which is a realistic portrayal. The literary constructions of these two archetypes imposed a male-generated conception of femininity on women. Feminist literary theorists began to deconstruct these images of women and to articulate their contradictions and their fallacies. The second phase of feminist literary theories entailed the questioning of the literary canon that failed to include the voices of women (Robbins, 1999). A third stage in the development of feminist literary theories questioned the prevailing aesthetic, and it challenged the notion that forms of literature often pursued by women, such as narratives, were in any way inferior to forms of literature often pursued by men (Rooney, 2006). The fourth phase of feminist literary theories focused on language itself as a constructor and a reinforcer of gender hierarchies (Morris, 1993). French feminists pointed out that women are often defined in terms of their deficiencies (e.g., lack of penis), and they speculated about the psychological toll this could inflict on women (Robbins, 1999).

According to Chaudhuri and Mukherji (2002), "Feminism is nothing if it is not a philosophy of action and engagement" (p. 1) where social change is both plausible and feasible (Robbins, 1999). Feminism, like other literary theories, is focused on action and the promotion of change where women can make a difference by shattering what was once assumed monolithic and leaving in its wake new possibilities to explore (Rooney, 2006). It acknowledges gender as a social construct that is a potent determinant of social existence and not as an organic trait by exposing the hidden patriarchal values that underpin gender as a binary construct (Chaudhuri & Mukherji, 2002). Feminist literary theories provide a strategy of reading that seeks to reexamine authority, question the formation of the self, bring to light repression, accept ambiguity and contradiction, and reform social structures (Chaudhuri & Mukherji, 2002). The following application provides an example of opening opportunities for exploration.

Literary Illustration

Gilbert and Gubar (1999) discuss a formidable challenge for women authors: transcending the Madonna/whore dichotomy, or what they refer to as the angel/monster dichotomy. Men's imposition of this dichotomy has been so pervasive, claim Gilbert and Gubar, that it has invaded women's sense of self-concept. To liberate their writing, women must liberate themselves. Women, these scholars argue, do not know themselves. Rather, patriarchal conceptions shape women's self-definitions. Though men have literary free reign, women are confined in a metaphorical prison built by men.

The authors frame their argument by using Elizabeth Barrett Browning's *Aurora Leigh*. In the poem, Aurora sees her dead mother as "Ghost, fiend, and angel, fairy, witch, and sprite;/ A dauntless muse who eyes a dreadful Fate;/ A loving Psyche who loses sight of Love;/ A still Medusa with mild milky brows" (Barrett Browning as cited in Gilbert & Gubar, 1999, p. 597). The authors draw attention to the extremities of the descriptions. On the one hand, the mother is described as a fiend, on the other, an angel. They point to the bipolarity of the descriptions as evidence that male self-definitions have altered the female narrator's outlook such that she sees the world through patriarchal eyes. To earn the moniker of angel, a woman exists solely to cater to men's needs, and she must be silent. To earn the moniker of monster, a woman asserts her autonomy, and she must be silenced. The male-imposed moniker of monster attempts to control the intransigence of a freely thinking woman. Thus, female characters are often doubly condemned, frozen in a no-win situation. Gilbert and Gubar (1999) write, "Either way, the images on the surface of the looking glass, into which the female artist peers in search of her *self*, warn her that she is or must be a 'Cypher,' framed and framed up, indited and indicted" (p. 609). To claim literary voices, argue the authors, women must rid themselves of male-imposed identity formation and construct their own identities. The dual tasks of deconstruction and reconstruction are also the focus of the next body of theory addressed: postcolonialism.

POSTCOLONIALISM

Like other theoretical orientations, postcolonialism is based on the premise that literature can be a tool of oppression and liberation; it strives to expose the oppressive capacities of literature and to harness its liberating abilities. Simply stated, postcolonialism resists the portrayal and the perpetuation of native persons as the Other (Ashcroft, Griffith, & Tiffins, 1995). As Parker and Starkey (1995) note, "Postcolonial writers have insisted that the colonized belong to the 'same world and are not absolutely other,' and have vigorously affirmed the rights of the silenced to be heard" (p. 6).

Postcolonial refers to a historical era (Mukherjee, 1996). However, the term is much more than a mere historical term; it includes an emancipatory process (Mukherjee, 1996). A colonial power was one that had large overseas holdings (Punter, 2000). Behind colonial powers were motivations of the exploitation of natural resources, the pursuit of European political dominance, the subjugation of native persons, and the spread of European culture (Punter, 2000). During the first part of the 20th century, the colonial system began to unravel given the unwieldiness of governing from afar and the rise of local resistance movements (Punter, 2000). Though the colonial system has unraveled, Punter (2000) argues that colonialism has not ended. He points to the powerful influence of the United States in the affairs of other nations, such as Iraq and Afghanistan, as well as its enormous voice in global institutions, such as the World Trade Organization.

Postcolonial theorists often characterize postcolonialism as a process that begins with the establishment of empires and not merely as the time proceeding the fall of empires. Theorists make this distinction because colonies were not subjugated by weapons and disease alone but rather by discourses deployed (both informally and institutionally) during the colonial era (Tiffin & Lawson, 1994), which permeated social consciousness and continue to persist. These discourses defined White persons as morally superior by denigrating native persons. In fact, native persons were portrayed as subhuman, and texts served to reify this portrayal by suggesting that the inferiority of native persons was somehow biological or organic (JanMohamed, 1995). The portrayal of natives as inferior afforded colonizers the opportunity to become blind to their identities as subjugators (JanMohamed, 1995). In other instances, the existence of native persons was entirely denied in texts, thereby, ideologically depopulating entire countries (Tiffin & Lawson, 1994). Thus, colonialist texts often served to squelch the voices of native persons.

Postcolonial theorists attempt to deconstruct assumptions and to decenter power by recognizing voices that emanate from localities rather than from the imperial center. Their strategies are multifaceted. Some have reexamined the Eurocentric literary canon (Parker & Starkey, 1995) by creating backstories of poorly portrayed native persons in texts, such as *Jane Eyre*. The backstories draw attention to the oppressive conditions imposed on native persons as well as the shortsightedness of European authors in failing to describe the oppressive conditions to the readers. The analysis of native persons as naive and lifeless extends to the contemporary media portrayal of persons residing in developing countries. For example, the media often depict Africans as passive and suffering and Africa as a continent in upheaval, which is in need of saving by former imperial powers (Parker & Starkey, 1995). Another strategy that postcolonial theorists use is the creation of a space for native voices that do not emanate from the imperial center (Mukherjee, 1996) or mimic Eurocentrism (Parker & Starkey, 1995). In fact, the voices of the marginalized are regarded in high esteem by postcolonial theorists by featuring the insights of those who have suffered from oppression (Mukherjee, 1996). Thus, oppression is reconstituted as a tool of empowerment (Mukherjee, 1996). Still other postcolonial theorists have argued that texts cannot be understood apart from geographical and historical contexts, thereby, debunking the European-universalist aesthetic norms, such as conformity to formal grammar (Mukherjee, 1996). The emphasis on plural aesthetic norms empowers the reader with authority to judge (Parker & Starkey, 1995).

As an action-driven theory, postcolonialism elevates local contexts as sites of political resistance (Mukherjee, 1996). It is argued that it would be a gross oversimplification to equate the circumstances of a native person in Australia with those of a person in India with those of a person in Kenya. Thus, postcolonialism provides an umbrella term to encapsulate a common struggle against oppression fought in many different cultural, political, social, and geographical contexts. This common struggle unfolds in different ways across time and space, but postcolonialism claims a stake in this struggle. Slemon (1995) urges his readers to use the insights gleaned from postcolonialism as a script for change rather than discussing theory for theory's sake (p. 52). The following example serves as a script for change by drawing attention to the unflattering depiction of Kolu adults.

Literary Illustration

In 1932, the Irish novelist Joyce Cary published *Aissa Saved*, a novel that details the conversion experience of an African girl to Christianity. Close inspection of the focus of *childhood* as a construct in the novel viewed through a postcolonial lens reveals the ability of language to marginalize when the colonizers' dominant status is threatened. In one part of the novel, the narrator praises the well-behaved Kolu children. The narrator states, "Kolu children of old-fashioned families like Makunde's were remarkable for their gravity and decorum; . . . they were strictly brought up and made to behave themselves as far as possible like grown-ups" (Cary as cited in JanMohamed, 1995, p. 21). In another part of the text, the narrator depicts Kolu adults who have converted to Christianity as

naughty children. Thus, in one instance, the narrator highlights the innocence of childhood, in another, the wantonness of childhood.

JanMohamed (1995) explains the disparate application of childhood through a postcolonial reading. Those identified developmentally as children pose little threat to colonialism because they are not fully grown physically, intellectually, emotionally, and so on. Thus, the author presents them in a positive, beneficent manner so that the narrator can draw "moral sustenance" (p. 21). The intent of the adults to convert to Christianity, however, threatens colonialism because it dares to eliminate a distinction between the colonizer and the Other. That is, colonialist discourses affirmed moral superiority of the colonizers based, in part, on their practice of Christianity in contrast to the practice of native religions, which were deemed to be inferior. In essence, the identity of the colonizer was dependent on opposition to and primacy over the Other. By depicting Kolu adults as metaphorical children, the narrator is able to maintain the hierarchy between the colonizer and the Other that threatened to be dissolved by sharing a religion. Reading the text through a postcolonial lens reveals the work that the text is doing to establish identity and to marginalize the Other. Without such a lens, this ideological operation and the self-contradictoriness of dominant discourse might not be apparent.

QUEER THEORY

Similar to the efforts of postcolonial theorists' attempts to deconstruct imperial discourses, queer theory attempts to deconstruct heteronormative discourses by splintering discourses about sexuality. *Queer* signifies potential differences, and it defies a singular, reductive definition (Goldman, 1999). Exploring these potential differences, queer theory encompasses race, gender, sexuality, and just about any marker of identity or community. Thus, queer can mean whatever its articulator desires so long as it resists the dominant and the legitimate form of discourse by using the first person (Hall, 2003). To grapple with queer theory, one has to acquiesce to its incomprehensibility (Hall, 2003). It emphasizes the multiplicity, the partiality, the contingency, and the malleability of human identity over time and across space (Hall, 2003). The focus on queer theory is on constant reformation and destabilization of itself and has led Judith Butler, a prominent scholar in the area, to argue that at some point queer theory will have to resign itself in order to usher in another theoretical orientation (Goldman, 1999).

Perhaps a riot spurred the movement that evolved into queer theory. The Stonewall riot of 1969 in Greenwich Village entailed a group of so-called sexual deviants banning against the New York police force as it raided a gay bar. Tired of the harassment, the bar patrons lobbed coins, stones, and parking meters at the police. From this riot emerged a gay and lesbian consciousness. The first gay and lesbian literary studies emerged as a set of counter-reading strategies (Pustianaz, 2000), or strategies that exposed the heteronormativity implicit in what was offered by dominant discourses as the "correct" reading of texts. These literary studies attempted to create a single political constituency in opposition to dominant discourses. They attempted to unveil the homosexual subtext of books already part of the literary canon and to create their own canon of gay and lesbian literature (Pustianaz, 2000). The homosexual and heterosexual binary embraced by initial gay and lesbian studies theorists had persisted in informing literary thinking until Michel Foucault published "The History of Sexuality" (1999).

Foucault's (1999) text, published as a series between 1976 and 1984, resisted the oversimplified distinction between homosexual and heterosexual. Foucault argued that sexuality must be understood in its political, social, and cultural context. He proposed a constructionist perspective of sexuality thereby challenging the essentialist discourse, or the medico-scientific understanding that there is a homosexual essence (Pustianaz, 2000). He examined how doctors created the homosexual as a case to be studied and treated and how homosexuality became a mental illness. What was at stake, according to Foucault, was not sexuality per se but instead a form of social control. Given the perceived sense of social unraveling, a fixation on normalizing certain forms of sexuality and marginalizing others protected the interests of an economic, political, and social order built upon a male-headed, two-parent, childbearing family as its basic unit. Rather than

focusing solely on the destructive power of the construction of homosexuality, however, Foucault also identified its productive power. By naming the homosexual, claimed Foucault, it opened up possibilities for sexuality through awareness that such a thing exists, and it also politicized a constituency against oppression. What was important to Foucault was to investigate the conditions that gave rise to the dichotomy of homosexuality and heterosexuality as an organizing social principle.

Successive queer theorists seized on Foucault's conception of sexuality as an organizing, albeit tenuous, construct of contemporary human existence. Eve Sedgwick highlighted the salience of sexuality as an organizing principle such that any theory of culture that does not take into account the imposed homosexual/heterosexual dichotomy is irreparably flawed (Sedgwick, 1999). She argues that the language of sexuality permeates other languages of identity and cuts across subjectivity (Goldman, 1999). Concomitantly, Butler emphasized the behavioral nature of sexuality. To sustain itself as a dominant discourse, claims Butler, heterosexuality must be practiced repetitively. With each performance and with each repetition, there is the possibility to rupture what is conceived of as natural and organic.

Though much of the discussion about queer theory has centered on a few notable academics, it is important to state that queer theory emerged from the streets and was later appropriated by academics (Hall, 2003). Organizations such as Queer Nation and AIDS Coalition to Unleash Power (ACT UP) fomented young activists who carried their ideas to the academy. It was these activists who decided to take up the term *queer* and to resignify its previously stigmatizing connotation (Hall, 2003). Their tongue-in-cheek use of *queer* drew attention to the ways in which language can marginalize (Hall, 2003).

Since queer theory is based on the experiences of daily life, it is always pushing boundaries, yet even it recognizes its self-enforcing sense of decorum and its upholding of certain normative practices (Hall, 2003). To push its boundaries, queer theorists have called for open and honest dialogue about highly sensitive issues, such as pedophilia and sadomasochism (Hall, 2003). Queer is about twisting and traveling across regimes of normal. It questions everything and assumes nothing. The subsequent example shows how a queer theorist read a text by bringing to the forefront something that had been avoided by other literary scholars. Stanivukovic (2000) pushed against what predecessors had offered as the "normal" reading of a Shakespearean poem.

Literary Illustration

Stanivukovic (2000) provides a queer reading of William Shakespeare's *Venus and Adonis*. In Shakespeare's rendering of the tale, the female Venus pursues the male Adonis. Adonis rebuffs Venus's advances because he claims that he has not reached sexual maturation, a claim that his subsequent "hunt" (i.e., seduction) of a boar calls into question. Adonis decides to go on the hunt for a boar, an animal that symbolizes male sexual potency. When he comes upon the boar, Adonis attempts to bestow a kiss on it. At the moment of the kiss, the boar fatally spears Adonis through the groin.

Stanivukovic brings a queer theory lens to bear on this text. First, he criticizes other literary scholars for not bringing attention to the homoerotic underpinnings of this poem. Other academics, claims Stanivukovic, either ignore or gloss over the death scene thereby avoiding the "queer question." Stanivukovic places the queerness of the text at the heart of his critique. He illustrates how Adonis's death serves to restore sexual and social order. Sexual relations between men do not result in procreation, thereby disrupting Elizabethan institutions of social order, such as the family. Thus, Adonis's death in the throes of homoerotic desire for the male boar serves to reinstill social organization. Stanivukovic also draws attention to the language employed throughout the text to describe Adonis's sex-related characteristics and his sexuality. In one scene, Venus describe Adonis as "no man, though of a man's complexion" (Shakespeare as cited in Stanivukovic, 2000, p. 91). In another scene, Adonis describes his sexual activities as "I know not love . . . nor will not know it" (Shakespeare as cited in Stanivukovic, 2000, p. 98). Thus, his gender and his sexual orientation are described in ambiguous and ambivalent terms. The lack of clarity in the text serves to clarify the sociohistorical contingency of sexuality. People living during the Elizabethan era,

unlike many living in the present day, did not think of sexuality in strictly binary terms. Shakespeare used open-ended adjectives and descriptions to avoid categorizing Adonis as either gay or straight. Invoking Butler, Stanivukovic shows how dissolving the binary opens up a multitude of ways to be and to do, simply stated. Having thusly examined concrete applications of four theories to texts, the paper now examines the social work profession's code of ethics through these four lenses.

TOWARD A SOCIAL WORK THEORY OF LANGUAGE

This article has outlined how scholars of literature systematically speak about social justice. Reading texts through the lenses provided by literary theories illuminates social injustices and opens opportunities for social justice. Literary theories work to bring about justice by examining how language functions to oppress based on lines of class, gender, race, nationality, ethnicity, and sexual orientation, among others. Literary theories locate agency with those who have been marginalized by affirming the power of their voices.

Like the aim of literary theories, social justice permeates the mission of social work. For example, the preamble of the *Code of Ethics* developed by the National Association of Social Workers (NASW, 2009) clearly articulates that social workers should align with the interests of people who are vulnerable and oppressed, and they should be "sensitive to cultural and ethnic diversity and strive to end discrimination, oppression, poverty, and other forms of social injustice" (para. 2). Literary theorists and social workers share concerns about the moral obligations to society, the promotion of social welfare, the encouragement of the voices of all people to participate in public institutions, and the need for social and political action.

The article concludes by considering how the ways in which literary scholars discuss social justice can inform social work practice to promote social justice. Given their congruence with the profession's ethical foundations, literary theories can inform the ways in which social workers use language. Synthesizing commonalities among the groups of theory discussed in this paper, the following social work theory of language is proposed.

Language matters. Language shapes realities, and realities shape language. For example, a mental health diagnosis can influence a client's self-perception. Or social policy that identifies families as being needy or lacking self-sufficiency can permeate understanding of oneself. Thus, social workers can reflect with clients on the power of language to shape realities.

Language is malleable. Though language may influence realities, it can also be used to change realities. Meanings fluctuate over time and over space. Words that oppress, such as queer, can be reappropriated to liberate. Thus, words can be tools of empowerment, and they are amenable to social work intervention.

Language can restore agency. Literary theories affirm that all people have voices with which to tell powerful stories. Regardless of personal circumstances, each voice deserves to speak and to be heard. Perhaps the people with whom a social worker interacts speak in broken English or a dialect of English not deemed "proper." A social work theory of language invites people to question what is meant by *proper* and affirms different ways of speaking.

Language can provide for self-definition. Upon reflection of its critical role in shaping realities, language can help people to define themselves in their own terms. People who frequent a social service agency, for example, may prefer to be called something other than client. Self-definition can be empowering and shape interactions in a positive, constructive manner.

Language can provide a symbolic resource toward empathic understanding. Language provides windows into others' lives that affirm a common humanity. Though each person has a different story to tell, disparate circumstances can give rise to shared joys or common struggles. Thus, language can serve as a reminder of human interconnectedness.

REFERENCES

Ashcroft, B., Griffiths, G., & Tiffin, H. (Eds.). (1995). *The post-colonial studies reader.* New York, NY: Routledge.

Chaudhuri, S., & Mukherji, S. (2002). Introduction. In S. Chaudhuri & S. Mukherji (Eds.), *Literature and gender* (pp. 1–12). New Delhi, India: Orient Longman.

Eagleton, T. (1996). Introduction: Part I. In T. Eagleton & D. Milne (Eds.), *Marxist literary theory* (pp. 1–15). Malden, MA: Blackwell.

Foucault, M. (1999). The history of sexuality. In J. Rivkin & M. Ryan (Eds.), *Literary theory: An anthology* (pp. 683–691). Malden, MA: Blackwell.

Gilbert, S., & Gubar, S. (1999). The madwoman in the attic. In J. Rivkin & M. Ryan (Eds.), *Literary theory: An anthology* (pp. 596–611). Malden, MA: Blackwell.

Goldman, J. (1999). Introduction: Works on the wild(e) side—Performing, transgressing, queering. In J. Wolfreys (Ed.), *Literary theories: A reader and guide* (pp. 525–536). New York: New York University Press.

Gubar, S. (2007). Introduction: Theory: On culture and gender. In S. M. Gilbert & S. Gubar (Eds.), *Feminist literary theory and criticisms: A Norton reader* (pp. 293–299). New York, NY: Norton.

Hall, D. E. (2003). *Transitions: Queer theories.* New York, NY: Palgrave Macmillan.

Haselett, M. (1999). Introduction: The politics of literature. In J. Wolfreys (Ed.), *Literary theories: A reader and guide* (pp. 99–108). New York: New York University Press.

Jackson, L. (1994). *The dematerialisation of Karl Marx: Literature and Marxist theory.* New York, NY: Longman.

JanMohamed, A. R. (1995). The economy of Manichean allegory. In B. Ashcroft, G. Griffiths, & H. Tiffin, (Eds.), *The post-colonial studies reader* (pp. 18–23). New York, NY: Routledge.

Mar, K., & Engels, F. (2004). *The Communist manifesto.* (Original work published 1848). Retrieved August 10, 2009, from http://www.marxists.org/archive/marx/works/1848/communist-manifesto/ch01.htm

Merriam-Webster Online. (n.d.). Literature. Retrieved August 10, 2009, from http://www.merriam-webster.com/dictionary/literature

Miller, D. (1976). *Social justice.* New York: Oxford University Press.

Milne, D. (1996). Introduction part II: Reading Marxist literary theory. In T. Eagleton & D. Milne (Eds.), *Marxist literary theory* (pp. 16–29). Malden, MA: Blackwell.

Mookerjee, R. N. (1988). *Art for social justice: The major novels of Upton Sinclair.* Metuchen, NJ: Scarecrow Press.

Morris, P. (1993). *Literature and feminism.* Cambridge, MA: Blackwell.

Mukherjee, M. (1996). Interrogating post-colonialism. In H. Trivedi & M. Mukherjee (Eds.), *Interrogating post-colonialism: Theory, text, and context* (pp. 3–12). Rashtrapati Nivas, Shimla, India: Indian Institute of Advanced Study.

National Association of Social Workers (NASW). (2009). *Code of ethics of the National Association of Social Workers.* Retrieved August 9, 2009, from http://www.socialworkers.org/pubs/code/default.asp

Parker, M., & Starkey, R. (1995). Introduction. In M. Parker & R. Starkey (Eds.), *Postcolonial literatures: Achebe, Ngugi, Desai, Walcott.* New York, NY: St. Martin's Press.

Punter, D. (2000). *Postcolonial imaginings: Fictions of a new world order.* Edinburgh, UK: Edinburgh University Press.

Pustianaz, M. (2000). Gay male literary studies. In T. Sandfort, J. Schuyf, J. W. Duyvendek, & J. Weeks (Eds.), *Lesbian and gay studies: An introductory, interdisciplinary approach* (pp. 146–153). Thousand Oaks, CA: Sage.

Rivkin, J., & Ryan, M. (1998). Introduction: "Starting with zero: Basic Marxism." In J. Rivkin & M. Ryan (Eds.), *Literary theory: An anthology* (pp. 231–242). Malden, MA: Blackwell.

Robbins, R. (1999). Introduction: Will the real feminist theory please stand up? In J. Wolfreys (Ed.), *Literary theories: A reader and guide* (pp. 49–58). New York: New York University Press.

Rooney, E. (2006). Introduction. In E. Rooney (Ed.), *The Cambridge companion to feminist literary theory* (pp. 1–26). New York, NY: Cambridge University Press.

Sedgwick, E. K. (1999). Between men. In J. Rivkin & M. Ryan (Eds.), *Literary theory: An anthology* (pp. 696–711). Malden, MA: Blackwell.

Slemon, S. (1995). The scramble for post-colonialism. In B. Ashcroft, G. Griffiths, & H. Tiffin, (Eds.), *The post-colonial studies reader* (pp. 45–52). New York, NY: Routledge.

Spikes, M. P. (2003). *Understanding contemporary American literary theory* (Rev. ed.). Columbia: University of South Carolina Press.

Stanivukovic, G. V. (2000). "Kissing the boar": Queer Adonis and critical practice. In C. Thomas (Ed.), *Straight with a twist: Queer theory and the subject of heterosexuality* (pp. 87–108). Urbana: University of Illinois Press.

Tiffin, C., & Lawson, A. (1994). The textuality of empire. In C. Tiffin & A. Lawson (Eds.), *De-scribing empire: Post-colonialism and textuality* (pp. 1–14). New York, NY: Routledge.

West, C. (1991). Theory, pragmatisms, and politics. In J. Arac & B. Johnson (Eds.), *Consequences of theory* (pp. 22–38). Baltimore, MD: Johns Hopkins University Press.

Wolfreys, J. (1999). Introduction: Border crossings, or close encounters of the textual kind. In J. Wolfreys (Ed.), *Literary theories: A reader and guide* (pp. 1–11). New York: New York University Press.

5

HISTORICAL PERSPECTIVES ON SOCIAL JUSTICE

SARAH ACCOMAZZO

INTRODUCTION

In the National Association of Social Worker's (NASW's) *Code of Ethics*, the term *social justice* is listed as one of the top five core values that serve as "the foundation of social work's unique purpose and perspective" (2009, p. 1). The *Code of Ethics* specifically states,

> Social workers pursue social change, particularly with and on behalf of vulnerable and oppressed individuals and groups of people. Social workers' social change efforts are focused primarily on issues of poverty, unemployment, discrimination, and other forms of social injustice (p. 5)

However, the code does not include a definition of *social justice*, leaving practitioners and educators to create their own meaning for the term (Longres & Scanlon, 2001). In 2007, the National Association of Scholars (NAS) noted that by teaching social justice as a core value,

> the NASW takes no notice of the existence of competing ideas but grants a privileged status to a single, arguable view. . . . NASW's emphasis on social justice,

when applied to academic programming, runs counter to the spirit and the principles of good educational practice, and normal scholarship. (p. 3)

The NAS also warns that "a social worker who is largely ignorant of American history faces an intellectually blinkered professional life in which there will be strong temptation to respond to problems according to the stereotypes and shibboleths of the moment" (p. 25). In order to respond to such critiques, it is important to develop a more nuanced understanding of the term *social justice* and what it means. It is helpful to look to other disciplines to see how social justice is defined and assessed.

This analysis focuses on the academic discipline of history and the different ways that historians have addressed the topic of social justice. At first glance, it may appear that historians have little to say about social justice because very few have written directly about the concept. However, a deeper analysis shows that historians, and the discipline of history, have made important contributions in the following three areas: (a) tracing the history of the usage and changing definition of the term *social justice*, (b) tracking the history of ideas related to social justice, and (c) expanding the discipline's subjects and methods, from the founding and professionalization period (1880s to the 1940s) that emphasized objectivity, science, political, event-driven history and the study of White men in power, to the modern period and a new social history (1940s–1970s) that describes "history from the bottom up" (or "history of the people"), then to postmodernism and the sociocultural turn (1980s–present), which questions the objective, scientific stance of history by using innovative methods that have resulted in new insights into history. Through this turn toward social and cultural history and to new methods and subjects, the discipline of history has contributed much to the efforts of many groups who have traditionally been viewed as fighting for social justice, including women, African Americans, minorities, people with disabilities, and gay, lesbian, bisexual, and transgender (LGBT) people. This analysis includes a case study of the history of the LGBT movement and how historians (using a social and cultural historical lens and postmodern methods and research) have changed the course of the LGBT movement and furthered its struggle for social justice.

SOCIAL JUSTICE IN A HISTORICAL CONTEXT

Historians and historical philosophers have placed the term *social justice* in a historical context in order to better understand its current usage. A large debate exists as to whether or not the term *social justice*, as we tend to understand it in contemporary times, is a modern innovation, or, whether the term meant something very different in previous times and contexts (Behr, 2003; Fleischacker, 2004; Jackson, 2005; Shields, 1941). This section describes some major scholars who have addressed this debate.

First, a few historians and historical philosophers have identified the origin of the term *social justice* (Behr, 2003; Shields, 1941). Shields (1941), a political philosopher, and Behr (2003), a historian, suggest that the term was first coined by a Jesuit priest named Luigi Taparelli D'Azeglio (1793–1862). Taparelli felt that Catholic teachings on social and moral issues had strayed and needed to return to the idea that humans are inherently social and thus have a right to the benefits of social groups; every large social group is made up of many smaller social groups, and social

justice required the large social groups to respect the rights of the smaller social groups, and vice versa (Behr, 2003). Taparelli had a direct influence on Pope Leo XIII (often credited with significant contributions to early discussions of social justice), who was one of his students at the Collegio Romano before assuming the position of pope.

Behr suggests that, when considering the historical context of Taparelli's life, Taparelli's concepts of social justice were fairly different from modern day conceptions of social justice. At his time, Italy was in as the midst of raging debates about Risorgimento (the unification of city-states into the country of Italy) and the place of the Catholic Church in this new country. In addition, Taparelli was concerned with the changes brought about by the Industrial Revolution in which society was disordered, different groups fought for power, and great inequalities existed between the elite and the average person. In response to a growing need, Catholic charities had expanded; however, this expansion was criticized as either overly reactionary or as covertly encouraging revolution among the lower classes. In light of this history, Behr sees Taparelli's ideas on social justice within the context of the early 19th century where local groups, charities, and governing bodies were dominated or ignored by larger bodies (such as monarchies, overly powerful families, and large-scale governments). As a Jesuit, Taparelli took a risk by stepping into a Catholic debate and advocating for smaller, more autonomous groups in order to promote social justice as an important aspect of society. While Taparelli greatly influenced future social justice and Catholic liberal doctrine, his use of the term social justice is different from modern day usages (Behr, 2003).

The modern usage of the term *social justice* is a post-18th-century conception (Behr, 2003; Fleischacker, 2004; Jackson, 2005; Shields, 1941). Historical philosopher Fleischacker, in *A Short History of Distributive Justice* (2004), writes that pre-18th-century ideas of social justice were based more on the ideas of charity and mercy than justice, and people without goods merited them only because of the virtues of charity and mercy and not because in a just society, everyone deserves a fair distribution of goods because they are humans.

Shields (1941) adds that pre-18th-century understandings of social justice drew mostly on ideas of legal justice or making sure that each is given their due under the current laws (but all are not necessarily due an equal amount).

Fleischacker (2004) builds his argument through the use of historical context that places thinkers and events (e.g., Aristotle, Aquinas, and the 17th-century English Poor Laws) in a new perspective since they refer to different concepts of social justice. For example, he states that when Aristotle describes distributive justice, he is referring to the distribution of political goods in the context of Roman government, not material goods. Aristotle also states that a just distribution of goods is based on a person's merit, not on an individual's humanity (acknowledging that unequal distribution is acceptable because not all humans merit the same distribution, thereby, justifying the class system that existed in Rome). He also gives the examples of 17th-century English Poor Laws that are often cited as one of the first examples of the state taking action in responding to poverty and regulating distribution of goods. However, Fleischacker argues that when placed in a historical context, it becomes clear that the Poor Laws were linked primarily to concepts of mercy and charity. The laws were actually regulated almost solely through the church, as opposed to the state, and goods were distributed in the name of the religious virtues of mercy and charity, not based on concepts of equality and equal rights. The poor were viewed as morally tarnished and deserving of poverty, and the rich and the government were given accolades for their virtuous contributions to the poor (Fleischacker, 2004).

Though Miller (1999), Shields (1941), and Fleischacker (2004) all trace modern conceptions of social justice to the 18th century, they trace the development of this modern conception of social justice to different causes. Fleischacker directly credits the Enlightenment, the French Revolution, and the development of the concept that humans have inherent rights to equality and a standard of living because they are humans (not based on merit) and that the state owes something to citizens in return for their support of government. Miller (1999) focuses on the development of the nation-state as a regulatory body that people can entrust

with the fair distribution of goods. Shields (1941) cites the influence of Catholic conceptions of obligations for caring for the poor and capitalism that involved industrialization and the rise of the class system. However, they agree that modern conceptions of social justice are built on the ideas that all humans deserve access to material goods because they are humans and that the state has a responsibility in distributing goods among members. A careful study of history shows that these ideas were unique to the 18th century, when a certain set of historical circumstances created an opportunity for these ideas to take hold. An understanding of the changing meaning of social justice over time and the historical circumstances that contributed to this change can provide deeper insight into today's struggles and debates about social justice.

HISTORY OF IDEAS
RELATED TO SOCIAL JUSTICE

Another way historians have contributed to an understanding of social justice is by tracing the history of ideas related to social justice, often called intellectual history, that includes history of philosophy, science, religion, and/or political, economic, or aesthetic thought (Southgate, 2003, p. 243). Beginning in the 1930s, historians traced the development of ideas over time, noting that ideas with the greatest influence on modern life were often the products of specific historical contexts, events, and people (Southgate, 2003).

Intellectual history has demonstrated insights into several concepts related to social justice. For example, Jones's book (2005), titled *An End to Poverty? A Historical Debate,* discusses how debates about poverty have evolved since the 1700s. Jones states that modern ideas about the eradication of poverty came into existence in the 1700s as (a) the Industrial Revolution increased disparities in wealth, (b) new immigrants poured into America, (c) the French Revolution and Enlightenment ideas spread, and (d) the relative peace and prosperity of the early 17th century gave people time to learn both the benefits and troubles of a market-driven society. Historical works have tended to focus on the above economic factors and to ignore that some key political figures at this time were calling for radical social reforms in order to eradicate poverty. As it turns out, universal health care is not a 20th-century idea; in fact, Jones suggests that several politicians and philosophers in France, including Marquis de Condorcet and Thomas Paine, called for some sort of universal health care and other federal reforms to alleviate poverty during the end of the 18th century. He also notes that Adam Smith, contrary to some interpretations, felt strongly that the federal government needed to take control of redistributing wealth equally (Jones, 2005).

Jones (2005) implies that an understanding of these debates is critical to understanding today's current political climate and legislative decisions made regarding poverty. Modern day politicians and economists have tended to forget the origins of the debate. Similar questions about poverty exist today as they existed in the 1700s, including an individual's accountability for poverty, what the federal government owes to impoverished citizens, and how individuals and governments should interact and overlap when working to eradicate poverty.

How Historians Have Furthered the Cause of Social Justice

Most historians would probably say that they do not consider themselves directly involved in social justice as part of their professional work. In fact, in a 2004 survey conducted by *Journal of American History* that included 1,047 readers (mostly historians working in academic settings) who responded to the question, "What value or worth do you experience in doing history?" only 4% picked "contribute to social justice" as an answer. In addition, 39% agreed that "Historians' political agendas drive their research too much" (Thelen, 1994, pp. 941, 945). There has long been an emphasis within the discipline that "historical research could or should be value-free" (Fulbrook, 2002, p. 16) and that an objective, scientific approach to reconstructing the past is based on the facts (Daddow, 2004; Fulbrook, 2002). Many current historians feel strongly that history written with the hope of changing policy is not proper history (Daddow, 2004).

Though historians strive for the most credible and fair interpretation of the facts and tend to avoid an activist agenda, the discipline of history has contributed to the causes of social justice by moving, over time, from methods and subjects that emphasized political history and the activities of rich, White elites to methods and subjects whose histories were previously ignored, thus, furthering the agendas of various movements for social justice. To illustrate these points, this analysis describes three time periods that capture the evolution of the discipline of history, along with the history of the LGBT movement and its advocacy for social justice.

Founding and Professionalization (1880s–1940s)

Historiography is defined by *Merriam-Webster Online* dictionary as having two components: "1) the principles, theories, and history of historical writing; 2) the product of historical writing and a body of historical literature" (*Miriam-Webster Online*, n.d.). The origins of the discipline of history, and historiography, can be traced to the beginning in the late 19th and early 20th centuries (Daddow, 2004; Lambert & Schofield, 2004). The "founding father of history" is generally considered to be German historian, Leopold Van Ranke (Daddow, 2004; Fulbrook, 2002; Lambert & Schofield, 2004). Ranke advocated for a more scientific, objective, hypothesis-driven, positivist approach to research in order to gain a unique and respectable standing within academia (Daddow, 2004; Lambert & Schofield, 2004; Ware, 1940). Historians considered themselves to be presenting a neutral, objective study of the facts that have no implications for policy or values; by using specific, scientifically driven methods that involved studying primary sources (documents written by people involved in the events being studied during the time period being studied) as opposed to secondary sources (others' interpretations of the events), historians hoped to avoid writing history that is overly ideological (e.g., Marx's interpretations of history are often cited as unreliable; see Daddow, 2004). Most historians during this period were very hesitant to use methods from other disciplines (such as ethnography in anthropology) and felt strongly that the official scientific, atheoretical presentation of facts by historians was a way for history to establish itself as an academic discipline in its own right (Cook & Glickman, 2008; Fulbrook, 2002; Ware, 1940).

In addition to using specific methods, historians during this early period tended to focus primarily on history "from the top down" that focused on specific research subjects (e.g., White people, Western political history, presidential history, wars, and intellectual and political leaders) (Cook & Glickman, 2008; Fulbrook, 2002; Lambert & Schofield, 2004; Stearns, 1983; Ware, 1940). Though this certainly reflected the biases and values of people in power during this time, it also was a strategy for professionalizing the discipline by focusing on the history of institutions that reflected both prestige and research funding. Groups such as the poor, working class, people of color, women, people with disabilities, and LGBT people were generally ignored by historians.

In contrast, there emerged during this time period an interest in history from the bottom up. In their book *The Cultural Turn in U.S. History* (2008), Cook, Glickman, and O'Malley credit historian Caroline Ware (1899–1990) as one of the most important, and often forgotten, historians who broke the traditional mold of historians of the time. In her book *The Cultural Approach to History* (1940), Ware urges historians to move away from the rigid ideals of the discipline, emphasizing a scientific method and the focus on convenient subjects and sources (mainly upper class, White men in power). She suggests that other disciplines have moved more quickly to adopt new methods and subjects of study (often outside the scope of traditional historians) and that historians have much to learn from these disciplines, particularly anthropology's study of culture. Ware insisted that historians must challenge the confines of traditional history and begin to address topics and subjects that had long been ignored, urging a new cultural approach to history (Ware, 1940; see also Cook & Glickman, 2008).

Interestingly, Ware attended Vassar College from 1916 to 1920 and first considered a career in social work (Fitzpatrick, 1991). Though Ware ultimately decided to pursue history, Fitzpatrick (1991) credits Ware's experience as a social work intern, in rural, upstate New York, working with poor immigrant families, as extremely influential in Ware's career. During this time, Ware gained an awareness that the lives of everyday people were not represented in traditional historical discourse. Ware's academic career illustrated her commitment to both academia and social activism, as she continued to study women, immigrants, people of color, and others who had rarely been represented in the discipline of history. Ware later taught in the social work program at Howard University. Though many historians officially deny that the study of history is influenced by values and political agendas, it is clear that early on, the movement toward new methods and subjects was influenced by a growing awareness of social justice.

During this early period, it was not surprising that very little was written specifically on gay and lesbian history for some of the following reasons: (a) The discipline of history concerned itself mostly with White people in power (with Ware and others as important exceptions), and (b) the gay rights movement in the 1960s and 1970s included people who identified their sexuality as something other than a traditional heterosexual one and did not constitute a recognized political category or comprise a cohesive group that could be studied.

THE MODERN PERIOD AND A NEW SOCIAL HISTORY (1940s–1970s)

The period from the 1940s to the 1970s was marked by a turn toward a new social history, "the most dramatic development in American historical research" that included increased attention to social justice (Stearns, 1983, p. 1). By this time, the discipline of history had achieved considerable standing as an established academic discipline and numbers of people entering the profession quintupled from 1940 to 1970 (Harrison, 2004). World Wars I and II had exposed Americans to the world, and the rise of Communism had forced new thinking on the role of the working class. Social movements gained momentum, and women, African Americans, immigrants, people with disabilities, and

LGBT people formed movements to advocate for their civil rights. In response to the historical context of the times, and also as a result of a growing appreciation for the advances of other disciplines, historians began to embrace new methods and subjects (Cook & Glickman, 2008; Lambert & Schofield, 2004; Stearns, 1983).

The new social history, as this movement was called, rejected the idea that rich, White males in power (usually political or war heroes and members of the elite classes) were the only worthwhile subjects for historical research. Instead, the new social history recognized that focusing on these traditional subjects had excluded the history of the majority of people in the world (Pudup, 2000). The new social history promised to capture a "total history," to get the story right and tell the real truth of a topic by studying what had been previously overlooked (Lambert & Schofield, 2004; Pudup, 2000; Stearns, 1983).

This change in historical subjects brought along a change in historical methods as well. Historians started to gain more appreciation for sophisticated qualitative, ethnographic methods (influenced greatly by the discipline of anthropology) that allowed them to focus on the cultural differences among groups (Stearns, 1983). Historians also studied a larger variety of sources than had ever been considered before, including oral histories, censuses, village birth and death records, diaries, and letters (Daddow, 2004; Stearns, 1983). In addition, people began to move into academia from different parts of society, such as poor people, rural people, and people of color, and brought with them new ideas for sources and subjects that had not been previously considered in the academic arena (Harrison, 2004). Historians took great risks in moving toward these new subjects and methods; for example, during the McCarthy hearings of the 1950s, many historians were labeled "subversive" in their work and were denied membership in the American Historical Society. Some historians admittedly used this new social history movement to try to raise awareness and empower groups that had been previously disempowered by older historical methods (Pudup, 2000). Others merely turned to social history as a way to carve out a niche for themselves in the ever-expanding field of history (Harrison, 2004). Whatever the case, the movement toward the new

social history helped further the cause of social justice for many groups.

For example, during these years, historians began to research the LGBT community. The growth of the gay rights movement had fostered a national, politicized group identity for people who had been isolated and seen as oddities or deviants within their individual communities. In responding to this new social movement, a few seminal historical works were written during this time, including Katz's *Gay American History* (1976). In the introduction to this nearly 700-page collection of primary sources written by and about LGBT people from as early as the 1500s, Katz wrote that due to the political climate of the 1970s and the rise of a gay rights movement after the Stonewall uprising in 1969, LGBT people

> have moved from various forms of self-negation to newfound outrage and action . . . starting with a sense of ourselves as characters in a closet drama . . . we experienced ourselves as initiators and assertive actors in a movement for social change . . . we experienced the change from one historical form of homosexuality to another. . . . We experienced homosexuality as historical. (p. 2)

Katz suggested that, for the first time, his collection brought together historical materials that demonstrate that homosexuals have both existed and been oppressed for hundreds of years. Along with the development of a personal and political identity, homosexual people needed to know their long and troubled history; Katz hoped that this book would help "in our present struggle to create a positive, rounded sense of self . . . and to abolish those social institutions that deny us" (1976, p. 5). Katz used the new social history's turn toward untraditional sources and new groups of subjects to publish a collection that he specifically hoped would not only contribute to the discipline of history but also would further the cause of social justice for LGBT people.

POSTMODERNISM AND THE SOCIOCULTURAL TURN (1980s–THE PRESENT)

From the 1980s to the present, one of the major debates in the discipline of history focused on the postmodern discrediting of previous historical methods and claims, especially challenging the Rankean notion of the historical, scientific objectivity. Postmodernists argue that historians always interpret history based on their own paradigm, beliefs, and political goals; in essence, the myth of objectivity is itself a paradigm and scholars must acknowledge that there is no absolute truth—every situation includes several truths (Fulbrook, 2002; McCullagh, 2004). In its extreme, postmodernism has even questioned the worth of the discipline of history, implying that other disciplines such as anthropology and sociology have more sophisticated methods and disciplinary goals (Stearns, 1983).

However, ultimately, the postmodern movement has helped clarify that, though it is impossible to determine a truly objective truth about any historical subject or event, some interpretations of history are clearly better than others. As McCullagh (2004) writes, "history is not simply a matter of opinion, for it can be rationally justified as credible and sometimes even fair" (p. 21). McCullagh emphasizes that the best accounts of history are those that present all sides and use rigorous research integrity in order to identify the most credible facts and the fairest interpretations of the facts.

Historians in the postmodern era come from diverse backgrounds and have often adopted nontraditional topics to study. Historians began to borrow from other disciplines, creating subfields, such as intellectual history, sociological history, and anthropological history. Historians have begun to acknowledge the limitations of their discipline in addition to the strengths. Though some historians have worried that history is now fragmented into multiple subfields (with no set methods or structure to guide historians), many historians have embraced these changes and see history as setting the path for new and creative ways of understanding the world (Fulbrook, 2002; McCullagh, 2004).

The strengths of history's postmodern period are exemplified in the ways that historians approached LGBT history during this time. From the 1980s to the present, LGBT history became an increasingly recognized subfield in history. Importantly, in 1990 the University of Chicago Press began publishing the *Journal of the History of Sexuality,* and in 1993, the *Journal of American History*

took the important step of officially establishing a subfield of studies titled "gay and lesbian history" (D'Emilio, 2002). The number of publications about LGBT history increased dramatically, and the contributions of LGBT historians have been influential. Historians have built on the new social and cultural movements and have sought to capture the history of LGBT people and the role of sexuality throughout time. Through their work, historians have challenged commonly held assumptions about gay people and thus helped support the LGBT civil rights movement.

First, it is often commonly assumed that the 1969 Stonewall uprisings, in which patrons at a gay bar in New York fought back after police raided the bar that led to 5 days of rioting, was the start of the gay civil rights movement. Stonewall is often presented as the ultimate beginning of LGBT people fighting for their own political identity (Carter, 2004; Chauncey, 1994; Duberman, 1993). However, using postmodern methods, sources, and subjects, historians have produced new insights into the lives of LGBT people before Stonewall and have demonstrated that LGBT people have been resisting discrimination and pushing for rights long before 1969 (D'Emilio, 1983, 2002). For example, the homophile movement existed throughout San Francisco and New York in the 1940s, 50s, and 60s. In 1955, Harry Hay published one of the first newsletters and/or magazines specifically for gay men (*The Mattachine Review*), with a national distribution of several thousand in its prime. This San Francisco magazine reflected significant courage on the part of its founders, considering the political climate in which being identified as a homosexual could result in beatings, imprisonment, and social condemnation. Though the homophile movement has been criticized as being too insistent that gay people are just the same as everyone else, it is clear by the example of *The Mattachine Review* that LGBT people were coming out of the closet and taking steps toward fighting for civil rights much before 1969 (D'Emilio, 2002).

Also, it is often assumed that there have always been two categories of sexuality, homosexuality and heterosexuality, and that the perception of homosexuality has been unchanged throughout history. In fact, many historians have carefully presented alternative interpretations of historical works and facts that suggest that this view is not accurate. D'Emilio and Freedmen's *Intimate Matters: A History of Sexuality in America* (1988) was one of the first books to insist that the binary categories of homosexual and heterosexual are 19th and 20th-century phenomena. The authors suggest that during the late 19th and early 20th centuries, medical practitioners started to learn more about the human body and created the categories of homosexuality and heterosexuality. Before the professionalization of the medical profession, the "category of sexuality" called homosexuality did not exist. Instead, men who had sex with men and women who had sex with women were quietly tolerated and ignored, not blatantly persecuted as became the case in the 20th century. Another factor in the creation of the category of homosexuality was a sexuality crisis experienced by men in the early 20th century. Brought on by industrialization and women's entrance into the workforce, men felt threatened in their sexuality and began to police sexuality by defining masculinity and identifying a subordinate "other" referred to as homosexual men. The authors suggest that these developments, in combination with the rise of a national gay identity, led to the rise of homophobia as a distinct phenomenon of modern society.

Chauncey, in his 1994 book *Gay New York*, combats various stereotypes by chronicling a highly visible gay male community that existed in New York from the 1890s through World War II. Using nontraditional sources (e.g., diaries, legal records, and oral histories), he demonstrates that a vibrant gay community existed in New York long before the stirrings of a national gay rights movement began in the 1950s. Though gay men were certainly persecuted before Stonewall, Chauncey suggests that society began to more openly and rigorously police homosexuality beginning in the 1950s. In fact, Chauncey demonstrates that before World War II, many New York citizens felt either indifferent or slightly curious about gay men and tolerated them as a part of the community, as opposed to treating them as hostile and threatening.

A final example of how historians have furthered social justice for LGBT people is the way that historians have demonstrated that "precedents" of sodomy laws do not hold up to accurate historical analysis. Conservative politicians have argued passionately that legalizing sodomy and gay marriage would go against centuries of wisdom that have upheld these laws, implying that without these laws, family values would be destroyed. In the 1986 court case of *Bowers v. Hardwick*, the United States Supreme Court upheld sodomy laws as constitutional based on "millennia of moral teaching" (as cited by Chauncey, 2008). However, in 2003, the Supreme Court ruled on *Lawrence v. Texas* and struck down the Bowers decision (and thus all sodomy laws); in a great moment for historians, the Court cited an amicus brief submitted to the Court by 10 historians that challenged the notion that sodomy laws have always had the same consequences. The brief demonstrated that though sodomy laws have existed for hundreds of years, they had most often been used to regulate "non-procreative sexual acts" between men, women, and animals and that they had not been applied specifically to homosexual sex acts until the 20th century. Second, the brief demonstrated that it was only in the late 19th century that a distinct category of sexuality titled "homosexual" emerged and that only in the early 20th century (particularly 1920–1950) did the federal government pass laws that explicitly regulated homosexual acts. In fact, a more careful examination of history (based on postmodern methods, resources, and subjects of study) demonstrated nearly the exact opposite of what the Bowers case cited as "historical fact" (Chauncey, 2008). The 2003 Supreme Court specifically credited the historical brief with influencing its decision to change precedent.

CONCLUSION

Historians have contributed to an understanding of social justice in several ways. First, through tracing the history of the term *social justice* and how it has been used over time, historians and historical philosophers have demonstrated that the meaning and usage of the term *social justice* has changed significantly since its inception in the early 1700s. Also, historians have addressed the intellectual history of ideas related to social justice. For example, by placing the debate about ending poverty in a historical context, it becomes clear that both historical economic and political factors must be taken into account in order to understand why discussions about welfare and universal health care did not regain credibility in the United States until the mid-20th century.

In addition, historians have furthered the cause of social justice through the discipline's expansion in the range of subjects covered and research methods used. Historians have moved from studying history from the top down (focusing on subjects that involved White, Western, rich, political people and events) and using methods that focused only on searching for objective, scientific "facts" to history from the bottom up in the form of social and cultural history (studying the poor and middle classes, people of color, women, LGBT people, etc.) using postmodern methods that included nontraditional sources, styles, and techniques. A case study of LGBT history demonstrates how historians have made significant contributions toward the cause of social justice through their work. Certainly, by placing social justice into a historical context and examining how historians have addressed this term, practitioners and researchers can expand their own understanding of social justice.

REFERENCES

Behr, T. (2003, January 1). Luigi Taparelli's natural law approach to social economics. *Journal Des Economistes Et Des Etudes Humaines, 13*, 213–234.

Carter, D. (2004). *Stonewall: The riots that sparked the gay revolution.* New York, NY: St. Martin's Press.

Chauncey, G. (1994). *Gay New York: Gender, urban culture, and the makings of the gay male world, 1890–1940.* New York, NY: Basic Books.

Chauncey, G. (2008). How history mattered: Sodomy law and marriage reform in the United States. *Public culture: Bulletin of the project for transnational cultural studies, 20*(1), 27–38.

Cook, J. W., & Glickman, L. B. (2008). Twelve propositions for a history of U.S. cultural history. In J. W. Cook, L. B. Glickman, & O'Malley, M. (Eds.), *The cultural turn in U.S. history: Past, present, and future* (pp. 1–57). Chicago, IL: University of Chicago Press.

Cook, J. W., Glickman, L. B., & O'Malley, M. (Eds.). (2008). *The cultural turn in U.S. history: Past, present, and future.* Chicago, IL: University of Chicago Press.

Daddow, O. (2004). The ideology of apathy: Historians and postmodernism. *Rethinking History, 8*(3), 417–437.

D'Emilio, J. (1983). *Sexual politics, sexual communities: The making of a homosexual minority in the United States, 1940–1970.* Chicago, IL: University of Chicago Press.

D'Emilio, J. (2002). *The world turned: Essays on gay history, politics, and culture.* Durham, NC: Duke University Press.

D'Emilio, J., & Freedman, E. B. (1988). *Intimate matters: A history of sexuality in America.* New York, NY: Harper & Row.

Duberman, M. B. (1993). *Stonewall.* New York, NY: Dutton.

Fitzpatrick, E. (1991). Caroline F. Ware and the cultural approach to history. *American Quarterly, 43*(2), 173. Baltimore, MD: Johns Hopkins University Press.

Fleischacker, S. (2004). *A short history of distributive justice.* Cambridge, MA: Harvard University Press.

Fulbrook, M. (2002). *Historical theory.* London, UK: Routledge.

Harrison, R. (2004). The "new social history" in America. In J. B. Gardner & G. R. Adams (Eds.), *Ordinary people and everyday life: Perspectives on the new social history* (pp. 3–22). Nashville, TN: American Association for State and Local History.

Jackson, B. (2005). The conceptual history of social justice. *Political Studies Review, 3*(3), 356–373.

Jones, G. S. (2005). *An end to poverty?: A historical debate.* New York, NY: Columbia University Press.

Katz, J. (1976). *Gay American history: Lesbians and gay men in the U.S.A.* New York, NY: Avon.

Lambert, P., & Schofield, P. R. (2004). *Making history: An introduction to the history and practices of a discipline.* London, UK: Routledge.

Longres, J. F., & Scanlon, E. (2001). Social justice and the research curriculum. *Journal of Social Work Education, 37*(3), 447–464.

McCullagh, C. B. (2004). What do historians argue about? *History and Theory, 43*(1), 18–38.

Merriam-Webster Online [dictionary]. (n.d.). Historiography. (11th ed.). Retrieved from http://www.merriam-webster.com/dictionary/HISTORIOGRAPHY.

Miller, D. (1999). *Principles of social justice.* Cambridge, MA: Harvard University Press.

National Association of Scholars (NAS). (2007). The scandal of social work education. Retrieved from http://www.nas.org/articles/The_Scandal_of_Social_Work_Education.

National Association of Social Workers (NASW). (2009). *Code of ethics of the National Association of Social*

Workers. Retrieved from http://www.socialworkers .org/pubs/code/default.asp

Pudup, M. B. (2000). The new, new social history? *Antipode, 32*(4), 505–507.

Shields, L. W. (1941). *The history and meaning of the term social justice.* Notre Dame, IN: Notre Dame.

Southgate, B. (2003). Intellectual history/history of ideas. In S. Berger, H. Feldner, & K. Passmore (Eds.), *Writing history: Theory & practice* (pp. 243–260). London, UK: Arnold.

Stearns, P. (1983). The new social history: An overview. In J. B. Gardner & G. R. Adams (Eds.), *Ordinary people and everyday life: Perspectives on the new social history* (pp. 3–22). Nashville, TN: American Association for State and Local History.

Thelen, D. (1994). The Practice of American History. *Journal of American History, 81*(3), 933–960.

Ware, C. (1940). *The cultural approach to history.* Port Washington, NY: Kennikat Press.

6

SOCIAL JUSTICE AND RELIGION

SARAH ACCOMAZZO, MEGAN MOORE, AND SIROJ SIROJUDIN

Most modern democratic nation-states have been generally successful in separating religion and the state. However, the substantive elements of law and justice systems that define the scope of freedom in the realms of social, economic, and human rights can be traced back to religious beliefs and the influence of organized religions. This chapter explores the concept of social justice within three world religions: Judaism, Christianity, and Islam. It explores how these religions define social justice and how to achieve it while recognizing the complexity of interpretation and arguments among different scholars and schools of thought. In the words of DeYoung (2008),

All of the major historic religions, if practiced authentically, share a core commitment to justice, reconciliation, and peace. . . . (When we focus) on the life story and legacy of a Christian pastor named Martin Luther King Jr. (over) forty years after his death, (we find) an exemplar of how religion inspires a life of activism for social justice. . . . Religion was the source of King's commitment to racial justice. Martin Luther King's Christian faith provided personal encouragement in difficult times. But it was also something more. King (noted that) any religion that professes to be concerned about the souls of men and is not concerned about the slums that damn them, the economic conditions that strangle them and the social conditions that cripple them is a spiritually moribund religion awaiting burial. (DeYoung, 2008, "How Religion Inspires Social Justice"; see also DeYoung, 2007)

As noted throughout the literature on social justice, the moral dimensions of justice are pervasive, namely, doing the right thing, doing right by others, or responding to injustices with righteous indignation. Much of the codified moral teachings can be traced to sources in organized religions. While reviewing the elements of all the religions in the world is beyond the scope of this chapter, the major sources of three historic religions were identified in order to describe a set of key social justice principles.

These sources include the Old Testament in Judaism, the New Testament in Christianity (in addition to the Catholic encyclicals), and the Qur'an in Islam. This chapter features the Judaic perspective of social justice related to three core principles (acts of loving-kindness, repairing the world, and righteousness acts), the seven major themes of Catholic social teaching (life and dignity of the human person; call to family, community, and participation; rights and responsibilities; option for the poor and vulnerable; dignity of work and the rights of workers; solidarity; and care for God's creation), and the four major Islamic teaching about social justice (fairness and balanced acts in the court, balanced acts in social relation, modesty of personal behavior, and sharing or equity) as interpreted by both the classical and the contemporary scholars (tribal, modernists, revivalists, and neo-modernists). This array of social justice concepts provides another perspective on the origins of social justice found in the humanities.

JUDAIC PERSPECTIVES ON SOCIAL JUSTICE

A study of the Jewish community's engagement with the term *social justice* can contribute to a deeper understanding of the meaning and applications of social justice, particularly because concepts related to social justice can be traced back to Judaism's most ancient holy texts and commentaries (Jacobs, 2009; Kliksberg, 2003; Rose, Green, & Klein, 2008; Schwarz, 2006; Vorspan & Saperstein, 1998). This section begins with a brief history of how the concept of social justice developed into a guiding principle among Reform Jews in America within the context of the universalism versus particularism debate. Next, several Jewish concepts related to social justice are examined in relationship to Jewish texts and commentaries. While not a comprehensive review of social justice and the history of Jews in America, this section highlights some of the major concepts that can increase current understandings of social justice.

Brief History of American Reform Judaism's Engagement With Social Justice

Traditional, Orthodox Judaism and a particularist emphasis. Due to the intense immigration patterns of the 19th century and the influx of Jewish immigrants into America, two specific strains of American Judaism emerged during this time: traditional Orthodox Judaism and Classical Reform Judaism (Jacob, 2002; Kaplan, 2002; Raphael, 2003; Sarna, 2004). The eastern European immigrants of the late 19th century brought an urgent sense of traditional ritual practice to American Jews. These Jewish immigrants had often faced anti-Semitism in other countries and identified strongly with a Jewish ethnicity. They formed professional trade organizations and community centers with others from the same European hometown. They maintained Yiddish as their primary language and practiced traditional orthodox ritual observances, such as the laws of keeping kosher, strict Sabbath and holiday observances, and separation of men and women in synagogues (Raphael, 2003; Sarna, 2004, p. 165).

Traditional orthodox Jewish practice during this time emphasized social justice concepts yet tended to take a particularist interpretation, in which Jews practiced social justice within their own communities but did not necessarily do social justice work outside of their communities (a more universalistic interpretation of Jewish social justice concepts). One major reason for this particularist social justice impulse was the experience of eastern European immigrants with anti-Semitism in their home countries; they had often been forced to live in segregated communities where the state did not take care of their needs and discriminated against them. Though traditional Judaism has always emphasized concepts related to social justice and Orthodox Jews continued to do so within their own communities in America, the term *social justice* was not commonly used in traditional, orthodox Jewish practice or in traditional orthodox literature and text during this time.

American Reform Jews and the universalist impulse. The term *social justice* came into common usage among American Jews during the 19th century as part of the Classical Reform movement emerging throughout the 19th and early 20th centuries in America (Jacob, 2002; Raphael, 2003; Sarna, 2004). Classical Reform Judaism, started in Germany in 1810 (Kaplan, 2002), reflected the more integrated, assimilated history and identity of these Jews in their European countries of origin, an identification with the nationality of their country of origin (and less of an identity with Judaism as a distinct ethnic identity), and thus a movement away from traditional, ritual practices. As these central and western European Jews immigrated to America, they brought Reform Jewish practices to America. Reform Judaism took on a life of its own in America during the 19th century, where it fit very well into other American historical trends, such as the Protestant Social Gospel movement and the melting pot, or assimilationist, ideal pushed in American politics and adopted by many immigrants (Kaplan, 2002; Raphael, 2003; Sarna, 2004).

During the 19th century and early 20th century, Classical Reform Jews in America adopted social justice as one of their major tenets, using the term *justice* specifically and emphasizing a more universalist application of the term. Though Jewish interpretations of holy texts from all denominations emphasize concepts related to social justice, and have done so for thousands of years, Classical Reform Jews in American were the first to adopt the term *social justice* and embrace its contemporary usage. Classical Reform Judaism moved away from traditional orthodox practices (e.g., keeping kosher, head coverings in synagogues, separating men and women in synagogues, and literal interpretations of holy texts; see Raphael, 2003; Sarna, 2004). Instead, the Reform movement emphasized (a) the universal connection of all humans intellectually and morally, (b) the need to leave behind old-fashioned rituals and practices that interfered with modernity, and (c) the idea of an "ethical monotheism" that emphasized a higher calling to fulfill certain moral obligations to humanity, in opposition to a ritual monotheism that emphasized religious affiliation based on ritual obligations (Kaplan, 2002; Sarna, 2004; Saperstein, 2008).

Reflecting these changes, a movement developed within Classical Reform Judaism during this time called "Prophetic Judaism," shifting emphasis from the Torah to the Neviim texts (detailing words of wisdom from 15 famous Jewish prophets, including Amos, Isaiah, Micah, and more) (Jacobs, 2008; Sarna, 2004). In Judaism, a prophet is typically defined as someone selected by God who thereby speaks the word of God (Jacobs, 2008). In the Neviim, the prophets often champion the poor and advocate for justness and righteousness, while de-emphasizing ritual practice. Prophetic Judaism placed ethical obligations over ritual obligations and was a way to connect a commitment to social justice to ancient textual sources, de-emphasizing Torah and ritual obligation and favoring a more universalist social justice focus.

By the late 19th century, Classical Reform Judaism had officially taken on justice as one of its major tenets (Raphael, 2003; Sarna, 2004). In 1885, at the Pittsburgh Platform, Reform Jewish clergy and practitioners came together for the first time and adopted a set of guiding principles that became the standards for Reform Judaism. Justice was listed as one of the main principles, as principle number 8 read, "in full accordance with the spirit of the Mosaic legislation, which strives to regulate the relations between rich and poor, we deem it our duty to participate in the great task of modern times, to solve, on the basis of justice and righteousness, the problems presented by the contrasts and evils of the present organization of society" (Central Conference of American Rabbis [CCAR], 2004, "The Pittsburgh Platform—1885," para. 8). In reflection of this Platform, Reform Jews became visibly involved in social justice causes throughout America; for example, David Einhorn, a famous abolitionist during the late 19th century, was greatly influenced by his Reform Jewish background and brought concepts from Judaism into his antislavery work (Jacob, 2002; Sarna, 2004).

In 1937, Reform Jewish rabbis came together again and issued the Columbus Platform, which indicated some major changes in other aspects of Reform American Jewish life, but it strongly reaffirmed Classic Reform Judaism's commitment to social justice, this time actually using the term *social justice* and devoting an entire paragraph to the principle in the Ethics section. Specific issues relevant to the time are listed as officially part of the Reform Jewish commitment to social justice. Continuing a trend set in 1885, American Reform Jews began to reflect the influence of eastern European immigrants by emphasizing Judaism as an ethnicity as well as a religion and taking a strong stance supporting the idea of a state of Israel. However, overall, they took a universalist stance about social justice and chose to emphasize moral and ethical responsibilities over traditional religious ritual.

A shift in American Reform Judaism toward a particularist Jewish social justice emphasis. During the mid-20th century, several major events contributed to a shift in American Jewish Reform movements from emphasizing universalist social justice values to a more particularistic social justice focus. First, the years leading up to World War II and the Holocaust contributed to an abiding sense among American Jews from all denominations that European Enlightenment principles had failed and that modernity and assimilation had failed to bring the safety, peace, and freedom from anti-Semitism that Jews had hoped for (Raphael, 2003; Sarna, 2004). American Reform Jews, who had particularly embodied a universalistic and more assimilationist belief system, began to question the universality sentiment and moved toward a view of Jews as a common people with a common history and future.

In the 1950s and 60s, many American Jews did keep their universalist social justice emphasis to some extent, as many from all denominations became involved in the civil rights movements for disenfranchised groups. For this group, injustices against any minority group could not be tolerated, because if one group was in danger, all groups were in danger. For example, Rabbi Abraham Heschel, an Orthodox Jewish immigrant from eastern Europe who is regarded as one of the most influential religious theologians of the 20th century, was an impassioned, outspoken advocate for the Black civil rights movement (Lerner, 2008; Sarna, 2004).

However, the movement in American Reform Judaism toward social justice particularism began in the 1950s and would continue to the end of the 20th century. Many events contributed to this shift. The creation of the state of Israel in 1948 had a significant impact; the American Jewish community, Reform, Conservative, and Orthodox alike, many of whom now had a strong financial basis in the United States, provided immeasurable financial support for this new country, indicating the recognition by American Jews of Judaism not just as a religion or moral creed but also as an ethnicity with a spiritual and national center with whom all Jews shared a common history and future interest (Sarna, 2004). Also, the civil rights movement allowed Jews to observe other groups finding solidarity in ethnic identity (sometimes to the point of making Jews feel less welcome), leading many Jews to focus inward and develop a group identity and consciousness of their own.

From the 1970s through 2000, the Reform Jewish community shifted dramatically from a more universalistic social justice focus to a more particularistic social justice focus (Raphael, 2003; Sarna, 2004).

The entire country moved toward an identity politics mind-set, and the Jewish community did the same. Social justice causes, such as Israel and helping free Soviet Jews, became a central focus of many Jewish social justice activists.

In 1999, the Central Conference of Reform Rabbis met, symbolically once again in Pittsburgh, and adopted a new set of guiding principles (CCAR, 2004, "Adopted in Pittsburgh—1999"; Sarna, 2004). The 1999 Platform, though still emphasizing a commitment to social justice as an integral aspect of Reform Judaism, couched a commitment to social justice in terms of a ritual and spiritual way of life. For the first time, a platform emphasized that social justice is specifically a partnership with God. Hebrew terms which were not previously part of a platform, such as *tikkun olam* and *tzedakah,* came into common usage. Some specific social justice acts are mentioned, but they are stated in much more vague terms than in the 1937 Platform. Reform Judaism had invested in connecting to traditional ritual and establishing a more inwardly focused, spiritual, vibrant Jewish community. Though still committed to social justice, this was couched in slightly different terms.

Jewish Social Justice Concepts

Jews from all over the world have identified concepts related to social justice as major tenets of Judaism for thousands of years (Jacobs, 2009; Schwarz, 2008; Vorspan & Saperstein, 1998). The contemporary era is no different; in fact, some argue that social justice is the main purpose of Judaism in the contemporary world. This section describes several key concepts that are often referenced today in contemporary discussions of social justice, namely, acts of loving kindness, repairing the world, and the pursuit of justice.

Chesed/gemilut chasidim. *Chesed* is often translated as "kindness" and *gemilut chasidim* is translated as "acts of loving-kindness" (Kanarek, 2008; Schwarz, 2006). Acts of chesed are immediate responses to immediate needs (Kanarek, 2008) and are ways that humans can act in God's image (Schwarz, 2006). The importance of chesed is symbolized by the fact that the Torah begins and ends with acts of chesed by God. In Genesis, God gives Adam and Eve clothing, an act of chesed, and at the end of the Torah, God buries Moses, also an act of chesed (Kanarek, 2008; Schwarz, 2006). These are particularly sacred because God did them without any expectation that the favor would be returned, and humans are expected to follow this example. Acts of chesed are considered some of the most sacred and holy responsibilities that the Torah imparts to the Jewish people, as expressed by an oft-quoted piece of writing in the Talmud, Pirkei Avot 1:2: "Simeon the Righteous used to say: 'On three things does the world stand: Torah, avodah (service), and gemilut chasidim (acts of loving kindness)'" (Kliksberg, 2003; Schwarz, 2006).

Tikkun ha'olam. An important distinction is made in the holy texts between acts of chesed and *tikkun olam*. Acts of chesed are present oriented and solve an immediate problem without any expectation of recip-rocation. However, tikkun olam represents the com-mitment to repair systematic injustices in the world and to help plan for a better future and is conceptually more related to social justice (Kanarek, 2008).

The phrase *tikkun ha'olam* may be translated from Hebrew to English as "repair the world" (Kanarek, 2008). However, due to the fact that bib-lical Hebrew did not contain vowels and so transla-tions can be slightly different depending on who did the translating, there are many different ways to interpret this phrase. *Tikkun* can also mean "to estab-lish" and *l'olam* can be taken to mean "eternity," referring to the physical, spiritual, emotional, or other types of eternity (Jacobs, 2009, p. 27). Though the phrase occurs in slight variations in the Aleinu prayer, one of the oldest and most holy Jewish prayers written in the second century CE, it seems to be first used to mean "repair the world" (its more contemporary interpretation) in the Mishnah, where it appears 10 to 15 times and is used by the rabbis to close loopholes or to justify a change in the legal system (Jacobs, 2009; Kanarek, 2008). The rabbis wrote that these changes should occur *mipnei tikkun ha'olam* or "because of tikkun ha'olam," and nearly all these situations have to do with changing laws in order to protect poor or vulnerable populations or to fix inequalities brought on by systemic injus-tice (Jacobs, 2009, pp. 30–31). For example, in the Mishnah, Gittin 4:2, it is written that a husband may not call a court of law and cancel a divorce docu-ment without the knowledge of his ex-wife "because of tikkun ha'olam"; commentary suggests that the rabbis outlawed this because it was unfair to the wife; if the wife does not know, she may still think she is divorced and do things that married women are not allowed to do (Kanarek, 2008).

However, it was during the 1950s, with the revival of a Lurianic Kabbalah story, part of Jewish mystic tradition, that the phrase tikkun olam was brought into commonly used American Jewish vocabulary, emphasizing the interpretation as "repair the world" (Jacobs, 2009; Kanarek, 2008). Rabbi Isaac Luria (1534–1572), in what is now Safed, Israel, told a creation story in which God took part of God's divine presence and replaced it with something finite and unholy—the world. As the story goes, God contained the divine part in holy vessels, how-ever, some of these vessels were too weak to hold the divine presence, and they shattered. Pieces of the divine presence got caught on the shards, and these shards scattered throughout the world, representing the introduction of evil in the world. It is the job of humans to find these pieces of a broken world and fit them back together in order to recreate God's divine presence on Earth (Jacobs, 2009; Kanarek, 2008). In the 1950s, American Jews began to use this story as a rallying cry for social justice work.

Tzedek/tzedakah. *Tzedek* and *tzedakah* both stem from a common root, and tzedek has been translated into many different meanings, including "just" or "justice" or "righteousness" or "loyalty" or "truth" or "courageous" (Jacobs, 2009). Rabbi Jill Jacobs (2009) argues that, ultimately, textual analysis of *tzedek* shows that *tzedek* is a relational term and is used mostly within the context of relationships to show a just, or right, or courageous way to interact with God and/or with other human beings, mostly encouraging humans to help the oppressed and vul-nerable. In a holy text often cited by contemporary Jewish social justice advocates, Deuteronomy 16:20 says, "*tzedek, tzedek tirdof*," translated as "jus-tice, and only justice, shall you pursue" (Coogan, Brettler, Newsom, & Perkins, 2001). Just before this verse, laws are being discussed about how to appoint fair judges, and God forbids the acceptance of bribes when picking judges, emphasizing that justice is achieved only in the fair, unbiased selection of judges. In another famous example of tzedakah, in the book of Genesis, God plans to strike down the entire cities of Sodom and Gomorrah, but Abraham challenges God and insists that the entire cities are not corrupted, and so it would be unjust to punish the innocent as if they were wicked, stating in Genesis 18:25, "Shall not the judge of all the earth do what is just?" (Coogan et al., 2001). Both of these examples support Jacobs's position that the term *tzedek* is specifically used in conjunction with describing relationships between the powerful and powerless and in supporting the needs of the oppressed population (Jacobs, 2008).

Variations on *tzedek*, with the same root, also shed light on the meaning of tzedek and its justice-focused, relational connotations. The term *tzedakah* is used in Jewish holy texts, starting in the first centuries of the common era, to denote financial gifts to the poor, made, not out of a sense of generosity but out of an obligation to address an unjust situation (Jacobs, 2009, p. 43). *Tzedakah* is thus very different from *charity*, because charity denotes a gift made out of kindness and generosity of the giver, without specifying the plight of the receiver (Jacobs, 2009, p. 43); in contemporary times, charity is often associated with a paternalistic attitude that the poor somehow deserve their lot (Vorspan & Saperstein, 1999). On the other hand, tzedakah is meant to be associated with a duty to address an unjust situation that is not the fault of the receiver of tzedakah; the giver of tzedakah gives because of an obligation to make a positive change to this unjust situation (Vorspan & Saperstein, 1999; Kliksberg, 2003, p. 21). For example, King David is considered an exemplar of someone who practiced tzedakah. In a story in the Babylonian Talmud (Sanhedrin 6b), King David is asked to punish, according to an existing law, a poor man who stole food; King David fines the man as the law requires, but because the man cannot pay the fine since he is poor, King David pays the fine out of his own pocket, thus, practicing both tzedakah, and justice (as told in Schwarz, 2006, p. 33). King David recognized that the poor man was not fully at fault for stealing food, as an unjust system left him without proper nourishment in the first place.

The term *tzedakah* is frequently used by American Jews today. For example, many Jewish organizations, synagogues, and households now have their own tzedakah boxes, where money is collected and then donated to a just cause. Many organizations list tzedakah as among their missions, such as Jewish Funds for Justice, a progressive Jewish organization that raises funds for social justice projects throughout the world, which includes in its mission statement, "The Jewish Fund for Justice is a national, publicly-supported foundation that acts on the historic commitment of the Jewish people to tzedakah (righteous giving) and tikkun olam (repair of the world). We believe that a commitment to combating poverty in the U.S., and the injustices underlying it, is an essential part of our core identity and values as Jews" (Jewish Fund for Justice, n.d., Mission Statement section, para. 1).

SOCIAL JUSTICE AND THE CATHOLIC PERSPECTIVES

Social justice is difficult to define. Considering the changing relationships between various social groups, any definition of social justice needs to be understood as fluid and variable depending on which group is defining it, the historical context, and on the nature of current social, economic, and political movements. The views of religious groups are of interest in this context due to the large influence they have on defining the moral basis of social justice in modern society.

A focus on the Roman Catholic Church is particularly important because Catholicism is the largest Christian faith, claiming approximately 1.1 billion members worldwide, or approximately 16% of the world population (Adherents, 2009). Catholic perspectives on social justice are illustrated by the following seven themes from Catholic social teaching: (a) life and dignity of the human person; (b) call to family, community, and participation; (c) rights and responsibilities; (d) option for the poor and vulnerable; (e) the dignity of work and the rights of workers; (f) solidarity; and (g) care for God's creation (U.S. Conference of Catholic Bishops, or USCCB, 2009). These themes are explored along with an example of social justice in action related to liberation theology.

CATHOLIC SOCIAL TEACHING

The seven themes of Catholic social teaching were derived from papal encyclicals, ecumenical councils, and other episcopal documents (USCCB, 2009). In particular, *Rerum Novarum* of 1891 (meaning "new things" in Latin) is acknowledged as the foundation of modern Catholic social teaching (Pope John Paul II, 1991). *Rerum Novarum* was Pope Leo XIII's encyclical that focused on capital and labor. It has been modified and expanded in modern times and serves as the basis for Catholic understanding of economic life and social justice. In addition, Catholic social teachings provide a modern guide for directing individuals toward social justice through social action (Windley-Daoust et al., 2008).

Scholars often interpret the social encyclicals and other church teachings to inform modern social and ethical debates. For example, the teachings have been applied to the social justice aspects of health care access (Langan, 1996), the commercialization of biotechnology (Cahill, 2001), poverty and globalization (Hollenbach, 2002), and foreign policy (Hehir, 1990). The encyclicals are also relevant to understanding Catholic interpretation of social welfare.

Criticism of Catholic social thought has also emerged in the literature. Cahill (2007) summarizes that the teachings have been called overly optimistic "about human nature," biased toward "moral and political authority," lacking in recognition of the solely "Western and Christian" applicability of some of its key concepts, lacking in "theological and philosophical-political" integration, and avoidant of addressing "racism and sexism" (p. 392). For example, the liberation theology movement began in the 1960s in Latin America and the Caribbean with a specific focus on addressing some of the social structural factors associated with poverty and inequality that were being marginalized within the Catholic teachings (Gutierrez, 1999). The proponents of liberation theology were challenged by the Church and continue to struggle to integrate their

message into the larger Catholic social teachings. This history is explored further in the final section.

Rooted in a belief in the Christian God, the seven themes of Catholic social teaching need to be viewed as part of a total picture of Catholic understanding of social justice (Windley-Daoust et al., 2008). The current Pope Benedict XVI (2009) affirmed that "there is a single teaching, consistent and at the same time ever new" (p. 12)[1], and this view applies to the seven themes that are highlighted in Table 6.1. The themes of family, community, and participation and the dignity of work along with the option for the poor and vulnerable are expanded upon in this analysis.

Call to family, community, and participation. Family is central to the social lives of Catholics and should therefore be supported (USCCB, 2009). With respect to community, Catholics are called upon to participate in their community and seek to improve the well being of "the poor and vulnerable" (USCCB, 2009). Participation has two concepts embedded in it, the common good and subsidiarity (Windley-Daoust et al., 2008).

The promotion of the common good calls for the promotion of the spiritual and physical growth of others (Langan, 1996). In 1967. Pope Paul VI articulated this message in *Populorum Progressio*. More recently, Pope Benedict XVI (2009) addressed this message by explaining that the church is promoting "integral human development" and needs to "operate in a climate of freedom" (p. 11). Authentic human development requires "development in every single dimension," including serving others (Pope Benedict XVI, 2009, p. 11). The "notion of development" is "the heart of the Christian social message . . . and Christian charity . . . [is] the principal force at the service of development" (Pope Benedict XVI, 2009, p. 13).

Quadragesimo Anno (1931), an encyclical of Pope Pius XI, introduced the idea of subsidiarity, affirming that while the state can provide human rights, problems should be resolved at the lowest or local level, using social networks before moving up to request formal help from a government entity (Langan, 1996). The state should follow both the

---

[1] As is the custom, the encyclicals are divided into numbered chapters rather than pages. Therefore, the numbers in parenthesis that refer to an encyclical represent the chapter number in which the quotation is located.

Table 6.1   The Seven Themes of Catholic Social Teaching

Theme	Description
Life and Dignity of the Human Person	Every person is created in the image of God, and every life is, therefore, inherently sacred. This core moral value underlies the church's social and political action against such controversial issues as abortion, euthanasia, cloning, embryonic stem cell research, the death penalty, and war (USCCB, 2009). Pope John XXIII (1963) affirmed his belief in universal human rights reflected in his encyclical *Pacem In Terris* (Langan, 1996). Modern interpretations of this principle suggest that these rights can be secured by modern welfare states (Langan, 1996).
Call to Family, Community, and Participation	Marriage and family are central to the social lives of Catholics and should therefore be supported (USCCB, 2009). Catholics are called upon to participate in their community (USCCB, 2009).
Rights and Responsibilities	All people have both rights inherent to their human nature and responsibilities to their family and community (USCCB, 2009). Each person is entitled to things necessary to sustain life (USCCB, 2009) and has the responsibility to maintain the rights of others to the extent that those with excess wealth are expected to give to others to ensure that they are fulfilled (Windley-Daoust et al., 2008).
Option for the Poor and Vulnerable	There is a need to care for the poor (USCCB, 2009). *Rerum Novarum* (1891) opposed violence and hatred and insisted that justice, with faith, could prevail over these evils to create a harmonious society (Pope John Paul II, 1991).
Dignity of Work and the Rights of Workers	Work is "a form of continuing participation in God's creation," and therefore, workers rights and dignity of work must be protected (USCCB, 2009). The right to ownership and private property must be protected (USCCB, 2009). The free market is part of fair participation.
Solidarity	We are all members of the human family and are called to protect each other. The pursuit of the common good involves contributing to the social conditions that promote the spiritual and physical growth of others (Langan, 1996). Supporting solidarity is viewed as an important counterbalance to the individualistic culture of our times (Langan, 1996). John Paul II (1988) affirmed the teaching of solidarity and authentic development in both economic and moral spheres where everyone should have access to modern science and technology (Langan, 1996).
Care for God's Creation	Moral obligation to care for the Earth, the environment, and all people.

principle of subsidiarity "by creating favorable conditions for the free exercise of economic activity and the principle of solidarity by defending the weakest" (Pope John Paul II, 1991, p. 15).

The church specifically addressed the welfare state by calling for public assistance to remedy poverty (Pope John Paul II, 1991). However, excesses in welfare are "the result of an inadequate understanding of the tasks proper to the State" (Pope John Paul II, 1991, p. 48). Subsidiarity means that a community of a higher order (e.g., the state) "should not interfere in the internal life of a community of a lower order (e.g., friends or family), depriving the latter of its functions, but rather should support it in the case of need and help to coordinate its activity with the activities of the rest of society, always with a view of the common good" (Pope John Paul II, 1991, p. 48). The church is called upon to continue to perform charity and welfare to this end (Pope John Paul II, 1991).

Dignity of work and the rights of workers. According to this theme, work is "a form of continuing participation in God's creation" and therefore workers rights must be protected (USCCB, 2009). In addition, the right to ownership and private property must be protected (USCCB, 2009). Dignity of work and the rights of workers to fair treatment should be protected; the free market and private ownership are part of fair participation.

The concepts of work and worker rights originated in *Rerum Novarum* (1891) and have had profound influence on the modern Catholic understanding of social justice and the welfare state. Therefore, this encyclical is explored in more depth with a focus on the following five major areas of economic social justice: (a) the market, (b) the distribution of goods, (c) duties and rights of workers and employers, (d) the role of the church in analyzing and commenting on the first three areas, and (e) the role of the state in regulating the first three areas.

Pope Leo XIII (1891) asserted that a free market creates social and economic balance based on the possession of private property. While the right to private property was affirmed, excess goods should be given to the poor because people naturally differ in their capacity and ability to participate in the market, and "unequal fortune is a necessary result of unequal condition" (p. 17). Those who have received a "large share of temporal blessings" are obliged to use them and then share material possessions "without hesitation when others are in need" (p. 22). Within the free market, both laborers and employers have rights and responsibilities. Workers were obliged to perform their work, never to injure their employer or his goods, and never to riot. Instead, workers were encouraged to participate in unions and utilize the strength of the group toward peaceful advocacy for their rights.

The state, or government, should have a role in ensuring social justice for workers. In fact, the wage-earning working class requires "special consideration" and state protection since it must rely on the government as a safety net and because it is so crucial to the well-being of society (Pope Leo XIII, 1891, p. 37). In addition, the state should support "free agreements" between employers and employees and private ownership should encourage, through policy, many to become owners (p. 45). The government should step in if free agreements are not upheld or in the case of unfair labor practices. The government should not excessively tax or regulate most private groups, such as unions. The government's role is to protect the poor while allowing individuals to freely strive for success in their work.

Modern interpretations support the intervention of the state in order to ensure justice, while allowing for freedom of the individual and family (Pope John Paul II, 1991). The state should not "control the means of production" but should determine "the judicial framework within which economic affairs are to be conducted" in order to protect the poor (Pope John Paul II, 1991, p. 15). It should guarantee security and human rights while allowing for individual freedom and creativity in the market. In effect, the church supports a regulated market. It recognizes "the positive value of the market and of enterprise, but . . . at the same time points out that these need to be oriented towards the common good" (Pope John Paul II, 1991, p. 43). Owning property or the means of production is just "if it serves useful work" but is unjust if it exploits the workers or does not contribute to the overall good of society (Pope John Paul II, 1991, p. 43). To this end, the church values "authentic democracy," also defined as democracy with morals (Pope John Paul II, 1991, p. 46).

Option for the poor and vulnerable. The Catholic church acknowledges that wealth disparity is growing, and there is a need to care for the poor who deserve special attention (USCCB, 2009). In *Rerum Novarum* (1891) Catholics are called upon specifically to care for the poor (Pope John Paul II, 1991). The church teaches that faith in God is the key to peace, social cooperation, and justice, and that the church's role is "preeminent" in preserving peace and providing a "necessary ethical foundation" for addressing social problems (Pope John Paul II, 1991, p. 60). The liberation theology movement expanded and took action on this social teaching.

Liberation Theology: Social Justice in Action

Exploring the roots of liberation theology provides another avenue for understanding and interpreting Catholic social justice. It has played a controversial role in defining modern Catholic social justice by emphasizing the use of political and social action to address the needs of the poor and vulnerable. The liberation theology movement began in the era of the civil rights movements of the 1960s by encouraging an action-based focus on options for the poor in Latin America. Gustavo Gutierrez, a Peruvian Roman Catholic priest and professor, is credited with championing the movement that focuses on the social and moral injustice of poverty and the direct action needed to create liberation for the oppressed and vulnerable groups in society (Rowland, 1999). In particular, liberation theology is a "contextual theology" whose proponents live and work among the poor and seek to address the unjust social and structural causes affecting those on the margins of society (see Hartnett, 2003). It is a reconciliation of faith in God and the church with the realities of the poverty affecting so many Catholics (Gutierrez, 1999).

There are special definitions of poverty and liberation within the context of liberation theology. Gutierrez (as qtd. in Hartnett, 2003) explains that the term "preferential option for the poor" originated in the Latin American Catholic Church in the 1970s as a core tenet of liberation theology and can be defined in the following way:

> The term poverty refers to the real poor. . . . The poverty to which the option refers is material poverty. Material poverty means premature and unjust death. The poor person is someone who is treated as a nonperson, someone who is considered insignificant from an economic, political and cultural point of view. The poor count as statistics; they are the nameless. But even though the poor remain insignificant within society, they are never insignificant before God. . . . [T]he word preferential [means] God demonstrates a special predilection toward those who have been excluded from the banquet of life. . . . In some ways, option is perhaps the weakest word in the sentence. In English, the word merely connotes a choice between two things. In Spanish, however, it evokes the sense of commitment. The option for the poor is not optional, but is incumbent upon every Christian. (as qtd. in Hartnett, 2003, "Do You Think the 'Preferential Option for the Poor'" section heading, para. 3).

Liberation theology seeks to address the situation of the poor through political, religious, personal, and social action.

Various types of liberation are included in this philosophy, such as political and social liberation, human liberation, and liberation from sin (Gutierrez, 1999). Political and social liberation address the social and economic structures that cause poverty, human liberation refers to changing anything else that "limit[s] their capacity to develop themselves freely," and liberation from sin means establishing "friendship" with God (Gutierrez, 1999, p. 26). These types of liberation call for working and living among the poor, community organizing with the church, and political advocacy by Catholic priests in order to directly effect local policy. Here, the concepts of praxis and "conscientization" infiltrate liberation theology. Praxis from this perspective means that first one must practice God's will and only after that can one reflect on God and faith (Gutierrez, 1999). Practice liberating the poor first, reflect on faith second (Gutierrez, 1999). Conscientization is a term linked to praxis and coined by Freire, an influential lay Catholic educator in Brazil (Brown, 1990). The term refers to gaining awareness of the social and economic structures that disempower the poor and becoming motivated to change these structures (Brown, 1990). In *Pedagogy of the Oppressed*, Paulo Freire linked conscientization back to praxis: "action and reflection . . . it is transformation of the world" (2000, p. 119). These two are inextricably linked in a symbiotic and reciprocal relationship.

This form of liberation work has been controversial and resulted in sanctions from the church. The Roman Catholic church's Congregation for the Doctrine of Faith (CDF), the group responsible for deciding and expressing the church's official interpretation of scripture and faith, published instructions on how liberation theology should be interpreted. In particular, the CDF initially condemned the "damaging" results of the concepts in liberation theology that are "borrowed from various currents of Marxist thought" (CDF, 1984). This interpretation was disseminated by Joseph Cardinal

Ratzinger, then prefect of the CDF and now Pope Benedict XVI. Gutierrez was called to Rome many times to defend his writing on the subject. He was called by the CDF to explain his work in detail so often that he is reported to have said, "The Sacred Congregation invented a new torture for me. They forced me to read many times my own books" (Brown, 1990, p. 137). In 1986, the CDF issued a second instruction that has been interpreted as much more positive toward the theology (Brown, 1990) and a survey of the members of the Pontifical Biblical Commission reported a more positive perspective (Rowland, 1999). However, in 2006, the CDF issued a critical notification regarding the works of liberation theologist and Catholic priest Jon Sobrino. The difficulties of integrating the ideas and philosophy of liberation theology within the more traditional views of the Roman Catholic faith remain. Despite this, Gutierrez, among others, remains an active member of the church and continues to work, teach, and preach liberation theology. The struggles between liberation theologians and Catholic leaders reflect the ongoing difficulty and fluidity of defining social justice.

Catholic Social Justice Defined

Despite ongoing debates within the church, the seven themes of Catholic social teaching have been consolidated into a definition of social justice. Catholic social justice can be defined as a combination of commutative, distributive, contributive, legal, achievement, and chance justice (Spiess, 2007). Drawing from the Pastoral Letter of the 1986 U.S. Conference of Catholic Bishops, Spiess (2007) identified the following six categories of social justice: (a) commutative justice (as in the demand for "fundamental fairness in all agreements and exchanges between individuals or private social groups," (b) distributive justice (emphasizing that the "allocation of income, wealth and power in society" has to be "evaluated in the light of its effects on persons whose basic material needs are unmet)," (c) contributive justice (representing on the one hand the obligation of all persons "to be active and productive participants in the life of society," and, on the other hand, society's duty to enable them to participate this way), (d) legal justice (as the

guarantee of fair proceedings in judgment regardless of "race," gender, social, denominational or any other differences), (e) the justice of achievement (as the obligation to consider individual achievement when allocating any of the goods mentioned above, both in order to recompense efforts by high capacity people and in order to compensate for the lower activity of low-capacity people), and (f) the justice of chances (as the demand that all persons should be guaranteed a real prospect of "participation in the life of the human community," which evidently refers to distributive and contributive justice (pp. 295–296).

Liberation theologists might add "action justice" or a type of justice that requires social action on behalf of the poor. Multiple values are rooted in these different types of justice. The emphasis on one or more of these types of justice can vary in any one of the seven themes of the social teaching and in the liberation theology movement.

Given the complexity of defining social justice, it is clear that there are multiple layers of social justice embedded in Catholic teaching. Understanding different approaches to defining social justice provides insights into the ways that various groups and religions perceive social problems, seek social services, and engage in advocacy.

ISLAM AND SOCIAL JUSTICE

This section explores the conceptualization of social justice in Islam and its continuous reinterpretation to address the ever-changing social conditions. Since social justice in Islam is situated in the interpretive domain of divine justice, Muslim scholars have formulated three perspectives of social justice (the modernist, the revivalist, and the neo-modernist) that are based on the problems facing the society and how they could be addressed.

The Islamic Divine Justice

The notion of justice can be differentiated between positive justice and divine justice. Positive justice assumes that societies are capable of accommodating both individual and collective interests in order to build an agreement on normative standards of acceptable or unacceptable behaviors. The normative institutions (law and justice system) grow out of the interactions between expectations and existing social conditions.

Divine justice, on the other hand, assumes that human beings and societies have limited capability to reach the highest standard of justice. Personal interests and human emotions are major impediments to producing an impartial justice that serves collective interests. Hence, the codes of conducts and justice should refer not to a social contract among individuals or societies but to a divine authority: namely, God. In the Hebrew, Christian, and Islamic traditions it is believed that God communicated about the ultimate justice through inspired prophets to all human society (Khadduri, 1984). Unlike the Aristotelian notion of "natural justice" that views justice as the product of natural forces, Christian and Islamic traditions assume that justice represents the will of God regarding the destiny of humankind (Khadduri, 1984, p. 2).

In the context of Islam, the prophet Muhammad communicated to his people the divine justice enshrined in the text, called al-Qur'an, known as the first authoritative textual source of God's will and justice. Prophet Muhammad was the first interpreter of God's will and justice; hence, his words and behavior were believed to be the most authentic interpretation of the divine in Islamic. The documentation of the sayings and behavior of Prophet Muhammad, called Sunna, or Hadith, became the second textual source of Islamic teaching. Both al-Qur'an and Sunna, or Hadith, are the primary sources of Islamic justice that contain absolute truth and provide the foundation for Muslim scholars to develop a legal and justice system to promote public order.

The notion of justice in the Qur'an is represented by two basic words: 'adl and qist. The two words denote "a balanced approach to all things, including life" (Ayoub, 1996) and the conditions characterized by equity and justice (Rahman, 1996). The balance principle applies to two moral codes that govern human behavior in relationship to other human beings, namely, (a) the relationship between human beings and nature, and (b) the spiritual relationship between human beings and God.

Despite the similarities in meaning, 'adl *and* qist can be applied in different contexts. 'Adl refers to the notion of legal fairness as related to a judge (*qadi*) and the testimony of witnesses while qist involves fairness that governs everyday human relations and economic transactions. While the balanced approach and the notions of fairness apply to both friends and enemy (Qur'an 60:8), they also apply to economic transactions of buying and selling goods and services and to gender relationships.

The core characteristics of the "balanced" approach are captured in the two subsidiary concepts: *Al-Nasf* refers to the practice of sharing and equity and *al-wasat* to the middle path. The notion of justice in Islam is built upon the assumption that taking the side of one of two extreme positions will not produce justice. Either side tends to negate the other. In essence, these two subsidiary concepts represent the inclusiveness that brings together the common elements of both sides to reach a state of sharing and equity (Rahman, 1996).

Besides the similarities in meaning, the concepts of 'adl and qist also have the opposite meaning called injustice (*zulm*) that apply to both institutions and individuals. The first meaning is a general condition of darkness, opaqueness, and gloom in which society or social organizations deprive individuals of their basic rights. A community or government can be promoting injustices if it does not treat individual members fairly and equally. The second meaning is an individual and institutional act of oppression resulting in the unlawful gain of a bigger share than others. Individuals can experience injustice if they violate the general norms of modesty and fairness. Therefore, any act that deviates from the middle course (e.g., greed or extravagance) contains risks of going beyond fairness and, hence, leads to injustice.

While the conception of justice in Islam is represented by the principles of procedural justice ('adl) and justice in social relations (qist), the core principles of the two terms seek to guide balanced behavior that features fairness and moderation and thereby govern individual and social behaviors that produce social order. How, then, can the basic concept of divine justice relate to social justice? The following section discusses social justice as a form of social well-being that is the ultimate objective of the Islamic justice system.

According to the classical scholar al-Syatibi as described by Masud (1977), the notion of social well-being (*al-maslaha*) is the ultimate objective of the Islamic justice system and the Islamic way of life (*syari'ah*). Social well-being is a condition in which the basic welfare necessities of every single individual are met and the opportunity to improve the quality of life beyond the basic necessities and the aspiration for a more meaningful and peaceful life is attainable. The basic necessity is called *al-daruriyat* and includes mental, spiritual, and material well-being: personal mental health, the security of the family (including elders and youngsters), the security of possessions and wealth, personal safety and life, and the safety of one's beliefs. The second type of social well-being in Islamic tradition is called *hajjiyat,* namely, the improvement of the quality of life beyond necessity. Individuals are allowed to improve their life both spiritually and materially. Finally, the third type of social well-being is called *tahsiniyat* and denotes the opportunity and the freedom for individuals to enjoy the best quality of life, including possessing luxurious goods and abundant wealth. The Islamic divine justice and the Islamic justice system are directed toward achieving social justice that is reflected in all three types of social well-being, or *maslaha* (Al-Raysuni, 2005).

Social Justice and Muslim Social Order

The implementation of the Islamic divine justice teaching in society and the way through which social well-being (al-maslaha) is achieved through the Islamic justice system vary greatly according to the contextual social conditions. The early period of Islam differs from the more recent colonial eras that included conflicting foreign ideas. In the precolonial period, the debate about justice in Islam included different theological schools of thought, philosophical traditions, economic policy, social policy, and politics. Among the classical ideas about social justice are those by Ibn Taimiya (d. 1325 CE) who envisioned the state institution as the most important mechanism for achieving the greater public interests and social well-being (maslaha). Based on the

constant threat from the Mongolian and Christian crusaders, he developed a strong argument for the integration of religion and state institutions where a system of checks and balances would be established between religious authority and government in the form of public policies. These policies maintained that every individual and family has the freedom to meet their basic needs and that the state institution needs to be viewed as the institutional power that ensures fairness, equality, and equity.

Since there are different ways of achieving social well-being, Khaldun (1958) describes two types of society, namely the nomadic (*ashabiya*) and urban (*Islamdom*) in order to develop an institutional framework to address the social forces beyond the control of the individual. Owing to kinship solidarity based in rural communal life, he notes that the close connection with a certain tribe determines the degree of social security of its members. Hence, the notion of social justice reflects the tribal perceptions of justice. In contrast, urban dwellers (*Islamdom*) experience social solidarity more through a formal justice system based on contractual social relations unlike the informal norms of rural dwellers. In urban society, social justice is defined as fairness and equality in the form of both religious law and the laws of the state without requiring the integration of state and religion as the only way to achieve well-being. Khaldun notes that well-being and public order could also be achieved through laws established by humans (secular law) and through a mixture of secular and religious laws. In essence, social well-being is not an absolute concept but a relative concept and dependent on the accepted system of public order.

The conceptualization of social justice was expanded during and after the colonial period, based on new perspectives adapted from Western tradition and the emergence of at least three strands of Islamic thinking: modernists, revivalists, and moderate (Rahman, 1979). The first two strands were intellectual reactions to Western colonial domination, and the moderate strand focused on a blend of both the Islamic and Western traditions.

The "modernist" perspective. The expansion of Western colonial empire into the centers of Muslim civilizations, such as Egypt, created different responses from Muslim scholars. For example, the exposure to the secular legal system of the French colonial government generated tremendous conflicts among Muslim scholars who were accustomed to the Islamic justice system, namely, a conflict between "reason" and "revelation." Two notable scholars, Jamal al-Din al-Afghani (1839–1897) and his student Muhammad Abduh (1849–1905), saw no reason to choose one over the other, especially in Iran, Turkey, and Egypt, and therefore advocated for combining both Islam and Western thinking, including in the political and social systems (Kerr, 1966; Sedgwick, 2009).

Both Afghani and Abduh noted that by adopting Western ideas of rational thinking and promoting individual freedom, Muslim society could regain its strength from the widespread social injustice and corruption among the remaining despotic Muslim rulers and the destructiveness of Western colonialism. Called Pan-Islamism, they asserted that Western liberal ideas could be used to eliminate the influence of despotic Muslim rulers as well as reduce the expansion of Western colonialism. This perspective was based on the view that human beings are honorable creatures who can be responsible for achieving perfection in this world even though despotism and colonialism can undermine this capacity.

From Afghani's point of view, social justice is the fulfillment of the highest quality of being human and requires the adoption of the virtues of self-restraint, trust, and truth that can contribute to righteousness (Keddie, 1972). The virtue of self-restraint (*al-haya*) is based on reducing the risks of committing negative actions that violate fairness. The virtue of trust (*al-amana*) is needed to produce fairness in social relations and serves as the foundation for cooperation. While telling the truth (*al-shiddiq*) can produce trustworthiness in social relations, the combination of the three virtues, according to al-Afghani, serves as the basis for building social justice.

The revivalist perspective. In contrast to the modernist approach to integrating elements of Western culture into Islamic culture, the Muslim revivalists called for the return to the Islamic tradition. They believed that the decline of Islamic civilization was due, primarily, to the deviation from the Islamic

standard and reviving the true Islamic standard was seen as the only way for Muslims to resurrect their civilization. The revivalist efforts were led by two influential organizations: the Islamic Group (*Jamaah al-Islamiyah*) in Pakistan under the leadership of Abu al-A'la al-Maududi (d. 1979) and the Muslim Brotherhood (*al-Ikhwan al-Muslimun*) in Egypt initiated by Hasan al-Banna (d. 1951). These two groups consistently called for the "return" to the pure source of Islamic civilization and urged total rejection of any Western culture and institutions. Instead of a democratic or a representative government system or adopting either socialism or capitalism or the Western justice system of Britain and France, these groups called for an Islamic State (*khilafah*) to promote the Islamic economic system by advocating for the use of divine Islamic law. In other words, the revivalist agenda was to reinstate an integrated Islamic social, political, and economic system.

The Egyptian revivalist scholar Sayyid Kotb (1906–1966) was affiliated with the Muslim Brotherhood in Egypt and had been subjected to political oppression by the Egyptian government. From exposure to Western thinking from his trip to the United States in the late 1940s, Kotb became a prolific writer and strong advocate for the reestablishment of Islamic principles of justice. His book *Social Justice in Islam* (first published in 1948) reflected his strong view about the superiority of Islam as a system of justice compared to any others. According to Kotb (1980), social justice in Islam is rooted in the view that humankind is part of the larger harmonious relations with the universe in which God, the Creator, provides the ultimate direction. This harmony produces the ideal balance between human strength and limitations, between individuals and groups and between the material and spiritual. Therefore, the fundamental ideal of Islamic justice is balance and harmony.

According to Kotb, Islamic social justice emerges from a liberation of self that allows for movement toward social solidarity (Kotb, 1980; Sheppard, 1996). Social justice means that every individual is free from serving anyone except God. More, every individual is liberated from fear and free from moral slavery in order to pursue wealth and ambitions. This inward liberation can lead to optimal human equality and thereby prevent inequality and oppression based on race, class, or gender. Furthermore, inward liberation and equality can produce social solidarity that promotes the balance between individual rights and social responsibility as well as legal protection for individuals and society. In his view, social justice is both a *condition* in which social solidarity is an expression of social justice and a *process* of the continuous struggle between the inward liberation of the individual and the collective responsibility of society.

To achieve social justice, Kotb identifies two important conditions: the application of a holistic Islamic legal system and the existence of an Islamic government. In the application of an Islamic legal system, economic activities are protected as long as they maintain balance with the responsibility to help the poor. In addition, the existence of an Islamic government includes the practice of checks and balances through consultation (*sura*) to ensure that the exercise of power is consistent with the divine wisdom (Sheppard, 1996). From his point of view, Islamic social justice can only be implemented in an Islamic state that utilizes an Islamic legal system.

The moderate perspective. The moderate scholars attempted to move beyond the apologetic views of the modernists and the rejectionist views of the revivalists, as reflected in the writings of Fazlur Rahman (1919–1988), a Pakistani, and Majid Khadduri (1909–2007), an Iraqi, both of whom held professorships in American Universities. Rahman (1979, 1982, 1996) envisioned Islam as an evolving religion in which the Qur'an is not a final divine product, and neither does it regulate every human behavior. While the Qur'an is viewed as a divine text that defines a way to seek truth, its essential divine wisdom needs to be separated from its contextual reference. For example, Rahman argues that the notion of social justice in Muslim society did not originate exclusively from the divine wisdom but rather as a hybrid of cultural interactions within Arabian societies and influences by multifaith and multiethnic communities. Even within the Qur'an, modernists acknowledged, Islam absorbed a large number of Judaic and Christian teachings, and the three faiths are descendants of the religion of Abraham. According to

Rahman, Muslims can still achieve social well-being (maslaha) without necessarily living in an Islamic state or being ruled by Islamic laws.

In his seminal book, the *Islamic Conception of Justice*, Khadduri (1984) examines the debate about Islamic justice within the context of politics, theology, philosophy, ethics, law, justice among nations, social justice, and the relation between Islam and human rights. Since he notes that there is no single dominant definition of Islamic justice, the ongoing debate among Muslim scholars suggests that the notion of justice is contextual. The concept of social well-being (maslaha), as the ultimate objective of Islamic pathway or the Islamic legal system, requires a public order in which the interpretation of divine wisdom will always be bounded by the context and the nature of public order.

Khadduri (1984) recognizes that the arguments advanced by both modernists and revivalists are not likely to be reconciled. Both arguments were built upon different assumptions, regarding the relations between Islamic and Western notions of justice. However, Khadduri sees the opportunity to integrate the principles of justice derived from both Islamic and modern principles (e.g., libertarian and egalitarian principles). In his view, social justice should serve both distributive justice in terms of promoting greater social and economic equalities and a greater degree of freedom, not only for individuals but also for nations. He asserts, "If social justice is to endure, it must depend ultimately on libertarian and not only on egalitarian principles" (Khadduri, 1984, p. 224).

In summary, the processes of achieving these ideals often requires culturally relevant knowledge and practices, despite the existence of universal ideals of social welfare (often expressed in United Nations reports; see Gray, Coates, & Bird, 2008; Midgley, 2008). From this perspective, both the liberal understanding of social justice and human rights in Islam and the established social justice tradition in the Western society can be mutually enriching and may eventually contribute to the construction of a contextual policy and practice of social welfare. In this respect, the competing perspectives of social justice and human rights among different Muslim groups can be understood as an opportunity for advancing social welfare in Muslim communities.

CONCLUSION

As can be seen in this review, three major world religions have all addressed social justice in some way through their religious teachings. However, the concept of social justice needs to be understood as fluid depending on which group is defining it, historical precedents, and current social and political movements. For example, the term *social justice* came into common usage in the American Jewish life in the post–World War II era of the 1950s and 1960s even though the concepts related to social justice have been part of ancient Jewish holy texts and commentaries for centuries. In Catholicism, there is no universal Catholic definition of social justice because there is disagreement about how to distribute justice in the social sphere and because the values underlying social justice principles are difficult to describe at any point in time because of constant societal change. Also, most Muslims have some degree of attachment to Islamic law through either personal beliefs or, in some countries, the formal application of law throughout the society; such law embedded in the culture of Muslim societies helps to define the meaning of social order with respect to time and place. While justice is absolute with respect to its divine source (God speaking through the prophet), it is also a relative concept that is subject to multiple interpretations among rulers and scholars throughout history.

This survey of religious perspectives on social justice suggests that though the three religions reviewed here all have addressed social justice in some form, religious perspectives on social justice are best understood through an examination of the particular historical and cultural moment. It is also clear that religions can serve as powerful rallying points for social justice if the timing is right.

REFERENCES

Adherents.com. (2009). Major religions of the world ranked by number of adherents. Retrieved from http://www.adherents.com/Religions_By_Adherents.html

Al-Raysuni, A. (2005). *Imam Al-Shatibi's theory of the higher objectives and intents of Islamic law*. London, UK: International Institute of Islamic Thought.

Ayoub, M. (1996). The Islamic concept of justice. In N. H. Barazangi, M. R. Zaman, & O. Afzal (Eds.), *Islamic identity and the struggle for justice* (pp. 19–26). Gainesville: University Press of Florida.

Brown, R. M. A. (1990). *Gustavo Gutierrez: An introduction to liberation theology*. New York, NY: Orbis Books.

Cahill, L. S. (2001). Genetics, commodification, and social justice in the globalization era. *Kennedy Institute of Ethics Journal, 11*(3), 221–238.

Cahill, L. S. (2007). Theological ethics, the churches, and global politics. *Journal of Religious Ethics, 35*, 377–399.

Central Conference of American Rabbis (CCAR). (2004). "Adopted in Pittsburgh—1999." Retrieved from http://www.ccarnet.org/rabbis-speak/platforms/

Central Conference of American Rabbis (CCAR). (2004). "Pittsburgh Platform—1885." Retrieved from http://www.ccarnet.org/rabbis-speak/platforms/

Congregation for the Doctrine of Faith (CDF). (1984). *Instruction of certain aspects of the "theology of liberation."* Retrieved from http://www.vatican.va

Coogan, M. D., Brettler, M. Z., Newsom, C. A., & Perkins, P. (2001). *The new Oxford annotated Bible: With the Apocryphal/Deuterocanonical books*. New York, NY: Oxford University Press.

DeYoung, C. P. (2007). *Living faith: How faith inspires social justice*. Minneapolis, MN: Fortress Press.

DeYoung, C. P. (2008). How religion inspires social justice: Lessons from the legacy of Martin Luther King, Jr. Retrieved from http://martinlutherking.fr/documents6.pdf

Freire, Paulo. (2000). *Pedagogy of the oppressed* (M. B. Ramos, Trans.). New York, NY: Continuum.

Gray, M., Coates, J., & Bird, M. Y. (Eds.). (2008). *Indigenous social work around the world: Towards culturally relevant education and practice*. Burlington, VT: Ashgate.

Gutierrez, G. (1999). The task and content of liberation theology (J. Condor, Trans.). In C. Rowland (Ed.), *The Cambridge companion to liberation theology* (pp. 19–38). Cambridge, UK: Cambridge University Press.

Hartnett, D. (2003). Remembering the poor: An interview with Gustavo Gutierrez. *America: The National Catholic Weekly*, February 3, 2003. Retrieved from http://www.americamagazine.org/gettext.cfm?articleTypeID=1&textID=2755&issueID=420#

Hehir, J. B. (1990). Papal foreign policy. *Foreign Policy, 78* (Spring), 26–48.

Hollenbach, D. (2002). *The common good and Christian ethics*. New York, NY: Cambridge University Press.

Jacob, W. (2002). Renewing Reform Judaism: From Pittsburgh to Pittsburgh. In D. Kaplan (Ed.), *Platforms and prayer books: Theological and liturgical perspectives on Reform Judaism* (pp. 81–92). Lanham, MD: Rowman & Littlefield.

Jacobs, J. (2008). A Jewish vision for economic justice. In O. Rose, K. Green, & M. Klein (Eds.), *Righteous indignation: A Jewish call for justice* (pp. 147–154). Woodstock, VT: Jewish Lights.

Jacobs, J. (2009). *There shall be no needy: Pursuing social justice through Jewish law & tradition.* Woodstock, VT: Jewish Lights.

Jewish Fund for Justice. (n.d.). Mission statement. Retrieved from http://www.just-tzedakah.org/shopexd.asp?id=59

Kanarek, J. (2008). What does tikkun olam actually mean? In O. Rose, K. Green, & M. Klein (Eds.), *Righteous indignation: A Jewish call for justice* (pp. 15–22). Woodstock, VT: Jewish Lights.

Kaplan, D. (2002). The Reform theological enterprise at work: Debating theory and practice in the American religious "marketplace." In D. Kaplan (Ed.), *Platforms and prayer books: Theological and liturgical perspectives on Reform Judaism* (pp. 81–92). Lanham, MD: Rowman & Littlefield.

Keddie, N. R. (1972). *Sayyid Jamal ad-Din "al-Afghani": A political biography.* Berkeley: University of California Press.

Kerr, M. H. (1966). *Islamic reform: The political and legal theories of Muhammad ʻAbduh and Rashid Rida.* Berkeley: University of California Press.

Khadduri, M. (1984). *The Islamic conception of justice.* Baltimore, MD: Johns Hopkins University Press.

Khaldun, Ibn. (1958). *Muqaddimah: An introduction to history* (F. Rosenthal, translated from the Arabic). Princeton, NJ: Princeton University Press.

Kliksberg, B. (2003). *Social justice: A Jewish perspective.* Jerusalem, Israel: Gefen.

Kotb, S. (1980). *Social justice in Islam.* New York, NY: Octagon Book.

Kugelgen, A. V. (2009). *Abduh, Muhammad.* In G. Krämer, D. Matringe, J. Nawas, & E. Rowson (Eds.), *Encyclopaedia of Islam,* Vol. 3. Leiden, Netherlands: E J Brill.

Langan, J. (1996). Catholic social teaching and the allocation of scarce resources. *Kennedy Institute of Ethics Journal, 6*(4), 401–405.

Lerner, M. (2008). The legacy of Abraham Joshua Heschel. In O. Rose, K. Green, & M. Klein (Eds.), *Righteous indignation: A Jewish call for justice* (pp. 38–44). Woodstock, VT: Jewish Lights.

Masud, M. K. (1977). *Islamic legal philosophy: A study of Abu Is aq Al-Sha ibi's life and thought.* Islamabad, Pakistan: Islamic Research Institute.

Midgley, J. (2008). Promoting reciprocal international social work exchanges: Professional imperialism revisited. In M. Gray, J. Coates, & M. Y. Bird (Eds.). *Indigenous social work around the world: Towards culturally relevant education and practice* (pp. 31–45). Burlington, VT: Ashgate.

Pope Benedict XVI. (2009). *Caritas in veritate* [In charity and truth: Encyclical of Pope Benedict XVI, promulgated on June 29, 2009]. Retrieved from http://www.vatican.va/holy_father/benedict_xvi/encyclicals/documents/hf_ben-xvi_enc_20090629_caritas-in-veritate_en.html

Pope John Paul II. (1991). *Centesimus Annus* [On the hundredth anniversary of *Rerum Novarum*: Encyclical of Pope John Paul II, promulgated on May 1, 1991]. Retrieved from http://www.vatican.va/holy_father/john_paul_ii/encyclicals/documents/hf_jp-ii_enc_01051991_centesimus-annus_en.html

Pope Leo XIII. (1891). *Rerum Novarum* [On capital and labor: Encyclical of Pope Leo XIII, promulgated on May 15, 1891]. Retrieved from http://www.vatican.va/holy_father/leo_xiii/encyclicals/documents/hf_l-xiii_enc_15051891_rerum-novarum_en.html

Rahman, F. (1979). *Islam.* Chicago, IL: University of Chicago Press.

Rahman, F. (1982). *Islam and modernity: Transformation of an intellectual tradition,* Chicago, IL: University of Chicago Press.

Rahman, F. (1996). Islam's origin and ideals. In N. H. Barazangi, M. R. Zaman, & O. Afzal (Eds.), *Islamic identity and the struggle for justice* (pp. 11–18). Gainesville: University Press of Florida.

Raphael, M. L. (2003). *Judaism in America (Columbia contemporary American religion series).* New York, NY: Columbia University Press.

Rose, O. N., Green, K. J. E., & Klein, M. (2008). *Righteous indignation: A Jewish call for justice.* Woodstock, VT: Jewish Lights.

Rowland, C. (1999). Introduction: The theology of liberation. In C. Rowland (Ed.), *The Cambridge companion to liberation theology* (pp. 1–16). Cambridge, MA: Cambridge University Press.

Saperstein, D. (2008). Religious leadership and politics. In O. Rose, K. Green, & M. Klein (Eds.), *Righteous indignation: A Jewish call for justice* (pp. 45–54). Woodstock, VT: Jewish Lights.

Sarna, J. D. (2004). *American Judaism: A history.* New Haven, CT: Yale University Press.

Schwarz, S. (2006). *Judaism and justice: The Jewish passion to repair the world.* Woodstock, VT: Jewish Lights.

Schwarz, S. (2008). Can social justice save the American Jewish soul? In O. Rose, K. Green, & M. Klein (Eds.), *Righteous indignation: A Jewish call for justice* (pp. 3–14). Woodstock, VT: Jewish Lights.

Sedgwick, M. (2009). *Muhammad Abduh.* Oxford, UK: Oneworld.

Sheppard, W. E. (1996). *Sayyid Qutb and Islamic activism. A translation and critical analysis of social justice in Islam.* Leiden, The Netherlands: E. J. Brill.

Spiess, C. (2007). Recognition and social justice: A Roman Catholic view of Christian bioethics of long-term care and community service. *Christian Bioethics, 13*(3), 287–301.

U.S. Conference of Catholic Bishops (USCCB). (2009). Washington, DC: USCCB. Retrieved from http://www.usccb.org

Vorspan, A., & Saperstein, D. (1998*). Jewish dimensions of social justice: Tough moral choices of our time.* New York, NY: UAHC Press.

Windley-Daoust, J., Kilmartin, L., Navarro, C. S., Hodapp, K. C., & Wilt, M. C. (2008). *Living justice and peace: Catholic social teaching in practice.* Winona, MN: St Marys Press.

7

SOCIAL JUSTICE FROM A HUMANITIES PERSPECTIVE:

A Synthesis to Inform Practice

BRYN KING AND MICHAEL J. AUSTIN

INTRODUCTION

> Rather than having a particular ideology about social justice . . . I maintain that social work scholarship, the definitions and application of social justice to professional and accreditation standards, the curriculum, and our practice environment suffer from a lack of clarity. . . . The profession uses the term *social justice* loosely, without a full understanding of the philosophies behind it. Social workers point to injustices and offer the social justice approach to eliminate exploitation, discrimination, and oppression. But are actions and rhetoric based more on intuition than on precision? What exactly does the profession mean by *social justice*? (Galambos, 2008, pp. 2–3)

In response to a growing debate about the profession's stated commitment to the ethical value of social justice in social work, the editor of the *Journal of Social Work Education* published a "call to action" to engage in a meaningful discourse about what is actually meant by social justice and the need to explore its philosophical and moral values (Galambos, 2008). Based on a review of social welfare policy textbooks (Austin, Branom, & King, this volume) and the study of social justice content in the teaching of social work research (Longres & Scanlon, 2001), it is clear that social justice reflects diverse concepts emerging from different theoretical traditions. As noted in Smith (this volume), the *Code of Ethics of the National Association of Social Workers* (NASW, 2009) provides only a limited context for understanding social justice because the term *social justice* is used multiple times and in a variety of contexts ranging from the expectation that social workers provide access to resources and opportunity to the exhortation to advocate for vulnerable populations at a political and legislative level. In spite of these different contexts, the code provides little detail on how social workers develop a perspective on what constitutes social justice and how they reconcile their own moral and philosophical ideals regarding equality and the distribution of resources with the vague prescriptions of the profession.

Hasenfeld (2010) notes that the human services context in which social workers practice operates on the basis of largely implicit individual and institutional moral values where decisions regarding access to services and supports are influenced by unspoken evaluations of client worth, as in the worthy, deserving poor. He maintains that much of the rationale for such determinations are embedded in organizational routines and service technologies and used by human service workers to shape, challenge, or manipulate this "institutional logic" without frequently examining the "moral assumptions" that underlie it (Hasenfeld, 2010). The idea of human service work as "moral work" has influenced the development of a social justice ethic in social work practice.

The chapters in this section of the volume provide the foundation for their synthesis that includes three components: (a) the philosophical and legal tensions inherent in defining social justice (Price Wolf, this volume; Smith, this volume), (b) the moral obligations and commitments found in Judaic, Catholic, and Islamic conceptions of social justice (Accomazzo, Moore, & Sirojudin, this volume), and (c) the application of different perspectives in the form of historical analysis, literary criticism, and liberation theology (Accomazzo, this volume; Accomazzo, Moore, & Sirojudin, this volume; Fitzgerald, this volume).

PHILOSOPHICAL AND LEGAL PERSPECTIVES OF SOCIAL JUSTICE

The foundation for the Western philosophical perspective of social justice can be found in the early Greek philosophers who conceived of justice as *virtue* where what is good (or virtuous) for society is also good for the rational self who is aligned with God (or Gods) (Smith, this volume). This idea of justice as virtue led to Aristotle's idea of justice as *supporting essential human capabilities* in which depriving individuals of the properties or capabilities that constitute humanity is considered unjust. Post-Enlightenment thinkers shifted their thinking about justice to a *social contract* where personal freedoms are sacrificed in exchange for social order as measured by the protection of individual property.

The extension of the social contract is the idea that a rational person can determine "just" actions that can then be applied to all circumstances where the conception of social justice is in the form of a *universal ethical maxim*. Other philosophers argued that justice should be measured by *consequences and outcomes* where the aggregate outcome of actions that maximize utility and happiness are more critical than any rational individual act. In essence, the trajectory of philosophical theorizing progressed from individual virtue to the social contract of the state that guarantees social justice.

The contemporary philosophical debates about social justice reflect a number of tensions; namely, what is the role of the market versus the role of the state? What is the responsibility of the state for redistributing wealth to ensure people's rights to some measure of equity or minimizing its involvement in property redistribution to ensure people's freedom to maximize opportunity and justly acquire such property? These reflect the debate between the liberal perspective and the libertarian. As Smith (this volume) notes, the essential question is, "How do we humans reconcile the conception of justice as a set of rights that may not be violated as opposed to a set of principles that we think will ensure the best outcome for the most number of people?" (p. 25). These questions ultimately focus on tensions between rights versus outcomes as well as individual justice versus communal justice.

In contrast to the philosophical perspective, the legal perspective relies upon the role of the state as the arbiter of distributive justice with respect to allocation and distribution of wealth, resources, and opportunity through government and social policies (Price Wolf, this volume). Distributive justice is concerned with the fairness of decision making and its outcomes, but conceptualizations of fairness are both subjective and contentious. According to Price Wolf, justice as *fairness* is often linked to the pioneering work of the philosopher John Rawls and is based on the egalitarian idea that all people should have access to a basic platform of rights and privileges. A corollary to this conception of fairness is the idea that social and economic inequality should exist only when such disparities are related to office or position (that can be achieved by anyone in society according to fair and equal opportunity) and when those privileges are utilized to benefit the most disadvantaged members of society.

Based on the ideas of "justice as fairness," Price Wolf (this volume) notes that tensions exist between the values of equality, personal liberty, moral relativism, and the role of government when seeking to ensure social justice for individuals and societies. The pluralistic theory of social justice as *complex equality* posits that there can be multiple coexisting and locally defined frameworks for distributing social goods. While inequalities in societies may exist, there needs to be localized methods for understanding and addressing systematic inequality. In contrast, the *equality of resources* theory is more universal in its conception of social justice based on the two principles of equal importance and responsibility for one's own success. This theory argues that inequalities should only arise as a result of individual differences in effort and ambition, while systematic and endowed inequalities should be controlled by the marketplace.

Another legal perspective on social justice can be found in *asset-based egalitarianism* that is concerned with the distribution of wealth along with an expectation of individual responsibility. An example of asset-based egalitarianism is the hypothetical "stakeholder society" where every citizen is given a sizable grant when they reach adulthood as an investment in future education or business. Related to the equality of resources theory is the *wealth maximization* theory that is a market-driven approach where wealth is distributed with minimal government involvement based on the freedom to pursue individual wealth. In an effort to address inequality and the distribution of wealth, these legal perspectives differ in terms of the role of individuals, communities, the state, or the market in promoting social justice.

MORAL PERSPECTIVES ON SOCIAL JUSTICE

The Abrahamic heritage of religions describes social justice as an integral theme in moral and spiritual teachings. Judaism, Christianity, and Islam all appear to agree that excesses of deprivation constitute injustice and ascribe a moral value to minimizing poverty while delineating obligations as guidelines for socially just actions. Each of these religious traditions differ slightly in the way that these commitments are conceptualized, but all emphasize the idea that social justice involves basic rights, responsibilities, and protections that reflect both individual morality and collective well-being.

Judaic Perspectives of Social Justice

The evolution of Judaic concepts of social justice reflects the transition from universalism to particularism within the Jewish community since the Holocaust and the establishment of the state in Israel (Accomazzo, Moore, & Sirojudin, this volume). In the context of balancing traditional religious ritual with a moral and ethical calling to universally connect and commit to all of humanity, the concept of social justice comprises one of the most fundamental tenets of Jewish life and spiritual practice as reflected in both historic and contemporary texts, debates, and discussion.

Three core concepts of Judaism that relate to concepts of social justice include kindness, healing the world, and charity (Accomazzo, Moore, & Sirojudin, this volume). The first concept is *chesed* and *gemilut chasidim* that translates from the Hebrew as "kindness" and "acts of loving kindness." This idea refers to generous acts in response to immediate needs where humans have the opportunity to act in the image of God. While *chesed* focuses on the present and immediate, the second concept of *tikkun olam* (e.g., healing the world by repairing systematic injustices) addresses the preparation for a more just future. This concept and value has served as a spiritual rallying point for advocates of progressive social action in the pursuit of social justice. The third concept is *tzedek or tzedekah* that denotes justness or righteousness in interactions with God and other human beings, particularly those who are poor, oppressed, or vulnerable. It also includes the moral obligation to make financial gifts to the poor as a commitment to address "an unjust situation."

Catholic Perspectives of Social Justice

Catholic social teaching also defines this issue of poverty in terms of morality and considers it a violation of human dignity, an affront to the presence of God in every person, and a threat to the overall good of society (Accomazzo, Moore, & Sirojudin, this volume). Seven themes related to distributive social justice can be drawn from papal encyclicals, ecumenical councils, and other documents produced by Catholic bishops to form an integrated concept of the Catholic perspective on social justice, rather than as separate and stand-alone statements.

The first value, *life and dignity of the human person*, refers to the idea that humans were created in the image of God and that human life is therefore sacred. This core value forms the foundation for the church's moral code and drives much of its social and political action that ranges from abortion to war. The second theme, *call to family, community, and participation*, is related to the primacy of marriage and family as well as the expectation to participate in the community in service of the poor and vulnerable. The two major concepts underlying this theme are the promotion of the common good through the encouragement of human development in all arenas and the concept of "subsidiarity" that maintains the importance of addressing social problems at the lowest level (within the family or the community) before appealing to more formal and higher level help (the church or the state). The notion of *rights and responsibilities* includes the idea that everyone is entitled to what is necessary to sustain life but is also responsible for maintaining the rights of others through charitable acts.

The fourth theme, *option for the poor and vulnerable*, relates to the responsibilities of Catholics to address the increasing wealth disparity by paying particular attention to the needs of the poor. The fifth theme, *dignity of work and the rights of workers,* includes the balance between the following competing forces: (a) the rights and responsibilities of workers and the distribution of goods, (b) the rights and responsibilities of employers and private businesses in a free market, and (c) the role of the church and the state in ensuring that all of these entities have the requisite freedom to achieve success and dignity. *Solidarity* refers to the commitment to the human family and the common good. And the last theme, *care for God's creation*, involves the moral obligation to care for the planet and all of its inhabitant creatures.

Muslim Perspectives of Social Justice

Social justice in Islam differs from much of the previously discussed religious, legal, and philosophical positions, as it relies less on a social contract with individuals or society and more on a divine contract with God where the codes of conduct and notions of justice are the manifestations of the will of God (Accomazzo, Moore, & Sirojudin, this volume). For example, in the Muslim holy text, the *Qur'an*, the notion of justice is characterized by the balance of two fundamental moral principles that govern relationships among human beings and with nature, as well as between human beings and God; namely, *adl* (judgment and fairness in the context of the legal system) and *qist* (fairness in social relations and economic transactions). The two terms represent the overall conception of justice in Islam, where both societies and people are ensured of the basic conditions for well-being or *al-daruriyat*. Injustice arises when one of these principles is out of balance and either individuals or institutions engage in unfair practices or deprive people of their basic rights.

Another aspect of Islamic social justice can be found in the following basic rights and protections that are included in the Islamic conceptualization of welfare: (a) spiritual and religious freedom; (b) the value of life (and the absence of life-threatening danger), including the protection of nature; (c) mental and intellectual health; (d) the protection of lineage and the obligation to care for the welfare of all generations of the family; and (e) the right to lawfully accumulate property or wealth. These basic protections represent the minimum level in the Islamic pathway to spiritual and social well-being.

The three major strands of Islamic thinking and conceptualizations of social justice can be found in the modernist, revivalist, and neo-modernist interpretations of social justice that emerged from Western incursion and colonization in Muslim lands. The modernists focus on the adoption of "rational" styles of governance and Pan-Islamism while the revivalists emphasize the reinstatement of a complete Islamic government where divine justice is achieved through the integration of both Islamic and Western principles. Efforts to reconcile these views of Islamic divine justice can be seen in the work of neo-modernists as they address the principles in the Universal Declaration of Human Rights, but all three strands of Islamic thinking provide a useful lens for understanding the diversity of social justice perspectives (Accomazzo, Moore, & Sirojudin, this volume).

FROM THEORY TO APPLICATION

The three perspectives included in this section seek to balance concepts of social justice with their application, emerging out of critical thinking and catalytic action. For the disciplines of history, literary theory, and liberation theology, social justice is defined by the beliefs and methodologies that constitute such practice. Much of this work is focused on exposing the realities of injustice, increasing attention to the experiences of the oppressed, and disrupting the power relations that reinforce unjust social structures.

Social Justice in the Discipline of History

The discipline of history approaches the concept of social justice in a number of different ways, including the process of promoting social justice (Accomazzo, this volume). As might be expected, the first approach includes the efforts of historians to describe the history of the term *social justice* and its usage within the social and political context of different eras. According to Accomazzo (this volume), historians trace the term *social justice* to the 19th century when it was based on the ideas of charity and mercy. The more modern usage is built on the principle that all persons deserve access to material and social goods distributed by the state. For example, the history of the debates about poverty and the redistribution of wealth is critical for understanding current struggles to achieve social justice.

The evolution of historical research (e.g., subjects and methods) has also helped to promote social justice as illustrated by the history of the lesbian, gay, bisexual and transgendered (LGBT) movement that includes the (a) *founding and professionalism period* where the goal was to remain objective by focusing on traditional subjects (those in power) and attracting funding and prestige, (b) *the modern period* that questioned the paradigm that there was one truth to be found by focusing on new subjects and sources using "bottom up" history that shifted attention to those who had long been ignored, and (c) the current *postmodernism era* where objectivity is seen as a myth in order to develop a more credible history that integrates diverse accounts and sources. During this current period, historians helped the Supreme Court overturn the Texas sodomy laws in 2003, a significant contribution to social justice for the LGBT community.

Social Justice and Literary Theory

Similar to the discipline of history, literary theorists provide another approach to engaging and promoting social justice (Fitzgerald, this volume). The systematic approach of literary scholars to promote social change involves exposing the values inherent in literature and its potential for challenging dominant ideologies. Like contemporary historians, literary theorists do not give priority or privilege to particular meanings over others by taking into account diverse contexts from which to interpret literature. Literary theorists define themselves in terms of the goal of improving the human condition and addressing different forms of oppression. As Fitzgerald (this volume) notes, four approaches to literary theory can be identified to help define the form of oppression, namely, social class, gender, colonial power, and heteronormativity.

To address social class and the role of capitalism, *Marxist literary theories* incorporate the political and social lens of Marxism to expose the contradictions of capitalism. The goal of literary Marxism is to uncover the reification of social conventions that subjugate the working class through the use of language that is consistent with the economic, political, and social order. Another goal is to raise the consciousness of readers in order to mobilize political engagement regarding issues of social class and the capitalist system. *Feminist literary theories* build on this method of criticism in order to deconstruct dominant images of women in literature, challenge gender discrimination regarding female authors, focus on language as both oppressor and liberator of women, and reconstruct and reform social structures. In a similar way, *postcolonial literary theories* call for both the capturing of a historical period along with a process of emancipation by engaging the voices of the marginalized and oppressed as a "script for change" in order to deconstruct and destabilize existing centralized (imperialist) powers. Last, the goal for *queer theory* is to subvert dominant discourses regarding the hetero/homo dichotomy (heteronormativity) by re-signifying queer as a nonstigmatized identity and reconstructing multiple notions of sexual identity.

Liberation Theology

Liberation theology emerges from the experiences of the oppressed and those committed to liberation, such as priests in Latin America who were confronting profound poverty that demanded a different response. The righteous indignation of young theologians to conditions of oppression contributed in the following ways to the evolution of liberation theology in the 1960s and 1970s: (a) the idea that the divinity (i.e., the face of God and Jesus) resides in the most oppressed, (b) the dialogue between these oppressed communities and clergy, and (c) the belief that the clergy is a political actor amid these conditions. The ideas of liberation theology in Latin America are based on the perceived failure of the Catholic Church to adequately respond to (a) the oppression and hardship experienced by parishioners under the "triple violence" of colonialism (internal colonialism, international trade, and private security forces and henchmen as agents of plantation owners and factory bosses), (b) extreme poverty, (c) government-sponsored torture, (d) mass displacement of rural peasants, (e) destruction and depletion of natural resources and habitat, and (f) U.S.-led military incursions (Boff & Boff, 1987; Rowland, 1999). Hennelly (1990) outlines

the following major components of liberation theology in Latin America: (a) Theology is only relevant after making a commitment to the oppressed, (b) theology involves an engagement with social reality, not detached observation, and (c) authentic Christian theology is developed only out of analysis, reflection, and practice that is called "praxis" (Accomazzo, Moore, & Sirojudin, this volume).

Another essential component of liberation theology is *conscientization* that includes the ultimate goal of disrupting power relations between the oppressed and the oppressor such that the oppressed are empowered to determine and achieve their own basic needs and life goals (Accomazzo, Moore, & Sirojudin, this volume). In terms of education, Freire (1972) sought to disrupt the traditional student–teacher power relationship by joining students and teachers to examine oppression together in order to liberate both people where only the oppressed could liberate themselves and oppressors needed to liberate themselves from the inhumanity of oppressing others. That is, he focused on only one form of liberation within the context of freeing learners to take charge of their own learning and for teachers to get out of the way to let this happen.

THE EMERGING SYNTHESIS

The social justice concepts drawn from the humanities can be organized to reflect a continuum of theory to application as illustrated in Figure 7.1. It begins with ideas from philosophy and legal perspectives that capture the theoretical tensions underlying the concept of social justice, namely, justice for the individual versus the community, the relative importance of freedom versus equality, and whether the state or the marketplace is responsible for ensuring a fair distribution of resources. The moral perspectives of social justice complement the philosophical and legal perspectives as seen in the Abrahamic traditions of Judaism, Christianity (represented by Catholicism), and Islam. The common themes in all three religious perspectives are the moral obligations that are integral to the believer's relationship with God. These obligations include commitments to (a) the family and the community, (b) ensuring basic rights and protections for all, and

(c) acting fairly and justly in all social relations. The third group of disciplines in the humanities includes history, literary theory, and liberation theology that reflect the active pursuit of social justice for oppressed populations. While these disciplines employ methodologies that help to define concepts of social justice, they are primarily concerned with the practices that expose the truth of injustice, raise awareness about the experiences of the oppressed, and disrupt existing power and social relations that seek to maintain such injustices.

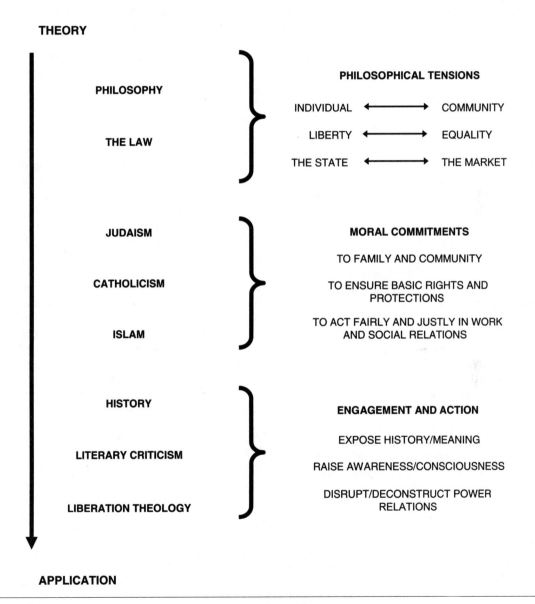

Figure 7.1   Synthesis of Key Perspectives From the Humanities

CONCLUSIONS AND IMPLICATIONS

The theoretical perspectives described in this volume will add much to the discourse on social justice in social welfare, but their diversity increases the complexity of this discussion. A singular definition of social justice that can be transcribed into an ethical mandate for the profession appears to be a challenging proposition given the tensions between competing ideological and moral values and commitments that may or may not be consistent with the de facto values of the profession. For example, a social worker could believe that poverty is essentially the result of a lack of responsiveness to the labor market and that the solution is to help poor people in low-income communities take advantage of existing opportunities. This social justice perspective is compatible with the equality of resources theory of social justice where inequalities emerge as a result of individual differences in effort and ambition, and the marketplace is responsible for managing systematic disparities (Price Wolf, this volume). Another example of this tension could be a Catholic social worker who has a passionate commitment to distributive social justice and an equally moral commitment to the rights of unborn fetuses (e.g., pro-life) that conflicts with the National Association of Social Workers' (NASW's) position supporting a woman's right to choose (National Association of Social Workers, *Social*, 2009). How are these social justice values reconciled, and how are these tensions engaged critically and meaningfully?

Unfortunately, a clue to this reconciliation is illustrated by the extreme case of Emily Brooker, a social work student at Missouri State University who was charged with discrimination and failure to adhere to social work ethics after refusing to sign a letter—as part of a social policy class assignment—to an elected official who was advocating for gay foster homes and adoption (National Association of Scholars, 2007). She argued that such an action violated her religious beliefs, but in order to graduate, she was forced to recant her position and adhere to the NASW's *Code of Ethics*. She graduated successfully but filed and won a civil lawsuit against the university. Rather than engaging Ms. Brooker in

a critical and supported debate that might clarify or expand her moral position, the actions of the social work faculty demanded a slavish compliance to an ideology that, as will be demonstrated in this volume, is not as universal as may be expected. While she may represent more of an outlier than is typical in the profession, there could be social workers who claim the mantle of social justice but have not yet examined their own ideology and moral development with respect to the clients and communities they serve.

As Hasenfeld (2010) argues, human service work is embedded in both individual and institutional moral values that have the power to determine the kind and quality of services clients receive. How do we help social workers examine, engage, and discuss these social justice perspectives in relationship to the values held by the profession as well as their own personal and religious values? As depicted in Figure 7.2, examining theories of social justice from the humanities can aid in the development of an individual framework for understanding and engaging in social justice work, a process that was clearly absent from the Brooker case. Identifying institutional patterns of injustice or being struck by a "spark of indignation" is often the beginning of the process. Based on the theories discussed in this volume, a next step would be to participate in a dialectic that includes a debate of philosophical and legal tensions and an examination of individual moral and spiritual commitments. This critical discussion informs how we understand and identify injustice and allows for the application of an integrated framework to practice and engagement in social justice work.

REFERENCES

Accomazzo, S. (2014). Historical perspectives on social justice. M. J. Austin (Ed.), *Social justice and social work: Rediscovering a core value of the profession* (pp. 55–64) [this volume, chapter 5].

Accomazzo, S., Moore, M., & Sirojudin, S. (2014). Social justice and religion. M. J. Austin (Ed.), *Social justice and social work: Rediscovering a core value of the profession* (pp. 65–82) [this volume, chapter 6].

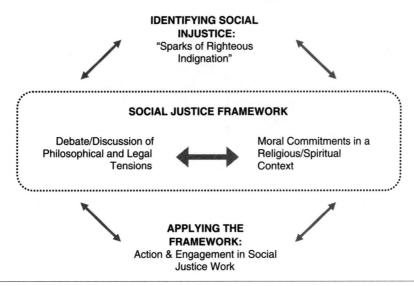

Figure 7.2   Moving From Theory to Application

Austin, M. J., Branom, C., & King, B. (2014). Searching for the Meaning of Social Justice. M. J. Austin (Ed.), *Social justice and social work: Rediscovering a core value of the profession* (pp. 1–18) [this volume, chapter 1].

Boff, L. & Boff, C. (Eds.). (1987). *Introducing liberation theology.* Maryknoll, NY: Orbis Books.

Fitzgerald, C.S. (2014). Literary theories and social justice. M. J. Austin (Ed.), *Social justice and social work: Rediscovering a core value of the profession* (pp. 43–54) [this volume, chapter 4].

Freire, P. (1972). *Pedagogy of the oppressed.* New York, NY: Continuum Press.

Galambos, C. (2008). A dialogue on social justice. *Journal of Social Work Education, 44*(2), 1–5.

Hasenfeld, Y. (2010). *Human services as complex organizations* (2nd ed.). Thousand Oaks, CA: Sage.

Hennelly, A. T. (Ed.). (1990). *Liberation theology: A documentary history.* Maryknoll, NY: Orbis Books.

Longres, J., & Scanlon, E. (2001). Social justice and the research curriculum. *Journal of Social Work Education, 37*(3), 447–463.

National Association of Scholars (NAS). (2007). The scandal of social work. Retrieved from http://www.nas.org/polArticles.cfm?doctype_code=Article&doc_id=26

National Association of Social Workers (NASW). (2009). *Code of ethics of the National Association of Social Workers.* Retrieved from http://www.socialworkers.org/pubs/code/default.asp

National Association of Social Workers (NASW). (2009). *Social work speaks: National Association of Social Workers policy statements, 2009–2012* (8th ed.). Washington, DC: NASW Press.

Price Wolf, J. (2014). Legal theories of social justice. M. J. Austin (Ed.), *Social justice and social work: Rediscovering a core value of the profession* (pp. 31–42) [this volume, chapter 3].

Rowland, C. (Ed.). (1999). *The Cambridge companion to liberation theology.* Cambridge, MA: Cambridge University Press.

Smith, R. J. (2014). The influence of Western philosophy on definitions of social justice. M. J. Austin (Ed.), *Social justice and social work: Rediscovering a core value of the profession* (pp. 21–30) [this volume, chapter 2].

PART II

THE SOCIAL SCIENCE PERSPECTIVES

Social Empathy—What Do We Need to Understand?

8

SOCIAL PSYCHOLOGICAL PERSPECTIVES ON MORALITY AND SOCIAL JUSTICE

CHRISTINA BRANOM

INTRODUCTION

Themes of social justice often emerge from the study of moral psychology. Specifically, some scholars in this subfield of psychology have concerned themselves with how individuals develop and express interests in social justice. For most psychologists, morality entails the rules of justice, rights, and welfare that define how people *should* treat one another (Gewirth, 1984). People make moral judgments regarding the actions of others in relation to these rules and use moral reasoning to determine their own actions (Haidt, 2001). Elements of social justice relevant to moral psychology include fair treatment, equal distribution of goods, and basic human rights. According to many psychologists, morality and concerns for justice and fairness codevelop. However, the connection between morality and justice is far from simple. For example, moral psychology can also show how both morality and immorality can lead to injustice. In addition, understandings of morality may vary by culture, which has implications for how different people value

social justice. Furthermore, moral psychologists differ in their understanding of moral development and expression. Therefore, the relationship between morality and social justice may change according to one's perceptions of morality and justice and the nature of different social and cultural contexts (Turiel, 1998). This review attempts to describe various understandings of morality and how it relates to justice and injustice.

METHOD

To examine the way in which social justice has been studied by moral psychologists, a search of all CSA Illumina Social Science databases was conducted using the keyword terms *moral psychology, morality, moral development, social justice, distributive justice, justice, equality, egalitarianism, fairness,* and *equity*. A search of the University of California (UC) library catalog focused on the tables of contents and indices in books related to moral psychology. The search also included articles by Haidt, a psychologist who has written about morality and social justice. Several additional psychologists in the field were consulted for recommended readings, one of whom (Dachner Keltner at UC Berkeley) responded with the names of relevant scholars (Haidt & Jost); the CSA Illumina database was then used to locate their articles. Finally, the reference lists in the articles and books were consulted for other relevant literature.

Although this search yielded numerous articles and books on the topic, the method used limited the scope of the literature reviewed as it did not include articles appearing in other databases. Furthermore, in the interest of space, this review will not address all conceptions of morality. For example, the subject has been studied in both psychology and philosophy, but this review is limited to work related to social justice of leading moral psychologists.

SOCIAL-COGNITIVE MORAL DEVELOPMENT AND JUSTICE

The study of morality and moral development began with Jean Claude Piaget's examination of child development. To understand moral development, Piaget studied how beliefs about right and wrong emerge through human interactions. At the beginning of moral development, children are bound by rules and authority, adhering to justice and fairness because adults have told them to (Piaget, 1932/1997). Piaget labeled this approach to morality "heteronomy," and indicated that it resulted from children's limited, egocentric cognitive abilities and their powerlessness in relation to adults. As children enter middle childhood (ages 7–8), however, they approach the "autonomous" stage of moral reasoning, in which greater cooperation and reciprocity emerge from understanding the perspectives of others. To study children's conceptions of justice, Piaget told children stories about young people and asked participants how the children should be treated based on their circumstances and actions. He found that young children (aged about 6–9) were preoccupied with pure justice (e.g., advocating punishment for children who had done wrong, regardless of the child's intent). Most older children (aged 10–13), on the other hand, supported treating

all children equally. The oldest of these actually took into account differing circumstances to establish equity (e.g., arguing that a small child should be given less to eat than a larger child by virtue of his or her size or that a poorer child should be given more to eat by virtue of his or her condition). In the early stages of development, most justice-oriented behaviors are motivated by fear of retribution rather than true concern for others. In contrast, older children will seek fair distribution of goods because this promotes social cohesion and cooperation.

Kohlberg elaborated on Piaget's work, agreeing with Piaget that moral development was driven by cognitive development and social interactions (Kohlberg as cited in Lapsley, 1996). Kohlberg (1969) defined his perspective as the "cognitive-developmental" approach to moral socialization and organized moral development into six stages. Each stage represents a more complete judgment of what is just and moral. Kohlberg (1969) was particularly concerned with justice, which, like Rawls (1971), he described as the foundation of morality and man's first virtue. For Kohlberg, justice was essentially conflict resolution for competing claims for goods. Stages 5 and 6 of Kohlberg's theory are especially relevant to social justice. In Stage 5, the individual recognizes that all humans have rights, even when society does not grant or acknowledge these rights. While a person in Stage 4 of morality is strictly concerned with upholding the law and maintaining the status quo, the person in Stage 5 cares more about what is moral than what is legal. For example, one might argue that during the civil rights era, those who upheld discriminatory practices simply because they were legal demonstrated Stage 4 moral thinking, while those who peacefully engaged in civil disobedience to support the rights of people of color demonstrated Stage 5 judgments. Stage 6 of Kohlberg's theory (which is now considered a hypothetical ideal as it has yet to be observed in reality) requires the individual to take what Rawls termed the "original position" (Rawls as cited in Kohlberg, 1969). That is, a person in this stage must imagine themselves in another's position as if that individual were entering the world prior to the existence of society. Next, the person must imagine others in this pre-society situation, vying for the same resources as the first individual. In this scenario, all claimants are completely stripped of their socially prescribed status and position. Consequently, Kohlberg argued, the person in Stage 6 is truly committed to pure, unbiased equality.

According to Kohlberg there are five ways people determine how to achieve justice (Lapsley, 1996). *Equality* assumes that everyone has a right to the same quantities of goods and all claims for goods should be considered equally. Social justice defined by equality would suggest social benefits (e.g., health care) should be universal. *Equity*, on the other hand, adjusts the distribution of goods depending on extenuating circumstances or preexisting inequalities. A just distribution of material resources in accordance with the equity principle would be means tested; those who are more affluent would receive less, while those who are poor would receive more. *Reciprocity* involves the exchange or distribution of goods based on how deserving one is (e.g., because of their efforts, talents, etc.). A true meritocracy, for example, would reward the hardest working, most talented, and highest performing citizens with wealth and status. The final two methods of obtaining justice, *prescriptive role-taking* and *universalizability*, use fair procedures to balance the claims of various people to the rights or benefits in question. Role-taking involves putting oneself in the shoes of those claiming the goods, while universalizability checks that the judgment can be applied to all people without bias. As one progresses through Kohlberg's stages, each of these justice operations becomes more refined and developed.

Justice operations are often used to establish distributive justice, or the fair allocation of goods. In studying the relationship between moral development and distributive justice, Damon (1975) proposed six developmental stages in which a child's use of various distributive justice criteria (equality, merit, equity, and self-interest) becomes progressively more sophisticated. By the final stage of development, the child adapts the principles of equality and reciprocity to the situation and the goals of the larger society. For example, if the goal is total financial redistribution, a person may decide to heavily tax all of the rich to redistribute the wealth to the poor. On the other hand, if the goal is to honor a particular group (e.g., veterans), a society may decide to provide that group with benefits not offered to others.

Few psychologists have empirically examined the relation between morality and social justice, but the existing evidence for this relationship is consistent with Kohlberg's theory. Researchers of one study asked participants to complete measures of moral reasoning and distributive and procedural justice (Wendorf, Alexander, & Firestone, 2002). They found that the early stages of moral development were correlated primarily with self-interest concerns (i.e., justice meant favorable outcomes for the self). However, by Kohlberg's Stage 4, participants were more concerned with consistent procedures and distributions (i.e., justice meant pure equality). Finally, the highest stages of reasoning were associated with procedural fairness and individual participation in decision making as a protection of human rights. The authors note that these results map closely onto the predictions made by Kohlberg's theory.

FEMINIST PERSPECTIVES ON MORAL DEVELOPMENT

While Kohlberg was a pioneer in moral psychology, other psychologists have challenged Kohlberg's theories. One prominent critic of Kohlberg's work is Gilligan, a feminist psychologist. She has argued that Kohlberg overlooked the female experience by giving too much attention to the role of justice in morality while ignoring the role played by the more feminine traits of caring and benevolence (Gilligan, 1982). Gilligan noted that Kohlberg's justice and human rights perspective fits well with the male objectives of individuation, autonomy, and separation, but it may conflict with the female's relational orientation. Whereas Kohlberg believed that the most ethical and moral decisions are made free from relationships, Gilligan suggests that women naturally prioritize human bonds. Thus, Kohlberg's stage theory devalues a woman's sense of morality. Instead, Gilligan conceptualized morality in terms of three levels, which incorporate the importance of human relationships for women. In Level 1, the focus is on the self and pure survival. That is, the person doesn't have the capacity to consider the rights and needs of others. In Level 2, the person engages in self-sacrifice, but her own needs are often ignored (e.g., a person in this stage may advocate intensely for the rights of a disenfranchised but allow others to infringe upon her own rights). At Level 3, this tension between care for self and care for others is resolved, and the person feels compelled to condemn all violence and exploitation. As one progresses through the levels, one begins to understand human interdependence and believe that caring for others benefits all, while violence hurts all.

From Gilligan's perspective, there are also gender differences in how individuals approach morality (Gilligan, 1982). While boys and men are more sensitive to inequality, girls and women find standards of care to be more salient. Some research has suggested that men and women consider both justice and caring when making moral judgments, but men tend to focus more on justice in their moral judgments, while women focus more on care (Gilligan & Attanucci, 1988a; Gilligan & Attanucci, 1988b; Vasudev, 1988). Others have found that men and women consider justice and care equally, but justice is perceived to be masculine, while care is perceived to be feminine (Ford & Lowery, 1986). Kohlberg countered Gilligan's criticism with the assertion that there are not two separate moral orientations (one concerned with caring and one concerned with justice), but both care and justice are needed to make moral judgments.

The Role of Emotions in Morality and Justice

Some researchers have also argued that Kohlberg's theory is limited by the fact that it does not give adequate credit to the role of emotions in moral reasoning and judgment. By extension, Kohlberg's theory also does not account for how emotions might motivate people to seek social justice. Other scholars have argued that moral behavior is in fact first triggered by emotions and later moral reasoning is used to justify or persuade others of one's beliefs (Haidt, 2003; Hoffman, 2001; Kagan, 1984). Haidt (2001) describes this model as social-intuitionist, as moral judgment is composed first of an intuition for which one searches ex post facto for a reason to justify it. The theory is partly based on the finding that many social judgments are made automatically,

rather than following deliberate conscious reasoning (Bargh, 1994; Wegner & Bargh, 1998). In addition, neuroimaging techniques have demonstrated that regions of the brain devoted to moral judgments are involved in integrating emotion with decision making, socioemotional processing, and affective imagery (Greene & Haidt, 2002).

According to Haidt (2003), emotions can be divided into many different components, but moral emotions can be viewed in terms of the elicitor of the emotion and the action tendency it inspires. The emotions most related to morality and justice tend to be easily evoked by situations involving persons other than the self and tend to strongly motivate prosocial action (i.e., actions which benefit others or society). Haidt clusters anger, elevation, guilt, and compassion as the most moral emotions according to these features, but he acknowledges that the division between moral and nonmoral emotions is blurred. Furthermore, each of the "moral" emotions can also be expressed in a highly self-interested manner and inspire antisocial actions. Nevertheless, the moral emotions are most often related to prosocial behavior.

One important moral emotion is anger, which is associated with the violation of rights or unjustified mistreatment (Haidt, 2003). Anger is often considered to be an immoral emotion and one that leads to selfish behavior. However, anger can be evoked by racism, oppression, and exploitation, even if the subject has no relation to the victims. Furthermore, anger fuels urges for retribution or compensation for the pain experienced by the victimized group (Haidt & Sabini, 2000, as cited by Haidt, 2003). Thus, pursuing social justice on behalf of a disadvantaged or oppressed group may be partly motivated by anger.

Social justice-oriented behavior may also be motivated by guilt, which is often elicited when persons other than the self have been harmed or have suffered (Hoffman, 1982a). More specifically, it occurs when a person senses responsibility for the harm or suffering that has transpired and fears that his or her social connection to the victims is threatened (Baumeister, Stillwell, & Heatherton, 1994). In general, guilt motivates individuals to make up for the wrongs they've done. For example, guilt may be felt by members of the dominant White majority for the years of discrimination and oppression against

African Americans. Such guilt may have motivated the introduction of affirmative action policies to help restore justice and accord with the African American population.

In addition to anger and guilt, individuals may pursue social justice because of their own distress at witnessing the suffering of others. Emotions, such as sympathy, compassion, and empathy, are elicited by the suffering of another person; furthermore, they motivate behavior intended to help, comfort, or alleviate the pain (Batson, O'Quin, Fultz, Vanderplas, & Isen, 1983; Batson & Shaw, 1991; Hoffman, 1982b). Compassion and anger may be felt simultaneously; one may feel compassion for people who have been treated unfairly and anger toward the perpetrators of the injustice (Goetz, Keltner, & Simon-Thomas, 2010). Compassion diminishes the focus on one's self and prepares one to respond to the suffering of others. In fact, numerous researchers have demonstrated the contribution of compassion to helping behaviors, including volunteerism (Batson & Shaw, 1991).

Hoffman (2001) has argued that social justice orientations may also depend on empathy. By empathy, he means the psychological processes that arise to match an individual's feelings with another's situation, rather than his or her own situation. Like Gilligan, Hoffman focuses his study of morality on a "caring" orientation. However, he argues justice is congruent with empathy. For example, one can empathically respond to violations of justice, creating a link between the empathic emotion felt and the moral principle of justice. He argued that all moral principles are "hot cognitions"; that is, they are cognitions associated with emotions. Those who are not empathetic think only of themselves and behave according to self-serving, egotistical principles. Those who are hardworking and not empathetic, for instance, will favor a system based on equity (which rewards them for their labor but not those who do not work hard), while those who are lazy and nonempathetic might prefer equality (so that they may receive benefits without exerting any effort). Conversely, those who are hardworking and empathetic think about the needs of others and therefore want equality for all or a distribution of resources based on need, despite the fact that they contribute disproportionately more to society. Studies have

found that empathy is often associated with helping behavior. For example, empathic college students are more likely than nonempathic students to volunteer and donate money to a philanthropic cause (Davis, 1983; Penner, Fritzsche, Craiger, & Freifeld, 1995). Although helping sometimes reduces the distress felt when confronted with the plight of others, this is not always the motivation for aiding the suffering (Batson & Shaw, 1991; Batson & Weeks, 1996). The pursuit of social justice may be stimulated by the prosocial emotion of empathy because it activates moral principles.

Finally, Haidt (2003) described *elevation* as an emotion that may encourage one to seek social justice. For Haidt, elevation is the sense of uplift and inspiration felt when one hears about acts of kindness or charity. Those experiencing elevation are motivated to serve others and follow the example of those who elicited the emotion. In one study, participants experiencing elevation were more likely to list prosocial objectives (e.g., donating to charity or volunteering) when asked to describe their life goals (Haidt, Algoe, Meijer, & Tam, 2002, as cited in Haidt, 2003). Therefore, elevation may inspire actions intended to restore or establish social justice.

SOCIAL DOMAIN THEORY OF MORALITY AND JUSTICE

The social domain theory provides yet another perspective on moral development. This theory contends that morality emerges from an interaction between an individual and his or her social environments (Turiel, 1998). The child develops moral reasoning through multiple social experiences, not simply from their parents. This view argues that cognitions take precedence over emotions in determining behavior. It is supported by evidence that people's judgments are not always emotionally based instincts that are simply justified later (Turiel, 2006). Instead, judgments can be intentional and deliberative. Unlike Kohlberg, social domain theory does not assume morality develops in easily defined, universal stages. Rather, the theory argues that moral judgments frequently take into account culture and context. It suggests that persons organize their social orientations into three domains (moral, conventional, and personal), and each domain influences social decisions (Smetana, 1995; Turiel, 1998). The moral domain is concerned with justice, welfare, and rights, while the conventional domain considers rules, traditions, norms, and authority. Finally, the personal domain concerns autonomy and personal choice. All three develop simultaneously and govern social behavior. Consequently, persons must resolve any conflict between domains when making social judgments (e.g., in some societies, considerations for the rights and fair treatment of commoners must be reconciled with the competing need to honor authority).

RESISTING INJUSTICE ON MORAL GROUNDS

Because morality is derived from a dynamic interaction between the individual and the environment and because individuals consider three domains in decision making, moral judgments and behaviors often depend heavily on situational factors (Turiel, 1998). For example, the reason or intent behind an action is usually considered when determining whether or not it is moral (e.g., hitting a child could be spanking in one situation or abuse in another). In addition, behavior that is usually considered immoral may sometimes be seen as both moral and necessary to achieve social justice. For instance, even when they value honesty and their parents' authority, adolescents deem it acceptable to lie to their parents if their parents are demanding that they do something morally wrong (e.g., not befriend someone of another race; Perkins & Turiel, 2007). Children will also resist following unjust rules (Laupa, 1991; Laupa & Turiel, 1986). Helwig and Jasiobedzka (2001) found that children as young as 6 believe that laws violating human rights, such as denying education to a class of persons, denying medical care to the poor, and discriminating against the aged, are morally wrong. Moreover, the children argued that it is appropriate to violate such laws. Children's evaluations of laws depended on the perceived justice of law, the socially beneficial purpose of the law, and the degree to which it infringed on individual freedoms or rights. Ultimately, they used notions of human rights and justice to determine whether or not they would comply with the stated law.

Like children, adults also believe it is not always right to adhere to rules, laws, or traditions that threaten justice, welfare, and human rights (Turiel, 2005). Although resistance is often seen as antisocial, it can be used to protest and overturn system inequalities. Turiel (2005) noted that Martin Luther King Jr., a social justice icon, protested against the practices of many psychologists who were trying to help individuals adapt to their conditions. He argued that it is not always morally beneficial to adapt to oppressive societal conditions and that some degree of tension and resistance to authority is needed for positive social change. Similarly, during the Holocaust, numerous individuals contributed to resistance movements by violating Nazi laws and lying to authorities in order to save Jewish lives (Bauer, 2001). As a result, illegal resistance can be considered morally acceptable or even desirable under conditions of inequality, injustice, and oppression.

Even in cultures in which deeply entrenched traditions allow injustice, inequality, and oppression to persist, many individuals within these cultures (often those of the oppressed group) resist traditions in favor of social justice. For instance, China is considered a collective society in which authority, hierarchy, and inequality take precedence over individual rights and autonomy (Markus & Kitayama, 1991). Nevertheless, Chinese adolescents tend to support fairness, voice, and majority rule (Helwig, Arnold, Tan, & Boyd, 2007). When asked about their preferences for democratic and nondemocratic forms of government, both Chinese and Canadian adolescents regarded democratic forms as more fair than nondemocratic forms and stated that they preferred democracy.

Scholars have also looked at attitudes toward inequality and injustice in India, which traditionally values family, tradition, and interdependence. In this society, men possess significantly more authority, autonomy, and freedom than women (Markus & Kitayama, 1991). When asked about norms and responsibilities for wives and husbands, Indian participants, as expected, emphasized more autonomy for husbands and interpersonal responsibility for wives (Neff, 2001). However there were some situations when a wife's autonomy was endorsed (e.g., when it was considered important for personal fulfillment). Some also expressed outright disagreement with the norms and traditions. Gender differences emerged, such that males allotted husbands more autonomy, while females were more egalitarian.

Even in the United States, men have traditionally been placed in positions of power and women in weaker, more subservient roles. These norms and traditions have been used to justify the unequal distribution of resources among men and women (Deaux & Kite, 1993). When middle school, high school, and college students were asked about power-related gender traits (e.g., leadership ability, dominance, and compliance) and attitudes toward sex-related inequality, participants who believed power-related traits were socially determined (as opposed to religiously or biologically determined) tended to hold more egalitarian views. Females also had more egalitarian views in general (Neff & Terry-Schmitt, 2002). Thus, views regarding morality (and specifically concerns about justice and equality) sometimes take precedence over traditions, norms, and authority.

OPPOSING JUSTICE ON MORAL GROUNDS

While morality is often seen as a positive attitude that encourages people to care for one another, views of morality can also be used to justify inequality, injustice, and oppression. Some have explained the relationship between morality and injustice by expanding the definition of morality (Haidt & Bjorklund, 2008; Haidt & Joseph, 2004), while others have described psychological techniques people use to preserve unjust or oppressive systems (Jost & Hunyady, 2005; Jost, Nosek, & Gosling, 2008; Jost, Pelham, & Carvallo, 2002). Unjust systems are no less a part of morality than those that promote social justice. Examining individual motives help explain how individuals who care about the well-being of others can nevertheless endorse policies and practices that establish or maintain injustice and inequality.

In contrast to many other psychologists, including Kohlberg and Turiel, Richard Shweder (1990) posited that there are three independent moral "ethics." The "ethic of autonomy" considers rights,

justice, and fairness. Second, the "ethic of community" supports the health and functioning of society and community. Finally, the "ethic of divinity" involves the protection and moral regulation of God-given bodies and souls. In most discourse on social justice, however, only the ethic of autonomy is considered. Haidt and Graham (2007) pointed out that moral considerations flowing from the ethics of community and divinity could be at odds with social justice. Consequently, certain individuals, particularly those with conservative views, may in fact oppose justice for moral reasons.

Based on Schweder's analysis of morality, Haidt and Bjorklund (2008) proposed five foundations of morality: *harm/care, fairness/reciprocity, in-group/ loyalty, authority/respect,* and *purity/sanctity*. They argued that moral psychologists and social justice advocates have traditionally focused only on harm/ care and fairness/reciprocity. The harm/care foundation suggests that people are sensitive to harm inflicted upon others and are often motivated to relive the harm. Witnessing human rights violations (e.g., female genital mutilation or dangerous working conditions) may inspire compassion and motivation to eradicate these problems. In contrast, the foundation of fairness/reciprocity encompasses feelings that motivate reciprocal altruism and a concern for fairness and justice (e.g., income inequality based purely on race or gender may cause individuals to protest the system's biases and demand equal pay for equal work). Haidt and Bjorklund's third foundation is in-group/loyalty, which includes loyalty, patriotism, trust, and cooperation within an in-group, and distrust of other groups. Performing rituals to build solidarity and define the in-group are valued. The fourth foundation, authority/respect, assigns more respect and greater rights to individuals in the upper ranks of a hierarchy. The final foundation, purity/sanctity, often involves feelings of disgust at those who are contaminated or diseased and those who give in to earthly passions (e.g., lust, gluttony, or greed). Piety and chastity are revered, while sins and sinful desires are condemned.

In order to explain how some individuals can oppose justice on moral grounds, Haidt and Graham (2007), applied the five foundations of morality to the agendas of liberals and conservatives. According to their *moral foundations hypothesis*, liberals only consider the first two moral foundations in their moral judgments. Conversely, they hypothesized that conservatives utilize all five foundations to make their moral evaluations. Thus, liberals are more likely to support social justice, while conservatives can oppose it because it conflicts with other moral values they hold. In support of their hypothesis, the authors note that most of the literature on social justice relates primarily to harm/care or fairness/reciprocity. Of the articles published in *Social Justice Research* between 2002 and 2005, 78% were linked to fairness/reciprocity and 65% were associated with harm/care. In contrast, fewer than half of the articles dealt with any one of the other three foundations. Moreover, the articles framed fairness, justice, care, and equality as positive, desirable, prosocial outcomes, whereas they rated the other three domains negatively. Activities designed to strengthen the in-group and maintain hierarchy, for example, were viewed as prejudicial, unjust, and oppressive, rather than helpful.

The moral foundations hypothesis was also supported by a study that used four different methods to assess the association between political orientation and concern for each moral foundation (Graham, Haidt, & Nosek, 2009). In one of the studies, participants were asked to directly rate how relevant various concerns were to them when making moral judgments. In a second study, participants were asked to make moral judgments about situations involving one of the five foundations. The third study examined how willing someone was to violate a particular taboo for money (each taboo was related to one of the moral foundations). The final study looked at the use of foundation-related terminology in religious sermons from liberal and conservative Christian denominations. The results of each study converged to show that liberals primarily endorse the harm/care and fairness/reciprocity foundations, while conservatives show evidence of morality based on all five foundations. Thus, conservatives are more likely to encounter conflicts between social justice and other moral concerns they have (e.g., conservatives may view equality or justice as threatening authority or weakening in-group bonds).

Therefore, Haidt and his colleagues suggest that understanding the five moral foundations may help liberals understand why conservatives sometimes resist social justice movements.

Like American conservatives, members of non-Western cultures often value elements of morality other than fairness/reciprocity and harm/care. Thus, some of their cultural practices may appear unjust but are not necessarily immoral. Specifically, non-Western cultures often endorse the ethic of community and ethic of divinity to a greater extent than Western cultures, identifying loyalty, patriotism, respect for authority, leadership, purity, and sanctity as moral virtues (Haidt & Joseph, 2008). In addition, many religious texts prescribe moral conduct surrounding food, clothing, sexuality, and gender relations, suggesting virtues in some religions are not limited to treating others with care and fairness. Researchers found that when presented with scenarios, Indian participants saw issues of respect, hierarchy, purity, or sanctity in situations where Americans saw only rights violations (e.g., when a husband beats his wife for disobedience) or saw no violation at all (e.g., someone eats foods considered impure in the Indian culture) (Shweder, Mahapatra, & Miller, 1987). Similarly, when asked to evaluate the morality of certain actions, Americans considered only those that violated harm, rights, and justice to be immoral, while poor participants in Brazil stated that disrespectful or disgusting actions were morally wrong even if no one was harmed (Haidt, Koller, & Dias, 1993). Equality is also not considered a moral virtue in some cultures. Instead, hierarchy is often valued (for examples, see Markus & Kitayama, 1991; Shweder et al., 1987). In fact, anthropologists note that egalitarian societies are relatively rare in history, and for millennia, humans have become more hierarchical than egalitarian (Boehm, 1999).

In any culture, moral justifications can be used to oppose justice in certain situations. Looking at morality through a Turiel lens, social judgments depend on an interaction between the individual and the circumstances (Turiel, 1998). As a result, unjust actions can be acceptable when they serve to enhance social relationships. Specifically, Killen and colleagues (2002) have found that children support the exclusion of individuals from social groups when such exclusion will improve group functioning or when the individual appeals to the ethic of autonomy (e.g., having the personal right to exclude someone). Participants in their study were likely to support their right to choose their individual friendships and the right of social groups to define group membership exclusively. However, they denounced the exclusion of certain groups from access to education. Thus, it may be appropriate to discriminate in certain situations (e.g., a women's support group should be open only to women) but not in others (e.g., when it denies certain individuals basic rights).

Another explanation for injustice and inequality comes from system justification theory. However, unlike other explanations for injustice, system justification theory does not argue that morality and injustice can be compatible. Instead, system justification theory posits that individuals constantly use cognitive, affective, and behavioral strategies to justify and perpetuate an unjust status quo (Jost & Banaji, 1994). According to the theory, people are motivated to believe the current social system is fair, legitimate, and necessary, even when it is unequal or oppressive toward certain groups. The following explanations can account for system justification: (a) the desire to reduce uncertainty and maintain shared reality with others (Hogg & Mullin, 1999; Wakslak, Jost, Tyler, & Chen, 2007), (b) the belief in a just world (Lerner, 1980), and (c) the influence of the mass media (Tyler & McGraw, 1986). In fact, some scholars argue that conservatives are generally happier than liberals, because their adherence to system justification helps them rationalize income inequality (Napier & Jost, 2008). System justification also occurs when people glorify or admire the poor in order to reduce their discomfort with the poor's financial circumstances. For example, one study found that support for the stereotypes "poor but happy" and "rich but miserable" was associated with higher scores on a measure of system justification (Kay & Jost, 2003). In contrast, exposure to noncomplementary stereotypes (e.g., that the rich are happier than the poor) implicitly raised concerns about social justice.

System justification tends to decrease emotional distress associated with exposure to social and economic inequality and may help explain why some oppose social justice causes. Conversely,

experiencing outward-focused emotional distress, described by scholars as "moral outrage," motivates some people to help the disadvantaged (Montada, Schmitt, & Dalbert, 1986). Wakslak and colleagues (2007) found that when system justification attitudes are induced (e.g., by telling participants "rags to riches" stories of people who have been independently successful), moral outrage declines and participants are less likely to support community service organizations that serve the needy. Some scholars also suggested that system justification reduced Americans' emotional distress following Hurricane Katrina (Napier, Mandisodza, Andersen, & Jost, 2006). They argued that a combination of victim blaming, internalization of inequality, and complementary stereotypes of the victims motivated people to continue to support the government, despite its failure to adequately protect and provide for the people most affected by the disaster (namely, the poor).

Even low status persons who are disadvantaged by current policies will engage in system justification. Some research has suggested that members of low status groups support the status quo, because they are ambivalent toward their own group and actually prefer the out-group (Glick & Fiske, 2001; Jost & Burgess, 2000). Data from five survey studies showed that underprivileged groups attempted to reduce cognitive dissonance by supporting the existing system to a greater extent than more affluent groups (Jost, Pelham, Sheldon, & Sullivan, 2003). That is, the underprivileged used system justification to resolve contradictory cognitions that (a) the system puts them at a disadvantage and that (b) they are in fact complicit in system maintenance. For example, low-income Latinos were found to trust in the government's motives to a greater extent than high-income Latinos. Similarly, low-income African Americans were more likely to believe inequality is legitimate and necessary than high-income African Americans and European Americans of all income levels.

System justification and injustice may be more likely when oppressed or disadvantaged individuals or groups are morally excluded. In other words, some individuals may be treated unfairly because they are considered to be outside the bounds of moral values, rules, and considerations (Opotow,

1990). Violations of human rights, discrimination, and other forms of oppression may be perceived as just or acceptable when others are viewed as undeserving, expendable nonentities. Throughout history, various groups, including slaves, women, Blacks, and Jews, have been excluded from the scope of justice. Moral philosophers have argued that membership in the human species is an appropriate boundary for social justice (e.g., Rawls, 1971), but the dominant group may define the boundaries more narrowly (Opotow, 1990), which suggested that conflict with an out-group and feeling disconnected from that group are associated with moral exclusion of the out-group. Like system justification, moral exclusion may be characterized by biased evaluations and victim blaming. However, moral exclusion can also include ordinary symptoms that occur in everyday life, such as condescension, normalization of violence, and psychological distancing, and exclusion-specific symptoms, such as dehumanization, fear of contamination from social contact, and desecration. The theory of moral exclusion notes that harm can be incurred by people within the moral community and outside the moral community, but it is only when it impacts the morally included that it is considered immoral.

Psychologists have shown how moral exclusion can lead to extreme forms of oppression and injustice. Bandura (2002), for example, described how disengagement of moral restraints can lead to harmful actions. Disengagement of moral restraints can occur when individuals redefine inhumane conduct as benign through moral justification; label their actions euphemistically; compare their actions to other, more harmful deeds; deny responsibility or blame others for their actions; minimize the deleterious impact of one's actions; and blame and dehumanize the victims. Bandura's moral justification is akin to Jost's system justification in that it is a cognitive mechanism used to make injustice seem personally and socially acceptable. However, the object of moral justification is an inhumane action rather than a static system. Euphemistic labeling involves "sanitizing language" or using an "agentless passive voice" when describing unjust conduct such that the damage or harm inflicted seems less objectionable (e.g., describing genocide of particular races as "ethnic cleansing") or seems to have been inflicted by a nameless, faceless entity (e.g., "the gun was fired at the prisoner's head" as opposed to "the guard fired a gun at the prisoner's head"). Unjust actions can also seem more legitimate when advantageously compared to the actions of others. For example, if a group of people is perceived to be contaminating or corrupting society, some will consider removal of them through murder or forced exile as justifiable and necessary to protect the "innocent" members. During World War II, this justification was used to purge European cities of their Jewish, homosexual, dissident, and criminal populations (Bauer, 2001).

Moral disengagement also occurs when individuals distance themselves from their role in creating or maintaining injustices. If unjust actions are legitimated by a law or other authority (e.g., a discriminatory employment policy), the agent of such actions feels he or she is only doing what is natural or expected. In the 19th and 20th centuries, for instance, science was used as a legitimating authority to justify racist beliefs (Watkins, 2005). Scientific racism or eugenics allowed people to argue that racial inequality and discrimination were only natural. In addition, moral disengagement is more likely if many others are involved in the unjust actions; when others are complicit, one feels less responsible for the outcome. Injustice is also easier to tolerate if the suffering it causes is not visible or perceived to be minimal. None of the Nazi death camps in World War II were in Germany (Bauer, 2001). Perhaps maintaining these camps far from German cities and towns helped the Nazis ensure the German people would remain ignorant of the suffering that Nazi victims endured, making them less likely to protest against government policies. Finally, empathy for victims tends to fade when they are dehumanized or portrayed as deserving of their suffering. If victims are perceived as subhuman objects, they are not granted the same rights as humans; thus, it is considered acceptable to treat them differently from humans. It is also easier for people mistreat others if the victims are believed to have provoked their perpetrator (e.g., made the perpetrator angry, resisted orders, or wronged the perpetrator). Each of these variants of moral disengagement is clearly a powerful tool people use to justify and tolerate injustice.

In addition to cognitive mechanisms, such as system justification and moral exclusion, some moral emotions may motivate injustice. For example, contempt is an emotion often associated with feelings of superiority (Ekman, 1994; Izard, 1977), which may solidify the separation of ranks or classes within a social hierarchy. In traditional, hierarchical societies, contempt is typically described as cool indifference felt by those of the upper ranks or classes toward those in the lower classes (Haidt, 2003). It causes those in the upper ranks to treat those in lower classes with less respect and consideration. Furthermore, Haidt (2003) argues that it may actually weaken prosocial moral emotions, like compassion. As a result, contempt may fuel unjust or oppressive campaigns against disadvantaged classes.

Like contempt, disgust is a moral emotion that can lead to injustice. It is a response to something revolting, primarily in relation to taste; however, it can also be elicited by anyone or anything that induces a similar feeling (Haidt, 2003). In some societies, disgust divides classes of people. For example, castes in India and racial segregation in the American South were reinforced by the disgust felt by the higher status groups for individuals in the lower classes (Haidt, 2003). Even bodily contact between classes was considered offensive in these cultures. Consequently, disgust can lead to the avoidance, ostracism, and exclusion of lower classes.

LIMITATIONS AND FUTURE DIRECTIONS

Although links can be drawn between conceptions of morality and social justice, few scholars to date have explicitly explored this relationship. As a result, this review has relied on the moral psychology concepts of caring, justice, fairness, and rights, values that are encompassed by social justice. However, the relationship between morality and social justice needs further exploration. Is advanced moral development needed to pursue social justice?

Are people more likely to advocate social justice when feeling certain moral emotions, like empathy and compassion? While this analysis suggests that moral development and moral emotions can promote social justice, few have formally tested these suppositions. Establishing the relationship between morality and social justice may help define a path to achieving greater social justice.

Even if a positive association between morality and social justice is found, several caveats need to be considered; namely, the term *social justice* is vague and can have multiple meanings, and conceptions of morality can vary according to culture and historical period. Multiple definitions and cultural relativity may preclude the establishment of broad, universal statements about the link between these two concepts. For example, morality and injustice can coexist when tradition and hierarchy are valued more than justice.

When both context and concepts are specifically defined and the views of various theorists are synthesized, a more nuanced understanding of morality and social justice may emerge (see Figure 8.1). Piaget and Kohlberg established the foundations of moral development and social justice, while later theorists elaborated on the role of emotion, cognition, and context-based views morality. Turiel, for example, suggested that social justice depends on contextual and cultural factors. From a feminist perspective, Gilligan argued that morality for women was about more than justice and fairness, while Haidt pointed out that social justice may conflict with other domains of morality. System justification theory explains why people support the status quo, even if it is oppressive or unjust. Finally, Bandura suggested that people are better able to tolerate injustice when it is inflicted on those who have been morally excluded. While each of these theories has been influential in understanding moral psychology, a clearer conceptualization of morality and social justice integrates the key components of these theories and takes into account the meaning of both morality and social justice. In addition, an extension of the existing theories may further explore the ways in which moral development and moral emotions directly impact social justice behavior.

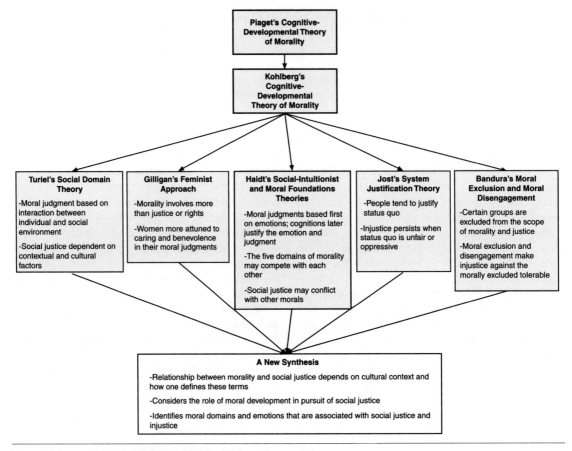

Figure 8.1 Morality and Social Justice Theory Concept Map

CONCLUSION

The concepts of morality and social justice both involve care for others. Understanding how moral reasoning and action develop over time helps explain how humans acquire the ability and motivation to seek social justice. However, understanding morality also provides insights into the dynamics of immorality. Moreover, moral and immoral positions can justify the existence of injustice. As this review has demonstrated, human psychology and social relations are complex; morality and justice depend on the interaction between individuals and their environments. Only by carefully examining individual thoughts, feelings, and motivations, as well as political, social, and cultural circumstances

can one fully appreciate the ways in which morality and social justice intersect.

REFERENCES

Bandura, A. (2002). Selective moral disengagement in the exercise of moral agency. *Journal of Moral Education, 31*(2), 101–119. doi:10.1080/0305724022014322

Bargh, J. A. (1994). The four horsemen of automaticity: Awareness, efficiency, intention, and control in social cognition. In R. S. Wyer Jr. & T. K. Srull (Eds.), *Handbook of social cognition* (2nd ed., pp. 1–40). Hillsdale, NJ: Erlbaum.

Batson, C. D., O'Quin, K., Fultz, J., Vanderplas, M., & Isen, A. M. (1983). Influence of self-reported distress and empathy on egotistic versus altruistic motivation to help. *Journal of Personality and Social Psychology, 45*(3), 706–718. doi:10.1037/0022-3514.45.3.706

Batson, C. D., & Shaw, L. L. (1991). Evidence for altruism: Toward a pluralism of prosocial motives. *Psychological Inquiry, 2*(2), 107–122. doi:10.1207/s15327965pli0202_1

Batson, C. D., & Weeks, J. L. (1996). Mood effects of unsuccessful helping: Another test of the empathy-altruism hypothesis. *Personality and Social Psychology Bulletin, 22*, 148–157. doi:10.1177/0146167296222004

Bauer, Y. (2001). *A history of the Holocaust*. Danbury, CT: Franklin Watts.

Baumeister, R. F., Stillwell, A. M., & Heatherton, T. F. (1994). Guilt: An interpersonal approach. *Psychological Bulletin, 115*(2), 243–267. doi:10.1037/0033-2909.115.2.243

Boehm, C. (1999). *Hierarchy in the forest: The evolution of egalitarian behavior*. Cambridge, MA: Harvard University Press.

Damon, W. (1975). Early conceptions of positive justice as related to the development of logical operations. *Child Development, 46*, 301–312.

Davis, M. H. (1983). The effects of dispositional empathy on emotional reactions and helping: A multidimensional approach. *Journal of Personality, 51*(2), 167–184. doi:10.1111/j.1467-6494.1983.tb00860.x

Deaux, K., & Kite, M. (1993). Gender stereotypes. In F. L. Denmark & M. A. Paludi (Eds.), *Psychology of women: A handbook of issues and theories.* (pp. 107–139). Westport, CT: Greenwood Press.

Ekman, P. (1994). Antecedent events and emotion metaphors. In P. Ekman & R. J. Davidson (Eds.), *The nature of emotion: Fundamental questions* (pp. 146–149). New York, NY: Oxford University Press.

Ford, M. R., & Lowery, C. R. (1986). Gender differences in moral reasoning: A comparison of the use of justice and care orientations. *Journal of Personality and Social Psychology, 50*(4), 777–783. doi:10.1037/0022-3514.50.4.777

Gewirth, A. (1984). Ethics. *Encyclopaedia Britannica* (Vol. 6, pp. 976–998). Chicago, IL: Encyclopaedia Brittanica.

Gilligan, C. (1982). *In a different voice: Psychological theory and women's development*. Cambridge, MA: Harvard University Press.

Gilligan, C., & Attanucci, J. (1988a). Much ado about . . . knowing? Noting? Nothing? A reply to Vasudev concerning sex differences and moral development. *Merrill-Palmer Quarterly, 34*(4), 451–456.

Gilligan, C., & Attanucci, J. (1988b). Two moral orientations: Gender differences and similarities. *Merrill-Palmer Quarterly, 34*(3), 223–237.

Glick, P., & Fiske, S. T. (2001). An ambivalent alliance: Hostile and benevolent sexism as complementary justification for gender inequality. *American Psychologist, 56*(2), 109–118. doi:10.1037/0003-066X.56.2.109

Goetz, J. L., Keltner, D., & Simon-Thomas, E. (2010). Compassion: An evolutionary analysis and empirical review. *Psychological Bulletin, 136*(3), 351–374. doi:10.1037/a0018807

Graham, J., Haidt, J., & Nosek, B. A. (2009). Liberals and conservatives rely on different sets of moral foundations. *Journal of Personality and Social Psychology, 96*(5), 1029–1046. doi:10.1037/a0015141

Greene, J., & Haidt, J. (2002). How (and where) does moral judgment work? *Trends in Cognitive Sciences, 6*(12), 517–523. doi:10.1016/S1364-6613(02)02011-9

Haidt, J. (2001). The emotional dog and its rational tail: A social intuitionist approach to moral judgment. *Psychological Review, 108*(4), 814–834. doi:10.37//0033-295

Haidt, J. (2003). The moral emotions. In R. J. Davidson, K. R. Scherer, & H. H. Goldsmith (Eds.), *Handbook of affective sciences* (pp. 852–870). Oxford, UK: Oxford University Press.

Haidt, J., Algoe, S., Meijer, Z., & Tam, A. (2002). *The elevation-altruism hypothesis: Evidence for a new prosocial emotion*. Unpublished manuscript, University of Virginia.

Haidt, J., & Bjorklund, F. (2008). *Social intuitionists reason, in conversation*. Cambridge, MA: MIT Press.

Haidt, J., & Graham, J. (2007). When morality opposes justice: Conservatives have moral intuitions that liberals may not recognize. *Social Justice Research, 20*(1), 98–116. doi:10.1007/s11211-007-0034-z

Haidt, J., & Joseph, C. (2004). Intuitive ethics. *Dædalus, 133*(4), 55–66.

Haidt, J., & Joseph, C. (2008). The moral mind: How five sets of innate intuitions guide the development of many culture–specific virtues, and perhaps even modules. In P. Carruthers, S. Laurence, & S. Stich (Eds.), *The innate mind* (Vol. 3, pp. 367–391). New York, NY: Oxford University Press.

Haidt, J., Koller, S. H., & Dias, M. G. (1993). Affect, culture, and morality, or is it wrong to eat your dog? *Journal of Personality and Social Psychology, 65*(4), 613–628. doi:10.1037/0022-3514.65.4.613

Haidt, J., & Sabini, J. (2000). *What exactly makes revenge sweet*. Unpublished manuscript, University of Virginia.

Helwig, C. C., Arnold, M. L., Tan, D., & Boyd, D. (2007). Mainland Chinese and Canadian adolescents' judgments and reasoning about the fairness of democratic and other forms of government. *Cognitive Development, 22*(1), 96–109. doi:10.1016/j.cogdev.2006.07.002

Helwig, C. C., & Jasiobedzka, U. (2001). The relation between law and morality: Children's reasoning about socially beneficial and unjust laws. *Child Development, 72*(5), 1382–1393. doi:10.1111/1467-8624.00354

Hoffman, M. L. (1982a). Affect and moral development. In D. Ciccetti & P. Hesse (Eds.), *New directions for child development: Vol. 16. Emotional development* (pp. 83–103). San Francisco, CA: Jossey-Bass.

Hoffman, M. L. (1982b). Development of prosocial motivation: Empathy and guilt. In N. Eisenberg (Ed.), *The development of prosocial behavior* (pp. 218–231). New York, NY: Academic Press.

Hoffman, M. L. (2001). *Empathy and moral development: Implications for caring and justice.* Cambridge, UK: Cambridge University Press.

Hogg, M. A., & Mullin, B. A. (1999). Joining groups to reduce uncertainty: Subjective uncertainty reduction and group identification. In D. Abrams & M. A. Hogg (Eds.), *Social identity and social cognition* (pp. 249–279). Oxford, UK: Blackwell.

Izard, C. E. (1977). *Human emotions.* New York, NY: Plenum.

Jost, J. T., & Banaji, M. R. (1994). The role of stereotyping in system justification and the production of false consciousness. *British Journal of Social Psychology, 33*(1), 1–27.

Jost, J. T., & Burgess, D. (2000). Attitudinal ambivalence and the conflict between group and system justification motives in low status groups. *Personality and Social Psychology Bulletin, 26*(3), 293–305. doi:10.1177/0146167200265003

Jost, J. T., & Hunyady, O. (2005). Antecedents and consequences of system-justifying ideologies. *Current Directions in Psychological Science, 14*(5), 260–265. doi:10.1111/j.0963-7214.2005.00377.x

Jost, J. T., Nosek, B. A., & Gosling, S. D. (2008). Ideology: Its resurgence in social, personality, and political psychology. *Perspectives on Psychological Science, 3*(2), 126–136. doi:10.1111/j.1745-6916.2008.00070.x

Jost, J. T., Pelham, B. W., & Carvallo, M. R. (2002). Nonconscious forms of system justification: Implicit and behavioral preferences for higher status groups. *Journal of Experimental Social Psychology, 38*(6), 586–602. doi:10.1016/S0022-1031(02)00505-X

Jost, J. T., Pelham, B. W., Sheldon, O., & Sullivan, B. N. (2003). Social inequality and the reduction of ideological dissonance on behalf of the system: Evidence of enhanced system justification among the disadvantaged. *European Journal of Social Psychology, 33*(1), 13–36. doi:10.1002/ejsp.127

Kagan, J. (1984). *The nature of the child.* New York, NY: Basic Books.

Kay, A. C., & Jost, J. T. (2003). Complementary justice: Effects of "poor but happy" and "poor but honest" stereotype exemplars on system justification and implicit activation of the justice motive. *Journal of Personality and Social Psychology, 85*(5), 823–837. doi:10.1037/0022-3514.85.5.823

Killen, M., Lee-Kim, J., McGlothlin, H., & Stangor, C. (2002). How children and adolescents evaluate gender and racial exclusion. *Monographs of the Society for Research in Child Development, 67*(4), vii–7. doi:10.1111/1540-5834.00218

Kohlberg, L. (1969). Stage and sequence: The cognitive-developmental approach to socialization. In D. A. Goslin (Ed.). *Handbook of socialization theory and research* (pp. 347–480). Chicago, IL: Rand McNally.

Lapsley, D. K. (1996). *Moral psychology.* Boulder, CO: Westview.

Laupa, M. (1991). Children's reasoning about three authority attributes: Adult status, knowledge, and social position. *Developmental Psychology, 27*(2), 321–329. doi:10.1037/0012-1649.27.2.321

Laupa, M., & Turiel, E. (1986). Children's conceptions of adult and peer authority. *Child Development, 57*(2), 405–412. doi:10.2307/1130596

Lerner, M. J. (1980). *The belief in a just world: A fundamental delusion.* New York, NY: Plenum.

Markus, H. R., & Kitayama, S. (1991). Culture and the self: Implications for cognition, emotion, and motivation. *Psychological Review, 98*(2), 224–253. doi:10.1037/0033-295X.98.2.224

Montada, L., Schmitt, M., & Dalbert, C. (1986). Thinking about justice and dealing with one's own privileges: A study of existential guilt. In H. W. Bierhoof, R. L. Cohen, & J. Greenberg (Eds.), *Justice in social relations* (pp. 125–143). New York, NY: Plenum.

Napier, J. L., & Jost, J. T. (2008). Why are conservatives happier than liberals? *Psychological Science, 19*(5), 565–572. doi:10.1111/j.1467-9280.2008.02124.x

Napier, J. L., Mandisodza, A. N., Andersen, S. M., & Jost, J. T. (2006). System justification in responding to the poor and displaced in the aftermath of Hurricane Katrina. *Analyses of Social Issues and Public Policy, 6*(1), 57–73. doi: 10.1111/j.1530-2415.2006.00102.x

Neff, K. D. (2001). Judgments of personal autonomy and interpersonal responsibility in the context of Indian spousal relationships: An examination of young people's reasoning in Mysore, India. *British Journal of Developmental Psychology, 19*(2), 233–257. doi:10.1348/026151001166056

Neff, K. D., & Terry-Schmitt, L. N. (2002). Youths' attributions for power-related gender differences: Nature, nurture, or god? *Cognitive Development, 17*(2), 1185–1202. doi:10.1016/S0885-2014(02)00094-1

Opotow, S. (1990). Moral exclusion and injustice. *Journal of Social Issues, 46*(1), 1–20. doi: 10.1111/j.1540-4560.1990.tb00268.x

Penner, L. A., Fritzsche, B. A., Craiger, J. P., & Freifeld, T.R. (1995). Measuring the prosocial personality. In J. Butcher & C. D. Spielberger (Eds.), *Advances in personality assessment* (Vol. 10, pp. 147–163). Hillsdale, NJ: Erlbaum.

Perkins, S. A., & Turiel, E. (2007). To lie or not to lie: To whom and under what circumstances. *Child Development, 78*(2), 609–621. doi:10.1111/j.1467-8624.2007.01017.x

Piaget, J. (1997). *The moral judgment of the child.* New York, NY: Free Press. (Original work published 1932)

Rawls, J. (1971). *A theory of justice.* Cambridge, MA: Belknap/Harvard University Press.

Shweder, R. (1990). In defense of moral realism: Reply to Gabennesch. *Child Development, 61*, 2060–2067. doi:10.1111/j.1467-8624.1990.tb03587.x

Shweder, R. A., Mahapatra, M., & Miller, J. (1987). Culture and moral development. In J. Kagan & S. Lamb (Eds.), *The emergence of morality in young children* (pp. 1–83). Chicago, IL: University of Chicago Press.

Smetana, J. G. (1995). Morality in context: Abstractions, ambiguities and applications. In R. Vasta (Ed.), *Annals of child development: A research annual* (Vol. 10, pp. 83–130). London, UK: Jessica Kingsley.

Turiel, E. (1998). The development of morality. In W. Damon & N. Eisenberg (Eds.), *Handbook of child psychology* (5th ed.)*: Vol. 3. Social, emotional, and*

personality development (pp. 863–932). Hoboken, NJ: Wiley & Sons.

Turiel, E. (2005). Resistance and subversion in everyday life. In L. P. Nucci (Ed.), *Conflict, contradiction, and contrarian elements in moral development and education* (pp. 3–20). Mahweh, NJ: Erlbaum.

Turiel, E. (2006). Thought, emotions, and social interactional processes in moral development. In M. Killen & J. G. Smetana (Eds.), *Handbook of moral development* (pp. 7–36). Mahweh, NJ: Erlbaum.

Tyler, T. R., & McGraw, K. M. (1986). Ideology and the interpretation of personal experience: Procedural justice and political quiescence. *Journal of Social Issues, 42*(2), 115–128. doi:10.1111/j.1540-4560.1986.tb00228.x

Vasudev, J. (1988). Sex differences in morality and moral orientation: A discussion of Gilligan and Attanucci study. *Merrill-Palmer Quarterly, 34*(3), 239–244.

Wakslak, C. J., Jost, J. T., Tyler, T. T., & Chen, E. S. (2007). Moral outrage mediates the dampening effect of system justification on support for the redistributive social policies. *Psychological Science, 18*(3), 267–274. doi:10.1111/j.1467-9280.2007.01887.x

Watkins, W. H. (2005). Race and morality: Shaping the myth. In L. P. Nucci (Ed.), *Conflict, contradiction, and contrarian elements in moral development and education* (pp. 173–192). Mahweh, NJ: Erlbaum.

Wegner, D., & Bargh, J. (1998). Control and automaticity in social life. In D. T. Gilbert, S. T. Fiske, & G. Lindzey (Eds.), *Handbook of social psychology* (4th ed., pp. 446–496). New York, NY: McGraw-Hill.

Wendorf, C. A., Alexander, S., & Firestone, I. J. (2002). Social justice and moral reasoning: An empirical integration of two paradigms in psychological research. *Social Justice Research, 15*(1), 19–39. doi:10.1023/A:1016093614893

9

SOCIAL JUSTICE AND ANTHROPOLOGY

From Observation to Activism

LEAH A. JACOBS

INTRODUCTION

To take action on injustice, one must believe in his or her stance on a matter and have the conviction that it is his or her responsibility to do something about that injustice. This proves to be a difficult feat for anthropologists who are divided between principles of universalism and principles of cultural relativism and unsure about their roles beyond the common definition of researcher as objective observer. Take the case of female genital mutilation (FGM), a consistently used example of universal injustice. From a relativist perspective, the parents who commit FGM do not intend to hurt their child but are instead following a deeply rooted cultural tradition out of love. From a universal perspective, FGM is a barbaric and oppressive act regardless of its cultural roots. If the anthropologist resigns herself to the idea that FGM is justified by its cultural nature, those who see FGM as a violation of human rights could consider the anthropologist a bedfellow of injustice. If the anthropologist raises awareness about this activity and promotes its criminalization, she risks being called ethnocentric or stepping beyond her role as researcher. These tensions exist

beyond the case of FGM and are at the root of divisions among anthropologists regarding the role of anthropologists in realizing social justice.

The use of anthropological knowledge to spur social change is reflected in the subfield of activist anthropology that has grown significantly over the course of the past 20 years. It has called into question many of anthropology's traditional theoretical underpinnings and spurred significant tensions within the field. The following discussion outlines the historical bases for activism in the field of anthropology as it relates to social justice, proposes a working definition of activist anthropology that draws upon multiple theorists, and discusses how activist anthropology has called into question anthropological canon and beliefs about universal human rights.

METHODS

The method used for exploring the topic of social justice and activist anthropology was an unstructured literature review. The starting point for the literature review was a search of the contents of the *International Encyclopedia of the Social and Behavioral Sciences* under the heading Anthropology and the subheading Subdisciplines, Theoretical Orientations, and Methods that yielded one article titled "Advocacy in Anthropology" (Sponsel, 2001) and an article titled "Gender and Feminist Studies in Anthropology" (Aretxaga, 2001). Next, in the *International Encyclopedia,* another foundational text titled "Anthropology of Colonialism" was found in the subsection Concepts. The next search was in the electronic database Anthropology Plus Detailed Record Index. The use of the search terms *anthropology* and *social justice* yielded 80 texts of which seven informed the development of this literature review. These texts provided a foundation from which the author was able to identify other relevant texts via a snowball methodology. All searches were conducted and texts accessed via the University of California, Berkeley library system.

In addition, the author conducted a Google search for college courses on activism in anthropology. This search yielded three courses. The author then obtained the syllabi for these courses and acquired any relevant readings listed on these syllabi to inform this literature review. This yielded six articles and books that contributed to the content of this review.

This literature review of anthropological theory provides a broad overview of the discipline of activist anthropology, including how it developed out of and differs from traditional scholarship. It does not include the considerable amount of literature that illustrates activist anthropology and therefore is not an exhaustive search. In addition, it is possible that the perspectives provided by the sources identified in this search exclude other sources that belong in this review. Finally, as a scholar outside of the field of anthropology conducted this review, it does not contain a comprehensive analysis of anthropological theory.

HISTORICAL AND DESCRIPTIVE ANALYSIS: UNDERSTANDING ANTHROPOLOGY

The leading organization of anthropologists worldwide, the American Association of Anthropology (AAA), simply defines anthropology as "the study of humans, past and present" (2010). The organization puts forth four major categories of anthropology, including sociocultural, physical, linguistic, and archeology, which together take on the complex task of understanding humanity. Anthropological research involves working closely with people and communities and using ethnographic and comparative methodologies. Influenced by both the content area and the nature of its methodologies, anthropology has a long history of internal tension regarding the optimal role of anthropologists in the field and in the world. Is the place of the anthropologist in the field or behind the walls of the ivory tower? Is the anthropologist's role to act as objective observer and objective scholar, or is the anthropologist responsible for putting scholarship to use in service of those that they study and the larger global community? If you ask one anthropologist, you may get a very different response from the next. As Stocking stated, "Despite anthropology's century as an academic discipline, its definition is in some respects more problematic today than at the time of its early institutionalization" (Stocking, 1983, p. 5). However, a brief historical analysis can shed light on the evolving definition and role of anthropology.

A BRIEF HISTORY OF ANTHROPOLOGY AND ITS ACTIVIST ROOTS

Anthropology has always played an active role in shaping social thought (Baker, 2004) and has a long history of advocating for social change (Sponsel, 2001). Anthropology began as a field that defined itself by objective observation and documentation and has moved toward a more critical awareness of the influence of the researcher on the observed environment, as well as the sociopolitical-cultural influences on the researcher (Aretxaga, 2001; Sponsel, 2001). While this recognition has been an evolutionary process, activism in anthropology is found not only in contemporary anthropology. It can also be viewed in the work of some of the field's most prominent scholars.

Predating the official creation of anthropology as a field of study, perhaps the first advocate anthropologist was Bartolome de las Casas (1474–1566); see Sponsel, 2001. Las Casas, a Franciscan priest, witnessed and documented extensively the impact of Spanish colonization on Latin America. In addition to witnessing and documenting, Las Casas advocated politically against human rights abuses of indigenous peoples of the Americas by Spanish colonists.

The work of Franz Boas (1858–1942), widely accepted as the father of modern anthropology, clearly illustrates the role of activism in early American anthropology. In his early career, Boas stated, "What I want to live and die for is equal rights for all, equal possibilities to learn and work for poor and rich alike! Don't you believe that to have done even the smallest bit for this, is more than all of science together?" (Boas as cited in Cole, 1983, p. 37). While clearly committed to social change, Boas was also deeply committed to advancing the field of anthropology. He wanted to push the field beyond racial and ethnic comparisons and would later extend this goal to society at large (Baker, 2004).

In his seminal texts *Changes in Bodily Form* and *The Mind of Primitive Man,* Boas argued that physical variations, especially cranial, were not an indication of evolutionary progress. Instead, Boas suggested that variations were due to environmental factors and, for this reason, cross-cultural generalizations regarding biologically based racial intellectual superiority cannot be made (Baker, 2004). Thus, although Boas did not name it as such, he coined the idea of cultural relativism, a critical philosophy within modern anthropology. This then lead to the methodological shift toward ethnography, which required the anthropologist to decrease their ethnocentrism by living with or spending extensive time with subjects under investigation. Ethnography allowed the anthropologist to understand the cultural context of these subjects.

In addition to Boas's scholarly contribution to anthropological theory and methods, his theory provided a critical foundation to arguments against racism and White supremacy both within and outside of academia. Boas was a "public scholar" and an active antinationalist and antiwar advocate (Baker, 2004). He contributed to social thought by crossing over the boundary of academia, appearing in *Time* magazine, and contributing to progressive magazines, such as the *Nation* (Baker, 2004). He also played a key role in the formulation of the "scientists manifesto" in 1938, which was a petition of over 1,200 scientists arguing against the conflation of race and moral character in the face of the Nazi takeover of Europe (Baker, 2004). Boas, having died in 1942, would not see the impact that World War II would have on the field of anthropology. World War II demarcates a qualitative shift in anthropology's focus (Paine, 1985). After the war, there was also a new interest in the well-being and future of anthropology's subjects (Paine, 1985). The field also became increasingly interested in Marxism and issues related to power and hegemony (Scott, 2001).

Competing with Boas for the title of father of modern anthropology, Claude Levi-Strauss is considered the most influential postwar anthropologist (Eriksen, 2001). Levi-Strauss's greatest contribution to the field of anthropology was the development of structuralism—a "universalist doctrine about the way human minds function" (Levi-Strauss as cited in Eriksen, 2001, p. 137). While Levi-Strauss argued that there were universal cognitive structures that guided human thinking and behavior, he was also a classic relativist with respect to culture. Levi-Strauss was criticized by scholars such as Derida for using universalism with a tinge of relativism to reduce cultural groups to "laboratory specimens" (Eriksen, 2001, p. 138). However, his text *Race et Histoire* (1961) played a key role in moving past racism and ethnocentrism. In the text, Levi-Strauss warns against genetic determinism, reveals the fallacies of ethnocentrism and oversimplifications of cultural evolution, and defends the rights of small societies to their cultural identities. In his other classic text, *Race et Culture* (1979), he argues that we overhomogenize racial groups that are different from our own and argues that race is a product of culture and against the idea that culture is a product of race. He views conflict arising from intercultural contact as inevitable and believes that it is a "dream that equality and brotherhood will one day rule among men" (as cited in Eriksen, 2001, p. 139). Despite promoting a universalist theory (structuralism), Levi-Strauss envisioned a world separated by culture and, as such, does not relate anthropological theory to the development of a human rights framework (Eriksen, 2001). However, Levi-Strauss was commissioned a number of times to write analyses on the nature of cultural variation by the United Nations Educational, Scientific and Cultural Organization (UNESCO) and has contributed significantly to contemporary social thought on ethnocentrism and race (Eriksen, 2001).

Having been mentored by Boas and witnessed the impact of World War II, Margaret Mead (1901–1978) would follow in the footsteps of Boas, and extend anthropology beyond the walls of academia into the public sphere (Dillon, 2001). Mead, most notably known for her statement, "Never doubt that a small group of thoughtful, committed citizens can change the world" (Mead as cited by Dillon, 2001, p. 447), in many ways embraced the idea of activism in anthropology. Mead was not opposed to providing commentary on public issues and spoke out against war and racism (Dillon, 2001). She also pushed the field toward advocacy when, as the president of the AAA, she passed a measure to declare certain weapons of war to be "offensive to human nature" (Mead as cited by Castile, 1975, p. 36).

The 1960s brought about significant change in anthropology. Heavily influenced by feminism and postcolonialist theory (Aretxaga, 2001; Scott, 2001), anthropologists began focusing on perceptions of gender and sexuality, and the impact of colonialism. According to Aretxaga (2001), feminist anthropology uncovered anthropology's allegiance to the Victorian concept of femininity and how it created the lens through which anthropologists interpreted their subjects. Similar to how we understood race, dominant gender expectations became the natural model of comparison. Feminist anthropologists put forth the idea that the terms *gender* and *culture* are not neutral or self-evident but are terms used to define regulatory practices between men and women as it was between the state and its people. Using gender as an example to illustrate the connection between the oppressor and the oppressed, feminist scholarship was closely linked to postcolonial scholarship.

According to Scott (2001), anthropology underwent an internal crisis in the 1970s. The field began to examine its relationship to the social and political world in which it existed and the role that it had played in colonialism. Anthropologists drew special attention to their role in American counterinsurgency efforts in Latin America and as cultural experts in the war in Indochina. This raised important questions regarding the responsibility of anthropology

to inquire into subjects related to oppression and justice and the role of anthropology in affecting social change. Soon, inspired by feminist anthropology and postcolonial anthropology, postmodern anthropology would take hold and call attention to the authority of the ethnographer (Aretxaga, 2001). It drew into question the impact of ethnography. According to Scheper-Hughes, "When anthropologists arrive in the field, everything local is said to dissolve into merged media images, transgressed boundaries, promiscuously mobile multinational industry and workers, and transnational-corporate desires and commodity fetishism" (1995, p. 417). Postmodern perspectives characterized people and cultures differently, and anthropology focused on becoming less of a tool of oppression (Paine, 1985; Scheper-Hughes, 1995). While some have argued that these shifts have somehow led to more justifications for anthropology's inaction, or even disappearance (Scheper-Hughes, 1995), it also appears to have laid the foundation for the emergence of overt activism in anthropology as well. While Boas and Mead demonstrated that advocacy has always played some role in anthropology, it was in this postcolonial and postmodern shift that the role of advocacy in anthropology was defined.

UNDERSTANDING ADVOCACY IN ANTHROPOLOGY

Activist anthropology, also referred to as "critical ethnography" (Chari & Donner, 2010), "barefoot" and "militant anthropology" (Scheper-Hughes, 1995), "advocacy anthropology" (Paine, 1985), and "responsible anthropology" (Messer, 1993), is an applied subtype of sociocultural anthropology. Activist anthropology finally emerged out of postcolonial criticisms of ethnocide and genocide and sought to increase the application and social responsibility of social science researchers (Scheper-Hughes, 1995; Sponsel, 2001). The differential quality of activist anthropology is that the anthropologist moves beyond "pure" scientific inquiry and observation to conducting research that can be put to use (Hale, 2001).

Activist anthropology focuses on "advancing the interests of a community, often as a practical plea on its behalf to one or more external agencies" (Sponsel, 2001, p. 204). It is aware of the power differential that exists between researchers and subjects (Chari & Donner, 2010). Hale (2001) suggests that the activist researcher is not an activist in the true sense of the word, but the activist researcher is one who acknowledges a political stance and how that political stance has framed the research. Hale also makes an important clarification that the word *activist* is used as an adjective to describe the way in which a research question is developed and research is carried out; it refers to research about or with people who are activists. According to Messer (1993), activist anthropology is drawn from a developing global human rights framework in order to achieve positive legal, political, and social results for communities of study.

The theoretical underpinning of activist anthropology is that the anthropologist has a moral or ethical obligation to move beyond observation, documentation, and publication and an obligation to work toward creating a more just world (Chari & Donner, 2010; Farmer, 2003; Messer, 1993; Scheper-Hughes, 1995). According to Madison, an "ethical responsibility" means

> a compelling sense of duty and commitment based on moral principles of human freedom and well-being, and hence a compassion for the suffering of human beings. The conditions for existence within a particular context are not as they *could* be for specific subjects; as a result, the researcher feels a moral obligation to make a contribution toward changing those conditions toward greater freedom and equity. (Madison as cited in Chari & Donner, 2010, p. 76)

Activist research forces the researcher to identify his political convictions and to ask research questions relevant to those convictions. This contradicts typical anthropological research training, which encourages the suppression of these convictions. Instead, Hale argues that the researcher should acknowledge how these convictions frame his or her research (Hale, 2001).

What Does Activist Research Look Like?

While the idea of researchers contributing directly to creating a more socially just world may have a certain moral appeal, it is still a fairly vague and nebulous notion. Models of practice and examples of scholarship can be reviewed in order to concretize activist anthropology. The following section describes Hale's model of activist research and illustrates how activist research has been conceptualized.

According to Hale (2001), activist research has three defining characteristics. First, it "helps us to better understand the root causes of inequality, oppression, violence and related conditions of human suffering." Second, it "is carried out, at each phase from conception through dissemination, in direct cooperation with an organized collective of people who themselves are subject to these conditions." Finally, it "is used, together with the people in question, to formulate strategies for transforming these conditions and to achieve the power necessary to make these strategies effective" (p. 13).

Hale (2001) also provides a practical guide to implementing activist research. He discusses five basic methodological steps to activist research. The first step is arriving at research questions and methods. This is a participatory process, which actively engages subjects and coincides with what these people think is important and should be prioritized in the study. The second step is data collection. Hale suggests that data collection should involve participation of interested subjects, allowing them to learn about the research process and to contribute to the collection of data. The third step is the interpretation and analysis of data, which should also be a participatory process involving stakeholders. The fourth step is the dissemination of research products. This step is an important fulfillment of the researcher's obligation to subjects. However, Hale recognizes that it can be challenging to produce findings in a way that is meaningful to both communities and scholars. The final step of this research process is the validation of results. This step involves not only peer review by scholars but also the determination of usefulness by community members.

Activist anthropology exists within different content areas of anthropological investigation. Some of the most common areas and prominent scholarship within these areas include the following:

- Medicine and health (see, for example, Farmer, 1992, 2003; Scheper-Hughes, 1993)

- Violence and war (see, for example, Sluka, 1999; McC. Heyman, 2010; Sanford, 2004)
- Globalization (see, for example, Lipman, 2005)
- Indigenous rights (see, for example, Sanford, 2004)

Clearly, this is not an exhaustive list. However, it demonstrates the different areas of study that activism scholarship has emerged within.

THEORETICAL DEBATES SURROUNDING ACTIVISM IN ANTHROPOLOGY

Over the course of the past 20 years, there has been an emerging body of literature on the content and methodology of activist anthropology. However, the role of activism in anthropology remains a contentious subject because it forces anthropologists to rethink foundational ideas behind their work as social scientists. As Scheper-Hughes explains, "The idea of active, politically committed, morally engaged anthropology strikes many anthropologists as unsavory, tainted, even frightening" (1995, p. 415). Activism in anthropology threatens core principles of positivism and relativism by questioning objectivity and promoting universal rights. As discussed next, these debates extend beyond philosophical rhetoric to practical issues such as the need for and content of the field's code of ethics and canons of practice, as well as the legitimacy of the Universal Declaration of Human Rights.

KEY DEBATE: SCIENCE OR ACTIVISM?

A significant part of the controversy related to activist anthropology revolves around whether or not activism delegitimizes anthropological scholarship. According to critics, advocacy marginalizes scientific objectivity for the sake of "social work or political action" (Elsass as cited in Sponsel, 2001, p. 205). Anthropology is based on scientific criteria, "objectivity through neutrality, and scholarship for the creation of knowledge; and advocacy on morality and the use of knowledge" (Elsass as cited in Sponsel, 2001, p. 205). The primary argument against activist anthropology is that it is not

methodologically sound because if the researcher has a vested interest in the outcome of the research, it is not objective.

In a 1975 article titled "The Unethical Ethic," Castile argues vehemently against anthropology's role in advocacy and the development of a code of ethics based on anthropology's obligation to advocate. Castile's primary objective is to maintain the legitimacy of anthropology as a science. He argues that when professional organizations make broad statements regarding the morality of certain actions (i.e., war crimes, political persecution, etc.), these claims are not founded in science but rather in personal emotions and opinions. For example, while he supports such claims as "there is no scientific basis for racial supremacy" because this has been proven through many years of anthropological investigation, he argues against Margaret Mead's declaration that certain weapons are offensive to humanity based on the idea that there is no scientific rationale for this assertion (p. 36).

Pro-activism scholars argue that advocacy in anthropology does not negate its scientific rigor. In fact, activist anthropologists argue that not only is activist anthropology a legitimate approach to research, but also it is even more complicated, relevant, and important than other forms of scholarship. According to Bourgois,

> Denouncing injustice and oppression is not a naïve, old-fashioned anti-intellectual concern or a superannuated totalizing vision of Marxism. . . . [I]t is a vital historical task intellectually, because globalization has become synonymous with military intervention, market-driven poverty, and ecological destruction. It is impossible to know what's going on without paying attention to the power dynamics that shape inequality everywhere. (as cited in Chari & Donner, 2010, p. 77)

Similarly, Chari and Donner (2010) suggest that bearing witness to the experience of the oppressed and recognizing their position within a power structure confirms a "commitment to ethnographic complexity" (p. 80). For Scheper-Hughes, anthropologists have a responsibility to include the manifestation of "evil" or injustice in their course of study, and simply because anthropologists are unsure about what to do with this injustice, it does not legitimize their inattention or inaction (1995, p. 416).

According to Hale (2001), "scientific rigor" is research that is methodologically sound (the evaluation of "better and less-good explanations") and an ability to convey results in a meaningful and utilitarian way (2001, p. 14). In other words, good scholarship is not based only on its academic merits. Hale argues that there are two reasons that activist research is not only a legitimate subfield of anthropology but also a priority in the field. First, Hale argues that the conflict between political commitment to solving a problem and rigorous scholarly work is a false dichotomy. Second, Hale argues that this commitment can lead to better research through a more thorough understanding of the problem and its theoretical implications. He also argues that it leads to better research because people are more invested in the research process when they have an active stake in the results of the process.

Another common argument for activism in research is that no science is apolitical or amoral, and even the decision not to act involves politics and morals (Sponsel, 2001). Hale connects this position to the constructivist perspective that all knowledge production exists within a political context (2001). However, he also notes that this does not equate to "radical relativism" (all knowledge is valid and justifiable) or "nihilistic deconstruction" (all knowledge is based upon "underlying power moves") (p. 14). Also, as Sponsel (2001) states, "All anthropologists are advocates in some sense," and many communities believe that the anthropologist is either part of the solution or part of the problem. In contrast to Castile's argument that activism will delegitimize anthropology as a social science discipline and thus lead to its demise, Sponsel suggests that without some commitment to the community under study, it will become increasingly difficult to gain entrance into communities.

Science Versus Advocacy and the Threat to Anthropology's Canon

The debate regarding whether or not the presence of activism in anthropology detracts from the fields scientific merit has played a significant role in shaping conversations within the field regarding anthropology's canon of practice and code of ethics. While there is currently a code of ethics that seems to have resolved this dispute, there are still diverse perspectives on the field's canon of practice. On one side of this debate are those who view the role of anthropology to be producer of bodies of knowledge solely for the advancement of human understanding. On the other side of this debate are individuals who recognize the harm done by anthropology and are committed to moving the field toward playing a more direct role in the betterment of humanity.

Wallman draws attention to the fact that there is no Hippocratic oath to anthropology (1985). Instead, there are implicit, traditional rules that guide anthropological work. Wallman describes four traditional rules of anthropology. The first, based on the Weberian idea that social science should be concerned with the means and not the ends, is "don't mess with the objectives" (p. 14). The second rule is the recognition of the inherent relativity of all things, or "don't be ethnocentric" (p. 14). The third is the process of asking, "what else is happening?" when investigating a specific cultural process, or "don't neglect context" (p. 14). The last rule is maintaining an objective distance, or "don't get involved" (Wallman, 1985, p. 14). Rules one, two, and four appear to conflict with the idea of activism in anthropology.

Similar to these principles, Castile (1975) argues that "pure" anthropology should only accept a code of ethics that protects the ability of the discipline to function. The field's code should not extend beyond this to discuss how the anthropologist can and should interfere with the larger community through his or her work. For Castile, it is dangerous ground to try and interfere with communities of study. He suggests that all societies will undergo change, and it is a reality that some societies and groups will have more of an "option" to change than others. However, he does not view this as a moral issue, but rather as a reality that large nation-states with advanced technologies and sophisticated systems of organization have superior means to influence other groups and nations. He astutely indicates that "the social sciences themselves are part of this superior equipment," that they are also an "ally of colonialism" (Castile, 1975, p. 38). He argues against the postmodern notions that ethnography, in and of its self, is "evil and exploitive" and that anthropologists owe some "debt based on racial guilt" (p. 37).

Castile (1975) urges anthropologists to avoid making judgments about the moral nature of what is being studied and suggests that "it is possible to proceed objectively and, while continuing to adhere to cultural relativism, to arrive at a perspective that allows positive action, serving the interests of the social groups involved, and promoting the well-being of mankind overall" (p. 38). According to Castile, this requires one fundamental position, one that is not ethnocentric but "speciocentric" where the ultimate survival of the species is good and ethics should be based on that assumption. Castile argues that the success of humanity depends on the adequacy of cultural response (from an evolutionary perspective). He suggests that maintaining diversity of cultural systems "as is practically consonant with their continued functioning" is fundamental to ensuring human survival (p. 38). He views pluralism as an important part of this (p. 38). Thus,

> the ethical obligation of the applied anthropologist . . . is to make plain to the power holders of the larger society the pattern of mutual benefit inherent in the procedure of stabilized pluralism since it is our contention that the most efficacious and perhaps only reliable means to achieve such stability is through an essentially nondirective approach to change in the smaller enclaved segment. (Castile, 1975, p. 38)

He references historical examples that illustrate the importance of autonomous decision making in community survival (e.g., the negative impact of government policies on the North American Native American communities). According to Castile (1975), by supporting pluralism, the rights of individual groups can be placed in their own hands. The anthropologist can provide information regarding what will happen if certain decisions are made, but he or she should not venture to say what *should* happen; the anthropologist is not an administrator or guide but instead provides the information needed to make informed decisions. In sum, Castile's "unethical ethic" argues for ethical neutrality in accord with the idea of relativism and in support of pluralism, which is most efficiently achieved by respecting self-determination or incorporation.

In contrast to these defined, elastic canons, Paine (1985) suggests that canons of anthropology should be reflective of current views on what social problems are and who they belong to, what public opinion indicates, and what the current theoretical underpinnings guiding the field suggest. Given that there has been significant change in current social thought, there also seems to have been a shift over the course of the past 20 years in views of what the content of anthropology's canon should be. Contemporary anthropology recognizes the oppression resulting from colonialism and how anthropologists have contributed to colonialism (i.e., counterinsurgency efforts in Vietnam [Messer, 1993]). It also takes into account the demand from indigenous groups and recognizes that participant observation has always meant getting involved (Messer, 1993; Wallman, 1985). In addition, as a result of globalization, the nature of social problems has changed from the problems of individual communities and nation-states to problems in the global community (Messer, 1993; Wallman, 1985). Anthropologists such as Farmer and Scheper-Hughes have argued that when anthropologists bear witness to human suffering, they have an ethical obligation to act in solidarity with those who are oppressed (Farmer, 2003; Scheper-Hughes, 1995). In a globalized world, the problem of "the other" is our problem.

Because of these historical and ideological shifts, the role of the anthropologist has shifted from the passive observer to the responsible researcher. This shift is exemplified by the American Association of Anthropology's (AAA's) current stance on a code of ethics. According to the AAA,

> Anthropologists collaborate closely with people whose cultural patterns and processes we seek to understand or whose conditions we seek to ameliorate. Understanding along with collaboration helps bridge social distances and gives wider voice to people and enables them to represent themselves in their own words. Because the study of people, past and present, requires respect for the diversity of cultures, societies, knowledge systems, and individuals that comprise [sic] humanity, the AAA adheres to a strong code of ethics. (AAA, 2010)

This supports not only a strong commitment to a code of ethics, but also this commitment is fueled not by the promotion of the field and its scientific pursuit, as Castile might hope, but by respecting the rights of the communities served and a sense of dedication to the global community.

PHILOSOPHICAL DEBATE: RELATIVISM OR UNIVERSALISM?

Like the debate between science and advocacy, the debate between cultural relativism and human universalism is fundamental to the field of anthropology and the approaches to anthropological investigation. Eriksen describes the navigation of this debate to maneuvering "in the muddy waters between the Scylla of nihilist cultural relativism and the Charybdis of supremacist universalism" (2001, p. 127). This debate has played an important role in anthropology's stance on universal human rights, which is inherently connected to activism.

Relativism has its philosophical routes in Herderian-Boasian classic concepts of culture (Eriksen, 2001). Herder, a philosopher, expanded on the Kantian idea that the interpretive process of the human mind mediates experience. He suggested that not only do individual interpretations mediate human experience, but so do cultural structures. As previously discussed, Boas applied these philosophical principles to anthropology and argued that human action and beliefs cannot be explained without acknowledging the cultural context. According to Hastrup, under relativism, "culture is the sole legitimate source of moral values" (Hastrup, 2001, p. 7008); thus, the potential for universal rights is negated.

Scheper-Hughes describes relativism as the "sacred cow" of anthropology that is used to justify inaction in the face of injustice (Scheper-Hughes, 1995). Dembour (2001) also critiques cultural relativism for being "indifferent," and he warns that under cultural relativism, culture becomes an excuse for abuse. According to Dembour, cultural relativism as a stance is flawed because it assumes that culture is clearly defined and universally applicable to members of a cultural group; it does not accept that cultural boundaries are gray and fluid. In addition, it overestimates the power of culture and the difference between Western and non-Western cultures.

Finally, anthropologists with this perspective also argue that universal rights are based on Western, individualistic ideas and practitioners of same do not recognize that even more communal cultures recognize the individual as deserving of protection. It obscures the fact that we humans live in a globalized world with a spreading modern state.

In contrast, universalism built on the philosophical principles of universal rights from the French enlightenment (Eriksen, 2001) is the argument that there are fundamental universal aspects to humanity and, as such, all humans have certain inalienable rights. Dembour (2001) critiques pure universalism as "arrogant" and urges us scholars to consider carefully that which we see as universal. She urges us to ask the following questions: universal for whom? What is "natural law"? Who determines natural law, and how is it formulated? Why is this person's reasoning thought to be unflawed? The essential criticism against universalism is that if certain universals are accepted, they risk falling to ethnocentrism.

Despite the seemingly disparate positions of universalism and relativism, Dembour argues that universalism and relativism are not necessarily mutually exclusive or irreconcilable stances. Instead, Dembour suggests that a person considering the two stances is always brought into a "pendulum motion" (2001, p. 56). She describes this as an inherently "unstable" position and recommends that law makers should recognize this motion with a willingness to let people move between the two ends of the spectrum of universalism to relativism and vice versa. Returning to the example of female circumcision, Dembour uses the example of FGM occurring in France among African immigrant communities to illustrate her point.

In France, a country considered a champion of human rights, legal decisions regarding FGM have vacillated in their degree of severity. There are three primary defenses used for parents charged with the offense. The first is that the parents are not criminals and that they did not intend to hurt their child. It was an act of love. Second, the parents were acting under the powerful constraint of culture. Last, imprisoning the mother only makes the situation worse for the child. Over time, the French courts have produced a variety of decisions in these cases. However, many of the cases have resulted in probation, a kind of middle ground between condemnation and acquittal. These decisions have not been made due to some shift in French public opinion; there has not been an adoption of the position that female circumcision is just. Instead, it appears to be possible to give these parents probation without taking an entirely culturally relative position (that they should be acquitted) or universalist position (that they should be sentenced to incarceration). Court decisions are constantly changing. The pendulum continues to swing because "general principles (whether phrased in legal language or in terms of human rights) do not do justice to the complex reality, and need to be 'relativized' in view of the circumstances of particular cases" (Dembour, 2001, p. 69). Dembour concludes that there are means of doing justice outside of a human rights framework, and the solution is to engage in a conversation with the "other" to understand their truth.

Implication for Social Justice and Human Rights

Dembour's argument for an individualized approach to ensuring social justice can appeal to anthropologists who investigate the complexities of individual circumstances of seemingly unjust situations. However, when the goal is to create a system for avoiding human rights violations on a global scale, Dembour's pendulum solution seems to lack utility. Initially, in support of principles of cultural relativism, the AAA rejected universal rights, arguing that different people have different rights and abide by different authorities (Messer, 1993). The Universal Declaration of Human Rights (UDHR) was criticized both for being ethnocentric and for having an enforcing body that was not truly sovereign (Messer, 1993). The argument was that anthropologists need to maintain respect for the cultural choices of varying groups, which is justified by the fact that there is no scientific manner of qualitatively evaluating culture; standards are a reflection of the values from the culture from which they are derived (Hastrup, 2001). Therefore, the declaration should not superimpose standards from external cultures.

According to Messer (1993), five anthropological conflicts exist within the human rights

framework that prevent its endorsement by anthropologists: (a) a universal declaration of human rights that is contrary to cultural relativism, (b) rejection of the idea that anthropology should be involved in advocacy, (c) applied anthropologists having been more involved in political and economic change versus change through human rights mechanisms, (d) the "political sensitivity" of field work and the risk of losing access to communities if critiques of governmental actions are made (p. 221), and (e) anthropologists typically concerning themselves with small cultural groups and their behaviors, not the behaviors of nation-states and laws.

More recently, scholars recognize that human rights concepts are culturally relative and require a search for the *essential* human rights (Messer, 1993). Messer (1993) argues that "it is possible to move from cultural relativism to universals" by examining commonalities and differences in judgment of acceptable behavior (p. 235). Anthropology has the ability to identify and interpret the underlying cultural principles of a culture, as well as the ways that values fit into shared human understanding of "good governance and respectable political action" (Hastrup, 2001, p. 7008). Another pro–human rights argument is that in the contemporary globalized world, groups of people are less dependent on local cultural ties for norms and a sense of belonging. Instead, people now look to laws to provide rules of social behavior, as well as an "increasingly strong culture of human rights" (Hastrup, 2001, p. 7009). This has increased the need for a UDHR.

A comprehensive UDHR is an amalgamation of cultural, political, and religious beliefs from throughout the world. It recognizes that nation-states are powered by and for citizens, but it also implies a larger global community. This global culture is represented in the courtroom via the formulated language of the UDHR (vs. a natural language). Legal thoughts and actions construct realities not just represent them. In turn, anthropologists are uniquely suited to help understand and construct this representation and construction of a global community. Messer (1993) explains that engaged anthropologists are contributing to the human rights framework in two ways: (a) conceptualizing what these rights are and who should be able to enjoy these rights, and

(b) "monitoring" the maintenance or abuse of those human rights (p. 221).

CONCLUSION

As this analysis and Figure 9.1 illustrate, activism in anthropology raises questions about the objectivity of the anthropologist, the existence of essential universal traits and rights, and the obligation of anthropologists to communities of study and the global community. While this review of the literature juxtaposes traditional anthropological canons against the theoretical underpinnings of activist anthropology, this is also an oversimplification of the debate regarding the role of activism in anthropology. As noted in Figure 9.1, there is a bidirectional arrow between nonactivist anthropology and activist anthropology to represent a continuum of activism that seeks to capture a spectrum of beliefs regarding the role of activism in anthropological scholarship.

When examining the dichotomy between objectivity and subjectivity, it is clear that activist anthropologists seek to conduct research that is objective through the use of rigorous methods, while also disclosing political and social beliefs up front in

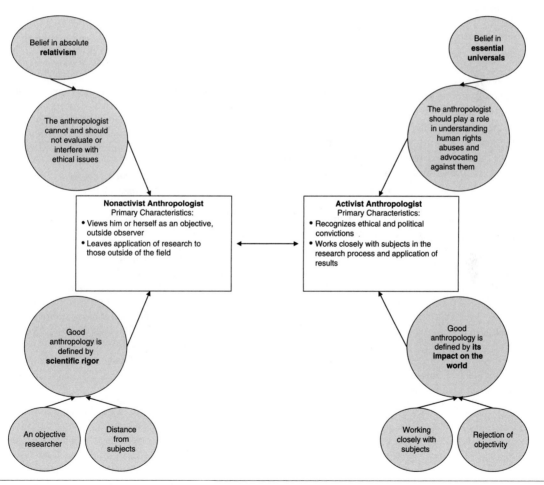

Figure 9.1   A Theoretical Continuum of Activist Anthropology

order to expose any bias that may exist. A closer examination of the continuum between universalism and relativism can capture the divergent views of most activist and nonactivist anthropologists.

Hale (2001) has called on the discipline of anthropology to move past discussions of the legitimacy of activism in anthropology toward a more systematic means for conducting such research by posing the following questions:

- What should the anthropologist do when studying groups of people in power with whom the anthropologist does not politically align?
- What should the anthropologist do when he or she uncovers results that could be detrimental to the group under study?
- What if the subjects and those in opposition to the subjects both want the anthropologist to be neutral and put aside his or her political convictions?

Therefore, the challenge of contemporary anthropology should not be to continue to defend the role of activism in research but to perfect it.

Over the course of the past several decades, the discourse on the role of activism in anthropology appears to have moved from exploring it as a possibility toward developing it as a field, including courses on activist research that seek to respond to postmodern changes in social thought and the social problems of a globalized world. When considering the history of activism within the discipline of anthropology (beginning with Boas in the early 20th century), it is clear that the process of articulating and developing the principles of activist anthropology represents a continuing "work in progress."

REFERENCES

American Association of Anthropology (AAA). (2010). What is anthropology? Retrieved October 22, 2010, from http://www.aaanet.org/about/WhatisAnthropology.cfm

Aretxaga, B. (2001). Gender and feminist studies in anthropology. In N. J. Smelser & P. B. Baltes (Eds.), *International encyclopedia of the social and behavioral sciences* (pp. 5915–5920). Amsterdam, Netherlands: Elsevier. doi:10.1016/B0-08-043076-7/00875-5

Baker, L. (2004). Franz Boas out of the ivory tower. *Anthropological Theory, 41*, 29–51.

Castile, G. P. (1975). The unethical ethic: Self-determination and the anthropological conscience. *Human Organization, 34*(1), 35–40.

Chari, S., & Donner, H. (2010). Ethnographies of activism: A critical introduction. *Cultural Dynamics, 22*(2), 75–85. doi:10.1177/0921374010380887

Cole, D. (1983). "The value of a person lies in his herzensbildung": Franz Boas' Baffin Island letter-diary, 1883–1884. In G. Stock (Ed.), *Observers observed: Essays on ethnographic fieldwork* (pp. 13–52). Madison: University of Wisconsin Press.

Dembour, M.-B. (2001). Following the movement of a pendulum: Between universalism and relativism. In J. K. Cowan, M.-B. Dembour, & R. A. Wilson (Eds.), *Culture and rights: Anthropological perspectives* (pp. 56–80). Cambridge, UK: Cambridge University Press.

Dillon, W. S. (2001). Margaret Mead (1901–1978). *Prospects: The quarterly review of comparative education, 31*(3), 447–461.

Eriksen, T. H. (2001). Between universalism and relativism: A critique of the UNESCO concepts of culture. In J. K. Cowan, M.-B. Dembour, & R. A. Wilson (Eds.), *Culture and rights: Anthropological perspectives* (pp. 127–148). Cambridge, UK: Cambridge University Press.

Farmer, P. (1992). *Aids and accusations: Haiti and the geography of blames*. Berkeley: University of California Press.

Farmer, P. (2003). *Pathologies of power: Health, human rights, and the new war on the poor*. Berkeley: University of California Press.

Hale, C. R. (2001). What is activist research? *Social Science Research Council, 2*(1–2), 13–15.

Hastrup, K. (2001). Human rights, anthropology of. In N. J. Smelser & P. B. Baltes (Eds.), *International encyclopedia of the social and behavioral sciences* (pp. 7007–7012). Oxford, UK: Pergamon. doi:10.1016/B0-08-043076-7/00888-3

Lipman, P. (2005). Educational ethnography and the politics of globalization, war, and resistance. *Anthropology & Education Quarterly, 36*(4), 315–328. doi:10.1525/aeq.2005.36.4.315

McC. Heyman, J. (2010). Activism in anthropology: Exploring the present through Eric R. Wolf's Vietnam-era work. *Dialectical Anthropology, 34*(2), 287–293. doi:10.1007/s10624-010-9186-6

Messer, E. (1993). Anthropology and human rights. *Annual Review of Anthropology, 22*, 221–249.

Paine, R. (Ed.). (1985). *Advocacy and anthropology, first encounters*. St. John's, Newfoundland, Canada: Institute of Social and Economic Research.

Sanford, V. (2004). *Buried secrets: Truth and human rights in Guatemala*. New York, NY: Palgrave MacMillan.

Scheper-Hughes, N. (1993). *Death without weeping: The violence of everyday life in Brazil*. Berkeley: University of California Press.

Scheper-Hughes, N. (1995). The primacy of the ethical: Propositions for a militant anthropology. *Current Anthropology, 36*(3), pp. 409–440.

Scott, D. (2001). Colonialism, anthropology of. In N. J. Smelser & P. B. Baltes (Eds.), *International encyclopedia of the social and behavioral sciences* (pp. 2232–2237). Oxford, UK: Pergamon. doi:10.1016/B0-08-043076-7/00826-3

Sluka, J. A. (Ed.). (1999). *Death squad: The anthropology of state terror*. Philadelphia: University of Pennsylvania Press.

Sponsel, L. E. (2001). Advocacy in anthropology. In N. J. Smelser & P. B. Baltes (Eds.), *International encyclopedia of the social and behavioral sciences* (pp. 204–206). Amsterdam, Netherlands: Elsevier. doi:10.1016/B0-08-043076-7/00784-1

Stocking, G. (Ed.). (1983). *Observers observed: Essays on ethnographic fieldwork*. Madison: University of Wisconsin Press.

Wallman, S. (1985). Rules of thumb. In R. Paine (Ed.), *Advocacy and anthropology, first encounters* (pp. 13–16). St. John's, Newfoundland, Canada: Institute of Social and Economic Research.

10

Perspectives of Social Justice in Sociology

Christina Branom

Introduction

Numerous contemporary scholars have argued that sociology was founded to make social changes that would eliminate or ameliorate oppressive social conditions (e.g., Fals-Borda, 1985; Feagin & Vera, 2001; Heller, 2003; Turner, 1995). However, some have argued that sociology lost its connection to issues of justice and rights in the 1930s, when it felt the need to establish itself as a legitimate academic discipline (Heller, 2003). During the 1960s and 1970s, the civil rights and feminist movements helped put social justice back in the center of sociological study. Although much of modern sociology remains biased toward empiricism and avoidant of social action, some sociologists have called for a return to the field's activist traditions (Feagin, 2001; Feagin & Vera, 2001; Heller, 2003; Turner, 1995). They draw upon the work of early social justice advocates to envision a world free from discrimination, oppression, and inequality. In contrast to mainstream sociology, their practice is sometimes termed *liberation sociology*.

The approach of liberation sociology stands in stark contrast to the narrow focus of the big three mainstream sociological theories:

structural-functionalism, conflict, and symbolic interactionism (Feagin & Vera, 2001; Macionis & Plummer, 2008). For example, scholars of the theory of structural-functionalism seek to explain societal dynamics in terms of a single organism composed of interdependent structures functioning together, with little attention to issues of race, class, and gender. Conflict theory, on the other hand, is a focus on the tendency of power differences to produce social discord, with little attention to the ways in which social cohesion can emerge from common values. Finally, symbolic interactionism features the dynamic interaction between individuals and their social surroundings, but often the approach shows a neglect of the impact of large structural forces on social relations (Macionis & Plummer, 2008). While there is a place for other sociological theories and methods, critical social theories and liberation sociology fill major gaps in the knowledge base of the social sciences.

This paper will explore the evolution of thought about social justice in sociology (see Figure 10.1). An exhaustive discussion of sociological theories of justice is beyond the scope of this review, but it outlines some of the major views of justice from the 19th century to the present day. It begins with the conceptions of justice proposed by the field's founding fathers, Karl Marx, Emilie Durkheim, and Max Weber. These scholars laid the foundation for 20th-century sociologists, who expanded the field's study of justice to include universal social rights of citizenship and state-sponsored social welfare, as well as the rights of minorities, women, and the urban poor. These efforts, along with the writings of Marx, Durkheim, and Weber, set the stage for an interdisciplinary discourse on justice, framed by critical social theory, feminism, and critical race theory. Together, social justice advocates across disciplines inspired contemporary sociologists in the liberation sociology movement, who promote methods and areas of study that emphasize empowerment, equality, diversity, and activism (Feagin & Vera, 2001).

METHOD

To examine the treatment of social justice in the sociology literature, several key databases were first consulted. The CSA Illumina Social Sciences and Google Scholar databases were searched using combinations of key words such as *sociology, justice, social justice, liberation sociology, morality, inequality, oppression, discrimination, feminism*, and *critical theory*. To explore the social justice viewpoints of key sociological figures, the key words *justice, social justice, inequality, morality*, and *oppression* were also entered into the databases with the names of significant sociologists (e.g., Durkheim, Weber, Marx, Du Bois, etc.). Finally, the reference lists of the resulting articles and books were scanned for other relevant literature.

IMPACT OF FOUNDING SOCIOLOGISTS ON THEORIES OF SOCIAL JUSTICE

Marx, Weber, and Durkheim are widely considered the three founding fathers of sociology (Altschuler, 1998; Hughes, Sharrock, & Martin, 2003; Hurst, 2000; Morrison, 2006; Pampel, 2000). Sociologists

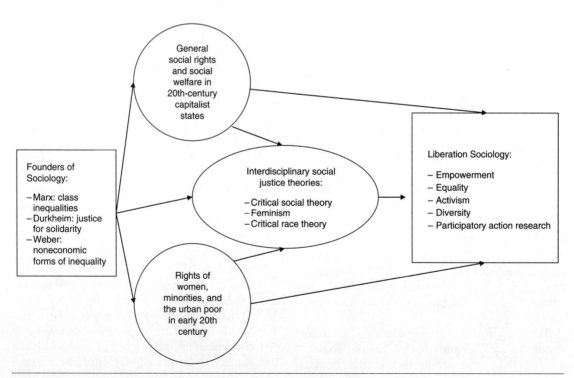

Figure 10.1   Evolution of Sociological Conceptions of Social Justice

are not in total agreement regarding their views about social justice or even if justice was a consideration in their theories. However, their work inspired and influenced later sociologists concerned with social justice (Feagin & Vera, 2001).

Karl Marx (1818–1883)

Although there is controversy over whether or not Karl Marx had a theory of justice, some sociologists consider him to have been among the first to actively address social inequality (Cole, 2001; Nielson, 1989). Marx openly critiqued concepts and theories of justice and rights, but several Marxist scholars have argued that he was not criticizing social justice, per se, but rather capitalist conceptions of justice (Arenson, 1981; Holmstrom, 1977; Husami, 1978; Peffer, 1990). In fact, his ideas have been critical to activist sociologists because he advocated for revolutionary social change in response to social inequality (Stoecker, 1996).

Marx's main concern was with the injustices of capitalism. He felt that modern capitalism oppressed the working class, creating wide disparities between laborers and their employers (Marx, 1906). He further believed capitalism dehumanizes and exploits the worker, who becomes just a cog in the industrial machine (Marx, 1906; Nielson, 1989). Marx argued that in capitalist societies, the proletariat (working class) lack (a) power over resources, (b) control over the means of production, and (c) access to social goods. In contrast, the capitalist earns a profit from the labor of the worker; in keeping that profit, Marx (1906, 1953/1973) reasoned, the capitalist robbed or cheated the laborer (Cohen, 1983; Marx, 1953/1973). Marx also criticized the capitalist view of equality, namely, that there should be "equal pay for equal work" (Marx, 1875/1972). Such a system is unfair, he argued, because it does not consider needs (e.g., if two laborers earn equal pay, only one of whom has a family to care for, the laborer without dependents is clearly at an advantage). Instead, Marx concluded that each should contribute according to his or her abilities and each should receive according to his or her needs (Parsons, 1971).

According to Marx, capitalist societies can never be democratic: They are founded on individualistic and egoistic principles and only the elite few hold economic power (Parsons, 1971). Liberty and equality are limited to the bourgeois (capitalist) class that enjoys economic opportunity and security. In contrast, Marx believed strongly in maximum equal freedom for all (Peffer, 1990). He conceived of freedom as power (Marx, 1906) and believed all had the right to both negative freedoms (i.e., freedom from the constraint or intrusion of others) and positive freedoms (i.e., full participation in decision-making processes and equal opportunity to attain social positions and social goods). For example, he advocated for universal suffrage, arguing that "only in unlimited voting, active as well as passive, does civil society actually rise to an abstraction of itself, to political existence as its true universal and essential existence" (Marx, 1843/1967, p. 202).

In Marx's view, socialism's system of communal property is morally superior to capitalism's system of private ownership (Marx & Engels, 1872/1987). He also considered socialism to be more democratic than capitalism because it provides maximum equal freedom and distributes power equally throughout society (Marx, 1906). In such a society, goods, services, and other resources are produced and distributed according to need, not for profit. Therefore, man is free to take charge over his own life rather than sell it to the capitalist (Marx, 1906). Furthermore, Marx believed that socialism would destroy bureaucratic privilege; while he acknowledged that there would not be perfect income equality in socialist societies, he concluded that the disparities between rich and poor would be much smaller than in capitalist societies (Peffer, 1990). Finally, Marx argued that overthrowing capitalism and developing a socialist state would require a revolution (Marx, 1906; Peffer, 1990).

While contemporary Marxists recognize the problems facing modern postcapitalist societies (e.g., human rights violations in China, Cuba, and the former Soviet Union), they contend that these problems do not derive from weaknesses in Marx's theory but rather from the failure of these societies to uphold Marx's egalitarian values (Peffer, 1990). Marxists agree that oppressive communist societies need to be democratized, but they argue that a reversion to capitalism, which inherently produces severe social inequalities, is not the solution. Despite the challenges in realizing Marx's ideals, it is clear from his writings that he hoped for social change in the pursuit of social equality. He was both revolutionary and progressive, believing that his theories should be applied to change society for the better.

Emilie Durkheim (1858–1917)

Durkheim was also concerned with social justice but, unlike Marx, did not feel the need for a structural and economic revolution (Schoenfeld & Mestrovic, 1989). Durkheim argued that suffering could be found among all classes, not just the proletariat, and believed that Marx overlooked the importance of merit in defining the dynamics of justice in social systems. He further maintained that justice could be incorporated into the existing capitalist system.

Although he did not call for revolutionary social change, Durkheim nevertheless recognized that the social conditions of his time were not ideal. He was concerned with the moral equality of human beings, feeling that people must be respected regardless of their position in society (Durkheim, 1893/1933). He noted that justice was, in fact, the basis of moral order and social solidarity in modern societies. Earlier societies had relied on *mechanical solidarity*, which depended on social homogeneity, but modern societies aimed for *organic solidarity* based on role differentiation and specialization. Justice was an important component of organic solidarity. Durkheim (1893/1933) wrote that "just as ancient people needed, above all, a common faith to live by, so we need justice" to make social relations equitable (p. 388).

Rather than total equality, Durkheim advocated for a distribution of resources based on equity (Durkheim, 1893/1933). It was important to Durkheim that individuals receive a fair reward for their efforts and accomplishments. Consequently, he believed it immoral to have an unequal distribution of resources due only to circumstances beyond the individual's control (e.g., political or economic crises or natural disasters). From Durkheim's perspective, a just society would reflect a close relationship between an individual's contributions to society and his or her social conditions and allow everyone the opportunity to fully develop and participate in the community.

Durkheim wanted to reduce human suffering, but he contended that it was unjust to provide resources and services without giving thought to the needs or deservedness of the recipients. As a result, Durkheim (1957/1992) opposed charity as the antithesis of justice. He noted that the problems with charity included the fact that people tend to be charitable primarily to people like themselves. Therefore, in diverse societies, in which solidarity depends on differentiation and specialization, charity would not successfully eliminate social inequalities. In fact, he believed that charity instead fueled social disorganization in such communities (Durkheim, 1893/1933). Rather than lifting the poor and oppressed out of their conditions, he saw charity breeding dependency and maintaining the status quo (Durkheim, 1928/1958). In addition, Durkheim viewed charity as an attempt to address the problems of the individual rather than the problems of the larger social structure. He believed that by focusing on justice, rather than charity, societies could successfully address abuses of power and privilege. Although Durkheim's view of justice has limitations, including the fact that he did not use it to probe deeply into the oppressive structures of his time, it inspired the social justice theories of more modern sociologists (Feagin & Vera, 2001).

Max Weber (1864–1920)

The positions taken by Weber on social justice are more ambiguous than those of Marx or Durkheim because he was more interested in researching specific social problems than addressing larger social issues (Stone, 2010). Nevertheless, he wrote about two topics that have contributed to discussions of inequality and justice, namely, social stratification and how diverse experiences shape perceptions of reality.

While Weber offered no clear moral judgment about the distribution of power in society, he argued that Marx's narrow focus on class ignored noneconomic bases of power (Holton & Turner, 1989). Instead, Weber proposed that power can be located in classes, status groups (based on social prestige), and parties (based on one's position in the political environment) (Brennan, 1997). He further argued that people have access to different types of power, depending on the kinds of resources they possess (e.g., political, social, financial, etc.). According to

Weber, different types of power fuel the ability to carry out one's own will, even against the resistance of others. He noted that domination is a special case of power that could be classified into one of two types, namely, domination in the market (derived from material resources and marketable skills) and patriarchal or magisterial authority.

Weber's writings on social stratification, power, and domination have influenced sociologists' views of justice, as they allow for the possibility of non-economic, status-based forms of social inequality, including racism and sexism (Holton & Turner, 1989). Weber (1968) also recognized that status groups are defined by social discrimination. Furthermore, he suggested that solidarity within status groups against outsiders deemed "inferior" remains strong even if there are other divisions within the status group (Bendix, 1974). Thus, social discrimination can be relatively fixed and impenetrable compared to other forms of discrimination.

Another contribution that Weber made to the study of social justice was his recognition that people can see society and history only from their own vantage point (Blum, 1944). Furthermore, he noted that that this perspective is influenced by various personal factors, such as age, gender, race, and religion. Consequently, he concluded, sociologists cannot "analyze reality 'without presuppositions'" (Weber, 1949, p. 78). While he thought that science could not be value free, he argued that it should be shielded from political influence. These ideas have lent support to the arguments of progressive sociologists that ethical sociology needs to move beyond research by and for the predominately White male academic elite to recognize the perspectives of women, minorities, the poor, and others who were previously ignored. In summary, Weber's work helped paved the way for future efforts to establish social justice, despite the fact that he did not propose remedies for social inequality and other social problems.

SOCIAL JUSTICE IN THE EARLY 20TH CENTURY

As mentioned, many 20th-century sociologists began to concern themselves with attaining prestige in the academy and in their attempts to gain scientific legitimacy, abandoned social change efforts. However, several social scientists during this period remained committed to issues of social justice. They were critical of the oppressive, discriminatory status quo and used their work to highlight disparities and demand more equitable, just societies.

Social Rights and Social Welfare

In Britain, several justice-oriented sociologists introduced the concepts of social rights and state-sponsored social welfare in response to the social problems of industrial capitalism. For example, Marshall (1950/1992) promoted the civil, political, and social rights that should be accorded all citizens. He described civil rights as the freedoms enjoyed by citizens (e.g., personal liberty, freedom of speech, freedom of religion, etc.) and political rights as those giving citizens a voice in the political process (e.g., through voting). Finally, Marshall's social rights included economic welfare and the resources necessary to participate fully in civilized society. He argued that these social rights need to be guaranteed by the education and social service systems of the modern nation-states. Marshall maintained that, while more traditional, less complex societies had blended and combined rights and supporting institutions, modern industrialized societies depended on this differentiation of rights and institutions.

Marshall (1950/1992) observed that the three rights of citizenship (which he believed would breed social equality) had not been upheld in England prior to the 20th century. The Elizabethan Poor Law, for example, had forced the poor into workhouses in order to claim state benefits. Marshall also noted that the interrelationship between the three types of rights that kept citizens deprived in one area of rights also kept them disadvantaged in the other two areas. For example, a lack of universal social rights in the 19th century also made the distribution of civil and political rights unequal (e.g., those who did not have the means to acquire property could not benefit from the right to own property).

Despite Marshall's criticism of 19th-century society, he maintained that policies established during this era had laid the foundation for social rights that were eventually realized in the 20th century

(Marshall, 1950/1992). These social rights grew from the public's emerging "conception of equal social worth" of all citizens (Marshall, 1950/1992, p. 24). Also, declining social inequality fueled popular demand for the complete eradication of social inequality. Marshall argued that achieving a socially just state would entail more than simply raising the minimum standard of living for the poor; it would require changing the entire system of inequality. However, he claimed that certain inequalities were legitimate as long as they were not too great or linked to "hereditary privilege." Marshall contended that social problems emerged when there was no pattern to the inequality and cases of inequality were extreme. He also believed that income equality was less important than social status equality that ensured all citizens would live enriched civilized lives, free from risk and insecurity.

Marshall's contemporary and fellow British sociologist Titmuss also wrote extensively on the need for a social welfare system to establish social justice in industrialized capitalist societies (Titmuss, 1969). He suggested that social policies are needed to address the inequalities created by capitalism in order to promote stable democracies. He observed that this was particularly true in modern society, where social changes (e.g., smaller families, extended dependencies of childhood and old age, and increasing division of labor) made social inequality more likely. He also criticized the distribution of social and economic benefits that favored those who had fewer responsibilities and greater wealth in writing that "the aims of equity, ostensibly set for society as a whole, become sectional aims, invariably rewarding the most favoured in proportion to the distribution of power and occupational success" (Titmuss, 1969, p. 55). For example, tax breaks, sick pay, and other employment benefits disproportionately rewarded more affluent and higher class workers thereby widening the gap between classes and occupations. Titmuss sought to counter the public image (reinforced by elite-controlled media) that the redistribution of resources from rich to poor had gone too far and that the poor were lazy and inferior to the wealthy.

Unlike Marx, Marshall (1950/1992) and Titmuss (1969) did not advocate for the overthrow of capitalism as a solution to social inequality. While the rise of citizenship (in which citizens were granted equal rights) coincided with the rise of capitalism (a system of inequality), they argued that society needed both the free market and public duty to the less fortunate. It was the role of social services to reduce and/or eliminate the risks and insecurities of capitalism as a way to promote social justice.

Rights of the Oppressed: Women, Minorities, and the Urban Poor

Sociologists around the world expanded the general discussion of social rights and social welfare to addressing the specific troubles facing women, minorities, and the urban poor. These scholars were influential in shaping contemporary theories of race, gender, class, and power.

In addition to advocating for social welfare benefits to establish greater economic equality, Titmuss (1969) praised the women's suffrage movement, arguing that it was proof that applied social science could be successful in producing social progress. At the same time, he criticized his fellow sociologists for neglecting to study how the status and role of women had changed as a result of social, economic, and technological changes. These changes included the fact that women had gained greater control over their reproductive activity, a development that contributed to "the process of 'democratizing' marriage" (Titmuss, 1969, p. 98). He also studied the movement of women into the workforce. While Titmuss lauded this progress toward gender equality, he warned that threats to social justice for women remained. Women still lacked access to many educational and occupational opportunities. Furthermore, women were experiencing increased responsibility in their dual roles as mothers and wage earners and yet were less financially secure than men. He argued that it was the state's role to address the fact that "mothers and wives are likely to be affected first by any rise in unemployment" (Titmuss, 1969, p. 103). Titmuss supported the establishment of a welfare state that would help struggling citizens make ends meet and participate fully in society.

As Titmuss discussed the rights of women in Britain, the Swedish sociologist Myrdal criticized the exploitation and oppression of Blacks in America. In *An American Dilemma*, Myrdal (1944/2009) pointed out the conflict between American liberal ideals and the poor treatment of Blacks. Blacks were a "problem" for White Americans, he claimed, because their situation contradicted the American creed of liberty, equality, and justice for all. Subjected to slavery, discrimination, prejudice, and poverty, Blacks had not been afforded the rights that the creed guaranteed to Whites.

Myrdal (1944/2009) also exposed flaws in Americans' justification for Black oppression. Myrdal suggested that White Americans saw biological inferiority as the cause of poor performance by Blacks in education and the workforce. Furthermore, he observed that Whites believed segregation was legitimate because Blacks presumably liked being on their own, and racial integration would presumably cause undue social friction. Myrdal reasoned that these false racial perceptions and beliefs served as a bridge between the American creed and the domination and exploitation of Blacks. Conversely, Myrdal argued that Blacks performed poorly in society because they lacked the resources and opportunities needed to advance (e.g., adequate education, health care, and other services). He noted that Blacks were ensnared in a vicious cycle in which "poverty itself breeds the conditions which perpetuate poverty" (Myrdal, 1944/2009, p. 208). Myrdal further warned of the adverse effects of inequality on society and called for social and economic equality among races.

The American sociologist Merton observed a similar cycle that maintained Blacks and other minorities in positions of low class. Merton (1968) maintained that Whites saw Blacks as "traitors to the working class" because they were considered desperate for wages, no matter how low. Consequently, Whites excluded Blacks from labor unions and thereby perpetuated the struggle of Blacks to make economic and employment gains. Furthermore, Whites viewed Blacks as uneducated and unskilled (and therefore inferior) and denied them educational opportunities to improve, arguing that their inferiority made them unworthy of educational support. As a result, Merton argued, Blacks were victims of a self-fulfilling prophecy.

Merton (1968) also noted that minorities were oppressed regardless of what they did (e.g., those who did not exhibit enough of the White American

virtues were considered inferior, and those who exhibited too much of these virtues were seen as a threat that needed to be controlled by discrimination). He was disturbed by the fact that ethnic prejudices were deeply embedded in American culture and argued that they needed to be addressed "by cutting off the sustenance now provided them by certain institutions of our society" (Merton, 1968, p. 490). He further advocated for the increased role of sociology in helping people become more accountable for social action by highlighting social problems and strategies for addressing them.

The rights of the poor, women, and minorities were also advocated by several female and Black sociologists, including Jane Addams, Florence Kelly, Ida B. Wells-Barnett, and W. E. B. Du Bois (Feagin, 2001). Addams was one of the first sociologists to address the social problems of U.S. cities. As cofounder and resident of Chicago's Hull House and leader of the settlement movement, she argued for democracy, social equality, and social reforms to improve the condition of the disadvantaged in urban areas (Addams, 2008). She wanted a true participatory democracy that included the perspectives of all members of society and practiced this value through the cooperative and democratic policies implemented at Hull House. She also actively involved herself in the antiwar, women's, and labor movements (Addams, 1905). Many academics saw her as a reformer and social worker rather than a sociologist (Deegan, 1988), but the research that she and other women at Hull House conducted contributed significantly to the social justice foundation of sociological knowledge (Feagin & Vera, 2001).

Du Bois also studied urban life, but he focused his work primarily on racial inequality and discrimination. He wrote about the ways in which Blacks were discriminated against in all areas of social life. For example, he noted that they were restricted from most jobs, suffered from more job competition and less job security than Whites, and experienced limitations to their civil and political rights. In response to the popular belief that Blacks were biologically inferior to Whites, Du Bois (1939) argued that race was a social construction and that racial inequality was due to social, economic, and historical factors (Katz & Sugrue, 1998). Thus, any improvement in the condition of Blacks would require changes in the social institutions and circumstances that perpetuated this inequality. Du Bois argued that social change was needed, not only because discrimination was immoral but also because it hurt Blacks and Whites alike (Du Bois, 1899/1996).

Du Bois admired Marx and agreed with him that a society's economic structure has a significant impact on its culture, politics, and institutions (DeMarco, 1983). Furthermore, he subscribed to Marx's view that socialism is more democratic and egalitarian than capitalism and that class conflict would stimulate social change (Du Bois, 1920, 1935). However, he argued that Marx overlooked the role of race in social relations and theorized that racism and capitalism worked together to perpetuate Black oppression. Although capitalism differentiated upper classes from lower classes, Whites of all classes were united in their "whiteness" (Du Bois, 1935). The privileged status of poor Whites in this racial hierarchy made their economic status more tolerable than that of Blacks. He further linked race and social class to colonialism and criticized the oppression of colonized peoples brought on by White imperialism (Du Bois, 1940, 1979).

Like other justice-oriented sociologists, Du Bois was more than just a teacher, scholar, and writer. He argued that the role of sociology is to improve conditions of society (Reed, 1997). Not content to merely study social problems, he was also a social activist who publicly fought for the rights of Blacks, women, Jews, and workers (Zuckerman, 2004).

SOCIAL JUSTICE IN CONTEMPORARY SOCIOLOGY

A revival of social justice as a prominent theme within sociology emerged with the civil rights and feminist movements of the 1960s and 1970s (Heller, 2003). Since this time, progressive sociologists have applied social justice values to the study of contemporary societies and crafted more culturally sensitive and emancipatory methods for researching and addressing issues such as inequality, prejudice, and oppression. Operating in a subfield sometimes referred to as liberation sociology (also known as humanist, activist, or countersystem sociology), sociologists concerned with social justice have

focused on issues facing the oppressed, particularly women, the poor, and minorities (Feagin & Vera, 2001). While devoted to conducting good science, their goal has been "not just to research the social world, but to change it in the direction of democracy and social justice" (Feagin & Vera, 2001, p. 1). In contrast to mainstream sociology, which tended to limit itself to the study of social *problems*, liberation sociology has attempted to offer *solutions* to the problems it documented (Feagin & Vera, 2001). Advocates of liberation sociology have claimed sociology is the social science discipline that is best positioned to address injustices because of its openness to interdisciplinary perspectives and the fact that its research methods capture the dynamics of human behavior and the social environment (Feagin, 2001). Consequently, Blackwell (1982) urged sociologists to contribute to the social justice agenda by educating the public and those in power about the need to eradicate injustice. He observed that "social scientists have yet to generate a strong sense of public appreciation for the utility of their research and its role in improving the human condition and helping to create a more just world society" (Blackwell, 1982, p. 340). He argued that young sociologists need to be educated to recognize their dual roles as scholars and advocates.

Critical Social Theories

Liberation sociology is rooted in various schools of thought, including critical social theories. These frameworks place oppression and power at the center of analysis but are fundamentally solution-oriented (Feagin & Vera, 2001). Critical social theories were developed, in part, by scholars associated with the Frankfurt school that focused on class exploitation and the Marxist critique of capitalism (Jay, 1996). Habermas (1971) was an important contributor to this school of thought who criticized sociology's positivist tradition of using physical science as a model for conducting research. He questioned the ability of sociologists to conduct value-neutral research and to gain any understanding of the world that was devoid of context. For the people to become liberated from their oppression, Habermas believed their situation and context needed to be understood. Furthermore, he argued that social progress and emancipation rely on human dialogue, or "communicative action," not simply observation (Habermas, 1987). He advocated for assessing the dialectical interaction between human actors and their natural social environments (Habermas, 1976).

Another critic of mainstream, positivist sociology was Alfred McClung Lee, who cofounded the Association for Humanist Sociology and served as president of the American Sociological Association (ASA) from 1976 to 1977 (Feagin, 2001). He praised sociologists who had questioned the methods and interests of the academic elite and lamented the fact that these innovative researchers (who recognized ways of knowing beyond the scientific method) were often marginalized or not taken seriously by the academy (Lee, 1976). Lee (1990) opposed traditional sociology for being elitist, supporting the status quo, and ignoring power, oppression, and domination. He believed many sociologists were hypocritical in their push for scientific objectivity, as they sought to be unbiased but, in actuality, were preoccupied with the mainstream observations of Western scientists. In contrast, Lee called for sociologists to be aware of their natural biases and to be more engaged in reflection on the ways in which their values and perspectives impacted the way they viewed the world (Friedrichs, 1987; Lee, 1986). To foster a diversity of perspectives, he supported the inclusion of more women and minorities in the ASA (Lee, 1976). Finally, Lee made it clear that sociology should be devoted to both accuracy and service to humanity (Lee, 1973). His approach to sociology viewed science as a tool to raise awareness of social problems (particularly exposing the fictions that hide social inequality) and seek social justice (Lee, 1990).

Gender and Power

Feminist theory has also made a significant contribution to liberation sociology by encouraging sociologists to focus on ways in which women have been oppressed. For example, Judith Stacey and Barrie Thorne noted that sociologists have begun to criticize the androcentric social structures that support the oppression and domination of women (Stacey & Thorne, 1996). Other feminist sociologists have looked at how reproductive and sexual relationships between men and women contribute

to and maintain gender-based power differences (MacKinnon, 1989).

To understand the oppression and domination of women, feminist sociologists have argued that the female viewpoint needs to be represented. Therefore, Smith (1990) introduced *stand-point theory*, which recommends conducting sociology from the point of view of women. Smith argued that even when women have participated in research, much of sociological theory has been "built up within the male social universe" (Smith, 1990, p. 13). She noted a major bifurcation or mismatch between the actual lived experiences of women and mainstream patriarchal ideal types. She advocated for diversity of perspectives in scholarly work in order to attain true democracy and emancipation.

Race and Power

Like feminism, critical race theory (or antiracist social theory) has played a central role in liberation sociology. While feminism has addressed gender relations, critical race theory has focused on racial inequalities in the distribution of power in society (Delgado & Stefancic, 2001). Those with this viewpoint have criticized institutionalized racism (Carmichael & Hamilton, 1967) and recognized that racism can be not only external to the victim but also manifest as internalized oppression (hooks, 1995). Furthermore, critical race theory has had an activist tradition, with individuals devoted to establishing a more just balance of power. Some scholars criticized the study of race because it is not a biological reality; these sociologists claimed that its inclusion in the scholarly literature only supports its legitimacy (Miles, 1982). Nonetheless, other scholars countered that race is an important focus of sociological analysis because humans treat race as real (Mason, 1994).

Scholars of race and power have noted the pervasive detrimental effects racism has had on the experiences of minorities. American sociologist Blackwell (1982), for example, observed that despite some improvement in the treatment of Blacks and other minorities in the last century, minorities still face numerous barriers to achieving economic and educational parity with Whites. He found that there are few minorities in graduate and professional education programs and that Blacks still have higher unemployment, lower incomes, and lower occupational positions than Whites. Blackwell illustrated how a history of racial isolation, oppression, and discrimination blocked the upward movement of minorities in educational, economic, and political life. Scholar and activist hooks (1995) further argued that White supremacy has damaged Black self-esteem. She suggested that being Black in America is viewed as a disadvantage because Blacks fail to live up to dominant societal norms and standards for beauty and success. According to hooks, widespread preference for White images and ideals has undermined Black self-determination.

In order to achieve justice for minorities, critical race theorists have asserted that there must be a radical change in racial power relations (Blackwell, 1982; Delgado & Stefancic, 2001). However, because the dominant group benefits from the status quo, it is motivated to avoid any disruptions in the power structure. Blackwell (1982) predicted that resistance to change will be particularly strong during periods of economic uncertainty, when minorities will be seen as a threat. Social justice can be attained and maintained only if policies to ameliorate inequality are eventually supported by the public and political leaders.

Race and Class

Some sociologists interested in the study of race have argued that the experience of minorities cannot be understood without a consideration of class. For instance, Newby (1988) suggested that it is insufficient to introduce "'race only' solutions to the situation of black people" (Newby, 1988, p. 77). Newby criticized capitalism for its injustices and advocated for a world that improved life conditions for all, regardless of race. In other words, he pointed out that social justice did not mean there would be an equal number of Blacks and Whites in poverty. On the contrary, he advocated for adequate levels of housing, income, health care, employment, and other resources for all races. By the same token, he supported the total elimination of corruption and domination; power should not simply be transferred from Whites to Blacks. A follower of Marx, he argued that "as long as you have capitalism, you will

have racism; and as long as you have capitalism, you will have sexism" (Newby, 1988, p. 78). Although concerned about the problems with capitalism, he also criticized traditional Marxists for failing to look at racial issues. His work examined Black oppression both on a racial and an economic level.

Race and Gender

Although the need for both racial and economic justice is critical, still other sociologists such as Collins and Baca Zinn have examined the intersection of race and gender. These sociologists have focused primarily on the stereotypes and discrimination against Black and Latina women (Baca Zinn & Dill, 1996; Collins, 1998). Collins (1998) argued that social theory has often reproduced existing power structures that disadvantage Black women. She contended that the elite, who have the means to produce and control social thought, have dominated academic sociology for years and throughout their reign have neglected the view of Black women. By including the voices of minority women, she believed social theory can support social justice (Collins, 1998). Baca Zinn and Dill (1996) similarly observed that women of color are negatively impacted by their subjugation in multiple social hierarchies. They asserted that there is no universal female experience. Instead, interlocking inequalities based on race, class, gender, and sexuality all define one's experience of injustice. Moreover, they argued that theories of race and gender must go beyond a binary model involving only Blacks and Whites. Social theory must recognize that Latinos, Asians, Native Americans, and other racial and ethnic groups occupy unique positions within the social structure.

Participatory Action Research

Mainstream sociologists have tended to avoid issues that cannot be studied with the conventional quantitative survey method (Feagin & Vera, 2001). However, even justice-oriented sociologists have done little to identify research methods that are in keeping with their democratic, justice-based values. As one of the founders of a nontraditional, egalitarian research approach known as participatory action research (PAR), Fals-Borda (1987) attempted to address this shortcoming with his work in Latin American communities. Like Habermas, Lee, Feagin, and other progressive sociologists, Fals-Borda took issue with sociology's exclusive dependence on the scientific method, asserting that the method is infused with the values of the elite scholars who produce it. Moreover, he noted that most sociologists maintain sole power and control over the knowledge they create, leaving communities empty handed at the end of the research process. He further argued that most sociologists consider communities as objects to be studied, placing their members in a position subordinate to the researcher.

Responding to what they viewed as exploitative positivist methods, Fals-Borda and others have applied the PAR model to their work as a way to alter the power relations between universities and communities so that knowledge and power are shared (Fals-Borda, 1987). Rather than being treated as passive objects, community members have been actively involved in the creation, implementation, and evaluation of PAR research projects. Furthermore, PAR scholars have done more than create knowledge; they have also demanded an action component designed to improve the lives of community partners. As Fals-Borda (1987) explained, in PAR, "the dominated, underdeveloped societies articulate their own socio-political position on the basis of their own values and capacities and act accordingly to achieve their liberation from the oppressive and exploitative forms of domination" (p. 331). Rather than simply advocating for the rights of the disadvantaged, sociologists using PAR have engaged in a humanistic, egalitarian practice that empowers people to overcome their oppression.

Future Directions

Despite the numerous efforts to promote social justice within sociology, room for progress remains. For example, Brekhus, Brekhus, and Galliher (2001) examined the scholarly journal *Social Problems*, which was originally dedicated to addressing social problems with recommended policies and programs. The articles Brekhus and colleagues sampled covered a range of issues from crime to poverty, with race as a primary focus. However, they also found

that few articles included policy implications, the authors' focus more on documenting social problems than offering solutions. Thus, despite their values and best intentions, even social justice-oriented sociologists struggle to take a more activist role. Future sociologists interested in social justice would benefit from examining the perspectives and emulating the methods of their activist predecessors.

CONCLUSION

The evolution of sociological theories of justice may be conceptualized in a roughly historical manner, beginning with three of the most significant founders of modern sociology: Marx, Durkheim, and Weber (see Figure 10.1). These three provided the foundation for modern discussions of power, oppression, and discrimination on the one hand, and equality and liberation on the other. Their writings have influenced the social justice work of social scientists across disciplines. However, other sociologists in the early 20th century noted that they were not attuned to the intersections of race, gender, and class in power relations. These sociologists expanded upon classic writings about power, oppression, and democracy to visualize a more just society for men and women of all races and classes. In addition, other 20th century theorists applied classical ideas of democracy and equality to the promotion of social rights of citizenship and state-sponsored social welfare as means to offset the insecurities and inequalities brought about by industrial capitalism. Finally, early conceptions of rights, welfare, equality, and solidarity influenced the formation of several interdisciplinary theories of social justice, including critical social theory, feminism, and critical race theory. Collectively, the ideas and efforts of progressive and activist social scientists inspired the development of liberation sociology, a subfield of sociology devoted to countering prejudice, oppression, and discrimination. Liberation sociology scholars and activists have questioned unequal power dynamics and advocated for equality, empowerment, diversity, and positive social change. As discussed above, the emancipatory methods of PAR is one promising research approach consistent with these social justice values.

Although not all sociologists have embraced their social justice roots, many have realized that the field's bias toward objectivity and scientific legitimacy left a hole in its understanding of social relations. Countersystem sociologists have noted that when people are reduced to statistics, their stories are not heard. In contrast, liberation sociologists aim to honor the experiences of communities studied and use the sciences to achieve just societies. Sociologists interested in pursuing social justice would profit from adopting the liberating and empowering approach of the field's activist scholars.

REFERENCES

Addams, J. (1905). *Democracy and social ethics*. London, UK: Macmillan.

Addams, J. (2008). *Twenty years at Hull House*. Stilwell, KS: Digireads.com.

Altschuler, R. (1998). *The living legacy of Marx, Durkheim, and Weber* (Vols. 1–2). New York, NY: Gordian Knot Books.

Arenson, R. J. (1981). What's wrong with exploitation? *Ethics, 91*(2), 202–227.

Baca Zinn, M., & Dill, B. T. (1996). Theorizing difference from multiracial feminisms. *Feminist Studies, 22*(2), 321–331.

Bendix, R. (1974). Inequality and social structure: A comparison of Marx and Weber. *American Sociological Review, 39*(2), 149–161.

Blackwell, J. (1982). Persistence and change in intergroup relations: The crisis upon us. *Social Problems, 29*(4), 325–346. Retrieved from http://www.jstor.org/stable/800023

Blum, F. H. (1944). Max Weber's postulate of "freedom" from value judgments. *American Journal of Sociology, 50*(1), 46–52. Retrieved from http://www.jstor.org/stable/2770341

Brekhus, W. H., Brekhus, K. L., & Galliher, J. F. (2001). Social problems in social problems: The theory and method of justice. *Social Problems, 48*(1), 137–143. Retrieved from http://www.jstor.org/stable/10.1525/sp.2001.48.1.137

Brennan, C. (1997). *Max Weber on power and social stratification*. Farnham, Surrey, UK: Ashgate.

Carmichael, S., & Hamilton, C. V. (1967). *Black power: The politics of liberation in America*. New York, NY: Random House.

Cohen, G. A. (1983). Review of Wood's Karl Marx. *Mind, 92*(367), 440–445.

Cole, M. (2001). Educational postmodernism, social justice and social change: An incompatible ménage a trios. *The School Field: International Journal of Theory and Research in Education, 12*(1–2), 87–94.

Collins, P. H. (1998). *Fighting words: Black women and the search for justice*. Minneapolis: University of Minnesota Press.

Deegan, M. (1988). *Jane Addams and the men of the Chicago school: 1892–1918*. New Brunswick, NJ: Transaction.

Delgado, R., & Stefancic, J. (2001). *Critical race theory: An introduction*. New York: New York University Press.

DeMarco, J. (1983). *The social thought of W. E. B. Du Bois*. Lanham, MD: University Press of America.

Du Bois, W. E. B. (1920). *Darkwater*. New York, NY: Harcourt, Brace, and Howe.

Du Bois, W. E. B. (1935). *Black reconstruction in America*. New York, NY: S.A. Russell.

Du Bois, W. E. B. (1939). *Black folk: Then and now: An essay in the history and sociology of the Negro race*. New York, NY: Holt, Rinehart, and Winston.

Du Bois, W. E. B. (1940). *Dusk of dawn: An essay toward an autobiography of a race concept*. New York, NY: Harcourt, Brace.

Du Bois, W. E. B. (1979). *The world and Africa*. New York, NY: International.

Du Bois, W. E. B. (1996). *The Philadelphia Negro: A social study*. Philadelphia: University of Pennsylvania Press. (Original work published 1899)

Durkheim, E. (1933). *The division of labour in society*. New York, NY: Free Press. (Original work published 1893)

Durkheim, E. (1958). *Socialism and Saint-Simon*. Yellow Springs, OH: Antioch Press. (Original work published 1928)

Durkheim, E. (1992). *Professional ethics and civil morals*. New York, NY: Routledge. (Original work published 1957)

Fals-Borda, O. (Ed.). (1985). *The challenge of social change*. Thousand Oaks, CA: Sage.

Fals-Borda, O. (1987). The application of participatory action research in Latin America. *International Sociology, 2*(4), 329–347. doi: 10.1177/026858098700200401

Feagin, J. R. (2001). Social justice and sociology: Agendas for the twenty-first century. *American Sociological Review, 66*, 1–20.

Feagin, J., & Vera, H. (2001). *Liberation sociology*. Boulder, CO: Westview Press.

Friedrichs, D. O. (1987). Bringing ourselves back in: The reflexive dimension in teaching a humanist sociology. *American Sociological Association, 15*(1), 1–6. Retrieved from http://www.jstor.org/stable/1317810

Habermas, J. (1971). *Knowledge and human interests.* Boston, MA: Beacon Press.

Habermas, J. (1976). The analytical theory of science and dialectics (G. Adey & D. Frisby, Trans.). In T. W. Adorno (Ed.), *The positivist dispute in German sociology* (pp. 131–162). London, UK: Heinemann Educational Books.

Habermas, J. (1987). *The philosophical discourse of modernity: Twelve lectures* (F. Lawrence, Trans.). Cambridge, MA: MIT Press.

Heller, P. L. (2003). Let's return to our roots: Sociology's original pursuit—The just society (2001 presidential address). *Sociological Spectrum, 23*(1), 3–25. doi: 10.1080/02732170309209

Holmstrom, N. (1977). Exploitation. *Canadian Journal of Philosophy, 7*(2), 353–369. Retrieved from http://www.jstor.org/stable/40230696

Holton, R. J., & Turner, B. S. (Eds.). (1989). *Max Weber on economy and society.* New York, NY: Routledge.

hooks, b. (1995). *Killing rage: Ending racism.* New York, NY: Henry Holt.

Hughes, J. A., Sharrock, W. W., & Martin, P. J. (2003). *Understanding classical sociology: Marx, Weber, Durkheim.* Thousand Oaks, CA: Sage.

Hurst, C. (2000). *Living theory: The applications of classical social theory to contemporary life.* Boston, MA: Allyn and Bacon.

Husami, Z. I. (1978). Marx on distributive justice. *Philosophy and Public Affairs, 8*(1), 27–64.

Jay, M. (1996). *The dialectical imagination: A history of the Frankfurt school and the Institute of Social Research, 1923–1950.* Berkeley: University of California Press.

Katz, M., & Sugrue, T. (Eds.). (1998). *W. E. B. Du Bois, race, and the city.* Philadelphia: University of Pennsylvania Press.

Lee, A. M. (1973). *Toward humanist sociology.* Englewood Cliffs, NJ: Prentice Hall.

Lee, A. M. (1976). Presidential address: Sociology for whom? *American Sociological Review, 41*(6), 925–936.

Lee, A. M. (1986). *Sociology for whom?* (2nd ed.). Syracuse, NY: Syracuse University Press.

Lee, A. M. (1990). *Sociology for the people: Toward a caring profession.* Syracuse, NY: Syracuse University Press.

Macionis, J. J., & Plummer, K. (2008). *Sociology: A global introduction* (4th ed.). Harlow, Essex, England: Pearson Education.

MacKinnon, C. A. (1989). *Toward a feminist theory of the state.* Cambridge, MA: Harvard University Press.

Marshall, T. H. (1992). Citizenship and social class. In T. H. Marshall & T. Bottomore (Eds.), *Citizenship and social class* (pp. 3–51). London, UK: Pluto Press. (Original work published in 1950)

Marx, K. (1906). *Capital: A critique of political economy* (Vol. 1), F. Engels (Ed.). New York, NY: Modern Library.

Marx, K. (1967). Critique of Hegel's *Philosophy of right.* In L. D. Easton & K. Guddat (Eds.), *Writings of the Young Marx on Philosophy and Society* (pp. 151–202). Garden City, NY: Doubleday. (Original work published 1843).

Marx, K. (1972). Critique of the Gotha Program. In R. Tucker (Ed.), *The Marx-Engels reader* (pp. 382–405). New York, NY: W. W. Norton. (Original work published 1875)

Marx, K. (1973). *Grundrisse.* New York, NY: Vintage. (Original work published 1953)

Marx, K., & Engels, F. (1987). Preface to the 1872 German edition of the manifesto of the communist party. In K. Marx & F. Engels (Eds.), *Karl Marx and Frederick Engels: Collected works* (Vol. 23, pp. 174–175). London, UK: Lawrence and Wishart. (Original work published 1872)

Mason, D. (1994). On the dangers of disconnecting race and racism. *Sociology, 28,* 845–859.

Merton, R. (1968). *Social theory and social structure.* New York, NY: Free Press.

Miles, R. (1982). *Racism and migrant labor.* London, UK: Routledge & Kegan Paul.

Morrison, K. L. (2006). *Marx, Durkheim, Weber: Formations of modern social thought.* Thousand Oaks, CA: Sage.

Myrdal, G. (2009). *An American dilemma: The Negro problem and modern democracy* (Vol. 1). New Brunswick, NJ: Transaction. (Original work published 1944)

Newby, R. G. (1988). The making of a class-conscious "race man": Reflections on the 1960s. *Critical Sociology, 15*(2), 61–78. doi:10.1177/089692058801500206

Nielson, K. (1989). *Marxism and the moral point of view: Morality, ideology, and historical materialism.* Boulder, CO: Westview Press.

Pampel, F. (2000). *Sociological lives and ideas: An introduction to the classical theorists.* New York, NY: Worth.

Parsons, H. L. (1971). *Humanism and Marx's thought.* Springfield, IL: Charles C. Thomas.

Peffer, R. G. (1990). *Marxism, morality, and social justice.* Princeton, NJ: Princeton University Press.

Reed, A. L. (1997). *W. E. B. Du Bois and American political thought: Fabianism and the color line.* New York, NY: Oxford University Press.

Schoenfeld, E., & Mestrovic, S. G. (1989). Durkheim's concept of justice and its relationship to social solidarity. *Sociological Analysis, 50*(2), 111–127.

Smith, D. E. (1990). *The conceptual practices of power: A feminist sociology of knowledge.* Boston, MA: Northeastern University Press.

Stacey, J., & Thorne, B. (1996). Is sociology still missing its feminist revolution? *Perspectives: The ASA Theory Section Newsletter, 18*(3), 1–3.

Stoecker, R. (1996). Sociology and social action: An introduction. *Sociological Imagination, 33*(1). Retrieved from http://comm-org.wisc.edu/si/stoecker1.htm

Stone, L. (2010). Max Weber and the moral idea of society. *Journal of Classical Sociology, 10*(2), 123–136. doi: 10.1177/1473325010370416

Titmuss, R. M. (1969). *Essays on the welfare state.* Boston, MA: Beacon Press.

Turner, B. S. (1995). Introduction: Symposium: Human rights and the sociological project. *Journal of Sociology, 31*(1), 1–8. doi: 10.1177/144078339503100201

Weber, M. (1949). *The methodology of the social sciences* (E. A. Shils & H. A. Finch, Trans.). New York, NY: Free Press.

Weber, M. (1968). *Economy & society.* G. Roth & C. Wittich (Eds.). New York, NY: Bedminister Press.

Zuckerman, P. (Ed.). (2004). Introduction. In *The social theory of W.E.B. Du Bois* (pp. 1–17). Thousand Oaks, CA: Pine Forge.

11

SOCIAL JUSTICE AND THE POLITICS OF CHILDREN'S RIGHTS

KELLY WHITAKER

INTRODUCTION

Children and adolescents are dependent on social structures, institutions, and families to support and advocate for their well-being and healthy development. However, adults and *social structures* (e.g., schools, laws, parents) responsible for protecting children's best interests often fail. In such instances, who is responsible for protecting children's rights? Usually legal rights take affect and perhaps a new guardian is identified. But is it possible for a child or adolescent to make choices regarding their own well-being? Is it possible for youth to participate in democratic processes (e.g., voting, sitting on a school board, or protesting injustices) or in divorce situations, choosing an adult to live with or deciding which school they would like to attend? In legal, policy, and educational arenas there are circumstances where youth are invited to participate in decisions regarding issues that directly affect them. However, in general, youth are excluded from political participation and denied full political rights. This exclusion is unnecessary and may be considered unjust. Recognizing youth as political entities and providing meaningful opportunities for

participation in the political sphere could empower youth to become more engaged citizens with a voice to protect and stand up for their own rights.

Although most theories of social justice in the field of political science have focused on *distributive justice*, related to the possession of material goods and social positions rather than social rules and relationships, Young in *Justice and the Politics of Difference* takes a different stance (1990). Young argues that distributive justice obscures other issues such as oppression and domination that are needed to understand the nature of social justice. She stresses, "A focus on the distribution of material goods and resources inappropriately restricts that scope of justice, because it fails to bring social structures and institutional contexts under evaluation" (Young, 1990, p. 20). Based on this view, Young (1990) offers an interpretation of justice that enables all to meet their needs and exercise their freedom. *Justice and the Politics of Difference* provides another theoretical framework of social justice and arguments surrounding children's rights.

Social justice is based in the concepts of human rights and equality. It is defined as "the view that everyone deserves equal economic, political, and social rights and opportunities" (National Association of Social Workers, 2012, "Social Justice"). Equality requires all members of society inclusion and participation in the major institutions and the opportunity to actively exercise their rights (Young, 1990). However, when it comes to children, there is a separate set of rights described in the UN Convention on the Rights of the Child (CRC) as well as a separate set of rules governing their participation (or lack thereof) in society's major institutions (United Nations [UN], 1989). This review of the literature explores the role of the CRC in order to gain a broader understating of children's rights. With this document as context, several major political science theories are described, including Young's politics of difference. The review concludes with ideas for including adolescents in the political process and implications for the rights of children.

METHODS

The initial literature search included the CSA Illumina database related to the CSA Worldwide Political Science Abstracts. The search was limited to peer-reviewed journal articles in English and included

the following keywords: *political, theory, rights, justice, representation,* and/or *child* or *family* in different combinations. The minimal results included six relevant articles. Political science faculty from the University of California, Berkeley, and Washington University, St. Louis, were consulted and provided citations on political theories of representation and children's rights. This review is not a comprehensive review of the literature but rather a mini-literature review based on 20 articles and four books related to social justice, political theories, and children's rights.

UNITED NATIONS CONVENTION ON THE RIGHTS OF THE CHILD

The United Nations (UN) Universal Declaration of Human Rights was created in 1948 to support general human rights for all human beings (UN, 1948). Almost forty years later, the UN decided that children deserved special protections and convened the Convention on the Rights of the Child (UN, 1989), as highlighted in Figure 11.1. This document outlined the specific protections for children and stated which rights were to be upheld and protected by adults (parents or the state when parents are

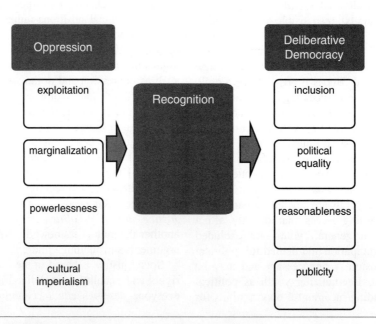

Figure 11.1   The Politics of Moving From Oppression to Social Justice

unable). Children are defined as any child between the ages of zero and 18. In the CRC document, basic rights include the right to life, to be named immediately following birth, and to be cared for by parents, including foster care and adoptive parents. Children are to be protected from violence, abuse, neglect, and exploitation. Article 12 "assures a child who is capable of forming his or her own views the right to express those views freely" (UN, 1989) and the right to be heard in judicial hearings either directly or through a representative. Other rights outlined in the CRC document include the right to health and health services, education, rest and leisure, freedom of expression, thought, religion, and association. Despite the breadth of these rights, they fall short of providing youth political rights.

The expansive debate on the rights of children often begins with whether or not children even possess rights of their own, the definition of those rights, and the theories used to explain the presence or absence of those rights. Embedded within these debates are the concepts of childhood and adolescence and how different levels of maturity and competence affect this discourse. There is a general consensus that infants have very different circumstances from a school-aged child who can read and write or from adolescents who can have a job or drive a car. Much of the debate focuses on the capability to reason and make good judgments and whether children have the ability to make choices in regard to rights. As noted in Figure 11.1, the complicated controversy regarding the nature of rights has led the United States to abstain from signing the CRC.

Throughout history, children have been purposely excluded from the political arena. They have been viewed as either parents' property, an extension of their parents, or incomplete adults who do not have the characteristics and capacities needed to function as full human beings (Archard & MacLeod, 2002). This type of thinking can be traced to the forefathers of moral and political philosophy (e.g., Aristotle, Locke, Hobbes, and Kant) who viewed children as being governed by parental authority (Archard & MacLeod, 2002). In addition, contemporary political theorists (e.g., Rawls, Nozick, Dworkin, Gauther) rarely include children or families in their theoretical work (Archard & MacLeod, 2002). Feminist political theorists have also noted the specific lack of attention to families, women, and children (Archard & MacLeod, 2002; Okin, 2004; Young, 1990).

The arguments for excluding children from the political sphere are similar to the reasons women were excluded prior to winning the right to vote at the beginning of the 20th century (Rehfeld, 2011). Rehfeld outlines three ways in which they are similar: first, children are viewed as a special group that needs its rights protected, similar to how women were viewed; second, children are seen to lack the emotional capacity to represent themselves just as women were once seen as politically immature; and third, children are considered represented by their parents, in a passive way, similar to the way a husband's vote was meant to represent his wife's interests as well (2011). The similarities between these arguments are quite surprising and suggest a closer look at reasons for excluding young people's voices and experiences from the public sphere.

THEORIES OF RECOGNITION

Theories of recognition have been subsumed under the larger umbrella of *identity politics*, which have highlighted oppression of certain groups (e.g., women, people of color, sexual minorities). As Markell notes, "To be recognized means to be seen or regarded—whether directly or through the mediation of social and political institutions" (2009, p. 450). Heyes observes, "What is crucial about the 'identity' of identity politics appears to be the experience of the subject, especially his or her experience of oppression and the possibility of a shared and more authentic or self-determined alternative" (2009, para 6). The two major theorists credited with beginning this discourse are—Charles Taylor in his 1994 work *The Politics of Recognition* and Axel Honneth in his 1996 work *The Struggle for Recognition* (see Markell, 2009). Theories of recognition are related to social justice in that "to be recognized means to be treated justly," while misrepresentation of a group's identity or lack of recognition of a group is to oppress (Markell, 2009, p. 455). Identity politics at the basic level contends that some social groups are oppressed and identity within an oppressed group makes one vulnerable to cultural imperialism (including stereotyping, erasure, or appropriation of one's group identity), violence, exploitation, marginalization, or power-lessness (Heyes, 2009; Young 1990). Young's work explores the oppression of marginalized social groups and a theory of social justice that calls for broader recognition of groups.

Justice and the Politics of Difference

In *Justice and the Politics of Difference*, Young (1990) argues that distributive justice, as described by contemporary political theorists, obscures other concepts such as oppression and domination, which would be better used to understand the nature of social justice. Based on this view, she proposes the "politics of difference" theory to explain how social structures constrain or enable social justice for populations, such as children whose participation in society is not entirely focused on equal access to goods and resources. The politics of difference theory makes the argument that the scope of justice is wider than distributive issues (1990). Young identifies how groups are excluded from decision making, cultural expression, and division of labor by noting that "sometimes recognizing particular rights for groups is the only way to promote their full participation" (Young, 1990, p. 11).

Oppression and domination can limit the promotion of social justice, especially when social groups are the subject of that oppression and domination through exclusion (Young, 1990). Young further classifies oppression into five categories: *exploitation, marginalization, powerlessness, cultural imperialism,* and *violence.* The presence of any one of these conditions can lead to oppression. Based on Marx's theory of exploitation, Young (1990) argues that "social rules about what work is, who does what for whom, how work is compensated, and the social process by which the results of work are appropriated operate to enact relations of power and inequality" (Young, 1990, p. 50). The concept of marginalization involved the exclusion from participation in the labor force as a way to limit full participation in society. Fraser (1995) defines the third concept of powerlessness as "the condition of having power exercised over one by others without oneself exercising power in turn; hence having to take orders but never oneself giving them" (p. 175). For example, cultural imperialism is the process of establishing group norms based on the dominant group in society and therefore "rendering invisible

the oppressed group's perspective, while simultaneously stereotyping that group as other" (Fraser, 1995, p. 175). Finally, oppressed groups are often oppressed through experiences of violence based on their vulnerability as a group. These five categories of oppression help us to understand the conditions that oppress different groups.

The central tenet to Young's theory of recognition is that the politics of difference is the remedy to cultural oppression (Fraser, 1995). As Young (1990) notes, "The politics of difference sometimes implies overriding a principle of equal treatment with the principle that group differences should be acknowledged in public policies and procedures of economic institutions, in order to reduce actual or potential oppression" (p. 11). From her perspective, ignoring difference can lead to oppression in three respects: first, failure to recognize ways that disadvantaged groups are different from mainstream and often privileged groups; second, a universal humanity which gives power to the dominant group in society and ignores other groups; and third, criticism of groups that do not fit the mainstream norm and forces them to assimilate leads to devaluation of the group (Young, 1990). The politics of difference as a theory of social justice leads to social equality through the full participation and inclusion of everyone in a society's major institutions.

Critiques of the theory. The several critiques of recognition theory and Young's *Justice and the Politics of Difference* are a call to remedy the conflicts between recognition and redistribution (Fraser, 1995). Fraser's critique seeks to refute Young's claim that redistribution is not an encompassing theory of justice and suggests that Young is actually creating "a new theory of justice that encompasses claims of both redistribution and recognition, of both equality and difference, of both culture and political economy" (Fraser, 1995). In fact, Young does not combine these two varying concepts of justice. Others have pointed out that identity politics can lead to essentialism in two ways; first, there is only one way to identify oneself in relation to only one group, and second, by belonging to that group, one must adopt the single identity of that group (Heyes, 2009). This obscures the prominence of groups and can limit the identity of individuals and can lead to further oppression of the group and individuals who identify with the group (Heyes, 2009).

Choice and Interest Theories

Rights theories tend to fall into two categories: either choice theory or interest theory (Archard, 2010; Goodin & Gibson, 1997). Choice theory is about actively participating in enforcing or refusing a right, such as the right to an education being enforced or refused (Archard, 2010). The interest theory, on the other hand, is based more on morality and entitlement where certain things are provided and protected such as providing education for all children. This distinction between choice and interest theories is of importance regarding children's rights because it stirs the debate regarding children's ability to make decisions in regard to their own welfare. Archard (2010) makes an argument for children as the holders of special rights and capacities based on choice and interest theories:

1. Rights are protected choices.

2. Only those capable of exercising choices can be right holders.

3. Children are incapable of exercising choice.

4. Children are not right holders.

5. Adults have duties to protect the important interests of children.

6. Rights and duties are correlative.

7. Children are right holders.

This argument is based on the idea that rights and capacities are related so that if children have rights but do not have the capacity to make choices for themselves, then adults have the responsibility to protect the interests of children. While children may not have the capacity to defend their own rights (choice theory), children's rights should be protected by adults (interest theory), and this line of reasoning suggests that children, in fact, do have rights (Archard, 2010).

Goodin and Gibson (1997) elaborate on the choice and interest theory in relation to moral capacities. They explain that the problem is not that all youth or elderly lack the capacity to make reasoned choices but that some do, including the very young or very old. As a result, the holders of rights have interests that are protected and "recognizable by others who are duly empowered, by the moral community in general, to press those claims on one's behalf" (Goodin & Gibson, 1997, p. 188).

Another aspect of this debate is the view that children should not have rights because they are incapable of making choices (Brighouse, 2002). This argument also distinguishes between interest rights and welfare rights. Brighouse (2002) critiques the interest and choice theory argument posed by noting that it is not possible to protect a person's fundamental interests but that welfare rights are rights that pertain to well-being. Brighouse (2002) further explains that there are two distinct types of welfare rights: immediate and future. Children are not capable of protecting their welfare rights because children are emotionally and physically dependent on others, and they are not well informed about their future choices, except as children age and as they become more capable of protecting their own interests.

It has been suggested that children's rights, which provide basic needs or protect their interests, do not change their status or empowerment because autonomy is needed (Arneil, 2002). "Autonomy is the freedom to make choices over one's life, a freedom that is restricted for children by both parents and the state" (Arneil, 2002, p. 80). Whereas increasing the rights of children to participate in decisions about their own life is related to their rational capacity (Arneil, 2002), especially when adolescent cognitive ability is similar to adults, there is more uncertainty regarding the capacity of very young children (Buss, 2004; Schrag, 2004). If adolescents have the necessary mental capacity to participate as citizens, then it is not clear why political and civil rights are not available to children.

Recognition Theory

Recognition theory is particularly relevant to the rights of children. Schrag argues that the exclusion of children from citizenship in democracy is unjust (2004). He uses the theory of democracy to explore the role of recognition, where people who are excluded entirely from any public role tend to be invisible, resulting in unequal treatment with respect to the one-person, one-vote rule (Schrag, 2004). With regard to the political and voting rights of children, Schrag (2004) identified the following reasons that the most vulnerable children are least likely to be represented by their parents: (a) Children have interests which are not shared by adults, (b) parents do not and often cannot adequately represent the rights of children through their votes, and (c) parents in the lowest social classes are least likely to vote. The lack of political rights for children has consequences for the underrepresentation of children's interests.

The CRC failed to include rights for children related to political participation. Kulynych (2001) argues that the discussion about the rights of children "tends to exaggerate children's current citizenship status, overemphasizing formal, legal interpretations of political participation, and obscures the crucial need for recognition in authorizing children's citizenship" (p. 232). She also notes, "Citizenship as political identity, for both adults and children, is central to genuine democracy. . . . It also entails a reciprocal recognition that one is politically relevant" (Kulynych, 2001, p. 241). Therefore, in order to change the political status of children, they need to be recognized as politically relevant citizens. To be recognized, they need to have a voice that is considered in the political sphere. According to Young's politics of difference, social justice requires full participation in order for groups to develop capacities and realize their choices (1990). Children constitute a social group with a particular social perspective that can improve democracy and is often failed to be considered (Kulynych, 2001).

Children have not been permitted to participate in political activities, such as voting, and are therefore kept from participating in society. Lecce (2009) views children as citizens with the moral right to an open future where they should be allowed to make choices rather than relying solely on their parents. He notes that the interests of children are neglected in policy and law because they are disproportionately powerless in relation to adults. This exclusion from the right to vote is problematic for the future of children and proposes that lowering the voting age would allow children to participate in democratic processes as a way to learn the values, processes, and results of political decision making (Lecce, 2009).

There is evidence that programs designed to promote youth participation merely provide another way for government to control youth (Bessant, 2003; Ginwright, Cammarota & Noguera, 2005). Yet youth have an important perspective and should be given a voice to contribute to policies and political processes. Ginwright et al. (2005) propose that youth civic participation could help to solve social problems noting,

Policymakers often view urban youth as [a] civic problem that should be controlled and contained, rather than problem-solvers who can contribute to community development and social justice. Public policy would better serve young people, and ultimately larger communities, by promoting opportunities for them to work for social justice and creating policies and programs that confront community problems that threaten their health and safety. (p. 26)

Developing an authentic avenue for youth participation in the political sphere is not without challenges. Adults do not always take children and their perspectives seriously. In order to create a system for youth participation, it is essential to recognize the different ways that young people are excluded from democratic practices (Bessant, 2003). The language and rhetoric surrounding young people and participation need clarification to ensure an honest and authentic process, especially when young peoples' diverse needs and capacities to think and act competently are captured in legislation (Bessant, 2003). Similar to the CRC's set of human rights, the political rights of children should be legislated in order to create legitimacy and clarity related to youth participation in the democratic process.

The Deliberative Model

To truly provide children with freedom from oppression and domination, it is essential to incorporate their choices and interests into the decisions and polices made on their behalf. Based on Young's politics of difference model, children constitute a social group that has been excluded from the democratic process, especially regarding policies that directly affect them (e.g., education, health care, and juvenile justice). Building on the politics of difference model, a new model known as *deliberative democracy* has emerged. According to Kulynych (2001), deliberative democracy offers a model of participation, which relies on a communicative process incorporating all relevant perspectives where those whose basic interests are affected by a decision are included in the deliberative democracy process.

In a more recent book by Young, *Inclusion and Democracy* (2002), she describes a new model based on deliberative democracy. Two ideals of social justice are outlined: self-development and self-determination. Self-development refers to "conditions for all persons to learn and use satisfying and expansive skills in socially recognized settings, and enable them to play and communicate with others or express their feelings and perspectives on social life in contexts where others can listen" (Young, 2002, p. 32). In contrast, self-determination is the second aspect of justice and "consists in being able to participate in determining one's action and the condition of one's action" (Young, 2002, p. 32). Therefore, Young (2002) defines social justice "as the institutional conditions for promoting self-development and self-determination of a society's members" (2002, p. 33). To achieve social justice for children, there must be avenues for participation in the democratic decision-making process for this societal group.

Young outlines a vision of social justice through deliberative democracy based on four main concepts: *inclusion, political equality, reasonableness,* and *publicity*; she notes that inclusion requires that a democratic decision is normatively legitimate only if all those affected by it are included in the process of discussion and decision making. She explains that although the normative definition of democracy literally means *political equality,* it must go further.

> Not only should all those affected be nominally included in decision-making, but they should be included on equal terms. All ought to have an equal right and effective opportunity to express their interests and concerns. All also ought to have equal effective opportunity to question one another, and to respond to and criticize one another's proposals and arguments. The ideal model of deliberative democracy, that is, promotes free and equal opportunity to speak. (Young, 2002, p. 23)

Not only is it necessary for each perspective to be heard, but there must also be openness to various perspectives. Young (2002) describes *reasonableness* as making an effort to understand the opinions of others, the willingness to change our own opinions based on the arguments of others, and suspending judgment long enough to allow that process to take place. Finally, she describes *publicity* as the interaction among participants in a democratic decision-making process where people hold one another accountable (Young, 2002). She describes a public as more than just the sum of members in society, in order to capture different individual and collective experiences, histories, commitments, ideals, interests, and goals needed to discuss collective problems under a common set of procedures (Young, 2002). The creation of authentic procedures and processes for the inclusion of children in the public political sphere will be not an easy task.

Young's work shown in *Justice and the Politics of Difference* helped to outline how children and adolescents can be considered an oppressed group. The oppression they experience is unjust, leaving them excluded from decision making and denied cultural expression. By recognizing youth as engaged political citizens through deliberative democracy, social justice can be revived. Through inclusion in politics, providing equal opportunities for their voices to be heard, making an effort to hear their voices, and developing meaningful interaction, deliberative democracy is a framework for moving from oppression to justice (Figure 11.1).

The Child as a Democratic Citizen

Although there are significant barriers to recognizing children as full participants in U.S. politics, several ideas have been presented to incorporate youth into the political arena. In his 2011 article, *The Child as a Democratic Citizen*, Professor Rehfeld identified three ideas to improve children's political participation: fractional voting, national electoral constituencies, and political spending accounts. Rehfeld suggests allowing children fractional voting rights, beginning at age 12. Fractional voting would provide adolescents one seventh of a vote at age 12, with an additional one seventh of a vote added each year until they are 18 (when they would have a full vote). Through fractional voting, they would have the opportunity to participate in their communities, develop their political maturity, and become politically engaged citizens. Schools' civic education curriculum could provide the structure for teaching adolescents about these rights in an applied way. Another idea to increase children's voices is to create a national electoral constituency organized by age group. This would allow children to have representation at the national level without the intimidation of parents or other adults. Finally, by creating political spending accounts for children, they would have more political capitol to actively engage in the political process (Rehfeld, 2011).

IMPLICATIONS AND CONCLUSION

Some of the tension regarding the failure of the United States to ratify the CRC is based on issues regarding the rights of parents in relationship to the rights of children. This tension is often found in the child welfare system. The rights of children are often neglected in the systems that are designed to protect their interests (e.g., juvenile justice, child welfare, and mental health) where children often do not have the right to basic due process (Mohr, Gelles & Schwartz, 1999). As Mohr et al. note (1999), "The child welfare system remains a system where the client is the parent, where the parent's legal rights are primary, and where a child's developmental best interests are rarely represented or given careful and appropriate weight" (p. 48).

Lack of clearly outlined rights for children leads to ambiguity about the different ways to protect their interests, the nature of the choices to be considered, and the structure of policies and programs that serve children. If the rights of children are not defined, how can we protect them? The ratification of the CRC by the United States would provide a starting point for specifying basic rights of children and ensuring that policies and programs are designed to provide and uphold those rights. In addition, recognizing youth as citizens with political rights to participate in processes that directly affect them would also be an important step in promoting social justice. Finally, the deliberative democracy process that takes youth seriously, welcomes their perspective in solving problems, and promotes changes in policies and programs could lead to significant improvement in social justice for youth.

APPENDIX 1: UNITED NATIONS CONVENTION ON THE RIGHTS OF THE CHILD[1]

Part I

Article 1: Definition of child

Article 2: Child's rights are ensured without discrimination

Article 3: State and private institutions shall protect children's interests, ensure protection, and care

Article 4: States shall implement children's rights

Article 5: States will respect parent rights and responsibilities

Article 6: States recognize child's right to life

Article 7: Child will be registered, named immediately after birth, and cared for by parents

Article 8: States respect child's identity, nationality, and name

Article 9: States ensure child is not separated from parents against his or her will, except in accordance with law and in the best interests of the child

Article 10: Family reunification will be positive, humane, and expeditious

Article 11: States parties shall take measures to combat the illicit transfer and nonreturn of children abroad

Article 12: Children's right to express views and right to be heard in judicial hearings

Article 13: Child right to freedom of expression

Article 14: Child right to freedom of thought, conscience, and religion

Article 15: Child rights to freedom of association and to freedom of peaceful assembly

Article 16: No child shall be subjected to arbitrary or unlawful interference with his or her privacy, family, home, or correspondence, nor to unlawful attacks on his or her honor and reputation

Article 17: Child access to information

Article 18: Parents are responsible for the upbringing and development of the child. States ensure that working parents have access to child care services

Article 19: State shall protect children from violence

Article 20: Children are entitled to special care by the state when they are temporarily or permanently deprived of their family environment

Article 21: State shall recognize and/or permit that the system of adoption shall ensure the best interests of the child

[1] Adopted and opened for signature, ratification, and accession by General Assembly resolution 44/25 of 20 November 1989: entry into force 2 September 1990, in accordance with article 49. The United States did not sign the resolution due to concerns about parents' rights. *Source:* From United Nations (1989). *Convention on the rights of the child (CRC).* Retrieved November 13, 2010, from http://www2.ohchr.org/english/law/pdf/crc.pdf. Reprinted with permission.

Article 22: States will provide appropriate measure for children seeking refugee status

Article 23: States shall recognize rights to a full and decent life for mentally or physically disabled children

Article 24: States recognize child's right to health, treatment of illness, and rehabilitation of health

Article 25: States recognize the right of a child who has been placed by the competent authorities, for the purposes of care, protection, or treatment of his or her physical or mental health, to a periodic review of the treatment provided to the child and all other circumstances relevant to his or her placement

Article 26: States recognize child's right to social security, including social insurance

Article 27: States recognize the right of every child to a standard of living adequate for the child's physical, mental, spiritual, moral, and social development

Article 28: States recognize child's right to education

Article 29: Education will develop children to their fullest potential while respecting children's rights and freedoms, cultural identity, language, values, and so on.

Article 30: In states where minority groups exist, child rights extend to culture, religion, and language

Article 31: States recognize the right of the child to rest and leisure, to engage in play and recreational activities appropriate to the age of the child, and to participate freely in cultural life and the arts

Article 32: States recognize child's right to be protected from economic exploitation

Article 33: States will protect children from illicit drug use and prevent the use of children in trafficking of such substances

Article 34: States will protect children from sexual exploitation and sexual abuse

Article 35: States will protect child abduction and trafficking

Article 36: State shall protect the child against all other forms of exploitation

Article 37: States will ensure that no child is subjected to torture or other cruel punishment

Article 38: States undertake and respect rules for international humanitarian law when in armed conflicts which are relevant to the child

Article 39: States shall take all appropriate measures to promote physical and psychological recovery and social reintegration of a child victim

Article 40: States recognize the right of every child alleged as, accused of, or recognized as having infringed the penal law to be treated in a manner consistent with the promotion of the child's sense of dignity and worth, which reinforces the child's respect for the human rights and fundamental freedoms

Article 41: Nothing in the present convention shall affect any provisions which are more conducive to the realization of the rights of the child and which may be contained in (a) the law of a state party or (b) international law in force for that state.

Part II

Article 42: States parties undertake to make the principles and provisions of the convention by appropriate and active means

Article 43: Establishment of a committee on the rights of the child

Article 44: States must report measures adopted by the established Committee on the Rights of the Child

Article 45: In order to foster the effective implementation of the convention and to encourage international cooperation in the field covered by the convention, the committee can request advice, make suggestions, transmit information, and otherwise interact with specialized agencies and state parties

Part III

Article 46: The present convention shall be open for signature by all states

Article 47: The present convention is subject to ratification

Article 48: The present convention shall remain open for accession by any state

Article 49: The present convention shall enter into force on the 30th day following the date of deposit with the secretary-general of the United Nations

Article 50: Any state party may propose an amendment

Article 51: The secretary-general of the United Nations shall receive and circulate to all States the text of reservations made by states at the time of ratification or accession.

Article 52: A state party may denounce the present convention by written notification

Article 53: the secretary-general of the United Nations is designated as the depositary of the present convention

Article 54: The original document of the present convention, as translated into the Arabic, Chinese, English, French, Russian, and Spanish texts, are equally authentic

REFERENCES

Archard, D. (2010). Children's rights. In E. N. Zalta (Ed.), *The Stanford encyclopedia of philosophy* (Winter ed.). Retrieved from http://plato.stanford.edu/archives/win2010/entries/rights-children/

Archard, D., & MacLeod, C. (2002). *The moral and political status of children*. Oxford, UK: Oxford University Press.

Arneil, B. (2002). Becoming versus being: A critical analysis of the child in liberal theory. In D. Archard & C. MacLeod (Eds.), *The moral and political status of children* (pp. 70–94). Oxford, UK: Oxford University Press.

Bessant, J. (2003). Youth participation: A new mode of government. *Policy Studies, 24*(2), 87–100.

Brighouse, H. (2002). What rights (if any) do children have? In D. Archard & C. MacLeod, (Eds.), *The moral and political status of children* (pp. 31–52). Oxford, UK: Oxford University Press.

Buss, E. (2004). Constitutional fidelity through children's rights. *Supreme Court Review, 2004*, 355–407.

Fraser, N. (1995). Recognition or redistribution? A critical reading of Iris Young's *Justice and the politics of difference. Journal of Political Philosophy, 3*(9), 166–180.

Ginwright, S., Cammarota, J., & Noguera, P. (2005).Youth, social justice, and communities: Toward a theory of urban youth policy. *Social Justice, 32*(3), 24–40.

Goodin, R. E., & Gibson, D. (1997). Rights, young and old. *Oxford Journal of Legal Studies, 17*(2), 185–203.

Heyes, C. (2009). Identity politics. In E. N. Zalta (Ed.), *The Stanford encyclopedia of philosophy* (Spring ed.). Retrieved from http://plato.stanford.edu/archives/spr2009/entries/identity-politics/

Kulynych, J. (2001). No playing in the public sphere: Democratic theory and the exclusion of children. *Social Theory and Practice, 27*(2), 231–264.

Lecce, S. (2009). Should democracy grow up? Children and voting rights. *Intergenerational Justice Review, 9*(4), 133–139.

Markell, P. (2009). Recognition and redistribution. In J. S. Dryzek, B. Honig, & A. Phillips, (Eds.), *The Oxford handbook of political theory* (pp. 450–469). Oxford, UK: Oxford University Press.

Mohr, W., Gelles, R. J., & Schwartz, I. M. (1999). Shackled in the land of liberty: No rights for children. *American Academy of Political and Social Science, 564* (July), 37–55).

National Association of Social Workers (NASW). (2012). *Social justice*. NASW. Retrieved February 12, 2012, from http://www.naswdc.org/pressroom/features/issue/peace.asp

Okin, S. M. (2004). The public/private dichotomy. In C. Farrelly (Ed.) *Contemporary political theory: A reader.* London, UK: Sage.

Rehfeld, A. (2011). The child as a democratic citizen. *Annals of the American Academy, 633*, 141–166.

Schrag, F. (2004). Children and democracy: Theory and policy. *Politics Philosophy Economics, 3*(3), 365.

United Nations (UN). (1948). *Universal declaration of human rights*. Retrieved November 23, 2010, from http://www.un.org/en/documents/udhr/index.shtml#ap

United Nations (UN). (1989). *Convention on the rights of the child (CRC)*. Retrieved November 13, 2010, from http://www2.ohchr.org/english/law/pdf/crc.pdf

Young, I. M. (1990). *Justice and the politics of difference*. Princeton, NJ: Princeton University Press.

Young, I. M. (2002). *Inclusion and democracy*. Oxford, UK: Oxford University Press. *Oxford Scholarship Online*. Retrieved December 2, 2010, from http://dx.doi.org/10.1093/0198297556.001.0001

12

SOCIAL JUSTICE IN POLITICAL THOUGHT

Examining the Rights of Parents

WENDY WIEGMANN

INTRODUCTION

According to the National Association of Social Workers (NASW) *Code of Ethics* (2009), social workers have a duty to challenge social injustice and to "promote social, economic, political, and cultural values and institutions that are compatible with the realization of social justice" (Preamble section). In addition, the code instructs social workers to "engage in social and political action," "be aware of the impact of the political arena on practice," and "advocate for changes in policy and legislation" (6.04 Social and Political Action section). It is clear from this code that social workers have an obligation to understand and be a part of the political discourse on social justice. This literature review identifies the major theoretical underpinnings of social justice in political thought, with a particular focus on issues of family and parental rights. The intent of the analysis is to explore social justice from a political science perspective, as well as identify the limitations of a political analysis of justice within

families. The review concludes with an exploration of the ways that political theory related to parental rights and social justice can be applied to the field of social welfare.

METHODS

To capture as much relevant literature as possible, the author conducted a search of published writings using the following databases: Academic Search Complete, Google Scholar, JSTOR, Hein Online, LexisNexis Academic, Philosophers Index, Social Service Abstracts, Social Science Abstracts, and Social Work Abstracts. The author also consulted the *Oxford Handbook of Political Science* as well as the *Routledge Encyclopedia of Philosophy* and the *Stanford Encyclopedia of Philosophy*. Seeking to join the three concepts which drive this paper—social justice, political theory, and family—the following search terms were used:

- Social justice: social justice, justice, distributive justice, procedural justice, social goals, social inequality, social reform, power;
- Political theory: political theory, theory, political philosophy, political science;
- Family: family, parents' rights, cultural differences, parenting rights, parental rights, multicultural rights, children's rights, right to rear, abuse, property rights.

As needed, search strings were used that linked several of the terms by using "AND" or "OR."

In addition to article database searches, the following political scientists were consulted: (a) Professor Wendy Brown of the University of California (UC), Berkeley Political Science Department and (b) Professor Sarah Song of UC Berkeley's Legal Studies and Political Science Departments. Both professors offered insights into "rights theory," social justice, and the political theory of protecting different classes of individuals. Professor Song also shared her course syllabus on political theory and individual rights.

Limitations of this analysis include the fact that while there are many political traditions (Marxism, feminism, egalitarianism, multiculturalism, to name a few) which discuss social justice and/or family, this analysis has focused exclusively on the concept of parents rights within Western liberal political theory. Furthermore, within the discussion of rights and families are many important attendant issues for which there was no space in this article. Issues such as equality and the rights of women within families, the rights of children within families, and the competing rights of parents within dissolved or broken families are just some of the most evident omissions. While these issues are certainly worthy of their own examination, in the interest of focusing attention on the interaction between the rights of parents and the intervention of the state, these issues have been excluded from this analysis.

FAMILY AND JUSTICE IN POLITICAL THEORY

Since the time of Socrates in 400 BCE, political theorists have considered the role of family in a just society, namely, the extent to which the family

is external to the state and how the rules of state should be imposed upon the family. In *The Republic,* Plato presents the family as an external hindrance to an idealized city, where all citizens must sacrifice themselves, and their family entanglements, to the ordering of society (Colmo, 2005). The family represents both a distraction for the republic's citizens and an expression of self-interest that can be detrimental to societal justice. In his discourse, justice is defined as harmony, efficiency, and moral goodness (Okin, 1977). Approximately 2,400 years later, Rawls presents the family as a central component of the basic structure of society and a key factor in determining whether an individual will experience justice. According to Rawls (2004), a happy family is necessary to a happy life, and the willingness of an individual to make an effort and earn society's benefits is also impacted by the nature of family life. In Rawls conception, then, family is not outside but an important internal element of a just society.

These theories reflect the tensions between the rights of individuals and the greater good of the state. The family represents a place that is both personal and interconnected with society. Decisions which address the tension between justice for individuals and the interest of the state in preserving harmony, efficiency, and moral goodness continue to be a focal point of political discourse. The central issues in this debate include, among other things, parental discretion in decisions affecting their children, rights of individuals to create families, and the protection of children within abusive and neglectful families.

The Autonomous Family

A discussion of the rights of parents logically begins with John Locke and the distinction between the private realm (where a person experiences liberty and freedom that is separate from the control of the state) and the public realm (where individuals consent to limiting their freedom in exchange for the protection of government in society) (Locke, 1988). For Locke, the distinction between the public and the private are essential to his idea of justice (Kelly, 2002). Locke conceived of humans as originally existing in a state of nature characterized by freedom and equality, which was also dangerous and disorganized. In exchange for the protecting and mediating powers of the state, Locke argues that individuals consented to relinquish some of their freedoms (Locke, 1988). This social contract is fully consensual and limited in its reach. Outside of the reach of the state, the domestic realm provides individuals with a space to realize their potential as rational, free beings even though they have consented to partial rule by government (Kelly, 2002). Locke argues that the state is not necessary in the private realm because a family does not require a neutral party to resolve disputes and enforce laws. Instead, the family is ruled by the father and is naturally peaceful and orderly (Kelly, 2002).

Locke goes on to argue that state interference within the family is not only unnecessary, but also it is antithetical to the state's purpose. Within the family, Locke argues, an individual should be fully at liberty to exercise free will and develop reason (Locke, 1988). These capacities are essential for individuals to distinguish themselves from the ignorant beings that existed within the state of nature. Within the family, the father teaches this ability to his children and cultivates it himself (Kelly, 2002). Locke further argues that the purpose of the state is to protect this space so that a father can fulfill his personal potential and his parental obligation to instill reason in his children. Justice, within this interpretation, is served when the state protects the individual and the family from outside forces but also from itself.

Right to Rear Children

Related to Locke's conception of protected family space are theories concerning the rights of parents to raise their families and make decisions according to their own judgments. Sometimes described as a "right to rear," these theories are based in liberal political thought, where justice depends on enumerated and inferred rights that protect the individual from unnecessary state interference (Waldron, 1998). Liberal theory is also based on the idea that adults are entitled to pursue their own conceptions of what is good and that political power should not be used to force a certain definition of good upon them (Gilles, 1996). In a liberal society, no one is allowed to coerce others with respect to choosing

values or beliefs unless they have a particular privilege to do so (Gilles, 1996).

The United States Supreme Court has applied right to rear theories in cases, thereby, protecting parental authority (*Meyer v. Nebraska,* 1923; *Pierce v. Society of Sisters,* 1925; *Prince v. Massachusetts,* 1944; *Stanley v. Illinois,* 1972; *Troxel v. Granville,* 2000; *Wisconsin v. Yoder,* 1972). In Meyer, for example, Justice McReynolds wrote that the 14th Amendment protects

> not merely freedom from bodily restraint, but also the right of the individual to contract, to engage in any of the common occupations of life, to acquire useful knowledge, to marry, establish a home and bring up children, to worship God according to the dictates of his own conscience, and, generally, to enjoy those privileges long recognized at common law as essential to the orderly pursuit of happiness by free men. (p. 396)

Despite a stated deference to parental rights, the Court has also delineated the circumstances under which those rights can be limited (*Prince v. Massachusetts,* 1944). In the Prince decision, Justice Rutledge wrote that while the Court should defer to parents in making decisions for their children, the state has "a wide range of power for limiting parental freedom and authority in things affecting the child's welfare; and that this includes, to some extent, matters of conscience and religious conviction" (p. 167). He went on to argue that the state has an interest in ensuring "that children be both safeguarded from abuses and given opportunities for growth into free and independent well-developed men and citizens" (p. 165). Thus, while the Court has recognized that parents have a right to rear their children according to their beliefs and customs, this right can also be limited if the Court sees a legitimate interest in doing so. According to the Prince decision, this obligation is most pertinent when it is designed to protect children from abuse.

Due Process

Following in the liberal tradition that protects individuals from the state are concerns about rights of due process, which are derived from political theories concerning the "rule of law" and procedural justice. Rule of law theories are based on the idea that justice is dependent on written legal codes and established laws. According to this theory, written law preserves justice because it is created by those whom it governs, but also it is because the law is available for all to see and is applicable to every citizen and the state (Allan, 1998). Under the rule of law, the state cannot create and apply arbitrary laws to its citizens. Furthermore, laws dictate the appropriate conduct of the state when it must interfere in the lives of citizens. In dealing with its citizens, rule of law theories hold that the state must follow guidelines of procedural and substantive fairness known as due process (Allan, 1998).

As applied to the rights of parents, due process and rule of law theories relate to the conduct of the state when it intervenes in the lives of families. In the United States, the Supreme Court has interpreted the due process clause of the 14th Amendment as protecting the rights of parents to the care, custody, and control of their children (*Meyer v. Nebraska,* 1923; *Pierce v. Society of Sisters,* 1925; *Prince v. Massachusetts,* 1944). Although the state may have legitimate reasons to intervene in the lives of families (*Prince v. Massachusetts,* 1944), a state cannot intervene unless it can demonstrate a compelling reason for doing so. The state's intervention must therefore be narrowly tailored to achieve the state's demonstrated objective.

In cases involving parental abuse and neglect, the state has a clear interest in intervening in family life. Even in these cases, however, the Supreme Court has held that the state must carefully protect the due process rights of parents (*Santosky v. Kramer,* 1982). In the majority opinion in the Santosky case, Justice Blackmun wrote:

> [T]he fundamental liberty interest of natural parents in the care, custody, and management of their child does not evaporate simply because they have not been model parents or have lost temporary custody of their child to the State. (p. 753)

Thus, while the Court has acknowledged that state intervention in family life is sometimes necessary, it also held that such intrusion must be limited by parents' due process rights.

Privacy

Political theories about social justice also include the concept of privacy. According to the utilitarian John Stuart Mill, a just society is one that attains the greatest amount of happiness for its citizens. In order to maximize happiness and promote well-being, Mill argues, individuals should be free to pursue self-development (Skorupski, 2005). Mill also argues that the function of the state is to help individuals achieve this end and the only reason that the state may exercise power over an individual is to prevent that individual from harming others (Skorupski, 2005). Similar to Locke, Mill contends that individuals have a right to private space where they can exercise self-determination and are free from state intervention.

Mill's conception of individual liberty is directly related to questions of privacy and is pertinent in debates about parental rights. Privacy rights bear on questions regarding birth control and abortion, same-sex relationships and marriages, and the rights of same-sex couples to start families. To some extent, these privacy issues have been debated by the Supreme Court. In 1965, the Supreme Court first articulated a constitutional right to privacy (*Griswold v. Connecticut,* 1965). In Griswold, the Court stated that within certain overlapping concepts of the Constitution (the "penumbra") are protections of privacy rights, where individuals are protected against state intrusion into private affairs. Justice Douglas, speaking for the Court wrote:

> We deal with a right of privacy older than the Bill of Rights. . . . Marriage is a coming together for better or for worse, hopefully enduring, and intimate to the degree of being sacred. (p. 486)

Since Griswold, the Court has expanded the rights of privacy to include family matters such as contraception and abortion (*Eisenstadt v. Baird,* 1972; *Planned Parenthood of Southeastern Pennsylvania v. Casey,* 1992; *Roe v. Wade, 1973*).

Despite initial judgments that state laws prohibiting homosexuality were legal (*Bowers v. Hardwick,* 1986), the Supreme Court has since ruled that laws prohibiting consensual homosexual intercourse violate the privacy protections of the Constitution (*Lawrence v. Texas,* 2003). In regards to the rights of homosexual individuals to have children, the

Supreme Court has been silent. Some state supreme courts have asserted their authority to intervene by relying on judgments about sexual conduct to deny gay men and lesbians custody and visitation rights to their biological children (*Bottoms v. Bottoms,* 1995). In addition, in Skinner and Kohler's view, because the adoption laws in several states require that parents be married, many state courts have denied same-sex adoption petitions.

Thus, while the courts have recognized the importance of privacy rights, they have also been inconsistent in their application of this theory. In controversial cases, such as the rights of homosexual couples, the Court has only recently recognized a right to privacy (*Lawrence v. Texas*, 2003). The Court has not yet determined its position with regard to homosexual parents.

Equal Protection

An analysis of social justice in political theory would not be complete without a discussion of equality. While there are many theories regarding the types of equality that can be attained, liberal theories are primarily concerned with the equality of individuals in relationship to the state. Political theories on equality hold that the law should apply equally to everyone and that all individuals should be treated the same. Such theories were prolific during the 17th and 18th centuries. Thomas Hobbes and Jean Jacques Rousseau wrote that individuals possessed equal rights in a state of nature. Emmanuel Kant and John Locke both argued that individuals have a natural and moral right to freedom (Gosepath, 2007). In American society, equality theories were codified in the 14th Amendment to the Constitution, asserting that all men are entitled to "equal protection of the laws" (Constitution of the United States, 1868).

In its application to parental rights, research has demonstrated that equality principles have not been adequately applied in child welfare cases (Dettlaff & Rycraft, 2010; U.S. Department of Health and Human Services, Administration for Children and Families, 2008). For instance, literature has established that children of color are overrepresented in child welfare systems, that minority parents have less access to services, and that minority children remain in foster care longer (Dixon, 2008). While the Supreme Court has not yet heard any cases regarding the disproportionality of minority children in child welfare systems, literature suggests that this is probably because these cases settle early or are dismissed on procedural grounds (Dixon, 2008). Regardless, to ensure that social justice is afforded to parents involved in the child welfare system, it is necessary to be aware of principles of equality and equal protection.

DISCUSSION AND CONCLUSION

Conceptual Framework

Figure 12.1 presents a conceptual map of parental rights. Within liberal political theory, the three most fundamental rights are those of liberty, equality, and the rule of law. As discussed previously, these three rights protect parents against undue state interference. The concept of liberty includes the ideas of the autonomous self and the autonomous family. As discussed by Mill and Locke, this theory protects the rights of parents to rear children according to their own beliefs and customs. The concept of equality further protects the rights of parents to rear children. The overlap between autonomy and equality reinforces the idea that the customs and values of any individual parent are equal and valid in comparison with other customs and values. They are also worthy of protection against the unnecessary intrusion of the state. Also secured in the overlap of liberty and equality are privacy rights within families and freedom for individuals to make their own choices regarding procreation, child rearing, and marriage.

Figure 12.1 also demonstrates the overlapping rights of liberty and rule of law. This combination of freedom and rules ensures that any state intervention in the family must be justified by a legitimate and important state interest, while respecting the due process rights of parents. Finally, the overlap of the rule of law and equality gives rise to the rights of parents to equal protection. The combination of these fundamental rights supports parents in their relationships with their children and protects them from outside interference. In the United States, these rights have been codified by the Constitution and supported by the Supreme Court.

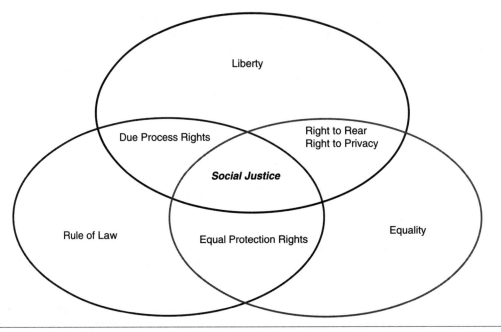

Figure 12.1   Concept Map of Parental Rights

Limitations to a Rights Analysis Within Families

Political theories on social justice have much to offer a discourse on parental rights. By providing a framework for balancing the liberties and protections of individuals against the interests of the state, political theories help clarify which rights are fundamental and deserving of protection. It is clear from the theoretical discussions alone, but also their application in Supreme Court cases, that parents have a right to privacy within their family and that they should be protected as much as possible from state intervention. It is also clear that in order for the state to interfere in the lives of families, it must have a legitimate and narrowly tailored interest in the protection of children. Furthermore, in its intervention in the lives of families, the state must adhere to the rule of law, make its purpose clear, and respect the due process and equal protection rights of individuals.

While political theories are useful in framing the discussion of state intervention and the rights of parents, conceptual problems arise out of a discussion of the rights of individuals within families because the family is viewed as a single entity when considering protections against state intrusion (Kelly, 2002). As the Supreme Court discovered in *Prince v. Massachusetts* (1944), however, there are times when individuals within a family need protection from other family members. A conception of parental rights based on the family as a single entity does not account for these circumstances.

Another criticism of a rights-based framework is that it creates an adversarial system under which the rights of individuals must be mediated. This is particularly problematic within families, especially in cases of abuse. Such a framework requires that the rights of one individual be limited so that the rights of another individual can be championed. It follows then that the rights of one family member (the abused) are in conflict with the rights of another (the abuser). The competing rights are then litigated in the adversarial environment of the courts, where both parties are provided with attorneys. This antagonistic process is generally harmful to families.

In addition, a preoccupation with the rights of the participants distracts attention from understanding and mitigating the complex circumstances that caused the harmful conditions in the first place. Particularly in child welfare cases, where the purpose of state intervention is to improve conditions for the entire family, a focus on the rights of individuals is not always helpful.

Application to Social Welfare

A discussion of the application of political theories to social welfare brings us back to the NASW *Code of Ethics*. Social workers have a responsibility to act politically and to protect families against injustices. Included in this social justice goal is the duty to protect individuals from undue infringement by the state. Social workers also have a responsibility to protect individuals from harming others. An appreciation for parental rights is useful in understanding how to balance these sometimes competing duties. Importantly, social workers are both helpers in society and agents of social control. Child welfare workers, in particular, have considerable authority in the lives of families, and it is important to remember that in this function, as representatives of the state, child welfare workers are subject to the same legal and political restraints placed on government. As such, social workers should remain ever vigilant about the rights of their clients and protect them from unnecessary interference, even from the workers themselves. As stated in the *Code of Ethics* (2009), social workers should "respect and promote the right of clients to self-determination" (1.02 Self-Determination section).

This analysis also serves as a reminder that principles of social justice are constant, even when circumstances make one wish otherwise. In cases of child abuse, it is tempting to ignore the legitimate rights of parents in order to protect children. As Justice Brandeis warned in Olmstead v. United States (1928), however,

> Experience should teach us to be most on our guard to protect liberty when the government's purposes are beneficent. . . . The greatest dangers to liberty lurk in insidious encroachment by men of zeal, well-meaning but without understanding. (p. 479)

Even when trying to protect maltreated children, workers need to take into account the principles of personal autonomy, privacy, due process, and equal protection. While social workers should not stop advocating for children, they need to actively take into account the rights of parents and thereby promote social justice for both parents and children.

REFERENCES

Allan, T. R. S. (1998). Rule of law (Rechtsstaat). In E. Craig (Ed.), *Routledge encyclopedia of philosophy*. London, UK: Routledge. Retrieved November 12, 2010, from http://www.rep.routledge.com/article/T022

Colmo, C. A. (2005, April 7). *Education and the family in Plato's Republic*. Paper presented at the annual meeting of The Midwest Political Science Association, Palmer House Hilton, Chicago, Ill. Retrieved from http://www.allacademic.com/meta/p86601_index.html

Constitution of the United States: Amendment XIV. (1868). Retrieved November 11, 2010, from http://www.archives.gov/exhibits/charters/constitution_amendments_11-27.html

Dettlaff, A. J., & Rycraft, J. R. (2010). Factors contributing to disproportionality in the child welfare system: Views from the legal community. *Social Work, 55*(3), 213–224.

Dixon, J. (2008). The African-American child welfare act: A legal redress for African-American disproportionality in child protection cases. *Berkeley Journal of African-American Law & Policy, 10*(2), 109–145.

Gilles, S. G. (1996). On educating children: A parentalist manifesto. *University of Chicago Law Review, 63*, 937–1034.

Gosepath, S. (2007). Equality. In E. N. Zalta (Ed.), *The Stanford encyclopedia of philosophy*. Palo Alto, CA: Stanford. Retrieved October 19, 2010, from http://plato.stanford.edu/entries/equality/

Kelly, K. A. (2002). Private family, private individual: John Locke's distinction between paternal and political power. *Social Theory and Practice, 28*(3), 361–380.

Locke, J. (1988). *Two treatises of government.* Cambridge, MA: Cambridge University Press.

National Association of Social Workers (NASW). (2009). *Code of ethics of the National Association of Social Workers*. Retrieved October 19, 2010, from http://www.naswdc.org/pubs/code/code.asp

Okin, S. M. (1977). Philosopher queens and private wives: Plato on women and family. *Philosophy and Public Affairs, 6*(4), 345–369.

Rawls, J. (2004). On justice as fairness. In M. Clayton & A. Williams (Eds.), *Social justice* (pp. 49–84). Malden, MA: Blackwell.

Skorupski, J. (2005). Mill, John Stuart. In E. Craig (Ed.), *Routledge encyclopedia of philosophy.* London, UK: Routledge. Retrieved November 11, 2010, from http://www.rep.routledge.com/article/DC054SECT12

U.S. Department of Health and Human Services, Administration for Children and Families. (2008). *The Adoption and Foster Care Analysis and Reporting System (AFCARS) report.* Washington, DC: U.S. Government Printing Office.

Waldron, J. (1998). Liberalism. In E. Craig (Ed.), *Routledge encyclopedia of philosophy.* London, UK: Routledge. Retrieved November 11, 2010, from http://www.rep.routledge.com/article/S035SECT1

COURT CITATIONS

Bottoms v. Bottoms, 457 S.E.2d 102 (Va. 1995).

Bowers v. Hardwick, 478 U.S. 186 (1986).

Eisenstadt v. Baird, 405 U.S. 438 (1972).

Griswold v. Connecticut, 381 U.S. 479 (1965).

Lawrence v. Texas, 539 U.S. 558 (2003).

Meyer v. Nebraska, 262 U.S. 390 (1923).

Olmstead et al. v. United States, 277 U.S. 438 (1928).

Pierce v. Society of Sisters, 268 U.S. 510 (1925).

Planned Parenthood of Southeastern Pennsylvania v. Casey, 505 U.S. 833 (1992).

Prince v. Massachusetts, 321 U.S. 158 (1944).

Roe v. Wade, 410 U.S. 113 (1973).

Santosky v. Kramer, 455 U.S. 745 (1982).

Stanley v. Illinois, 405 U.S. 645 (1972).

Troxel v. Granville, 530 U.S. 99 (2000).

Wisconsin v. Yoder, 406 U.S. 205 (1972).

13

Economic Theories of Social Justice

Anupama Jacob

Introduction

The continuing debates on the diverse and competing conceptualizations of "social justice" are shaped by underlying values, political ideologies, and economic conditions. The inherent moral dimension of social justice is reflected in opposing views about the nature of a "good" or "just" society. These views are often based on what people consider to be an equitable distribution of rights and responsibilities, income and resources, as well as capacities and entitlements. The challenges inherent in these debates relate to defining an equitable distribution and *who* should decide what is fair.

The idea of social justice also includes economic justice that focuses on a fair distribution of the benefits obtained from economic resources. Economic justice can be said to be guided by three principles. The first emphasizes equality of opportunity to engage in productive work and own property and other assets. The second principle emphasizes the right of every individual to be rewarded in proportion to his or her contribution. The third principle focuses on removing the barriers (such as monopolies or exploitation of certain groups of individuals) to establishing a fair economic order for all

members of society (Center for Economic and Social Justice, n.d.).

Economists have remained divided on how to define a just society and how to attain and sustain one. Mainstream economic theory has generally avoided questions of fairness by taking a value-neutral stance and maintaining that "economics deals with ascertainable facts; ethics with valuations and obligations. The two fields of inquiry are not on the same plane of discourse" (Robbins, 1932/2007, p. 132). Economists have instead argued that when rational individuals are free to pursue their own economic self-interest, the common good is maximized in the form of economic growth and improvements in living standards for the nation as a whole.

Economists also differ in their views on the role of the market in promoting a good society and the function of the government in this regard. One group of economists strongly favors a market economy with minimal government intervention. This group believes that the welfare of society is enhanced when individuals are offered economic incentives to succeed through the market. Another group contends that there are times when the government needs to step in and direct the market in order to address market failures. They argue that free markets cannot be considered just and that a just society must address economic and social disparities among its members (Sandel, 2009). Debates continue as to whether an equitable distribution of resources requires a free market approach, government intervention, or some combination of the two.

Sen, a Nobel Prize winning economist, pioneered what he called the "capability approach" that emphasizes the ability of individuals to develop capabilities to realize their potential and lead valued lives. The ability to develop capabilities in turn is dependent on an individual's access to resources and opportunities. Sen (1970, 1993) argues that the customary narrow focus of standard economic theory on the self-interest of individuals overlooks what they actually want, need, or are capable of realizing.

The main objective of this analysis is to present an overview of economic theories of justice by drawing attention to the free market versus intervention approach and then discussing Sen's capability approach. The "living wage" movement is used as a case study for exploring the economic arguments for and the social justice dimensions of a living wage. The chapter concludes with a conceptual map that shows integration of the economic perspectives.

Economic Theories of Social Justice

The concepts of fairness and justice do not form the basis of standard economic theory. Economic ideologies, however, shape the environment in which economic and social rights are debated. Since economists vary in their beliefs on the nature of a good or fair society, this section provides an overview of three economic approaches to the idea of justice or welfare, namely, the free market approach, the intervention approach, and the capability approach. Each of these approaches reflects underlying beliefs about how the economy should be organized, the role of the government, and the design of policies that seek to address economic and social inequities.

The Free Market Versus Intervention Approach

Adam Smith (1723–1790) is one of the earliest advocates of a market economy with minimal government intervention. Smith opposed the prevailing ideas of mercantilism in the 17th and 18th centuries that regulated the markets to serve the interests of merchants and the revenues of the crown (Stabile, 2008). Instead, he believed that in a free market in which individuals are free to pursue their own economic self-interest, the so-called invisible hand of the marketplace will maximize the common good in the form of economic growth and improvements in living standards for the nation as a whole. Smith also argued that a free market would result in the production of goods that would benefit society. In one of his most well-known quotes, Smith notes that "it is not from the benevolence of the butcher, the brewer or the baker, that we expect our dinner, but from their regard for their own interest" (Smith 1776/1976, p. 18). Smith believes that the government's role in promoting a flourishing economy should be limited to maintaining a "competitive environment," guaranteeing protection from external and internal threats or disorder, and investing in public goods, such as roads and education (Pressman, 2006, p. 37).

Two of the most well-known proponents of the free market philosophy in the 20th century are Austrian economist Friedrich von Hayek (1899–1992) and American economist Milton Friedman (1912–2006). Echoing Smith's sentiments, Hayek argues in favor of individual choice and minimal government interference in the economy. In his famous book, *The Road to Serfdom*, Hayek (1944) contends that government planning and expanding collectivism ultimately leads to a totalitarian system that devalues individual liberty. The inherently coercive nature of the welfare state thus entails a reverting to serfdom. Both Hayek and Friedman believe that economic freedom is an integral part of individual freedom.

Friedman (1962/2002) maintains that while political freedom means "the absence of coercion of a man by his fellow men," economic freedom can be realized only through a free market (p. 15). He further notes that "by removing the organization of economic activity from the control of political authority, the market eliminates this source of coercive power. It enables economic strength to be a check to political power rather than a reinforcement"

(p. 15). A democracy, argues Friedman (1998), not only promotes political freedom but also requires a free market to thrive because an individual whose livelihood is not independent of government cannot possibly make political decisions freely.

By interfering in the economy, governments simply exacerbate economic problems. Hayek (1944) further argues that no individual could fully understand the complex nature of the market economy, making interventionist economic policies inherently faulty. Hayek also argues against the idea of a "middle way," stating that planning and competition are "alternative principles used to solve the same problem, and a mixture of the two means that neither will really work and the result will be worse than if either system had been consistently relied upon" (p. 42). Hayek notes that his main critique is that planning is not a substitute for competition.

Hayek (1944) also believes that the idea of government providing equal economic opportunity is misleading because equality before the law acts as a safeguard against the coercive capacity of the government. Hayek further argues against the idea of fairness because what the state determines to be fair may in fact be at odds with the rights of individuals to property or freedom. If planning, wealth distribution, and competition fall under the state's domain, then the state becomes the final authority of what is right and wrong in a society. Despite their emphasis on a residualist role for government, Hayek and Friedman both acknowledge that a free market does not completely remove the need for government to maintain law and order, protect property rights, impose the "rules of the game," regulate competition, and protect against the creation of monopolies (Friedman, 1962/2002, p. 15).

Hayek and Friedman's ideas were especially popular among conservative political leaders (such as Margaret Thatcher in Britain and President Reagan in the 1980s to mid-1990s) who endorsed cutbacks in wasteful government welfare expenditures, privatization of services, and more effective management of the economy (Stewart, 2000). During this period, some critics also argued that welfare programs had worsened social conditions rather than improving the general standard of living. One such vociferous critic is American libertarian political scientist Charles Murray (1984) whose main thesis in his well-known book, *Losing Ground*, is that government social policies that were designed to help the poor in the 1960s and 1970s succeeded only in further worsening the problem of poverty.

The almost universal acceptance of the free market approach was challenged in the 1930s with the onset of the Great Depression. The 20th century saw ideas of government intervention express themselves through a word called *planning*, particularly in the form of concrete government economic policies. The main purpose of intervention was not only economic planning and development but also the promotion of people's welfare. In the West, William Henry Beveridge (1879–1963) and John Maynard Keynes (1883–1946), both British economists, are two of the most well-known interventionists of this period who support capitalism as the best economic system but at the same time recognize the "human implications of capitalism" (George & Wilding, 1976, p. 43). These interventionists did not believe in egalitarianism, but they were similar in their confidence in "the benevolent potentialities of government action" (p. 52). Their core argument was that the state must step in to ensure the efficient functioning of the system as well as correct for the harmful effects of market failure, with particular emphasis on unemployment.

Beveridge has been called the "father of the welfare state" (Berend, 2006, p. 231). He believed that the powers of the state should be used to fight what he called the five giant evils that jeopardized individual liberty: want, disease, ignorance, squalor, and idleness (George & Wilding, 1976). Beveridge (1942) stressed the role of government in pursuing a national minimum below which no citizen should be allowed to fall, although he did not support complete state control of the economy to achieve this goal. To achieve such a national minimum, Beveridge advocated for the use of insurance. Beveridge, however, did not believe that it was the government's responsibility to provide more than the minimum, arguing that there should be room for individuals to include voluntary insurance to enhance the state provided minimum (George & Wilding, 1976). A modified version of his 1942 report was adopted by the British Labor party in 1945 and included the National Health Service, family allowances, social security, and education and housing programs (Handel, 1982). As public funding of services and benefits became legitimized, support for government intervention and public outlays soon took hold in Western Europe, leading to the postwar European welfare state (Berend, 2006).

Keynes (1936/2009) was extremely critical of the classic economic theory of market equilibrium and the notion that the market was self-regulating. Although Keynes did not think it necessary to nationalize the economy, he contended that the government must intervene to stimulate employment and promote economic development. According to Keynes, there were particular times for the government to step in and direct the market. For example, government intervention in the form of increased spending or lower taxes could promote consumption and investment during a recession. Keynes's ideas provided the theoretical foundation for government policies to end the Great Depression in the 1930s (Pressman, 2006). With Keynes, economic policy came to stand side by side with social policy. Although Keynes did not directly push the concept of "rights," his ideas provided a foundation for the establishment of institutions and policies that sought to support the realization of economic and social rights (Williams, 1989). Although Keynesian ideas began to lose their sway, starting in the 1970s, the fundamental debate continues: Is the welfare of society best promoted through government intervention or a laissez-faire, minimalist free market approach?

The Capability Approach

Sen (1983, 1992, 1999, 2006) laid the groundwork for a paradigm shift in the way human development and welfare is conceptualized. Sen (2009) argues that "the question 'what is a just society' is not a good *starting point* for a useful theory of justice" and not a "plausible *end-point* either" (p. 105, italics added). Criticizing standard economic theory, Sen contends that income and standards of living matter only because they are the means to what is truly important, namely, a person's capability to function in society. Sen (1985, 1993) employs the terms *functionings* and *capabilities* to articulate his

ideas. The term *functionings* refers to an "achievement" and can vary from basic nourishment and good health to attaining self-respect and social integration. Individuals differ in the value they place on each type of functioning. The term *capabilities* refers to, on the other hand, what individuals are able to achieve ("doing" or "being") based on the choices available to them.

The capability approach is concerned with the "fair distribution of capabilities—the resources and power to exercise self-determination—to achieve well-being" (Morris, 2002, p. 368). In other words, a person's quality of life is determined by the "capability to achieve valuable functionings" (Sen, 1993, p. 31) and the freedom to choose between different ways of life. For example, having an education provides individuals with the freedom to achieve what they want, including receiving an income that allows them to sustain a lifestyle of their choice. Income or lifestyle is then the outcome or functioning that the capability—education—allows them to achieve. Education, however, may also be considered intrinsically valuable because of its relative importance to an individual or society in terms of the opportunities that education offers for individual or societal well-being (Wagle, 2008). Similarly, if individuals value good health (a functioning), a question to ask is if they have the capabilities needed to achieve this goal in the form of clean water, sanitation facilities, access to health care, and protection from infections? Capabilities are thus dependent on individual characteristics, social and economic arrangements, and political and civil liberties (Sen, 1999).

Although Sen (1992) acknowledges that the lack of economic means continues to influence a person's ability to pursue well-being, income is just one of many possible influences on capability deprivation. It is not enough to look at the goods an individual can effectively acquire. It is more important to examine how well individuals can function based on the goods and services available to them (Clark, 2005). Further, the effect of income on capabilities will likely vary among individuals, households, and communities (Kanbur & Squire, 1999). Sen acknowledges that structural factors, such as class, race, discrimination, and disability, can act as barriers to the ability of an individual to achieve their capabilities. The idea of social justice based on the capability approach rests on the belief that such barriers must be addressed in order to help those individuals who might need additional resources to develop their capabilities. For example, if a person faces discrimination in the job market because of a disability, it prevents them from developing the capability to function in ways that are meaningful to them.

Another example Sen (1983) provides is that of a bicycle. An individual may be interested in a bicycle (a commodity or resource), not so much for its physical characteristics but because it provides a cheap and convenient means of transport. However, a person cannot derive utility from the bike if he or she cannot use it to be mobile due to individual constraints (such as lack of balance), social constraints (such as women not being allowed to bike), or environmental constraints (such as lack of proper roads or bike paths). Mobility in this example would be the functioning that the capability, being able to bike, provides the individual. Thus, owning the commodity, in this case a bicycle, alone does not tell us what utility an individual can derive from it. The bicycle example illustrates that economic resources may be key to promoting certain capabilities. However, capabilities also depend on individual characteristics, social and economic organization, cultural norms, as well as political and civic freedoms and rights.

Sen does not endorse any fixed or predetermined set of capabilities, although he does suggest examples of intrinsically valuable capabilities (such as longevity, good health, and literacy) that also form the basis of the Human Development Index (HDI) and the Human Poverty Index (HPI) developed by the United Nations Development Program (UNDP) in 1990. Human development can be defined as "a *process* of enlarging people's choices and the *level* of their achieved well-being" (*Human Development Report* [*HDR*], 1990, p. 10, italics in original). There are thus two components to human development. The first focuses on capabilities such as education or health. The second focuses on how individuals use their capabilities in terms of work or leisure activities. The HDI is said to take a "conglomerative perspective" that concentrates on the improvements made by all groups of a society. The HPI, on the other hand, takes a "deprivational perspective" that assesses advances made by the poor and deprived in a given society. The HPI also distinguishes between the quality of life in developing (HPI-I) and developed (HPI-2) countries.

In order to measure the overall quality of life, these measures focus on three key elements: life expectancy at birth, literacy, and standard of living. To measure standard of living, the HDI uses purchasing-power adjusted real GDP per capita. The HPI-1 uses percentage of population with access to health services and safe water, and, percentage of malnourished children under age 5, while the HPI-2 uses percentage of population below 50% of median household disposable income (*HDR*, 1990, 1997; UNDP, n.d.).

One major drawback of composite measures like the HDI or HPI is that they omit several other elements that can be considered essential to human development, including political freedom, protection against discrimination or violence, and physical environment. In other words, while the HDI includes essential dimensions, such as health and education, it still fails to account for the various aspects of "economic, political, and civic or cultural exclusion" (Wagle, 2002, p. 162). Another drawback is that the measures can be used to rank countries around the world, but the distinctions or overlaps in the individual dimensions cannot be isolated.

The UNDP's 2010 *Human Development Report* introduced the Multidimensional Poverty Index (MPI). Developed by two economists, Sabina Alkire and James Foster at the University of Oxford, the MPI is a new international measure of poverty that is to replace the HPI. Grounded in the capability approach, the MPI complements income poverty measures by directly measuring the number of deprivations a poor person faces simultaneously with respect to education, health, and living standard. While most appropriate for developing countries, the MPI makes it possible to get a clear picture of people living in poverty, both across countries, regions, and the world and within countries by ethnic group, urban or rural location, and other key household characteristics (*HDR*, 2010).

Sen has been praised for bringing the focus back to individuals as the ends themselves and recognizing that different individuals and societies are likely to have different values and goals (Clark, 2005).

At a fundamental level, the capability approach views human beings as individuals with agency who should have the freedom to make choices about what they want to be or do and how to utilize the resources that they are able to access (Lister, 2004). The capability approach connects with notions of well-being and quality of life by focusing on the kind of life every individual should be able to achieve in order to flourish.

The capability approach uses terms such as *freedom, choice, values*, and *opportunities* (Wagle, 2008). The approach focuses on the elements of a good life for an individual and how the capability framework can help build a more just society (Sugden, 1993). Sen (1985) maintains that a just society emerges when individuals have the freedom to freely decide on the type of life they want to lead, what they can and cannot do, and what they can and cannot be.

In summary, Each of the three economic approaches discussed in this section have different takes on the idea of justice or welfare, how it is to be promoted in a society, and what the role of the state should be in this regard. The free market approach strongly favors individual choice and minimal government involvement in the economy. Advocates of the free market argue that if the government is to decide what is fair, then the state becomes the final authority of what is right or wrong in a society. Further, interventionist policies are considered inherently faulty because no individual can fully comprehend the working of the market economy. Proponents of this approach argue that it is only when individuals are free to pursue their own economic self-interest that the so-called invisible hand of the market maximizes the common good in the form of improved standards of living for society as a whole.

Interventionists counter the free market approach by arguing that government take an active role in planning and implementing concrete economic policies. They maintain that the main goal of government involvement was not economic growth alone but also to improve people's welfare. The underlying belief is that government action can mitigate the impact of market failures on individual well-being.

This group thus pushes for the establishment of policies that promote economic and social rights.

Criticizing standard economic theory, the capability approach stresses that income and standards of living matter only because they are the means to what is truly important, namely, a person's ability to function and participate on an equal basis with mainstream society. By building on the nature of economic and social needs, this approach can help inform the debate on the political, social, and economic framework that helps individuals develop the capacity to function and promotes their overall well-being in a particular society.

How can a society help individuals, particularly low-income workers, achieve the kind of life they wish to lead? From an economic perspective, individuals must be able to earn a wage that allows them to meet not only their basic needs but also offer opportunities for them to improve their overall well-being. The next section discusses the living wage movement as an example of one way individuals can be enabled to become self-sufficient and productive citizens.

SOCIAL JUSTICE AND THE LIVING WAGE: A CASE EXAMPLE

The concept of a living wage has existed since the onset of industrialization and the growth of wage labor. The ideological roots of this concept continue to endure despite the trend toward market-determined wage levels. A living wage is defined as a wage rate that allows workers to meet their "basic needs." Although there is no consensus as to what the term *basic needs* includes, there is some consensus that a living wage should provide a certain minimum standard of living that goes beyond mere physical sustenance (Shelburne, 1999). This belief can be traced back to the writings of Adam Smith (1776/1976) who notes that if future generations are to survive, a person's work and earnings must be able to sustain not only the individual but also his or her family. The principal objective of a living wage is to enable individuals to be self-supporting and sufficient to lift families out of poverty. However, it is not clear when a person becomes self-supporting or when an individual is "out" of poverty, but these hotly contested issues are beyond the scope of this chapter (Quigley, 2003).

It was the living wage movement that spurred the enactment of the first national minimum wage laws in the form of the Fair Labor Standards Act in 1938 that established the standard of a decent living wage standard (Neumark, 2002; Pollin, Brenner, Wicks-Linn, & Luce, 2008). Reflecting the acceptance of the Keynesian idea that government can play a positive role, the minimum wage was seen as a strategy to increase the income of the poor (Waltman, 2008). The current federal minimum wage is $7.25. Eighteen states have minimum wages higher than the federal rate (including California), 23 states have minimum wages that equal the federal rate, four states have minimum wages less than the federal rate, and 5 states do not have any minimum wage requirements (Department of Labor, 2011). It is interesting to note here that full-time minimum wage labor has failed to help individuals escape from below the federal poverty line in more than a decade. Yet the minimum wage is taken as the starting point for discussions on living wages that have yet to occur at the federal government level in the development of actual policy (Quigley, 2003). If the social justice goal is to enable individuals to become self-reliant through employment, it is important to consider what it would take to achieve this goal.

The methodological and operational challenges in determining an appropriate wage level or minimum acceptable standard of living reflect the inherently subjective nature of such a task. Despite attempts to ascertain such a level using "objective," or scientific means, the efforts are frequently influenced by underlying ideologies, social norms, and economic conditions. Glickman (1997) defines a living wage as "a wage level that offers workers the ability to support families to maintain self-respect and to have both the means and the leisure to participate in the civic life of the nation" (p. 66). In this definition, a living wage includes an element of decency that clearly takes social needs into consideration. Adam Smith understood this concept in 1776 when he wrote,

> By necessaries I understand not only the commodities which are indispensably necessary for the support of

life but whatever the custom of the country renders it indecent for creditable people, even of the lowest order, to be without. A linen shirt, for example, is strictly speaking not a necessity of life. . . . But in the present time . . . a creditable day labourer would be ashamed to appear in public without a linen shirt. (Smith as cited in Lister 2004, p. 26).

While Glickman and Smith's ideas of a decent wage do not specify a wage level, they do reflect Sen's capability approach. Being more interested in the development of human capabilities, Sen (1999) notes that living wages are more than just income because society needs not only competent workers but also productive citizens; in essence, "human beings are not merely the means of production, but also the end of the exercise" (pp. 295–296). The focus then turns to the question of how living wages can help individuals, particularly low-income workers, develop their capabilities to achieve what they value.

Local Living Wage Ordinances

In the United States, the living wage movement has typically focused on increasing the minimum wage at the local level. Local living wage ordinances also tend to be tied to the federal poverty line that has long been considered outdated and flawed (Besharov & Couch, 2009; Citro & Michael, 1995). The city of Baltimore was the first to pass a living wage ordinance in 1994. Since then, around 50 jurisdictions have adopted living wage ordinances, and another 75 are participating in living wage movements (Quigley, 2003).

While living wage rates vary greatly across localities due to variations in local costs-of-living, they exceed both national and state-level minimum wage rates. However living wage laws, unlike minimum wage legislation, have limited coverage because they are limited to businesses that are on contract with the city (Fairris & Reich, 2005; Neumark, 2002). For example, the living wage ordinance in San Francisco includes businesses operating on property owned by the city and county government, such as an airport or marina (Fairris & Reich, 2005). The living wage coalition in San Francisco began in 1998 and included labor unions, community groups, and religious organizations. The coalition declares that a full-time worker should be able to support his or her family without governmental aid or charity. For that reason, the coalition campaigns for economic justice and seeks to promote "a more prosperous, healthier and livable community" (San Francisco Living Wage Coalition, n.d.).

The grassroots campaign led to the approval of the living wage laws, known as the Minimum Compensation Ordinance (2000) and the Health Care Accountability Ordinance (2001). Businesses contracting with the city to provide services were required to pay a minimum living wage rate of $11.54 an hour as well as provide 12 paid vacation days and health care coverage. The city estimates that the living wage ordinance has benefited over 30,000 workers (San Francisco Living Wage Coalition, n.d.).

The living wage calculator, developed by Pennsylvania State University, estimates the living wage in the city and county of San Francisco for a single earner in a family of two adults and two children to be $32.70 an hour by accounting for food, housing, transportation, child care, medical, and miscellaneous expenses. A living wage rate of even $11.54 then falls far short of its goal to help families become self-sufficient using the federal poverty threshold of $22,113 for a family of two adults with two children under the age of 18 (U.S. Census Bureau, 2010).

Some of the items listed in the coalition's strategic plan for the future include the following: (a) increasing the base wage rate in the Minimum Compensation Ordinance where $32 per hour is a long-term goal; (b) expanding coverage of health benefits to include dependents, spouses, and domestic partners of employees; (c) extending coverage of the Minimum Compensation Ordinance to workers on other city property; and (d) ensuring adequate funding to organize community-based education and outreach on the wage and benefit laws (San Francisco Living Wage Coalition, n.d.).

Arguments For and Against the Living Wage

The idea of setting a minimum wage floor has its share of supporters and critics whose arguments reflect underlying beliefs about the role of the market and the state in helping individuals achieve self-sufficiency. Those in favor of a living wage contend that a living wage is an essential component of economic justice. Critics, however, counter this argument by noting that standard economic theories do not rely on the concepts of justice and fairness. It is also difficult to reach a consensus on what constitutes a living wage and why one should be provided to workers. Consequently, government intervention in determining a minimum wage floor goes against the principles of the free market school (Stabile, 2008). This section presents some of the key arguments for and against a living wage.

At the employee level, critics argue that living wages interfere with the incentive structures embedded in the market system. Advocates of the free market approach maintain that individuals should be free to choose to pursue activities they believe provide the best opportunities for economic well-being in relation to the value they add to a market economy. In other words, market wages are believed to reflect the individual worker's value-addition to the economy. The quest for a higher standard of living accordingly acts as an incentive to engage in or pursue more productive ventures by, for instance, investing in more training or education to find a job with higher earning potential. A living wage impedes the efficiency of this value-adding process by interfering with the entrenched incentive structure of the market economy (Stabile, 2008).

In contrast, supporters of a living wage argue that higher wages can stimulate more consumption in the economy by increasing the spending capacity of low-wage workers. Higher wages can also encourage workers to be more productive and efficient. Employers stand to gain only from the increased productivity of their workers. Even from a purely economic point of view, the economy cannot function properly if workers are "overused" and are unable to earn enough to support themselves and their families. For example, the lack of adequate nourishment or inability to access proper health care due to a lack of medical insurance can inhibit the productivity and earning potential of low-wage workers, limiting the individual's capability to achieve a better life. Proponents of a living wage recognize that negative outcomes, such as poor health, resulting from insufficient means can affect not only low-wage workers but also the rest of society in the form of overflowing social costs. In this case, a living wage would not only improve the standard of living for the most vulnerable members of society but also would help to address the social costs arising from the negative social and economic outcomes of low wages on the rest of society (Stabile, 2008).

At the employer level, advocates of the free market approach argue that wages are based on the value assigned by the market for certain skills and jobs. As a result, lower wages reflect the lower productivity of such workers. An artificial increase in wages might consequently result in employment losses by lowering the number of available low-wage jobs in the market. Employers might also fire low-wage workers in favor of workers with better skills or move to areas with lower wages as a response to the mandated higher wages. Businesses might also respond by passing on the higher labor costs to consumers in the form of higher prices on consumer products (Pollin et al., 2008).

In contrast, proponents of the living wage argue that higher wages might mean lower turnover rates for businesses. This could mean lower costs to administer, hire, and train new workers. In addition, businesses (particularly large ones) may not react to a wage increase by instantly moving to a different location but rather look for alternative ways to absorb the higher costs and still make a profit. Businesses may also try to offset the higher labor costs by becoming technologically more efficient or making technological advances (Bernstein, 2002; Pollin et al., 2008).

In summary, free market economists are not against the setting of a minimum level of security for members of a society. However, they caution against letting this minimum standard interfere with market-generated outcomes or the functioning of the market. The definition of this minimum level is perceived to be linked to the wealth of a society and its willingness to support poverty alleviation programs through the use of taxes (Stabile, 2008). It was in this context that Hayek (1944) viewed social justice as a deceptive concept because no one individual or organization can determine the economic outcome for a particular group of people beforehand (Morison, 2003). These ideas continue to reflect the concerns of those who argue that living

wages will lower the demand for low-skilled labor, increase prices, and result in unnecessary government interference in the economy. There is little evidence, however, that raising the minimum wage will negatively impact employment or price levels in any significant way (Card & Kreuger, 1994; Neumark, 2002; Quigley, 2003).

Supporters of the living wage have blurred the boundaries between the market economy and the moral economy. However, they need to be clear about where they draw the line on what constitutes a living wage and why. Bernstein (2002) notes that the living wage movement

> forces you to step back from the narrow economic arguments for and against the living wage and ask yourself the following question: Why does America, the largest and one of the most productive economies in the world, need to subsidize wages so that full-time, adult workers performing essential tasks can achieve a dignified life style? ("The Living Wage Movement")

According to Bernstein, it is time to critically examine how our policies can be better designed to encourage businesses to positively contribute to the economic life of the communities. It is here that "the living wage movement, by pointing the way to the high road, offers a timely and progressive alternative route" (Bernstein, 2002, "The Living Wage Movement," last para.).

DISCUSSION AND CONCLUSION

This chapter describes the contested nature of the concept of social justice among economists, namely, its meaning, its outcome measurement, and the role of government. Since the idea of justice is shaped by economic conditions as well as by the social and cultural norms of a society, it is difficult to define the characteristics or goals of a just or good society at a particular point in time. The definition of a just society is influenced by three schools of thought in the field of economics: the free market approach, intervention approach, and the capability approach as illustrated in Figure 13.1.

The figure highlights the core beliefs of each school of thought. The concept of the living wage reflects the core values of the intervention and

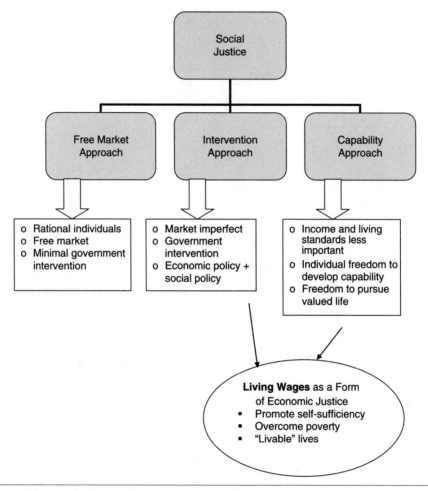

Figure 13.1   Mapping the Economic Theories of Social Justice

capability approaches in that there is a role for the state in ensuring that families have the opportunity to achieve self-sufficiency and a sense of overall well-being. The free market economists favor individual choice and minimal government intervention based on the belief that the common good or welfare of a society is best promoted by allowing rational individuals to pursue their self-interest. The interventionists, on the other hand, believe that the state must intervene to correct for market failures and ensure the efficient functioning of the system. They call for the establishment of institutions and policies that support the realization of both economic and social rights. The capability approach views income

and standards of living as a means to enhancing a person's capability to function in society where the economic and social arrangements help individuals achieve self-sufficiency.

The concept of a living wage aligns most closely with the capability approach. The central goal of the living wage movement is to help individuals and families become self-supporting and overcome poverty. A major advantage of a localized living wage movement is that it can take into account local costs-of-living as well as more clearly identify the local stakeholders. However, the coverage of workers is limited to businesses that have service contracts with the city. While the living wage is higher than the federally stipulated minimum wage, it still appears to fall short of enabling families to become fully self-sufficient. In San Francisco, the living wage coalition has made strides in improving the lives of some workers, but it continues to campaign for improved coverage of workers and benefits. Living wage movements have been mostly at the state and local level and have yet to take hold at the federal level in terms of major policy or legislation.

By providing a living wage, it is also hoped that individuals will not only be able to better meet their basic needs but also have opportunities to lead "livable" lives. The capability approach can in this context provide a framework for social justice. This approach acknowledges that a living wage is not a silver bullet and that the need for government intervention in addressing structural barriers could hinder an individual's ability to achieve the capabilities associated with self-sufficiency. By building knowledge about the nature of economic and social needs, the capability approach provides a political, social, and economic framework that can help individuals develop the capacity to function and promote an overall sense of well-being in a particular society.

REFERENCES

Berend, I. T. (2006). *An economic history of twentieth-century Europe.* New York: NY: Cambridge University Press.

Bernstein, J. (2002, March 4). The living wage movement—Viewpoints. Economic Policy Institute. Retrieved December 27, 2011, from http://www.epi.org/publication/webfeatures_viewpoints_lw_movement/

Besharov, D. J., & Couch, K. (2009). European measures of income, poverty, and social exclusion: Recent developments and lessons for U.S. poverty measurement. *Journal of Policy Analysis and Management, 28*(4), 713–752.

Beveridge, W. (1942). *Social insurance and allied services.* London, UK: H. M. Stationery Office.

Card, D., & Krueger, A. B. (1994). Minimum wages and employment: A case study of the fast-food industry in New Jersey and Pennsylvania. *American Economic Review, 84*(4), 772–793.

Center for Economic and Social Justice. (n.d.). *Defining economic justice and social justice.* Retrieved October 1, 2011, from http://www.cesj.org/thirdway/economicjustice-defined.htm

Citro, C. F., & Michael, R. T. (Eds.). (1995). *Measuring poverty: A new approach.* Washington, DC: National Academy Press.

Clark, D. A. (2005). *The capability approach: Its development, critiques and recent advances* (Report No. GPRG-WPS-032). Oxford, UK: Global Poverty Research Group.

Department of Labor. (2011). Minimum wage laws in the states—January 1, 2011. Retrieved October 5, 2011, from http://www.dol.gov/whd/minwage/america.htm#Consolidated

Fairris, D., & Reich, M. (2005). The impacts of living wage policies: Introduction to the special issue. *Industrial Relations, 44*(1), 1–13.

Friedman, M. (1998). Classical liberal as economic scientist. In W. Breit & R. L. Ransom (Eds.), *The academic scribblers* (pp. 223–260). Princeton, NJ: Princeton University Press.

Friedman, M. (2002). *Capitalism and freedom.* Chicago, IL: University of Chicago Press. (Original work published 1962)

George, V., & Wilding, P. (1976). *Ideology and social welfare.* London, UK: Routledge & Kegan Paul.

Glickman, L. (1997). *A living wage: American workers and the making of consumer society.* Ithaca, NY: Cornell University Press.

Handel, G. (1982). *Social welfare in Western society.* New York, NY: Random House.

Hayek, F. A. (1944). *The road to serfdom.* London, UK: Routledge.

Human Development Report 1990 (HDR). (1990). Defining and measuring human development. In *Concept and measurement of human development* (pp. 9–16). New York, NY: Oxford University Press.

Human Development Report 1997 (HDR). (1997). Poverty in the human development perspective: Concepts and measurement. In *Human development to eradicate poverty* (pp. 15–23). New York, NY: Oxford University Press.

Human Development Report 2010 (HDR). (2010). Innovations in measuring inequality and poverty). In *The real wealth of nations: Pathways to human development* (pp. 85–100). New York, NY: Oxford University Press.

Kanbur, R., & Squire, L. (1999, September). *The evolution of thinking about poverty: Exploring the interactions.* Retrieved November 1, 2009, from http://unstats.un.org/unsd/methods/poverty/edocuments.htm

Keynes, J. M. (2009). *The general theory of employment, interest, and money.* New York, NY: Classic Books America. (Original work published 1936)

Lister, R. (2004). *Poverty.* Cambridge, UK: Polity Press.

Morison, S. T. (2003). A Hayekian theory of social justice. *NYU Journal of Law & Liberty*. Retrieved September 30, 2011, from http://www.law.nyu.edu/ecm_dlv/groups/public/@nyu_law_website__journals__journal_of_law_and_liberty/documents/documents/ecm_pro_060892.pdf

Morris, P. (2002). The capabilities perspective: A framework for social justice. *Families in Society: The Journal of Contemporary Human Services, 83*(4), 365–373.

Murray, C. (1984). *Losing ground: American social policy, 1950–1980*. New York, NY: Basic Books.

Neumark, D. (2002). Raising incomes by mandating higher wages. *NBER Reporter*. Retrieved October 3, 2011, from http://www.nber.org/reporter/fall02/higherWages.html

Pollin, R., Brenner, M., Wicks-Linn, J., & Luce, S. (2008). *A measure of fairness: The economics of living wages and minimum wages in he United States*. Ithaca, NY: Cornell University Press.

Pressman, S. (2006). *Fifty major economists* (2nd ed.). New York, NY: Routledge.

Quigley, W. P. (2003). *Ending poverty as we know it: Guaranteeing a right to a job at a living wage*. Philadelphia, PA: Temple University Press.

Robbins, L. (2007). *An essay on the nature and significance of economic science*. London, UK: Macmillan. (Original work published 1932)

San Francisco Living Wage Coalition. (n.d.). *It's time for a living wage*. Retrieved September 21, 2011, from http://www.livingwage-sf.org/

Sandel, M. J. (2009). *Justice: What's the right thing to do?* New York, NY: Farrar, Straus, & Giroux.

Sen, A. K. (1970). The impossibility of a Paretian liberal. *Journal of Political Economy, 78*(1), 152–157.

Sen, A. K. (1983). Development: Which way now? *Economic Journal, 93*(372), 745–762.

Sen, A. K. (1985). *Commodities and capabilities*. Amsterdam, North-Holland, Netherlands: Elsevier Science.

Sen, A. K. (1992). *Inequality reexamined*. Cambridge, MA: Harvard University Press.

Sen, A. K. (1993). Capability and well-being. In A. Sen & M. Nussbaum (Eds.), *The quality of life* (pp. 30–53). Helsinki, Finland: United Nations University.

Sen, A. K. (1999). *Development as freedom*. New York, NY: Random House.

Sen, A. K. (2006). Conceptualizing and measuring poverty. In D. Grusky & R. Kanbur (Eds.), *Poverty and inequality* (pp. 30–46). Stanford, CA: Stanford University Press.

Sen, A. (2009). *The idea of justice*. Cambridge, MA: Belknap Press of Harvard University Press.

Shelburne, R. C. (1999). *The history and theory of the living wage concept*. Washington, DC: Division of Foreign Economic Research, U.S. Department of Labor.

Smith, A. (1976). *An inquiry into the nature and causes of the wealth of nations* (2 vols.). Chicago, IL: University of Chicago Press. (Original work published 1776)

Stabile, D. R. (2008). *The living wage*. Northampton, MA: Edward Elgar.

Stewart, J. (2000). Social policy. In M. Davies (Ed.), *Blackwell encyclopaedia of social work* (pp. 322–324). Oxford, UK: Blackwell.

Sugden, R. (1993). Welfare, resources, and capabilities: A review of inequality reexamined by Amartya Sen. *Journal of Economic Literature, 31*(4), 1947–1962.

U.S. Census Bureau. (2010). Poverty thresholds for 2010 by size of family and number of related children under 18 years. Retrieved January 6, 2012, from http://www.census.gov/hhes/www/poverty/data/threshld/thresh10.xls

United Nations Development Programme (UNDP). (n.d.). Statistics. Retrieved April 1, 2010, from http://hdr.undp.org/en/statistics/indices/hpi/

Wagle, U. (2002). *Rethinking poverty: Definition and measurement*. Paris, France: UN Educational, Scientific and Cultural Organization (UNESCO).

Wagle, U. R. (2008, June). *Capability and income poverty in the United States A comparative analysis of the measurement outcomes and poverty profiles between 1994 and 2004* (Working Paper Series, No. 08-09). Ann Arbor, MI: National Poverty Center.

Waltman, J. L. (2008). *Minimum wage policy in Great Britain and the United States*. New York, NY: Algora.

Williams, F. (1989). *Social policy: A critical introduction*. Cambridge, UK: Polity Press.

14

THEORIES OF ORGANIZATIONAL JUSTICE

Interdisciplinary Social Science Perspectives

HYUN SOO KWON

INTRODUCTION

Justice issues in organizations usually refer to matters affecting employees in the workplace that relate to the human resource management aspects of achieving productivity and profitability. Organizational justice concerns are related to individuals and human rights as well as organizational regulations and policy making (Sheppard, Lewicki, & Minton, 1992). In for-profit organizations, organizational justice issues often involve fairness of human resource policies, for example, hiring, evaluating and rewarding, and solving interpersonal disputes and conflicts (Greenberg, 1987). Greenberg (2009) identified some of the following reasons for renewed interest in organizational justice: (a) The maintenance of justice in the workplace provides benefits to the organizations by increasing positive commitment of employees to organizations (e.g., when fairly treated, workers tend to participate in their work with high levels of commitment to the organization, resulting in high performance and low

turnover [Dailey & Kirk, 1992]), (b) fair treatment can promote the perception of individual value and improve self-worth of employees in organizations, and (c) promoting justice in the workplace is important because it is a moral benefit.

The study of organizational justice is also part of the broader field of social justice research, and the focus of this chapter is to identify the theoretical foundations of organizational justice in order to develop a conceptual framework to increase our understanding of workplace justice. The chapter is organized around three traditional domains of organizational justice, namely, distributive justice, procedural justice, and interactional justice (interpersonal and informational justice). In addition, several concepts related to low-status workers are explored, including the related concepts of equity, stratification, and wage disparity, as well as perceptions of trust and fairness and organizational culture and norms.

The chapter begins with definitions of organizational justice related to distributive justice, procedural justice, and interactional justice (inter-personal and informational justice). Additional perspectives are identified in relation to both individual and group-level theories as well as the use of hypothetical reasoning (e.g., referent cognitions theory, fairness theory, and multifocal approaches). The chapter concludes with implications of organizational justice for practice.

JUSTICE IN AN ORGANIZATIONAL CONTEXT

From a social science perspective, organizational justice is often related to fair and unfair employment conditions within a social context of rewards and punishments (Folger & Cropanzano, 1998). Within an organizational context, justice is associated with rules and social norms that control outcomes of workers, define the distribution and procedures for decision making in organizations, and regulate the human dimension of organizational life (Folger & Cropanzano, 1998).

Philosophers have identified the prescriptive or normative concepts underlying organizational justice (Fortin & Fellenz, 2008). In essence, the goal of justice is to achieve "the flourishing of all members of the community" (Fortin & Fellenz, 2008, p. 419). For example, those who consider both equality and freedom tend to solve the unfair distribution of economic resources through democratic socialism, while those who value freedom more than equality tend to adopt free market capitalism to solve the same problem. In essence, organizational justice is defined as perceived justice, often perceived differently by all relevant stakeholders—managers, employees, and other interest groups, for example (Fortin & Fellenz, 2008).

The principles of balance and correctness provide another approach to perceiving justice in organizational contexts (Sheppard et al., 1992). The judgment of balance is applied in order to compare one action with another. The concept of balance is closely connected to the notion of organizational equity and outcome. In contrast, correctness relates to evaluating a decision, action, or procedure in order to make judgments about "rightness" in terms of "consistency, accuracy, clarity, procedural thoroughness, and compatibility with the morals and values of the times" (Sheppard et al., 1992, p. 11). From this relationship, balance (equity) and correctness are important elements to determine outcomes, procedures, and systems. It is clear that the nature of organizational justice is rooted in human behaviors that are governed by outcomes, procedures, and systems.

MAJOR FORMS OF ORGANIZATIONAL JUSTICE

The nature of organizational justice based on individual perceptions of fairness in the workplace has been defined over the years in terms of distributive justice, procedural justice, and interactional justice. All three theoretical approaches focus on the outcomes of justice and the procedures guiding the distribution of outcomes.

Distributive Justice and Equity Theory

Distributive justice is defined as "perceived fairness of the outcome or allocations that an individual receives" (Folger & Cropanzano, 1998, p. xxi). Distributive justice is about whether rewards or resources are fairly distributed to the members in the workplace as measured by the relative contributions of participants in an organization where the *outcome distribution* can be explained in terms of equity (Greenberg, 2011; Sheppard et al., 1992).

According to Adams (1963), equity theory relates to efforts by workers to assess the ratio of their contribution as work inputs and view rewards as the corresponding outcome with respect to expectations about "equal ratios" between themselves and others in the organization. Therefore, the assumption underlying the equal ratio is that fair considerations have been given to the contributions of their work to the workplace. In the equity theory, the lower ratio relates to the perception of being underpaid (with accompanying feelings of anger), and the high ratio involves perceptions of being overpaid (with accompanying feelings of guilt). Therefore, unequal ratios do not create balance and therefore can provoke dissatisfaction that calls for a realignment of inputs or outcome. For example, the lower paid people tend to decrease their inputs and the overpaid people tend to increase their performance (Greenberg, 1982).

Scholars have also criticized equity theory, especially related to highly paid workers and their behaviors. It was assumed that high-paid workers would generate high productivity to justify their compensation. That is, the workers who earn more than their apparent or perceived contribution to the organization may work hard to justify their salaries and maintain their self-esteem (Greenberg, 2011).

In sum, understanding justice in an organizational context involves making the connection between *equity* and *balance* regarding the fair distribution of rewards based on the contributions of each participant toward common goals.

Reactive-Proactive Studies

The reactive and proactive studies are an approach to examining distributive justice and equity theory based on individual behaviors. Greenberg (1987) applied this reactive-proactive approach to the study of equity theory with respect to distributions of outcome. While reactive studies of justice theory seek to identify how people react to avoid unfairness in the distribution of outcome and resources, proactive studies focus on how people attempt to promote fairness in a given situation (Chan, 2000; Greenberg, 1987). The reactive behavior of individuals in terms of equity involves the negative emotions emerging from the unequal ratio of input and outcome. It is assumed that low-paid workers are less productive and high-paid workers are more productive in comparison with those who are paid at the equilibrium level (Greenberg, 1987). In other words, these perceptions of unfair rewards are used to justify behaviors that help people deal with these unfair conditions (e.g., union organizing vs. board member defense of high corporate salaries). Another reactive approach to the unequal distribution of rewards is the relative deprivation framework described by Martin (1993). It is designed to determine the inequity of outcomes by comparing the contributions and rewards of individuals.

In contrast with the reactive approach, proactive concepts and theories focus on the more positive behaviors of individual workers related to making equitable outcomes. In this approach, workers are perceived as people who create fair rewards and distributive justice based on two theoretical frameworks, namely, the *justice judgment model* and the *justice motive theory*.

The proactive justice judgment model was developed by Leventhal (1976) based on three justice rules: the contributions rule, the needs rule, and the equality rule (Chan, 2000). The justice judgment model is based on the argument that implementing reward allocation, following the contribution rule, relates to promoting high productivity and work performance (Leventhal, 1976). The needs rule relates the welfare needs of individuals regardless of contribution. And finally, the equality rule involves equal distribution of outcomes. According to Leventhal (1976), the outcome distributors tend to use equality rule when they pursue social consensus. In other words, people tend to justify fairness in outcome distribution based on the three major justice rules of contribution, needs, and equality. The justice judgment model is complemented by the justice motive theory where outcome distribution is based on the interrelationship of competition (allocations based on performance outcomes), parity (equal allocations), equity (allocations based on contributions in relationship to others), and Marxian justice (allocations based on needs) that closely relate to the needs rule of the judgment model (Greenberg, 1987).

In sum, this interdisciplinary perspective examines the relationship between unequal rewarding and the notion of relative deprivation that can be used to address the problem and impact of wage disparities. While the reactive approach focuses more on *equity issues*, the proactive approach places more emphasis on the determinants of outcome distribution related to equity, equality, and need.

PROCEDURAL JUSTICE

Procedural justice is another form of perceived fairness related to the determination of outcome, especially decision making that involves outcome distribution or *dispute resolution* (grievance resolution) in an organization (Folger & Cropanzano, 1998).

According to Thibaut and Walker (1975), procedural justice includes the concepts of *process control* and *decision control*. The use of decision control in the dispute resolution could involve decisions made by a third party. While decision control features control over outcomes, process control relates to the control that individuals have over the decision-making process of the dispute resolution (Greenberg, 1990). Thibaut and Walker (1975) note that the adversary system in the United States represents a high degree of process control that includes the right to select an attorney. They found that there is positive relationship between the level of process control and the fairness in the resolution procedure.

On the other hand, Folger (1977) suggested that the concept of *voice* is more appropriate for explaining organizational justice than the notion of process control because the concept of voice includes an array of communication mechanisms, beyond the legal context, in which *fair-process effects* can be generated. In essence, voice provides people with an opportunity to express opinion about their interests and concerns.

Another attempt to conceptualize procedural justice is referred to as the *six justice rules* that can be summarized as a fair procedure that is (a) consistent, (b) unbiased, (c) accurate, (d) correctable in case of a mistake, (e) representative of the interests of all concerned parties, and (f) in accordance with personal standards of ethics and morality (Chan, 2000). These six rules and other concepts previously noted (e.g. decision control, process control, and voice) can be used to promote fair procedures in organizational decision processes. In general, the control framework emerges from reactive process theories, whereas the six justice rules reflect proactive process theories (Chan, 2000; Greenberg, 1987).

In sum, process-oriented fairness deals with how those decisions related to outcome distribution and dispute resolution were settled along with the policies and procedures used for the decisions. Procedural justice relates to the fairness of organizational regulations for workers and the effective control of decision making. With regard to procedural justice, it is important to note that fair organizational procedures can influence the perceptions of other forms of justice; that is, people may accept unfavorable outcomes if procedural justice is fair (Folger, 1977). For example, fair procedures can positively impact worker job performance (Greenberg, 2011).

INTERACTIONAL JUSTICE

Interactional justice is based on the idea that the style of interpersonal communication can affect the perception of fairness in organizations (Greenberg, 2011). It is assumed that people can recognize fairness in the manner that others explain outcomes or procedures in an organizational context (Bies & Moag, 1986). Therefore, interactional justice is understood as "the quality of the interpersonal treatment they receive during the enactment of organizational procedures" (Bies & Moag, 1986, p. 44).

Interactional justice includes two separate concepts, namely, interpersonal justice and informational justice. Interpersonal justice involves treating people with respect and dignity, and informational justice relates to the provision of fair and adequate explanations shared in a timely manner (Chan, 2000; Greenberg, 2011). While the unfair treatment of people can provoke undesirable behaviors (e.g., theft, workplace aggression, or retaliation), people tend to accept inappropriate outcomes when informational justice (fair rationale) is provided (Beugre & Baron, 2001; Chan, 2000).

The different forms of organizational justice—distributive, procedural, and interactional (interpersonal and informational) justice—can reflect different organizational cultures and sectors (public, nonprofit, and for-profit). Nevertheless, interactional (interpersonal and informational) justice appear most frequently in organizations representing all three sectors because both the patterns of interpersonal communication and the means of information delivery for rational decision making helps to create more workplace justice.

CONTEMPORARY THEORIES OF ORGANIZATIONAL JUSTICE

Group Values and Relational Approaches to Justice

The recent development of organizational justice theories addresses the group values that underlie the theories of procedural justice. Individuals who pursue their own self-interests and rewards from their work are often concerned with decision control in procedural justice (Chan, 2000; Lind & Tyler, 1988). Procedural justice provides instrumental value to people and fair procedures contribute to securing long-term benefits (Greenberg, 2011). However, there are limitations to the self-interest model when people work as a group and therefore focus more on process control rather than decision control (Lind & Tyler, 1988).

The group value model can inform the procedural justice process when group members are concerned with fair treatment, for example, the opportunity to state his or her opinion in decision-making processes and to be treated with a consistent, respectful, and unbiased manner (Greenberg, 2011; Tyler, 1989). The group value model involves fair treatment for its members, often utilizing the six rules of procedural justice noted earlier in order to promote consistent long-term associations as well as a rationale for following the procedures, cooperating, and supporting group cohesion (Lind & Tyler, 1988). In essence, the commitment of individuals to group involvement is often less related to self-interest and economic benefits and more related to the values of the group and the perception of organizational fairness as measured by the following three elements of interpersonal relationships: procedures for open and unbiased decision making (neutrality), the behaviors of decision makers that take into account the interests of other members (trust), and respecting the values of individuals in group decision making (standing) (Greenberg, 2011; Tyler, 1989).

The three theoretical concepts of neutrality, trust, and standing as part of the group value perspective can be illustrated in several ways. A person with authority can obtain trust by maintaining *fairness* through unbiased decision making and thereby gain legitimacy that can convince group members to accept the decision of the person in authority and the fairness of the system (Tyler & Lind, 1992). In sum, people assess fair treatment by persons in authority by determining their legitimacy and the nature of respect from authority figures.

The group value models related to organizational justice have been expanded to include concepts of group engagement and the factors associated with encouraging people to participate in groups (Tyler & Blader, 2003). The concepts of group engagement include *psychological engagement* and *behavioral engagement* (Tyler & Blader, 2003). For example, when people in a group share intrinsic interests, they are displaying psychological engagement, and when others comply with mandatory or discretionary expectations and citizenship behavior, they are displaying behavioral engagement (Greenberg, 2011; Tyler & Blader, 2003). As Greenberg (2011) noted, the evolving nature of *social identity* is a key aspect of the group engagement perspective. In essence, procedural and interactional justice within a group can contribute to and possibly promote group membership identity.

Referent Cognitions Theory

In an effort to integrate different or relevant theories, scholars of organizational justice have introduced referent cognitions theory (RCT) as a way to interpret fairness by using counterfactual or hypothetical approaches to *what might have been* but did not actually occur (Chan, 2000; Greenberg, 2011).

Scholars of referent cognitions theory seek to integrate the organizational justice concepts of distributive, procedural, and interactional justice. RCT scholars use the assumption that people would react to hypothetically unfair situations that "might have been" by referencing group experiences (Greenberg, 2011). Folger (1987) identified two different reactions, namely, resentment (a process-associated reaction) and dissatisfaction (an outcome-based reaction). In other words, imagining alternative procedures to obtain related outcomes can lead to high levels of resentment where people believe that they would have earned more rewards if poorly implemented procedure had not been used (Greenberg, 1990). Using caution about the possibility of manipulating referent cognitions, Cropanzano and Folger (1989) found that such manipulation can occur when inadequate explanations about procedures are provided. Conversely, it is also likely that fair and transparent procedures can reduce or eliminate the resentment of individuals who experienced unfair outcomes. In sum, research on referent cognitions theory suggests that negative reactions like resentment can be traced to the interactive effect between unfair processes and outcomes.

Fairness Theory

Fairness theory can be viewed as a critical element of organizational justice, especially the interrelationship between distributive justice, procedural justice, interactional justice, relational approaches, and referent cognitions that reflect the theme of *moral obligations* (Folger & Cropanzano, 1998). Fairness theory focuses on accountability for fair judgment as it seeks to define who is responsible for the unfair treatment that damages the well-being of others (Folger & Cropanzano, 2001). While accountability is implicit in existing justice theories, a clear example can be seen in the *group value model of authority* where individual-related interests of an authority is involved in the decision-making process (Lind & Tyler, 1988). Using the three rules of the group value model (trust, neutrality, and standing), Folger and Cropanzano (2001) note that the intention of the rules, is directly related to accountability in the same way that the interactional justice concept of blame relates to the accountability of the behaviors of a person in authority and how they impact the welfare of others. While none of the existing theories of justice clearly addresses the process of assessing accountability, Folger and Cropanzano (2001) suggest that fairness theory can be used to explore how a person in authority can be held accountable for inequities using both equity theory and referent cognitions theory (Chan, 2000; Folger & Cropanzano, 1998).

Moral accountability, a key element of fairness theory, is based on the interrelationships between conditions of well-being, discretionary actions, and the principles guiding actions. For example, fairness theory can be used to address the following: (a) the emergence of a negative circumstance and a person accountable for the unfavorable situation, (b) the intentions of the person accountable for the cause of the negative conditions, and (c) the ways that unfavorable behaviors bring about moral or ethical issues in connection with a normative standard of justice (Folger & Cropanzano, 2001).

Fairness theory can also be used in connection with referent cognitions theory; namely, "what *would* and *could* the person in authority do differently to identify what *should* have been done?" (Chan, 2000; Folger & Cropanzano, 1998; Folger & Cropanzano, 2001; Greenberg, 2011). In essence, while the "would" component functions to assess the unfavorable conditions, the "could" and "should" components define the feasibility and morality components of accountability.

Fairness theory attempts to address both aspects of "behavioral reactions" and "adverse emotional reactions" because unfair outcomes alone provide insufficient explanation of an individual's response to injustice (Greenberg, 2011, p. 287). There can also be a negative relationship between the perceived organizational justice capacities of an authority person and the accountability for adverse outcomes; for example, the more a person in authority considers unfavorable outcomes, the more that the perceived injustice can be assessed (Greenberg, 2011). From the philosophical perspective, scholars studying fairness theory tend to emphasize the deontological perspective (e.g., requirement-based, moral rule-following reasons for action), more than the instrumental viewpoint—interpersonal interactions, for example (Cropanzano, Goldman, & Folger, 2003; Greenberg, 2011; Leventhal, 1980).

MUTLIDIMENSIONAL APPROACH TO ORGANIZATIONAL JUSTICE THEORY

While the traditional approaches to organizational justice include distributive, procedural, and interactional justice (interpersonal and informational), there is growing interest in a multidimensional approach to understanding the source of justice in the workplace (Cropanzano, Byrne, Bobocel, & Rupp, 2001). This new approach is based on the assumption that employees perceive many parties in organizations (e.g., managers and others) as being related to their assessment of fair treatment in the workplace, especially since the different forms of justice (i.e., distributive, procedural, interpersonal, and informational justice) reflect different sources and investments in workplace justice (Rupp & Cropanzano, 2002). For example, Lavelle, Rupp, and Brockner (2007) found that supervisors and managers are often the source of interpersonal injustice and organizations as a whole are also the source of procedural justice where workers perceive fair or unfair treatment throughout the organization. They also noted two other sources of internal and external justice, namely, internal coworkers (peers) as team members (including self-managed teams) and external customers (e.g., sources of unfair information as well as unfair treatment).

IMPLICATION OF ORGANIZATIONAL JUSTICE IN PRACTICE

Theories of organizational justice focus on the connections between human resource management and social justice. Drawing primarily on the social science discipline of organizational psychology, theories of organizational justice using social science concepts related to human behavior and the social environment can help to explain the reactions of workers to fair or unfair conditions.

Organizational context is critical to understanding perceptions of justice by individuals who work under different workplace conditions and organizational cultures (nonprofit, public, and for-profit). Organizational justice involves issues of ethics in relationship with respect to human resource management as reflected in the rules and regulations of organizations at different stages of development, especially with respect to the breadth and depth of their administrative systems. Organizational justice often requires clear rules and procedures, mechanisms that support the fair distribution of resources (e.g., salary scales), and transparent information sharing and interpersonal opportunities for perception-checking discussions among members of the organization.

With respect to the degree of the workplace justice, the relationship between union and management is also important. Some of the scholars studying organizational justice often address the importance of grievance systems and the roles of unions in the process of addressing grievances in the workplace. Grievance systems are designed to address procedural justice related to the interpersonal processes of labor-management relations. While organizations are set up with functional systems to support justice in the workplace, workers may be required to accept unfair outcomes related

to using procedural justice systems (Gordon & Fryxell, 1993). In addition to the political aspects of the union activities and management operations that can influence grievance systems, there are external factors outside of the workplace that can affect the effectiveness of the organizational systems designed to promote workplace justice (e.g., bankruptcy, budget reductions called for by funders, etc.). Different types of organizations would perceive the impact of these variables in carrying out organizational justice.

CONCLUSION

A conceptual map of organizational justice theories is illustrated in Figure 14.1 as a way to highlight the interrelationships between the theories and concepts. The major forms of organizational justice theories (distributive, procedural, and interactional justice) are based on individual perceptions of fairness in the workplace. Building on equity theory, the theory of distributive justice includes reactive approaches (seeking to avoid unfairness) and proactive approaches (seeking to promote fairness). The proactive approach draws upon the justice judgment model and justice motive theory. Second, procedural justice is another approach to fairness and uses the concepts of decision control for resolving disputes, process control related to the use of outside advisors, and voice with respect to expressing opinions. The six control rules of procedural justice include consistency, accuracy, absence of bias, correctable situations, representation of interests of all, and use of personal standards of morality and ethics. Third, interactional justice is related to two concepts of interpersonal justice (treating people with respect and dignity) and informational justice (fair and adequate explanations shared in a timely manner).

The group values model evolved from the individual concepts of procedural and interactional justice and includes the concepts of neutrality, trust, and standing, as well as psychological and behavioral engagement. Scholars of referent cognitions theory (RCT), recognized as a counterfactual or hypothetical approach, seek to integrate the three major forms of organizational justice (distributive, procedural, and interactional) related to the issues of

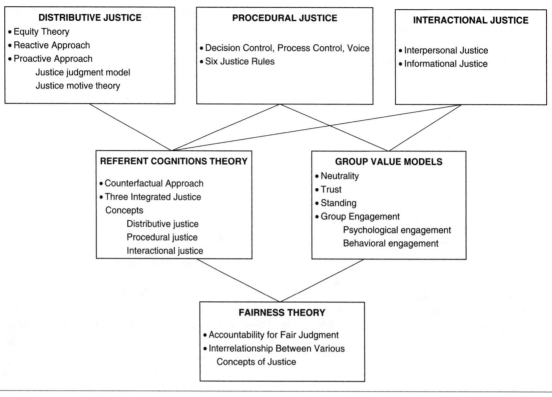

Figure 14.1   Theories of Organizational Justice

resentment, dissatisfaction, and perceived manipulation. Finally, fairness theory is a critical theoretical framework, explaining the interrelationship between various concepts of organizational justice discussed in previous sections. In particular, fairness theory emphasizes accountability for fair judgment.

Organizational justice is primarily about the fair treatment of workers within the context of human resource management systems. Concerns about justice in the workplace have led to the development of theoretical frameworks designed to inform the determination of performance and rewards. Distributive justice is a means to address the balance between equity, equality, and need in allocating rewards to workers. Procedural justice addresses perceived fairness by focusing on how decisions are made rather than on the distribution of rewards.

It is notable that procedural justice provides more concrete theoretical grounds to explain justice in the workplace, not only by demonstrating the procedures of outcome determination but also by offering the grounds of expanding the relevant concepts that account for following justice theories. Folger (1977) notes that procedural justice plays a central role in organizational justice because the fairness of procedures tends to affect the perceptions of other forms of justice in organizations (distributive and interpersonal). In addition to the legal issues emerging out of labor-management relations (e.g., layoffs and grievance procedures), entitlements are involved that relate to individual power (e.g., status or title in the workplace) and collective power (e.g., unions). Furthermore, distributive justice and procedural justice also define the behavioral responses of workers to fair or unfair treatment in organizations. These responses also lead to derivative theories of justice based on the use of reactive or proactive behaviors (e.g., group values and referent cognitions and fairness).

In addition to distributive and procedural justice, interactional justice (interpersonal and informational) is most closely related to organizational culture. While the three (or four) central forms of justice—distributive, procedural, and interactional (interpersonal and informational) justice—explore justice from an individual perspective, the scope of organizational justice is expanded to include the group values and relational approaches. The expansion of theories about organizational justice is rooted in procedural justice and the concepts of rules, neutrality, trust, standing, and authority as they relate to workplace justice. Efforts to integrate some of these concepts can be seen in referent cognitions theory (RCT) and fairness theory. While the referent cognitions theory incorporates outcome and process related to unfair circumstances, fairness theory combines the concepts of distributive justice, interactional justice, relational approaches, and referent cognitions. This form of integration features moral obligations and accountability as well as behavioral and emotional reactions. In essence, scholars use the theories of procedural justice seek to reconcile different theories of organizational justice.

The history of thinking about organizational justice illustrates the complexity and multidimensionality of justice (Colquitt, Greenberg, & Zapata-Phelan, 2005). An individual's perception of fairness in the workplace may vary depending on work conditions, management styles of authority figures (e.g., managers or supervisors), and the organizational culture itself. The sources of justice and organizational culture related to dealing with unfair conditions influences the proactive and reactive behaviors of workers. In sum, acquiring an understanding of organizational justice involves the use of concepts and frameworks that reflect both multidimensional and multidisciplinary approaches.

REFERENCES

Adams, J. S. (1963). Toward an understanding of inequity. *Journal of Abnormal and Social Psychology, 67,* 422–436.

Beugre, C., & Baron, R. (2001). Perceptions of systemic justice: The effects of distributive, procedural, and interactional justice. *Journal of Applied Social Psychology, 31*(2), 324–339.

Bies, R., & Moag, J. (1986). Interactional justice: Communication criteria of fairness. In R. Lewicki,

B. Sheppard, & M. Bazerman (Eds.), *Research on negotiation in organizations: A biannual research series* (pp. 43–55). London, UK: JAI Press.

Chan, M. (2000). Organizational justice theories and landmark cases. *International Journal of Organizational Analysis, 8*(1), 68–88.

Colquitt, J., Greenberg, J., & Zapata-Phelan, C. (2005). What is organizational justice? A historical overview. In J. Greenberg & J. A. Colquitt (Eds.), *Handbook of organizational justice* (pp. 3–56). Mahweh, NJ: Erlbaum.

Cropanzano, R., Byrne, Z. S., Bobocel, D. R., & Rupp, D. E. (2001). Moral virtues, fairness heuristics, social entities, and other denizens of organizational justice. *Journal of Vocational Behavior, 58,* 164–209.

Cropanzano, R., & Folger, R. (1989). Referent cognitions and task decision autonomy: Beyond equity theory. *Journal of Applied Psychology, 74,* 293–299.

Cropanzano, R., Goldman, B., & Folger, R. (2003). Deontic justice: The role of moral principles in workplace fairness. *Journal of Organizational Behavior, 24,* 1019–1024.

Dailey, R. C., & Kirk, D. J. (1992). Distributive and procedural justice as antecedents of job dissatisfaction and intent to turnover. *Human Relations, 45,* 305–316.

Folger, R. (1977). Distributive and procedural justice: Combined impact of "voice" and improvement on experienced inequity. *Journal of Personality and Social Psychology, 35,* 108–119.

Folger, R. (1987). Distributive and procedural justice in the workplace. *Social Justice Research, 1,* 143–160.

Folger, R., & Cropanzano, R. (1998). *Organizational justice and human resource management.* Thousand Oaks, CA: Sage.

Folger, R., & Cropanzano, R. (2001). Fairness theory: Justice as accountability. In J. Greenberg & R. Cropanzano (Eds.), *Advances in organizational justice* (pp. 1–55). Stanford, CA: Stanford University Press.

Fortin, M., & Fellenz, M. (2008). Hypocrisies of fairness: Towards a more reflexive ethical base in organizational justice research and practice. *Journal of Business Ethics, 78,* 415–433.

Gordon, M. E., & Fryxell, G. E. (1993). The role of interpersonal justice in organizational grievance systems. In R. Cropanzano (Ed.), *Justice in the workplace: Approaching fairness in human resource management* (pp. 231–255). Hillsdale, NJ: Erlbaum.

Greenberg, J. (1982). Approaching equity and avoiding inequity in groups and organizations. In J. Greenberg & R. L. Cohen (Eds.), *Equity and justice in social behavior* (pp. 389–435). New York, NY: Academic Press.

Greenberg, J. (1987). A taxonomy of organizational justice theories. *Academy of Management Review, 12*(1), 9–22.

Greenberg, J. (1990). Organizational justice: Yesterday, today, and tomorrow. *Journal of Management, 16*(2), 399–432.

Greenberg, J. (2009). Everybody talks about organizational justice, but nobody does anything about it. *Industrial and organizational psychology, 2,* 181–195.

Greenberg, J. (2011). Organizational justice: The dynamics of fairness in the workplace. In S. Zedeck (Ed.), *APA handbook of industrial and organizational psychology: Vol 3. Maintaining, expanding, and contracting the organization* (pp. 271–327). Washington, DC: American Psychological Association.

Lavelle, J., Rupp, D., & Brockner, J. (2007). Taking a multifoci approach to the study of justice, social exchange, and citizenship behavior: The target similarity model? *Journal of Management, 33,* 841–866.

Leventhal, G. S. (1976). Fairness in social relationships. In J. W. Thibaut, J. T. Spence, & R. C. Carson (Eds.), *Contemporary topics in social psychology* (pp. 211–239). Morristown, NJ: General Learning Press.

Leventhal, G. S. (1980). What should be done with equity theory? New approaches to the study of fairness in social relationships. In K. Gergen, M. Greenberg, & R. Willis (Eds.), *Social exchange: Advances in theory and research* (pp. 27–55). New York, NY: Plenum Press.

Lind, E. A., & Tyler, T. R. (1988). *The social psychology of procedural justice.* New York, NY: Plenum.

Martin, J. (1993). Inequality, distributive injustice, and organizational illegitimacy. In J. K. Murnighan (Ed.), *Social psychology in organizations: Advances in theory and research* (pp. 296–321). Englewood Cliffs, NJ: Prentice-Hall.

Rupp, D., & Cropanzano, R. (2002). The mediating effects of social exchange relationships in predicting workplace outcomes from multifoci organizational justice. *Organizational Behavior and Human Decision Processes, 89,* 925–946.

Sheppard, B., Lewicki, R., & Minton J. (1992). *Organizational justice: The search for fairness in the workplace.* New York, NY: Lexington Books.

Thibaut, J., & Walker, K. (1975). *Procedural justice: A psychological analysis.* Hillsdale, NJ: Erlbaum.

Tyler, T. R. (1989). The psychology of procedural justice: A test of the group-value model. *Journal of Personality and Social Psychology, 57,* 830–838.

Tyler, T. R., & Blader, S. L. (2003). The group engagement model: Procedural justice, social identity, and cooperative behavior. *Personality and Social Psychology Bulletin, 7,* 349–361.

Tyler, T. R., & Lind, E. A. (1992). A relational model of authority in groups. In M. P. Zanna (Ed.), *Advances in experimental social psychology* (Vol. 25, pp. 115–191). San Diego, CA: Academic Press.

15

INTERDISCIPLINARY SOCIAL SCIENCE PERSPECTIVES

Key Concepts to Inform Practice

JASMIN SERIM

INTRODUCTION

The concept of social justice has historically been of great importance to social workers, despite vague and at times conflicting definitions. While the National Association of Social Workers (NASW) *Code of Ethics* cites social justice as a core value, the code provides a relatively brief description of this value, with little guidance for application. For the NASW, social justice is tied to the ethical principle that social workers "challenge social injustice" (NASW, 2009, p. 4). However, definitions of social injustice are no more universal than definitions of social justice. While the *Code of Ethics* includes poverty, unemployment, and discrimination as examples of social injustice, the structural causes of these forms of injustice are not defined. The ability of social workers to challenge social injustice in a meaningful way requires attention to the root causes of injustice in order to guide future interventions. The NASW in its *Code of Ethics* clearly states that social workers work "with and on behalf of vulnerable and oppressed groups" in order to "promote sensitivity to and knowledge about oppression and cultural and ethnic diversity" and to "ensure access to needed information, services and resources; equality of opportunity, and meaningful participation for all people" (NASW, 2009, p. 4).

The preceding chapters have drawn from the social science disciplines of social psychology, sociology, anthropology, economics, organizational management, and political science to identify major theories relevant to social justice. This synthesis chapter draws upon concepts from these disciplines to explore the following five themes: conceptualizations of justice, psychosocial aspects of social justice, political and economic perspectives, research perspectives, and the relationship between knowledge production and participatory practices. Conceptualizations of justice include distributive, procedural, and interactional justice frameworks, as well as concepts of fairness, equality, and equity. While the preceding chapters focused on concepts of justice rather than injustice, the two are inextricably related. As such, a brief discussion of theories of injustice from the social sciences will be included in this section. Psychosocial aspects of social justice include concepts related to morality and moral development as well as responses to social injustice. As related to distributive and procedural justice, discussion of political and economic perspectives explores the role of government intervention, reviewing democratic principles from liberal political theory and contrasting interventionist and free market economic theories. As a powerful branch of social science disciplines and the social work field, research is described in terms of its relationship to institutionalized power and the role of scientific legitimacy. Finally, an examination of the role of knowledge production includes a description of objective versus subjective knowledge, universalism versus cultural relativity and participatory practices.

Conceptualizations of Justice

Within social science disciplines, justice has been described in terms of fairness in the distribution of income and resources, procedures that ascribe rights and responsibilities, and the recognition of capacities and entitlements (Branom, 2014a; Branom, 2014b; Jacob, 2014; Kwon, 2014; Whitaker, 2014; Wiegmann, 2014). Conceptualizations of injustice have conversely related to inequity in the distribution of power and resources and the limitation of freedom or the capacity to intervene (Jacob, 2014; Kwon, 2014; Whitaker, 2014; Wiegmann, 2014). This section reviews the various conceptualizations of both justice and injustice. Fairness is explored in relationship to equality, equity, and need in ways that inform distributive, procedural, and interactional justice. Injustice is explored as oppression and the limitations to liberty, capacity, and freedom.

Fairness and Justice

The concept of fairness relates to the treatment of individuals and groups, the distribution or allocation of resources, and procedures for resolving conflicts (Branom, 2014a; Branom, 2014b; Kwon, 2014; Whitaker, 2014; Wiegmann, 2014). However, within each of these applications, different and conflicting philosophies inform specific criteria for determining what constitutes "fair." Within the justice judgment model, resources may be distributed on the basis of equality (sameness), contributions (equity), or need (difference) (Kwon, 2014; Whitaker, 2014). The concept of equality suggests that everyone should receive the same treatment, have equal access to resources, and be subject to the same procedure, frequently referred to as due process and equal protection in liberal political theory (Wiegmann, 2014). Equity, on the other hand, is based on receiving benefit in accordance with one's contribution (Kwon, 2014). For example, in the organizational context, workers receive varied amounts of pay. Workers may perceive this difference as fair, as long as the ratio of contribution to compensation appears equal (Kwon, 2014). A third approach also focuses on difference, but it suggests that resources be distributed on the basis of need rather than contribution (Branom, 2014a; Branom, 2014b; Kwon, 2014; Whitaker, 2014). This model, as explained by Young, promotes "overriding a principle of equal treatment with the principle that group differences should be acknowledged . . . in order to reduce actual or potential oppression" (as cited in Whitaker, 2014, p. 142). These concepts of equality (sameness), equity (contribution), and need (difference) can be seen as the foundation for understanding both distributive and procedural justice.

Distributive justice. Distributive justice can be understood as "the *perceived fairness of the outcome or allocations* that an individual receives" (Foger & Cropanzano, qtd. in Kwon, 2014, p. 170). Within the organizational studies context, distributive justice most directly relates to whether resources, rewards, or punishment are distributed to workers in a way that is perceived as fair. In this context, theories of both equality and equity come into play. The theory of equity would suggest that workers who are compensated at higher levels work harder, which may fail to motivate workers who are compensated at a lower rate (Kwon, 2014). In sociology, theorists such as Durkheim believed that justice hinged upon equity, allowing individuals to be rewarded for their achievements (Branom, 2014a). Karl Marx, on the other hand, argued vehemently for equality as the basis of justice and democracy (Branom, 2014a).

However, in Marx's view, the outcome of equality was far more complex than "equal pay for equal work" (Marx, as cited in Branom, 2014a, p. 101). Distributive justice, according to Marx, was based not on achievement but rather on the contribution of resources based on ability and the distribution of resources based on need (Branom, 2014a). While the liberal political tradition focuses primarily on equality (Whitaker, 2014; Wiegmann, 2014), critics have cautioned that justice is not wholly served through a focus on distribution of resources and goods, which fails to facilitate a larger, structural critique of social and institutional inequities (Whitaker, 2014).

Procedural justice. Procedural justice refers to the *perceived fairness of a process*, particularly one that resolves a dispute or conflict (Kwon, 2014). Two key components of procedural justice are decision control (as related to the outcome) and process control (as related to the means by which the outcome is reached) (Kwon, 2014). Fairness, in this context may rely more on the principle of equality, as related to the value placed on *consistent* procedures that apply to all (Branom, 2014b, Wiegmann, 2014). This is evident in the legal concept of due process that seeks to promote justice in three ways: The law is (in theory) created by those who are subject to it, all citizens have access to it, and it applies to all citizens equally (Allan, as cited in Wiegmann, 2014). Evaluating the fairness of process can also involve the "six justice rules," which dictate that a fair process is "(a) consistent, (b) unbiased, (c) accurate, (d) correctable in case of a mistake, (e) representative of the interests of all concerned parties, and (f) in accordance with personal standards of ethics and morality" (Kwon, 2014, p. 172).

Interactional justice. This more micro-level approach focuses on interpersonal interactions and individual perceptions of fair treatment (Kwon, 2014). Two components of interactional justice are interpersonal and informational justice. The former relates to the role of respect and dignity in the way individuals are treated, while the later refers to the timeliness and adequacy of explanations provided (Kwon, 2014). Each of these plays a role in shaping perceptions of justice when evaluating undesired outcomes. For

example, when an individual does not have process or decision control, they still may be able to accept the results when they are treated respectfully and provided with an adequate explanation.

Capabilities and freedom. Amartya Sen has argued that determining what is fair or just is only valuable in so far as these concepts apply to an individual's capability to function within the social order, namely, addressing a range of needs from basic nutrition to social integration and self-respect (Sen as cited in Jacob, 2014). This view informs the "capability approach" in which a "just society" is one in which individuals have the capacity and freedom to exercise choice in creating what they see as a "good life" as well as accessing the necessary resources (Jacob, 2014). From an economic perspective, this means that "human beings are not merely the means of production, but also the end of the exercise" (p. 163). It is clear that the achievement of a just society in which all participants have *equal* self-determination would require redistribution of resources to those with disproportionate need (Marx, as cited in Branom, 2014a). Political theorists have characterized a just society as "one that attains the greatest amount of happiness for its citizens" and does so by ensuring that individuals are "free to pursue self-development" (Mill, as cited in Wiegmann, 2014).

Conceptualizations of injustice. One central challenge to developing an operational definition of social justice may be the variety of ways in which social injustice is understood. While injustice is not the focus of the preceding chapters, two frameworks of injustice are mentioned and briefly described here to inform further discussion of social justice work: Beveridge's notion of the five evils that jeopardize liberty (as cited in Jacob, 2014) and Young's theory of oppression (as cited in Whitaker, 2014).

Obstruction of self-determination. Beveridge, referred to as "the father of the welfare state," believed that it was the responsibility of government to intervene and protect citizens from "the five giant evils," or conditions, that inhibited self-determination and liberty (Berend, as cited in Jacob, 2014, p. 159).

These conditions included want, disease, ignorance, squalor and idleness. Beveridge argued that the government should provide insurance to ensure that no citizen fell below a minimum standard, in order to protect them against the five evils (Jacob, 2014). As attached to a welfare state framework, the five evils represent symptoms to be treated through the provision of government assistance. This orientation does not necessarily promote equal access to resources, but it suggests that it is unjust to deny citizens a minimum level of self-determination.

Oppression. Young identified five components of oppression, including powerlessness, exploitation, marginalization, cultural imperialism and violence (Young, as cited in Whitaker, 2014). In a general sense, powerlessness can be seen as a theme that underlies all aspects of oppression, as one group holds power over others. Exploitation identifies this powerlessness in the context of labor conditions; when the conditions surrounding labor are regulated in such a way as to maintain domination of one group over another, this can be understood as exploitation (Whitaker, 2014). In this form of oppression, the oppressed group is denied the full benefits of its labor, which are instead appropriated by the oppressor group. While exploitation relates to the products of participation in the workforce, marginalization relates to the process of participation (Whitaker, 2014). When a marginalized group is prevented from participating in the labor force, the economic impact on this group is detrimental, creating conditions in which civic participation is also limited. Cultural norms shape group and individual perspectives on what constitutes both justice and injustice. When social norms of one group become dominant in a society, the norms of others become subjugated and invisible. This process can be understood as cultural imperialism (Whitaker, 2014). Finally, violence can be understood as a critical aspect of oppression, as the dominant group enforces conditions that are not in the interest of the oppressed. The oppressed individuals do not simply give up their rights or power willingly but rather resist. To maintain oppressive conditions, this resistance is often met with violence (Gil, 1998).

Psychosocial Aspects of Social Justice

Social science perspectives on social justice have in many cases addressed socialization and cognitive development. These psychosocial aspects of social justice include concepts of morality and moral development, as well as responses to injustice (Branom, 2014b; Jacob, 2014; Jacobs, 2014).

Concepts of Morality

Similar to the concept of "fairness," morality has been described as "the rules of justice, rights, and welfare that define how people *should* treat one another" (Branom, 2014b, p. 95). The concept of morality as an imperative to work toward creating a more just society is featured in social psychology, anthropology, and political science (Branom, 2014b; Jacobs, 2014; Wiegmann, 2014).

Cognitive development and processes. Some researchers have explored morality in terms of cognitive development and socialization, identifying progressive stages through which morality is developed (Branom, 2014b). In his study of child development, Jean Claude Piaget noted that young children approach morality as dictated by the rules and authority of adults and have "limited, egocentric cognitive abilities" whereas older children develop the capacity for moral reasoning and are able to understand the perspectives of others (Branom, 2014b, p. 96). Further, throughout childhood, notions of justice shifted from an absolute focus on equality to a more nuanced, equity-based approach, incorporating circumstances and needs of the individuals involved. Building on Piaget's work, Lawrence Kohlberg developed a six-stage framework of moral development centered around cognitive development and socialization. As in Piaget's model, Kohlberg asserts that as individuals progress through the stages, moral reasoning becomes more nuanced and dependent on the ability to see things from alternate perspectives (Branom, 2014b). A third model was developed by Carol Gilligan, who critiqued Kohlberg's framework as male-centric, identifying the objectives with a masculine orientation that obscured a female perspective. In Gilligan's view, the female perspective placed higher value on relationships and bonds with others and less on autonomy and separation (Branom, 2014b). However, like Piaget and Kohlberg, Gillian posits the earliest stage of moral development as one in which the individual lacks the capacity to take others needs or perspectives into account (Branom, 2014b). As the individual progresses, understanding of the needs of others is developed, and in the final stage, self-care is balanced with care and concern for others (Branom, 2014b).

Moral accountability. Within the organizational justice context, moral accountability has been recognized as an element of fairness theory that incorporates conditions, actions, and the principles that guide actions (Kwon, 2014). Moral accountability comes into play to assess the nature of a harmful situation in the workplace and identify the person or persons responsible, the intentions involved, and the moral or ethical issues that are raised in relationship to "a normative standard of justice" (Kwon, 2014, p. 174).

Responses to Injustice

System justification. System-justification theory suggests that "individuals constantly use cognitive, affective and behavioral strategies to justify and perpetuate an unjust status quo" (Branom, 2014b, p. 103). Even when particular groups within a society are systematically oppressed, members of that society (both oppressed and oppressors) can be led to believe that the existing social structure is fair and even necessary (Branom, 2014b). System justification is facilitated through the combination of a desire to minimize uncertainty and protect a shared sense of reality with others (the belief that the world is just) and the use of mass media (Branom, 2014b). The notion of system justification also aligns with cultural imperialism, as described by Whitaker, in which the perspective of the oppressed group is obscured and the group is stereotyped "as other."

Moral outrage and ethical responsibility. Moral outrage has been defined as an "outward-focused emotional distress" that occurs when a group or individual recognizes conditions that undermine their sense of fairness or morality (Branom, 2014b, p. 103). Moral outrage can be related to ethical responsibility, described as "a compelling sense of duty and commitment based on moral principles of human freedom and well-being, and hence a compassion for the suffering of human beings. The conditions for existence within a particular context are not as they *could* be, for specific subjects; as a result, the researcher feels a moral obligation to make a contribution toward changing those conditions toward greater freedom and equity" (Madison, as cited in Jacobs, 2014, p. 115). If ethical responsibility relates to a moral imperative to act on behalf of "specific subjects," identity politics, as described by Whitaker, represent an approach to political theory driven by firsthand experience of oppression as the subject (2014).

Recognition theory and identity politics. Shared identity and a focus on the experience of the subject allow for shared understanding of the nature of oppression and provide a catalyst for resistance. Citing Markell, Whitaker notes that "misrepresentation of a group's identity or lack of recognition of a group is to oppress" (2014, p. 141). As such, the recognition of oppressive conditions, oppressed groups, and the validity of their experiences and perspectives is a necessary antecedent to social action. As system-justification serves to protect the status quo, recognition serves to compel groups and individuals to act, shifting existing relations to alleviate suffering and promote justice.

POLITICAL AND ECONOMIC PERSPECTIVES

In previous chapters, justice has been depicted both as protection from and protection by the government. The government, particularly in relation to the marketplace, holds regulatory power over the distribution of resources and is charged with maintaining conditions that promote equality, equity, and individual freedom (Wiegmann, 2014). Economic and political circumstances shape the material realities faced by members of a society and can either maintain relations of inequity or provide pathways for meaningful change. Since the social sciences operate within these political and economic contexts, institutionalized power can directly influence their theoretical perspectives and substantially impact the relationship between researcher and subject (Branom, 2014a; Jacobs, 2014).

Government and the Marketplace

Social scientists have viewed the role of government in creating or inhibiting social justice in several ways. Liberal political theory and economic theories provide a range of approaches that can guide the role of government when intervening to promote and protect the interests of the individual and society as a whole, especially in relationship to rights, freedoms, and public versus private space.

Rights. Sociologists and political theorists have focused a great deal of attention on the importance of rights. Sociologist T. H. Marshall argued that citizenship should provide individuals with three types of rights that would serve to promote social equality, namely, civil rights (freedoms such as speech and religion), political rights (political voice), and social rights (resources and support to fully participate in society) (Branom, 2014a). Rights have also been conceptualized as "protected choices," related to capacity where those who have the capacity to exercise choice are afforded rights and corresponding duties (Whitaker, 2014, p. 143). Within liberal political thought, rights have also been conceptualized as protection of the individual from "unnecessary state interference" (Waldron, as cited in Wiegmann, 2014). However, there are also limitations to the rights-based framework. The function of rights as protection of the individual against state intrusion does not translate well when the rights of two individuals are in conflict; instead, state intervention here will prioritize the rights of one individual over another, in what can be a traumatic and harmful process (Wiegmann, 2014). Further, the rights-based framework is criticized as ethnocentric, as concepts of human rights differ between cultures, including the many cultures subsumed under "protection" of one government (Jacobs, 2014).

Protection versus freedom. The balance between protecting the rights of the individual and the interests of the state is an acknowledged tension in political discourse (Wiegmann, 2014). According to Locke, pre-governed society was chaotic and dangerous, but it allowed absolute freedom. Members of a society have thus traded a degree of freedom in exchange for the protection provided by government, namely, the prevention of harm to citizens by other citizens or outside forces. However, within a democracy, laws are meant to ensure that citizens are protected from potential harm inflicted by the state as well (Wiegmann, 2014). The principle of equal protection is meant to ensure that the laws are equally applicable to all citizens and that they protect equal rights. However, adoption and marriage rights for same-sex couples serve as examples of the many instances in which this protection is not upheld (Wiegmann, 2014).

Public versus private. Within liberal political thought, the distinction between public and private spaces defines the appropriate boundaries of government intervention. The private sphere is where citizens are able to "exercise self-determination" and freedom from the state "intervention" (Wiegmann, 2014). While this is meant to ensure fundamental rights associated with the family and childrearing, it fails to protect individuals who are subject to abuse by a family member (Whitaker, 2014; Wiegmann, 2014). Here again, the private sphere becomes a site where the rights of one individual are pitted against the rights of another (Wiegmann, 2014).

Capitalism and the marketplace. As fairness and justice have moral connotations, they have not been articulated focal points of economic theory, which aims to deal exclusively with objective matters (Jacob, 2014). However, economic theories and realities have significant influence over the disparate conditions that social justice efforts seek to address. The rules of capitalism dictate many aspects of how goods are distributed, manufactured, and consumed. As a sociologist and economist, Marx argued that capitalism negated democracy by concentrating economic power among an elite few and thus promoting economic disparity (Branom, 2014a). In contrast, Friedman and Hayek, two proponents of free market capitalism, stressed the centrality of the free market to the future of democracy (Jacob, 2014). Friedman argued that individuals could not exercise political freedom when their livelihoods were dependent on government (Jacob, 2014). "If planning, wealth distribution, and competition fall under the state's domain, then the state becomes the final authority of what is right and wrong in a society" (Jacob, 2014, p. 159). The economic philosophy of the free market posits that the pursuit of economic self-interest with minimal government intervention is most beneficial to society as a whole (Jacob, 2014). Within this view, government intervention inhibits democracy and runs the risk of creating a totalitarian system (Jacob, 2014). Thus, it is not the role of government to promote equal economic opportunity among citizens but simply to ensure a competitive environment (Jacob, 2014). The implications of this view of government include opposition to government welfare expenditures and support for the privatization of services (Jacob, 2014). In contrast, the philosophy of government intervention in the form of planning can help to regulate the marketplace as well as enhance the welfare of the people (Jacob, 2014). Government interventionists, such as Beveridge and Keynes, did not necessarily oppose capitalism but simply recognized "human implications" by arguing that "the state must step in to ensure the efficient functioning of the system as well as correct for the harmful effects of market failure, with particular emphasis on unemployment" (Jacob, 2014, p. 159). Similarly, sociologist Richard Titmuss argued that capitalism produced inequalities; as such, governmental intervention in the form of social policies was necessary to maintain stable democracies (Branom, 2014a).

RESEARCH PERSPECTIVES

Institutionalized Power and Research

Throughout history, social science theories and research methodologies have included approaches that support the maintenance of social inequities (Branom, 2014a; Jacobs, 2014). In anthropology, the assertion has been made that the discipline should only adhere to a code of ethics that serves to further the discipline itself rather than engaging in advocacy (Castile, as cited in Jacobs, 2014). As an anthropologist, Castile recognized that some societies possessed more power and influence than others and recognized the social sciences as a tool of this

power and an "ally of colonialism" (Castile, as cited in Jacobs, 2014, p. 117). Further, other anthropologists have recognized the power of government in allowing access to studied communities, noting that if anthropological research critiques government action, there may be a risk of losing access to the communities involved (Messner, cited in Jacobs, 2014). However, as an "applied subtype of sociocultural anthropology," activist anthropologists take a different approach to institutionalized power. Emerging from the postcolonial studies of ethnocide and genocide, activist anthropology is focused on promoting the interests of the community studied (Jacobs, 2014). In doing so, activist anthropologists recognize the power dynamics that exist not only between oppressed communities and their oppressors but also between researchers and their subjects (Jacobs, 2014). Similar approaches have emerged in sociological research. Branom cites sociologist Orlando Fals-Borda who recognized that "most sociologists maintain sole power and control over the knowledge they create, leaving communities empty handed at the end of the research process" and further asserted that sociologists viewed communities "as objects to be studied, placing their members in a position subordinate to the researcher" (Fals-Borda, as cited in Branom, 2014a, p. 135). It was this recognition that lead Fals-Borda, along with others, to develop the participatory action research approach.

Scientific or professional legitimacy. The concept of legitimacy has often been at odds with the pursuit of social justice in the social sciences. Modern sociology has been described as "biased toward empiricism and avoidant of social action" (Branom, 2014a, p. 125), and in anthropology, scientific objectivity and neutrality have been conceptualized by some as at odds with advocacy or social action (Wallman, as cited in Jacobs, 2014). Some researchers express concern that criticism of government action can limit research access, while others assert that the purpose of an ethical code should be to serve the needs of the social science discipline rather than the needs of communities studied (Jacobs, 2014). Finally, it has been argued that claims about morality cannot be based on scientific evidence but on "personal emotions and opinions" and thus undermine the legitimacy of scientific disciplines or professional organizations (Castile, as cited in Jacobs, 2014).

CULTURAL NORMS AND KNOWLEDGE PRODUCTION

In many social science disciplines, there is epistemological conflict over the role of perspective in the production of legitimate, scientific knowledge. While objectivity and the reduction of bias remain central to many scientific methodologies, some schools of thought call into question whether true objectivity is possible. If it is not, who determines standards for what is just or unjust, what cultural norms inform these standards, and whose interests are served? For social justice work, there are significant implications for the value placed on various types of knowledge and the perspectives that inform them.

Objective Versus Subjective

The standard of objectivity is prized in many social science disciplines as a means to eliminate bias and ensure neutrality (Branom, 2014a; Jacobs, 2014). However, some social scientists argue that positivism and the scientific method are "infused with the values of the elite scholars who produce it" (Branom, 2014a, p. 135). Habermas suggested that the positivist approaches used in physical science do not fit with those of sociology, questioning the feasibility and utility of value-neutral research in developing knowledge of groups and communities without taking context into account (Branom, 2014a). Weber argued that views of society and history are position specific, influenced by race, gender, age, religion, and other personal factors (Branom, 2014a). For scholars and practitioners who believe that the influence of their own position cannot be eliminated from their work, one solution has been to openly acknowledge that position by describing one's political stance and the impact that it can generate on one's research (Jacobs, 2014). As Whitaker (2014) notes, identity politics (when focused on the knowledge of oppressed groups) reflects "the experience of the subject" thus relying on subjective knowledge for an accurate understanding of the nature of oppression (Whitaker, 2014, p. 141).

Cultural Relativism Versus Universality

As pointed out by Jacobs (2014), cultural relativism and universality do not necessarily represent disparate positions but make up two ends of a continuum in interpreting standards of justice across cultures. The cultural relativist approach places value on the intention behind the act, acknowledging that what constitutes a violent or unjust act according to the norms of one culture can signify love, belonging, and other positive values in another (Jacobs, 2014). The philosophical underpinning of cultural relativism is that experience is mediated by interpretation, which is a function of both individual and cultural processes (Jacobs, 2014). As such, "Culture is the sole legitimate source of moral values" (Hastrup, as cited in Jacobs, 2014, p. 119). Cultural relativism has been critiqued as "indifferent" and as a justification for inaction in response to injustice (Jacobs, 2014). It can also obscure the conflicting interests and heterogeneity of norms that may be found within a given culture, suggesting instead a common perspective among all members of a cultural group (Dembour, as cited in Jacobs, 2014). Thus, cultural imperialism can be bolstered by the cultural relativist approach, as the voices and perspectives lost within each group are likely to belong to those who are most marginalized.

Universality, on the other hand, dictates that certain standards can be applied to all acts as a way of determining whether they are just or unjust, regardless of cultural context or intention (Jacobs, 2014). This position is based on the notion that "there are fundamental universal aspects to humanity, and, as such, all humans have certain inalienable rights" (Jacobs, 2014, p. 119). Universalism has also been subject to critique as arrogant and ethnocentric. When rights or standards of justice are conceptualized as "universal," the perspective that informed their construction is obscured (Jacobs, 2014).

Participatory Practices—Voice and Representation

In response to the perceived dichotomy between cultural relativism and universality, a proposed alternative approach is "to engage in a conversation with the 'other' to understand their truth" (Jacobs, 2014, p. 120). Similarly, "communicative action," rather than observation alone, has been suggested as an antecedent to social change (Branom, 2014a, p. 133). Whether in the context of political process, law, theory, or research, this approach points to a need to bring the subject into the process in a meaningful way.

Democracy and political participation. Within a democracy, the "one person, one vote" rule is meant to ensure equal representation. However, when addressing the rights of children, the exclusion from political participation results in a lack of recognition that can lead to unequal treatment (Schrag, as cited in Whitaker, 2014). For example, there are unique challenges to facilitating political participation for youth, based on their diverse needs and capacities (Whitaker, 2014). If political decisions are to be made by adults on behalf of youth, it is critical that there are viable ways to incorporate the interests of youth into these decisions and policies (Whitaker, 2014). The model of deliberative democracy offers one framework for participation based on four central concepts: inclusion, political equality, reasonableness, and publicity (Whitaker, 2014). In this model, the legitimacy of a democratic decision is based on the successful inclusion of those affected through a communicative decision-making process (Whitaker, 2014).

Voice within organizational procedures. In the organizational justice context, *voice* has been recognized as a critical component of procedural justice. As cited in Kwon, Folger notes that voice may be more important than "process control" because it includes a broader array of mechanisms for communication and representation (Folger, cited in Kwon, 2014). Organizational justice is enhanced when organizational procedures support the expression of people's interests and concerns (Kwon, 2014).

Participatory action research. Sociologist Orlando Fals-Borda, along with others, founded participatory action research (PAR), a methodological approach that involves research subjects in every step of the research process. Fals-Borda explains that in PAR, "dominated, underdeveloped societies articulate their own socio-political position on the basis of their own values and capacities and act

accordingly to achieve their liberation from oppressive and exploitative forms of domination" (as cited in Branom, 2014a, p. 135). This participatory approach enables researchers to go beyond observation or even advocacy on behalf of subjects in order to empower subjects in shaping the knowledge produced about their communities and circumstances. Central to this approach is the value placed on the knowledge and perspectives of those experiencing social injustice.

CONCLUSION AND IMPLICATIONS FOR PRACTICE

Conceptual Map

The social justice concepts reviewed in this chapter can be arranged as an interactional web, as illustrated in Figure 15.1. Conceptualizations of social justice include distributive, procedural, and interactional justice frameworks that are based on notions of morality and fairness. As noted, morality can also be linked to injustice (Branom, 2014b). Both socialization and cognitive development contribute to responses to injustice, such as system justification and moral outrage (ethical responsibility). The system justification response serves to reinforce social injustice, while the moral outrage response, or sense of ethical responsibility to act, can call for broader participation and representation of oppressed groups and individuals. Fairness can be based on principles of equality or equity, and equity may indicate attention to need or contribution. As reviewed in the previous chapters, distributive and procedural justice provide the foundation for economic and political justice. While organizational justice also incorporates these concepts, the focus is primarily on procedural and interactional justice. Under ideal democratic conditions, the role of government can be understood as supporting political justice, promoting equality through due process and equal legal protection, and providing equity through the provision of resources to those most in need. Also noted in Figure 15.1 is the role of the researcher who can bolster system justification or be driven by a sense of ethical responsibility to create a more just society. Finally, practices to promote participation and representation can be exemplified by social science concepts, such as participatory action research, voice, and civic participation that can be found in the disciplines of sociology, organizational psychology, and political science respectively.

Implications for Social Work Practice

The concepts explored in this chapter have several implications for social work practice. Ensuring access to information, services, and resources relies on theories of distributive justice, just as equal opportunities and meaningful participation rely on procedural and interactional justice. When advocating for social justice, are we promoting equality or equity? Further, the sense of ethical responsibility that compels social workers to challenge existing conditions may draw from differing stages of moral development; do social workers advocate simply for stricter adherence to existing laws or develop a more nuanced approach to justice based on understanding and engaging the perspectives of a broad range of stakeholders? To what degree does our work identify and respond to injustice and to what degree do we justify existing systems, thereby, maintaining the status quo? When social workers are employed by, funded by, and interacting with governmental programs, they need to examine how their interventions promote self-determination, rights, and the limitations of these frameworks. In a similar way, social workers engaged in research also need to examine the role of institutional power and scientific or professional legitimacy in shaping their relationship to research subjects; how does social work research support "meaningful participation and decision making" when working "with and on behalf of vulnerable and oppressed individuals and groups" as called for in the *Code of Ethics* (NASW, 2009, p. 4)? Finally, in the production of social work knowledge, whether in the form of scholarly research, professional education, or policy, social workers need to pay attention to the involvement (or lack thereof) of groups and individuals with firsthand experience of oppression and injustice.

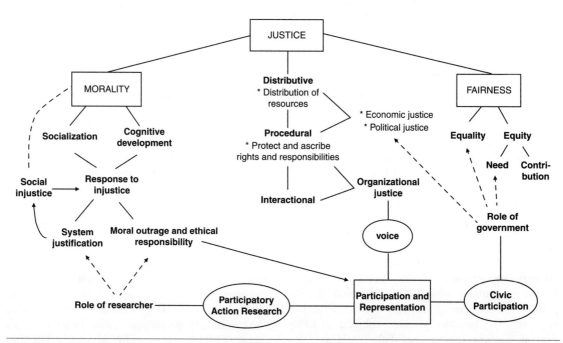

Figure 15.1   Key Concepts From the Social Sciences

REFERENCES

Branom, C. (2014a). Perspectives of social justice in sociology. (ch 10) In M. J. Austin (Ed.), *Social justice and social work* (pp. 125–138). Thousand, Oaks, CA: Sage.

Branom, C. (2014b). Social psychological perspectives on morality and social justice. (ch 8) In M. J. Austin (Ed.), *Social justice and social work* (pp. 95–110). Thousand, Oaks, CA: Sage.

Gil, D. G. (1998). *Confronting injustice and oppression: Concepts and strategies for social workers.* New York, NY: Columbia University Press.

Jacob, A. (2014). Economic theories of social justice. (ch 13) In M. J. Austin (Ed.), *Social justice and social work* (pp. 157–168). Thousand, Oaks, CA: Sage.

Jacobs, L. A. (2014). Social justice and anthropology: From observation to activism. (ch 9) In M. J. Austin (Ed.), *Social justice and social work* (pp. 111–124). Thousand, Oaks, CA: Sage.

Kwon, H. S. (2014). Theories of organizational justice: Interdisciplinary social science perspectives. (ch 14) In M. J. Austin (Ed.), *Social justice and social work* (pp. 169–178). Thousand, Oaks, CA: Sage.

National Association of Social Workers (NASW). (2009). *Code of ethics of the National Association of Social Workers.* Washington, DC: NASW.

Whitaker, K. (2014). Social justice and the politics of children's rights. In M. J. Austin (Ed.), *Social justice and social work* (pp. 139–148). Thousand, Oaks, CA: Sage.

Wiegmann, W. (2014). Social justice in political thought: Examining the rights of parents. In M. J. Austin (Ed.), *Social justice and social work* (pp. 149–156). Thousand, Oaks, CA: Sage.

16

SOCIAL JUSTICE FOR ACTIVE CITIZENSHIP

RHONDA Y. WILLIAMS

How did the theme of social justice emerge in Case Western Reserve University's (CWRU's) 5-year strategic plan, Forward Thinking (2008–2013), as one of the university-level academic priority areas? This CWRU study describes the journey of an idea from an individual proposal, to incorporation into the campuswide strategic plan and, ultimately, the beginning stages of institutionalization in the form of the newly created Social Justice Institute.

INSTITUTIONAL CONTEXT

Case Western Reserve University (CWRU) is a private, research-one institution in Cleveland, Ohio. Founded in 1826 and federated in 1967, CWRU began as two institutions, the Case Institute of Technology and Western Reserve University. CWRU borders Cleveland Heights, the City of East Cleveland, as well as the Cleveland neighborhoods of Glenville, Hough, and Fairfax—the latter four are composed primarily of African American residents. The university comprises the College of Arts and Sciences and seven professional schools—law, nursing, medicine, dental medicine, engineering, social

work, and business management. The university has about 10,000 students with 40% undergraduates and the remainder graduate and professional students. Currently, the majority of the university's undergraduates receive their degrees through the College of Arts and Sciences and the School of Engineering. The business management and nursing schools also have undergraduate programs.

In 2007 to 2008, with a newly hired university president, Barbara R. Snyder, CWRU launched a university-wide planning process. The university had not engaged in such a strategic planning process in more than a decade. Nor had the university, which was suffering a budget deficit, launched a development campaign in many years. The planning process was envisioned as an opportunity to assess, innovate, enhance, potentially connect, and better align the various parts of a decentralized university. It began with the reconsideration of CWRU's mission and identifying a set of priorities and goals that would ideally reenergize the faculty and lay a foundation for an eventual development campaign.[1]

The university's strategic planning process evolved on multiple levels. Different academic units at the departmental, school, and college levels formed their own planning teams to develop priorities and lobby for their needs. These visioning processes not only provided strategic focus for those academic units but also influenced, and were influenced by, discussions at the university level. This multilevel approach incorporated faculty, interdisciplinary program and center directors, academic department chairs, the deans of the seven schools and the college, university administrators from undergraduate and graduate studies, student affairs, development and fundraising, campus facilities and physical plant, the offices of the provost and the president, as well as other administrators, staff, and undergraduate and graduate and professional students.

IN THE BEGINNING:
THE EMERGENCE OF SOCIAL JUSTICE

In spring 2008, I joined the university-level planning team in my capacity as the chair of the President's Advisory Council on Minorities (PACM). With the top leadership position in the diversity office open, I would also soon serve, at the request of the university president, as the chair of the search committee for CWRU's inaugural vice president for Inclusion, Diversity & Equal Opportunity. By spring 2008, the strategic planning process already had been underway for a semester, but no one from PACM—as had been agreed upon by the then provost—had been appointed to the university-level team. I stepped into the gap, at the request of PACM.

Assessing and advocating for diversity measures and accountability at CWRU was then (and remains now) among the primary goals of PACM. PACM had created a robust diversity statement that was adopted by the university in May 2007.[2] As part of their ongoing advisory and advocacy work, PACM members believed that diversity also must be visible in CWRU's new strategic plan. This meant not only declaring diversity a core value but also explicitly articulating diversity as a strategic goal—with aims, initiatives, and measures of success. Doing this would reinforce and elevate diversity's importance by signaling to university members the need for community responsibility. We also hoped that the incorporation of diversity as a strategic goal would result in empowered action, more financial and

human resources, and the establishment of coordinated pathways of actualization. This is how I found myself on the university strategic planning team and in a place to witness silences that ultimately provided what I viewed as an opportunity to introduce another issue into the strategic planning conversation, namely, social justice.

The discussions about academic and research priorities focused significantly on science, medicine, and engineering. This was not a surprise, given the university's identity and the tremendous strengths in those fields, but for me, it revealed a significant gulf—one that laid bare the ongoing concern of many faculty members in the humanities, arts, social sciences, and related professions who often found themselves and their scholarly contributions eclipsed by this particular CWRU trinity. How could we spotlight and advance the often overlooked, but extremely exciting and significant, fields of inquiry, education, and creativity?

I also pondered: How could faculty members do that in a way that elevated the conversation about diversity and inclusion from the individual and interpersonal levels to a connected and more expansive examination of systemic oppression and structural impediments to advancement. Prejudice, discrimination, and inequality are not only institutional matters—that is, they are not confined to campus-based discussions of representation, climate, and university processes (though critically important). These matters also required scholarly investigation; and yet, at the same time, these issues should not be bound by the arguably protective scaffolding of scholarly debate. As individuals, as members of an academic community, as a university, we are also part of a local community and society. Injustices existed around us on- and off-campus. Undoubtedly, the local neighborhoods had human and institutional assets, rich histories, grounded knowledge, and founts of promise and hope. But there is also no disputing that these neighborhoods continued to experience and struggle with the legacies and contemporary manifestations of exclusion, marginalization, and disinvestment. How do we as scholars and faculty members understand this history and the present-day circumstances, and what is our and the university's relationship to it all?

This led to the idea of suggesting social justice as an "academic priority" or "alliance" area. The theme, study, and advocacy of social justice had the potential to build a community of scholars; bridge seemingly unrelated research, scholarship, teaching, and other creative projects and initiatives; and promote more holistic thinking with regard to analyzing and addressing social issues. A social justice focus also could result in increased attention to the humanities, arts, social sciences, and other related professions. The following statement was included in a 2008 proposal that I drafted in 2008 to make the initial case for social justice as a university-wide academic priority:

> Creating a university-wide Social Justice Institute at CWRU—where critical inquiry into such enduring questions are not only valued, but also seen as a crucial part of the knowledge process that generates policies and enacts programs to address disparities and inequalities—can truly distinguish the university from its peer and aspirant institutions. The development of such an institute also can help realize the university's stated goal of truly creating a research university that values all of its scholars and recognizes its place in society. . . . It is a bold move.

THE INITIAL PROPOSAL

As part of the established strategic planning process, ideas for university-level academic priority areas had to initially be submitted at the school or college level. The fact that academic priority areas had to originate in the schools and the college reflected both an attempt to pay attention to the priorities emerging in each academic unit as well as to the existence of "silos" of the university. In fact, the effort to identify university-wide academic priorities was articulated as a deliberate attempt to promote innovative initiatives and break down silos by seeking ways to bring faculty together as colleagues and intellectual thought leaders. This was not an easy task at CWRU where science, medicine, and engineering seemed to rule the day (proposing alternatives or unabashedly stating a desire to move beyond these foci could often raise eyebrows). Nor is it an easy task at any university, particularly a highly decentralized one, where the budgets, tuition streams, appointments, and promotion and tenure structures do not necessarily provide incentives or long-term benefits for multidisciplinary or multischool collaborations.

While submitting university-wide proposals at the college and school levels may have seemed contrary to the goal of breaking down silos, the process did not, a priori, have to replicate silos, reify a decentralized model, or feed into internecine institutional politics. There were valid reasons for seeking counsel and gaining support for academic priorities at the college and school levels. If proposals did not garner enough backing at these levels, then securing even broader buy-in of those ideas as university-level priorities might be difficult. Moreover, the thinking was that the submission of the proposal through a school or college would encourage faculty and administrators to consider how the proposal reflected, incorporated, or built upon strengths; how it had the potential for innovation as well as addressed the gaps (since thinking outside the box was encouraged); or how it aligned with the priorities and goals of numerous academic units.[3] Finally, initial endorsement of an idea through a school or the college was viewed as a minimal way of ensuring that there would be some "appeal" to build upon whether, for instance, it was linked to already identified research or teaching priorities, faculty enthusiasm, or the likelihood of institutional commitment of resources. The proposed ideas needed able explainers and ardent advocates; finding champions and galvanizing interest were imperative. This procedure potentially had a democratic (even if arguably extinguishing) impulse as well. Academic units that often were or felt marginalized at CWRU might have a better chance of bringing forward ideas that may not have otherwise emerged.

Submitting a proposal through a school or the college, however, could also lead to problems. For example, a proposal could be dismissed prematurely for various reasons, including intellectual and/or institutional politics, without first gaining a broader hearing from others across the university. A proposal also could be crafted to align with already established university academic emphases in order to gain traction and resources and, in this way, harbored the potential for quenching or chilling originality, as well as ignoring discussions about the lack or imbalance of resources available for some academic units. In fact, by the time I joined the strategic planning team, it seemed to me that at the university level, the ideas that consistently seemed to gain traction tended to reinforce the already established brand of the university. This is why it is so important, alongside establishing the necessary mechanisms for vetting ideas during a strategic planning process, to also pay attention to and be intentional about who is at the table. Diverse voices, among the usual suspects, can make a profound difference.

I am not sure what other models for submitting an idea for consideration had been discussed. Having joined the team with the process barreling ahead, this is the procedure that I followed. I can say this, however. I tended to think in terms of the potential benefits that designating social justice (which had not emerged in discussions up to that point) as a university-wide priority might garner: that is, an endorsement of critically studying and teaching about the concepts, stances, and praxis of social justice on campus and in community; of adding depth and value to the university mission; and of promoting a multilayered intellectual and creative enterprise that could enrich real-world impact. Once social justice became a part of university-level discussions about selecting academic priority areas, representatives from different schools who saw potential benefits for and linkages to their work supported the idea. This included the College of Arts and Sciences, the School of Law (which had recently established a center for social justice), and the Mandel School of Applied Social Sciences (which mentions social justice in its mission).

An equally important rationale for choosing social justice as an academic priority was this: Just imagine the potential transformational impacts that giving deliberate attention to, and university-level support for, social justice could have on CWRU's campus and the greater community—local, national, and even international. For me, social justice was connected to the mission of universities, critical pedagogy, and even goals echoing around campus. In 2000, for instance, I piloted my City as Classroom course, which focuses on a select social justice issue

(e.g., education or criminal injustice), is taught off campus at a community home, and requires students to engage in change activism in cooperation with community partners. Developed with the support of a University Center for Innovation in Teaching and Education (UCITE) Glennan Fellowship, the City as Classroom course has a philosophy grounded in the critical pedagogy of Paulo Freire and bell hooks.[4] The course philosophy statement reads:

> In the tradition of critical pedagogy, education and learning should be "relevant and emancipatory" and based upon a humanist agenda. It is my belief that the study and application of history should be part of a broader liberation project—one that arms students and scholars with the necessary analytical tools and information to combat social, cultural, and political myths and to address historical and contemporary issues.[5]

My research reflects this interest as well by focusing on race, class, gender; urban history; and liberation struggles.[6]

In considering social justice as a strategic university-level academic priority, the following questions came to mind in the Spring of 2008: Shouldn't we teachers and researchers be educating students and members of the university in an increasingly global world about the critical issues of our society? Shouldn't we be paying attention to the role of entrenched systems of inequality that structure people's life chances, social relationships, and political, economic, and other opportunities—or the lack thereof? What about inequality and oppression? How do we as scholars perpetuate it, how do we challenge it, how do we use our expertise and knowledge to create different, more just situations? From my perspective, social justice as an issue and goal was a valid area of study and intellectual endeavor and a worthy and necessary realm of praxis.

Society is full of social injustices. Far from a society that openly accepts and appreciates differences, historical, systemic, and contemporary prejudice and discrimination devalue and oppress people. My life's journey, academic pursuits, and engagement as a scholar-activist have involved identifying and revealing such systems of inequality through the incorporation of voices of people struggling to improve the quality of life. Rigorous intellectual work—inquiry, research, and critical analysis—is crucial for recognizing, understanding, and challenging inequalities and oppression.

Moreover, for me, social injustice has been embodied. My own experience as an African American woman (at CWRU and elsewhere) has involved navigating what is now called conscious and unconscious bias, personal and systemic inequality, and culturally insensitive situations often exposed in the very positioning of being the "only," one of a few, or, still in the 20th and 21st centuries, a "first." I was the first Black salutatorian in my undergraduate institution's 187-year history, and in 2004, I was the first Black person tenured in CWRU's history department. This represents progress *and* exemplifies the unfinished business before us. Moving closer to social justice means developing approaches and strategies for identifying, analyzing, and addressing lack of access and injustices—including the horrid, dehumanizing "isms"—through the power of education, dialogue, collaboration, and action. The way in which people understand the breadth and depth of injustice is a critical crossroad en route to a socially just society or social justice.

Even as the idea of social justice was gaining traction as an academic priority area, it remained amorphously defined. And, yet, clearly those two words resonated. They meant something—at its most basic, to bring attention to injustice and to improve people's lives. Social justice, paired with ethics, was included in the strategic plan as one of the four academic priorities, or pillars, of the university.[7] In June 2008, the CWRU Board of Trustees approved the university's 5-year strategic plan Forward Thinking, and this also meant endorsing diversity as a core value *and* a strategic goal and social justice as an academic priority area.

BUILDING ALLIANCES AND IMPLEMENTING AN EXPANDED PROPOSAL: AN ITERATIVE PROCESS

The incorporation of social justice into CWRU's strategic plan as a pillar of research and scholarship heralded a critical first step. It brought recognition, affirmation, and a level of commitment. Moving

from idea to action required further planning, champions, human and financial resources, and vigilance. While awaiting the board of trustees' vote on the strategic plan and having been invited to shepherd the social justice idea into reality, I enthusiastically charged ahead, invigorated by the prospect of working with others to institutionalize social justice.

Early in the process, the social justice initiative benefited from seed money from the Office of the President. I also received support in the form of a number of committed faculty searches from the dean of the College of Arts and Sciences, Cyrus Taylor, who became an enthusiastic supporter of the initiative in its conceptual stage (and remains so).

I began meeting with other deans and faculty colleagues. I wanted to know what others found exciting about this opportunity. What might they envision as the pitfalls? What were the possibilities for collaboration? How did they picture their schools as part of such a university-wide initiative? Would they, too, be willing to commit resources?

Receiving ongoing input (sometimes solicited, other times volunteered; sometimes with enthusiasm, other times measured), I expanded the initial proposal, including a review of CWRU's heritage, assets, and gaps; national context and distinctiveness; and the relationship of social justice to diversity and inclusion as well as community bridge building. The expanded proposal suggested a structure as well and identified potential research foci and programmatic elements. In other words, it suggested a way to operationalize and institutionalize social justice. I recommended creating a university-wide Social Justice Institute as a home, informational clearinghouse, and hub of innovation and support for alliance-based activities, including faculty research and scholarship, programs and events, curriculum innovation, and civic engagement. While the institute would build alliances across the existing schools and college, it would also operate with its own budget and leadership.

In order to foster further buy-in, collaboration, and support for the social justice initiative, as well as the other academic priority and alliance areas, faculty from different disciplines and schools were proactively approached and brought together into working groups. After a semester of meeting with some deans and faculty and sharing the draft proposal, the social justice working group began meeting. The social justice initiative approach, which I advocated, was on institutionalizing the alliance, that is, evolving social justice from "idea" to "action" to a "sustainable entity."

Not all the university-wide faculty alliance leaders and working groups decided to follow this route in their own academic priority areas. There existed a continuum of approaches. Some alliance areas (for instance, culture-creativity-design and health) functioned as "umbrellas" for programs or projects that existed independently. Other alliance areas envisioned their role as a federation of faculty, departments, or programs that coalesced for specific projects or as endorsers of proposals, but not as developers of an institutionalized entity. Some faculty members who did suggest establishing a center or institute imagined those enterprises as situated within a particular school or as drawing upon their own discipline or unit while seeking input from faculty appointed in different schools. The model proposed for social justice was differently ambitious not only in its desire to establish a university-wide institute but also in its vision to provide a home and hub for social justice-related work that was tied to, but not focused only on, research.

Interestingly enough, the challenges that have accompanied launching the institute were not the result of hesitancy on the part of university leadership, because substantial financial support and faculty searches had been committed to help launch it. Initial (and ongoing) challenges included institutional culture, getting buy-in from some departmental and school-level representatives, vying for the time of very busy people, and navigating turf claims and a decentralized bureaucratic structure. Some schools were worried about supporting their ongoing enterprises versus starting new ones or, alternately, controlling new resources. For instance, some colleagues involved in the social justice initiative implementation process did not believe an institute should be developed. There were conversations about whether a formalized structure and independent entity, especially in a time of limited university resources, should be created. A couple faculty members argued that whatever resources were available should be used to support existing centers and projects.

The real thorny issues of how to allocate existing and new financial resources provoked feelings of a zero-sum game for some—no matter the priority area. The fear that disciplines would be ignored or their academic units or offices would not have access to the resources they already craved or needed or wanted, were real. During a period of scarcity and mounting deficits, some CWRU faculty and deans were less apt to see the potential, or this situation, as an occasion for creating or expanding opportunities not more firmly under their control. This situation persisted despite the fact that other universities had already begun recognizing the rich possibilities of establishing multidisciplinary frameworks, professorships, and research collaborations, and competitive granting agencies increasingly required collaboration. However, others believed that the diversity of participation, and the strength that comes from that, could potentially bring more attention and increase resources and impact.

The existence of silos and turf presented challenges as well. I was viewed by some as chiefly a history department faculty member in the college rather than as someone promoting the ideas undergirding a university-wide social justice initiative. In my mind, whoever led the initiative had to have a "home" somewhere in the university. Moreover, as a member of the university-level planning team, I consciously wore a university-wide hat and had imagined the establishment of an entity that served as a campuswide hub that also encouraged and supported the promotion of social justice as theory, lens, and praxis throughout the seven schools and college and their many departments and programs. I viewed the collaborative approach as powerful, exciting, and transformative.

Not oblivious to the silos and bureaucratic constraints, I took seriously the university strategic planning challenge to "think outside of the box" and believed that if enough of us worked together, we might just begin to change the institutional culture. The university was not known for social justice, nor was it articulated as a university-wide priority. This had the potential to open up new opportunities for faculty, as well as staff and students, to come together to generate, initiate, and implement programs and projects. I had imagined the creation of an intellectual and social space of support and synergy where the whole was greater than the sum of its parts. Despite the challenges, as director of the initiative, I just kept pushing against small and large barriers that kept emerging in our discussions. While some colleagues probably viewed this approach as stubborn or rigid, I call it holding the vision.

In 2009, the Office of the Provost made additional funds available to the social justice alliance area to hire a consultant to help in expanding buy-in, in navigating politics, and in developing and refining our ideas in the form of a strategic plan. Having an outside consultant to help facilitate the dialogue and the social justice strategic planning process was a tremendous help, and it showed a commitment on behalf of the Office of the Provost to the collaborative process and social justice effort. Over the summer of 2009, the consultant, Jackie Acho, and I met together and separately with individual stakeholders on campus and in the community. It was important to build investment in the process and to identify distinctive ways that we could work together across departmental or professional school boundaries. Moreover, these strategic interviews also provided an additional foundation for introducing the social justice initiative to community members. Some of these interviews have led to partnerships and collaborations with internal and external partners thereby supporting a critical element of the Institute's alliance-based concept and generating enthusiasm and attention around social justice issues.[8]

During Fall 2009, after recruiting some new participants from the faculty and staff, the working group embarked upon a rigorous planning process that included simultaneously thinking about potential grants that we might apply for to underwrite social justice work. This included applying for a major external grant which ultimately was unsuccessful, as well as an internal interdisciplinary alliance investment grant (IAIG) from the Office of the Provost. The strategic planning process was time and labor intensive, but the working group had some dedicated and thoughtful faculty who committed themselves to the process. The social justice working group met once a week and completed our strategic plan that included proposals for staff support, a collaboratively developed idea for a community-based research project, a plan to innovate social justice curriculum, an outline for a talent plan that included hiring faculty and identifying mechanisms for supporting and growing social change leaders, and suggestions for launching robust programming and minigrant competitions. We used the strategic plan as the basis for our IAIG proposal, and in Spring 2010, we received notice of our award and began the implementation process.

Developed through an iterative process, the proposals incorporated a myriad of voices and reflected the creativity and concerns of different constituents, laid the foundation for the institute's strategic plan, investment grant proposal, and subsequently its alliance-based work. In particular, the working group collaboratively developed the institute's mission statement: "Working toward equal access to opportunity for all people through understanding and addressing the root causes of social injustice and developing innovative solutions." Our working group's overarching goals are to provide a space for promoting and supporting alliance-based social justice-related research, scholarship, and teaching; for building trust with and improving our community and society; and for training social change leaders.

In thinking about a research agenda, three preliminary thematic areas were identified, taking into consideration the pressing concerns of the day, as well as the possible areas of faculty strength and growth. The following themes continue to guide the Social Justice Institute's collaborative efforts: (a) subject identities (e.g., race, gender, class, and sexuality), (b) political and economic inequalities, and (c) spatial and geographical inequality. Finally, the strategic plan for the Social Justice Institute also identified the necessity for permanent, full-time administrative and project staff to support social justice initiatives. Not all of these components have been implemented, nor is it clear how many will remain as we continue to develop the institute.

THE INSTITUTE'S LAUNCHING

A successful IAIG proposal accompanied by additional resources did not eliminate the bureaucratic, political, and human resource challenges, and new challenges would emerge. However, the leadership team expanded to incorporate new faculty and staff representing offices such as the Center for Community

Partnerships and the Center for Civic Engagement and Learning. By the Fall of 2010, the Social Justice Institute launched its public face. Compiling ideas from the leadership team and other university constituents, and supported by a design team from the university marketing and communications office, the institute conceived and unveiled its website.

With volunteer staff support (the institute had not yet hired a dedicated staff person), the institute held its inaugural public programs and signature events.[9] In Fall 2010, a two-day conference titled Social Justice, Race, and Profiling: An Intergenerational Think Tank featured local and national scholars as well as nonprofit and grassroots practitioners. The panels included such topics as criminal injustice, from redlining to housing foreclosure, and immigration. And the first College of Arts and Sciences faculty member hired as part of the social justice faculty recruitment initiative in Chicana/o & Social Justice History, Dr. John Flores, gave a presentation as part of the think tank. For 2 days (and in the spirit of the Charles S. Johnson Race Relations Institute at Fisk University), the CWRU Social Justice Institute think tank featured local and national scholars, thought leaders, and activists including John A. Powell, Dr. Bernice Johnson Reagon, Ms. Xernona Clayton, and Donald Freeman. During Spring 2011, the institute also launched its second signature event with the help of an appointed subcommittee of faculty, student, institute teams members, and external partners.[10] Titled the Jean Donovan International Social Justice Conference: "Repression, Resistance & Transformation in Central America," this 2-day event marked UN World Social Justice Day and honored a management school alumna who was one of the four martyred church women killed by a military hunta in El Salvador 30 years ago in December 1970. On this weekend, even with the university officially closed because of a blizzard, this event proceeded successfully, conveying the excitement generated by the event and the appeal for social justice-related programming.

In Spring 2011, with its investment grant funding, the institute was able to hire its first administrative staff member, a part-time department assistant (who became full time in February 2012). The institute launched a search for a research associate–project coordinator for its debut community bridge-building

and research project titled the Voicing and Action Project, and ran its second tenure-track faculty search in the College.[11] The power to define faculty positions lie with the institute's director and members of the leadership team. Run as an interdisciplinary search, the chosen candidate would be appointed in the department most reflective of her or his area of study and discipline—if the department's faculty voted positively. To search for a teacher in the subject area of urban inequality and social justice, a search committee was intentionally composed not only to represent multiple departments in the College of Arts and Sciences but also to include a faculty member from outside the college. There were seven committee members; four of them also served on the institute's leadership team. The search ended in the successful hire of Timothy Black who started the Center for Social Research at the University of Hartford and wrote the award-winning book *When Heart Turns Rock Solid: The Lives of Three Puerto Rican Brothers on and off the Streets*.

Most of the institute's projects and initiatives (several of which still remain to be launched) either promote or are developed or implemented through a collaborative, alliance-based process that seeks to expand faculty, staff, and external networks and collaborations to move forward the work of social justice.[12] This includes the institute's community-based Voicing and Action Project, which has been inaugurated in and with East Cleveland, a predominantly Black inner-ring suburb where efforts to organize bases of community power and promote revitalization are underway.[13] The Voicing and Action Project has a steering committee of university, institute, and community partners and has trained East Cleveland residents and stakeholders as community researchers to conduct interviews for the first phase of its "voicing" work. The project has been featured in the *Neighborhood Voice*, recognized for creating a collaborative and inclusive approach to engaging community in the institute's work.[14]

A CWRU STUDY WITHIN A CWRU STUDY: DEVELOPING SOCIAL JUSTICE CURRICULUM

Another vital element of the institute's work has been curriculum development. There was extensive discussion and debate about how our working group should approach curricular innovation and implement what we developed. During the Fall 2009 social justice strategic-planning process, the group decided to give priority to establishing a university-wide social justice minor, with an aspiration toward a major. Our working group also decided that it would like to develop a series of graduate and professional courses or even a program or degree.

During Fall 2010, the institute established a subcommittee to begin creating the social justice minor. The investment funds secured from the Office of the Provost allowed us to provide incentives—research and travel stipends—to encourage faculty to participate in the curriculum planning process. In addition to members from the different disciplines within the college (including history, sociology, and political science), participators included the vice president of Inclusion, Diversity & Equal Opportunity (also a faculty member in English) and faculty members from the schools of engineering, management, nursing, law, social work, and medicine.[15] (The planning process is still ongoing.)

The curriculum planning team discussions began with faculty members sharing their course syllabi (or if they had not taught a related course, they shared an article) that conveyed how they defined, framed, approached, and viewed social justice. The planning team then engaged in a provocative dialogue about how best to define social justice for the curricular program, as well as about whether other terms (such as *social change* or *justice* without the "social") might serve to describe the minor program. We also looked at minor programs at other colleges and universities, explored the history and philosophy of social justice itself, examined how different disciplines probed social justice as theory and praxis, and how social justice as a concept related to other familiar terms, such as *inequality, disparities, fairness, equity*, and *oppression*, as well as the tension between promoting critical analysis, advocacy, or both. In addition, as part of an assignment for a diversity-and-design class taught by the subcommittee's management school faculty representative, a few students held focus groups to ferret out potential student interest in a social justice minor. The students presented the information they'd gathered to the subcommittee, providing yet another input of information. Like the

institute proposal itself, the social justice minor also incorporated an iterative process.

Beginning in mid-Fall 2010, the curriculum subcommittee met every other week. Over the next 18 months, participating faculty on the subcommittee developed the institute's justification for a social justice minor. The subcommittee provided an intellectual purpose that focused on educating future social change leaders:

> Drawing inspiration from the root meaning of education—*e-ducere*, "to lead out"—we envision a truly unprecedented, university-wide curricular program designed to equip and empower people to become agents of change in our world, not just as "doers of good" but as informed, critically minded promoters of social justice, both on and off campus.

In addition to developing a justification for the minor, the subcommittee spent a significant amount of energy developing its curricular mission and objectives that are also used to address the merits of elective courses as part of the minor. The curricular mission reads as follows:

> The Social Justice Program prepares students across the university to address national and global inequities. The curriculum will emphasize history, theory and practice of social justice; the distribution of power, resources and opportunities; and appropriate individual and collective remedies for social injustices. Through cross-disciplinary study, dialogue, research, active community engagement, and advocacy and leadership development, the curriculum promotes understanding of one's place in and responsibility to community, country, and planet.

The curricular objectives elaborate on the mission. The curriculum planning subcommittee developed three concentrations: (a) ethics, politics, and economics; (b) inequality and discrimination, and (c) social movements and social change. These are all reflected in the introductory social justice "signature" core course.

In Spring 2012, the institute piloted its signature introductory course (see course highlights in Figure 16.1). SJUS100: Introduction to Social Justice is divided into three segments: concept, issues, and remedies, and it takes a case study approach. Each week, students have a reading that either presents a dilemma—hypothetical or actual—that encourages students to wrestle with definitional, theoretical, and situational questions related to social justice. The instructional model includes at least two professors in the classroom throughout the entire course; the other faculty on the subcommittee who also helped to design the minor and the course serve as lecturers during the semester. As of this writing, Fall 2012, the institute is completing its assessment of elective courses for potential inclusion into the social justice minor and preparing to submit its application to establish the minor.

[SJUS100]—Syllabus as of February 20, 2012

Co-Instructors:

Dr. Rhonda Y. Williams and Dr. Diana Lynn Morris

"Never doubt that a small group of thoughtful, committed people can change the world. Indeed, it is the only thing that ever has." ~ Margaret Mead

Course Description:

Concepts and quests for justice and struggles against injustice have shaped human understanding, relationships, and behavior for centuries. Individuals operate within community contexts created through interactions and relationships structured by sociability, belonging, and responsibility. Probing broad questions, this signature core course encourages students to think critically and expansively about the social world and the conditions of humanity. The course provides a foundational exploration of social justice concepts, issues, and remedies thereby developing the necessary analytical tools and information to assess inequality and injustice and address historical and contemporary issues. Based on a cross-disciplinary, case study approach, featuring faculty from different schools and departments at CWRU, this course also provides students with multiple frameworks for understanding the interconnections between what are often perceived as disparate and disconnected fields of study and inquiry. The three primary questions that guide the course are, What is social justice (concepts)? Why does social justice matter (issues)? What can be done (remedies)?

Course Objectives:

- Expose students to a wide range of academic literatures focused on inequity and discrimination.
- Familiarize students with the overarching historical and theoretical "concepts" and frameworks of social justice.
- Introduce students to key topics and/or issues exposing social injustice and critically analyze and problem solve around them.
- Introduce students to social justice remedies or "tools" to combat injustice, such as individual resistance, policy, advocacy and social action, and collective struggle.

Required Readings:

The Immortal Life of Henrietta Lacks
A Raisin in the Sun
No Fear

Figure 16.1   Highlights of Introduction to Social Justice

Course Schedule

SOCIAL JUSTICE CONCEPTS (Weeks 1–4)

WEEK 1: Introduction

Who are you?
What is social justice?
What is dialogue?

CWRU Study: "The Cake"
CWRU Study Facilitator: Dr. David Crampton, Mandel School of Applied Social Sciences

Reading:

David Bohm, Chapter 2: "On Dialogue," in *On Dialogue* (New York: Routledge, 1996), pp. 6–47.

WEEK 2: Equality, Equity, and Fairness

How am I connected, and to whom do I have an obligation?

CWRU Study: Amartya Sen, "The Flute"
CWRU Study Facilitator: Dr. Rhonda Y. Williams, Director, Social Justice Institute; History Department, College of Arts and Sciences

Readings:

Michael J. Sandel, Chapter 1: "Doing the Right Thing," in *Justice: What's the Right Thing to Do?* (FSG, 2009), pp. 3–30
Amartya Sen, "Introduction: An Approach to Justice," in *The Idea of Justice* (Cambridge: Belknap Press, 2009), pp. 6–27.

WEEK 3: Rights, Ethics, and the Collective Good, Part I

CWRU Study: Toni Morrison, "Recitatif"
CWRU Study Facilitator: Dr. Marilyn S. Mobley, Vice President, Inclusion, Diversity & Equal Opportunity; English Department, College of Arts and Sciences

Readings:

Audrey Thompson, "Caring and Colortalk: Childhood Innocence in White and Black"
Garrett Albert Duncan, "The Play of Voices: Black Adolescents Constituting the Self and Morality," in *Race-ing Moral Formation: African American Perspectives on Care and Justice*, edited by Vanessa Siddle Walker and John R. Snarey (New York: Teachers College Press), pp. 23–54
Beverly Daniel Tatum, "The Resegregation of Our Schools and the Affirmation of Identity," in *Can We Talk About Race? And Other Conversations in an Era of School Resegregation* (Boston: Beacon Press, 2007), pp. 1–38.

WEEK 4: Rights, Ethics, and the Collective Good, Part II

CWRU Study: Henrietta Lacks
CWRU Study Facilitator: Dr. Diana Morris, Executive Director, University Center on Aging and Health; Florence Cellar, Associate Professor of Gerontological Nursing

Readings:

Excerpts from Rebecca Skloot, *The Immortal Life of Henrietta Lacks* (New York: Random House, 2009)

Figure 16.1   Continued

(Continued)

Paul Farmer, Chapter 9: "Rethinking Health and Human Rights," (pp. 213–246), in *Pathologies of Power: Health, Human Rights, and the New War on the Poor* (Berkeley: University of California Press, 2005).

SOCIAL JUSTICE ISSUES (Weeks 5–8)

WEEK 5: Discrimination, Privilege, and Power, Part I

CWRU Study: *A Raisin in The Sun,* a play by Lorraine Hansberry (Read in its entirety)
CWRU Study Facilitator: Dr. Rhonda

WEEK 6: Discrimination, Privilege, and Power, Part II

CWRU Study: "The Case of Julie Franklin Powell"
CWRU Study Facilitator: Dr. Sue Hinze, Department of Sociology, College of Arts and Sciences

Readings:

Peggy McIntosh, "White Privilege: Unpacking the Invisible Knapsack," *Peace and Freedom,* July/August, (1989): 10–12
Excerpts from Jonathan Kozol, *Savage Inequalities* (New York: Crown, 1991).

WEEK 7: Race, Ethnicity, and Class

CWRU Study: "The Case of Undocumented Mexican Immigrants"
CWRU Study Facilitator: Dr. John Flores, Department of History, College of Arts and Sciences

Readings:

Samuel Huntington, "The Hispanic Challenge," *Foreign Policy* (2004)
Mike Davis and Justin Akers Chacon, "Conquest Sets the Stage," "Neoliberalism Consumes the 'Mexican Miracle,'" and "From the Maquiladoras to NAFTA: Profiting From Borders," in *No One Is Illegal: Fighting Violence and State Repression on the U.S.-Mexico Border* (Chicago: Haymarket Books, 2006)
Jonathan Walters, "How Immigrants Are Organizing for Workers Rights: Your Hands Make Them Rich: Justice for Janitors (JforJ)" (2004), The Electronic Hallway and Research Center for Leadership in Action: www.wagner.nyu.edu/leadership/tools/files/JusticeforJanitors.pdf

WEEK 8: Local Issue in the News

CWRU Study: TBD
CWRU Study Facilitators: Dr. Rhonda and Dr. Morris

Readings: TBD

SOCIAL JUSTICE REMEDIES (Weeks 9–13)

Week 9: Legal Solutions and Limits

CWRU Study: "The Case of Alvin Atkins"
CWRU Study Facilitator: Jonathan Entin, J.D., Law and Political Science, School of Law

Reading:

Joseph Tussman and Jacobus tenBroek, "The Equal Protection of the Laws," *California Law Review* 37, no. 3 (Sept. 1949): 341–381.

Figure 16.1   Continued

(Continued)

Week 10: Policy

CWRU Study: "Allocating Public Money"
CWRU Study Facilitator: Dr. Susan Case, Department of Organizational Behavior, Weatherhead School of Management

Reading:

Susan S. Case and J. Goosby Smith, "Contemporary Application of Traditional Wisdom: Using the Torah, Bible, and Qur'an in Ethics Education," in *Handbook of Research on Teaching Ethics in Business and Management Education,* edited by Charles Wankel & Agata Stachowicz-Stanusch (Hershey, PA: IGI Global, 2012)

Week 11: Individual Resistance and Social Action, Part I

CWRU Study: "Whistle-Blowing: Bunnatine Greenhouse"
CWRU Study Facilitator: Dr. Marc Buchner, Department of Electrical Engineering, School of Engineering

Reading:

Marsha Coleman-Adebayo, *No Fear: A Whistleblower's Triumph Over Corruption and Retaliation at the EPA* (Chicago: Lawrence Hill Books, 2011)

Week 12: Individual Resistance and Social Action, Part II

Potential Guest Speaker: Marsha Coleman-Adebayo, of the No Fear Coalition

Reading:

Finish Coleman-Adebayo, *No Fear*

Week 13: Protest Movements and Collective Struggle

CWRU Study: Occupy Wall Street
CWRU Study Facilitators: Dr. Rhonda and Dr. Morris

Readings:

Website: occupywallst.org
Select ten (10) news reports that together will allow you to (1) assess the movement over time, (2) reflect diverse political perspectives and news analyses, and (3) convey the voices of those engaged in the protest.

Week 14: Sharing Group Project Reports (in-class)

Figure 16.1   Continued

ORGANIZATIONAL LESSONS LEARNED

An "idea" has to be championed into action. This case reveals the power of vision, intellectual stewardship, and impassioned commitment. It also reveals the necessity of securing multiple levels of buy-in and university resources. This particular institutionalization and change process was facilitated by key faculty and administrators and nourished by the intellectual and creative energy, as well as the time, of other faculty, staff, and community partners. In Fall 2012, the institute will have operated 2 years in the public sphere. Given this relatively short time frame and the various events already held and programs underway, recognition of this milestone and the people who helped to make it happen is in order.

This case also exposes the challenges and potential pitfalls that need to be navigated or handled when moving from ideas to action to institutionalization. New ideas can take root and grow. However, such change is rarely smooth or conflict free, particularly when it comes to social justice. Moreover, the pace of institutional change can be glacial, and the bureaucratic structures and politics that provide the context for implementing new ideas can be both liberating and exasperating. Finding the pathways to get ideas heard and moving those ideas into action require not only personal commitment and passion but also learning how bureaucratic structures operate, gaining greater understanding of institutional politics, and identifying champions (not simply "allies") who will help navigate rough and often shifting terrains as well as internal institutional contradictions.

Allies, "Worker Bees," and Engagement

Those who enact and sustain organizational change benefit not only from the existence of champions but also from learning about who is an ally, why, and in what way. It is imperative to understand (as much as any of us can) why people are at the table and the nature of their self-interests. We humans all have them. Moreover, thinking through who one's allies are, versus merely presuming certain people to be allies, is equally necessary. Such intense work, particularly starting enterprises from scratch or the ground up, also requires "worker bees" who are asked about their interests, what they see as their value-added skills, and how much time they can commit. The underlying consideration here is, How do you effectively involve the talents of others as well as effectively maximize the use of their time when time in academe is a scarce competitive resource.

Bringing onboard dedicated support staff is critical to the success and sustainability of an initiative of this magnitude. Although depending primarily on the faculty director, volunteer leadership team members, and even volunteer staff support to initially advance the institute's initiatives might work in the short term, sustaining an institute with multiple objectives and initiatives calls for several astute and loyal administrative staff members who can oversee the daily administrative tasks. Such talent can free up more time for the faculty director and leadership team members to focus on the intellectual enterprise and community-based praxis, as well as issues of sustainability. In the case of the Social Justice Institute, this includes developing a plan for identifying internal and external grant and operational resources that can support the initiative. While the institute received substantial "seed" money, it does not yet have a guaranteed annual budget. This represents a critical next phase of institutionalization—one that incorporates shoring up and sustaining the human and financial resources necessary to carry out the mission and multiple goals of the institute.

Reflection and Rejuvenation

Taking the time to reflect upon what has worked and what has not worked is necessary. Reflecting, adjusting, retooling—all these are critical to social justice pedagogy and praxis. As critical thinkers and practitioners, we scholars need to reflect upon the meaning of being a social change agent operating within and from the academy. This type of reflection includes regularly appraising personal and collective goals, institutional contexts, power dynamics, available resources, moral compass and integrity, and the role that all of these play in advancing, or potentially destabilizing, the work. Reflection also must be accompanied by dedicated time for rejuvenation.

A Future Direction

There are many tasks ahead, including implementing, even as committee members reassess the elements of the strategic plan. This includes launching curricular and research competitions, filling positions, recalibrating the institute's metrics, and developing a sustainability plan. In particular, a critical future aim is to work with development and foundational relations to secure philanthropic, corporate, and foundational support that can ultimately result in an endowment.

ENDNOTES

1. In 2011, Case Western Reserve University (CWRU) announced the launching of its $1 billion fundraising campaign guided by some of the priorities established in its 5-year strategic plan, "Forward Thinking."

2. For CWRU's diversity statement, see http://blog.case.edu/case-news/2007/05/03/diversity

3. Not surprisingly, the processes did not always work as thought.

4. See hooks, b. (1994). *Teaching to transgress: Education as the practice of freedom.* (New York, NY: Routledge); Freire, P. (2000). *Pedagogy of the oppressed* (30th anniversary ed.). (Harrisburg, PA: Continuum). Original work published 1970.

5. Rhonda Y. Williams, City as Classroom course syllabus.

6. For instance, see Williams, R. Y. (2004). *The politics of public housing: Black women's struggles against urban inequality.* New York, NY: Oxford University Press; Williams, R. Y. (2009). "Something's wrong down here": Low-income Black women and urban struggles for democracy. In K. L. Kusmer & J. W. Trotter (Eds.), *African American urban history since World War II* (Historical Studies of Urban America, pp. 316–330). Chicago, IL: University of Chicago Press; Williams, R. Y. (2010). The pursuit of audacious power: Rebel reformers & neighborhood politics in Baltimore, 1966–1968. In P. E. Joseph, *Neighborhood rebels: Black power at the local level.* New York, NY: Palgrave Macmillan; Williams, R. Y. (2011). "To challenge the status quo by any means": Community action & representational politics in 1960s' Baltimore. *The War on poverty and struggles for racial & economic justice: Views from the grassroots.* Athens: University of Georgia Press; Williams, R. Y. (2012). "We refuse!": Privatization, housing, and human rights. In C. Heatherton & J. T. Camp (Eds.), *Freedom now! Struggles for the human right to housing in L.A. and beyond* (pp. 12–23). Freedom Now Books: http://freedom-nowbooks.wordpress.com/about/

7. One of the four major pillars identified as an academic priority area in the 5-year strategic plan was social justice and ethics. CWRU already had established an endowed center, the Inamori Center for International Ethics and Excellence, directed by Dr. Shannon French. The existence of this center, as well as relatedness but not sameness of social justice and ethics as concepts, resulted in the pairing of social justice and ethics as an alliance area. Dr. French serves as the alliance leader for ethics, and Dr. Williams serves as the director for the alliance-based Social Justice Institute. While they operate different programs and have established their own missions and agendas, the two leaders work to regularly update each other, support each unit's work, and also intentionally sponsor a couple events together each academic year, in addition to sharing thoughts and advice. Also of note is that the Social Justice Institute's curricular minor program has three focus areas—one of which is ethics, politics, and economics. (See provided syllabus for SJUS100.) As the Social Justice Institute (SJI) curricular subcommittee developed the minor, members decided that including ethics as concept or building block was important. Members also agreed, however, that while ethics as a point of departure can encourage us to examine moral dilemmas in order to analyze and prescribe personal and interpersonal dynamics and praxis, this discussion can happen without necessarily addressing issues of the "collective good," power, hierarchy, access, and oppression.

8. For instance, during these interviews, I met Randall McShepard, the cofounder and executive director of PolicyBridge, an African American think tank in Cleveland, Ohio. During the institute's inaugural year, Randy McShepard supported the institute by facilitating a plenary session during our inaugural think tank, and then, during Spring 2011, the Institute cosponsored a PolicyBridge event featuring MacArthur Fellow, CEO of Growing Power, and biodiversity expert, Will Allen. Since then, I have been asked to serve on the PolicyBridge board, and our organizations continue to seek opportunities for collaboration.

9. See the CWRU Social Justice Institute website: www.case.edu/socialjustice

10 This team included Dr. Marixa Lasso, a scholar of Latin America at CWRU, who originally suggested holding an event to mark the 30th anniversary of the martyred women, particularly Jean Donovan, a CWRU alumna. Dr. Shannon French, the director of the Inamori International Center, shared with me information on UN World Social Justice Day. The two ideas were bridged to create this signature event.

11. The research associate and project coordinator position was filled in November 2012.

12. According to the 2011 CWRU Social Justice Institute director's report, about 40 faculty or staff members and about 35 external constituents either engaged in the planning of or participated in institute initiatives.

13. The central community organizing group in East Cleveland, the Northeast Ohio Alliance for Hope (NOAH), is also a community partner of the Social Justice Institute. Additional SJI community partners who are involved with the institute's Voicing and Action Project include residents and institutional stakeholders representing city hall, seniors, parks and recreation, and the business and arts community.

14. Perry, M. LaVora. (2011, August). East Cleveland voices hope: CWRU's social justice institute to record residents' histories. *Greater University Circle Neighborhood Voice*. LaVora Perry serves on the institute's Voicing and Action Project steering committee and participated as a member of the research associate subcommittee. She and two of her teenaged children also have decided to train as community researchers-interviewers for the Voicing and Action Project.

15. The original faculty subcommittee members were Marc Buchner (engineering), Susan Case (management), David Crampton (social work), Jonathan Entin (law), John Flores (history), Scott Frank (public health), Susan Hinze (sociology), Jennifer Madden (graduate student), Marilyn S. Mobley (English; vice president, Inclusion, Diversity & Equal Opportunity), Diana Morris (nursing), Elliot Posner (political science), and Rhonda Y. Williams (history; founder and director, Social Justice Institute). In Fall 2012, Susan Hinze and Diana Morris became cochairs of the subcommittee.

PART III

Social Injustice Outside and Inside Human Service Organizations

17

PREDATORY LENDING

MARY E. A. CAPLAN

INTRODUCTION

How do these people meet their financial needs?

- With only $100 in the bank, a single mother suffers a car break down, and payday is still 2 weeks away.
- A couple with poor credit would like to buy into the American Dream of homeownership.
- An elderly homeowner on Social Security needs a new roof but cannot afford it.
- An 18-year-old without medical insurance needs to pay to get his aching wisdom teeth removed.

If they have several financial alternatives, such as the ability to borrow money from friends and family, use credit cards or bank loans, or have enough assets to provide for their needs, then they will most likely be fine. However, if they do not have such options, where do they look?

Without financial resources, people with poor or no credit often turn to predatory lenders who can be coercive, manipulative, usurious, and sometimes abusive. Even the term *predatory* connotes an unequal power dynamic (e.g., the ruthless nature of predators and prey). This analysis of predatory lending includes definitions, practices, and prevalence in the United States by focusing on two types of subprime services, namely, payday lending and

subprime mortgage lending. Predatory lending is a major contemporary social problem that calls for considerable public attention.

It is difficult to define predatory lending because there is no widely accepted definition or practical boundary between a predatory and nonpredatory practice (Caskey, 2003; Engel & McCoy, 2002; Karger, 2005; Lord, 2005; Renuart, 2004; University of Pennsylvania Wharton Financial Institutions Center, 2000). Similar to the problem of defining pornography, where two observers may differ over whether a picture is obscene, observers may also differ over whether a particular practice is abusive (University of Pennsylvania Wharton Financial Institutions Center, 2000, p. 5). As Karger (2005) writes, "If a broad definition is applied that includes high-interest home refinancing and credit cards, then the fringe economy is used as frequently by the financially troubled middle class as by the poor" (p. 5).

According to Engel and McCoy (2002), the following provides the common language used to define predatory lending:

> [It's] a syndrome of abusive loan terms or practices that involve one or more of the following: 1) loans structured to result in seriously disproportionate net harm to borrowers; 2) harmful rent seeking; 3) loans

involving fraud or deceptive practices; 4) other forms of lack of transparency in loans that are not actionable as fraud; and 5) loans that require borrowers to waive meaningful legal redress. (p. 1260)

A U.S. Department of Housing and Urban Development (HUD) Report (HUD, 2000) also highlights the centrality of coercion and deception as follows:

Predatory lending—whether undertaken by creditors, brokers, or even home improvement contractors—involves engaging in deception or fraud, manipulating the borrower through aggressive sales tactics, or taking unfair advantage of a borrower's lack of understanding about loan terms. These practices are often combined with loans terms that, alone or in combination, are abusive or make the borrower more vulnerable to abusive practices. (p. 1)

Lord (2005) describes a type of predatory lending known as subprime mortgages simply as, "high interest, high fee loans to people who can't or don't go to banks" (p. x). Hill and Kozup (2007) found that a predatory lender (a) "victimized consumers with few other options," (b) "induced consumers to assume additional debt" beyond what they could afford, (c) "hid essential information from consumers," and (d) "used unfair and aggressive collection practices" (pp. 44–45). Common among these practices are the concepts of deception and coercion, which are used to force people with few options to pay unfair and sometimes usurious rates that are above and beyond any actual risk to the lender. These practices reflect a well-documented history of systematic exclusion of poor people from the mainstream financial services sector (Caplovitz, 1967).

This chapter examines an element of the financial services industry known as predatory lending that is part of *fringe banking, second-tier banking*, or *subprime lending*, terms that reflect the primary and secondary levels of banking in the United States. The first level includes services provided by commercial banks, savings and loan institutions, title companies, and credit unions. The second level of services includes check cashing, payday loans, subprime mortgages, rent-to-own, and other loans provided by pawn shops that are primarily used by people who have bad credit, no credit, or do not

qualify for financial services provided by first-level financial institutions. While first-level establishments may use predatory practices, the incidence of these practices within the second level is so high that the term *predatory lending* is often synonymous with the services provided by second-level lenders. While not all subprime lending is predatory, there is a much higher incidence of predatory lending in second-level services.

Although pawn shops, check-cashing establishments, and rent-to-own stores reflect predatory practices, it's the predatory practices related to payday loans and subprime mortgages that illustrate the range of loan amounts, from small payday loans (e.g., $50–$300) to large subprime mortgages of thousands of dollars. These two financial services are similar in that they both engage in usurious practices that are often coercive, deceptive, and/or designed implicitly or explicitly to take advantage of people who have limited economic resources.

Conditions Contributing to Predatory Lending

By identifying predatory practices as a social injustice, it is important to identify the major contributing conditions that include a lack of financial alternatives, consumer vulnerability, and the deregulation of mainstream financial services.

The lack of financial alternatives includes limited options for increasing one's income, borrowing money from family or friends, managing a history of bad credit, and/or having limited access to loans for emergencies (e.g., car repairs, lack of food stamps, and victim of theft). Assuming that people are rational and would not pay more for financial services than they need to and that people will do what they need to in order to meet their financial needs, people use payday loans because they do not have other viable options to get money to pay for the things they cannot afford.

The lack of alternatives can lead to *consumer vulnerability*, defined as the failure of consumers "to understand their own preferences and/or lack the knowledge, skills, or freedom (i.e., personal prerogatives and marketplace options) to act on them" (Ringold, 2005, p. 202), especially the elderly, immigrants, and the poor. In this context, it is important to focus on the conditions that produce consumer vulnerability rather than just the experiences with consumer vulnerability. Ringold (2005) proposes a new definition based on the interaction between (a) individual characteristics (e.g., mental and/or physical status, psychological states, as in grief or mood), (b) external conditions (e.g., discrimination and stigmatization), and (c) a person's experience of vulnerability in the marketplace, where "they lack control and experience an imbalance in the exchange process" (p. 136). While it is not clear how specific populations differ in their vulnerability, different adaptive mechanisms are often employed in different contexts.

Historically, predatory lending practitioners have been able to operate outside the bounds of U.S. usury laws. First, there is a well-documented history of "redlining" in the United States that was an unintended consequence of the GI Bill for World War II veterans seeking assistance with homeownership. While the homeownership programs and provisions outlined by the bill did not discriminate by race, mortgage firms were able to draw red lines around neighborhoods and thereby discriminate against non-Whites seeking to buy homes in those areas (Squires, 1993, 2003).

A second historical contributor to predatory lending was the deregulation of the banking industry in the 1980s and 1990s, especially the Financial Services Modernization Act of 1999 (FSMA), that replaced the Glass-Steagall Act of 1933 (preventing banks from providing wholesale and retail banking). As a result, large financial services corporations (e.g., Citibank and the Traveler's Group) were created in the form of "the world's first trillion-dollar financial services conglomerate" (Manning, 2000, p. 198) that affected predatory lending. For example, when big banks withdrew from low-income and working-class communities (i.e., less profitable) and created a vacuum for much-needed financial services, predatory lenders quickly filled the vacuum. Despite major pieces of legislation aimed at addressing discrimination in housing and lending (e.g., the 1968 Fair Housing Act, the 1974 Equal Credit Opportunity Act, and the 1975 Home Mortgage Disclosure Act), the 1977 Community Reinvestment Act (CRA) held federally regulated banks accountable for meeting the credit needs of communities in which they reside (with special attention to

low-to-moderate-income communities) (Apgar & Duda, 2003). Over time, the CRA has been systemically undermined by predatory lending practices.

Poverty and Predatory Lending

The relationship between predatory lending and poverty is evident in the United States, where use of fringe financial services are more expensive for the poor than for those who utilize mainstream banks and other lenders. Payday loans can be the way that people in poverty generate income to address the necessities of life (e.g., paying rent or paying for medical bills, paying for food, or paying for car repairs). The charges associated with payday loans are often very high and can exacerbate personal financial crises.

Another way that predatory lending and poverty are linked lies in loan repayment. In this case, assets can be quickly drained from the individual and family in the form of high interest, fees, and other charges. In addition to the individual losing equity in the foreclosed home, the surrounding community also loses when multiple foreclosures contribute to neighborhood blight and abandonment.

Finally, the twin issues of consumerism and consumption affect people of all income and asset levels where social pressures to consume are met with the inability to satisfy desire with luxuries out of reach. This issue becomes especially problematic for poor or low-wage working families who often cannot meet basic needs, not to mention luxury items. There is also very little research on the extent to which low-income or poor people use payday loans to purchase what they consider to be "luxuries." In the case of subprime mortgages, a low-income person may have been able to purchase a home with the help of subprime loans based on the mortgage deals that may seem too good to pass up. If the mortgage terms are predatory (e.g., significant late fees or monthly rate increases), then people with limited financial resources will not be able to keep up payments and will eventually lose their homes.

Payday Loans

Payday loans are typically small short-term loans (e.g., $100–$300 over 2 to 4 weeks) that often require evidence of a checking account as well as a job that offers direct deposit. The borrower writes a post-dated check and is given cash minus a transaction fee (usually $15–$30 per $100 loaned); then, the lender cashes the check and recoups the loan plus the fee on the borrower's "payday."

The problem arises when the borrower does not have enough money to cover the post-dated check that originated the loan. In this case, he or she pays another visit to the payday lender and writes another post-dated check to cover the one that is about to overdraw his or her bank account and quickly deposits the money into the checking account. Again, the borrower pays the loan fee in order to "roll over" the loan. The industry claims that rollover loans are not the intended service of a payday loan (Community Financial Services Association of America [CFSA], 2012). In fact, in states that prohibit rollovers, companies repackage the loan by closing out the original loan and issuing a new one. This is called "back-to-back" lending and provides a way to work around the law (Coclanis, 2001).

Historically, payday lending is not a new process as it operates in a similar way to pawn shop lending, store-owner lending (layaway), and the use of credit at company stores in the rural South (Coclanis, 2001). While payday loan shops barely existed prior to 1990, today there are over 22,000 shops in the United States, more than McDonald's, Burger King, Sears, J.C. Penney, and Target stores combined (Bair, 2005; Karger, 2005). No state regulatory data were collected on payday lenders before 1995 (Caskey, 2003). First-tier banks do not offer the type of small short-term loans that payday lenders provide, but major banks do partner with payday lenders. For example, Wells Fargo partners with Cash America, one of the leading payday lenders in the country (Manning, 2000). While there is no reliable research on how many people use payday lenders, it is estimated that approximately 5% of people in the United States (or over 15 million) have taken out at least one payday loan (Stegman, 2007).

Payday lenders tend to be located in low- and middle-income neighborhoods, especially neighborhoods with migrant or military populations (Apgar & Herbert, 2006). An extensive study on the geographic location of 15,000 payday lenders shows that they are concentrated around military bases (Peterson & Graves, 2005). Estimates of the number of military families who have taken out a payday loan range from 7% to 25% (Henriques, 2004). According to the Pentagon Federal Credit Union, soldiers and their families have increased financial stress because of deployments, time gaps in pay, low pay compared with civilians, and gaps in financial literacy (Stevens, 2007). Most of the borrowers are young recruits (often financially inexperienced) who become "enmeshed in a cycle of debt" (Dean & Bland, 2006, p. 2). As a result, predatory lending can "undermine military readiness, harm the morale of the troops and their families, and add to the cost of fielding an all-volunteer fighting force" (Dean & Bland, 2006, p. 4).

The Community Financial Services Association of America (CFSA) makes the claim that borrowers becoming enmeshed in a cycle of debt is a "myth" (CFSA, 2012) and notes:

> A 2010 survey by the American Payroll Association found that 71.6 percent of American employees are living paycheck to paycheck, a situation in which a family may be unable to absorb unexpected expenses without short-term loans. The vast majority of Americans, undeniably, use payday advances responsibly and, as intended, for short-term use. State regulator reports and public company filings confirms that more than 90 percent of payday advances are repaid when due and more than 95 percent are ultimately collected (n.p., "Myth").

In a similar way, Steve Grow, the President of the North Carolina Association of Check Cashers puts it succinctly (Coclanis, 2001):

> The payday cash advance service allows consumers to choose a short-term financial product for a short-term fee because of the time-limited nature. You could take a taxi from Raleigh [NC] to Cary [NC]—or you could take that same taxi from Raleigh to Seattle for exactly the same rate, but the total expense would be ridiculous. It would be much cheaper to fly. The same is true for cash advance. It would be silly for a cash advance customer to take a single cash advance for an entire year. We cannot always control consumer behavior. (p. 15)

In a study of 4,832 transactions by 322 customers over one year, a little over half of transactions were rollover or same-day advances (Stegman & Faris, 2003). While not technically a rollover loan, 26% of customers took out loans one day to 2 weeks after repaying the last loan. While payday loan fees are not inherently usurious, they become usurious when a borrower constantly rolls over the loan. Rolling over a payday loan can produce compounded interest resulting in hundreds or thousands of dollars (Stegman & Faris, 2003). As one payday loan customer describes, "I was behind in my car payment. It was just that one time I didn't have the money. But I never did have the $300 to go on and pay the payday lender, so I kept renewing—just for that one time. Now I know that I spent more than $2,000 over a two-year period, just for that one $261 loan" (Coclanis, 2001, p. 7). Another experience of a payday loan borrower appeared on the front page of *The Dallas Morning News* as follows (Case, 2010, p. A01):

On July 2, a 74-year-old Dallas widow named Yvonne Sands received her monthly Social Security check of $1,360. Shortly after 7:30 a.m., she withdrew money from the bank and drove off to renew four payday loans with annual percentage rates of about 250 percent to more than 300 percent. Sands can't afford to pay back the loans all at once, and they come due every month. So each month, she takes out new loans to pay for the old ones, shelling out nearly $400 in fees in the process. Over the last year, Sands has paid more than $4,200 in fees on those four loans—far more than the $1,850 she received in principal. And that's not counting fees on two other loans she paid off earlier this year, one of which carried an annual rate of about 660 percent. "I'm just trying to dig myself out of this hole I'm in," Sands said.

The payday loan industry claims to provide a necessary service: "payday lenders provide a short-term emergency liquidity insurance to people who have no better alternative" (Caskey, 2003). One company even goes so far as to say that a loan made for people with bad credit is "a gift to mankind":

Bad credit payday loans are one of the best finance management tools that modern society has formulated to help mankind. Hat off to the brains that have come up with such a compassionate instrument when the whole world is running after only materialistic things with very less consideration about moral values. (Easy Payday Loans, 2012a).

Payday loans are also described as a way to restore self-respect:

A good thing about bad credit payday loan is that it gives you a sense of satisfaction that there are people, who despite your poor credit history have faith in you. Having bad credit history, in no way, makes you ineligible for borrowing this type of payday loan. After all, destiny doesn't differentiate bad credit people from those that have good credit history. Unexpected events may happen to any one and even people with bad credit may need some cash urgently to manage such situations. (Easy Payday Loans, 2012b)

As Coclanis (2001) documented, a community activist in South Carolina by the name of Octavia Rainey noted that even for people with good credit, there often is no choice between mainstream and alternative banks:

In a neighborhood like ours, where you don't have a bank within walking distance, you will see within a three-block radius four payday lenders. I've noticed the check cashers have turned over (changed their services) to payday lending because they get more regular business: you go in this Friday and borrow money, and then in two weeks you're right back in again. (p. 17)

Subprime Mortgage Lending

The subject of subprime mortgage lending has dominated the U.S. news since 2007 when the subprime mortgage industry began to collapse. But years before the crisis began, scholars revealed how dangerous this financial sector was. Apgar and Herbert (2006) produced a report for the U.S. Department of Housing and Urban Development (HUD) on predatory lending that noted the lack of national data on the number of subprime foreclosures, but several smaller regional studies found an increase of foreclosures. For example, in five large cities (Baltimore, Atlanta, Boston, Rochester, and Chicago), the subprime mortgage foreclosures nearly tripled between 1990 and 1999. Based on 6 million subprime loans made between 1998 and 2004, 2.2 million were expected to fail (Scholoemer, Li, Ernst, & Keets, 2006). Bunce and colleagues (2000) reported subprime refinance loans increased by 10 times during the 5-year period between 1993 and 1998. One of the unintended consequences of the Tax Reform Act of 1986 is the allowance of converting nonmortgage debt into tax-deductible mortgages.

While not all subprime loans reflect predatory practices, they are designed for people who have poor or no credit history for use in the purchase, or refinance, of a home. According to Fishbein and Bunce (2000), the four mechanisms of predatory subprime lending include (a) loan flipping that reflects a pattern of refinancing loans within a short time period that incurs high fees; (b) excessive fees that are charged in excess of what would be reasonable, even for a subprime loan; (c) lending without regard to the borrower's ability to repay; and (d) outright fraud and abuse (p. 281).

In a report for the Department of Housing and Urban Development (HUD), Apgar and Herbert (2006) found that subprime mortgages and foreclosures are more likely to be in low-income and African American neighborhoods. In addition, Immergluck and Smith (2005) found that foreclosures of subprime mortgage loans are much higher than for prime loans, especially for the elderly and African American elderly as noted below:

> Another factor in the growth and concentration of subprime lending has been the growth in the elderly population, including many relatively isolated homeowners—especially in minority neighborhoods—who are generally unfamiliar with mortgage products. . . . Many older Blacks purchased their homes in an era when financial institutions, especially banks, were not at all interested in making loans to them. Elderly homeowners tend to have substantial equity in their homes, making them ideal targets for lenders wishing to extract large amounts of fees via "equity stripping" practices. (p. 365)

The Coalition for Responsible Lending attempted to quantify the cost of predatory mortgage lending and concluded that Americans lose $9.1 billion annually (Stein, 2001). The costs are related to (a) "equity stripping" related to charging excessive interest and fees through deceptive and coercive means that are incorporated into the loan and result

in a net loss of equity of a property, (b) "rate-risk disparities" involving the charging of interest in excess of the borrower's actual risk, and (c) loans made without regard to the borrower's ability to pay.

Subprime mortgages on homes are more likely to be in predominantly African American neighborhoods (Apgar & Herbert, 2006). Even though there is no statistical difference in the average level of bad credit among White and Blacks, Ards and Myers (2001) found that African Americans still believe that their credit is bad, a possible legacy from the days of redlining. It is clear that groups excluded in the past from mainstream banking are being targeted by subprime mortgage brokers in ways that may not serve the best interest of these groups. Squires (2003) called this phenomenon "the new redlining" and "reverse redlining" where targeting practices perpetuate long-standing discrimination against such groups.

Elders are another population that is vulnerable to predatory lending. Walters and Hermanson (2001) found that elders carrying subprime mortgages were less likely to understand loan terms, the mortgage process, and loan rates than elders who have prime loans. In a later study (Walters & Hermanson, 2002), older people were found to be three times more likely than younger people to have a subprime mortgage where older people with a subprime mortgage were more likely to have reported a decrease in income or have major medical expenses than their younger counterparts. Even though subprime borrowing is considered "the loan of choice" for those with poor credit, 11% of older subprime borrowers had very good credit. Kim-Sung and Hermanson (2003) studied the origination of refinance mortgage loans and found that 49% of older borrowers have lender-originated refinance loans and of these, 21% did not feel they received a loan that was the best for them and 19% did not feel that the brokers were honest with them about the terms of the loan. An example on the front page of *The Washington Post* reveals the human aspect of this process (Powell, 2005, p. A01):

> A few years ago, Ruth Watt walked into a utility office to pay an overdue electric bill. A widow, she retired from American Express in the 1980s and lives in a handsome house in southeastern Queens, a

neighborhood of black homeowners. The customer service rep, Calvin Norwood, told Watt that he had a side business—real estate—and that he could lower her home costs by refinancing her mortgage. Later Norwood introduced her to an elderly partner, Odell Wilson, who was about Watt's age. They talked of family, religion and race—the men and Watt are black. Wilson promised to get Watt a refinancing loan of about 6 percent. At the loan closing, Wilson introduced Watt to a lawyer, Bruce Weiner. Watt said that Weiner, who is white, placed a pile of papers in front of her and advised her to start signing. No one told Watt that the closing costs on her refinanced mortgage were $18,206, which is about triple the typical costs. Her interest rate rose from 8 percent to 11.25 percent and her mortgage payment jumped from $992.32 to $2,214, according to papers provided by the St. John's Elder Law Clinic.

Another high-profile article on the perils of subprime mortgage lending tells the story of 82-year-old Mary Lee Ward, an African American resident of Brooklyn who took out a subprime loan in 1995 (Lennard, 2011, p. A17):

> Fifteen years ago, Ms. Ward says, she needed money for a lawyer to help keep her great-granddaughter from being put up for adoption. Like many others in her neighborhood, she turned to a subprime lender. . . . She borrowed $82,000 against her house, but claims she only ever received a payment of $1,000. . . . In 1999 and 2000, several state and federal agencies sued Delta Funding, accusing the company of predatory lending practices directed at elderly members of minority groups throughout Queens and Brooklyn. Those suits were settled with Delta denying wrongdoing. Lawyers from Common Law say the lender sent a letter to Ms. Ward in 2001 informing her that they were canceling her loan, but the loan never was canceled. Instead, the mortgage passed from financial institution to financial institution over the last 10 years. Unable to pay the growing debt, Ms. Ward was issued a judgment of foreclosure in 2008 and the property was put up for auction that July. The winning bidder, the real estate investment company 768 Dean Inc., has been trying to evict Ms. Ward ever since.

Squires (2003) cites the following example of elders who signed subprime loans under duress or without fully understanding the terms of the loan:

> Take the case of Florence McKnight, an 84-year-old Rochester widow who while heavily sedated in a hospital bed signed a US $50,000 contract for a loan secured on her home for new windows and other home repairs, worth only US $10,000. The terms of the loan called for US $72,000 in payments over 15 years at which point she would still owe a US $40,000 balloon payment. Her home is now in foreclosure. (p. 5)

One of the most prominent community organization efforts to combat predatory lending was led by the Association of Community Organizations for Reform Now (ACORN), a nation-wide grassroots community organizing nonprofit. It was "the largest community organization of low and moderate-income families in the United States. ACORN [had] an active membership of over 160,000 families, organized into more than 750 neighborhood chapters in more than 60 cities across the country" (SourceWatch.org, 2010).

In 1999, ACORN launched a campaign against predatory mortgage financing, using strategies such as member education, use of the media, legislative advocacy, communication of personal stories to policymakers in Washington D.C., and staging a series of campaigns across the country, targeting individual predatory mortgage lenders. The core of ACORN's strategy was to tell the stories of hundreds of people who had been harmed by predatory mortgage lending policies to share with the media, legislators, and the commercial industry (Hurd & Kest, 2003). For example, ACORN engaged in demonstrations at Household Finance offices (one of the nation's biggest subprime lenders) in order to generate media coverage to expose Household's predatory lending practices and to file a successful $484 million class action suit requiring Household to change policies to prevent predatory practices (Hurd, Donner, & Phillips, 2004). Pressure from ACORN during this campaign was responsible for the Federal Trade Commission examination of 19 lenders for possible predatory lending violations. In 2008, ACORN successfully lobbied Congress to ensure that the 2008 housing bill had a $600 million trust fund for affordable housing and another $4 billion in grants to restore housing in areas hardest hit by subprime mortgage foreclosures (Atlas, 2010).

In 2009, ACORN became embroiled in a scandal of its own and filed bankruptcy in 2010.

EXPERIENCES OF PREDATORY LENDING

When accounting for the subjective experiences of people who have taken out subprime mortgages, involving predatory practices, Hill and Kozup (2007) identified three major themes: (a) "the friendly veneer" in the initial stages of the lending relationship in the form of "courtesy," "availability," speed of the transaction, and lack of full disclosure where borrowers feel respected and empowered, despite their poor credit (e.g., rushing the closing process to avoid full disclosure of the loan package; (b) "the rules of engagement" that included the avoidance of questions (e.g., not asking questions when the interest rate was higher at closing than initially discussed); borrowing more over time (e.g. encouraging increased spending and thereby expanding the loan that was initially agreed upon) and making payments on time where breaking the rules was perceived to be threatening to the relationship, and (c) "an aggressive response," that was characterized by changing the loan package, blaming the victim, and fake claims. One informant, who had breast cancer and temporarily could not work, tried unsuccessfully to use the credit insurance she purchased with her mortgage to make up for lost income. As Hill and Kozup (2007) summarize,

> The resulting thematic structure reveals practices by predatory lenders designed to provide vulnerable classes of consumers with easy access to financial resources. In exchange for this opportunity, borrowers were expected to ask few questions about their loan packages, expand their borrowing without a complete understanding of the agreements, and continue making increasingly larger monthly payments. Failure to meet these obligations caused the lenders' demeanor to change from responsive and helpful to negligent and aggressive. This metamorphous led to an assault on borrowers that involved modifying contracts without their knowledge, blaming them for discrepancies between understood and actual terms, and harassing and verbally abusing them when they failed to meet imposed liabilities. (p. 43)

Ferguson and King (2006) examined the experiences of African American women who advocated on behalf of their elder family members and friends when they were victims of predatory mortgage lending. Overwhelmed by frustration, these women found that predatory lenders "are capable of giving unmitigated attention to the multiple court appearances, legal meetings, correspondences, and requisite documentation. They have the further advantage of unlimited legal council and expertise, as well as knowledge of the world of finance and lending" (p. 161). In addition to personal frustration, they found that their community was being unfairly targeted by predatory mortgage lenders where "the most marginal were being steamrollered by the wheels of economic greed" (p. 159). In the Ferguson and King (2006) study, one advocate tells of meeting a "magistrate's" secretary in the bathroom right before she and the elder would attend court.

> She stated that she had processed some 1,200 cases in the first six months of this year and all but ten of them involved middle-aged African-American women fighting for an elder family member who had been hoodwinked out of their homes. She said there was something spooky, racial, and discriminatory going on and that no one was willing to talk about it. After she dried her hands and left, I just stood there barely able to breathe. (p. 163)

In addition to institutional racism, the financial strain of debt can lead to poor mental health outcomes. In a study of 2,812 people over the age of 65 living in New Haven, Connecticut, Mendes de Leon, Rapp, and Kasl (1994) found a significant relationship between financial strain and depression. In addition, Chiriboga, Black, Aranda, and Markides (2002) found that chronic financial strain was associated with depressive symptoms in a sample of 3,050 Mexican Americans, when over 55% of the sample said that they could not pay monthly bills some or most of the time. It is clear that the experience of acute and chronic economic strains can contribute to depressive symptoms. Mirowsky and Ross (1999) found that depression associated with economic hardship seems to decrease with older age; however, having a disabling illness or not having any income increases depression associated with economic hardship. In a study on the relationship between credit card debt, stress, and health, Drentea and Lavrakras (2000) found that a high debt-to-income ratio was associated with stress and poorer health. Despite these studies, it is unclear if debt and financial strain have a direct impact on mental health.

Reframing Subprime Lending as a Solution

The payday loan and subprime mortgage industry argues that subprime lending is a solution, not a problem, because it provides financial services for a range of people who live in neighborhoods without bank branches, have bad credit, and need a convenient, fast, and easy way to get money. The industry also claims that people should be free to exercise control over financial decisions without government regulation or interference where subprime mortgage lending enables more people to purchase homes that they might not otherwise be able to afford (Elliehausen & Staten, 2004).

Responses to Predatory Lending

On a policy level, states have responded to predatory practices by laws prohibiting or limiting predatory lending. The laws exempt predatory lenders by referring to "fees" and "leasing" services instead of loans (Lord, 2005). North Carolina enacted a time-limited law that capped interest rates on payday loans and other predatory practices, but research shows that this has had no effect on the rate of homeownership (Quercia, Stegman & Davis, 2004). On a federal level, the Talent-Nelson Amendment prohibits lenders from charging over 36% on loans and prohibits mandatory arbitration clauses that thereby prevent class action lawsuits (Dean & Bland, 2006).

The industry response has been primarily from community credit unions that have developed alternatives to payday lenders. To date, federations of credit unions in Pennsylvania, New York, and Wisconsin have created loan packages that combine features of payday loans, such as small loan amounts and terms that are short, with low interest rates, financial education, and savings account incentives (Walsh, 2006). In a collaborative effort between the government and a private foundation, the California Community Foundation has partnered with the Pentagon Federal Credit Union to expand an emergency debt relief program for military families, called ARK: Asset Recovery Kit (Pentagon Federal Credit Union Foundation, 2012). This program provides interest-free emergency loans and counseling to military borrowers who are mired in debt from payday loans. In addition to financial education, prevention programs for youth provide an early warning approach to the problem of predatory lending, especially in relationship to asset-building programs (Lucey & Giannangelo, 2006; Sherraden & Johnson, 2007).

Conclusion

It is clear that people who need credit but who do not qualify for it, or who think they do not qualify for it, will use the options that the fringe market provides. As Hill and Kozup (2007) so aptly conclude,

> The need for fiscal services among vulnerable members of our society will remain, requiring that ethical lenders step forward and provide credit opportunities where they do not currently exist. Any other solution leaves the door open for the return of unethical practices since unfulfilled important and legitimate needs will always seek some form of satisfaction. (p. 45)

These conclusions raise the following questions:

1. What is the essence of the problem with predatory lending? Is it poverty? An unregulated market? Financial exclusion? Materialism and consumption?

2. Who bears the responsibility for this problem? Individuals, the market, the government?

3. To what extent should consumers be protected from exploitative business practices? How shall people be protected, and who shall do the protecting? What might be some unintended consequences of consumer protection?

The answers to these questions call for a thoughtful examination of the social values and underlying assumptions of the social injustices associated with predatory lending in order to guide future actions.

REFERENCES

Apgar, W., & Duda, M. (2003). The twenty-fifth anniversary of the Community Reinvestment Act: Past accomplishments and future regulatory challenges. *Federal Reserve Bank of New York Economic Policy Review, 9*, 169–191.

Apgar, W. C., & Herbert, C. E. (2006). *Subprime lending and alternative service providers: A literature review and empirical analysis.* Cambridge, MA: U.S. Department of Housing and Urban Development, Office of Policy Development and Research.

Ards, S. D., & Myers, S. L., Jr. (2001). The color of money. *American Behavioral Scientist, 45*(2), 223–239.

Atlas, J. (2010). *Seeds of change: The story of ACORN, America's most controversial antipoverty community organizing group.* Nashville, TN: Vanderbilt University Press.

Bair, S. (2005). *Low-cost payday loan: Opportunities and obstacles.* Baltimore, MD: Annie E. Casey Foundation.

Bunce, H. L., Gruenstein, D., Herbert, C. E., & Scheessele, R. M. (2000). Subprime foreclosures: The smoking gun of predatory lending? In *Housing policy in the new millennium* (pp. 257–268. Washington, DC: U.S. Department of Housing and Urban Development.

Caplovitz, D. (1967). *The poor pay more: Consumer practices of low income families.* New York, NY: Free Press.

Case, B. (2010, July 25). Poor get the loans, lenders get the payday. *The Dallas Morning News*, p. A01.

Caskey, J. P. (2003). *Fringe banking a decade later.* Manuscript in preparation.

Chiriboga, D. A., Black, S. A., Aranda, M., & Markides, K. (2002). Stress and depressive symptoms among Mexican American elders. *Journal of Gerontology: Psychological Sciences, 57*(6), 559–568.

Coclanis, P. (Ed.). (2001). *Too much month at the end of the paycheck: Payday lending in North Carolina.* Chapel Hill: Community Reinvestment Association of North Carolina, Center for Community Capitalism, Frank Hawkins Kenan Institute of Private Enterprise, University of North Carolina at Chapel Hill.

Community Financial Services Association of America (CFSA). (2012). Myth vs. reality. Retrieved from http://cfsaa.com/aboutthepaydayindustry/myth-vs-reality.aspx

Dean, S., & Bland, J. (2012). *Congress acts against predatory lending and mandatory arbitration for members of the military and their families.*

Drentea, P., & Lavrakas, P. J. (2000). Over the limit: The association among health, race and debt. *Social Science and Medicine, 50*, 517–529.

Easy Payday Loans. (2012a). *Bad credit payday loans—A gift to mankind.* Retrieved from http://sites.google.com/site/easypaydayloans/badcreditpaydayloans-agifttomankind3

Easy Payday Loans. (2012b). *People have faith in you.* Retrieved from http://easypaydayloans.googlepages.com/badcreditpaydayloan-peoplehavefaithinyou

Elliehausen, G., & Staten, M. E. (2004). Regulation of subprime mortgage products: An analysis of North Carolina's Predatory Lending Law. *Journal of Real Estate Finance and Economics, 29*(4), 411–433.

Engel, K. C., & McCoy, P. A. (2002). The CRA implications of predatory lending. *Fordham Urban Law Journal, 29*, 1571.

Ferguson, S. A., & King, T. C. (2006). Taking up our elders' burdens as our own: African-American women against elder fraud. *National Women's Studies Journal, 18*(2), 148–169.

Fishbein, A., & Bunce, H. (2000). Subprime market growth and predatory lending. In *Housing policy in the new millennium* (pp. 273–288). Washington, DC: U.S. Department of Housing and Urban Development.

Henriques, D. B. (2004, December 4). *Seeking quick loans, soldiers race into high-interest traps.* New York Times. Retrieved from http://www.nytimes.com/2004/12/07/business/07military.html

Hill, R. P., & Kozup, J. C. (2007). Consumer experiences with predatory lending practices. *The Journal of Consumer Affairs, 41*(1), 29–46.

Hurd, M., Donner, L., & Phillips, C. (2004). Community organizing and advocacy: Fighting predatory lending and making a difference. In G. Squires (Ed.), *Why the poor pay more: How to stop predatory lending* (pp. 133–152). Westport, CT: Praeger.

Hurd, M., & Kest, S. (2003). Fighting predatory lending from the ground up: An issue of economic justice. In G. Squires (Ed.), *Organizing access to capital: Advocacy and the democratization of financial institutions* (pp. 119–134). Philadelphia, PA: Temple University Press.

Immergluck, D., & Smith, G. (2005). Measuring the effects of subprime lending on neighborhood foreclosures: Evidence from Chicago. *Urban Affairs Review, 40*, 362–389.

Karger, H. (2005). *Shortchanged: Life and debt in the fringe economy*. San Francisco, CA: Berrett-Koehler.

Kim-Sung, K., & Hermanson, S. (2003). Experiences of older refinance mortgage loan borrowers: Broker- and lender-originated loans. *AARP Public Policy Institute Digest*, Number 83, 1–4. Washington, DC: American Association of Retired Persons.

Lennard, N. (2011, August 20). Community gathers to fight a great-grandmother's eviction. *The New York Times*, p. A17.

Lord, R. (2005). *American nightmare: Predatory lending and the foreclosure of the American dream*. Monroe, ME: Common Courage Press.

Lucey, T. A., & Giannangelo, D. M. (2006). Short changed: The importance of facilitating equitable financial education in urban society. *Education and Urban Society, 38*(3), 268–287.

Manning, R. (2000). *Credit card nation: The consequences of America's addiction to credit*. New York, NY: Basic Books.

Mendes de Leon, C. F., Rapp, S., & Kasl, S.V. (1994). Financial strain and symptoms of depression in a community sample of elderly men and women: A longitudinal study. *Journal of Aging and Health, 6*, 448–468.

Mirowsky, J., & Ross, C. E. (1999). Economic hardship across the life course. *American Sociological Review, 64*, 548–569.

Pentagon Federal Credit Union Foundation (2012). How ARK works. Retrieved from http://www.pentagonfoundation.org/site/PageServer?pagename=ark_index

Peterson, C. L., & Graves, S. M. (2005). *Predatory lending and the military: The law and geography of "payday" loans in military towns*. Retrieved December 11, 2007, from http://ssrn.com/abstract=694141

Powell, M. (2005, July 29). Hot housing market opens doors for fraud: Dream of homeownership is preyed upon. *The Washington Post*, p. A01.

Quercia, R. G., Stegman, M. A., & Davis, W. R. (2004). *Assessing the impact of North Carolina's Predatory Lending Law*. Chapel Hill, NC: Fannie Mae Foundation.

Renuart, E. (2004). An overview of the predatory mortgage lending process. *Housing Policy Debate, 15*(3), 467–503.

Ringold, D. J. (2005). Vulnerability in the marketplace: Concepts, caveats, and possible solutions. *Journal of Macromarketing, 25*(2), 202–214.

Scholoemer, E., Li, W., Ernst, K., & Keest, K. (2006). *Losing ground: Foreclosures in the subprime market and their cost to homeowners*. Center For Responsible Lending. Retrieved from http://www.responsiblelending.org/pdfs/foreclosure-paper-report-2-17.pdf

Sherraden, M. S., & Johnson, E. (2007). From financial literacy to financial capability among youth. *Journal of Sociology and Social Welfare, 34*(3), 119–146.

SourceWatch.org. (2010). *Association of Community Organizations for Reform Now (ACORN)*. Retrieved from http://www.sourcewatch.org/index.php?title=Association_of_Community_Organizations_for_Reform_Now

Squires, G. D. (1993). *From redlining to reinvestment: Community responses to urban disinvestment*. Philadelphia, PA: Temple University Press.

Squires, G. D. (2003). The new redlining: Predatory lending in an age of financial service modernization. *Race Relations Abstracts, 28*(3/4), 5–18.

Stegman, M. A. (2007). Payday lending. *Journal of Economic Perspectives, 21*(1), 169–190.

Stegman, M. A., & Faris, R. (2003). Payday lending: A business model that encourages chronic borrowing. *Economic Development Quarterly, 17*(8), 8–32.

Stein, E. (2001). *Quantifying the economic cost of predatory lending*. Durham, NC: Coalition for Responsible Lending.

Stevens, M. L. (2007, March 1). *Asset recovery kit (ARK) Emergency Relief Program to receive major grant to expand services* [PR Newswire document]. Alexandria, VA: Pentagon Federal Credit Union Foundation.

University of Pennsylvania Wharton Financial Institutions Center. (2000). *Another view of predatory lending*. Philadelphia, PA: J. Guttentag.

U.S. Department of Housing and Urban Development (HUD). (2000). *Curbing predatory home mortgage lending*. Washington, DC: U.S. Department of Housing and Urban Development.

Walsh, K. (2006, October 19). Credit unions offer better choice alternative to predatory payday loans; First statewide program in U.S. to help cash-strapped working families avoid costly debt traps. *PR Newswire*. Retrieved from www.patreasury.org

Walters, N., & Hermanson, S. (2001). Subprime mortgage lending and older borrowers. *AARP Public Policy Institute Digest*, Number 57. Washington, DC:

American Association of Retired Persons. Retrieved from http://www.aarp.org/work/retirement-planning/info-2001/risk_preferences_and_the_investment_decisions_of_older_americans.html

Walters, N., & Hermanson, S. (2002). Older subprime refinance mortgage borrowers. *AARP Public Policy Institute Digest*, Number 74 (pp. 1–4). Washington, DC: American Association of Retired Persons.

18

THE INJUSTICES OF INTIMATE PARTNER VIOLENCE

KATHERINE E. RAY

"Congress also learned that 'women are victims of violence simply because they are women.' Every fifteen seconds, a woman in the United States is battered by her husband or boyfriend; every six minutes, a woman is raped."

—Then-Senator Joseph Biden, 2000

Violence against women includes many types of gender-based violence. A particularly insidious form of social injustice is called intimate partner violence (IPV) that encompasses several types of violence, from the mildest psychological abuse to murder. While IPV could appear to be a personal issue, in recent decades, it has become recognized as a significant public health problem. This analysis describes the prevalence of intimate partner violence perpetrated against women as a form of oppression and social injustice.

The brutality and lethality of intimate partner violence needs to be understood as a visceral reality, often described by outmoded terms such as *battered women*. IPV means bruises, bludgeons, and scarred self-esteem. It involves trips to the emergency room late at night with tired, frightened children and in the worst case can lead to death. While IPV is a system of violence that affects women disproportionately,

the uniqueness of each woman's situation should be kept in mind, especially its occurrence in an intimate setting.

DEFINING INTIMATE PARTNER VIOLENCE

Intimate partner violence is by definition violence that occurs between partners. It has historically been referred to as wife battery and domestic violence, but IPV is the more encompassing term that is in use today (Frieze & Chen, 2010). Wife battery implies a female gender victim-survivor and a marital relationship, while domestic violence implies cohabitation. Sokoloff and Dupont (2005) describe battery as "physical, emotional, psychological, and sexual violence and control against women" (p. 1). And Jaaber defines it as a "purposeful course of action buttressed by familial, institutional, social, and cultural practices" (as qtd. in Sokoloff & Dupont, 2005, p. 1). In essence, IPV can be perpetrated by anyone and experienced by anyone. Intimate partner violence varies in its degree of brutality, from pushing to severe forms of violence, and it can be unidirectional (one partner abusing the other) or bidirectional (mutual abuse) (Frieze & Chen, 2010). Given the existence of bidirectional violence, as well as gay and lesbian partner violence, intimate partner violence can be understood as aggression that is perpetrated by anyone of any gender and in any kind of relationship. Nonetheless, gender is not a neutral factor in domestic violence, no more so than race, ethnicity, class, sexual orientation, immigration status, or ability.

The Battered Woman

In traditional feminist discourse on the subject of violence against women, the experience of the battered woman was advanced as a model for understanding "domestic violence." This model places gender in a more prominent role than age, race, or sexual orientation. Its dissemination in public policy and public health led to the popularization of "partner violence" as occurring with a male batterer and female victim (Frieze & Chen, 2010). It is clear that there are many other factors that are captured in the *intersectionality* approach that is described later. While IPV is not a monolithic phenomenon of the experiences of the battered woman, it is still a useful description of some types of intimate partner violence experienced by some women. The battered woman, then, is a victim-survivor who is located in a severely violent relationship. She is, by definition, a woman who experiences severe intimate partner violence perpetrated by a man. Battered women's syndrome is not the most common instance of IPV but is the most commonly researched type of violence (Frieze & Chen, 2010). In this type of IPV, the male partner can be severely physically violent, as well as psychologically abusive. Along with the physical and psychological abuse, issues with drugs, alcohol, coercion, and surveillance of the woman are often present (Frieze & Chen, 2010).

As a way of capturing the multiple factors related to IPV, Figure 18.1 illustrates Pence and Paymer's power and control wheel that is based on research done with more than 200 victim-survivors at a Duluth domestic violence shelter and includes confirmation from perpetrators of violence (Chavis & Hill, 2008). Intimate partner violence is complicated by the notion that perpetrators utilize tactics (or behaviors and actions) that maintain power and control over the victim-survivor (Chavis & Hill, 2008). The eight "tactics" noted in Figure 18.1 are used to gain and maintain control, often supported by physical and sexual violence. The tactics include intimidation; emotional abuse; isolation; minimizing, denying, and blaming; using children; using male privilege; economic abuse; and coercion and threats (Chavis & Hill, 2008). This power and control model is heavily gender based and presupposes a male perpetrator and female victim. It is widely used with both victim-survivors and batterers and demonstrates the intersection of both psychological control and physical violence (Chavis & Hill, 2008).

RIGHTS OF WOMEN

From the early days of public advocacy for battered women in the 1970s, awareness began to grow around violence against women, culminating over several decades in federal legislation called the Violence Against Women Act (VAWA) of 1994. It included provisions that criminalized acts of gender-based violence and allocated funding for prevention, response, and treatment (Biden, 2000). Cho and Wilke (2005) refer to this act as a "consolidation" of existing state laws that were passed prior to the federal law. Prior to the signing of this significant federal act, crimes against women were perceived as "anything *but* crime" (Biden, 2000, p. 4). The passage of the Violence Against Women Act (VAWA) of 1994 signaled a major cultural shift in the way intimate partner violence and related crimes were viewed. The VAWA was first introduced with the intention of increasing legal protections in the judicial system by Senator Biden in

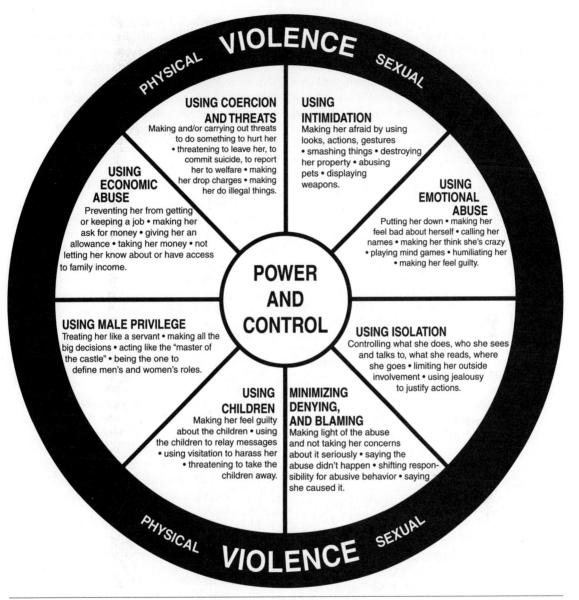

Figure 18.1   The Duluth Model, the Power and Control Wheel, Developed by Survivors of Intimate Partner Violence

Source: Domestic Abuse Intervention Project, 202 East Superior Street, Duluth, MN 55802; 218-722-2781; www.theduluthmodel.org.

1990 and was signed into law by President Clinton 4 years later (Biden, 2000).

The passage of VAWA was the result of a 4-year inquiry by Congress that established the gender-based nature of these crimes and highlighted disturbing statistics and trends. The VAWA was an attempt to rectify the existing state of affairs at the time, in which violent crimes against women were under-recognized and not treated seriously. Indeed, not only was wife battery not recognized as a crime, but it was also an institutionalized practice, illustrated by the historical "rule of thumb" law that stipulated husbands should not beat their wives with anything wider than a thumb (Biden, 2000). As Biden wrote about the congressional inquiry,

> This legislative record demonstrated that violence against women is a national problem of the highest order—a problem that Congress found seriously impeded women from participating fully in the commercial life of the nation and one that state legal systems had proven unable and unwilling to remedy. The evidence reflected that violence is the leading cause of injury to women ages fifteen to forty-four. (Biden, 2000)

Biden further describes the appalling statistics on violence against women in the United States that were used to lead the legislative effort to pass the federal act. As a result, the criminal justice system has increased police notification and perpetrator arrest (Cho & Wilke, 2005).

From a Private Matter to a Public Health Concern

A key paradigm shift occurred with the congressional inquiry and passage of VAWA where IPV and related forms of violence were no longer viewed as private matters but rather as a pervasive public health problem. The law codified the efforts of advocates since the 1970s, as well as instituted a cultural shift in thought about the problems facing battered women (Biden, 2000). The transformation of the public perception of violence against women into a public health problem was due largely to the dissemination of an early feminist message about IPV, specifically "that domestic violence is

common, that it is based in gender inequality and oppression of women, and that it affects women of all social standings, effectively cutting across stratifications of ethnicity and socioeconomic status" (Nixon & Humphreys, 2010, p. 138). While efforts to gain recognition of IPV as a public health problem have succeeded, there has been less success in measuring the severity and mutuality of IPV beyond the research of Williams and Frieze (2010).

Disproportionate Impact on Women

The disproportionate impact of intimate partner violence on the oppression of women clearly constitutes a social injustice. Simply stated, women are more likely to be victim-survivors of IPV, particularly severe forms, and they experience worse outcomes compared to male victim-survivors as a result (Tjaden & Thoennes, 2000). Several national surveys have identified women as the primary recipients of intimate partner violence, including the 2000 *National Violence Against Women Survey* (Tjaden & Thoennes, 2000) and the 2011 White House report on *Women in America: Indicators of Social and Economic Well-Being.*

These national reports document the disparate effect of intimate partner violence. The significantly greater incidence of women being victimized by intimate partners over the course of a lifetime held true across different types of violence, including rape, physical assault, and stalking (Tjaden & Thoennes, 2000). Even more disturbing are the findings:

> Moreover, the survey found that differences between women's and men's rates of physical assault by an intimate partner become greater as the seriousness of the assault increases. For example, women were two or three times more likely than men to report that an intimate partner threw something that could hurt them or pushed, grabbed, or shoved them. However, they were 7 to 14 times more likely to report that an intimate partner beat them up, choked or tried to drown them, or threatened them with a gun or knife. (Tjaden & Thoennes, 2000, p. 17)

In addition, women make up 70% of all victims killed by an intimate partner (U.S. Department of Commerce [DOE], 2011), and intimate partners were responsible for 26% of all violence against females and only 5% of all violence against males. Women are also at much greater risk of being raped (a dramatically underreported crime) as well as stalked (DOE, 2011).

While there has been a major focus in our society on women as victims of crimes (DOE, 2011), women can also perpetrate intimate partner violence at lower rates against male or female partners, as well as committing other crimes. In fact, since 2000, women in America were incarcerated at an increased rate. While an examination of the meaning of these statistics is outside of the scope of this analysis, they do illustrate the presence of female perpetrated violence and crime. While both nonfatal violent crimes and femicides (murder of women) declined between 1993 and 2008, "sexual victimization and intimate partner violence disproportionately affect women" (DOE, 2011, p. 53).

OUTCOMES OF INTIMATE PARTNER VIOLENCE

Numerous negative outcomes have been associated with intimate partner violence perpetrated against women, including effects that include the physical, psychological, financial, and reproductive. As Plichta (2004) notes, the negative physical health consequences experienced by women suffering from intimate partner abuse include poor communication with their health care providers and increased risk of female mortality where intimate partners represent 41% of known perpetrators of this type of murder. A Kansas City, Missouri, study reports that "almost one half of victims of femicide had prior visits to the ER for injuries because of IPV" (Plichta, 2004, p. 1300). In addition, 13% to 24% of all pregnancy-associated deaths are attributable to femicide where death occurs during or within one year of delivery or the termination of the pregnancy (Plichta, 2004).

Women experiencing intimate partner violence are at greater risk of minor life threatening injuries, especially injuries to the head, neck, and face. Long-term detrimental effects include traumatic brain injury, strangulation, disability, chronic pain, and declining maternal health during pregnancy. Finally, there are indirect effects on the health of women

(e.g., poor general physical health), increased risk of sexually transmitted diseases and urinary tract infections, and poor health behavior (e.g., smoking, drug use, and poor nutrition) (Plichta, 2004).

Another dimension of negative health outcomes stemming from the coercive control that often accompanies intimate partner violence is negative consequences on the reproductive health of victim-survivors. Pregnancy is a time of increased risk of violence where, according to Moore, Frohwirth, and Miller (2010), "male reproductive control" contributes to poor sexual and reproductive health outcomes and intimate partner violence is associated with "unwanted pregnancy, women not using their preferred contraceptive method, sexually transmitted infections including HIV/AIDS, miscarriages, repeat abortion, a high number of sexual partners, and poor pregnancy outcomes" (p. 1737).

Male reproductive control constrains women's reproductive freedoms related to forced sex, a partner's refusal to use contraception, a lack of negotiating power on the part of the victim-survivor, interference with contraception, and the abusive partner's refusal to pay for contraception (Moore et al., 2010). Male reproductive control includes one or more of the following tactics: intimidation, threats, and/or actual violence. Not only does this form of control negatively impact the health of victim-survivors, but it also denies the autonomy of women (Moore et al., 2010).

The poor psychological effects of intimate partner violence include heightened rates of depression, anxiety disorder, post-traumatic stress disorder (PTSD), substance abuse, and cognitive disturbance (e.g., hopelessness, low self-esteem, and suicidality) (Jordan, Campbell & Follingstad, 2010). While Jordan et al. (2010) view sexual violence, psychological aggression, and stalking separately from intimate partner violence, all three can occur along with IPV and produce negative health outcomes that need to be viewed holistically (especially the combination of PTSD, depression, and substance abuse disorders). Observable psychological traits that do not meet the threshold of a mental health diagnosis are also seen in female victim-survivors (e.g., low self-esteem and self-blame for the abuse) (Jordan et al., 2010).

These injurious health outcomes and limited access to services in the mental health system are further complicated by inadequate service provider knowledge. As Jordan et al. (2010) note, "If there is one consistency in reviews of clinical outcome research related to IPV, sexual assault, and other forms of violence against women, it is that the extant literature is inadequate" (p. 617). This lack of empirical data compounds the following issues: (a) Mental health services are most commonly accessed by Caucasians, with women of color turning to informal sources of support; (b) lack of health insurance of victim-survivors creates a barrier to care; (c) perpetrators may try to prevent victim-survivors from seeking care; and (d) once in the mental health system, women may not be identified victim-survivors (Jordan et al., 2010).

The impact of detrimental physical and psychological effects can be most vividly seen in women engaged in paid work outside the home. Physical and mental health issues resulting from IPV are often associated with poor work outcomes. Banyard, Potter, and Turner (2011) cite high levels of victimization among working women in the forms of stalking and job interference. They found that experiences of interpersonal victimization were linked to poor work outcomes as reflected in an inability to concentrate, inability to go to work, difficulty problem solving at work, and job loss. These findings demonstrate that mental and physical health outcomes of intimate partner violence can impact other aspects of women's lives.

In addition to physical and psychological outcomes of IPV, financial barriers are both a risk factor and a negative outcome for female survivor-victims. Studies have shown very poor and homeless women to be at increased risk of intimate partner violence (Frieze & Chen, 2010). The challenges include difficulties in retaining employment and the actions of abusers that keep the women dependent. The financial vulnerability of these women predisposes them to more detrimental financial outcomes (Frieze & Chen, 2010). For example, the impact on access to public benefits can be seen in the current requirements for public assistance that can make it difficult for some women to use some assistance to build job experience or even to gain assistance in meeting basic needs (Frieze & Chen, 2010). For women who leave their abusive partnerships, this often leads to financial difficulty and strain associated with the costs of setting up a new household and managing debts incurred during the violent relationship (Frieze & Chen, 2010). A final compounding factor is the sense of isolation and the lack of adequate support networks for women experiencing severe violence (Frieze & Chen, 2010).

INTERSECTIONALITY AND INTIMATE PARTNER VIOLENCE

The singular lens of gender is insufficient to understand the varied experiences of IPV as a form of social injustice since no lens is neutral, each privileging a certain experience of intimate partner violence. While the gender-based view of IPV as a social injustice stems from an early feminist systemic construct (e.g., wife battery or domestic violence based on the assumptions and social location of the most vocal advocates, namely, upper-middle class White women). As Bograd (1999) noted, "I privileged the dimension of gender over others because it seemed to offer parsimonious explanatory power and clinical direction" (p. 276). Since then, much has changed in the articulation of violence against women.

New perspectives include greater insight into differences among human experiences and diverse cultures. Based on these differences, Bograd (1999) makes the case for an intersectional approach in which intimate partner violence is considered a form of oppression and social control, based on the social contexts in which people live, namely, the intersections between systems of power and oppression in the form of prejudice, class stratification, gender inequality, and heterosexist bias. These systems can compound one another. Bograd (1999) notes that "gender inequality itself is modified by its intersection with other systems of power and oppression" (p. 277). It has become increasingly apparent that experiences of IPV require multiple lenses of oppression and power.

Chavis and Hill (2008) operationalized an intersectional approach (e.g., multicultural power and control wheel) to address the lack of attention to issues of diversity in the IPV literature, especially the "experiences of immigrants and racial/ethnic minorities, elderly victims, those with low incomes, victims with disabilities, those in same-sex relationships, or the role of religion/spirituality in relationships where IPV is present" (p. 122). They argue that an individual's social location at certain intersections of oppression and power may result in greater entrapment by violence. Women are viewed in their full heterogeneity that includes sexual orientation, age, race or ethnicity, disability, religion or spirituality, and class. The use of multiple intersectional lenses makes it possible to encompass multiple dimensions of identity and oppression as well as account for power and control tactics specific to each intersection of identity (Chavis & Hill, 2008). For example, emotional abuse that is racial in character could be "making her feel like she is betraying her race" while using intimidation in an ageist manner might be "instilling fear with greater physical strength" (Chavis & Hill, 2008, p. 140).

THREE INTERSECTIONS OF
OPPRESSION AND INTIMATE PARTNER VIOLENCE

As a way of demonstrating the intersectional nature of IPV, three different groups of women were selected for focus, despite the overlapping nature of these three groups, namely, women with disabilities, immigrant women, and lesbian partners. One commonality is the way in which identity and oppression shape the abuse experience and constrain options for escape thereby compounding the social injustice. The inequities of ableism, immigrant policy, and heterosexism also create new opportunities and vulnerabilities for perpetrators to exploit, as well as unique barriers to legal help and social services. Higher rates of IPV were found in each group, despite the limited amount of research on IPV among these three groups over the past decade (Copel, 2006; Erez, Adelman, & Gregory, 2009; Fortunata & Kohn, 2003; Hassouneh & Glass, 2008; Ingram, Mclelland, Martin, Caballero, & Mayorga, 2010; Mays, 2006). Just as intimate partner violence against women has come out of the private sphere

into the public realm, so are these intersections being drawn into the light of day.

Disability and Intimate Partner Violence

Research focusing on the specific experiences of victim-survivors of IPV with disabilities emerged in the 1980s when disability and abuse were generally treated separately in the literature (Copel, 2006). It was not until the 1990s that large-scale studies in the United States and Canada highlighted the issue of violence against people with disabilities that is linked to "historical, social, political, and economic dimensions, such as systemic inequality" (Mays, 2006, p. 147). A specific form of inequality related to IPV is a form of discrimination called *ableism* that privileges the able-bodied in a society and systematically oppresses those with disabilities (Chavis & Hill, 2008). In an ableist society, different ability is construed in such a way that marginalizes those with disabilities (Mays, 2006). This marginalization emerging at the intersection of gender and ability is just beginning to be documented in research on IPV and disability.

At the intersection of gender and ability, women with disabilities can be at greater risk of intimate partner violence because it can persist for longer periods of time (Copel, 2006). Not only are husbands and partners potential perpetrators, but women with disabilities also face abuse at the hands of health care workers and personal care attendants (Copel, 2006). The most frequent form of abuse of women with disabilities is usually perpetrated in the home by a male partner (Chavis & Hill, 2008). Furthermore, certain types of abuse are disability specific, such as tampering with assistive devices or unwanted sexual touching during caregiving activities (Chavis & Hill, 2008). Disabled women's firsthand accounts of experiences of abuse include stressors that exceed their ability to cope. For example, the use of economic abuse occurs when perpetrators enforce power and control over survivor-victims with disabilities, especially since disabled women have higher rates of poverty and unemployment than their nondisabled peers (Mays, 2006). Other risk factors include social isolation and the lack of credibility experienced by women when they seek to report abusers (Copel, 2006). The myth that women with disabilities are asexual and would therefore not have intimate partnership makes invisible the widespread crisis of abuse as well as limits their access to IPV resources, especially legal services, social services, and economic self-sufficiency (Chavis & Hill, 2008; Mays, 2006).

Immigrant Women and Intimate Partner Violence

At the intersection of immigration and other identities, intimate partner violence is experienced in ways that are unique to immigrant women in the United States. As noted by Erez et al. (2009), "Rather than consider immigration as a variable or static category within race, we consider immigration as part of the multiple grounds of identity shaping the domestic violence experience" (p. 33). Immigration status, then, is another dimension of power, oppression, and identity that can help to explain the prevalence and impact of IPV. The status of being an immigrant brings with it an array of vulnerabilities, barriers, and special considerations in the realm of IPV.

In spite of the longer history of domestic violence research and advocacy, research on intimate partner violence against immigrant women only began to emerge in the early 2000s (Ingram et al., 2010). Immigrants and immigrant women face special risk factors because they are inhibited from escaping from IPV due to their legal status (Erez et al., 2009). In fact, immigration laws are considered a "trap" for immigrant women because they can increase the danger of IPV (Erez et al., 2009). Under U.S. immigration law, the legal status of women often depends on the sponsoring spouse, with married couples being treated as a single legal entity (Erez et al., 2009). The dependence on husbands can create extreme vulnerability (Erez et al., 2009). Existing gender inequality, whether in the country of origin or in the United States, is intensified by the circumstances under which wives often immigrate. This dependency gives rise to new forms of intimate partner violence as illustrated in the form of (a) destroying their spouse's immigration papers, (b) threatening to withdraw their petitions for immigration, or (c) threatening to call immigration authorities and have

them deported (Ingram et al., 2010). M. Ingram et al. (2010) noted that 72% of citizen or legal resident spouses who are abusive do not file immigration petitions for their wives.

As a result of cultural expectations, immigrant women are at greater risk of intimate partner violence as a result of patriarchy and collectivism that can exacerbate the increased risk already present in their dependency status (Ingram et al., 2010). Further intensification of IPV occurs when immigrant women find themselves socially isolated in a new country and facing financial insecurity (Ingram et al., 2010).

When VAWA was passed in 1994, it included provisions for undocumented immigrant women by allowing them to self-petition for citizenship or to request suspension of deportation when experiencing abuse. However, it failed to protect those immigrant women abused by U.S. citizens and lawful resident boyfriends and fiancés, as well as immigrant spouses. The VAWA Reauthorization Act of 2000 created immigration relief for the children of victim-survivors and the VAWA Reauthorization Act of 2005 expanded protections further (Conyers, 2007).

Even in successful cases of self-petitioning, the women described many barriers, especially the hesitancy to file the petition based on the fear that it might be rejected and result in deportation. Immigrant women often described self-petitioning as a final resort (Ingram et al., 2010). Once the decision to file the application has been made, additional hurdles include (a) reliving their emotions through the required personal statement, (b) coping with the insecurity of having to wait for an outcome, (c) experiencing confusion about the process, intensified by their emotional state, (d) amassing the amount of evidence needed to demonstrate eligibility, (e) financial hardship due to the length of time spent waiting for employment authorization, and (f) being separated from family due to the stipulation that they must remain in the United States throughout the application process (Ingram et al., 2010).

Many immigrant women, often the most impoverished, do not make it through the process of filing an application, making it even more difficult to escape their abusers (Villalón, 2010). Lacking knowledge about their right to self-petition under

VAWA, immigrant women whose immigration status depends on their husbands' sponsorship will not leave their abusers out of fear (Erez et al., 2009). In addition, immigrant women often lack access to financial resources that could help them escape their abuser who often becomes increasingly abusive and controlling due to frustrations with finances (Erez et al., 2009).

Lesbian Partner Abuse

While it is difficult to measure the prevalence of lesbian partner violence due to the limited amount of research, the lowest estimate in the best study available is that 11.4% of the lesbian partners experience, over a lifetime, the presence of female same-sex intimate partner violence (FSSIPV) (Hasssouneh & Glass, 2008). Some research shows that lesbian rates of FSSIPV are similar to those rates of heterosexual couples where physical, social, and psychological violence occurs (Eaton, Kaufman, Fuhrel, Cain, & Cherry, 2008). However, the National Violence Against Women Study identifies a much higher lifetime prevalence rate of IPV among lesbian women (35.4 %) than heterosexual women (20.4%) (Klostermann, Kelley, Milletich, & Mignone, 2011). The paucity of clear and accurate information on female same-sex IPV may be due to the homophobia that inhibits lesbian, bisexual, and transgender women from reporting violence (Klostermann et al., 2011). Another barrier to recognizing IPV in same-sex relationships can be traced to the battered women's movement that framed IPV in terms of a male perpetrator and a female victim (Hassouneh & Glass, 2008).

The limited research on risk factors related to FSSIPV makes it difficult to apply heterosexual models of IPV to FSSIPV (Hassouneh & Glass). However, it is well recognized that substance abuse, especially alcohol, is a risk factor for IPV among heterosexuals (Eaton et al., 2008; Klostermann et al., 2011). Furthermore, higher rates of problematic drinking behaviors are increasingly shown to be present in homosexual populations, potentially increasing the risk of IPV (Klostermann et al., 2011). Klostermann et al. (2011) noted that "it is plausible that higher rates of alcohol misuse may contribute to partner violence among sexual

minorities" (p. 116). While another related factor may be sexual risk behaviors, little research is available on the link between sexual risk behaviors and female SSIPV, despite the link in heterosexual populations. Eaton et al. (2008) suggest that this may be due to the constraints of a heterosexist culture and the ignorance of the medical community that fail to recognize the risk of sexually transmitted disease among lesbians.

Gender role stereotyping and homophobia impact women's experiences of intimate partner violence based on a system of heterosexism that oppresses sexual minorities and interacts with other identities (e.g., gender) that shape lesbian experiences of IPV (Hardesty, Oswald, Khaw, & Fonseca, 2011; Hassouneh & Glass, 2008). According to Hardesty et al. (2011),

> Heterosexism refers to the institutionalization of a belief system that denigrates and invalidates sexual minorities. Heterosexism is a salient part of our current formal support systems, which often assume heterosexuality, offer limited to no services specific to sexual minorities, and include providers who are homophobic. (p. 29)

Hassouneh and Glass (2008) identify the following ways in which gender role stereotyping exacerbates FSSIPV and creates barriers to help seeking by placing lesbian, bisexual, transgender (LBT) women at greater risk: (a) the myth that "girls don't hit other girls," (b) the myth that there is a lesbian utopia in which IPV does not exist, (c) the myth that abuse is merely a "cat fight," and (4) the myth that women are not perpetrators.

In focusing on the impact of this type of stereotyping, Hassouneh and Glass (2008) note that there is a reluctance on the part of the battered women's movement and the LBT community to recognize FSSIPV and concluded that "this reluctance has place battered LBT women at a severe disadvantage, leaving them with extremely limited access to vital social, health, and community services that meet their needs" (p. 312). Even when lesbian women reach out to social services, for example, they face barriers to receiving assistance due to stereotyping. In a study of crisis center staff, same-sex domestic violence calls tended to be rated as less serious than opposite-sex domestic violence calls (Brown & Groscup, 2008). Lesbian women are often reluctant to report IPV due to the barrier of homophobia that impedes women from seeking help through the legal and social service system. Reporting IPV may also place lesbian women at risk of losing custody or visitation rights of their children (Eaton et al., 2008; Hardesty et al., 2011). Lesbian women who have experienced IPV report distrust of law enforcement and the courts (Eaton et al., 2008).

FUTURE DIRECTIONS

The Utility of Defining Gender-Based Violence

Is there any ongoing value in defining violence against women as a form of gender-based violence? Given the historical influence of early feminism on the discourse about intimate partner violence as a gender-based form of social injustice (e.g., the VAWA 1994), it is still difficult for lesbians to recognize and seek help for intimate partner violence when gender stereotypes block our perceptions and understanding of female-perpetrated intimate partner violence. Indeed, there are some who would argue for a "personality-based" definition of perpetrators that discounts gender (Eaton et al., 2008). How can we use the intersectional approach to negotiate a more multidimensional analysis that moves us beyond gender-based violence?

Employing the Intersectional Framework

To what extent does the inclusion of an intersectional analysis inform practice? How might the application of this approach make vital treatment more accessible to many underserved groups? Given the limited nature of the research on intersectionality and the multiple dimensions of identity and oppression related to IPV, it seems important to find ways for this approach to be applied in clinical settings. What would the implementation of the intersectional framework look like in a treatment context? How would this be achieved given disparities in the resources allotted to research on diverse populations and their access to social services?

The commonalities seen across the domains discussed in this analysis raise the possibility of a systematic analysis across discrete forms of identity. To what extent do individuals with multiple marginal identities experience greater risk for IPV that compounds the effects of multiple identities and forms of oppression? Also, how should we interpret and address the unique forms of IPV that perpetrators devise at these intersections, as in the case of abuses related to immigration status? Do these unique patterns, seen at different intersections, form a useful model that could inform policy related to social and legal services?

CONCLUSION

Intimate partner violence is well established as a form of gender-based violence and a social injustice that disproportionately affects women. The movement to end this form of violence has evolved from discourses on "wife battery" and "domestic violence" to intimate partner violence. The early feminist perspective on violence against women led to successful efforts to raise public consciousness about the issue and the passage of the Violence Against Women Act of 1994 but also created limitations in our understanding of IPV. Developing since the 1990s, the intersectional approach to IPV helps to highlight intersections of experience and oppressions in the lives of women who reflect differences in race, ethnicity, religion, ability, sexual orientation, and immigration status. As demonstrated by the examples of women with disabilities, immigrant women, and female same-sex intimate partner violence, the state of the research on intersectionality and IPV is still evolving and needs to be applied to public policy and social service interventions. The intersectional approach holds great potential for refining our response to this social injustice of violence against women.

REFERENCES

Banyard, V., Potter, S., & Turner, H. (2011). The impact of interpersonal violence in adulthood on women's job satisfaction and productivity: The mediating roles of mental and physical health. *Psychology of Violence, 1*(1), 16–28.

Biden, J. (2000). The civil rights remedy of the Violence Against Women Act: A defense. *Harvard Journal of Legislation, 437*, 1–44.

Bograd, M. (1999). Strengthening domestic violence theories: intersections of race, class, sexual orientation, and gender. *Journal of Marital and Family Therapy, 25*(3), 275–289.

Brown, M. J., & Groscup, J. (2008). Perceptions of same-sex domestic violence among crisis center staff. *Journal of Family Violence, 24*, 87–93.

Chavis, A., & Hill, M. S. (2008). Integrating multiple intersecting identities: A multicultural conceptualization of the power and control wheel. *Women and Therapy, 32*(1), 121–149.

Cho, H., & Wilke, D. J. (2005). How has the Violence Against Women Act affected the response of the criminal justice system to domestic violence? *Journal of Sociology and Social Welfare, 32*(4), 125–139.

Conyers, J. (2007). The 2005 reauthorization of the violence against women act: Why Congress acted to expand protections to immigrant victims. *Violence Against Women, 13*(5), 457–468.

Copel, L. C. (2006). Partner abuse in physically disabled women: A proposed model for understanding intimate partner violence. *Perspectives in Psychiatric Care, 42*(2), 114–128.

Eaton, L., Kaufman, M., Fuhrel, A., Cain, D., & Cherry, C. (2008). Examining factors co-existing with interpersonal violence in lesbian relationships. *Journal of Family Violence, 23*, 697–705.

Erez, E., Adelman, M., & Gregory, C. (2009). Intersections of immigration and domestic violence: Voices of battered immigrant women. *Feminist Criminology, 4*(32), 32–56.

Fortunata, B., & Kohn, C. S. (2003). Demographic, psychosocial, and personality characteristics of lesbian batters. *Violence and Victims, 18*(5), 557–568.

Frieze, I. H., & Chen, K. (Ed.). (2010). *Intimate partner violence: Perspectives from racial/ethnic group in the united states.* New York, NY: Springer.

Hardesty, J. L., Oswald, R. F., Khaw, L., & Fonseca, C. (2011). Lesbian/bisexual mothers and intimate partner violence: Help seeking in the context of social and legal vulnerability. *Violence Against Women, 2009, 17*(1), 28–45.

Hassouneh, D., & Glass, N. (2008). The influence of gender role stereotyping on women's experiences of female same-sex intimate partner violence. *Violence Against Women, 14*(3), 310–325.

Ingram, M., Mclelland, D. J., Martin, J., Caballero, M. F., & Mayorga, M. T. (2010). Experiences of immigrant women who self-petition under the violence against women act. *Violence Against Women, 16*(8), 859–880.

Jordan, C. E., Campbell, R., & Follingstad, D. (2010). Violence and women's mental health: The impact of physical, sexual, and psychological aggression. *Annual Review of Clinical Psychology, 6*, 607–628.

Klostermann, K., Kelley, M. L., Milletich, R. J., & Mignone, T. (2011). Alcoholism and partner aggression among gay and lesbian couples. *Aggression and Violent Behavior, 16*, 115–119.

Mays, J. M. (2006). Feminist disability theory: Domestic violence against women with a disability. *Disability and Society, 21*(2), 147–158.

Moore, A. M., Frohwirth, L., & Miller, E. (2010). Male reproductive control of women who have experienced intimate partner violence in the united states. *Social Science and Medicine, 70*, 1737–1744.

Nixon, J., & Humphreys, C. (2010). Marshalling the evidence: Using intersectionality in the domestic violence frame. *Social Politics: International Studies in Gender, State and Society, 17*(2), 137–158.

Plichta, S. B. (2004). Intimate partner violence and physical health consequences: Policy and practice implications. *Journal of Interpersonal Violence, 19*(11), 1296–1323.

Sokoloff, N. J., & Dupont, I. (2005). Domestic violence: Examining the intersections of race, class, and gender—An introduction. In N. Sokoloff (Ed.), *Domestic violence at the margins: Readings on race, class, gender, and culture* (pp. 1–11). New Brunswick, NJ: Rutgers University Press.

Tjaden, P., & Thoennes, N. (2000, July). *Extent, nature, and consequences of intimate partner violence: Findings from the National Violence Against Women Survey* (Report No. NCJ-181867). Washington, DC: U.S. Department of Justice, National Institute of Justice.

U.S. Department of Commerce (DOE), Economics and Statistics Administration, Executive Office of the President Office of Management and Budget. (2011). *Women in America: Indicators of social and economic well-being.* Washington, DC: Author.

Villalón, R. (2010). Passage to citizenship and the nuances of agency: Latina battered immigrants. *Women's Studies International Forum, 33*, 552–560.

Williams, S. L., & Frieze, I. H. (2010). Patterns of violent relationships, psychological distress, and marital satisfaction in a national sample of men and women. *Sex Roles, 52*(11/12), 771–784.

19

SOCIAL INJUSTICES EXPERIENCED BY CHILDREN OF INCARCERATED PARENTS

JENNY VENTURA

INTRODUCTION

The children of prisoners are guaranteed nothing. They have committed no crime, but the penalty they are required to pay is steep. They forfeit, too often, much of what matters to them: their homes, their safety, their public status and private self-image, their primary source of comfort and affection. Their lives and prospects are profoundly affected by the multiple institutions that lay claim to their parents—police, courts, jails and prisons, probation and parole—but they have no rights, explicit or implicit within any of these jurisdictions. Children of incarcerated parents experience injustice at all junctures of their parent's incarceration, from arrest to release. (Bernstein, 2005, p. 4)

Across the nation, researchers, child-advocates, service providers, and those working in public policy are beginning to pay attention to a population of vulnerable children who have been historically overlooked: children of incarcerated parents. Those concerned with the well-being of children are beginning to understand the unique challenges that this population faces and how these challenges are often exacerbated or ignored during different junctures of their parent's incarceration process, including arrest, sentencing, visitation, and community reentry. The San Francisco Children of Incarcerated Parents Partnership (SFCIPP, 2005) is dedicated to promoting the child's perspective during a parent's incarceration process by publishing the widely disseminated document called *Children of Incarcerated Parents: A Bill of Rights* that includes the following:

1. I have the right to be kept safe and informed at the time of my parent's arrest.

2. I have the right to be heard when decisions are made about me.

3. I have the right to be considered when decisions are made about my parent.

4. I have the right to be well cared for in my parent's absence.

5. I have the right to speak with, see and touch my parent.

6. I have the right to support as I face my parent's incarceration.

7. I have the right not to be judged, blamed or labeled because my parent is incarcerated.

8. I have the right to a lifelong relationship with my parent. (SFCIPP, 2005)

This chapter uses the bill of rights as a framework to highlight the various social injustices experienced by children of incarcerated parents at each juncture of their parents' incarceration.

Globally, the United States has the highest number of incarcerated individuals in both absolute and per-capita terms (McLeigh & Sianko, 2010; The Pew Center on the States, 2008). By 2008, nearly one in 100 adults were incarcerated, representing a 700% increase since 1970 (The Pew Center on the States, 2008). Over half of the individuals incarcerated in the United States are parents of children under the age of 18, and it is estimated that there are now 2.7 million children with a parent currently behind bars (The Pew Charitable Trusts, 2010). In addition, it is estimated that over 10 million children have parents who were imprisoned at some point in their lives (Hirsche et al., 2002). Children of color are disproportionately affected by parental incarceration. African American children (11.4%) are nearly six and a half times more likely than White children (1.8%) to have an incarcerated parent and Hispanic children (3.5%) are nearly two times more likely than White children to have an incarcerated parent (The Pew Charitable Trusts, 2010).

Another important nationwide trend is the fact that the rate of incarcerating women has increased faster than the rate of incarcerating men, although the number of incarcerated men is still roughly 10 times the number of incarcerated women (Makariev & Shaver, 2010). The impact of this trend is illustrated by the fact that the number of children with incarcerated mothers has grown more rapidly (131%) than the number of children with incarcerated fathers (79%) between the years 1991 and 2007 (Murray & Murray, 2010). The overall high rates of female incarceration are of great concern because nearly three quarters of women incarcerated are single parents of minor children thereby threatening the structure and functioning of families (Cassidy et al., 2010; Dallaire, 2007). The incarceration of a mother is much more likely to disrupt care arrangements for children, as many of these children lose

their primary caregiver in the process (Murray & Murray, 2010). While the vast majority of children with incarcerated fathers live with their mothers during the incarceration period, children of incarcerated mothers are more likely to live with their grandparents, other family members, or in foster care (Poehlmann, Dallaire, Loper, & Shear, 2010).

There is substantial evidence to suggest that children of incarcerated parents may be in need of services, including economic, emotional, and social support. For example, Murray and colleagues (2009) found that children of prisoners have about twice the risk of antisocial behavior (externalizing behavior) and poor mental health outcomes (internalizing behavior) compared to children without imprisoned parents. Although there is a lack of sufficient evidence to suggest that parental imprisonment is a *causal* risk factor, having a parent in prison correlates with an increased probability that children will experience antisocial behavior and poor mental health outcomes (Murray, Farrington, Sekol, & Olsen, 2009). Some of these children's antisocial behaviors include high rates of truancy, increased drug use, displays of physical aggression, delinquency, disruptive behaviors, and, eventually, higher incarceration rates than that of their peers (Adalist-Estrin, 2006; Allard & Greene, 2011; Wagner, 2006). Poor mental health outcomes include the experience of anxiety and depression, as well as feelings of fear, loss, anger, guilt, resentment, and sadness (Adalist-Estrin, 2006; Allard & Greene, 2011; Wagner, 2006).

It is important to note that the consequences of incarceration on children and families are multifaceted and complex. Incarceration can have both positive and negative effects on a family. For example, if the incarcerated individual was violent, removing this person may decrease violence in the household while causing stress to the remaining family members, financially and socially. The effects on children are not universal. While some children and families cope successfully with the experience of parental incarceration, it is clear that a substantial portion of these children would benefit from additional support.

The factors that contribute to the unique challenges and risks faced by many children of incarcerated parents exist on several levels. On the first level, when one or both parents of a child are incarcerated, the child will likely experience dramatic disruption and uncertainty. These include (a) a loss of secure attachments and undermined sense of stability and safety, (b) threats to his or her family's economic security, (c) a compromised sense of connectedness and worthiness, as well as possible social stigmatization (Allard & Greene, 2011; La Vigne, Davies, & Brazzel, 2008). While these children may already face other risk factors, such as living in poverty, studies have shown that the removal of a parent through incarceration represents a risk factor that directly correlates with antisocial behavior and poor mental health (La Vigne et al., 2008).

In addition, the unique needs of children of incarcerated parents are often not met because systemically this population often goes unidentified, resulting in a lack of direct services to support these children as well as limited data on the number of children of incarcerated parents (La Vigne et al., 2008; Wagner, 2006). With limited coordination of the various institutions that handle accused offenders (e.g., police, courts, jails, prisons, and probation departments), it is not surprising that these agencies do not inquire about the existence of children, much less address their needs and care (Adalist-Estrin, 2006).

Finally, the number of children with incarcerated parents is increasing due to the growing number of people incarcerated nationwide. The expansion of the prison system in the United States is related to the increased number of children facing the unique risks and challenges that result when one or both of their parents are incarcerated.

The injustices experienced by these children stem from a lack of understanding about this population and its needs; from the stigma often associated with incarceration; from current policies and practices that create barriers to a healthy, safe, and just experience for children; and from a lack of alternative policies and practices that take the children's experience into account. This chapter describes the injustices experienced by children of incarcerated parents at each juncture of their parents' involvement in the criminal justice system. More specifically, it explores the child's experience in relationship to arrest, sentencing, stigma, alternative care, visitation, and community reentry.

BILL OF RIGHTS 1: I HAVE THE RIGHT TO BE KEPT SAFE AND INFORMED AT THE TIME OF MY PARENT'S ARREST

A nine-year-old burns his hand trying to make breakfast for himself and his baby brother. The two have been alone in an empty apartment for almost two weeks, since police removed their mother without explanation. Eventually, a neighbor will notice the boy out pushing a stroller by himself and call Child Protective Services. (Bernstein, 2005, p. 1)

It is difficult to imagine the trauma associated with the arrest of one's parent. For many children, the trauma of a parent's arrest is unnecessarily exacerbated by the lack of police department policies for dealing with an arrest in which children are present. In a national survey by the American Bar Association Center on Children and the Law, the researchers found that only one third of officers will handle an arrest differently if children are present; only one in 10 will take special care to protect the needs of the children (Smith & Elstein, 1994).

A lack of protocols on how to handle the arrest of a parent can negatively affect children. Witnessing the arrest is, in itself, a traumatic experience. Police officers are not systematically trained to address the trauma created by parental arrests, nor are they taught alternative approaches to minimize that trauma (Nolan, 2003; Smith & Elstein, 1994). In interviews with 30 children each of whom had witnessed his or her mother's arrest, C. Kampfner (1995) found that these children exhibited symptoms of post-traumatic stress disorder (PTSD), including nightmares and flashbacks of the arrest.

This traumatic event is often aggravated by police conduct and arrest protocols, including arresting and restraining individuals in front of their children and routinely conducting arrests at night with guns drawn (Nieto, 2002). In a national study, it was found that 70% of children present while their parents were arrested watched their parents get handcuffed and 30% were confronted with drawn weapons (Smith & Elstein, 1994). This same survey showed that many police raids were conducted in the middle of the night, when the suspects were usually at home with their families, forcing children to awaken to the sound of sirens and strangers breaking into their homes (Bernstein, 2005; Smith & Elstein, 1994).

For children who have one or both custodial parents arrested, an alternative caregiving arrangement needs to be made. Most law enforcement agencies lack training and protocols on how and where to place children when a parent is arrested and incarcerated (Nieto, 2002). Routinely, arrested mothers are not given access to a phone to secure a safe caregiver for their children at the time of the arrest (Bernstein, 2005). This increases the chances of children being transported in police cars to the police station and then into foster care or an emergency shelter, with no familiar faces and little understanding of what is happening. In many interviews with children of the incarcerated, Bernstein (2005) found that children often felt like they were being arrested when they were transported in police cars. Due to lack of protocol, children may also be left home alone to fend for themselves, or, placed in unsafe environments because officers hurriedly identify caregivers without any knowledge of their histories and background (Annie E. Casey Foundation, 2001; Bernstein, 2005; Nolan, 2003).

Even if children are not present at an arrest, there is still potential for unnecessary harm. Arresting officers are not required to inquire about the existence of offenders' children, much less concern themselves with the children's care. As a result, children may come home to an empty house where they are left to fend for themselves, sometimes for days or weeks, without knowledge of their parent's whereabouts and condition (Bernstein, 2005; Nolan 2003).

After an arrest is made, information about where the parent is being taken and how to arrange visitation is not routinely given to children and their alternative caregivers. This can result in children being unable to reconnect with their parent for weeks after the arrest (Bernstein, 2005). For children, the effects of this separation can be quite traumatic, especially considering that they may be unaware of their parent's condition, their location, and when they can expect to make contact with their parent again. This lack of knowledge can produce high levels of anxiety, PTSD-like symptoms, bad dreams, and other negative experiences for children of incarcerated parents (Nolan, 2003).

Coordination of services between the police department and social services is sorely lacking in cases of parental arrest. Surveys of child welfare agencies reported a lack of written policies regarding staff response to law enforcement for requests for assistance with minor children at the time of arrest. Surveys also revealed that these very agencies do not have guidelines or consistent policies governing placement of children after their parent's arrest (Nolan, 2003). Based on these findings, it is clear that "current policies and practices . . . are insufficient to ensure the safety and well-being of children affected by parental arrest" (Nolan, 2003, p. 13).

BILL OF RIGHTS 3: I HAVE THE RIGHT TO BE CONSIDERED WHEN DECISIONS ARE MADE ABOUT MY PARENT

Beginning in the 1970s, the United States underwent a shift in thinking about the purpose of incarceration, by moving from rehabilitation to punishment (Bernstein, 2005). At that time, political conservatives pointed to rising crime rates and research findings that questioned the effectiveness of rehabilitation and called for sentencing reforms as a way to "crack down" on criminals (Travis, Solomon, & Waul, 2001). Part of this shift included the introduction of mandatory sentencing laws that required judges to impose legislatively prescribed sentences for a particular offense, rather than using judicial discretion when deciding on the sentence (Bernstein, 2005; Travis et al., 2001). These mandatory sentencing laws have contributed to the rapid increase in women in the prison population. Bernstein (2005) notes that

> according to the federal general accounting office, their numbers increased more than sevenfold between 1980 and the end of 2003. Most of this increase can be traced to "tough on crime" measures such as mandatory sentencing, rather than to an increase in female criminality. (p. 33)

As more and more women find themselves incarcerated for longer lengths of time, more children are feeling the effects of losing their primary caregiver.

Sentencing reform has contributed to both the increase in imprisonment rates and the soaring prison population as many individuals are serving much longer sentences without the option of earned release. Bernstein (2005) notes that the number of individuals serving life sentences has more than tripled in the past two decades and today one in every 11 federal and state prisoners is doing a life sentence while one in four is serving a sentence of 20 years or more.

Are these mandatory sentencing policies helping to reduce crime and drug abuse rates? A study by the RAND Corporation (Caulkins, 1997) concluded that drug treatment is nearly eight times more effective than are mandatory minimum sentences in reducing drug consumption. However, only 18% of the soon-to-be released prison population with substance abuse problems received treatment while incarcerated (Travis et al., 2001). The nation's shift in philosophy from rehabilitation to punishment has created a situation where parents with substance abuse problems are not only being separated from their children for longer lengths of time but also are returning to the community and to their families without having received the treatment necessary to overcome their disorder and care for their children.

In addition, research indicates that high incarceration rates also impact neighborhoods, making them more crime ridden by breaking up families, destabilizing communities, and damaging the credibility of the law and its enforcers (Bernstein, 2005, p. 56). Children of incarcerated individuals often find themselves growing up in these destabilized communities.

BILL OF RIGHTS 7: I HAVE THE RIGHT NOT TO BE JUDGED, BLAMED OR LABELED BECAUSE MY PARENT IS INCARCERATED

> I used to be the coach of my daughter's softball team. She's played softball all her life and she's always loved it. It was something we did together until I went in. When my daughter was in grade ten, she decided not to play softball anymore. My wife said she would get teased about her father by other players on the team. (Allard & Greene, 2011, p. 20)

While society in general and psychologists, educators, and doctors in particular recognize the significant pain that a child experiences when a parent is lost to death or divorce, the same recognition is not consistently given to those children who lose their parent due to incarceration (Allard and Greene, 2011). These children often suffer from social stigma. As Allard and Greene (2011) note, "unlike children of the deceased or divorced who tend to benefit from society's familiarity with the acceptance of their loss, children of incarcerated parents too often grow up and grieve under a cloud of low expectations and amidst a swirling set of assumptions that they will fail, that they will themselves resort to a life of crime or that they too will succumb to a life of drug addiction" (p. 5).

With the potential for a "self-fulfilling prophecy," social stigma experienced by children of incarcerated parents as a result of bullying, teasing, and biased treatment could actually lead to a higher risk of these children resorting to criminal behavior (Allard & Greene, 2011, p. 7).

Feeling stigmatized by the community, family, and friends may also result in children feeling deeply alienated, along with low self-esteem and an inability to connect with people in their lives (Allard & Greene, 2011). Children who feel stigmatized may respond in one of two unhealthy ways, namely, by exhibiting antisocial behaviors or by isolating themselves and suffering from depression and sadness.

BILL OF RIGHTS 4 AND 6: I HAVE THE RIGHT TO BE WELL CARED FOR IN MY PARENT'S ABSENCE AND I HAVE THE RIGHT TO SUPPORT AS I FACE MY PARENT'S INCARCERATION

Losing a parent to incarceration often creates a state of financial instability or economic hardship for those left to care for the children. Most parents (71%) in state prison were employed either full- or part-time in the month preceding their arrest (Mumola, 2000). Sixty percent of fathers had a full-time job prior to imprisonment, and 68% of them were the primary source of income for their families. Incarcerated mothers relied primarily on wages (44%) and public assistance (42%) as primary sources of family income (Mumola, 2000). When a parent is incarcerated, these sources of income are terminated, leaving a significant economic burden on the alternate caregiver for his or her children (Travis, Cincotta, & Solomon, 2006). Allard and Greene (2011) cite a study that compared the financial circumstances of children whose parents had been imprisoned with those of their peers. After controlling for parental substance use, mental health, education and race, the study found that children of incarcerated parents are 80% more likely to live in households that face economic strain.

This economic strain may be due, in large part, to the fact that substitute parents for children of incarcerated parents typically assume unexpected burdens without compensation. When these substitute parents are relatives, they are especially likely to go uncompensated or undercompensated for their additional child care responsibilities (Allard & Greene, 2011). Growing up in a household with caregivers who are experiencing severe economic strain can affect the children of that household. Research shows that poverty and economic loss diminish the capacity for supportive, consistent, and involved parenting. This substantial influence on the caregiver's behavior toward the child may adversely affect the child's socioemotional functioning.

In addition to affecting the economic environment that a child is raised in, parental incarceration can create a shift in caregiving arrangements. The extent to which parental incarceration impacts living arrangements of children is related to whether the incarcerated parent was the child's exclusive caregiver. Ninety percent of the children who lived with their father prior to his incarceration continue to live with their mother during their father's incarceration (Travis et al., 2006). When a mother is incarcerated, 70% of the time her children go to live with grandparents or other relative caregivers, and most are low-income maternal grandparents over the age of 50 (Bloom & Steinhart, 1993; Johnston, 1995).

As the rate of incarcerating women increases, more children are being cared for by their elderly and often low-income grandparents. For most relative caregivers, the caring for these children often comes as an unexpected experience that they are not equipped to handle (Phillips & Bloom, 1998). Children may have challenging behavioral

issues from coping with a parent's incarceration. Grandparents may have limited energy or health problems that make it hard to provide parental guidance (Allard & Greene, 2011). In addition, when these caregiving arrangements are voluntary and informal, children of incarcerated parents are not eligible to access mental health services that are available for children who enter foster care.

Grandparents often lack the financial resources needed to raise their grandchildren. Despite being eligible for numerous public services (i.e., TANF, food stamps, and Medicaid) many children in kinship arrangements do not receive them (Ehrle, Geen, & Clark, 2001). This may be due to a lack of knowledge and understanding on the part of kinship caregivers that these resources are available to them.

Bill of Rights 5: I Have the Right to Speak With, See and Touch My Parent

Murray and Murray (2010) connect the experience of parental incarceration with the theory of attachment as follows:

> According to attachment theory, a key influence on a child's sense of security is availability of the attachment figure. Availability depends on children believing that there are open lines of communication with the attachment figure, that there is physical accessibility, and that the attachment figure will respond sensitively if called upon to help. All three aspects of availability might be challenged by parental incarceration, in which visits are difficult, communication about parental absence can be suppressed or distorted, and parents are held, against their will, in a situation in which active and responsive parenting is almost impossible to perform. Thus, there are strong theoretical reasons to suppose that separation by parental incarceration may be a particularly threatening kind of separation for children. (pp. 295–296)

Attachment theory is based on the idea that every child needs a consistent and responsive primary caregiver, especially during infancy and early childhood (Byrne, Goshin, & Joestl, 2010). If a parent served as a child's primary caregiver prior to incarceration, this parent is most likely to have served as the child's primary attachment figure. Since incarceration separates the child from this figure who has served as their secure base, this kind of separation (according to attachment theory) is likely to be traumatic and to have lasting, adverse effects (Dallaire, 2007; Makariev & Shaver, 2010). Research suggests that children who lack secure attachments to their caregivers are more likely than secure children to have difficulties with anxiety, anger, aggression, depression, and mental disorganization (Cassidy et. al., 2010; Makariev & Shaver, 2010).

According to researchers, ensuring a continued, healthy relationship between children and incarcerated parents calls for consistent visitation in a child-friendly and welcoming environment and supplemental and alternative activities to in-person visits, such as letter writing and phone calls (Allard & Greene, 2011; Eddy & Poehlmann, 2010; Murray & Farrington, 2006).

According to a recent survey, 58% of incarcerated women did not see their children during their entire incarceration, and only 6% of incarcerated parents have weekly visits with their children (Glaze & Maruschak, 2008). One of the barriers to visitation (reported by incarcerated individuals) was the location of the prison that was too far away from where their children live (La Vigne, Naser, Brooks, & Castro, 2005). As the distance between prison and one's family member increases, the number of face-to-face visits decreases (Hoffmann, Byrd & Kightlinger, 2010). The fact that there are fewer female facilities than male facilities across the country means that women are usually farther away from their children, an average of 160 miles farther from families than men (Hoffmann et al., 2010; Laughlin, Arrigo, Blevins, & Coston, 2008).

Current caregivers have significant control over the child's ability or inability to visit a parent. As Poehlmann et al. (2010) note, "Caregivers often function as gatekeepers of children's contact. Whereas some caregivers of young children support the parent-child relationship by fostering contact, other caregivers limit contact" (p. 586). While most children of incarcerated mothers live with grandparents, other family members, or friends, about 10% of children are placed in foster care (Dallaire, 2007). Foster parents are under no obligation to facilitate visits or contact with incarcerated parents (Laughlin et. al, 2008).

Even when caregivers are willing and able to support visitations, there are environmental factors within the facility that can prevent the visit from being child friendly. Various institutions have different policies regarding visits and offer a range of opportunities, from visits with physical contact to "barrier visits" which occur through or across a barrier, such as plexiglass (Poehlmann et al., 2010). Poehlmann and colleagues (2010) found that most jails employ barrier visits that can undermine the well-being of young children. In interviews with caregivers at a county jail, participants noted that the inability of children to touch their family members was distressing for the children, and the lack of contact affected the well-being of the children (Arditti, 2003). As one formerly incarcerated mother noted, "If you put a glass barrier between a child and a parent, it's crazy-making for the children. They feel they can't get to the person they love—there's this wall between them and they don't understand" (Bernstein, 2005, p. 80). Even though jails are generally located much closer to family members (often within the same county) as compared to prisons, the visitation environment can be very distressing to young children.

There also exists a large degree of variability in the quality of child-centered environments within facilities that do offer contact visitation. Some facilities make no special efforts to tailor the experience to children and create an unfriendly environment for children that includes long lines and waits with no access to bathrooms or water, disrespectful treatment by staff, lack of age-appropriate games and toys, and a lack of children's activities (Arditti, 2003; Hairston, 2003; Poehlmann et. al, 2010).

When looking at supplemental or alternative forms of contact, one frequently cited barrier is the cost of telephone calls and their limited duration. Because distance creates barriers to in-person visits, incarcerated individuals rely heavily on phone calls as a means to communicate with family. The system is set up in such a way that phone companies pay substantial fees to the prison system in order to have exclusive contracts. Incarcerated individuals are not able to receive calls and typically can place only collect calls. Recipients of the phone calls (i.e., the family or caregiver of the children) then pay very high rates, as much as twenty times that of standard collect calls. In addition, phone calls are usually limited by the prison to 15 minutes in duration, making conversation with multiple family members or children quite difficult (Bernstein, 2005). The burden of the cost of phone calls often makes it virtually impossible for many incarcerated individuals to maintain contact with their children. For many children who live a great distance from where their parent is incarcerated, a lack of phone conversation denies children the only viable means of contact with their parent.

BILL OF RIGHTS 8: I HAVE THE RIGHT TO A LIFELONG RELATIONSHIP WITH MY PARENT

Whereas the volume of offenders released from prison increased dramatically from 1980 to 2000 (from about 170,000 to 585,000), this increase was reduced in the 1990s when the number of prisons continued to expand, and prisoners found themselves serving longer sentences (Lynch & Sabol, 2001). As a result of these longer sentences, formerly incarcerated individuals may be less attached to jobs, their families. and the communities to which they return (Travis et al., 2001). Incarcerated individuals facing release often feel anxious about reestablishing family ties, finding employment, and managing finances once they return to the community (Travis et al., 2001). For those incarcerated individuals who are also parents, their ability to reintegrate successfully into their family and community is a crucial step in reestablishing a relationship with and reassuming the care of their children. These children are depending on their parents to return from prison prepared to handle the responsibilities of life. It is not clear whether the criminal justice system and society at large aids or hinders the ability of formerly incarcerated individuals to successfully reintegrate into their communities.

PRISONS, PAROLE, AND THE LAW

Facility Programming

While the philosophical shift from rehabilitation to punishment has translated into harsher sentencing laws and prison expansion, it has also led to a decrease in programming within prisons (Lynch & Sabol, 2001). In 1996, nearly $22 billion was spent nationwide to build facilities and expand staff in order to maintain and house individuals in state prisons. Of this amount, about 6% was used to support in-prison programs, such as vocational programs, educational programs, and substance abuse treatment (Travis et al., 2001). It is not surprising that the low-priority given to in-prison programming has translated into low rates of participation in these programs. For example, in 1997, only 12% of soon-to-be released individuals participated in "prerelease" programming.

In-prison programming has been shown to reduce recidivism, improve the chances of successful reintegration, and benefit an incarcerated individual's family networks and community (Travis et al., 2001; Travis et al., 2006). By giving low priority to in-prison programming related to individuals who will resume responsibility for their children upon release, society is not only hindering individuals' chances of successful reentry but also hindering the chances that their children will be successfully reunited with healthy and able mothers and fathers.

Post-Incarceration Support

The transformation of the parole system in the United States has led to increased caseloads and an increased focus on surveillance rather than support and rehabilitation (Travis et al., 2001). Released individuals are encountering fewer resources to help them secure employment, access substance abuse services, and reestablish family and community ties (Travis et al., 2001). Research has shown that providing services to families of recently released individuals results in the positive outcomes of lower rates of physical, mental, and emotional problems and drug use and recidivism (Travis et al., 2006). A lack of postrelease support services often contributes to increased chances of former offenders reentering the system, leaving their children to repeatedly experience the trauma and effects of losing a parent to incarceration.

Laws

In the United States, there are laws that "undermine the nation's commitment to justice and fairness, creating roadblocks to the basic necessities for hundreds of thousands of individuals who are trying to rebuild their lives, support their families, and become productive members of communities" (Legal Action Center, 2004). Since the early 1980s, Congress and state legislatures have created new restrictions on the eligibility of ex-offenders to receive food stamps, public assistance, public housing, student loans, and driving licenses, while further expanding barriers to employment, parenting, and voting (Legal Action Center, 2004).

As Travis et al. (2001) point out, "There is a complex relationship between crime and employment" (p. 7). While having a legitimate job lessens the chances of re-offending, released prisoners face significant challenges in their efforts to secure employment when they have limited educational backgrounds and vocational skills (often due to the lack of educational and vocational programs offered in prisons) and face discrimination from potential employers (Legal Action Center, 2004; Travis et al., 2001; Travis et al., 2006).

Securing housing is also challenging for several reasons. As Hirshe et al. (2002) point out, "Safe, decent and affordable housing is critical to the well-being of parents and children" (p. 7). Many parents must secure housing in order to regain custody of their children. However, incarcerated individuals returning to the community rarely have the financial resources to secure housing in the private housing market, and federal law bars many formerly incarcerated individuals from public housing and federally assisted housing programs (Travis et al., 2001). While some of these restrictions have been repealed at the federal level, there are still significant institutional barriers to housing, employment, and public assistance for individuals with felony convictions. Expecting incarcerated individuals who return to their communities to become responsible citizens and capable parents yet at the same time creating significant barriers to securing legitimate employment and safe housing, can set both parents and their children up for failure.

For some parents whose children enter the foster care system as a result of their incarceration, the option to resume a caregiving role is eliminated before they are released from prison. The 1997 Adoption and Safe Families Act (ASFA) authorizes

states to initiate termination of parental rights proceedings when a child has been placed in foster care for 15 out of the past 22 months (Bernstein, 2005; Travis et al., 2006). Bernstein (2005) notes that the enactment of ASFA, combined with the trend toward longer sentences, has resulted in an increase in termination rights among incarcerated individuals. While a number of Supreme Court cases have established that incarceration is not sufficient evidence of a parent's inability to care for his or her children, 34 states now have statutes that use parental incarceration as a criterion for termination of parental rights (Bernstein, 2005).

CONCLUSION

From policy decisions that allow phone companies to charge exorbitant phone call rates to the families of incarcerated individuals, to the general societal tendencies to stigmatize families involved in the criminal justice system, children of incarcerated parents suffer social injustices on numerous levels and throughout each phase of their parent's incarceration, from arrest to reentry.

There are significant obstacles and barriers that exist for those interested in addressing the needs and improving the experiences of children of incarcerated parents. Perhaps the most significant challenge is in identifying and understanding the needs of this population. There is no system in place, even within the department of corrections, to consistently track whether incarcerated individuals have children or to collect information about those children (Eddy & Poehlmann, 2010). In addition, there is no governmental system that is responsible for addressing the needs of this population (unless children are placed into foster care or become involved themselves with the criminal justice system). This gap introduces many challenges and inadequacies, especially the lack of governmental funding to support services for these children.

Efforts to successfully identify and understand this population and its needs will benefit from considering the Bill of Rights 2: "I have the right to be heard when decisions are made about me" (SFCIPP, 2005). No one can describe the injustices experienced by children of incarcerated parents more accurately than the children themselves. The ability of researchers, practitioners and community members to listen to this population can help to promote a more socially just experience, as well as reduce the stigma associated with incarceration.

Many social injustices experienced by children of incarcerated parents are the result of existing protocols, policies, and laws, namely, punitive sentencing laws, anxiety-and-stress-producing visitation protocols, and policies that inhibit a formerly incarcerated individual's ability to successfully reintegrate into society. These "human-made" barriers call for a reevaluation of the various social systems using a child-centered perspective.

Future protocols, policies, and laws are needed to create a more socially just experience for children of incarcerated parents. Efforts of this sort are beginning to spread across the country, as various agencies, counties, and states consider possibilities such as developing police protocol for the arrest of a parent and providing rehabilitative alternatives to incarceration for mothers of young children.

In our efforts to make the experience of children of incarcerated parents more tolerable, we humans must not lose sight of the fact that long-standing, deep-rooted societal support for a punitive approach to criminal activity led to soaring rates of incarceration. Moving the pendulum from punishment to rehabilitation can help to decrease incarceration rates and lead to fewer children coping with parental incarceration.

References

Adalist-Estrin, A. (2006). Providing support to adolescent children with incarcerated parents. *Prevention Researcher: Adolescents with Incarcerated Parents, 13*(2), 7–10.

Allard, P., & Greene, J. (2011). *Children on the outside: Voicing the pain and human costs of parental incarceration.* Brooklyn, NY: Justice Strategies.

Annie E. Casey Foundation, Women's Prison Association & Home Inc. (2001). *Partnerships between corrections and child welfare: Collaboration for change, part two.* Retrieved from http://www.aecf.org/upload/publicationfiles/partnerships%20between%20corrections.pdf

Arditti, J. A. (2003). Locked doors and glass walls: Family visiting in a local jail. *Journal of Loss and Trauma, 8,* 115–138.

Bernstein N. (2005). *All alone in the world: Children of the incarcerated.* New York, NY: New Press.

Bloom, B., & Steinhart, D. (1993). *Why punish the children: A reappraisal of the children of incarcerated mothers in America.* San Francisco, CA: National Council on Crime and Delinquency.

Byrne, M. W., Goshin, L. S., & Joestl, S. S. (2010). Intergenerational transmission of attachment for infants raised in a prison nursery. *Attachment and Human Development, 12,* 375–393.

Cassidy, J., Ziv, Y., Stupica, B., Sherman, L. J., Butler, H., Karfgin, A., . . . Powell, B. (2010). Enhancing attachment security in infants of women in a jail-diversion program. *Attachment and Human Development, 12,* 333–353.

Caulkins, J. P. (1997). *Mandatory minimum drug sentences: Throwing away the key or the taxpayers' money?* Santa Monica, CA: RAND Drug Policy Research Center.

Dallaire, D. H. (2007). Children with incarcerated mothers: Developmental outcomes: Special challenges, and recommendations. *Journal of Applied Developmental Psychology, 28,* 15–24.

Eddy, J. M., & Poehlmann, J. (Eds.). (2010). *Children of incarcerated parents: A handbook for researchers and practitioners.* Washington, DC: Urban Institute Press.

Ehrle, J., Geen, R., & Clark, R. L. (2001). *Children cared for by relatives: Who are they and how are they faring?* Washington, DC: Urban Institute.

Glaze, L. E., & Maruschak, L. M. (2008). *Parents in prison and their minor children.* Washington, DC: U.S. Department of Justice, Bureau of Justice Statistics.

Hairston, C. F. (2003). Prisoners and families: Parenting issues during incarceration. In J. Travis & M. Waul (Eds.), *Prisoners once removed: The impact of incarceration and reentry on children, families, and communities.* (pp. 259–284). Washington, DC: Urban Institute Press.

Hirsche, A. E., Dietrich, S. M., Landau, R., Schneider, P. D., Ackelsberg, I., Bernstein-Baker, J., & Horhenstein, J. (2002). *Every door closed: Barriers facing parents with criminal records.* Washington, DC: Center for Law and Social Policy.

Hoffmann, H. C., Byrd, A. L., & Kightlinger, A. M. (2010). Prison programs and services for incarcerated parents and their underage children: Results from a national survey of correctional facilities. *Prison Journal, 90*(4), 398–416.

Johnston, D., (1995). The care and placement of prisoner children. In K. Gabel & D. Johnston (Eds.), *Children of incarcerated parents* (pp. 103–123). New York, NY: Lexington Books.

Kampfner, C. J. (1995). Post-traumatic stress reactions in children of imprisoned mothers. In K. Gabel & D. Johnston (Eds.), *Children of incarcerated parents* (pp. 89–102). New York, NY: Lexington Books.

Laughlin, J. S., Arrigo, B. A., Blevins, K. R., & Coston, C. T. M. (2008). Incarcerated mothers and child visitation: A law, social science, and policy perspective. *Criminal Justice Policy Review, 19*, 215–238.

La Vigne, N. G., Davies, E., & Brazzel, D. (2008). *Broken bonds: Understanding and addressing the needs of children with incarcerated parents.* Washington, DC: Urban Institute.

La Vigne, N. G., Naser, R. L., Brooks, L. E., & Castro, J. L. (2005). Examining the effect of incarceration and in-prison family contact on prisoners' family relationships. *Journal of Contemporary Criminal Justice, 21*, 314–355.

Legal Action Center. (2004). *After prison: Roadblocks to reentry: A report on state legal barriers facing people with criminal records.* Retrieved from http://www.lac.org/roadblocks-to reentry/upload/lacreport/LAC_PrintReport.pdf

Lynch, J. P., & Sabol, W. J. (2001). *Prisoner reentry in perspective.* Washington, DC: Urban Institute.

Makariev, D. W., & Shaver, P. R. (2010). Attachment, parental incarceration and possibilities for intervention: An overview. *Attachment and Human Development, 12*(4), 311–331.

McLeigh, J. D., & Sianko, N. (2010). Where have all the children gone? The effects of the justice system on America's children and youth. *American Journal of Orthopsychiatry, 80*(3), 334–341.

Mumola, C. J. (2000). *Incarcerated parents and their children* (Report No. NCJ 182335). Washington, DC: U.S. Department of Justice, Bureau of Justice Statistics. Retrieved from: http://bjs.ojp.usdoj.gov/content/pub/pdf/iptc.pdf

Murray, J., & Farrington, D. P. (2006). Evidence-based programs for children of prisoners. *Criminology and Public Policy, 5*(4), 721–736.

Murray J., Farrington, D. P., Sekol, I., & Olsen, R. F. (2009). *Effects of parental imprisonment on child antisocial behaviour and mental health:*

A systematic review. Campbell Systematic Reviews 2009:4. doi:10.4073/csr.2009.4 Retrieved from www.campbellcollaboration.org/lib/download/683/

Murray, J., & Murray, L., (2010). Parental incarceration, attachment, and child psychopathology. *Attachment and Human Development, 12*(4), 289–309.

Nieto, M. (2002). *In danger of falling through the cracks: Children of arrested parents* (Report No. CRB 02-009). Sacramento: California State Library: California Research Bureau. Retrieved from http://www.library.ca.gov/crb/02/09/02-009.pdf

Nolan, C. (2003). *Children of arrested parents: Strategies to improve their safety and well-being.* Sacramento: California Research Bureau.

The Pew Center on the States. (2008). *One in 100: Behind bars in America in 2008.* Washington, DC: Pew Charitable Trusts.

The Pew Charitable Trusts. (2010). *Collateral costs: Incarceration's effect on economic mobility.* Washington, DC: Pew Charitable Trusts.

Phillips, S., & Bloom, B. (1998). *In whose best interest? The impact of changing public policy on relatives caring for children with incarcerated parents.* Washington, DC: Child Welfare League of America.

Poehlmann, J., Dallaire, D., Loper, A. B., & Shear, L. (2010). Children's contact with their incarcerated parents: Research findings and recommendations. *American Psychologist, 65*, 575–598.

San Francisco Children of Incarcerated Parents Partnership (SFCIPP). (2005). *Children of incarcerated parents: A bill of rights.* Retrieved from http://www.sfcipp.org/ images/brochure.pdf

Smith, B., & Elstein, S. (1994). *Children on hold: Improving the response to children whose parents are arrested and incarcerated.* Washington, DC: American Bar Association, Center for Children and the Law.

Travis, J., Cincotta, E. M., & Solomon, A. L. (2006). *Families left behind: The hidden costs of incarceration and reentry.* Washington, DC: Urban Institute. Retrieved from www.urban.org/publications/310882.html

Travis, J., Solomon, A. L., & Waul, M. (2001). *From prison to home: The dimensions and consequences of prisoner reentry.* Washington, DC: Urban Institute.

Wagner, J. O. (2006). *Children of incarcerated parents* (Youthwork Information Brief No. 15). Columbus, OH: LearningWork Connection.

20

THE SOCIAL INJUSTICES EXPERIENCED BY THE LESBIAN, GAY, BISEXUAL, AND TRANSGENDER COMMUNITY

ELIZABETH WHITE

Since the Stonewall Rebellion in 1969, lesbian, gay, bisexual, and transgender (LGBT) people and communities have made tremendous social and civil rights gains. However, despite these gains, LGBT people continue to live as second-class citizens in the United States. One need just look at today's news, current events, or political debates to see topics about LGBT people at the forefront. For example, it is next to impossible to witness a debate between political candidates that does not address same-sex marriage or gays in the military. Given their marginalized status and a significant increase in attention (both positive and negative), the LGBT movement is the major civil rights movement of the 21st century. With public opinions ranging from welcoming and inclusive to fearful and disgusted, LGBT people are one of the most hotly contested and discussed minority groups in the United States.

While LGBT people have been organizing and meeting since the beginning of the 20th century (some examples are the Mattachine Society and Daughters of Bilitus), the Stonewall Rebellion is largely recognized as the beginning of the modern gay rights movement. The Stonewall Rebellion ignited an ongoing and continuing battle for LGBT recognition, inclusion, and protection when lesbians, gay men, drag queens, transvestites, and transsexuals rose up against police harassment and violence. Since 1969, LGBT people and communities have organized and won major victories in the ongoing battle to procure rights and protections. LGBT people, like many minorities, have seen tremendous gains for their rights in the past four decades, from the removal of "homosexuality" from the psychiatric *Diagnostic and Statistical Manual of Mental Disorders (DSM)* in 1973 to addressing federal inaction during the AIDS epidemic in the 1980s to the abolition of sodomy laws in 2003. However, despite these historical shifts that have defined and propelled the LGBT community into today's limelight, LGBT people still face a number of laws, personal beliefs, institutional structures, and social prejudices that maintain their marginalized status.

Three years after the Stonewall Rebellion came another critical development that critically altered the psychological perceptions of homosexuals and helped to coalesce the political and social movement for gay rights. In 1972, George Weinberg in *Society and the Healthy Homosexual* popularized the term *homophobia* to mean the personal fear of homosexuals. While Weinberg did not coin the term, he identified the concept of "homophobia" as located "not in homosexual people, but in heterosexuals who were intolerant of gay men and lesbians" (Herek, 2004, p. 8). By naming the source of prejudice and discrimination experienced by LGBT people, the identification of homophobia played a critical role in laying the groundwork for the social and political gains made by LGBT people over the decades. Despite the critical role that the term *homophobia* played in identifying and describing the minority status of LGBT people, current literature has suggested that *heterosexism* is a more appropriate term to describe the pervasive, structural inequalities that face LGBT people (Elze, 2006; Herek, 2004).

While homophobia focuses on the marginalization of LGBT people as well as an individual's personal and even irrational fear of homosexuals, heterosexism addresses an individual's personal belief in the inherent superiority of heterosexuality and identifies the ideological system that denies rights to nonheterosexual people (Elze, 2006). Heterosexism is both cultural (in the heterosexual privilege that pervades societal customs, expectations, and legal protections) and psychological (in the widespread personal condemnation of LGBT people). Heterosexism not only prescribes expectations around sexuality but also prescribes normative gender roles. Feinberg (1998) argues that sexual orientation and gender presentation are intimately entwined. Men and women who cross gender boundaries, regardless of their sexual orientation, face an increased risk of abuse. Both sexism and heterosexism play a dual role in outlining and policing the rigid expectations for men and women and their relationship with each other—these expectations form the social prejudices and injustices impacting LGBT people. It is through these concepts of heterosexism and homophobia that we can understand the external structures that perpetuate injustices experienced by LGBT people and communities.

Antigay prejudice, which informs personal interactions as well as public policies and laws, has a number of consequences for both LGBT and heterosexual people. Antigay prejudice influences behavior in such a way as to encourage LGBT people to hide their sexual orientation or gender identity. Antigay prejudice is also reflected in overt victimization of LGBT people through hate crimes, vulnerability, and punishment for failing to fit into heterosexual society. Finally, many heterosexuals limit and monitor their own behavior in order to distance themselves from any threat of experiencing the stigma attached to LGBT people (Herek, 1995). Antigay prejudice has a far-reaching impact on the physical, social, and emotional health of LGBT individuals.

While many books have been written on the impact of heterosexism on the current social and political landscape in the United States, this analysis briefly describes some major areas of inequality currently experienced by the LGBT community before describing some of the populations within LGBT communities.

Hate Crimes and Violence

LGBT people often face significant threats of physical violence due to their second-class status and lack of protection. One of the most notorious examples of violence is the 1998 murder of Matthew Shepard (a student at the University of Wyoming) who was beaten, tortured, tied to a fence post, and left to die by his murderers. Matthew's death and the subsequent trial of his assailants drew much attention and publicity—both from the LGBT movement, calling for expanded hate crimes protections, and from antigay conservatives, protesting Matthew's funeral. In 2008, Lawrence King, a 15-year-old boy, was shot and killed for being gay by his 14-year-old classmate right outside their junior high school in Oxnard, California.

In the end, Matthew's death, and many like his, launched a successful campaign to expand hate crimes legislation to include LGBT victims. In 2009, President Obama signed LGBT-inclusive hate crimes protections into law, marking the first ever LGBT-inclusive federal law. While this marked a tremendous win for the LGBT community, the hate crimes expansion drew much attention from conservative lawmakers and antigay organizations that argued against the need to protect the LGBT community, highlighting the ongoing prejudice and discrimination that permeates our political institutions.

Research has identified some of the psychological motivations of sexual prejudice that manifest into violent behavior toward LGBT populations. For some heterosexual people, sexual prejudice results from negative interactions (often superficial and stereotypical) with LGBT people. For other heterosexual people, prejudice is rooted in deeply held fears of LGBT people. For others, prejudices may be reflective of in-group norms (i.e., reflecting "good Christian" behavior). Another source of prejudice is rooted in the belief that gay people represent values and morals that directly conflict with one's personal values (Herek, 2000). Studies have shown that sexual prejudice correlates with violent, antigay behavior, but many varied factors also mitigate and influence that correlation.

Antihomosexual Conduct Laws

As recently as 2003, thirteen states had "sodomy laws," or antihomosexual conduct laws, which outlawed consensual sexual interactions between same-sex adults—at the same time protecting similar sexual interactions between opposite-sex adults. These sodomy laws explicitly prohibited and monitored same-sex behavior, literally outlawing it in several states. Sodomy laws also played an essential role in discriminatory policies and practices directed at LGBT people, such as the prohibition against same-sex adoption (Lambda Legal, 2010). In the 2003 *Lawrence v. Texas* ruling on unconstitutional "homosexual conduct" laws, the U.S. Supreme Court established, for the first time, that lesbians and gay men share the same fundamental right to private sexual intimacy with other adults.

Antidiscrimination Protection

Nondiscrimination laws ensure that LGBT people have access to the same opportunities and protections as other people. This includes, but is not limited to, employment protection, equal access to housing, public accommodation, medical care, and education. As of June 2011, only 15 states, including the District of Columbia, ban discrimination based on sexual orientation and gender identity or expression. Six other states ban discrimination based on sexual orientation. The rest, 29 states, offer no protection against discrimination (National Gay & Lesbian Task Force [NGLTF], 2011b), and LGBT people live in fear of discrimination by their landlords, employers, medical practitioners, and social workers.

Partnership Recognition

Through marriage or other relationship recognition laws (e.g., civil unions or domestic partnerships), partnership recognition is critical to supporting LGBT couples and families. Due to the privileging of heterosexual relationships, LGBT people are often excluded from partaking in legal protection and recognition of their families in a majority of states. Six states and the District of Columbia have full marriage equality. Eight states have broad relationship recognition laws such as civil unions or domestic partnerships (NGLTF, 2011a). While progress is being made in the quest for relationship recognition, an overwhelming majority of states limit or prohibit same-sex relationships (e.g., 17 states prohibit same-sex marriage, and 21 states prohibit marriage and any other relationship recognition); see NGLTF, 2009.

Even though a few states extend marriage rights to LGBT people, the Defense of Marriage Act (DOMA) prohibits federal recognition of same-sex marriages. While married same-sex couples may access all the state's rights of marriage, they are excluded from the federal benefits and privileges associated with marriage. A 2004 report shows that there are 1,138 of these federal rights granted to married, opposite-sex couples but denied to married, same-sex couples (U.S. Government Accountability Office, 2004).

These examples are just a few of the areas in which LGBT people are explicitly or implicitly denied support, rights, and equality. Oppression, rejection, threats of violence, and discrimination are shown to have significant negative effects on the physical and mental health of LGBT people. While all marginalized groups suffer from "minority stress," LGBT people often do not have the safety and protection provided by their family and community of origin. Many LGBT people are raised in communities that do not reflect their identities and offer little to no positive support or role models for their development.

Before exploring some specific characteristics of the LGBT community, it is important to recognize that the category of LGBT includes very diverse types of sexual minority individuals who are also members of other oppressed groups (e.g., people of color, people with disabilities, and low-income people). The reaction to stigmatization and minority stress varies greatly depending on the experience of an LGB and/or T identity with the intersection of multiple marginalized identities. Without ignoring the vast diversity of LGBT experience, this analysis is an introduction to some prominent themes that underlie some of the injustices faced by marginalized groups within the LGBT community. While there are many different aspects of the LGBT community, the purpose of this analysis is to focus on only three groups within the community: LGBT youth, LGBT people of color, and transgender people.

QUEER YOUTH—(UN)SAFE FAMILIES AND SCHOOLS

In 1995, 14-year-old Derek Henkle was in the Gifted and Talented Education (GATE) program in a Reno, Nevada, high school. Despite facing ongoing bullying and harassment for being openly gay, he had aspirations of graduating and attending college. After two boys "strung a lasso" around Derek's neck and threatened to drag him from their pickup truck, school officials responded by transferring Derek to an alternative high school for students with behavioral or academic problems. The principal there told Derek to "stop acting like a fag." He was transferred again for his safety. In 1996, two school police officers witnessed Derek being beaten by another student, doing nothing to break up the fight. Following this incident, Derek quit school (Horn, 2008).

In September 2010, after enduring years of school bullying and harassment for being gay, 13-year-old Seth Walsh committed suicide by hanging himself in his family's backyard in Tehachapi, California. Despite acceptance of his sexual orientation by his family, friends and relatives report that teachers and school administrators were aware of the bullying Seth faced at school yet failed to intervene, sometimes participating in the harassment. Seth's suicide along with the suicides of four other LGBT youth over a short period of time (Tyler Clementi, freshman at Rutgers University; Billy Lucas, 15-year-old in Greensburg, Indiana; Asher Brow, 13-year-old in Houston, Texas; Raymond Chase, sophomore at Johnson and Wales University) contributed to increased national attention to the pressures and injustices that LGBT youth face in schools and communities (McKinley, 2010).

These examples highlight the pressures that LGBT youth experience every day in a country that fails to acknowledge their identities, value their lives, and protect them. Unlike other minority youth, LGBT youth are not raised in communities where they can see themselves in their neighbors, community leaders, and family members. Early on, they witness numerous negative LGBT stereotypes and language and, subsequently, often internalize the homophobia and heterosexist messages they receive.

Family Violence and Homelessness

Family and family support play a critical role in adolescent development as, typically, they can encourage a youth's identity development, resilience, independence, and connection. Unfortunately, many LGBT youth often lack supportive and loving family relationships as they may face open rejection of their sexual orientation or gender identity. One study found that coming out or being discovered as gay by family or friends, along with gay-related harassment, produced the most common gay-related stressors among youth (D'Augelli, 1996). The same study also showed that only 11% of gay and lesbian youth experienced supportive responses from their parents after coming out, while 20% of mothers and 28% of fathers were rejecting or completely intolerant. Hunter (1990) found that more than 60% of violence perpetrated against a sample of gay and lesbian youth had been inflicted by family members (as cited in Morrow, 2006).

Based on the high rates of family rejection and violence that LGBT youth experience, it is no surprise that LGBT youth make up a large proportion of the homeless youth population. Available research suggests that between 20% and 40% of all homeless youth identify as LGBT (Ray, 2006). One study found that 50% of gay teens experience a negative reaction from their parents when they come out and 26% were kicked out of their homes (Remafedi, 1987). Given this high prevalence of homelessness among LGBT youth, this population suffers not only from a lack of family security and support but also from the negative consequences of homelessness.

LGBT homeless youth are particularly vulnerable to mental health issues, such as depression, loneliness, social problems, and delinquency (Ray, 2006). The daily stressors of life on the streets can lead to drug and alcohol abuse for many homeless youth, a risk that is even greater for those youth who identify as LGBT (Ray, 2006). Homelessness for LGBT youth also increases the prevalence of risky sexual behavior. A study of homeless youth in Canada found that LGBT youth were three times more likely than their heterosexual peers to engage in survival sex (Gaetz, 2004). Life on the streets also brings LGBT youth into more contact with juvenile and criminal justice systems, traditionally unsafe environments for sexual minority and gender-nonconforming youth. Although there is little research on the experiences of LGBT youth in the criminal justice systems, preliminary findings suggests LGBT youth are disproportionately victims of harassment and violence, including rape, within these systems (Ray, 2006).

Unsafe Schools

In addition to families, schools play a central role in the lives of youth and adolescents. The lack of safety experienced by LGBT youth in schools can negatively affect their physical and mental well-being (as illustrated in the harrowing impact that school bullying had on Seth Walsh who was otherwise supported by his family). The Gay, Lesbian, and Straight Education Network's (GLSEN's) 2009 National School Climate Survey showed that 84.6% of youth were verbally harassed at school because of their sexual orientation and 63.7% because of their gender expression. Even more striking is the finding that as many as 40% of respondents were physically harassed because of their sexual orientation and 27% because of their gender expression (Kosciw, Greytak, Diaz, and Bartkiewicz, 2010).

Unlike other marginalized students, LGBT students often lack a support structure in their families, needed to develop resilience against such bullying and harassment. Youth who are not "out" to their families often do not share their experiences of victimization and harassment for fear of being forced to tell their parents about their sexual orientation or gender identity (D'Augelli, 1998). This often leaves LGBT youth without important adult supports to face unsafe circumstances in schools.

Since a safe place to learn is necessary for school achievement, LGBT students often face a decrease in school performance as a result of school-based bullying and harassment. LGBT students are more likely than straight students to miss school, obtain lower grades, and have fewer aspirations for pursuing post-secondary education (Kosciw et al., 2010). In addition, the high levels of victimization lead to higher levels of depression and anxiety and lower levels of self-esteem (Kosciw et al., 2010).

Prevalence of Suicide

As this section began with the sad reality of youth suicide and depression as a result of prejudice and harassment, it is important to recognize the rash of suicide that impacts LGBT youth who often lack the resources to identify support for their despair. Research suggests that 30% to 40% of LGBT youth have attempted suicide as compared to 8% to 13% for presumed heterosexual youth (as cited in Morrow, 2006). This substantial disparity between rates of depression and suicidal ideation for LGBT youth and their heterosexual counterparts can frequently be attributed to the pervasiveness of heterosexism in our social messages, cultural values, and legal policies, clearly contributing to the feelings of despair that lead LGBT youth to suicide.

LGBT PEOPLE OF COLOR

LGBT people of color (LGBTPOC) suffer from invisibility in their communities as they reflect multiple marginalized identities. Heterosexism in communities of color may discourage LGBT people from coming out to their families and communities. In addition, racism within the LGBT community precludes LGBTPOC from interacting and engaging within that community. While the invisibility certainly exists, it is important to acknowledge the contributions that LGBT people of color have made to the LGBT movement and community and other civil rights movements (Moradi, DeBlaere, & Huang, 2010). A classic example is the relatively invisible accomplishments of Bayard Rustin, an openly gay African American man who played a leading role in the U.S. civil rights movement alongside Dr. Martin Luther King Jr.

LGBTPOC must navigate between three worlds: the LGBT world, their community of color, and the dominant culture (White, straight). This form of navigation requires the ability "to transverse many social and cultural boundaries and multiple social roles and expectations" and thereby endures multiple stressors (Walters & Old Person, 2008, p. 46). Within their community of color, they experience sexism and heterosexism as gay, lesbian, or bisexual and/or transphobia as a transgender person. Within LGBT communities, they experience racism, and within the dominant culture, they experience heterosexism and racism.

Identity Development and Negotiating Conflicting Allegiances

Psychological research has shown that many LGBT people of color suffer from stressors in negotiating their racial and sexual identity development process (Walters, Longres, Han, & Icard, 2003). Many LGBTPOC feel as though they must decide between being an open part of the LGBT community or their community of color (Harper, Jernewall, & Zea, 2004). This sense of divided allegiances may result in attempts by LGBTPOC to hide certain aspects of their identities when in different environments. The duality of this role increases the stressors that impact LGBTPOC in their identity development. In contrast, Crawford and colleagues (2003) found that the ability to achieve a positively integrated identity as an LGBT person of color may result in healthier functioning and improved well-being (Crawford et al. as cited in Harper et al., 2004).

As a result of negotiating conflicting allegiances between the LGBT community and communities of color, LGBT people of color often face marginalization at the hands of both communities. The LGBT community's social and political causes oftentime alienate LGBTPOC by ignoring the needs of this population, because the "causes" are often defined by White, middle-class LGBT activists. For example, criticism of the LGBT community's focus on marriage equality argues that other issues (e.g., immigration reform and universal health care) better meet the needs of the extremely marginalized within the LGBT community (e.g., low-income people, people of color, people with disabilities, etc.).

Another example of marginalization occurs when LGBTPOC face heterosexism within their communities of color when coming out as LGBT is considered an abandonment of the fight against racial and cultural oppression. Oftentimes, LGBTPOC are accused of assimilating into White, Western culture when they come out to their families and communities. While coming out is considered a politically valuable and psychologically healthy thing to do in the White, LGBT community, coming out is not necessarily aligned with collectivist values in some communities of color (Walters et al., 2003).

Economic Disparities

While popular media tends to portray same-sex couples as rich and affluent, research has documented the inaccuracy of this myth (Lee Badgett, 2001). In addition, findings from Census 2000 show that same-sex couples of color face even greater economic disparity than White same-sex couples. While Black and Latino same-sex couples are twice as likely as White same-sex couples to be raising children, they earn significantly less than their White counterparts. For example, Black, female same-sex couples earn $21,000 less than White, female same-sex couples (Dang & Frazer, 2004). The largest disparity exists between Latino same-sex male couples and their White counterparts, where they earn $27,000 less than that of White, male same-sex couples (Cianciotto, 2005).

Immigration is also an important factor for non-White same-sex couples; for example, same-sex couples where both male partners were Hispanic are 17 times more likely than White, male same-sex couples to report that they are not U.S. citizens (Cianciotto, 2005). The lack of federal recognition of same-sex relationships increasingly ignores the plights of binational same-sex couples who, many times, are not able to live with their partners and families due to immigration issues. While marriage equality certainly plays a role in obtaining these rights for LGBT people and couples, many within the LGBT community (specifically LGBTPOC) advocate for a larger focus on immigration rights by LGBT activists and leaders.

Health Disparities

LGBT people of color are likely to feel the compounded effect of their ethnic and sexual minority statuses with regard to their health where they can experience poorer health outcomes when compared to White LGBT populations. P. Wilson and Hi Yoshikawa (2007) found the following three factors play a role in this health disparity: (a) the negative impact of discrimination on health and risk behavior, (b) racism and heterosexism in the health care system, and (c) immigration experiences and their effect on health care. The combined effect of stigma and psychological stress related to ethnic minority and sexual minority status poses significant health consequences (acute and chronic) to LGBTPOC (Wilson & Yoshikawa, 2007). For example, researchers have linked experiences of discrimination and racism to risky sex behavior in various populations of ethnic men who have sex with men (Wilson & Yoshikawa, 2007).

Communities of color have long-standing histories of discrimination at the hands of health care providers, as do LGBT people. For example, Blanchard and Lurie (2004) found that 14% of African Americans, 19% of Latinos, and 20% of Asian and Pacific Islanders (APIs) reported being treated with disrespect by health providers, compared to 9% of Whites (as cited in Wilson & Yoshikawa, 2007). As such, a fervent distrust and nonutilization of the health care services are prevalent for both communities and compounded for LGBTPOC.

Immigration status and citizenship also play a significant role in access to health care by people of color. Findings from a national survey suggest that Black, Latino, and API immigrants are much more likely to be uninsured than their citizen counterparts (Ku & Waidmann, 2003). Also, noncitizen immigrants are more likely to work in low-income jobs that do not include health insurance benefits and are

more concerned about accessing public health care programs when it might jeopardize their undocumented status (Wilson & Yoshikawa, 2007). As such, immigration status may compound the other health care challenges facing LGBT people of color.

Pitting LGBT and Communities of Color Against Each Other

In addition to negotiating membership in two marginalized communities, LGBT people of color must also contend with the increased polarization between the communities fueled by antigay activists and religious conservatives. Capitalizing on opportunities to pit two marginalized groups against each other, the religious right has portrayed the LGBT community and communities of color as mutually exclusive (Cahill, 2009). For example, an antigay group in Miami distributed a flyer claiming that Martin Luther King, Jr. "would be outraged if he knew that homosexualist extremists were abusing the civil rights movement to get special rights based on their behavior" (as cited by Cahill, 2009, p. 222). LGBT rights are portrayed as "special rights" that threaten the civil rights of people of color. This assertion obviously ignores the reality that some people of color experience discrimination also based on their sexual orientation and gender identity.

The antigay, religious right is not the only perpetrator of homophobic or racist propaganda that can pit these communities against each other. In the fallout over the passage of California's Proposition 8, that sought to amend the state constitution to limit marriage between a man and a woman, many LGBT individuals were angered by the suggestion in the media that African Americans voted overwhelmingly in support of Prop 8.[1] The racist reaction within the LGBT community similarly ignored the investment of LGBT people of color in campaigning against the proposition and affiliating with communities of color.

LGBT people of color constantly face the push and pull of their intersecting, marginalized identities. In a society that labels people under one category, the inability to recognize and honor the often

---

[1] Data were later clarified, illustrating that religious affiliation played a much larger role in voting for Proposition 8 than racial identity.

complicated identities of individuals can have harmful effects on the physical, emotional, and social health of LGBT people of color.

TRANSGENDER[2] PEOPLE

The combining of LGBT communities can overlook the differences between people and the inequity between the groups. Bisexual and transgender members of the community face increased marginalization because their identities do not fit neatly in the binary distinctions of gender and sexuality prominent in U.S. culture (i.e., there are two genders, male and female, and two sexual orientations, heterosexual and homosexual). Bisexual and transgender people challenge these binaries and often face marginalization in the LGBT community as well as in the mainstream culture.

Transgender people are the most visible and vulnerable in the gay community (Minter, 2006) and as a result are most likely to face violence, housing and employment discrimination, and labels of deviant and criminalized. Due to this vulnerability, it is no surprise that transgender individuals played a large role in the Stonewall Rebellion. Despite this historical link to gays and lesbians, the current mainstream gay rights movement defines itself by embracing gender-conformity (Minter, 2006).

Historically, the root of same-gender attractions and relationships were intricately tied to gender nonconforming presentation in the late 19th and early 20th centuries—when same-sex attraction was less about a sexual orientation and more about reversing one's gender. However, in the mid-20th century, middle-class gays and lesbians began to distance themselves from working-class gays and lesbians whose gender transgressions were viewed as politically "unsavory" in the strictly gendered society of the 1940s and 1950s (Minter, 2006). As such, the older model of homosexuality as gender inversion has evolved into the contemporary model of sexual object choice. Consequently, despite the historical link between same-sex attraction and gender variation, the modern gay rights movement has changed to an articulation of a strict division between the fight for gay and lesbian rights and the fight for transgender rights. While all the large, national LGBT rights organizations have expanded to include transgender people and communities, many within the modern gay rights movement view political power and resources as limited and, as such, the transgender movement is often seen as a threat to the promotion of gay rights.

The medicalization and pathologizing of transgender people plays a critical role in disempowering the transgender community. While homosexuality was viewed as a psychological disorder by a large segment of the population, many people and medical practitioners now recognize homosexuality as a concrete identity. In contrast, the perception of a transgender identity is still associated with a disease as Dean et al. (2000) note, "Prejudice against transgendered individuals is pervasive within American medicine. . . . Most U.S. medical providers and researchers, as well as the public at large, believe that transgendered behavior is pathological. This, in itself, constitutes one of the most significant barriers to care" (Dean et al, as qtd. in Davis, 2008, p. 97).

The medical model framing the care of transgender people began with the endocrinologist, Harry Benjamin, who began treating those seeking sex reassignment in the 1950s and published *The Transsexual Phenomenon* in 1966. He defined transsexualism and a treatment model widely used to "treat" gender nonconforming people throughout the 1990s. To qualify for treatment, individuals needed to report gender dysphorias (such as feeling out of place in one's own body) from an early age, document a history of playing with toys associated

---

[2] The term *transgender* refers to individuals whose gender identity or expression does not conform to the social expectations of their assigned sex at birth. I use *transgender* in this chapter (except in situations where another term is explicitly used in the literature) as an umbrella term to include many different and varying expressions of gender nonconformity, including but not limited to transsexuals, transvestites, cross-dressers, gender queers, et cetera. Like LGBT, the experiences of those who identify as transgender or any of the included identities vary considerably.

with the non-natal sex, report sexual attractions exclusively with the same biological sex, and display the potential to pass successfully as the desired sex (Denny, 2006). This medical model ensured that access to treatment was explicitly the purview of professionals who operated with a set of biases and assumptions about transgender people.

However, in 1991, transgender activist and educator, Holly Boswell, challenged the long-standing Benjamin model by arguing that the best "fit" for many gender-variant people was along a continuum of gender variance (somewhere between cross-dressing and transsexualism) (Denny, 2006). While not the first to use the term *transgender*, Boswell's article and books by Kate Bornstein (1994) and Martine Rothblatt (1994) helped popularize the term. The new transgender model legitimated those individuals who did not fit comfortably into the limited, prescriptive categories largely monitored by medical providers.

With the momentum of the newly popularized transgender identity came the inevitable demands for political equality and justice as reflected by several important events that coalesced transgender organizing in the 1990s. For example, the Michigan Womyn's Music Festival excluded a transgender woman from the festival when it was discovered that she had male genitalia. Transgendered activists gathered at the entrance of the festival to protest the event and educate attendees about transgender identity.

The tragic deaths of Brandon Teena and Tyra Hunter in the 1990s gave publicity and a face to the countless acts of violence experienced by many transgender people. Brandon Teena was a transgender man who was raped and murdered in Nebraska in 1993 and depicted in the Academy Award winning film, *Boys Don't Cry*. In 1995, Tyra Hunter was injured in a car accident in Washington, D.C. When the emergency medical technicians (EMTs) cut off her clothes and discovered she was a transgender woman, they suspended care while she continued to bleed with technicians looking on and making jokes. Tyra later died in the hospital emergency room (Davis, 2008). Examples of violent acts against transgender people still continue to this day. For example, Gwen Araujo was a teenage transgender woman beaten to death by a group of young men

in Northern California in 2003. Attorneys for the perpetrators argued that her murder was justified because of her "deception" based on not disclosing her transgender identity.

In 2011, the National Center for Transgender Equality (NCTE) and the National Gay & Lesbian Task Force (Grant et al., 2011) published findings from their National Transgender Discrimination Survey, documenting the experiences of 6,450 transgender individuals from across the United States and its territories. The findings range from economic disparity and homelessness to experiences of suicide and police harassment. The survey found that transgender people live in extreme poverty with study respondents nearly four times more likely to have a household income of less than $10,000 per year compared to the general population. Respondents had twice the rate of unemployment compared to the general population. A substantial number (90%) reported experiencing harassment, mistreatment, or discrimination on the job or taking actions to hide their identities to avoid discrimination. In addition to experiencing homelessness at some point in their lives due to their transgender identity (19%), respondents reported on the need to teach their medical providers about transgender care (50%), on police harassment (22%), and on attempted suicide (41% compared to 1.6% of the general population) (Grant et al., 2011, pp. 2–9; see also NGLTF, 2011b). These findings highlight the prejudicial experiences that transgender individuals face and the significant barriers to care and equality described in more detail in the next sections.

Health Issues

Transgender individuals face multiple barriers when accessing health and mental health care services. These barriers range from lack of insurance coverage to the unwillingness of providers to work with transgender clients (Lombardi & Masen Davis, 2006). For example, *Southern Comfort* is a documentary depicting the last year in the life of Robert Eads, a female-to-male transsexual who died from ovarian cancer after being unable to find a medical provider willing to treat a transgender patient (Davis, 2000). Most geographical areas lack trans-positive health and mental health providers and the absence of services often force transgender youth and adults to go long periods of time without regular health checkups and to acquire services such as access to hormones from the street.

Transgender people, especially transgender women, face high rates of HIV infection and substance abuse (Lombardi & Masen Davis, 2006). While the research is varied, the risky behaviors of transgender women and the perception that transgender men have low risks put both groups at risk for HIV infection. HIV/AIDS prevention programs are often not designed to target transgender people, especially transgender men (Lombardi & Masen Davis, 2006). While there is little research on transgender populations, there is strong evidence that transgender people are at a heightened risk for substance abuse (Hughes & Eliason, 2002). Similar to HIV/AIDS prevention programs, treatment programs are rarely geared toward transgender people and, as such, transgender people lack access to needed treatment resources.

Economic Barriers

One of the largest barriers to economic security that transgender people face is the lack of protection against employment discrimination. Only 15 states protect against discrimination based on gender identity and, in 36 other states, transgender people can be fired from their job if it is discovered that they are transgender or if they make the transition while on the job. It also means that transgender job candidates may be discriminated against during hiring processes. The absence of protection means that transgender people are severely economically disadvantaged, have less access to employee paid health care, and may be forced to resort to the underground economy (such as sex work or selling drugs) for income.

During the recent debate over the Employment Non-Discrimination Act (ENDA), leaders in the LGBT rights movement opted to exclude transgender people from legal protections in exchange for more politically viable legislation. Essentially, LGBT leaders opted to exclude the population most in need of employment protection. In an unprecedented response, LGBT activists and community members responded by calling on the leaders to require transgender inclusion in the bill. While the future for the inclusion of transgender populations in ENDA remains uncertain, the willingness to exclude the transgender population for "political viability" illustrates the barriers that transgender people face, even within the LGBT community.

Structural Barriers to Social Services

While biases and invisibility may create substantial barriers to transgender health care, the structures and requirements of social services actively exclude transgender people from these services, resulting in either inappropriate and/or harmful referrals (Spade, 2006). For example, within the adult or juvenile justice system, transgender individuals are often labeled *sex offenders* even if their criminal offense was not sex-related. Most institutions that provide social services (jails, homeless shelters, domestic violence shelters, group homes, drug treatment facilities, etc.) are segregated by gender, often based on the gender designation reflected in legal documents. In many locales in the United States, changing these legal documents can be cost prohibitive and/or require surgery. Subsequently, transgender people are often assigned to facilities that are inappropriate and can be very dangerous due to inexplicitly sanctioned violence against transgender people.

CONCLUSION

Greene (1996) wrote, "The very act of defining the experiences of all lesbians and gay men by the characteristics of the most privileged and powerful members of that group is an act of oppression" (p. 62). It was this observation that led to the focus in this analysis on three marginalized populations within a larger LGBT community in order to shed light on often overlooked groups, while recognizing that the brevity required may not allow for as comprehensive and nuanced an analysis as this diverse community deserves.

By highlighting the inequalities faced by these marginalized groups, it was possible to capture the varied experiences of prejudice and oppression faced by LGBT individuals. Certainly, members of the LGBT community can relate to all three subcommunities (e.g., transgender youth of color).

Also, the experience of social injustice is impacted by the intersection of an individual's experiences with prejudice based on her or his sexual orientation or gender identity with other marginalized statuses.

It is also necessary to highlight and recognize the critical advocacy and movement building that the LGBT community has achieved in a relatively short period of time. Even more impressive is recognizing this achievement against the extensive backdrop of historical discrimination and prejudice the community has faced. LGBT political leaders are being elected to public office. Local LGBT communities are banding together for fund-raising and to provide community health services for those who cannot afford traditional health care. LGBT youth and parents are advocating for inclusive school curriculum within their local school districts. These are some of the critical examples of community activism and advocacy that the LGBT community has achieved to combat the experiences of prejudice and heterosexism.

With that in mind, this analysis seeks to highlight and address some of the prejudices faced by LGBT people as a result of structural injustices embedded in social institutions. Certainly, these are not unique to each subpopulation, but each population (youth, people of color, and transgender people) introduces common institutions that regularly discriminate and exclude LGBT people. These institutions are schools, religion, and health care. Considering the day-to-day functioning of U.S. citizens, these three institutions play a considerable role in the ability to contribute to culture and society. Only by recognizing the sources of injustice and the role that every person plays in supporting these institutions can we hope to address and combat the inequalities that the LGBT community faces.

In depicting the pervasive negative experiences that LGBT people suffer in schools, religions, and health services, two common themes emerge. In all three institutions, personal beliefs and biases materialize into official practice and protocol within the environments. Additionally, there is a gapping absence of legal protections to protect this marginalized group when served by these institutions. As outlined in the introduction of this analysis, essential protection against discrimination based on sexual orientation or gender identity is dramatically overdue for the LGBT community.

These institutions become negative and harmful environments for LGBT people when personal and individual beliefs become policy and practice. Schools acquiesce to individually held beliefs by ignoring and permitting school bullying. Religions become so embroiled in persecuting homosexuality in society at large that they lose sight of their primary role—supporting and growing faith and commitment to a higher deity. Health care services depend entirely on the one-on-one relationships between practitioner and patient, which can be influenced and damaged by either's personal biases. In all cases, service providers need to be educated and challenged to separate their personal biases from their provision of services. Also, laws and policies must be put in place to protect LGBT people from personal biases, especially in public sectors, such as schools and health care services.

In that vein, the laws and protections that limit personal prejudice against LGBT people in these three institutions is woefully behind the protection of other marginalized groups. While the bullying of protected classes, such as African Americans and Jewish Americans, still happens throughout schools in the United States, anti-LGBT bullying is far more pervasive and tolerated by school officials than other forms of bullying. Today, we are disturbed by the past role religion played in supporting widespread discrimination of ethnic minorities, and yet religious institutions are currently playing a significant role in debates over public policy and legal protections of LGBT people. Intolerance against different marginalized groups manifests itself in differing ways; however, protection against LGBT prejudice is not only absent in U.S. laws that protect other groups, but also injustice is maintained and perpetrated by many U.S. laws and policies.

At the root of all of this is the burning question that continues to fuel injustice against LGBT people: How do we really change personal beliefs and biases? Is it a catch-22? Do personal prejudices fuel the lack of legal protections that continue to permit and allow personal prejudices? The argument has long been that, as heterosexuals get to know and have relationships with LGBT individuals, their attitudes and beliefs shift to more supportive and positive views of the community in general (Barth & Perry, 2009). However, how directly do these personal interactions with LGBT individuals convert to support inclusive policies? For example, P. Egan and K. Sherrill (2009) found that three quarters of California voters in 2008 reported knowing friends or family members who were lesbian or gay and yet about one half of those voters supported Proposition 8. Where do we really achieve social justice for LGBT people—in questioning and reforming personal biases or in fighting for legal and political gains?

For LGBT people, the pervasive social morals and biases that perpetrate negative and violent attitudes against LGBT people and communities are intricately linked to the limitations and exclusions of U.S. policies and laws. In essence, the greatest argument against extending protections and equality to LGBT people is the general population's extensive ignorance about and biases against this marginalized community. Antigay leaders have created entire careers out of campaigning against people based on their sexual orientation and gender identity.

Fighting for equal inclusion and protection under the law plays an important role in changing those stereotypes. However, the permissive nature of the culture, regarding an individual's beliefs and morals, continues to allow for the growth and perpetuation of bigotry. The goal of this chapter is to document and illustrate the injustice experienced by LGBT people and the need for providers of human services (e.g., health care providers, educators, social workers, and others) to understand the nature of these social injustices and to advocate for justice and equality for the LGBT community.

REFERENCES

Barth, J., & Parry, J. (2009). 2 > 1 + 1? The impact of contact with gay and lesbian couples on attitudes about gays/lesbians and gay-related policies. *Politics & Policy, 37*(1), 31–50.

Bornstein, K. (1994). *Gender outlaw: On men, women, and the rest of us*. New York, NY: Routledge.

Boswell, H. (1991). The transgender alternative. *Chrysalis Quarterly, 1*(2), 29–31.

Cahill, S. (2009). The disproportionate impact of antigay family policies on Black and Latino same-sex couple households. *Journal of African American Studies, 13*, 219–250.

Cianciotto, J. (2005). *Hispanic and Latino same-sex couple households in the United States: A report from the 2000 census*. New York, NY: National Gay and Lesbian Task Force Policy Institute and the National Latino/a Coalition for Justice.

Dang, A., & Frazer, S. (2004). *Black same-sex households in the United States: A report from the 2000 census*. New York, NY: National Gay and Lesbian Task Force Policy Institute and the National Black Justice Coalition.

D'Augelli, A. R. (1996). Enhancing the development of lesbian, gay and bisexual youths. In E. Rothblum & L. Bonds (Eds.), *Preventing heterosexism and homophobia* (pp. 124–150). Newbury Park, CA: Sage.

D'Augelli, A. R. (1998). Developmental implications of victimization of lesbian, gay and bisexual youths. In. G. Herek (Ed.), *Stigma and sexual orientation: Understanding prejudice against lesbians, gay men, and bisexuals* (pp. 187–210). Thousand Oaks, CA: Sage.

Davis, C. (2008). Social work practice with transgender and gender nonconforming people. In G. P. Mallon (Ed.), *Social work practice with lesbian, gay, bisexual, and transgender people* (pp. 83–112). New York, NY: Routledge.

Davis, K. (2000). *Southern comfort*. New York, NY: Q-Ball.

Denny, D. (2006). Transgender communities of the United States in the late twentieth century. In P. Currah, R. M. Juang, & S. P. Minter (Eds.), *Transgender rights* (pp. 171–191). Minneapolis: University of Minnesota Press.

Egan, P. J., & Sherrill, K. (2009). *California's Proposition 8: What happened, and what does the future hold?* New York, NY: National Gay and Lesbian Task Force Policy Institute.

Elze, D. E. (2006). Oppression, prejudice, and discrimination. In D. F. Morrow & L. Messinger (Eds.), *Sexual orientation and gender expression in social work practice* (pp. 43–77). New York, NY: Columbia University Press.

Feinberg, L. (1998). *Trans liberation: Beyond pink or blue*. Boston, MA: Beacon.

Gaetz, S. (2004). Safe streets for whom? Homeless youth, social exclusion, and criminal victimization. *Canadian Journal of Criminology and Criminal Justice, 46*(4), 423–456.

Grant, J. M., Mottet, L. A., Tanis, J., Harrison, J., Herman, J. L., & Keisling, M. (2011). *Injustice at every turn: A report of the national transgender discrimination survey, executive summary*. Washington, DC: National Center for Transgender Equality and National Gay and Lesbian Task Force.

Greene, B. (1996). Lesbians and gay men of color: The legacy of ethnosexual mythologies in heterosexism. In E. D. Rothblum & L. A. Bond (Eds.), *Preventing heterosexism and homophobia* (pp. 59–70). Thousand Oaks, CA: Sage.

Harper, G. W., Jernewall, N., & Zea, M. C. (2004). Giving voice to emerging science and theory for lesbian, gay, and bisexual people of color. *Cultural Diversity and Ethnic Minority Psychology, 10*(3), 187–199.

Herek, G. M. (1995). Psychological heterosexism in the United States. In A. R. D'Augelli & C. J. Patterson (Eds.), *Lesbian, gay, and bisexual identities over the lifespan: Psychological perspectives* (pp. 321–346). New York, NY: Oxford University Press.

Herek, G. M. (2000). The psychology of sexual prejudice. *Current Directions in Psychological Science, 9*(1), 19–22.

Herek, G. M. (2004). Beyond "homophobia": Thinking about sexual prejudice and stigma in the twenty-first century. *Journal of the National Sexuality Resource Center, 1*(2), 6–24.

Horn, S. (2008). Leaving LGBT students behind: Schools, sexuality and rights. In C. Wainryb, J. Smetana, & E. Turiel (Eds.), *Social development, social inequalities, and social justice* (pp. 131–154). New York, NY: Erlbaum.

Hughes, T. L., & Eliason, M. (2002). Substance use and abuse in lesbian, gay, bisexual and transgender populations. *Journal of Primary Prevention, 22*(3), 263–298.

Kosciw, J. G., Greytak, E. A., Diaz, E. M., & Bartkiewicz, M. J. (2010). *The 2009 National School Climate Survey: The experiences of lesbian, gay, bisexual and transgender youth in our nation's schools*. New York, NY: Gay, Lesbian, and Straight Education Network.

Ku, L., & Waidmann, T. (2003). *How race/ethnicity, immigration status and language affect health insurance coverage, access to care and quality of care among the low-income population*. Washington, DC: Kaiser Family Foundation.

Lambda Legal. (2010, April 13). Summary: Lawrence v. Texas. Retrieved from http://www.lambdalegal.org/in-court/cases/lawrence-v-texas.html

Lee Badgett, M. V. (2001). *Money, myths, and change: The economic lives of lesbians and gay men*. Chicago, IL: University of Chicago Press.

Lombardi, E., & Masen Davis, S. (2006). Transgender health issues. In D. F. Morrow & L. Messinger (Eds.), *Sexual orientation and gender expression in social work practice* (pp. 343–363). New York, NY: Columbia University Press.

McKinley, J. (2010, October 3). Suicides put light on pressures of gay teenagers. *The New York Times*. Retrieved from http://www.nytimes.com/2010/10/04/us/04suicide.html

Minter, S. P. (2006). Do transsexuals dream of gay rights? Getting real about transgender inclusion. In P. Currah, R. M. Juang, & S. P. Minter (Eds.), *Transgender Rights* (pp. 141–170). Minneapolis: University of Minnesota Press.

Moradi, B., DeBlaere, C., & Huang, Y. (2010). Centralizing the experiences of LGB people of color in counseling psychology. *Counseling Psychologist, 38*(3), 322–330.

Morrow, D. F. (2006). Gay, lesbian, bisexual and transgender adolescents. In D. F. Morrow & L. Messinger (Eds.), *Sexual orientation and gender expression in social work practice* (pp. 177–195). New York, NY: Columbia University Press.

National Gay & Lesbian Task Force (NGLTF). (2009, June 30). [Map illustration of state laws]. *State laws prohibiting recognition of same-sex relationships*. Retrieved from http://thetaskforce.org/reports_and_research/issue_maps

National Gay & Lesbian Task Force (NGLTF). (2011a, June 14). *Relationship recognition for same-sex couples in the U.S* [Map illustration of state relationship recognition laws]. Retrieved from http://thetaskforce.org/reports_and_research/issue_maps

National Gay & Lesbian Task Force (NGLTF). (2011b, June 14). *State nondiscrimination laws in the U.S* [Map illustration of state nondiscrimination laws]. Retrieved from http://thetaskforce.org/reports_and_research/issue_maps

Ray, N. (2006). *Lesbian, gay, bisexual and transgender youth: An epidemic of homelessness*. New York, NY: National Gay and Lesbian Task Force Policy Institute and the National Coalition for the Homeless.

Remafedi, G. (1987). Male homosexuality: The adolescent perspective. *Pediatrics, 79*(3), 326–330.

Rothblatt, M. (1994). *The apartheid of sex: A manifesto on the freedom of gender*. New York, NY: Crown.

Spade, D. (2006). Compliance is gendered: Struggling for gender self-determination in a hostile economy. In P. Currah, R. M. Juang, & S. P. Minter (Eds.), *Transgender rights* (pp. 217–241). Minneapolis: University of Minnesota Press.

U.S. Government Accountability Office. (2004). *Defense of marriage act: Update to prior report* (GAO Publication No. GAO-04-353R). Washington, DC: U.S. Government Printing Office.

Walters, K. L., Longres, J. F., Han, C., & Icard, L. D. (2003). Cultural competence with gay and lesbian persons of color. In D. Lum (Ed.), *Cultural compe-tent practice: A framework for understanding diverse groups and justice issues* (pp. 310–342). Pacific Grove, CA: Brooks/Cole—Thomson Learning.

Walters, K. L., & Old Person, R. L., Jr. (2008). Lesbians, gays, bisexuals, and transgender people of color: Reconciling divided selves and communities. In G. P. Mallon (Ed.), *Social work practice with lesbian, gay, bisexual, and transgender people* (pp. 41–68). New York, NY: Routledge.

Wilson, P. A., & Yoshikawa, Hi. (2007). Improving access to health care among African-American, Asian and Pacific Islander, and Latino lesbian, gay, and bisexual populations. In I. H. Meyer & M. E. Northridge (Eds.), *The health of sexual minorities* (pp. 607–637). New York, NY: Springer Science + Business Media.

21

PROCEDURAL INJUSTICES IN CHILD WELFARE

WENDY WIEGMANN

INTRODUCTION

Child welfare agencies assess families for child abuse and neglect. They also coordinate and provide prevention and intervention services. In cases where the courts are involved, child welfare agencies make recommendations to the courts about whether abuse or neglect has occurred, where a child should live, and what services children and parents should receive to improve family functioning. In addition, in cases where children have been removed from the home and parents are not able to reunify, child welfare agencies make recommendations regarding a permanent plan for the child.

Path of a Child Welfare Case

In most child welfare jurisdictions, services are provided to families through an array of service units that vary in their involvement based on the trajectory of the case. During the investigatory phase, a family is referred to a child welfare worker from the Emergency Response or investigatory unit who assesses the allegations of child abuse or neglect and whether or not children are safe in their home. During the initial phase, the social worker is also responsible

for stabilizing the child and family, setting up visits, and initiating the process of arranging services for families. Following the investigatory phase, a family is generally assigned to a different unit and a different social worker who carries the case during the adjudication and disposition hearings. Although this social worker continues to be responsible for providing referrals and services, the social worker's role is also to make the case in court that the child's parents have abused or neglected the child and that the child should be placed in out-of-home care. Following the adjudication and disposition phase of the case, the family is assigned to another ongoing or continuing worker. This worker is primarily responsible for providing the supports and services necessary to make families safe and stable, and, if possible, to return children placed in out-of-home care to their biological parents. In addition, this worker is responsible for initiating the process of concurrent planning for the child by establishing the placements and legal procedures necessary to place the child in an adoptive home if the biological parents are unable to reunify. In cases where children do not reunify with their parents, the case generally goes to a permanency planning or adoption unit that provides long-term care services exclusively to the child.

This chapter describes a number of circumstances within the child welfare system that may lead parents to perceive the system as procedurally unjust. It begins with the concept of procedural justice and research literature on the relationship of justice to effective client services. Based on this introduction, a more detailed description of the path of a child welfare case is provided by featuring a number of policies and practices that are perceived to be unjust to families and which may undermine the cooperation and collaboration necessary for child welfare staff to work effectively with parents. The chapter concludes with a discussion of how an awareness of procedural injustices within the field of child welfare can help child welfare workers better advocate for their clients.

Street Level Bureaucracy

In his book, *Street-Level Bureaucracy: Dilemmas of the Individual in Public Services*, Lipsky (2010) defines street-level bureaucrats as the teachers, social workers, police officers, and other civil servants who perform the specific tasks with which the government is charged. Lipsky argues that an essential component of the work carried out by a street-level bureaucrat is the ability to exercise discretion and serve clients according to their individual needs. Lipsky points out, however, that due to lack of time, information, and resources, many bureaucrats do not practice effective decision making. Rather, he found that bureaucrats often find ways to routinize their work and simplify the needs of their clients. Lipsky concludes that this simplification and "mass processing" of clients carries negative implications for the quality of services clients receive as bureaucrats develop lower expectations for themselves, their clients, and public policy (p. xii). Street-level bureaucrats often accept the maxim that they are doing the best that they can under the prevailing circumstances but that there is little that they can do to significantly change the lives of the clients that they serve.

Organizational and Procedural Justice

Lipsky's findings relate directly to the concepts of organizational and procedural justice as workers seek to actively and diligently strive toward fair processes and outcomes for their clients. Organizational justice refers to people's perceptions about fairness within organizations (Greenberg, 1987). According to Greenberg (1987), there are at least two perspectives of organizational justice: (a) procedural justice, defined as the fairness of the processes used to make decisions, and (b) content justice, defined as the fairness of the resulting decisions. Given that the task of a child welfare worker is to assist parents with the dual processes of assessment and case plan completion, this analysis focuses on the application of procedural justice to the field of child welfare.

Thibaut and Walker (1975) developed a theory of procedural justice based on a series of investigations into mediation and dispute resolution where they compared reactions of people to simulated procedures that differed in terms of two types of control: control over the procedures used to make decisions (process control) and control over the outcomes (decision control). Their research consistently found that decisions, resulting from procedures where participants believed themselves to have process control, were considered fairer and were better accepted than identical decisions made when participants did not feel they had process control (Thibaut & Walker, 1978; Walker, Lind, & Thibaut, 1979). These findings were replicated by other researchers who examined various courtroom and dispute-resolution settings (Casper, Tyler, & Fisher, 1988; Houlden, 1980; Lind, Kurtz, Musante, Walker, & Thibaut, 1980; Lind & Tyler, 1988; Tyler, 1987).

The findings of Thibaut and Walker have also been applied to noncourt settings where attitudes of fairness are deemed to be important. For example, Tyler and his associates found that reactions to encounters with police officers (Sunshine & Tyler, 2003; Tyler, 1990; Tyler & Huo, 2002), politicians (Tyler & Caine, 1981; Tyler, Rasinski, & McGraw, 1985), and teachers (Tyler & Caine, 1981) were heavily influenced by perceptions about the fairness of authorities. In the field of child welfare, researchers have also found the perceptions of fairness to be important to child welfare clients (Ashford, 2006; Ashford & Faith, 2004; Ashford & Holschuh, 2006). In essence, when people are satisfied that procedures and decisions are made in a fair manner, they are more likely to be satisfied with the decision. Research has also demonstrated that this theory holds even when decisions are unfavorable (LaTour, 1978; Lind et al., 1980; Tyler, 1990; Tyler & Huo, 2002).

The purpose of this analysis is to identify examples of how child welfare services have become routinized in ways that are unjust and thereby undermine many of the fairness assumptions deemed critical to clients. Although the original intent of services is to help children and families or to improve the efficiency of the child welfare system, this review identifies ways in which procedures have inadvertently resulted in unfair or unfavorable consequences for child welfare clients. Thus, instead of improving the child welfare system, these procedures have made the efforts of child welfare workers more difficult by discouraging clients and limiting the potential for cooperation. This analysis is also designed to help identify the unintended consequences of child welfare procedures and highlight bureaucratic impediments to effective service delivery. It is important to note that child welfare injustices do not arise out of negligence or blatant disregard for the rights of men, women, and children. Rather, they have evolved over time, despite good intentions, as a result of oversimplification and routinization that can result in injustices for the children and families served by child welfare staff.

INVESTIGATIONS

The involuntary involvement of parents with the child welfare system begins when an agency receives a report of suspected child neglect or abuse (sometimes called "child maltreatment"), that triggers an investigation. Child maltreatment is defined by the Child Abuse Prevention and Treatment Act (CAPTA, 1974) as an act or failure to act by a parent or caregiver that results in serious physical or emotional harm, sexual abuse or exploitation, or death. Reports of maltreatment, often received on hotlines, are referred to a local child welfare agency for investigation.

Depending on the allegations in the case, investigations are normally initiated within 24 hours, although response times vary from state to state (DePanfilis & Salus, 2003). During a typical investigation, the child welfare worker speaks to the person who made the report, conducts an in-person interview with the child or children in question, interviews "collaterals" (other people who may have information on the case), and sometimes interviews the parents who are accused of perpetrating the abuse (U.S. Department of Health and Human Services [USDHHS], Child Welfare Information Gateway, 2010). At the conclusion of the investigation, the child welfare worker determines whether the case is substantiated, inconclusive, or unsubstantiated, although these terms vary by state (USDHHS, Child Welfare Information Gateway, 2010). Typically, a finding of *unsubstantiated* means there is insufficient evidence for the worker to conclude that a child was abused or neglected or that the situation does not meet the legal definition of child abuse or neglect. A finding of *substantiated* often means that the worker believes an incident of child abuse or neglect, as defined by state law, has occurred. A finding of *inconclusive* indicates that there was not enough information for the worker to determine whether abuse or neglect took place (USDHHS, Child Welfare Information Gateway, 2010).

As part of an investigation, a parent is likely to encounter requests by child welfare workers to enter his or her home, go to a child's school, or interview the child alone. Many parents also receive demands that they grant permission for other interviews with family members or service providers (Moynihan, Forgey, & Harris, 2001). These requests and demands are often made of parents under the implied threat that the child may be removed from the parent's care and that the information gained may be used to convince the court of the alleged abuse or neglect (Hardin, 1988). Despite the potential for self-incrimination, child welfare workers conducting investigations rarely present a search warrant or fully inform parents that they have a right to deny the requests (Dickson, 2009; Hardin, 1988). Instead, many parents are informed that a lack of participation and cooperation may be presented as evidence that parents are hiding something or that they are generally uncooperative. As such, the first set of impressions developed by parents of child welfare agencies often include perceptions of demanding child welfare workers who interfere and intrude into their personal lives without any demonstrated legal right to do so. In this process, parents often feel confused, powerless, and overlooked, creating a sense of procedural injustice that can impede cooperation and collaboration (Diorio, 1992; Haight et al., 2002; Kapp & Propp, 2002).

The investigative processes used by child welfare workers do not necessarily reflect carelessness or indifference. Instead, many of the procedures are derived from ambiguous definitions and procedures that inform child welfare practice. Since workers fill in the gaps created by procedural ambiguity with actions that are expedient and seemingly most protective of children, this ambiguity can breed poor practices over time. Every state has laws that dictate the circumstances (definitions of child abuse and neglect) and procedures under which a child welfare agency may intervene in the life of a family. Unfortunately, the language used in such laws is often broad and considerably more vague than language used in other laws (Huxtable, 1994).

Studies have demonstrated that the vagueness of child welfare laws makes the work of child welfare workers more difficult. Research by Van de Luitgaarden (2009) has demonstrated that ambiguous, missing, or contradictory information can impair the judgment of even highly skilled workers. Furthermore, Drury-Hudson (1999) found that many child welfare workers operated with a lack of awareness (and often confusion) about organizational policies and procedures thereby shaping their practice according to the worker's experience and the agency culture. Unfortunately, the result of child welfare ambiguity is inconsistency and low reliability in decision making (Arad-Davidzon & Benbenishty, 2008; Lindsey, 1992; Rossi, Schuerman, & Budde, 1999; Ruscio, 1998; Schuerman, Rossi, & Budde, 1999). Research suggests that the decisions made by child welfare workers in evaluating families may be influenced more by their own views than by the facts of the case, raising serious concerns about the accuracy, fairness, and procedural justice of child welfare investigations.

The ambiguous nature of child welfare law is not the result of inattention or antiquated statutory language. To the contrary, child welfare laws and procedures are updated regularly to reflect current customs, court decisions, or promising practices. Why, then, are the procedures guiding child welfare practice so vague? Some authors have argued that the vagueness of child welfare statutes is necessary to allow for worker and judicial flexibility to assess each individual case with sensitivity in relationship to local community standards (Katz, 1975). Other authors suggest that greater worker discretion is necessary to ensure that children are protected (Polansky, Chalmers, Buttenwieser, & Williams, 1981). They assert that due to the variety of child welfare abuses, narrow definitions within child welfare statutes could prohibit child welfare workers from protecting children in situations where it is necessary, especially considering the difficulties in children's testimony (Huxtable, 1994). It has also been argued that since child welfare law does not involve the same restrictions on liberty as criminal law, it is not as necessary to narrowly define the laws to prevent abuses (Sinden, 1999). However, the ambiguity in child welfare law can result in intrusive investigations into the lives of families without sufficient assurances of procedural fairness (Hutchison, 1987). Not only do workers conduct investigations that appear on their surface to violate typical search-and-seizure protections, but workers are also often not equipped with sufficient information to fully inform families about the process. Given the complexity of explaining their processes to parents, workers proceed in their investigations with a presumption of authority that can be difficult to adequately justify. While the intent of ambiguity in child welfare law is certainly aimed at protecting children and promoting an environment where workers and judicial officers may exercise as much flexibility as possible, the unintended consequences include alienating families, tarnishing the worker-family relationship with suspicion, and creating a sense of injustice. To improve the procedural fairness of child welfare investigations, procedures need to be explicitly stated, easily explained, and uniformly practiced.

ADJUDICATION AND DISPOSITION

Following an investigation resulting in substantiation, a child welfare worker appears in court to formally inform the judge and the family about the charges of abuse that are being filed and the whereabouts of a child removed from the family's care (USDHHS, Child Welfare Information

Gateway, n.d.). These court hearings (called the adjudication and disposition hearings) are necessary to protect the due process rights of the parents (Chill, 2004; Sinden, 1999). During this phase of a case, the child welfare agency must properly notify the parents about the child welfare proceedings and prove parental unfitness with clear and convincing evidence (USDHHS, Child Welfare Information Gateway, n.d.). In addition, the child welfare worker must offer recommendations for the placement of the child and prepare a service plan designed to enable the parents to reunify with the child (USDHHS, Child Welfare Information Gateway, n.d.).

Child welfare courts (often called family or dependency courts) differ in many ways from criminal and civil courts (Sinden, 1999). Since dependency cases are considered civil matters, not all states require that parents have access to appointed legal counsel (Outley, 2004). While most states appoint counsel in practice, some states only require that an attorney be provided in hearings related to the termination of parental rights (Abel & Rettig, 2006; Outley, 2004; Rhode, 2009; Sankaran, 2007). For clients with an appointed attorney, contact with counsel appears to be infrequent, with attorneys meeting their clients briefly, and often in the lobby or outside of the courthouse just before the hearing (Sankaran, 2007).

Child welfare courts also employ a more informal or relaxed atmosphere in their courtrooms. Believing an informal process to be better able to empower parents, engender trust, build rapport, and resolve issues through a process of cooperation, mediation, and shared goals, most child welfare courts employ a nonadversarial, informal process (Sinden, 1999). Supporters of an informal process claim that by removing the adversarial character from the courtroom, participants are more likely to be open and honest and less intimidated by the court setting (Sinden, 1999). Despite the beneficial intent, however, some authors argue that this type of informality does more harm to child welfare clients than good. In her article, "Why Won't Mom Cooperate? A Critique of Informality in Child Welfare Proceedings," Sinden (1999) argues that the current informal court procedures in child welfare cases interfere with two fundamental due process goals: first, to promote accurate decision making and, second, to provide the best opportunity for

parties to be heard. Specifically, Sinden argues that by removing many of the procedural components of a formal courtroom (such as evidentiary requirements, the exclusionary rule against illegally obtained evidence, rules regarding prejudicial information, standards for expert testimony, and a process of cross-examination), an informal courtroom increases the admission of biased and inaccurate information.

Sinden (1999) also argues that there is a substantial power disparity between the child welfare agency and the parent in child welfare proceedings. Because of this disparity, instead of offering up additional information honestly and eagerly, parents are often discouraged from expressing their true opinions or opposition or introducing new information that may help their case. Instead, parents are often compelled to cooperate in order to make their case go easier and to satisfy the authorities:

> In child welfare cases, where the individual is pitted against the vast power and resources of the state, the power imbalance is particularly extreme. Parents frequently come to court unfamiliar with the system, unversed in the prevailing professional discourse, unaware of their legal rights, eager to prove themselves respectable, rational, reasonable, and cooperative, and eager to please the agency social worker, whom they (rather accurately) perceive as enormously powerful. . . . Even where coercion is not intentional on the part of the social worker, parents are often too quick to accede to the agency social worker's suggested resolution of their case, resulting in false agreements that do not accurately reflect either the result that would have been achieved in court or our society's chosen balance between intervention and family privacy. (p. 385)

Thus, although the original intent of the current courtroom environment was to empower, welcome, and support parents, the unfortunate result is a system of informal hearings, where the assessment of the child welfare agency is largely unchallenged (Sankaran, 2007; Sinden, 1999). Within such a context, it is easy to see how parents may feel that they are not being fairly treated and that the process by which their parenting is being evaluated is unjust and flawed. As many authors have noted, a different, and perhaps more adversarial, court may be necessary to ensure parents that their procedural rights are being protected.

OUT-OF-HOME PLACEMENT

After the court has determined that children should be placed in out-of-home care, the family becomes formally involved with the juvenile or dependency court system. The courts, having declared that the child is a ward or dependent of the court and asserting the government's *parens patriae* right to protect the child, charges the child welfare agency with the responsibilities of providing for the child's safety and welfare and placing the child in a safe home (Badeau & Gesiriech, 2003). As will be illustrated, however, maintaining the appropriate balance between the state's legitimate interest in protecting and caring for children, and the rights of family members to make decisions about the child become significantly more complicated once a child is placed in out-of-home care. Furthermore, placing a child outside parental custody can carry many additional consequences for families which may undermine perceptions of procedural justice.

Children With Mental Health and Behavioral Problems

According to the National Alliance on Mental Illness (NAMI, 2003), 20% of children and adolescents in the United States (approximately 7.5 million) suffer from a mental illness. Providing care for a child with mental illness can be very challenging for parents in the following ways: (a) feeling shunned by neighbors and friends because of their children's illnesses, (b) blamed for their children's conditions, (c) forced to change jobs or quit in order to take care of their children, (d) pushed to the emotional breaking point, (e) disturbed by severely stressed marriages, and/or (f) siblings negatively affected by a child's mental illness, putting further strain on the family (National Alliance for the Mentally Ill [NAMI], 1999).

In addition to the social and emotional toll, caring for a child with mental illness carries enormous financial costs. In many cases, the costs of care for mentally ill children force parents to relinquish their children to child welfare agencies. As reported by Goodman (2004), the average middle-class family has an income too high to receive Medicaid yet too low to be able to pay out-of-pocket for childhood

mental health services (Giliberti & Schulzinger, 2000). According to the NAMI study (1999), 66% of responding parents reported that their health insurance did not provide adequate coverage for their children's mental health disorders. Forty-nine percent reported that lack of coverage impeded needed services for their children. In addition, nearly half of the respondents indicated that managed care organizations limited or denied access to needed treatment for their children to the detriment of their child's health. Parents that may be able to afford treatment for their child still face limited options because many residential facilities serve only children who are in state custody (Giliberti & Schulzinger, 2000).

With nowhere else to go, many parents turn to the child welfare system to obtain services for their mentally ill children. Once there, many parents are surprised by what they are told. According to the NAMI survey (1999), 23% of respondents reported that they were instructed to relinquish custody of their children if they wanted to access needed services, and 20% reported that they ultimately did so in order to get care for their children. According to Inglish (2010), many state child welfare jurisdictions erroneously believe that they are ineligible for federal funding to assist with mental health care unless the child is a ward of the state. Thus, through no fault of their own, many parents become involved in the child welfare system simply to address the mental health needs of their children. Whether due to the costs of treatment for their child or the specific policies of residential facilities, parents feel compelled to place their children in foster care to treat a child's mental health needs.

During the 1970s, many child welfare agencies maintained a two-tiered foster care system (Barth, 2009). With one level designed for children without behavior problems who needed protection from maltreatment and a second tier created for children with behavioral and mental health problems, this system allowed for a unique approach to placing and treating mentally ill children (Fanshel as cited in Barth, 2009). In 1980, the Adoption Assistance and Child Welfare Act made federal funding of child welfare services contingent upon parental incapacity or abuse (Barth, 2009). Despite the act, many children continue to enter care because of emotional and behavioral problems (Barth, Wildfire,

& Green, 2006). Regardless of the fact that these cases come into child welfare due to child behavior or mental illness, many are defined or reclassified as cases of abandonment or caregiver incapacity in order to meet funding requirements (Barth et al., 2006; Ervin, 1999). In these cases, child welfare workers write court petitions that describe the inability of the parents to care for the child, or they present the facts of the case in a way that focuses on the inadequacies of the parents (Ervin, 1999). Following the child welfare petition, the court handles the case as one of parental abandonment or incapacity and emphasizes the parent's compliance with their case plan and cooperation with the child welfare agency (Goodman, 2004). Parents involved in this system may wonder why so much attention is focused on their efforts when the original reason for child welfare involvement was to care for the specific needs of their children. Furthermore, all parents involved in the child welfare system are constrained by the provisions of the Adoption and Safe Families Act (1997) that limits the length of time that services can be provided to a reunifying parent, meaning that if parents are unable to reunify with their children within the mandated guidelines,[1] they risk losing their children permanently (Ervin, 2007; USDHHS, Child Welfare Information Gateway, 2010).

In recent years, public policy and legal efforts have been made to keep families intact when a child has a serious mental disability, by providing services and supports to families to ensure that children can remain at home (Goodman, 2004; Inglish, 2010; Stefan, 2008). Despite these efforts, and the fact that the original intent of child welfare involvement was to provide services to children desperately needing care, the procedure for providing mental health care to children through the child welfare system commonly involves charging parents in court with being abusive, neglectful, or inadequate to meet their children's needs. Under these circumstances, parents not only lose decision-making control regarding their children, but also they are routinely ordered to comply with a case plan and threatened with the termination of services if they cannot reunify within a specified period of time. The tragic result of these procedures is that instead of feeling supported by the child welfare system, many parents perceive the system as unfairly blaming them, as well as interfering in their family in ways that are neither helpful nor just. These types of initial engagements do not lead to cooperative or supportive relationships between child welfare workers and parents. Instead, it often creates a confrontational environment where parents feel as though they must defend themselves against procedural injustices. Significantly, these procedures also shift the focus of child welfare and court processes from the needs and status of the child to an assessment of parental fitness, further impeding the success of child welfare efforts.

The Interstate Compact on the Placement of Children (ICPC)

Another complication that can arise once a child is placed in out-of-home care involves the Interstate Compact for the Placement of Children (ICPC). ICPC guidelines were originally designed to facilitate interjurisdictional placement of children into foster care or adoptive homes (Secretariat to the Association of Administrators of the Interstate Compact on the Placement of Children [SAAICPC], 2002). Within the policy, each state and territory in the United States maintains its own foster care system for children in the state's custody. If a child welfare agency in one state wishes to place a child with a parent, relative, foster parent, or potential adoptive parent in another state, officials in the "sending state" must cooperate with officials in the "receiving state" to assess the appropriateness of the placement and to oversee the delivery of any needed services. Importantly, the ICPC also mandates that a receiving state maintains the right to approve or deny placement of a child in its jurisdiction. Created as a result of unfortunate practices where children were placed in different states and forgotten, with no protections for their safety, the ICPC process was designed to ensure that children are placed in safe homes, assessed by child welfare agency staff, and that their safety and well-being are safeguarded

---

[1] Under the act, state agencies are required to seek termination of the parent-child relationship when a child has been in foster care for 15 of the most recent 22 months (USDHHS, Child Welfare Information Gateway, 2010).

following the placement (Colyer, 2009; Freundlich, Heffernan, & Jacobs, 2004).

Despite the intentions of its design, the ICPC has long been criticized as a barrier to the timely placement of foster children into permanent homes (Colyer, 2009; Dalberth, Hardison, & Gibbs, 2006; Freundlich, 1997). The most common problems are lengthy delays due to coverage of education and medical expenses, conduction of criminal background checks, facilitating collaboration between states, and issues related to staffing and workload (American Public Human Services Association, 2002; Dalberth et al., 2006). For noncustodial biological parents residing in different states, the process is even more complicated. These situations often arise when a parent who was living apart from the child learns that the child has been placed in foster care due to allegations of abuse or neglect against the custodial parent (Sankaran, 2006). In the process of petitioning the court to place the child in his or her custody, the noncustodial parent is often told that a home-study must be conducted by the receiving state under an ICPC agreement prior to placement of the child in the noncustodial parent's home (Sankaran, 2006). In these cases, the ICPC agreement mandates that until out-of-state approval is received, the court is prohibited from placing the child with the parent or approving a visit of over 30 days (SAAICPC, 2002).

Sankaran (2006) argues that the application of the ICPC process to biological parents is unjust, particularly when it comes to determining whether or not to approve placement of children with noncustodial parents. According to Sankaran (2006), caseworkers in a receiving state may consider the following factors when assessing a family's home: caregiver's income, preferred form of discipline, the safety of the neighborhood, the proposed school for the child, sleeping arrangements, housekeeping standards, and school performance of other children in the home. While all of these factors are not mandated, they are suggested in ICPC policy guidelines and prove to be more demanding than considerations commonly applied to parents within their own jurisdiction. Sankaran argues that because the ICPC guidelines do not specifically address assessments of biological parents, a vast number of appropriate placements have been unfairly denied under ICPC arrangements.

Furthermore, since ICPC guidelines do not include a provision for judicial review of decisions made by child welfare workers and few states have an administrative review of decisions, parents may be unfairly denied placement of their children without any recourse (Sankaran, 2006).

While the original intent of the Interstate Compact was to improve the efficiency of interstate placements and monitor the safety of children once they were placed in a different jurisdiction, the result is a process that is procedurally unjust to parents and often detrimental to children. Parents involved in this process often feel as though they are being punished for the faults of the custodial parent and denied access to their child without adequate reason. In addition, many children remain in foster care placements in their original jurisdictions, while biological parents eagerly seek, and are denied, placement in other states.

Financial Aid and Housing

In many cases, when children are removed from the care and custody of their parents, bureaucratic procedures may result in the family losing financial and housing assistance provided by the state (Courtney, 1998; Eamon & Kopels, 2004). Under these circumstances, family reunification may be more difficult (or even impossible) since parents must contend not only with the original causes of maltreatment but also with new problems arising out of homelessness and lack of financial stability. According to Courtney (1998), under the Personal Responsibility and Work Opportunity Reconciliation Act (1996) legislation that mandates the terms and conditions of public assistance, families may be denied cash assistance if the child for whom the family is receiving support is absent from the home for 45 days. Despite this language, Courtney (1998) also points out that states have considerably more flexibility than usually assumed and that, if certain procedures are followed, states may actually provide assistance during an absence of up to 6 months. Although this additional assistance is generally predicated on the efforts of states to coordinate communications between child welfare agencies and the state's welfare program, California and other states have begun the process of integrating the child welfare and welfare services to improve this collaborative process (Berns & Drake, 1999; Berrick, Frame, Langs, & Varchol, 2006; Ehrle, Scarcella, & Geen, 2004). In a similar fashion, proactive work on the side of the child welfare agency may also encourage state housing programs to grant extensions and exemptions to families who have lost temporary custody of their children, allowing them to stay in their homes during their reunification.

Research has documented the crucial connection between financial stability and housing for families involved in the child welfare system. Wells and Guo (2003) demonstrated that children placed in out-of-home care reunified more quickly when a family's welfare benefits were consistent during the child welfare case. In another study, Shook & Testa (1997) compared child welfare outcomes for parents who did not receive cash assistance with parents whose benefits continued; they found that parents who continued to receive cash assistance were less likely to have children placed in out-of-home care and were more likely to be reunified with their children more quickly than families who did not receive assistance.

Numerous housing studies have demonstrated that when families receive housing assistance, they are more likely to experience successful family reunification. For example, a recent study by Choi and Ryan (2007) demonstrated that mothers with substance abuse problems who received housing services were more likely to achieve family reunification than mothers who did not receive such services. For families involved in child welfare, housing stability is a key factor in family reunification (Hoffman & Rosenheck, 2001; Ryan & Schuerman, 2004). In addition, when families with housing needs receive housing assistance, the risk of subsequent maltreatment is also decreased (Ryan & Schuerman, 2004).

The involvement of child welfare workers and subsequent placement of children in foster care is meant to be a temporary and ameliorating intervention in the lives of families. Unfortunately, when child welfare agencies and workers are not alert and attentive, child welfare involvement can also have serious negative consequences for families who lose desperately needed financial assistance and housing due to out-of-home placement. Furthermore, parents who lose financial and housing assistance when their children are placed in care may not understand the difference between child welfare and public welfare, and they may wonder why the agency is making it as difficult as possible for them to reunify with their children. In order to preserve financial and housing stability as a result of child welfare involvement, child welfare workers need to recognize and understand the procedural implications of their practice and to ensure that their clients are not unduly affected by their interventions.

FAMILY REUNIFICATION

In moving from out-of-home care to family reunification, most parents must participate in a case plan of services designed to mitigate the circumstances under which the child was removed. Under the Adoption Assistance and Child Welfare Act (1980), a written case plan must be on file for any child receiving federal foster care assistance. In most states, the child welfare agency must also include the parent or guardian in the case planning process unless compelling circumstances prevent participation of the parents (USDHHS, Child Welfare Information Gateway, 2008). Under Title IV-E of the Social Security Act, case plans must also describe the type of home or institution where the child is placed, provide a plan for ensuring that the child receives safe and proper care, and describe the ways that appropriate services will be provided to the parents, child, and foster parents (USDHHS, Child Welfare Information Gateway, 2008). In addition, many states require a specific arrangement of goals, objectives, and timelines to improve the safety and well-being of a family's home. Some states also require that the case plan include a schedule of visitation between children and their parents and siblings (USDHHS, Child Welfare Information Gateway, 2008).

The Adoption Assistance and Child Welfare Act (1980) requires that states review a child's case at least every 6 months after foster care placement in order to determine whether the placement continues to be necessary and appropriate, whether the case plan is being properly and adequately followed, and whether the family has made progress in mitigating the problems that led to out-of-home placement (USDHHS, Child Welfare Information Gateway, n.d.). The review hearings also consider whether a family can be reunified and establishes a target date for the child's return home, adoption, or other permanent placement (USDHHS, Child Welfare Information Gateway, n.d.).

Case Planning

The development of the child welfare case plan is one of the most important processes in a family reunification case. During this process, the child welfare worker often consults with the family to determine the unique circumstances that led to abuse and neglect and the services and supports that the family will need to ensure that maltreatment does not recur. Parental involvement in case planning is essential in order to match services and supports with the specific needs of the family. It also demonstrates to the parents that the agency believes them to be capable of achieving the case plan goals (Hatton, Brooks, & Hafer, 2008). Research on parental case plan involvement finds that people who are asked to participate in decision making are more likely to follow through with the plans and decisions that are made (Maddux, 2002).

Despite these findings, engagement of parents in case planning is neglected by child welfare workers approximately 50% of the time (USDHHS, Children's Bureau, 2010). Based on state program improvement plans, common concerns among state child welfare agencies include inconsistent matching of services to needs, failure to involve parents and children in case planning, inadequate caseworker visits with children and parents, and failure to engage fathers (USDHHS, Children's Bureau, n.d.). As Berrick (2009) notes:

> Parents' stories about the path to reunification suggest a lonely experience that speaks largely to issues of compliance and less to changes in real-life experiences. The large majority of parents are given case plans that include parent education, drug treatment, and sometimes therapy—services that may match some of their needs but may also be less directly related to their parenting experience. (p. 31)

With such lack of engagement, it is no surprise that parents fail to reunify with their children approximately 50% of the time (USDHHS, Children's Bureau, 2010). Child maltreatment recurrence rates of 20% to 30% also suggest that many parents are unable to sustain lasting change (DePanfilis & Zuravin, 1999; Drake, Jonson-Reid, Way, & Chung, 2003; Fluke, Shusterman, Hollinshead, & Yuan, 2008; Marshall & English, 1999). If child welfare workers are to successfully promote reunification, meaningfully protect children from abuse and neglect, and ensure procedural fairness for parents, effective case planning processes are needed to address the unique needs of each family.

Providing Services and Feedback

In order to assist families in reunifying, child welfare agencies must make "reasonable efforts" to mitigate the circumstances that necessitated a child's placement in out-of-home care (Adoption Assistance and Child Welfare Act, 1980). This policy is based on the assumption that families can improve their caregiving and adequately protect children from abuse and neglect if provided with targeted and effective services. Despite this mandate, many child welfare agencies simply refer parents to a standard array of services without consulting the parents during the case planning process, and with little proof that the services are beneficial or helpful in addressing the problems faced by these families (Barth, 2008; Berrick, 2009; USDHHS, Children's Bureau, 2010).

Some advocates have argued that the standard services offered by child welfare agencies do not even come close to addressing the complex problems that bring children into the foster care system (Wells & Marcenko, 2011). Research demonstrates that parents with substance abuse problems are less likely to reunify (Brook & McDonald, 2007; Eamon, 2002; Green, Rockhill, & Furrer, 2007; Mapp & Steinberg, 2007; McDonald, Poertner, & Jennings, 2007), as are parents with low incomes (Courtney, 1994; Courtney & Wong, 1996; Eamon, 2002; Kortenkamp, Geen & Stagner, 2004; Wells & Guo, 2003), inadequate housing (Courtney, McMurtry & Zinn, 2004), or mental health problems (Courtney, 1994; Eamon & Kopels, 2004; Grella, Needell, Shi, & Hser, 2009; Potter & Klein-Rothschild, 2002; Rockhill, Green, & Furrer, 2007). By not addressing deep-seated and entrenched causes such as addiction, poverty, and mental health problems, researchers argue that child welfare agencies underserve families and run the risk of setting them up for the recurrence of abuse and neglect (Wells & Marcenko, 2011).

Considering some of the difficult problems that parents must address in reunifying with their children, the promotion of procedural justice calls for workers to adequately monitor the case plan as well as track and reward the progress made by parents (Saint-Jacques, Drapeau, Lessard, & Beaudoin, 2006). The essential process of monitoring and tracking progress provides families with an ongoing source of motivation and assistance with making progress toward reunification. In addition, the case plan helps to document the areas of family life that need continued work and improvement, and it provides an opportunity, when necessary, to revise the reunification plan (Gambrill & Stein, 1985). Regular feedback on clear objectives and outcome indicators helps parents to see that the child welfare process is designed to reunify them with their children. It also encourages parents who are making progress to see areas that need additional support. This is essential to providing families with adequate service (Gambrill & Stein, 1985).

DISCUSSION AND CONCLUSIONS

This analysis provides a review of procedural injustices experienced by parents involved in the child welfare system. While it is not exhaustive (societal and system-based injustices are too numerous to mention), it identifies many procedural injustices that have arisen out of policies and procedures that were created with good intentions but have resulted in detrimental and unjust outcomes. By highlighting the unintended consequences of such policies, experienced and novice child welfare workers should be able to find ways to change, work around, and adapt policies to serve clients in ways that are fairer, more responsive, and just.

According to the National Association of Social Workers (NASW, 2009), social workers have an ethical responsibility to "challenge social injustice" by pursuing "social change, particularly with and on behalf of vulnerable and oppressed individuals

and groups of people" (*Code of Ethics*). Therefore, child welfare workers need to be active in changing or modifying policies and procedures that are unfair to child welfare clients, by challenging existing policies and documenting the detrimental outcomes that call for reform.

Since child welfare workers are perceived as authorities and their own actions carry serious implications for the people they serve, they do not need to wait until policy changes are made in order to improve the procedural justice perceptions of their clients. As research has documented, judgments about procedural justice are often influenced by the interpersonal communications that clients receive from decision makers (Lind & Tyler, 1988; Tyler, 1990; Tyler & Huo, 2002). These judgments include respectful treatment (Bies, 2001; Bies & Moag, 1986), fully explained decisions (Bies & Moag, 1986; Tyler & Bies, 1990), and the trust engendered by the transparency of the authority figures (Tyler & Huo, 2002). Thus, child welfare workers have an opportunity to conduct themselves in ways that create perceptions of fairness on a daily basis. Child welfare workers can give clients the sense that they are being treated fairly and honestly when they (a) take time to clearly explain legal and administrative decisions to clients, (b) speak honestly with parents about the authority and responsibility of their role, and (c) communicate clearly about the decisions clients can make as well as the consequences of those decisions. Proactive workers can also engage families in the case planning process, address underlying causes, and provide encouragement and concrete feedback about progress. Of equal importance, child welfare workers need to avoid the oversimplification and routinization that can impede their ability to address the unique circumstances faced by their clients by remembering that each family faces unique challenges that require tailored responses and services.

In summary, the role of a child welfare worker is to engage parents in a shared process that will improve the safety and well-being of children. Whether through reunification or adoption, the accomplishment of this goal requires the help and cooperation of the child's parents. The key to this cooperation is ensuring fairness for parents involved in the child welfare process.

REFERENCES

Abel, L. K., & Rettig, M. (2006). State statutes providing for a right to counsel in civil cases. *Clearinghouse Review Journal of Poverty Law and Policy, 40,* 252–262.

Adoption and Safe Families Act of 1997, Pub. L. No. 105-89, 111 Stat. 2115 (1997).

Adoption Assistance and Child Welfare Act of 1980, Pub. L. No. 96-272, 94 Stat. 500 (1980).

American Public Human Services Association. (2002). *Understanding delays in the interstate home study process.* Retrieved from http://icpc.aphsa.org/Home/Doc/resources/home_study_report.pdf

Arad-Davidzon, B., & Benbenishty, R. (2008). The role of workers attitudes and parent and child wishes in child protection workers' assessments and recommendations regarding removal and reunification. *Children and Youth Services Review, 30*(1), 107–121.

Ashford, J. B. (2006). Comparing the effects of judicial versus child protective services relationships on parental attitudes in the juvenile dependency process. *Research on Social Work Practice, 16*(6), 582–590.

Ashford, J. B., & Faith, R. L. (2004). Testing models of justice and trust: A study of mediation in child dependency disputes. *Social Work Research, 28*(1), 18–27.

Ashford, J. B., & Holschuh, J. (2006). Fairness issues in law and mental health: Directions for future social work research. *Journal of Sociology and Social Welfare, 33*(4), 131–152.

Badeau, S., & Gesiriech, S. (2003, July 28). *A child's journey through the child welfare system.* Retrieved from http://pewfostercare.org/docs/index.php?DocID=24

Barth, R. P. (2008). The move to evidence-based practice: How well does it fit child welfare services. *Journal of Public Child Welfare, 2*(2), 145–171.

Barth, R. P. (2009). Preventing child abuse and neglect with parent training: Evidence and opportunities. *Future of Children, 19*(2), 95–118.

Barth, R. P., Wildfire, J., & Green, R. (2006). Placement into foster care and the interplay of urbanicity, child behavior problems, and poverty. *American Journal of Orthopsychiatry, 76*(3), 358–366.

Berns, D. A., & Drake, B. J. (1999). Combining child welfare and welfare reform at the local level. *Policy & Practice of Public Human Services, 57*(1), 26–34.

Berrick, J. D. (2009). *Take me home: Protecting America's vulnerable children and families.* New York, NY: Oxford University Press.

Berrick, J. D., Frame, L., Langes, J., & Varchol, L. (2006). Working together for children and families: Where TANF and child welfare meet. *International Journal of Policy Practice 5*(2/3), 27–42.

Bies, R. J. (2001). Interactional (in)justice: The sacred and the profane. In J. Greenberg & R. Cropanzano (Eds.), *Advances in organizational justice* (pp. 89–118). Palo Alto, CA: Stanford University Press.

Bies, R. J., & Moag, J. S. (1986). Interactional justice: Communication criteria of fairness. In R. J. Lewicki, B. H. Sheppard, & M. H. Bazerman (Eds.), *Research on negotiation in organizations* (pp. 43–55). Greenwich, CT: JAI Press.

Brook, J., & McDonald, T. P. (2007). Evaluating the effects of comprehensive substance abuse intervention on successful reunification. *Research on Social Work Practice, 17*(6), 664–673.

Casper, J. D., Tyler, T. R., & Fisher, B. (1988). Procedural justice in felony cases. *Law and Society Review, 22*(3), 483–507.

Child Abuse Prevention and Treatment Act (CAPTA) of 1974. Pub. L. No. 93-247 (1974).

Chill, P. (2004). Burden of proof begone: The pernicious effect of emergency removal in child protective proceedings. *Family Court Review, 42*(3), 540–553.

Choi, S., & Ryan, J. P. (2007). Co-occurring problems for substance abusing mothers in child welfare: Matching services to improve family reunification. *Children and Youth Services Review, 29*(11), 1395–1410.

Colyer, C. J. (2009). Delayed placement: An analysis of the interstate compact for the placement of children in West Virginia. *Children and Youth Services Review, 31*(7), 768–774.

Courtney, M. E. (1994). Factors associated with the reunification of foster-children with their families. *Social Service Review, 68*(1), 81–108.

Courtney, M. E. (1998). The costs of child protection in the context of welfare reform. *Future of Children, 8*(1), 88–103.

Courtney, M. E., McMurtry, S., & Zinn, A. (2004). Housing problems experienced by recipients of child welfare services. *Child Welfare, 83*(5), 389–392.

Courtney, M. E., & Wong, Y. I. (1996). Comparing the timing of exits from substitute care. *Children and Youth Services Review, 18*(4/5), 307–334.

Dalberth, B., Hardison, J., & Gibbs, D. (2006, September). *Interjurisdictional placement of children in the child welfare system: Improving the process.* Retrieved from http://www.hunter.cuny.edu/socwork/nrcfcpp/downloads/IJReport.pdf

DePanfilis, D., & Salus, M. K. (2003). *Child protective services: A guide for caseworkers,* 2003. Retrieved from http://www.childwelfare.gov/pubs/usermanuals/cps/cpse.cfm

DePanfilis, D., & Zuravin, S. (1999). Epidemiology of child maltreatment recurrence. *Social Services Review, 27*(2), 218–223.

Dickson, D. T. (2009). When law and ethics collide: Social control in child protective services. *Ethics and Social Welfare, 3*(3), 264–283.

Diorio, W. D. (1992). Parental perceptions of the authority of public child welfare caseworkers. *Families in Society: The Journal of Contemporary Human Services, 73*(4), 222–235.

Drake, B., Jonson-Reid, M., Way, I., & Chung, S. (2003). Substantiation and recidivism. *Child Maltreatment, 8*(4), 248–260.

Drury-Hudson, J. (1999). Decision making in child protection: The use of theoretical, empirical and procedural knowledge by novices and experts and implications for fieldwork placement. *British Journal of Social Work, 29*(1), 147–169.

Eamon, M. K. (2002, May 20). *The effect of economic resources on reunification of Illinois children in substitute care.* Retrieved from http://www.cfrc.illinois.edu/publications/rp_20020520_TheEffectOfEconomicResourcesOnReunificationOfIllinoisChildrenInSubstituteCare.pdf

Eamon, M. K., & Kopels, S. (2004). "For reasons of poverty": Court challenges to child welfare practices and mandated programs. *Children and Youth Services Review, 26*(9), 821–836.

Ehrle, J., Scarcella, C. A., & Geen, R. (2004). Teaming up: Collaboration between welfare and child welfare agencies since welfare reform. *Children and Youth Services Review, 26*(3), 265–285.

Ervin, C. L. (1999). Parents forced to surrender custody of children with neurobiological disorders. *New Directions for Mental Health Services, 54,* 111–116.

Fluke, J. D., Shusterman, G. R., Hollinshead, D. M., & Yuan, Y. T. (2008). Longitudinal analysis of repeated child abuse reporting and victimization: Multistate analysis of associated factors. *Child Maltreatment, 13*(1), 76–88.

Freundlich, M. D. (1997). Reforming the interstate compact on the placement of children: A new framework for interstate adoption. *University of Pennsylvania Journal of Law and Social Change, 4,* 15–54.

Freundlich, M., Heffernan, M., & Jacobs, J. (2004). Interjurisdictional placement of children in foster care. *Child Welfare, 83*(1), 5–26.

Gambrill, E. D., & Stein, T. J. (1985). Working with biological parents: Important procedural ingredients. *Children and Youth Services Review, 7*(2/3), 173–189.

Giliberti, M., & Schulzinger, R. (2000, March). Relinquishing custody: The tragic result of failure to meet children's mental health needs. Retrieved from http://www.bazelon.org/LinkClick.aspx?fileticket=-hWbIbUX5v8%3D&tabid=104

Goodman, G. (2004). Accessing mental health care for children: Relinquishing custody to save the child. *Albany Law Review, 67*(1), 301–330.

Green, B. L., Rockhill, A., & Furrer, C. (2007). Does substance abuse treatment make a difference for child welfare case outcomes? A statewide longitudinal analysis. *Children and Youth Services Review, 29*(4), 460–473.

Greenberg, J. (1987). A taxonomy of organization justice theories. *Academy of Management Review, 12*(1), 9–22.

Grella, C. E., Needell, B., Shi, Y. F., & Hser, Y. I. (2009). Do drug treatment services predict reunification outcomes of mothers and their children in child welfare? *Journal of Substance Abuse Treatment, 36*(3), 278–293.

Haight, W. L., Black, J. E., Mangelsdorf, S., Giorgio, G., Tata, L., Schoppe, S. J., & Szewczyk, M. (2002). Making visits better: The perspectives of parents, foster parents, and child welfare workers. *Child Welfare, 81*(2), 173–202.

Hardin, M. (1988). Legal barriers in child abuse investigations: State powers and individual rights. *Washington Legal Review, 63*(3), 493–605.

Hatton, H., Brooks, S., & Hafer, N. (2008, December). *Participatory case planning in child welfare services.* Retrieved from http://humanservices.ucdavis.edu/Academy/pdf/FINAL2PCPVersion.pdf

Hoffman, D., & Rosenheck, R. (2001). Homeless mothers with severe mental illness and their children: Predictors of family reunification. *Psychiatric Rehabilitation Journal, 25*(2), 163–169.

Houlden, P. (1980). The impact of procedural modifications on evaluations of plea bargaining. *Law and Society Review, 15*(2), 267–292.

Hutchison, E. D. (1987). Use of authority in direct social work practice with mandated clients. *Social Service Review, 61*(4), 581–598.

Huxtable, M. (1994). Child protection: With liberty and justice for all. *Social Work, 39*(1), 60–66.

Inglish, J. A. (2010). Preventing custody relinquishment for youth with mental health needs: Implications for the state of Utah. *Journal of Law and Family Studies, 12*(1), 237–249.

Kapp, S. A., & Propp, J. (2002). Client satisfaction methods: Input from parents with children in foster care. *Child and Adolescent Social Work Journal, 19*(3), 227–245.

Katz, S. (1975). Child neglect laws in America. *Family Law Quarterly, 9,* 1–372.

Kortenkamp, K., Geen, R., & Stagner, M. (2004). The role of welfare and work in predicting foster care reunification rates for children of welfare recipients. *Children and Youth Services Review, 26*(6), 577–590.

LaTour, S. (1978). Determinants of participant and observer satisfaction with adversary and inquisitorial modes of adjudication. *Journal of Personality and Social Psychology, 36*(12), 1531–1545.

Lind, E. A., Kurtz, S., Musante, L., Walker, L., & Thibaut, J. (1980). Procedure and outcome effects on reactions to adjudicated resolutions of conflicts of interest. *Journal of Personality and Social Psychology, 39*(4), 643–653.

Lind, E. A., & Tyler, T. R. (1988). *The social psychology of procedural justice.* New York, NY: Plenum.

Lindsey, D. (1992). Reliability of the foster care placement decision: A review. *Research on Social Work Practice, 2*(1), 65–80.

Lipsky, M. (2010). *Street-level bureaucracy: Dilemmas of the individual in public services.* New York, NY: Russell Sage Foundation.

Maddux, J. E. (2002). Self-efficacy. In C. R. Snyder & S. J. Lopez (Eds.), *Handbook of positive psychology* (pp. 277–287). New York, NY: Oxford University Press.

Mapp, S. C., & Steinberg, C. (2007). Birthfamilies as permanency resources for children in long-term foster care. *Child Welfare, 86*(1), 29–51.

Marshall, D., & English, D. (1999). Survival analysis of risk factors for recidivism in child abuse and neglect. *Child Maltreatment, 4*(4), 287–296.

McDonald, T. P., Poertner, J., & Jennings, M. A. (2007). Permanency for children in foster care: A competing risks analysis. *Journal of Social Service Research, 33*(4), 45–56.

Moynihan, A., Forgey, M. A., & Harris, D. (2001). Achieving justice: Parents and the child welfare system. *Fordham Law Review, 70,* 287–335.

National Alliance for the Mentally Ill (NAMI). (1999, July). *Families on the brink: The impact of ignoring children with serious mental illness.* Retrieved from http://www.nami.org/Content/ContentGroups/CAAC/Families_on_the_Brink.pdf

National Alliance on Mental Illness (NAMI). (2003, February). Broken promises and the health care crisis in the children's mental health system. Retrieved from http://www.nami.org/Template.cfm?Section=Issues_Spotlights&Template=/Content/ContentGroups/Youth/Broken_Promises_and_the_Health_Care_Crisis_In_the_Childrens_Mental_Health_System.htm

National Association of Social Workers (NASW). (2009). *Code of ethics of the National Association of Social Workers.* Retrieved from http://www.naswdc.org/pubs/code/code.asp

Outley, A. (2004, June 1). *Representation for children and parents in dependency proceedings.* Retrieved from http://www.pewtrusts.org/our_work_report_detail.aspx?id=49014&category=370

Personal Responsibility and Work Opportunity Reconciliation Act of 1996. Pub. L. No. 104-193 (1996).

Polansky, N. A., Chalmers, M. A., Buttenwieser, E., & Williams, D. P. (1981). *Damaged parents: An anatomy of child neglect.* Chicago, IL: University of Chicago Press.

Potter, C. C., & Klein-Rothschild, S. (2002). Getting home on time: Predicting timely permanence for young children. *Child Welfare, 81*(2), 123–150.

Rhode, D. L. (2009). Whatever happened to access to justice? *Loyola of Los Angeles Law Review, 42,* 869–912.

Rockhill, A., Green, B. L., & Furrer, C. (2007). Is the adoption and safe families act influencing child welfare outcomes for families with substance abuse issues? *Child Maltreatment, 12*(1), 7–19.

Rossi, P. H., Schuerman, J., & Budde, S. (1999). Understanding decisions about child maltreatment. *Evaluation Review, 23*(6), 579–598.

Ruscio, J. (1998). Information integration in child welfare cases: An introduction to statistical decision making. *Child Maltreatment, 3*(2), 143–156.

Ryan, J. P., & Schuerman, J. R. (2004). Matching family problems with specific family preservation services: A study of service effectiveness. *Children & Youth Services Review, 26*(4), 347–372.

Saint-Jacques, M. C., Drapeau, S., Lessard, G., & Beaudoin, A. (2006). Parent involvement practices in child protection: A matter of know-how and attitude. *Child and Adolescent Social Work Journal, 23*(2), 196–215.

Sankaran, V. (2006). Out of state and out of luck: The treatment of non-custodial parents under the Interstate Compact on the Placement of Children. *Yale Law & Policy Review, 25*(1), 63–94.

Sankaran, V. (2007). Procedural injustice: How the practices and procedures of the child welfare system disempower parents and why it matters. *Michigan Child Welfare Law Journal, 11*(1), 11–19.

Schuerman, J., Rossi, P. H., & Budde, S. (1999). Decisions on placement and family preservation. *Evaluation Review, 23*(6), 599–618.

Secretariat to the Association of Administrators of the Interstate Compact on the Placement of Children (SAAICPC). (2002). *Guide to the Interstate Compact on the Placement of Children.* Retrieved from http://icpc.aphsa.org/Home/Doc/Guidebook_2002.pdf

Shook, K., & Testa, M. (1997, December). *Cost-savings evaluation of the Norman Program: Final report to the Department of Children and Family Services.* Chicago: Illinois Department of Children and Family Services.

Sinden, A. (1999). "Why won't mom cooperate?" A critique of informality in child welfare proceedings. *Yale Journal of Law and Feminism, 11,* 339–396.

Stefan, S. (2008). Accommodating families: Using the Americans with Disabilities Act to keep families together. *St. Louis University Journal of Health Law & Policy, 2,* 135–175.

Sunshine, J., & Tyler, T. R. (2003). The role of procedural justice and legitimacy in shaping public support for policing. *Law and Society Review, 37*(3), 555–589.

Thibaut, I., & Walker, L. (1975). *Procedural justice: A psychological analysis.* Hillsdale, NJ: Erlbaum.

Thibaut, I., & Walker, L. (1978). A theory of procedure. *California Law Review, 66*(3), 541–566.

Tyler, T. R. (1987). Conditions leading to value expression effects in judgments of procedural justice: A test of four models. *Journal of Personality and Social Psychology, 52,* 333–344.

Tyler, T. R. (1990). *Why people obey the law: Procedural justice, legitimacy, and compliance.* New Haven, CT: Yale University Press.

Tyler, T. R., & Bies, R. J. (1990). Beyond formal procedures: The interpersonal context of procedural justice. *Applied social psychology and organizational settings, 77,* 98.

Tyler, T. R., & Caine, A. (1981). The role of distributional and procedural fairness in the endorsement of formal leaders. *Journal of Personality and Social Psychology, 41,* 642–655.

Tyler, T. R., & Huo, Y. J. (2002). *Trust in the law: Encouraging public cooperation with the police and courts.* New York, NY: Russell-Sage Foundation.

Tyler, T. R., Rasinski, K., & McGraw, K. (1985). The influence of perceived injustice on support for political authorities. *Journal of Applied Social Psychology, 15,* 700–725.

U.S. Department of Health and Human Services (USDHHS), Child Welfare Information Gateway. (2008). *Case planning for families involved with child welfare agencies: Summary of state laws.* Retrieved from http://www.childwelfare.gov/system-wide/laws_policies/statutes/caseplanning.cfm

U.S. Department of Health and Human Services (USDHHS), Child Welfare Information Gateway. (2010). How the child welfare system works: Factsheet. Retrieved from http://www.childwelfare.gov/pubs/factsheets/cpswork.cfm#one

U.S. Department of Health and Human Services (USDHHS), Child Welfare Information Gateway. (n.d.). *Overview of the civil child protective court process.* Retrieved from http://www.childwelfare.gov/pubs/usermanuals/courts_92/courtsd.cfm

U.S. Department of Health and Human Services (USDHHS), Children's Bureau. (2010). *The AFCARS report: Preliminary FY 2009 estimates as of July 2010(17).* Retrieved from http://www.acf.hhs.gov/programs/cb/stats_research/afcars/tar/report17.pdf

U.S. Department of Health and Human Services (USDHHS), Children's Bureau. (n.d.). *52 Program improvement plans.* Retrieved from http://www.acf.hhs.gov/programs/cb/cwmonitoring/index.htm#cfsr

Van de Luitgaarden, G. (2009). Evidence-based practice in social work: Lessons from judgement and decision-making theory. *British Journal of Social Work, 39*(2), 243–260.

Walker, L., Lind, E. A., & Thibaut, J. (1979). The relation between procedural and distributive justice. *Virginia Law Review, 65*(8), 1401–1420.

Wells, K., & Guo, S. (2003). Mothers' welfare and work, income and reunification with children in foster care. *Children and Youth Services Review, 25*(3), 203–224.

Wells, K., & Marcenko, M. O. (2011). Introduction to the special issue: Mothers of children in foster care. *Children and Youth Services Review, 33*(3), 419–423.

22

ELDER MISTREATMENT

A Social Justice Perspective

AMANDA J. LEHNING

INTRODUCTION

While the World Health Organization (WHO) recently described elder mistreatment as a "violation of human rights" (2002, p. 3), elder mistreatment has rarely been viewed through a social justice lens. Indeed, until the mid-1970s, researchers, policymakers, and social work practitioners did not view elder mistreatment as a problem (Fulmer, 2008). To date, research has focused on identifying individual-level risk factors for, or individual-level impacts of, elder mistreatment (e.g., Acierno et al., 2010; Wolf, 2000). The causes of elder mistreatment, including the societal and structural factors contributing to the mistreatment of an older adult or the most effective interventions for older adults and potential perpetrators, are not well understood. Moreover, according to Anetzberger (2005), the majority of existing elder mistreatment interventions, including federal legislation, state mandatory reporting laws, and county adult protective services (APS), were established without any empirical basis and in some cases

contradict the limited research findings. In addition, despite the mission of social work to address the well-being of the most vulnerable members of society, as noted in the *Code of Ethics of the National Association of Social Workers* (NASW, 2009), social work practitioners intervene primarily at the individual level as APS investigators and play a peripheral role in policy and programmatic responses to elder mistreatment (Anetzberger, 2007).

This chapter presents elder mistreatment as a form of social injustice perpetrated on the most vulnerable older adults. It begins with an overview of elder mistreatment, including its definition, prevalence estimates, and a brief summary of interventions in the United States. It then describes how elder mistreatment can be viewed as stemming from the conditions that contribute to the vulnerability of older adults. Specifically, these conditions include societal ageist beliefs and attitudes; race, ethnicity, and gender; the risk of social isolation; and physical and cognitive impairments that often occur in old age.

BACKGROUND

Elder mistreatment is defined as "(a) intentional actions that cause harm or create a serious risk of harm, whether or not intended, to a vulnerable elder by a caregiver or other person who stands in a trust relationship to the elder or (b) failure by a caregiver to satisfy the elder's basic needs or to protect the elder from harm" (Bonnie & Wallace, 2003, p. 39). Elder mistreatment includes (a) physical abuse (i.e., physical coercion, restraint, or infliction of pain and injury), (b) psychological or emotional abuse (i.e., verbal or nonverbal acts that lead to mental distress or pain), (c) sexual abuse (i.e., any nonconsensual sexual act), (d) financial exploitation (i.e., improper or illegal use of financial resources), (e) neglect (i.e., failure to provide the necessities of life or fulfill caregiving obligations), and (f) abandonment (i.e., desertion by an individual who has taken responsibility for an elder) (National Center on Elder Abuse [NCEA], 1999). Elder mistreatment may also include self-neglect, which occurs when an older adult engages in behavior that threatens her or his own health and safety, such as the refusal of food, water, or shelter (NCEA, 1999.). A review of substantiated APS reports suggests that neglect is the most common form of elder mistreatment (37.2% for self-neglect and 20.4% for caregiver neglect), followed by psychological or emotional abuse (14.8%), financial exploitation (14.7%), physical abuse (10.7%), sexual abuse (1%), and other (1.2%) (NCEA, 2006).

Estimates regarding the prevalence of elder mistreatment vary widely and are complicated by a number of factors. The National Elder Abuse Incidence Study reported that almost 450,000 adults aged 60 and older were mistreated in 1996 (NCEA, 1998). It is likely, however, that this study underestimated the extent of elder mistreatment, as it gathered data from APS agencies and state units on aging and not directly from older adults. In the 1980s and 1990s, studies of community-dwelling elders reported a prevalence of between 3% and 6% (Comijs, Pot, Smith, & Jonker, 1998; Pillemer & Finkelhor, 1988; Pot, van Dijck, Jonker, & Deeg, 1996). Current studies suggest that approximately 1 in 10 older adults experience mistreatment (Acierno et al., 2010; Laumann, Leitsch, & Waite, 2008). Given that more than 57 million Americans were aged 60 or older in 2010 (U.S. Census Bureau, 2010), it appears that elder mistreatment could be a major social problem affecting over 5 million Americans.

Elder mistreatment is typically perpetrated by someone the older person knows, generally a relative (Pillemer & Finkelhor, 1988; O'Keefe et al., 2007). For example, results from the recent National Elder Mistreatment Study indicate that approximately 76% of perpetrators of physical abuse, 74% of perpetrators of neglect, and 57% of perpetrators of emotional abuse are family members of the older victim (Acierno, Hernandez-Tejada, Muzzy, & Steve, 2009). Theories that seek to explain the existence of elder mistreatment therefore tend to focus on understanding why family members abuse an older relative. A brief summary of six major theories of elder mistreatment is provided in Table 22.1. Empirical support for these theories is currently limited, as few studies have attempted to test their propositions, and those that do test them often rely on small samples and ill-defined outcome variables thereby limiting their generalizability and comparability (Anthony, Lehning, Austin, & Peck, 2009). In particular, theories that do not take into account the larger social, cultural, and environmental context (i.e., web of dependency, psychopathology of the abuser, and transgenerational violence) have not been supported by research (Quinn & Tomita, 1997). While all of these theories highlight that elder mistreatment is a social problem that emerges predominantly through social relationships, they fail to adequately explain the causes of elder mistreatment.

According to Acierno and colleagues (2010), the authorities are aware of very few incidents of elder mistreatment, and Bonnie and Wallace (2003) believe that for every case that is reported, at least five more cases go unreported. Barriers to the self-reporting by elderly victims include a lack of knowledge of elder mistreatment laws, impaired cognitive capacity, cultural beliefs about what is and is not mistreatment, and feelings of shame or blame (Dayton, 2005; Donovan & Regehr, 2010; Gelles, 1997). Elder mistreatment by a family member or caregiver presents additional obstacles to disclosure,

Table 22.1   Theories of Elder Mistreatment

Theory	*Major Assumptions*
The web of dependency	Caregiver is dependent on the elder for housing and money; elder is dependent on caregiver for daily activities (due to poor health).
Psychopathology in the abuser	Alcohol or drug abuse by the abuser and or/mental illness among family members are risk factors for abuse.
Transgenerational violence	Children who are victims of abuse or witness abuse between their parents are more likely to become perpetrators of violence when they reach adulthood.
Caregiver stress	Increasing care needs (or problematic behavior) combined with caregiver feeling forced to care for unwanted elder or external stress for caregiver contribute to abuse.
Caregiving context	Factors such as social isolation, shared living arrangement, lack of close family ties, and lack of community support or access to resources contribute to abuse.
Sociocultural climate	Factors such as inadequate housing, recent relocation and adaptation to American culture, loss of support systems, and the decline of stature within the family create a climate that supports abuse.

Source: Jones, Holstege, & Holstege (1997).

such as familial norms regarding the discussion of family problems with outsiders, a fear of being admitted to a long-term care facility, and feelings of love or protection toward the perpetrator (Dayton, 2005; Wahl & Purdy, 2002). Even in states that have mandatory reporting laws for certain professionals (e.g., social workers or physicians), many cases are not reported (Wolf & Li, 1999). This may be due to the lack of awareness of elder mistreatment by mandated reporters, especially since abuse tends to occur in the home and out of the sight of others (Kosberg, 1988). The detection of elder mistreatment is further complicated by common chronic illnesses in older adults, such as chronic heart failure, diabetes, or hypertension, which can obscure or mimic the signs and symptoms of elder mistreatment (Lachs & Pillemer, 1995; Lachs, Williams, O'Brien, Hurst, & Horwitz, 1996).

Prior research has documented a number of negative effects associated with elder mistreatment, including increased psychological distress, such as anxiety, fear, guilt, and learned helplessness; decreased psychological well-being; and a higher risk of mortality (Lachs, Williams, O'Brien, Pillemer, & Charlson, 1998; Luo & Waite, 2011; Wolf, 2000). Therefore, elder mistreatment is a social and public health problem that impacts a significant proportion of the older adult population and can result in both poor short-term outcomes (e.g., injury and illness) and long-term outcomes (e.g., mortality). Current interventions in the United States, however, appear to be ill-equipped to prevent, detect, or ameliorate the effects of elder mistreatment.

Federal legislation did not begin to address elder mistreatment until 1975, when Title XX of the Social Security Act permitted states to use a portion of funding from the Social Services Block Grant for services and advocacy for vulnerable elders (Nerenberg, 2006). Currently, the Violence Against Women Act authorizes the attorney general to allocate funding to enhance elder mistreatment services, conduct training for community-based services, and develop multidisciplinary collaborations to address elder mistreatment (Dong & Simon, 2011). The Older Americans Act (OAA) targets elder mistreatment for community-dwelling older adults by funding the National Center on Elder Abuse (NCEA), which offers grants to states to develop elder mistreatment interventions, and through its funding of state units on aging and area agencies on aging, which offer elder mistreatment services. In addition, the OAA supports the long-term care ombudsmen program, which investigates allegations of mistreatment in institutions. Finally, the Elder Justice Act (EJA), which became law in 2010 as part of the federal health care reform bill, will enhance the role of the federal government in elder mistreatment interventions through training, services, demonstration programs, and the establishment of an Elder Justice Coordinating Council to prepare reports and recommendations to Congress. Total federal spending on elder mistreatment from all sources (i.e., Administration on Aging, National Institute of Justice, Department of Justice Civic Division, National Institutes of Health, Office for Victims of Crime, and Office on Violence Against Women) was $11.9 million in 2009 (U.S. Government Accountability Office, 2011), compared to $12.4 billion in total federal spending for child abuse and neglect in 2006 (DeVooght, Allen, & Geen, 2008). While funding to prevent, detect, and ameliorate child abuse is also inadequate to address the need, federal funding for elder mistreatment is miniscule compared to funding for child maltreatment.

State and local efforts to prevent, detect, and treat elder mistreatment also started in 1975, as Title XX of the Social Security Act led to the development of Adult Protective Services (APS), the state and county programs responsible for investigating allegations of elder mistreatment and arranging for services (Nerenberg, 2006). State mandatory reporting laws also began in the 1970s and by the 1980s, the majority of states required certain professionals and paraprofessionals to report suspected cases of elder mistreatment (Fulmer, 2008). Because federal legislation has focused primarily on funding rather than on coordinating services or developing guidelines for reporting systems and intervention strategies, there is a great deal of variation across states and counties in terms of the assessment and treatment of elder mistreatment (Nerenberg, 2006). Moreover, states differ on the types of mistreatment covered (e.g., some exclude psychological or emotional abuse) and the types of older adults covered (e.g., some exclude those living in long-term care facilities); see the American Bar Association, 2005. A lack of adequate funding has also been a challenge to states and counties, and a recent report that 60% of APS programs are experiencing budget cuts at the same time that the majority are experiencing an increase in reports of elder mistreatment suggests that this challenge will be even greater in the future (Leadership Council of Aging Organizations, 2011).

Another challenge to the ability of APS to intervene in cases of elder mistreatment is the need to accommodate the tension between the obligations to protect vulnerable older adults and the commitment to respect an individual's right to self-determination (Donovan & Regehr, 2010). In contrast, child protective services workers can initiate interventions, such as removal from the home, without the consent of the maltreated child. Older adults, however, have the legal right to refuse any intervention; currently, there are no clear guidelines for APS workers regarding the appropriate balance between respect for autonomy and protection from harm (Anthony et al., 2009). While Bergeron (2006) argues that the duty to protect vulnerable elders should take precedence over respect for self-determination, a recent study in Canada indicates that in practice, APS workers typically give a higher precedence to respect for self-determination (Beaulieu & Leclerc, 2006).

There is therefore a great deal of confusion regarding elder mistreatment. The absence of coordination and leadership has resulted in inconsistent definitions of elder mistreatment by policymakers, researchers, and practitioners (Quinn & Tomita, 1997). Current prevalence estimates are questionable given the lack of uniformity in definitions and the failure of older adults and mandated reporters to notify the authorities of the majority of cases. Understanding the extent to which elder mistreatment is a problem is further hampered by the absence of a national data collection project, an initial component of the Elder Justice Act that was removed from the final version (Dong & Simon, 2011). This confusion is compounded by limited research on the causes of elder mistreatment, how to identify instances of mistreatment, or the most effective interventions for older adults and their families. As noted by Anetzberger (2005), recently proposed research agendas, such as that put forth by the National Research Council's Panel to Review Risk and Prevalence of Elder Abuse and Neglect (2003), differ minimally from research agenda recommendations made two decades ago, suggesting that there has been little progress in these aspects of elder mistreatment research. However, there has been progress in terms of identifying the risk factors that make older adults particularly vulnerable to mistreatment (Bugental & Hehman, 2007).

CONDITIONS OF VULNERABILITY

Models of risk for elder mistreatment typically include status inequality, power dynamics, social relationships, and individual-level factors (Fulmer et al., 2005).

Status Inequality: Ageism

The term *ageism* was coined by the gerontologist Robert Butler (1969), who defined it as discrimination against and stereotyping of older people because of their age. Levy and Banaji (2002) further delineate ageism as "an alteration in feeling, belief, or behavior in response to an individual's or group's perceived chronological age" (p. 50). These altered feelings or beliefs, which in part stem from societal values that rank economic productivity above all else, may be used to justify behaviors, such as elder mistreatment (Phelan, 2008; Thornton, 2002).

While ageism has not received a great deal of attention in the research literature, there is empirical evidence that older adults are often relegated to a devalued social status (Kite, Stockdale, Whitley, & Johnson, 2005). While aging stereotypes can be either negative (e.g., incompetent, weak, sickly, dependent, unproductive, frail) or positive (e.g., kind, warm, friendly, happy, dependable), they all lead to the perception that older adults are somehow less than other age groups (Bugental & Hehman, 2007). It has been proposed that all older adults are ultimately viewed as more feminine and less masculine (Kite, Deaux, & Miele, 1991), a perception that could further reduce their social status. Ageism is committed not only by the young: Research using implicit measures (i.e., automatic and potentially unconscious reactions) suggests that both younger and older adults produce more negative reactions to the elderly (Dasgupta & Greenwald, 2001). Since older adults can internalize these negative reactions, the response could impact their health and functioning. For example, Hess and colleagues (2003) found that the performance of older adults on a memory test decreased after they were exposed to negative age stereotypes.

Age discrimination and stereotypes contribute not only to elder mistreatment but also create a barrier to the detection and treatment of instances of abuse (Phelan, 2008). For example, the devalued status ascribed to older adults may foster a tolerance or acceptance of abusive behaviors toward elders that would be unacceptable if they were perpetrated toward children. Furthermore, federal laws regarding child abuse are far more comprehensive than those for elder mistreatment because, for example, they cover protective services and shelters for victims (Donovan & Regehr, 2010). In addition, research on child abuse far outpaces research on elder mistreatment. This includes greater attention to the need to establish uniform definitions and eligibility criteria across jurisdictions (Wolf & Li, 1999). A little over 13% of children in the United States are estimated to be victims of abuse (Finkelhor, Ormod, Turner, & Hamby, 2005), which is only slightly higher than the 10% of elders believed to experience elder mistreatment (Laumann et al., 2008). Therefore, while elder mistreatment should receive a level of attention from policymakers, researchers, and social work practitioners on par with child maltreatment, it has yet to do so.

Power Dynamics:
Double Jeopardy Hypothesis

The *double jeopardy* hypothesis, originally proposed by the National Urban League in 1964 to describe the situation of aging African Americans, posits that members of an oppressed minority group face even greater losses in old age than those in more advantaged groups (Salmon, 1994;

Dressel, Minkler, & Yen, 1999). The double jeopardy hypothesis is typically employed to explain disparities in health and well-being (e.g., Ferraro & Farmer, 1996). For example, the proportion of African Americans with limitations in activities of daily living (ADLs) is higher than that of Whites (Dunlop, Song, Manheim, Daviglus, & Chang, 2007). The African American elderly population has higher rates of stroke (He, Sengupta, Velkoff, & DeBarros, 2005) and lung cancer than Whites, while obesity plagues both African Americans and Hispanics more than other groups (Satariano, 2006). Obesity has been linked to Type 2 diabetes, and Hispanics and African Americans also have a higher prevalence of this disease than Whites (He et al., 2005). These health disparities are, in part, the result of disparities in income and education levels between racial and ethnic groups (Fuller-Thompson, Nuru-Jeter, Minkler, & Guralnik, 2009). In 2003, while 76% of non-Hispanic Whites aged 65 and older had at least a high school diploma, only 52% of African Americans and 36% of Hispanics in this same age group had completed high school (He et al., 2005). Across all age groups, more members of racial and ethnic minorities find themselves in a deprived economic position compared to their White counterparts; in 2004, the poverty rate for non-Hispanic Whites was 8.6%, while 24.7% of African Americans and 21.9% of Hispanics lived below the poverty line (DeNavas-Walt, Proctor, & Lee, 2005).

The risk of abuse appears to be higher for minority elders than for White elders, suggesting that the double jeopardy hypothesis is applicable to elder mistreatment as well. For example, in the mid-1990s, the National Elder Abuse Incidence Study found that 10% of the reports to APS involved Hispanic or Latino elders, 18.7% African American, and 66.4% White (NCEA, 1998). These data were unexpected given that the general older adult population was 4.1% Hispanic or Latino, 8.3% African American, and 85.8% White at the time (U.S. Census Bureau, 1992). Other studies conducted over the past two decades have also reported an overrepresentation of minority elders in allegations of elder mistreatment to APS (Beach, Schulz, Castle, & Rosen, 2010; Lachs, Berkman, Fulmer, & Horwitz, 1994; Lachs,

Williams, O'Brien, Hurst, & Horwitz, 1997; Wolf & Li, 1999). Higher rates of mistreatment among African American and Hispanic or Latino elders may be due to physical or cognitive impairment, discussed in greater detail below. In addition, the association between low incomes and an increased risk of a report of elder mistreatment suggests that the mechanisms linking race and ethnicity with elder mistreatment are similar to those linking race and ethnicity with health disparities (Wolf & Li, 1999).

Researchers and commentators have also applied the double jeopardy hypothesis to understand the disadvantages experienced by older women (Gibson, 1996). In terms of elder mistreatment, a number of studies have documented that women are more likely to be the victims of elder mistreatment (Biggs, Manthrope, Tinker, Doyle, & Erens, 2009; Laumann et al., 2008; Lowenstein, Eisikovits, Band-Winterstein, & Enosh, 2009; NCEA, 1998; O'Keefe et al., 2007). In contrast, men are more likely to be the perpetrators of elder mistreatment, comprising 83% of those committing abandonment, 63% of physical abuse, 60% of psychological or emotional abuse, and 59% of financial exploitation (Bugental & Hehman, 2007). While racial and ethnic disparities in elder mistreatment may be the result of both socioeconomic and health differences, women's vulnerability to elder mistreatment may be predominantly related to their increased likelihood of impaired health and social isolation. Compared to their male counterparts, older women are more likely to be widowed and live alone (Federal Interagency Forum on Aging-Related Statistics, 2006). In addition, a larger percentage of women need assistance with personal care (e.g., dressing, feeding) and routine care (e.g., shopping, household chores) than men (Centers for Disease Control, 2007). Furthermore, women make up nearly two thirds of all diagnosed cases of Alzheimer's disease and other dementias in the United States (Alzheimer's Association, 2011).

While one recent study using a nationally representative sample found no evidence of gender or racial and ethnic differences in the risk of elder mistreatment (Acierno et al., 2010), the preponderance of evidence indicates that the social injustices enacted against women and minorities throughout the life course, including poverty and violence, continue or perhaps even accelerate in old age, increasing their risk of experiencing physical abuse, neglect, and other forms of elder mistreatment.

Social Relationships

Social isolation and the absence of social support have been identified as risk factors for elder mistreatment (Acierno et al., 2010; Comijs, Penninx, Knipscheer, & van Tilburg, 1999; Dong & Simon, 2008; Fulmer et al., 2005; Hawes & Kimbell, 2009; Luo & Waite, 2011). Having a large and diverse social network is beneficial because it can increase access to resources and social support (Antonucci & Akiyama, 1995), including informational support, emotional support, and tangible assistance (Krause, 2006). Both social support and social integration are associated with a number of positive outcomes, including better mental health, improved quality of life, decreased risk of mortality, higher self-rated health, and fewer depressive symptoms (Andrew, 2005; Antonucci, Fuhrer, & Dartigues, 1997; Borglin, Jakobsson, Edberg, & Hallberg, 2006; Krause, 1997; Uchino, 2004).

As individuals grow older, however, they tend to experience a reduction in the size and frequency of contact with social network members (Barnes, Mendes de Leon, Bienias, & Evans, 2004; Schnittker, 2007; Shaw, Krause, Liang, & Bennett, 2007). This can lead to social isolation, both in terms of physical separation from others (e.g., living in a rural area, living alone) or subjective feelings of loneliness (Golden et al., 2009). Among adults aged 65 and older, between 15% and 45% report at least occasional feelings of loneliness (Golden et al., 2009; Lauder, Sharkey, & Mummery, 2004; Prince, Harwood, Blizard, Thomas, & Mann, 1997), and approximately half of those aged 80 and over often feel lonely (Pinquart & Sorensen, 2001). Elders who have low socioeconomic status, mobility limitations, and difficulty performing activities of daily living are more likely to report loneliness (Pinquart & Sorensen, 2001). Older adults therefore are at an increased risk of social isolation, which in addition to elder mistreatment is associated with negative outcomes, such as depressive symptoms, feelings of hopelessness, and an increased risk for morbidity and mortality (Golden et al., 2009; Patterson & Veenstra, 2010; Tomaka, Thompson, & Palacios, 2006).

It has been proposed that the presence of sources of social support deters potential perpetrators of elder mistreatment because of the fear of being caught or punished (Lachs & Pillemer, 2004), but researchers and theorists propose that the quality of social relationships, and not merely their presence, is important. For example, a recent study using a nationally representative sample of older adults found that criticism from close social ties increased the odds for elder mistreatment (Luo & Waite, 2011).

Individual-Level Factors: Physical and Cognitive Impairment

Previous studies indicate that elder mistreatment is more likely to be experienced by older adults with impaired physical (Beach et al., 2010; Biggs et al., 2009; Fulmer et al., 2005; Laumann et al., 2008) and cognitive functioning (Burgess, Dowdel, & Prentky, 2000; Dyer, Pavlik, Murphy, & Hyman, 2000; Fulmer et al., 2005). The relationship between health and elder mistreatment is further substantiated by the high number of reported cases of mistreatment for elders aged 85 and older, the ages at which the majority of individuals require assistance with personal care or suffer from dementia (Administration on Aging, 2008). While individuals aged 80 and over compose only 19% of the U.S. elderly population, they make up 48% of reported cases of financial exploitation, 41% of psychological or emotional abuse, 52% of neglect, and 44% of physical abuse (NCEA, 1998).

It is clear that a significant proportion of current and future older adults will be vulnerable to elder mistreatment. The current cohort of older adults has less disability and fewer limitations in physical functioning compared to previous generations of older adults, reflecting advances in medical treatment and diagnosis as well as improvements in education and socioeconomic status (Crimmins, 2004). Data from the National Long Term Care Surveys show that the chronically disabled elderly population declined from 26.2% to 19.7% between 1982 and 1999 (Manton & Gu, 2001). Because of an increase in the size of the elderly population, the number of older adults with a chronic disability remained unchanged at about 7 million during this same time period. However, the percent of older Americans requiring assistance with routine care activities (e.g., shopping and taking care of everyday household chores) decreased, while the percent of older adults requiring assistance with personal care activities (e.g., walking, bathing, transferring, dressing, toileting, and eating) did not (Schoeni, Freedman, & Wallace, 2001). Furthermore, there is evidence that recent trends of declining disability rates will reverse in the future. First, limitations in ADLs increase with age, and the 85 and older population is expected to increase from 5.4 million in 2008 to 19 million in 2050 (U.S. Census Bureau, 2008). This population growth has implications particularly for rates of cognitive impairment, as the number of new annual cases of Alzheimer's disease is expected to more than double from 377,000 in 1995 to 959,000 in 2050, and about 60% of these new cases will be among those 85 and older (Hebert, Beckett, Scherr, & Evans, 2001). Second, older baby boomers approaching retirement are reporting more chronic illness, pain, and difficulties in physical functioning compared to those approaching retirement in the previous decade (Soldo, Mitchell, Tfaily, & McCabe, 2006). Younger baby boomers also appear to be in poorer health than the current cohort of older adults: In the mid-1990s, as disability rates decreased among older adults, they increased by 40% among those in their 40s (Lakdawalla, Bhattacharya, & Goldman, 2001).

In some cases, the impact of physical and/or cognitive impairment in an aging relative on family members may lead to elder mistreatment, as hypothesized by many of the theories of elder mistreatment described above. In other cases, physical and/or cognitive impairment may lead to mistreatment because these health conditions are associated with self-neglect, guardianship, and institutionalization.

Self-Neglect

Self-neglect is defined as "the inability (intentional or nonintentional) to maintain a socially and culturally accepted standard of self-care with the potential for serious consequences to the health and well-being of the self-neglecter and perhaps even to their community" (Gibbons, Lauder, & Ludwick, 2006, p. 16). Typically, self-neglect occurs when an older adult refuses or fails to provide him or herself with basic necessities, including food, water, shelter, medication, or basic hygiene. Estimates of the prevalence of self-neglect are a little more than one million cases per year (Dong, Tang, Gorbien, & Evans, 2008; NCEA, 1998). Self-neglect accounts for the largest percentage of reports to adult protective services (Fulmer, 2008) and has been found to occur at a rate three times higher than physical abuse or neglect (Pavlik, Hyman, Festa, & Dyer, 2001). Older adults who self-neglect have an increased risk for morbidity and mortality (Dong et al., 2009; Dong, Simon, Fulmer et al., 2011; Lachs, Williams, O'Brien, & Pillemer, 2002).

Proposed risk factors for self-neglect include neighborhood conditions (e.g., safety) and limited transportation and mobility options (Paveza, VandeWeerd, & Laumann, 2008). Based on the empirical evidence, race may play a factor, as a recent study in Chicago found that nearly 22% of African American elders in the sample had self-neglected, compared to 5.3% of Whites (Dong, Simon, Fulmer et al., 2011). Elders who self-neglect also tend to live alone (Naik, Burnette, Pickens-Pace, & Dyer, 2008), have few sources of social support (Burnette et al., 2006; Choi & Mayer, 2000), and show signs of depression (Dyer et al., 2000; Abrams, Lachs, McAvay, Keohane, & Bruce, 2002). At the individual level, impairments in physical functioning and cognitive functioning increase one's risk for elder self-neglect (Abrams et al., 2002; Dong et al., 2009; Dyer et al., 2000; Longres, 1995). According to G. Paveza and colleagues (2008), cognitive impairment is the most important condition leading to self-neglect.

The presence of physical or cognitive impairment may be the determining factor in detecting cases of elder self-neglect that require intervention. Active or willful self-neglect reflects an individual's choice to live a certain way and engage in certain behaviors (Gibbons et al., 2006; Longres, 1995). This type of self-neglect may result from conflicting beliefs between dominant community values and an elder's self-determination about maintaining appropriate living conditions (Iris, Ridings, & Conrad, 2009). Passive self-neglect, however, reflects an inability to care for oneself due to physical, cognitive, or financial limitations (Gibbons et al., 2006; Longres, 1995). In these cases, concern for an elder's safety typically overrides respect for autonomy, increasing the likelihood that APS will intervene even in instances in which the elder does not want them to do so.

Guardianship

Similarly, the decision to take away an individual's rights and place them under legal guardianship depends on the elder's capacity to engage in self-care (American Bar Association, 1996). Older adults placed in guardianship lose the right to make the most important decisions in their life, including the right to refuse medical treatment, get married, live where they would like to live, and a host of lifestyle choices (Bugental & Hehman, 2007).

Flaws in legal guardianship statutes across the United States, including questionable definitions of diminished capacity and poor monitoring practices, increase the risk of elder mistreatment associated with legal guardianship (Bugental & Hehman, 2007). Legal guardianship is created through a court proceeding to assess the older adult's ability to comprehend information and make informed decisions about their personal care and safety (American Bar Association, 1996). States vary, however, in terms of how an elder's abilities are assessed, with 30 states requiring a clinical evaluation from a physician, psychologist, or other health care professional; 15 states allowing the court to make its own determination of capacity; and five states providing no instructions whatsoever (Moye, Butz, Marson, & Wood, 2007). In 15 states, having a diagnosed medical condition or even just being older is ground for legal guardianship (Anderer, 1990). Furthermore, in a recent national survey of those working in the legal guardianship field, more than one third reported that no one from the court verifies reports or testimonies submitted to determine an individual's capacity and only 16% reported that court staff substantiates every report (Karp & Wood,

2006). These inconsistencies in verification and monitoring continue after an elder has been placed in a legal guardianship. For example, the same national survey found that regular visits to the incapacitated individual occur in only approximately 25% of jurisdictions, and no one makes any visits in over 40% of jurisdictions. As with other aspects of elder mistreatment (e.g., APS), this may be due to insufficient funding, as only about 11% of those surveyed reported that there are adequate funds to engage in monitoring practices, such as responding to complaints, imposing sanctions, reviewing the need to continue a legal guardianship, and providing assistance to guardians.

Institutionalization

Physical and cognitive impairment is associated not only with an increased likelihood of admission to a long-term care facility (Banaszak-Holl et al., 2004; Bharucha, Pandav, Shen, Dodge, & Ganguli, 2004; Yaffe et al., 2002) but also with an increased likelihood of experiencing mistreatment in such settings (Burgess et al., 2000; Dyer et al., 2000). A recent report by the U.S. House of Representatives (2001) indicated that 30% of nursing homes in this country have been cited for the mistreatment of elder residents. Because assisted living facilities (ALFs) are regulated by the states and not by the federal government and state statutes vary in terms of mandated annual inspections, it is difficult to estimate the prevalence of mistreatment in ALFs. Phillips and Guo (2011) postulate that incidents of abuse may be even higher in ALFs because the majority of staff members are unlicensed and untrained. Underreporting may be particularly widespread in long-term care institutions because of the lack of alternative residential settings in some communities, fears of retaliation or recrimination by staff and management, lack of knowledge of reporting procedures, and impaired memory of victims or other resident witnesses (Hawes & Kimbell, 2009; Hirst, 2002; McCarthy, 2002).

Patterns of elder mistreatment in long-term care facilities differ from those in the community. For example, physical abuse is the most common form of mistreatment in long-term care institutions, and the majority of perpetrators of this type of abuse are male employees (Payne & Civokic, 1996). Sexual abuse also occurs more frequently in institutions, accounting for nearly 9% of reported cases in nursing homes (Payne & Civokic, 1996), compared with 1% of reports of mistreatment for community-dwelling elderly (NCEA, 2006). Victims of sexual abuse living in an institution tend to be older women with impaired cognitive functioning (Burgess et al., 2000; Teaster, 2002). Furthermore, the majority of perpetrators of sexual abuse are fellow residents, making up 70% of perpetrators in a recent study across the state of Virginia (Teaster & Roberto, 2004). The high proportion of perpetrators who are residents has been blamed for the extremely low rates of prosecution in cases of sexual abuse in institutions.

CONCLUSION

This chapter was aimed at highlighting the many ways in which elder mistreatment is a form of social injustice imposed on the most vulnerable older adults in this country. While policymakers, researchers, and social work practitioners have recognized elder mistreatment as a social problem for four decades, the state of knowledge remains quite limited. Variation in terms of definitions of abuse across states and empirical investigations has served as a barrier to understanding the causes, prevalence, and effective interventions for elder mistreatment. Tensions between respect for autonomy and protecting a vulnerable older adult complicate the detection and treatment of elder mistreatment. Insufficient funding further limits prevention, education, and intervention efforts. In part, the lack of adequate attention to elder mistreatment stems from the vulnerability and lack of power of its victims in this country. First, ageist attitudes and beliefs, whether conscious or unconscious, lead to the perception of older adults as less important than other age groups. Second, among older adults, the most vulnerable to elder mistreatment are those who are most vulnerable to a host of social injustices across the life course, including those who are women, racial and ethnic minorities, socially isolated, and afflicted with physical or cognitive impairments. Viewing elder mistreatment through this social justice lens

highlights how the current focus on the individual, in terms of research and interventions, fails to address the multifaceted aspects of physical abuse, neglect, psychological and emotional abuse, abandonment, sexual abuse, and self-neglect of older adults.

REFERENCES

Abrams, R., Lachs, M., McAvay, G., Keohane, D. J., & Bruce, M. L. (2002). Predictors of self-neglect in community-dwelling elders. *American Journal of Psychiatry, 159*, 1724–1730.

Acierno, R., Hernandez, M. A., Amstadter, A. B., Resnick, H. S., Steve, K., Muzzy, W., & Kilpatrick, D. G. (2010). Prevalence and correlates of emotional, physical, sexual, and financial abuse and potential neglect in the United States: The National Elder Mistreatment Survey. *American Journal of Public Health, 100*, 292–297.

Acierno, R., Hernandez-Tejada, M., Muzzy, W., & Steve, K. (2009). *Final report: The National Elder Mistreatment Study.* Retrieved October 5, 2011, from https://www.ncjrs.gov/pdffiles1/nij/grants/226456.pdf

Administration on Aging (2008). A profile of older Americans: 2008. Retrieved August 21, 2011, from http://www.aoa.gov/AoARoot/Aging_Statistics/Profile/index.aspx

Alzheimer's Association (2011). 2011 Alzheimer's disease facts and figures. Retrieved August 24, 2011, from http://www.alz.org/downloads/Facts_Figures_2011.pdf

American Bar Association (1996). *A professional's guide to capacity and guardianship.* Washington, DC: American Bar Association.

American Bar Association, Commission on Law and aging (2005). *Information and laws related to elder abuse.* Newark, DE: National Center on Elder Abuse.

Anderer, S. (1990). *Determining competency in guardianship proceedings.* Washington, DC: American Bar Association.

Andrew, M. K. (2005). Social capital, health, and care home residence among older adults: A secondary analysis of the Health Survey for England 2000. *European Journal of Ageing, 2*, 137–148.

Anetzberger, G. J. (2005). Moving forward on elder abuse and guardianship: Will it take a thesis or a scream? *Gerontologist, 45*, 279–282.

Anetzberger, G. J. (2007). Responding to elder abuse: Interdisciplinary cooperation or leadership void? [Book review]. *Gerontologist, 47,* 711–715.

Anthony, E. K., Lehning, A. J., Austin, M. J., & Peck, M. D. (2009). Instruments for assessing elder mistreatment: Implications for Adult Protective Services. *Journal of Gerontological Social Work, 52*, 815–836.

Antonucci, T. C., & Akiyama, H. (1995). Convoys of social relations: Family and friendships within a life span context. In R. Blieszner & V. H. Bedford (Eds.), *Handbook of Aging and the Family* (pp. 355–371). Westport, CT: Greenwood.

Antonucci, T. C., Fuhrer, R., & Dartigues, J. (1997). Social relations and depressing symptomatology in a sample of community-dwelling French older adults. *Psychology & Aging, 12*, 189–195.

Banaszak-Holl, J., Fendrick, A. M., Foster, N. L., Herzog, A. R., Kabeto, M. U., Kent, D. M., . . . Langa, K. M. (2004). Predicting nursing home admission: Estimates from a 7-year follow-up of a nationally representative sample of older Americans. *Alzheimer Disease and Associated Disorders, 18*(2), 83–89.

Barnes, L. L., Mendes de Leon, C. F., Bienias, J. L., & Evans, D. A. (2004). A longitudinal study of Black-White differences in social resources. *Journals of Gerontology: Social Sciences, 59*, S146–S153.

Beach, S. R., Schulz, R. S., Castle, N. G., & Rosen, J. (2010). Financial exploitation and psychological mistreatment among older adults: Differences between African Americans and non-African Americans in a population-based survey. *Gerontologist, 50*, 744–757.

Beaulieu, M., & Leclerc, N. (2006). Ethical and psychosocial issues raised by the practice in cases of mistreatment of older adults. *Journal of Gerontological Social Work, 46*, 161–186.

Bergeron, L. R. (2006). Self-determination and elder abuse: Do we know enough? *Journal of Gerontological Social Work, 46*, 81–102.

Bharucha, A. J., Pandav, R., Shen, C., Dodge, H. H., & Ganguli, M. (2004). Predictors of nursing facility admission: A 12-year epidemiological study in the United States. *Journal of the American Geriatrics Society, 52*, 434–439.

Biggs, S., Manthrope, J., Tinker, A., Doyle, M., & Erens, B. (2009). Mistreatment of older people in the United Kingdom: Findings from the first national prevalence study. *Journal of Elder Abuse & Neglect, 21*, 1–14.

Bonnie, R., & Wallace, R. (2003). *Elder mistreatment: Abuse, neglect and exploitation in an aging America.* Washington, DC: National Academies Press.

Borglin, G., Jakobsson, U., Edberg, A., & Hallberg, I. (2006). Older people in Sweden with various degrees of present quality of life: Their health, social support, everyday activities and sense of coherence. *Health and Social Care in the Community, 14,* 136–146.

Bugental, D. B., & Hehman, J. A. (2007). Ageism: A review of research and policy implications. *Social Issues and Policy Review, 1*, 173–216.

Burgess, A. W., Dowdel, E. B., & Prentky, R. A. (2000). Sexual abuse of nursing home residents. *Journal of Psychosocial Nursing and Mental Health Services, 36*, 10–18.

Burnette, J. Regev, C., Pickens, S., Prati, L. L., Aung, K., Moore, J., & Dyer, C. B. (2006). Social networks: A profile of the elderly who self-neglect. *Journal of Elder Abuse and Neglect, 18*, 35–49.

Butler, R. (1969). Ageism: Another form of bigotry. *Gerontologist, 9*, 243–246.

Centers for Disease Control. (2007). *Trends in health status and health care use among older women.* Retrieved September 14, 2011, from http://www.cdc.gov/nchs/data/ahcd/agingtrends/07olderwomen.pdf

Choi, N., & Mayer, J. (2000). Elder abuse, neglect, and exploitation: Risk factors and prevention strategies. *Journal of Gerontological Social Work, 33*, 5–25.

Comijs, H. C., Penninx, B. W. J. H., Knipscheer, K. P. M., & van Tilburg, W. (1999). Psychological distress in victims of elder mistreatment: The effects of social support and coping. *Journal of Gerontology: Psychological Sciences, 54B*, P240–P245.

Comijs, H. C., Pot, A. M., Smith, J. H., & Jonker, C. (1998). Elder abuse in the community: Prevalence and consequences. *Journal of the American Geriatrics Society, 46*, 885–888.

Crimmins, E. M. (2004). Trends in the health of the elderly. *Annual Review Public Health, 25*, 79–98.

Dasgupta, N., & Greenwald, A.G. (2001). On the malleability of automatic attitudes: Combating automatic prejudice with images of admired and disliked individuals. *Journal of Personality and Social Psychology, 81*, 800–814.

Dayton, C. (2005). Elder abuse: The social worker's perspective. *Clinical Gerontologist, 28*, 135–155.

DeNavas-Walt, C., Proctor, B., & Lee, C. (2005). *Income, poverty, and health insurance coverage in the United States: 2004* [U.S. Census Bureau, Current Population Reports]. Washington, DC: U.S. Government Printing Office.

DeVooght, K., Allen, T., & Geen, R. (2008). *Federal, state and local funding to address child abuse and neglect in SFY 2006.* Retrieved August 23, 2011, from http://www.childtrends.org/Files/Child_Trends-2009_02_17_FR_CWFinancePaper.pdf

Dong, X., & Simon, M. (2008). Is greater social support a protective factor against elder mistreatment? *Gerontology, 54*, 381–388.

Dong, X., & Simon, M. A. (2011). Enhancing national policy and programs to address elder abuse. *JAMA, 305*, 2460–2461.

Dong, X., Simon, M., Fulmer, T., Mendes de Leon, C. F., Rajan, B., & Evans, D. A. (2009). Physical function decline and the risk of elder self-neglect in a community-dwelling population. *Gerontologist, 50*, 316–326.

Dong, X., Simon, M. A., Fulmer, T., Mendes de Leon, C. F., Hebert, L. E., Beck, T., . . . Evans, D. A. (2011). A prospective population-based study of differences in elder self-neglect and mortality between Black and White older adults. *Journal of Gerontology: Medical Sciences, 66A*, 695–704.

Dong, X., Tang, Y., Gorbien, M., & Evans, D. (2008). Personality traits and elder self-neglect severity among community dwelling population. *Journal of the American Geriatrics Society, 56*, S105.

Donovan, K., & Regehr, C. (2010). Elder abuse: Clinical, ethical, and legal considerations in social work practice. *Clinical Social Work Journal, 38*, 174–182.

Dressel, P., Minkler, M., & Yen, I. (1999). Gender, race, class, and aging: Advances and opportunities. In M. Minkler & C. Estes (Eds.), *Critical Gerontology: Perspectives From Political and Moral Economy*.

Dunlop, D. D., Song, J., Manheim, L. M., Daviglus, M. L., & Chang, R. W. (2007). Racial/ethnic differences in the development of disability among older adults. *American Journal of Public Health, 97*, 2209–2215.

Dyer, C., Pavlik, V., Murphy, K., & Hyman, D. J. (2000). The prevalence of depression and dementia in elder abuse and neglect. *Journal of the American Geriatrics Society, 48*, 205–208.

Federal Interagency Forum on Aging-Related Statistics. (2006). *Older Americans update 2006: Key indicators of well-being.* Washington, DC: U.S. Government Printing Office. Retrieved from http://www.agingstats.gov/Main_Site/Data/2006_Documents/OA_2006.pdf

Ferraro, K. F., & Farmer, M. M. (1996). Double jeopardy, aging as leveler, or persistent health inequality? A longitudinal analysis of White and Black Americans. *Journal of Gerontology: Social Sciences, 51B*, S319–S328.

Finkelhor, D., Ormod, R., Turner, H., & Hamby, S. (2005). The victimization of children and youth: A comprehensive national survey. *Child Maltreatment, 10*, 5–25.

Fuller-Thompson, E., Nuru-Jeter, A., Minkler, M., & Guralnik, J. M. (2009). Black-White differences in disability among older Americans: Further untangling the role of race and socioeconomic status. *Journal of Aging and Health, 21*, 677–698.

Fulmer, T. (2008). Barriers to neglect and self-neglect research. *Journal of the American Geriatrics Society, 56*, S241–S243.

Fulmer, T., Paveza, G., VandeWeerd, C., Fairchild, S., Guadagno, L., Bolton-Blatt, M., & Norman, R. (2005). Dyadic vulnerability and risk profiling for elder neglect. *Gerontologist, 46*, 525–534.

Gelles, R. J. (1997). *Intimate violence in families* (3rd ed.). Thousand Oaks, CA: Sage.

Gibbons, S., Lauder, W., & Ludwick, R. (2006). Self-neglect: A proposed new NANDA diagnosis. *International Journal of Nursing Terminologies and Classifications, 17*, 10–18.

Gibson, D. (1996). Broken down by age and gender: "The problem of old women" redefined. In V. Minichiello, N. Chappell, H. Kendig, & A. Walker (Eds.), *Sociology of Aging: International Perspectives*, (pp. 16–30). Melbourne, Australia: International Sociological Association Research Committee on Aging.

Golden, J., Conroy, R. M., Bruce, I., Denihan, A., Greene, E., Kirby, M., & Lawlor, B. A. (2009). Loneliness, social support networks, mood and wellbeing in community-dwelling elderly. *International Journal of Geriatric Psychiatry, 24*, 694–700.

Hawes, C., & Kimball, A. M. (2009). *Detecting, addressing and preventing elder abuse in residential care facilities.* Retrieved July 27, 2011, from https://www.ncjrs.gov/pdffiles1/nij/grants/229299.pdf

He, W., Sengupta, M., Velkoff, V., & DeBarros, K. (2005). *65+ in the United States: 2005.* [United States Census Bureau, Current Population Reports, P23-209]. Washington, DC: U.S. Government Printing Office.

Hebert, L. E., Beckett, L. A., Scherr, P. A., & Evans, D. A. (2001). Annual incidence of Alzheimer disease in the United States projected to the years 2000 through 2050. *Alzheimer Disease and Associated Disorders, 15*, 169–173.

Hess, T. M., Auman, C., Colcombe, S. J., & Rahhal, T. A. (2003). The impact of stereotype threat on age differences in memory performance. *Journals of Gerontology: Psychological Science, 58B*, 3–11.

Hirst, S. P. (2002). Defining resident abuse within the culture of long term care institutions. *Clinical Nursing Research, 11*, 267–284.

Iris, M., Ridings, J. W., & Conrad, K. J. (2009). The development of a conceptual model for understanding elder self-neglect. *Gerontologist, 50*, 303–315.

Jones, J. S., Holstege, C., & Holstege, H. (1997). Elder abuse and neglect: Understanding the causes and potential risk factors. *American Journal of Emergency Medicine, 15*, 579–583.

Karp, N., & Wood, E. (2006). *Guardianship monitoring: A national survey of court practices.* Washington, DC: AARP Public Policy Institute.

Kite, M. E., Deaux, K., & Miele, M. (1991). Stereotypes of young and old: Does age outweigh gender? *Psychology and Aging, 6*, 19–27.

Kite, M. E., Stockdale, G. D., Whitley, B. E., & Johnson, B. T. (2005). Attitudes toward younger and older adults: An updated meta-analytic review. *Journal of Social Issues, 61*, 242–262.

Kosberg, J. I. (1988). Preventing elder abuse identification of high risk factors prior to placement decisions. *Gerontologist, 28*, 43–50.

Krause, N. (1997). Received support, anticipated support, social class, and mortality. *Research on Aging, 19*, 387–422.

Krause, N. (2006). Social relationships in late life. In R. H. Binstock & L. K. George (Eds.), *Handbook of aging and the social sciences* (6th ed., pp. 181–200). Burlington, MA: Academic Press.

Lachs, M. S., Berkman, L. F., Fulmer, T., & Horwitz, R. I. (1994). A prospective community-based pilot study of risk factors for the investigation of elder mistreatment. *Journal of the American Geriatrics Society, 42*, 169–173.

Lachs, M. S., & Pillemer, K. A. (1995). Abuse and neglect of elderly persons. *New England Journal of Medicine, 332*, 437–443.

Lachs, M. S., & Pillemer, K. A. (2004). Elder abuse. *Lancet, 364*, 1263–1272.

Lachs, M. S., Williams, C., O'Brien, S. Hurst, L., & Horwitz, R. (1996). Older adults: An 11 year longitudinal study of adult protective service use. *Archives of Internal Medicine, 156*, 449–453.

Lachs, M. S., Williams, C., O'Brien, S., Hurst, L., & Horwitz, R. (1997). Risk factors for reported elder abuse and neglect: A nine-year observational cohort study. *Gerontologist, 37*, 469–474.

Lachs, M. S., Williams, C. S., O'Brien, S., & Pillemer, K. A. (2002). Adult protective service use and nursing home placement. *Gerontologist, 42*, 734–739.

Lachs, M. S., Williams, C. S., O'Brien, S., Pillemer, K. A., & Charlson, M. E. (1998). The mortality of elder mistreatment. *Journal of American Medical Association, 280*, 428–432.

Lakdawalla, D. N., Bhattacharya, B., & Goldman, D. P. (2001). *Are the young becoming more disabled?* (NBER Working Paper No. 8247). Cambridge, MA: National Bureau of Economic Research.

Lauder, W., Sharkey, S., & Mummery, K. (2004). A community survey of loneliness. *Journal of Advanced Nursing, 46*, 88–94.

Laumann, E. O., Leitsch, S. A., & Waite, L. J. (2008). Elder mistreatment in the United States: Prevalence estimates from a nationally representative study. *Journal of Gerontology: Social Sciences, 63B*, S248–S254.

Leadership Council of Aging Organizations (2011). Letter to Chairman Harkin and ranking member Cochran/ Chairman Obey and ranking member Tiahrt. Retrieved July 21, 2011, from http://www.nasuad .org/documentation/policy_priorities/Signed_onto_ letters/ElderJusticeAct.pdf

Levy, B. R., & Banaji, M. R. (2002). Implicit ageism. In T. D. Nelson (Ed.), *Ageism: Stereotyping and prejudice against older persons* (pp. 49–76). Cambridge, MA: MIT Press.

Longres, J. F. (1995). Self-neglect among the elderly. *Journal of Elder Abuse and Neglect, 7*, 87–105.

Lowenstein, A., Eisikovits, Z., Band-Winterstein, T., & Enosh, G. (2009). Is elder abuse and neglect a social phenomenon? Data from the first national prevalence survey in Israel. *Journal of Elder Abuse & Neglect, 21*, 253–277.

Luo, Y., & Waite, L. J. (2011). Mistreatment and psychological well-being among older adults: Exploring the role of psychosocial resources and deficits. *Journal of Gerontology: Social Sciences, 66B*, 217–229.

Manton, K. G., & Gu, X. (2001). Changes in the prevalence of chronic disability in the United States Black and nonBlack population about age 65 from 1982 to 1999. *Proceedings of the National Academy of Sciences, 98*, 6354–6359.

McCarthy, M. (2002). Report finds abuse in US nursing homes goes unreported and unpunished. *Lancet, 359*, 850.

Moye, J., Butz, S. W., Marson, D. C., & Wood, E. (2007). A conceptual model and assessment template for capacity evaluation in adult guardianship. *Gerontologist, 47*, 591–603.

Naik, A., Burnette, J., Pickens-Pace, S., & Dyer, C. B. (2008). Impairment in instrumental activities of daily living and the geriatric syndrome of self-neglect. *Gerontologist, 48*, 388–393.

National Association of Social Workers (NASW). (2009). *Code of ethics of the National Association of Social Workers.* Retrieved August 22, 2011, from http:// www.socialworkers.org/pubs/code/code.asp

National Center on Elder Abuse (NCEA). (1998). *The National Elder Abuse Incidence Study.* Washington, DC: American Public Human Services Association.

National Center on Elder Abuse (NCEA). (1999). *Types of elder abuse in domestic settings* [Elder Abuse Information Series]. Washington, DC: Author.

National Center on Elder Abuse (NCEA). (2006). *The 2004 survey of state adult protective services: Abuse of adults 60 years of age and older.* Washington, DC: Author.

Nerenberg, L. (2006). Communities respond to elder abuse. *Journal of Gerontological Social Work, 46,* 5–33.

O'Keefe, M., Hills, A., Doyle, M., McCreadle, C., Scholes, S., Constantine, R., . . . Erens, B. (2007). *UK study of abuse and neglect of older people.* London, UK: National Center for Social Research and King's College.

Patterson, A. C., & Veenstra, G. (2010). Loneliness and risk of mortality: A longitudinal investigation in Alameda County, California. *Social Science & Medicine, 71,* 181–186.

Paveza, G., VandeWeerd, C., & Laumann, E. (2008). Elder self-neglect: A discussion of a social typology. *Journal of the American Geriatrics Society, 56,* S271–S275.

Pavlik, V., Hyman, D., Festa, N., & Dyer, C. (2001). Quantifying the problem of abuse and neglect in adults—Analysis of a statewide database. *Journal of the American Geriatrics Society, 49,* 45–48.

Payne, B., & Civokic, R. (1996). An empirical examination of the characteristics, consequences, and causes of elder abuse in nursing homes. *Journal of Elder Abuse and Neglect, 7,* 61–74.

Phelan, A. (2008). Elder abuse, ageism, human rights and citizenship: Implications for nursing discourse. *Nursing Inquiry, 15,* 320–329.

Phillips, L. R., & Guo, G. (2011). Mistreatment in assisted living facilities: Complaints, substantiations, and risk factors. *Gerontologist, 51,* 343–353.

Pillemer, K., & Finkelhor, D. (1988). The prevalence of elder abuse: A random sample survey. *Gerontologist, 28,* 51–57.

Pinquart, M., & Sorensen, S. (2001). Influences on loneliness in older adults: A meta-analysis. *Basic and Applied Social Psychology, 23,* 245–266.

Pot, A. M., van Dijck, R., Jonker, C., & Deeg, D. J. H. (1996). Verbal and physical aggression against elderly by informal caregivers in the Netherlands. *Social Psychiatry and Psychiatric Epidemiology, 31,* 156–162.

Prince, M. J., Harwood, R. H., Blizard, R. A., Thomas, A., & Mann, A. H. (1997). Social support deficits, loneliness and life events as risk factors for depression in old age: The Gospel Oak Project VI. *Psychological Medicine, 27,* 323–332.

Quinn, M. J., & Tomita, S. K. (1997). *Elder abuse and neglect: Causes, diagnosis, and intervention strategies.* New York, NY: Springer.

Salmon, M. (1994). *Double jeopardy: Resources and minority elders.* New York, NY: Garland.

Satariano, W. (2006). *Epidemiology of aging: An ecological approach.* Sudbury, MA: Jones and Bartlett.

Schnittker, J. (2007). Look (closely) at all the lonely people: Age and the social psychology of social support. *Journal of Aging and Health, 19,* 659–682.

Schoeni, R. F., Freedman, V. A., & Wallace, R. B. (2001). Persistent, consistent, widespread and robust? Another look at recent trends in old-age disability. *Journals of Gerontology: Social Sciences, 56,* S206–S218.

Shaw, B., Krause, N., Liang, J., & Bennett, J. (2007). Tracking changes in social relations throughout late life. *Journals of Gerontology: Social Sciences, 62B,* S90–S99.

Soldo, B. J., Mitchell, O. S., Tfaily, R., & McCabe, J. F. (2006). *Cross-cohort difference in health on the verge of retirement* (NBER Working Paper No. 12762). Cambridge, MA: National Bureau of Economic Research.

Teaster, P. B. (2002). *A response to abuse of vulnerable adults: The 2000 Survey of State Adult Protective Service.* Retrieved July 26, 2011, from http://www.ncea.aoa.gov/Main_Site/pdf/research/apsreport030703.pdf

Teaster, P. B., & Roberto, K. A. (2004). Sexual abuse of older adults: APS cases and outcomes. *Gerontologist, 44,* 788–796.

Thornton, J. E. (2002). Myths of aging or ageist stereotypes. *Emotional Gerontology, 28,* 301–312.

Tomaka, J., Thompson, S., & Palacios, R. (2006). The relation of social isolation, loneliness, and social support to disease outcomes among the elderly. *Journal of Aging and Health, 18,* 359–384.

Uchino, B. N. (2004). *Social support and physical health: Understanding the health consequences of relationships.* New Haven, CT: Yale University Press.

U.S. Census Bureau. (1992). *General population characteristics.* Washington, DC: Author.

U.S. Census Bureau. (2008). *An older and more diverse nation by midcentury.* Retrieved June 19, 2009, from http://www.census.gov/Press-Release/www/releases/archives/population/012496.html

U.S. Census Bureau. (2010). *United States: Profile of general population and housing characteristics: 2010.* Washington, DC: Author.

U.S. Government Accountability Office. (2011). Stronger federal leadership could enhance national response to elder abuse. Retrieved July 21, 2011, from http://aging.senate.gov/events/hr230kb2.pdf

U.S. House of Representatives. (2001). *Abuse of residents is a major problem in U.S. nursing homes.* Special Investigation Division, Committee on Government Reform. Retrieved July 27, 2011, from http://www.hospicepatients.org/ilaswan/nursinghomesabuse.pdf

Wahl, J., & Purdy, S. (2002). *Elder abuse: The hidden crime.* Toronto, Ontario, Canada: Advocacy Center for the Elderly and Community Legal Education Ontario.

Wolf, R. S. (2000). The nature and scope of elder abuse. *Generations, 24,* 6–12.

Wolf, R. S., & Li, D. (1999). Factors affecting the rate of elder abuse reporting to a state protective services program. *Gerontologist, 39,* 222–228.

World Health Organization. (2002). *Toronto declaration on the global prevention of elder abuse.* Retrieved July 21, 2011, from http://www.who.int/ageing/projects/elder_abuse/alc_toronto_declaration_en.pdf

Yaffe, K., Fox, P., Newcomer, R., Sands, L., Lindquist, K., Dane, K., & Covinsky, K. E. (2002). Patient and caregiver characteristics and nursing home placement in patients with dementia. *Journal of the American Medical Association, 287,* 2091–2097.

23

Social Justice and the Injustices Experienced by People With Mental Health Disabilities

Juliene Schrick

Mental illnesses are difficult to describe in a way that adequately captures the vast spectrum of thoughts, feelings, and behaviors that are markers of these disorders. Adding to this complexity is the fact that the etiology of mental illnesses is not clear and is debated within mental health communities. The lack of accurate information regarding mental health problems has added to the stigmatization and discrimination experienced by people who have been labeled as having a mental illness. In an effort to decrease stigma, many advocacy groups focus on educating the public on evidence that some disorders are linked to biological roots and are responsive to psychotropic medications. Equating mental health problems with physical health problems will, it is hoped, increase people's willingness to seek mental health services as well as decrease the marginalization of people living with a serious mental illness. However, framing mental illness within a medical paradigm while ignoring environmental context fortifies inaccurate representations of mental health disabilities and the people who experience them, thus, setting the stage

for further discrimination. A balanced and flexible analysis of both biological and environmental factors and their interactions over time is needed in order to increase the understanding of mental health and illness. As more accurate knowledge is disseminated, the opportunity to decrease stigma and discrimination grows, allowing more people to seek the mental health services they feel they may need and allowing individuals who live with a mental health disability to have more opportunities in order to live a dignified life.

Along with the complexity of defining mental illnesses, the tools to diagnose and treat them remain imperfect. Nevertheless, it is apparent that across the globe in all cultures and classes, a percentage of people have similar experiences that are classified as mental disorders. These illnesses do not occur in an all or none manner, and individuals move along a continuum of mental wellness to mental unwellness where all people have a potential for recovery. The Substance Abuse and Mental Health Services Administration (SAMHSA) defines *recovery* as "a journey of healing and transformation enabling a person with a mental health problem to live a meaningful life in a community of his or her choice while striving to achieve his or her full potential" (*National Consensus Statement*, 2009). While there are similarities among the various types of mental illnesses, there are differences in the severity in which people experience a disorder and its impact on the person's life. Stefan (2001) describes two distinct groups of mental health consumers, "overcomers" who may have a diagnosed mental illness but have been able to maintain their role in their families, to retain a stable job, and to "pass" in the community as someone who does not experience mental health problems. Stefan labels the other group as "cripples" who are individuals that rely on the public mental health system, often living in poverty with a high risk of homelessness and incarceration. They experience more direct discrimination due to the visibility of their mental illness; thus, few have stable employment, safe and secure housing, or meaningful involvement in community or family activities.

From a different perspective, Lonnie Snowden (class lecture, February 2, 2009) describes three worlds of mental health consumers: (a) The cripples are individuals diagnosed with a form of serious mental illness, (b) the overcomers who typically face misperceptions in the community are seen as having either "gotten over" their mental health disorder or are not believed to have a true mental health problem to begin with (Stefan, 2001), and (c) a growing number of people who do not necessarily meet the criteria for diagnosis but receive mental health services by choice for assistance with "problems with living," such as the death of a loved one or after being fired from a job. However, most individuals with a diagnosable mental disorder do not receive treatment (Kessler et al., 2005).

The substantial prevalence of major mental illness is not widely understood by the general public. The World Health Organization (WHO) identified mental illness as the leading cause of disability worldwide. It estimates that mental illnesses cause almost 25% of all disabilities in industrialized countries wherein the prevalence of mental disorder was generally higher than that of any other class of chronic illness. Additionally, the WHO found that mental disorders have a greater impact on role functioning than many other serious chronic conditions (U.S. Department of Health and Human Services [HHS], 2003). Furthermore, suicide worldwide is the third leading cause of death for 15- to 34-year-olds and accounts for 875,000 deaths per year. In the United States, approximately half of all people will meet the criteria for a *Diagnostic and Statistical Manual of Mental Disorders,* fourth edition (DSM-IV) disorder sometime during their lives with the onset most likely in childhood or adolescence (Kessler et al., 2005). Within the population, approximately 5.4% of adults are labeled as having a *serious* mental illness (SMI). This term is defined by federal regulations and is applied to disorders that interfere with at least one area of social functioning. Half of those who have SMI are said to be even more affected and are said to have "severe and persistent" mental illness. Among this group is the approximate 0.5% of the population who receive Social Security benefits due to their mental health disability (U.S. Department of Health and Human Services [HHS] and colleagues, 1999). However, epidemiological studies do not include homeless and institutionalized populations and do not represent an accurate reflection of individuals who are overrepresented in these groups (e.g., African Americans). Another factor that limits such studies is that interviews and surveys are often conducted in English only, systematically excluding a large group of people who do not have the fluency in English to respond.

This chapter focuses on the small percent of individuals with serious mental disorders who receive services through the public mental health system based on the fact that the majority of mental health policies, laws, and public mental health systems have developed over time in response to the discrimination, abuses, and abandonment experienced by this group. The aim of this chapter is to bring to light how people who live with a serious mental illness experience social injustices and, ultimately, to project the voices of people who are impacted by discrimination based on a mental health disability, so they may increase their influence within mental health research, clinical practice, and mental health systems change.

THE RIGHTS OF PEOPLE LIVING WITH A MENTAL ILLNESS

Ethics of Civil Commitment Laws

To understand discrimination experienced by people who have a serious mental illness, it is necessary to first understand how their rights have been defined. The most arduous debate, concerning the liberties of people with mental disabilities, is in regard to involuntary commitment. During the beginning half of the 19th century, public concern grew over the inappropriate placement of sane individuals into psychiatric institutions. In 1845, Massachusetts Supreme Court Chief Justice Lemuel Shaw decided that a person may be restrained only if they are a danger to themselves or others and only if the restraint is supportive of the individual's return to a safe state. This new precedent became the foundation for most of today's civil commitment statutes (Mechanic, 2008). Despite the intention of this ruling, over time, it was used as a means to warehouse large numbers of individuals in institutions where many of them stayed for extended periods of their lives without mechanisms to contest their confinement.

Stories of abuse and neglect attracted civil liberties lawyers in the 1960s and 1970s to take up the cause of involuntary placement in mental hospitals. Two landmark developments, the Lanterman-Petris-Short Act in California, which passed in 1969, and Wisconsin's 1972 *Lessard* decision made stringent criteria for involuntary hospitalization, set specific time periods for commitment, and developed procedures for reviewing such commitment on regular intervals (Mechanic, 2008). These changes had pervasive effects on the civil commitment laws in other states, and today, the criteria in all states for involuntary treatment requires that an individual have a combination of a mental illness and dangerousness to self or others (Olsen, 2003). Many states also include "grave disability" as a criterion for commitment, a legal determinant that a person, due to a mental illness, is unable to provide for their own food, clothing, or shelter. This can be seen as an extension of dangerousness to self.

Civil commitment laws require government agencies to define the situations when the right to individual freedom can be superseded by the state. This has created a fierce and polarizing debate between those who hold individual liberty as a right above all else and those who defend the right-to-treatment. Different models of ethical decision making have been used to support the perspective that the state has a legitimate right to use coercive power to protect people from safety and health risks. Zolnierek (2007) describes the differences between two distinct methods of decision making: the *rights-based* model, rooted in the core principles of bioethics and the *relation-based* model, stemming from two central themes of mutual interdependence and emotional responsiveness. The currently dominant rights-based approach applies the core of bioethics: values of *autonomy*, *beneficence*, and *nonmaleficence* in order to justify involuntary commitment.

Autonomy is highly valued throughout the dominant American culture, and respect for an individual's liberty is an integral component of ethical guidelines for those in the medical and social service fields who work directly with consumers of mental health services. In order to justify denying the autonomy of another individual, the person must lack sound judgment. Some would argue that having a serious mental illness can be equated with having a lack of agency; thus, the principle of autonomy cannot apply to people who are mentally disabled. Zolnierek describes two perspectives on the autonomy of people with mental illness. Matthews (2000) concludes that a person with mental illness cannot make choices that are one's own due to the nature of the illness, while Szasz (2005) strongly argues for the absolute autonomy of people who have been labeled as having a mental disorder (Matthews; Szasz, as cited in Zolnierek, 2007). While there is a lack of consensus on how to apply the concept of autonomy, there is an implication of incompetence that accompanies a label of *mental illness* within the dominant culture. Thus, the determination of a mental disorder usually removes the necessity for further evidence of incapacitation, providing a foundation for justifiably impeding another's autonomy (Olsen, 2003).

The second principle, beneficence, is used to support the limiting of autonomy when the overall benefit to the individual outweighs the costs expended to achieve it. This perspective has been called "Alan Stone's thank you theory" of civil commitment and is illustrated by a study conducted where 17 of 24 patients in a psychiatric facility believed strongly that it was correct to commit them against their will for treatment and that if they were to become unwell again they should be treated involuntarily if necessary (Rosenson, 1993). As a result, the act of involuntarily committing a person who is of unsound mind is viewed as ethical in accordance with medical paternalism, as long as the commitment will result in the person's returning to sanity. Ironically, Olsen (2003) cites two studies that point to conflicting findings where, in the first, 40% of involuntary patients reported (after discharge) that they would never commit another person and, in a second study, 12 out of 24 patients interviewed one week after seclusion stated that the seclusion was inappropriate and unnecessary.

The third principle in the rights-based model is nonmaleficence and relates to preventing harm to the individual or another person. This principle shifts the intention of the person making the ethical decision from doing good to preventing harm where the decision to treat rests upon an assessment of risk and not on the individual's need for treatment (Olsen, 2003). Commitment laws require that the danger to self or others needs to be immanent, but it is difficult for clinicians and police officers to predict the likelihood of harm. Family and friends of people with serious mental illness often complain that this statute withholds treatment to people who need it, forcing them to decompensate (fall apart mentally and emotionally) and thereby worsen their illness and increase the stress on others connected with the person.

In contrast, the relation-based model for ethical decision making is built on the following three assumptions: (a) All clinical relationships involve one-way influence from the clinician to the client-consumer, (b) the level of intensity of the clinician's influence varies in contrast to the dichotomous rights-based model, and (c) the clinician or person making the decision is an integral part of the situation since all decisions are subjective (Olsen, 2003). Zolnierek (2007) and Olsen (2003) contend that the relational model allows clinicians (or others

involved in this decision-making process) to take into account the complex and unique context of each situation so that the decision to use power over another individual arises out of the relationship between the client and practitioner. Thus, it moves the concern away from justifying the use of coercion to maintaining an ethical relationship with the individual (Olsen, 2003).

While the relational and rights models differ in perspectives, they both focus on the individual's capacity and/or potential to harm self or others. The relational model seeks to reflect the experiences of those involved, while the rights-based model relies on specific legal categories with less emphasis on the uniqueness of the situation or the diversity of human experiences. Finally, another key difference in the approaches emerges when ethical concerns in the rights-based model arise when the use of coercion comes into question, whereas the relation-based model obligates the clinician to integrate ethical dimensions into the therapeutic relationship on an ongoing basis (Olsen, 2003).

Long-Term Care and the Americans With Disabilities Act

A person who has met the criteria for involuntary commitment is taken to a psychiatric facility for a specified amount of time, commonly 72 hours. For some, a temporary hold may turn into long-term care in an institution or residential facility. For individuals with serious mental illnesses, using public mental health services, long-term congregate care is common along with the "revolving door" between levels of care. While the effects of living in an institution may not be deleterious for all tenants, being treated as a group rather than as an individual with almost all facets of life controlled by bureaucratic procedures can negatively impact most residents. Individuals who live in institutions for long periods of time can become apathetic and experience a loss of interest, initiative, and self-maintenance (Mechanic, 2008).

While commitment laws have developed mechanisms to prevent inappropriate long-term placement, there are still many individuals who live in institutions and congregate facilities who would prefer to live independently in the community with relevant supports. For example, in 2001, there were 237,133 people in psychiatric institutions (and another 2 million are admitted each year) along with 1.5 million Americans with disabilities who reside in nursing homes. (Stefan, 2001). The primary reason this segregation continues is the lack of alternative housing and support services in communities. The Americans with Disabilities Act (ADA) of 1990 sought to make community living accessible to all people with a disability. Title II of the ADA, which prohibits discrimination from a public entity, has been the most influential piece of the act in the lives of people who have mental disorders due to its direct challenge to inappropriate institutionalization.

Congress viewed the ADA as a way to prohibit segregation caused by discrimination based on disability status. In the 1998 case of *Olmstead v. L.C.*, two individuals who were residing in Georgia Regional Hospital brought a suit against the institution, alleging that they were being segregated inappropriately and that the hospital was in violation of the ADA. The court rejected the hospital's argument that insufficient funding made community placement an impossibility (Petrila, 2009). As a result, the right to receive services in the *least restrictive environment* has become a fundamental principle in today's mental health systems. In essence, the "least restrictive environment" is preferred over the "most facilitative environment" (Ridgway & Zipple, 1990).

Involuntary Outpatient Treatment

As more individuals with serious mental illnesses live in the community with shrinking resources for acute care, the debate over involuntary treatment has expanded to include outpatient treatment for those living in independent, supported, or congregate housing in the community. Today, the majority of states have some form of involuntary outpatient commitment (OPC), but its definition, eligible participants, and implementation vary widely. Generally, OPC provides treatment to individuals who do not meet the criteria for involuntary commitment but are likely to decompensate to become a danger to themselves or others (Mechanic, 2008). Advocates for mandated outpatient treatment describe it as a device

for ensuring that people who lack insight into their illness will obtain treatment and prevent increased disability and high costs of emergency care, while opponents maintain its use reflects inappropriate coercion and control.

Petrila, Ridgely, and Borum (2003) describe three categories of OPC: (a) Conditional release allows psychiatric hospitals to impose treatments that the individual must follow (with the consequences of a forced to return to the hospital if they are broken), (b) a person who meets inpatient commitment criteria may be treated on an outpatient basis, and (c) unique state guidelines for situations when mandated outpatient treatment may be ordered. For example, New York's statute for OPC, known as Kendra's Law, includes more details than its description of inpatient involuntary commitment by specifying that the person needs to have been treated in the past and rehospitalized or threatened harm within a specified time prior to the petition of OPC (Petrila et al., 2003).

The crux of the involuntary outpatient treatment debate revolves around the public duty to provide treatment to individuals who are resistant to such treatment rather than protecting the rights of individuals from inappropriate state intervention. Opponents view OPC as an expansion of the state's coercive practices, and many have stated that if an adequate community mental health treatment system existed, mandatory treatment would not be needed. The other side of the debate contends that some individuals have a biological component called anosognosia that prevents them from recognizing that they have a mental illness (Torrey & Zdanowicz, 2001).

New York passed Kendra's Law in 1999 after a woman was killed by a man with untreated schizophrenia. Prior to Kendra's death, the man sought out mental health treatment, but it had been denied due to a lack of resources. The same scenario took place in Washington, where a person with a mental illness sought treatment, was denied it, and shortly thereafter caused the death of another person (Mechanic, 2008). Both of these incidents were followed by the passage of outpatient commitment laws. It is interesting that both states responded to these tragedies by broadening the law's power to control individual treatment compliance, while making little effort to increase the amount of services available.

Can the State Fail to Provide Treatment?

There has been at least one case in which the police were charged for failing to involuntarily commit an individual who was obviously suffering from a mental disability. The case was dismissed, as the judge found that failing to segregate a person based on disability is not a violation of the ADA (Stefan, 2001). However, many advocates argue that allowing people to leave their mental illness untreated is a deeper violation of the person's rights and reflects the public's abandonment of people who have serious mental disorders. "To die with their rights on" was a phrase coined by psychiatrists, reacting to the emerging civil commitment laws of the 1960s and 70s (Mechanic, 2008). Rosenson (1993) refers to the rights of a mentally ill person to refuse treatment as inhumane, and Torrey and Zdanowicz (2001) describe the failure to provide psychiatric medications as neglect. In contrast, the consumer movement strongly advocates for the minimal use of involuntary interventions and only as a last resort after all other alternatives have been explored. The National Coalition of Mental Health Consumer/ Survivor Organizations views any use of force as a failure of the mental health system to provide adequate services, and they claim that if such services were available, there would be no need to use involuntary methods of intervention (*Countering Discrimination and Stigma*, 2007).

The debate over the rights of people with mental illnesses has broadened from focusing on an individual's ability to refuse treatment to include how structural violence impedes the lives of people with serious mental illnesses. Farmer, an anthropologist and medical doctor describes "structural violence" as rights violations that are symptoms of "deeper pathologies of power and are linked intimately to the social conditions that so often determine who will suffer abuse and who will be shielded from harm" (Farmer, 2005, p. 7). While Farmer focuses on international human rights abuses, his perspective can be applied to the treatment of people with mental health disabilities by linking political, social, and economic rights.

In addition, Arboleda-Florez (2008) contends that in order to address discrimination of mentally ill people, it is necessary to first recognize that realities have changed since the original commitment laws were developed. Statutes focusing on institutionalization, due process, and the right to autonomy do not protect people with serious mental illnesses from systematic neglect and structural violence. Mechanic (2008) describes this phenomena as a part of a larger social process whereby the community finds alternative means to separate and confine others they judge to be lesser than themselves. Thus, if hospitalization becomes difficult, other means of confinement or segregation, such as incarceration or homelessness, are used.

The next segment of this chapter discusses violations of rights in the domains of housing, employment, and health care and is followed by a look at how this discrimination has influenced the criminalization of people with mental health disabilities. A variety of perspectives, including voices of consumers, practitioners, researchers, and policymakers are described in order to gain insight into the processes through which social injustices frame the lives of individuals with mental health disorders.

EMPLOYMENT DISCRIMINATION

Until recently, people with a serious mental illness were told to give up any hopes of working, going back to school, or maintaining a professional life. Today, practitioners often respond to a client's desire to work with concerns about the increased stress that could trigger a relapse or about the increased income that may disqualify the person from receiving her benefits. Providing support to a stigmatized group of individuals trying to join the labor force often involves employment discrimination. Best practices are reviewed for both decreasing employer discriminatory behavior and increasing the long-term employability of people who have a serious mental illness.

Employment discrimination is both widespread and severe. As Stefan (2001) found, 55% of the participants reported experiencing employment discrimination, and when asked to identify the category where they experienced the worst discrimination,

33% of respondents replied their worst experiences with discrimination were in relation to their work life. For people living with a serious mental illness, making a meaningful contribution to one's community is one of the pillars of the recovery model. Cook, one of the contributors to the 2003 president's New Freedom Commission on Mental Health, describes the results of four national surveys conducted between 1989 through 1998. One of them found that those who had high levels of a disabling mental illness had employment rates ranging from only 22% to 40% (Cook, 2006).

Nearly two fifths, or 38%, of workers with a mental health disability had jobs that paid near minimum wage compared to one fifth, or 20%, of people who did not have a disability (Cook, 2006). Compared to others working with physical disabilities, individuals with mental health disorders experience the strongest stigma, lowest employability rankings, and largest productivity-adjusted wage differences (Baldwin & Marcus, 2006). Despite these realities, most people with psychiatric disabilities desire to be employed, and half of all working-age adults with a serious mental illness, who were not employed, considered themselves able to work if provided appropriate supports (Cook, 2006).

In order to understand this discrepancy, it is important to note the internal and environmental factors impacting employability for people with serious mental illnesses. The age of onset of most serious mental illnesses occurs during a person's teenage years or young adulthood (reducing the individual's total education and marketability as a worker). Additionally, cognitive difficulties related to the mental illness itself can impact productivity. Cook (2006) reports that a person with bipolar disorder experienced an average annual loss of $9,619, while those with major depression had a loss of $4,426 per employee. According to projections, this amounts to a total loss of $50.7 billion per year in the U.S. labor force from bipolar and major depression.

Another factor relates to public policies where programs of the Social Security Administration and Medicaid and Medicare intertwine in such a way as to inhibit beneficiaries from returning to work. Individuals who rely on Supplemental Security Income (SSI) or Supplemental Security Disability Income (SSDI) and thus Medicaid and/or Medicare

are reluctant to return to work due to the possibility of losing their benefits and health insurance. Despite recent efforts to increase the amount of money participants can make while keeping their benefits, the National Council advocacy group found that only 8% of individuals who returned to full time jobs received mental health insurance coverage (*Meaningful Employment*, 2009).

A severe lack of effective vocational services constitutes another element contributing to the low rates of employment and disproportionate pay for people with serious mental illnesses. Traditionally, mental health systems have not perceived vocational rehabilitation as part of their service responsibility. While this view is changing, it was recently found that only 23% of people with schizophrenia in a stratified random sample of persons in two states received any kind of vocational rehabilitation (Cook, 2006). Until Medicaid makes vocational services reimbursable, the vast majority of people in the public mental health system will not receive them despite their vital importance in the recovery process. A fifth component of disproportionate employment rates can be seen as the failure of protective legislation to be effective in preventing and responding to discriminatory practices in the workplace. The Supreme Court interpreted the ADA with increasing restriction after its passage, making it extremely difficult for people with legitimate disabilities to prove that they qualify. The ADA Amendment Act was created explicitly to rectify the original intent of the law (Petrila, 2009). Other legislation such as the Workforce Investment Act of 1998 and the Ticket to Work and Work Incentives Act of 1999 attempted to increase vocational options for people at the same time as reducing government spending on people with disabilities (Cook, 2006). Nevertheless neither program has been successful in improving employment conditions for individuals with serious mental illnesses.

Last, the fact that people relying on public mental health systems are often trapped in poverty may be the most substantial obstacle blocking people with serious mental disorders from gaining employment. In 2006, the maximum federal SSI benefit was 75% of the federal poverty line. In 2004, a person with SSI income assistance received $564 per month, while the national average for a one bedroom apartment cost $676. Thus, an SSI beneficiary had an average annual income of only 18.4% of the average non-disabled person's median household income (Cook, 2006). With an income this low, basic needs, such as food and shelter, may be unattainable at times, making the possibility of job searching and job training far from reach. As a result, poverty may have a larger influence on labor force participation than having a mental illness (Cook, 2006). Discrimination based on disability can be difficult to separate due to intertwining injustices of racism, sexism, heterosexism, abelism, and poverty-based discrimination. It has been repeatedly documented that people who are members of ethnic or racial minority groups and who have a serious mental illness have far greater problems with finding and keeping work than their White counterparts or members of ethnic or racial minorities who do not have a mental illness (Stefan, 2001). More research with consumers who face multiple levels of injustices and how this impacts their relationship to the labor force is sorely needed.

While individuals with mental disabilities astutely recognize discrimination in interviews, on the job, and when getting fired, research is now able to support the validity of their claims. Baldwin and Marcus (2006) explain the methods that economists use to quantify the role that stigma plays in determining the wages of minority groups. Their research shows that functional limitations account for only a portion of wage differences in the population of people with serious mental illnesses. The results also reflect that self-reports of stigmatizing experiences are consistent with the econometric measures used to quantify how much stigma plays a part in their wages (Baldwin & Marcus, 2006).

Cook (2006) reports two surveys representing the experiences of discrimination by mental health consumers. Out of a national survey of more than 1,300 individuals with disabling mental disorders, almost a third reported that they were turned down for a job for which they felt qualified after disclosing their mental illness. Other reported experiences included being fired, laid off or told to resign, refused a transfer, refused a promotion, or refused a training opportunity because of their mental disorder (Cook, 2006). As a result, in 2004, people with disabling mental disorders filed a fifth of all U.S. court cases alleging employment discrimination.

With all of this evidence, it seems logical to ask what measures are being taken with employers to decrease the discrimination against people with mental disabilities in the workplace. In two studies conducted in California, employers were asked whom they would hire for a retail sales job. People with mental health disorders were seen as equally undesirable as ex-convicts, and the only group that employers stated they were more wary of hiring were individuals with active tuberculosis (Thornicroft, 2006). This fear of hiring people with a serious mental illness can also be found in the results of a survey conducted in the southern United States where only 15% of business participants had specific policies for implementing the ADA (Thornicroft, 2006). When asked what helps businesses hire and retain people with mental health disabilities, it was found that companies that were in compliance with the ADA had received formal training or had received a threat of legal sanctions (Thornicroft, 2006).

More innovation and forward movement is occurring on the consumer side of the issue, where practitioners are becoming increasingly aware of employment programs that provide support for people with psychiatric disabilities who are seeking and maintaining competitive employment. Cook (2006) describes a randomized, controlled trial where 55% of those receiving services from evidence-based supported employment services were those hired for a competitive job, compared to 34% of the control group who were receiving services as usual. While few longitudinal studies have been published on the long-term results of the Supported Employment Services program, one 10-year follow-up study found mixed results. While individuals with a mental disability receiving supported employment services were successful in obtaining competitive and long-term jobs, very few people transitioned to full-time employment with health insurance (Cook, 2006).

HOUSING DISCRIMINATION

Housing is an essential element in creating a safe place for healing but has not received sufficient attention by mental health systems. In identifying the link between housing discrimination and people with mental health disabilities, Carling (1990) noted that individuals with a serious mental illness are at risk of losing their housing, living in substandard housing, or being placed in inappropriate housing. Housing discrimination operates on three levels: (a) national policies, (b) organizational structures of mental health systems, and (c) interpersonal level interactions that include landlords and neighbors. These descriptions are followed by a look at alternative housing models that are more in line with the recovery and wellness model and have shown to have promising results in reducing rates of incarceration and hospitalization.

At the broadest level, federal policies governing Supplement Security Income (SSI) and Housing and Urban Development (HUD) do not provide adequate resources to sustain a healthy lifestyle. These programs provide minimal resources and inadvertently cause most of this population to live in poverty with inadequate housing options. At the mental health systems level, services are linked to housing in a disempowering all or none relationship. Individuals relying on the public mental health system are likely to lose their home if they are hospitalized or choose to no longer receive treatment. And finally, on the interpersonal level, exchanges between landlords, neighbors, and family around housing-related issues are often characterized by mistrust, negative expectations, and exclusion.

Of all the people eligible for federally subsidized housing, people with disabilities have the highest level of unmet need (*Position Statement on Housing*, 2005). The inadequate supply of affordable housing is a main contributor to an environment where housing discrimination of people with mental disabilities is commonplace and overlooked. Between 1980 and 1990, nearly 80% of federally assisted housing for low-income and special needs groups were cut (Carling, 1990). In response to the lack of options, the mental health system developed housing for people with mental health disabilities in the form of a continuum of care. People using this model of housing must adjust to group-living environments at the same time as preparing to move to the next housing level where there will be decreased supervision and support. These constant changes in housing accommodations place enormous stress on the person and exacerbate difficulties the person may already be experiencing such as loose social support. Moreover, individuals do not necessarily recover in a linear fashion within a predetermined time period (Ridgway & Zipple, 1990).

This causes limited options along the continuum in terms of bed availability and results in persons being placed wherever a bed is empty, often in a setting that is inappropriate, such as a higher level of care when they are clearly ready to move to a more independent environment. It is also common for people to be pushed out of acute settings prematurely. Several consumers report having to choose between where they want to live or getting the services they need. Others describe feelings of powerlessness when faced with the "decision" to either accept medications that they do not want or becoming homeless (Ridgway & Zipple, 1990).

On an interpersonal level, individuals relying on the public mental health system experience housing discrimination through unfair treatment by landlords and NIMBYism, where neighborhoods organize to prevent the development of housing for people with mental health disabilities. For example, when a couple attempted to convert a house into a home for people moving from state hospitals into the community, neighbors responded out of fear of violence and loss of property values by bringing legal action against the couple. When the assessor of the property spoke in court, he used a malodorous factory and a sewage works plant as comparisons to a board and care home for people with mental disorders. The case was taken to a higher court that allowed the couple to go ahead with their plans on the grounds that the public interest of providing community care outweighed the claims of the neighbors (Thornicroft, 2006).

Accurately accessing the number of homeless people and the subgroup that have a mental illness is complex. The National Law Center on Homelessness and Poverty (NLCHP) in 2007 found that approximately 3.5 million people were likely to experience homelessness in a given year, which translates to roughly 1% of the U.S. population (NLCHP, as cited in Nichols, 2008). Out of this group, 40% to 45% have a major mental illness, which equates to 150,000 to 200,000 individuals. Despite these overwhelming numbers, progress is being made in certain areas around the country. For example, Main Street Housing, Inc. is a consumer-operated housing development that opened its doors in Maryland in 2002 and has rented approximately $2 million worth of property to those who have a mental health disorder (Wireman, 2007). This program uses a form of supported housing called the "housing only" model where the only requirement for tenancy is that the individual show evidence of a disability. Participants found that taking on a role in the community other than that of being a mental health client brought about a significant change in self-perception (Wireman, 2007). The supported housing model views housing as a right and is based on three core principles: (a) consumers choosing their own living situation, (b) living in "normal" community housing that is not associated with a mental health program, (c) and consumers having access to the services and supports they need in order to maximize their opportunities for success (Carling, 1990). Another approach to supported housing is the housing-first model for addressing the needs of individuals who are both homeless and have a mental illness. For example, Pathways to Housing (PTH) is a program where individuals are given housing that is immediate, independent, permanent, and not contingent on treatment compliance. A study examining the success of the housing-first model found it resulted in increased levels of housing stability and cost savings (Padgett, Gulcur, & Tsemberis, 2006).

DISCRIMINATION IN MEDICAL CARE

The Physical Health of People with SMI

People who have a mental health disability die approximately 25 years earlier than Americans overall. While individuals with SMI generally have higher suicide and accident rates, three out of five die from preventable diseases, and the vast majority of them live with at least one chronic medical condition (Elias, 2007). A study conducted in Maine reports 70% of people with a mental health disability have at least one chronic physical health condition, 45% have two, and 30% have three or more (Kim et al., 2007). Explanations of increased mortality include the convergence of many factors including cigarette smoking and a lack of exercise, substance abuse, damaging side effects of prescribed medications, and inaccessible and poor quality health care. Lasser et al., (2000) found that Americans with mental illnesses are almost twice as likely to smoke cigarettes as people without mental illness. Another element related to the poor health outcomes for people with mental health disabilities is inactivity. Negative symptoms of schizophrenia and signs of major depression (such as loss of motivation and social withdrawal) compound with environmental factors of low social support and societal exclusion often leading to a lifestyle of limited physical activity or exercise.

Antipsychotic medications have always had serious physical side effects with some first generation drugs causing irreversible damage, such as Tardive Dyskinesia and Parkinsonian symptoms. While the newest generation of antipsychotics has increased medication compliance through decreasing the severity of associated side effects, they have also developed a new class of side effects that cause cardiovascular disease and diabetes (Elias, 2007).

While psychiatric symptoms, lifestyle choices, and medications all have a direct impact on a person's well-being, it is the social determinants of health, such as economic inequality, discrimination, and crime and safety, that have been identified as playing the largest role in health outcomes (*Health Status Report*, 2007). For example, people with mental health disabilities are victims of crime at a higher rate than other groups at the same time as they experience isolating stigma and discrimination in housing, employment, and community life. These factors interact to compound their adverse impact on both the physical and mental well-being of the individual.

Experiences of Discrimination in Medical Care

Other obstacles to health involve discrimination against people with mental illness when they try to get their medical needs met. There is strong evidence that people who have a diagnosed mental illness have less access to physical health care and receive poorer quality care despite their higher rates of illness and premature death (Thornicroft, 2006). Stefan (2001) found two categories of discrimination: prejudiced treatment by hospital and clinic staff and systemic neglect maintained by the organizational structure of the health care system.

The most common interpersonal experience of discrimination that could be clearly traced to mental health disability was the loss of credibility when attempting to communicate medical problems (Stefan, 2001). This manifests itself when medical professionals disregard the physical health complaints of people with a mental illness and attribute them as simply false, attempts at attention seeking, or psychosomatic symptoms of the mental health disorder. This can result in people in need of medical attention being turned away. The misinterpretation of physical symptoms as psychiatric symptoms has also resulted in the inappropriate commitment of individuals to mental health facilities (Stefan, 2001). Stefan (2001) also found overt hostility from medical providers who were responding to physical injuries sustained during a mental health crisis. For example, an individual who attempted suicide by cutting her wrists was taken to the emergency room where her wounds were stitched without anesthetic, and she was told by medical staff that the lack of anesthetic was an incentive so she would not repeat the behavior again. Mental health consumers are not the only ones who recognize these injustices. Both mental health professionals and emergency room professionals acknowledge that the medical complaints of people with psychiatric disabilities are often not taken seriously (Stefan, 2001).

Structural inequalities within health care systems also perpetuate discrimination based on mental health disability. The medical care provided inside inpatient mental health facilities is often inadequate and of poor quality. There are also disproportionate placements of do not resuscitate (DNR) orders in the charts of people with serious mental illnesses who reside in inpatient facilities. Last, patient "dumping" or the "economically motivated transfer" of an individual to another facility is disproportionately used with patients who have a diagnosed mental illness (Stefan, 2001).

Beyond interpersonal and health service system-based discrimination, federal health policies incentivize the continued segregation of mental health consumers. The reimbursement structures of Medicaid create fiscal incentives for hospitals and other facilities to maintain individuals with mental health disabilities inside institutions rather than in the community despite the passage of the ADA (Stefan, 2001). Medicaid's exclusion related to state mental hospitals is the mechanism through which this discrimination is carried out. The home and community-based waiver program was developed to enable people with disabilities living in institutions to move to the community. It requires states to show that Medicaid would be spending more money on a person's care inside an institution than they would if the person were receiving support services in the community. However, since Medicaid does not pay for adult care in state mental hospitals, it is impossible to meet the cost-neutrality rule for people with serious mental illnesses. Thus, people with other types of disabilities (nonmental health) have been able to greatly decrease the segregation they experience and integrate into communities through the use of this waiver. At the same time, these Medicaid rules have contributed to the increase of people with serious mental illnesses in nursing homes (Stefan, 2001). Without changes in these federally imposed fiscal incentives, there are few options that will allow facilities and service providers to assist people with all types of disability to be able to live as they desire in their communities.

CRIMINALIZATION AND DISCRIMINATION

The result of marginalization in employment, housing, medical care, and other life domains leaves people with serious mental illnesses with few options to pursue the kind of life they desire. The increasing incarceration of this population has been a concern over the past three decades and reflects the cyclical nature of mental health reforms in the United States. Prior to the development of psychiatric hospitals in the mid-19th century, advocates such as Dorothea Dix campaigned for the rights of people with mental illnesses, so they could move out of jails and into asylums. Approximately 140 years later, in 1972, Abramson first noted that people with serious mental illnesses were increasingly processed through the criminal justice system rather than the mental health system (Lurigio, Fallon, & Dincin, 2000). Today, this recriminalization of people who live with a psychiatric disability is explained from different and converging perspectives. While some analysts point to the failure of deinstitutionalization, increasing restrictions in civil commitment laws, and the severe lack of community mental health and support services, others contend that interactions with law enforcement are among the causes for the increase of people with mental disorders in jails and prisons. Others argue that the incarceration of people with mental illnesses is more a reflection of the increasing criminalization of the general population, especially individuals with low incomes.

According to Lamb (2009), about 360,000 to 500,000 people with a major mental illness were living in jails and prisons in 2007. There was a dramatic increase in the rates of incarceration of people with a mental disorder in federal prisons and state jails from 209 per 100,000 in 1978 to 708 per 100,000 in 2000 (Lamb & Weinberger, 2005). The U.S. Department of Justice reports that half of all inmates in prisons and jails had mental health problems, and 42% of all inmates in state prisons and 49% in local jails had both a mental disorder and a problem with substance use (Lurigio et al., 2000).

The interactions between police and people with mental illnesses have been cited as a factor in the increase in criminalization of this population. Law enforcement has been labeled as the "system that cannot say no" (Lamb & Weinberger, 2005). Police officers, having to respond to all calls, become "street corner psychiatrists" and "gatekeepers" to mental health services due to the inadequate numbers of mental health workers and treatment options for people with a serious mental illness (Lamb, Weinberger, DeCuir, 2002). This can be problematic for a variety of reasons. For example, officers may not recognize the signs of mental illness and therefore attribute the individual's behavior to drugs or alcohol use instead of to symptoms of a serious mental health disability, potentially escalating the situation rather than diffusing it. Other times, an officer may choose to make a "mercy booking" where the person with a serious mental illness is arrested as a means of protection due to their extreme vulnerability on the streets or in cases where mental health services are more accessible in jail than in the community (Lamb et al., 2002).

An alternative view of the causes of increased criminalization of people with mental health disabilities looks beyond the mental health system to the national policies that disproportionately impact people in lower socioeconomic classes. As Draine, Salzer, Culhane, and Hadley (2002) note, focusing solely on the increase in incarceration of people with mental illness ignores the fact that the number of inmates in the United States has grown sixfold between 1970 and 2006 and continues to rise substantially each year. Today, the United States leads the world in incarceration rates with approximately 2.3 million people in federal and state prisons and local jails. This equates to more than 1 adult American in 100 who resides behind bars, according to the U.S. Department of Justice (2009).

Building on the role of social disadvantage, Junginger, Claypoole, Laygo, and Crisanti (2006) report that increased incarceration of people with mental illness is largely due to the war on drugs where nonviolent drug convictions account for more than half of new prison sentences made between 1985 and 2000. Thus, it was found that substance abuse is more likely to lead to criminal offenses than serious mental illness. Other elements of social disadvantage include poverty, homelessness, unemployment, lack of social support, and limited education. It is widely known that African American and Latino males face higher rates of incarceration. For example, at midyear of 2008, the U.S. Department of Justice (DOJ) reported a total of 4,777 Black male inmates per 100,000 Black males in federal and state prisons and local jails. This is compared to 1,760 Hispanic male inmates per 100,000 Hispanics males and 727 White male inmates per 100,000 White males (DOJ, 2009). Thus, the factors of race and ethnicity, economic status, mental health disorder, and others converge to contribute to the increased likelihood of arrest and incarceration.

The Eighth Amendment of the Constitution protects the rights of inmates and detainees to treatment for acute medical problems, including psychiatric problems (HHS, 2003). Nevertheless, inadequate behavioral health care for inmates is widespread across the country where the magnitude of the need overwhelms the ability to provide appropriate care. In the 1980 case of *Inmates of the Allegheny County Jail v. Pierce* in the Third Circuit Court of Appeals, it was ruled that inmates are explicitly entitled to mental health care. While it is necessary to provide treatment, it is also important that mental health programs for inmates do not encourage police, judges, and others to see jails as venues for long-term care for people with serious mental illnesses (Lurigio et al., 2000). Increased coordination between systems has improved and will continue to develop as mental health practitioners and law enforcement personnel work through differing orientations toward clients, disparate organizational cultures, and obstacles in the accessibility to sharing client information.

Those who view the social context as a more significant factor in the criminalization of people with mental illness see the need for extensive changes in health, drug, and corrections policies in order to adequately address the increasing rate of incarceration of people living with a mental disorder. Draine et al. (2002) assert that without major changes in drug policy, mental health systems change will be more difficult, more expensive, and less effective. The criminalizing trajectory of the United States, including people with mental illness, needs to be addressed before rates of incarceration can be expected to decrease. Furthermore, discrimination based on class, race, and other intertwining markers of difference also need to be addressed within this context in order to move toward a society where the forced removal of people from communities is exercised in a more just manner.

CONCLUSION

Few other conditions have such far-reaching effects on individuals as major mental illnesses. These disorders impact every facet of life from the most personal and fundamental concepts of self to the more public areas of interpersonal relationships and professional roles. At the same time, the disorders themselves do not account for the level of burden that is associated with them. Instead, prejudiced attitudes with regard to people who have a mental illness permeate our social lives as well as the policies and systems of care that have been built to serve people with mental health disabilities.

The advancement of social justice continues to be a slow, nonlinear path in the field of mental health. Increased human and capital investments are required to implement the kinds of changes that are known to be efficacious and in line with the recovery process. Research scholars of numerous reports have made recommendations, calling for the transformation of the mental health system, such as those in the 2003 *New Freedom Commission Report* and in the 1999 *Report of the Surgeon General*. However, the political will to maintain mental health reform as a priority among so many other competing concerns has been lacking.

Reviewing a variety of the social injustices experienced by people with mental health disabilities allows for a more contextualized understanding of this population. It also calls for researchers to make space in order for people with mental illnesses to participate in driving the direction of future research. The lack of discussion on intertwining social injustices needs to be addressed, especially the physical and psychological impacts of co-occurring racism, classism, sexism, heterosexism, and abelism.

In the realm of clinical practice it is important to examine the embedded biases toward people with mental illnesses especially the perception that people with mental health disabilities have limited potentials and require others to exercise judgment for them. In their work with all clients, mental health practitioners can integrate strengths-based and culturally appropriate treatment models.

In the area of systems change, the mental health field practitioners can learn from populations of people with other types of disability. The independent living movement for people with physical disabilities and assisted living models for older adults have helped make progress in integrating these groups into communities. When looking to transform the current mental health system, individuals need to examine the organizational structures of programs, facilities, systems of care, and the coordination between systems. The mechanisms within these structures that perpetuate discrimination need to be identified and addressed.

Listening to people with mental illnesses describe their experiences of discrimination is a first step toward advancing social justice in the mental health field. While mental health systems are becoming more consumer and family centered, they remain constrained by larger structures that prevent people with serious mental illnesses from developing a secure base from which to redevelop their life roles (e.g., adequate income, safe shelter, freedom from violence, and access to health care). Without meeting these basic needs, the steps involved in the recovery process lie further from reach for most people who use the public mental health system. The policies that perpetuate poverty need to be addressed in order for recovery-oriented systems to be effective. At the same time, stigmatizing public perceptions of mental health disabilities also needs to be challenged while accurate information regarding mental illnesses should be disseminated broadly. The tenant of the disability rights movement, "nothing about us without us," needs to be strengthened and kept central as individuals and groups with and without disabilities continue to work on decreasing mental health discrimination and increasing opportunities for people living with a serious mental illness.

REFERENCES

Arboleda-Florez, J. (2008). Mental illness and human rights. *Forensic Psychiatry, 21*(5), 479–484.

Baldwin, M. L., & Marcus, S. C. (2006). Perceived and measured stigma among workers with serious mental illness. *Psychiatric Services, 57*, 388–392.

Carling, P. J. (1990). Major mental illness, housing, and supports: The promise of community integration. *American Psychologist, 45*, 969–975.

Cook, J. A., (2006). Employment barriers for persons with psychiatric disabilities: Update of a report for the president's commission. *Psychiatric Services, 57*, 1391–1405.

Countering discrimination and stigma by promoting mental health recovery and resiliency. (2007). National Coalition of Mental Health Consumers/Survivor Organizations. Retrieved from http://www.ncmhr.org/downloads/NC_Countering_Disc_Stigma_by_Promoting_MH_R_R.pdf

Draine, J., Salzer, M. S., Culhane, D. P., & Hadley, T. R. (2002). Role of social disadvantage in crime, joblessness, and homelessness among persons with serious mental illness. *Psychiatric Services, 53*, 565–573.

Elias, M. (2007, May 3). Mentally ill die 25 years earlier, on average. *USA Today.* Retrieved from http://usatoday30.usatoday.com/news/health/2007-05-03-mental-illness_N.htm

Farmer, P. (2005). *Pathologies of power: Health, human rights, and the new war on the poor.* Berkeley: University of California Press.

Health status report. (2007). City of Berkeley, Department of Health and Human Services. Retrieved from http://www.ci.berkeley.ca.us/ContentDisplay.aspx?id=28084

Junginger, J., Claypoole, K., Laygo, R., & Crisanti, A. (2006). Effects of serious mental illness and substance abuse on criminal offenses. *Psychiatric Services, 57*, 879–882.

Kessler, R. C., Berglund, P., Demler, O., Jin, R., Merikangas, K. R., & Walters, E. E. (2005). Lifetime prevalence and age-of-onset distributions of DSM-IV disorders in the National Comorbidity Survey Replication. *Archives of General Psychiatry, 62*, 593–602.

Kim, M., Swanson, J., Marvin, S., Bradford, D., Mustillo, S., & Elbogen, E. (2007). Healthcare barriers among severely mentally ill homeless adults: Evidence from the Five-Site Health and Risk Study. *Mental Health Services Research, 34*, 363–375.

Lamb, H. R. (2009). Reversing criminalization. *American Journal of Psychiatry, 166*, 8–10.

Lamb, H. R., & Weinberger, L. E. (2005). The shift of psychiatric inpatient care from hospitals to jails and prisons. *Journal of the American Academy of Psychiatry Law, 33*, 529–534.

Lamb, H. R., Weinberger, L. E., & DeCuir, W. J., Jr. (2002). The police and mental health. *Psychiatric Services, 53*, 1266–1271.

Lasser, K., Boyd, J., Woolhandler, S., Himmelstein, D., McCormick, D., & Bor, D. (2000). Smoking and mental illness: A population-based prevalence study. *Journal of the American Medical Association, 284*, 2606–2610.

Lurigio, A. J., Fallon, J. R., & Dincin, J. (2000). Helping the mentally ill in jails adjust to community life: A description of a postrelease ACT program and its clients. *International Journal of Offender Therapy and Comparative Criminology, 44*, 532–548.

Meaningful employment for individuals with mental illness (Issue Brief). (2009). National Council for Community Behavioral Healthcare. Retrieved from http://www.thenationalcouncil.org/cs/employment_housing#issue%20briefs

Mechanic, D. (2008). *Mental health and social policy: Beyond managed care.* San Francisco, CA: Pearson Education.

National consensus statement on mental health recovery. (2009). Substance Abuse and Mental Health Services Administration. Retrieved from http://mentalhealth.samhsa.gov/publications/allpubs/sma05-4129/

Nichols, M. (2008, October 15). A national shame: The mentally ill homeless. *Anxiety, Panic, & Health: Living with Health, Wellness and Wholeness.* Retrieved from http://anxietypanichealth.com/2008/10/15/a-national-shame-the-mentally-ill-homeless/

Olsen, D. (2003). Influence and coercion: Relational and rights-based ethical approaches to forced psychiatric treatment. *Journal of Psychiatric and Mental Health Nursing, 10,* 705–712.

Padgett, D. K., Gulcur, L., & Tsemberis, S. (2006). Housing first services for people who are homeless with co-occurring serious mental illness and substance abuse. *Research on Social Work Practice, 16,* 74–83.

Petrila, J. (2009). Congress restores the Americans with Disabilities Act to its original intent. *Psychiatric Services, 60,* 878–879.

Petrila, J., Ridgely, M. S., & Borum, R. (2003). Debating outpatient commitment: Controversy, trends, and empirical data. *Crime & Delinquency, 49,* 157–172.

Position statement on housing and supports for individuals with mental illness. (2005). National Association of Mental Health Program Directors. Retrieved from http://www.nasmhpd.org/

Ridgway, P., & Zipple, A. (1990). The paradigm shift in residential services: From the linear continuum to supported housing approaches. *Psychosocial Rehabilitation Journal, 13*(4), 11–31.

Rosenson, M. (1993). Social work and the right of psychiatric patients to refuse medication: A family advocate's response. *Social Work, 38,* 107–112.

Stefan, S. (2001). *Unequal rights: Discrimination against people with mental disabilities and the Americans with Disabilities Act.* Washington, DC: American Psychological Association.

Thornicroft, G. (2006). *Shunned: Discrimination against people with mental illness.* London, UK: Oxford University Press.

Torrey, E. F., & Zdanowicz, M. (2001). Outpatient commitment: What, why, and for whom. *Psychiatric Services, 52,* 337–341.

U.S. Department of Health and Human Services (HHS), Substance Abuse and Mental Health Services Administration, Center for Mental Health Services, National Institutes of Health, National Institute of Mental Health. (1999). *Mental health: A report of the surgeon general.* Retrieved from http://www.surgeongeneral.gov/library/mentalhealth/summary.html

U.S. Department of Health and Human Services (HHS), New Freedom Commission on Mental Health (Final report). (2003). *Achieving the promise: Transforming mental health care in America.* Rockville, MD. Retrieved from http://govinfo.library.unt.edu/mentalhealthcommission/reports/FinalReport.htm

U.S. Department of Justice (DOJ). (2009). Bureau of Justice statistics. Retrieved from http://www.ojp.usdoj.gov/bjs/prisons.htm

Wireman, K. R. (2007). Preventing homelessness: A consumer perspective. *Journal of Primary Prevention, 28,* 205–212.

Zolnierek, C. D. (2007). Coercion and the mentally ill: Ethical perspectives. *American Psychiatric Nurses Association, 13,* 101–108. doi:10.1177/107839030730310

PART IV

Embedding Social Justice in Social Work Practice

24

CLIENT VOICE AND EXPERTISE IN PROMOTING SOCIAL JUSTICE

JASMIN SERIM

INTRODUCTION

The role of client voice in the formation and provision of social services can be understood in many ways: as a catalyst for empowerment, a guide for improving services, and a means for greater service accountability. Client voice can be incorporated into social services at the interpersonal level (between client and practitioner), at the program level (between groups of clients and social service agencies), and at the organizational level (research, planning, and policy). The common theme at each of these levels is the recognition of client expertise about the services she or he uses and needs. The capacity to capture and utilize this expertise has significant implications for both the ethics and efficacy of social work practice.

At their most effective, social work practices designed to amplify and respond to client voice can empower clients, improve the quality of services, and ensure that vital resources are reaching their intended recipients. At their least effective, efforts to involve clients can be tokenizing, misleading, and/or disappointing for both clients and agencies

(Beresford et al., 2011; Rutter, Manley, Weaver, Crawford, & Fulop, 2004; Woodford & Preston, 2011).

This chapter explores several approaches to client participation in social service organizations in terms of its utilization in the design, delivery, and evaluation of services as well as several implications for the training and education of future social work practitioners. It begins with two major references to client voice that appear in the *Code of Ethics of the National Association of Social Workers* (NASW, 2009) and in guidelines for effective evidence-based practice (EBP). The next section focuses on the meaning of client voice within the context of client participation by identifying common modalities and benefits as well as ideological approaches. While there is a growing body of literature on client participation in the United States, there is even more in the United Kingdom. Despite differing political and social contexts between the United States and the United Kingdom, there are many commonalities among the efforts to incorporate client perspective into social services. This chapter draws upon both in order to identify client voice implications for social work practice and education. The chapter concludes with a review of promising practices and several challenges facing client participation.

Definitions and Background

This chapter utilizes several terms that can be defined multiple ways, as well as some borrowed from critical theory. The meaning of social justice is discussed in reference to its place as a standard in the National Association of Social Workers (NASW) *Code of Ethics*. However, in a broader sense, client voice is linked to the promotion of social justice, conceptualized as an endeavor to identify and eradicate sources of oppression and injustice and facilitate the redistribution of resources to those who have historically been denied and disenfranchised. To alter the power dynamics that create and support systemic oppression, it is necessary for oppressed individuals and groups to gain greater access to resources, a process that will be further discussed as *empowerment*. Terms borrowed from critical theory include *marginalization* and *agency* as a way to enhance discourse around social services. Marginalization refers to the process by which a powerful dominant group controls access to resources through exclusion and stigmatization of other groups. Marginalization both stems from and is perpetuated by systemic oppression, and it speaks directly to the destructive effects of exclusion from dominant discourse. The ability of marginalized groups and individuals to challenge or confront oppressive forces and create viable change is known as *agency*, or the degree to which they are able to act as *agents* in their collective empowerment. In social work literature, it is important to note that "agency" is frequently used to describe organizations that provide social services. To avoid confusion, this chapter uses the term *organization* when referring to entities that provide social services.

Throughout this chapter, references are made to professionalized social work and professionalized knowledge. It is important to recognize that within the field of social work, there are multiple schools of thought that inform social workers ideas of the purpose of their work and the strategies they employ. These varying approaches to social work hold differing implications for client voice and participation, particularly as they relate to the value placed on client expertise. For many, Dr. Abraham Flexner's famed 1915 assertion that social work was not a profession represented a critical challenge: to gain legitimacy for social work practice by developing and identifying a unique body of knowledge and technical skills. Schools of social work functioned as a mechanism to provide this knowledge and skill set, distinguishing graduates as professionals and experts. However, as this chapter will discuss, some of this formalization has failed to address the expertise of clients, gained through lived experience.

It is necessary to note that throughout the social work history, there have also been movements that relied heavily on client expertise. The settlement house movement serves as an early example, in which social workers as providers of resources created spaces within impoverished communities to allow community members to define the services and resources they needed and to educate social workers on the nature and causes of the suffering they experienced. Social services developed through grassroots community organizing have historically relied largely on volunteers rather than paid professionals to identify and fight for rights, resources, and services based on the articulated needs of community members. Self-help agencies within the community mental health field have maintained that the design, delivery, and oversight of services by mental health consumers lead to effective practice and empowerment on the individual and community level.

This background is provided to acknowledge that within social work as a field, the concepts of client voice and participation are not new. However, their incorporation and implementation in more professionalized practice represent an area in which there is considerable room for development. This chapter will highlight client participation practices in a range of human service contexts, some more professionalized than others. Professionalism will be referenced where it carries direct implications for the usage of or barriers to client participation.

CLIENT VOICE AND SOCIAL WORK PRACTICE

Professionalized social work has long been concerned with the production of a unique body of knowledge and expertise to guide practice.

This approach seeks to ensure the provision of effective and ethical services through the creation of formalized principles, standards, and practices for social workers. Examples of this endeavor can be found in both the NASW's *Code of Ethics* and the growing attention to evidence-based practice (EBP). However, there remains a significant gap between the articulated interest in ethics and efficacy, and, the implementation of practices that are well informed and suited to meet the needs of clients (Gambrill, 2001, 2008). As the profession engages in ongoing efforts to define standards for effective and ethical practice, the importance of incorporating client perspectives holds a constant, if contentious, place in the discussion. The notion of clients as experts can be viewed by some as a challenge to professional expertise and by others as the hallmark of social services that are focused on meeting client needs.

The current interest in evidence-based practice (EBP) calls for increased accountability in the social work profession by formalizing expertise and identifying the elements of effective services based on three sources of information, namely, evidence from research, the tacit and explicit knowledge of practitioners, and the preferences and actions of the client (Gambrill, 2008; Sackett, Straus, & Richardson, 1997). Adapted from evidence-based medicine (EBM), EBP strives to ensure that interventions utilized with clients are as effective and individually appropriate as possible. While considerable attention has been given to deriving evidence from research and the professional expertise of the provider (Gambrill, 2008; Sackett, 1997), each of these sources gains its validity through the involvement of clients in participatory research and direct consultation (Sackett, 1997). In essence, the inclusion of the client perspective is intrinsic to the provision of evidence-based services according to the original concept of EBP. However, the incorporation of results from empirical research and clinical understanding of client characteristics receive far more attention in EBP than does client participation. The task of accessing and operationalizing client voice remains a challenge to both practitioners and researchers.

Throughout the history of social work, there has been great concern for the ethical nature of services provided to vulnerable populations. In creating the

Code of Ethics, the National Association of Social Workers (NASW) sought a comprehensive set of values, principles, and standards that could be used to train new social workers and ensure accountability of existing practitioners (Reamer, 1998). Given the broad spectrum of services that social workers provide, the *Code of Ethics* is unable to provide specific applications of its values, principles, and standards. Service standards do not, and possibly cannot, dictate the degree to which clients influence their services or specify mechanisms by which client perspectives are to be solicited, offered, or utilized. However, it is clear that client involvement is intrinsically linked to ethical practice.

Ethical Principles

Among the many values and ethical principles included in the *Code of Ethics*, "social justice" and "dignity and worth of the person" speak most directly to the need to incorporate client voice. The ethical principle associated with social justice reads as follows:

> Social workers pursue social change, particularly with and on behalf of vulnerable and oppressed individuals and groups of people. . . . These activities seek to promote sensitivity to and knowledge about oppression and cultural and ethnic diversity. Social workers strive to ensure access to needed information, services, and resources; equality of opportunity, and meaningful participation in decision making for all people. (NASW, 2009, p. 4).

If professional social workers are to accurately promote knowledge about oppression, it follows that their work needs to be informed by the lived experience of those who are oppressed. Client voice can be instrumental in identifying the information, services, and resources that are needed. As social workers "strive to ensure access," they rely on client perspectives to ensure that the information, services, and resources they provide effectively address the needs of their clients. It is clear that the *Code of Ethics* (NASW, 2009) includes within the principle of social justice "meaningful participation in decision making" as an integral mechanism by which those who have been marginalized gain access to necessary resources.

Similarly, the following value, "dignity and worth of the person," suggests that clients are to be treated with respect with regard to their individual preferences and differences and that their self-determination is to be promoted. In directing social workers to "seek to enhance clients' capacity and opportunity to address their own needs" (NASW, 2009, p. 4), it is clear that social workers are expected to work not only on behalf of clients but also in support of clients as they articulate and combat the injustices they experience. Many other stated values, including "importance of human relationships," also promote the idea that clients are not simply passive recipients of services but partners in the process of service delivery.

Ethical Standards

In addition to ethical principles, the NASW *Code of Ethics* identifies standards for service, many of which refer to the responsibilities of social workers to their clients, especially the promotion of client well-being and interests as the primary responsibility of social workers. The standard on "self-determination" calls for clients to retain the power to identify their own treatment or service goals, with the exception of instances in which a "serious, foreseeable and imminent risk" is posed to themselves or others (NASW, 2009, p. 5). While professional judgment of social workers regarding the definition of risk supersedes client self-determination, the goal is to assist clients in working toward client-defined outcomes. The "cultural competence" and "social diversity" standards suggest that social workers not only respect the cultural differences among clients but also are prepared to provide "culturally sensitive" services (NASW, 2009). While considerable diversity exists among both client groups and social work practitioners, it is important to recognize that there are often great sociodemographic differences between clients and social workers, particularly in more professionalized settings. Ensuring that individual practitioners are aware of cultural norms and meanings held by clients is an ongoing process in which the expertise of clients needs to be incorporated into the training of providers. While some approaches to "cultural competency" have suggested that providers gain expertise through

rigorous study of cultures and societies as groups, this approach has been criticized for its inability to capture the heterogeneity that exists within groups (Clark, 2000). Instead, it is suggested that social workers "adopt the stance of the learner" (Clark, 2000, p. 7) as opposed to that of the expert, remaining open to the valuable insight offered through client voice. This approach to culturally sensitive practice has also been referred to as "cultural humility," and it depends on responsive human service organizations that actively seek out client views of what constitutes culturally sensitive service.

Defining Client Participation

Beyond the ethics and evidence-based practices associated with worker-client interaction, the involvement of clients in the design, implementation, and evaluation of services has received increasing attention in both the United States and United Kingdom. The implications, benefits, and logistics of client involvement have been explored from many vantage points. Despite the lack of consensus on what constitutes client participation (Beresford & Croft, 2008; Beresford et al., 2011), government mandates tied to various social services in the United States and United Kingdom have required that organizations involve clients and community members in decision-making processes. Table 24.1 reviews the terminology and benefits associated with common modalities of client participation in social work practice, education, and research.

As illustrated in Table 24.1, the terms *patient, client, consumer*, and *service user* have different connotations as to the degree of service recipient empowerment in public, for-profit, and nonprofit organizations. The role of the patient is generally thought of as passive, receiving diagnosis and treatment from an expert professional. *Client*, on the other hand, can be viewed as a more neutral term for individuals accessing services, but it also reflects a level of powerlessness, as there is a lack of consensus on the rights of clients to define their services (Mizrahi et al., 2009). *Consumer* is a term that has intentionally replaced *client* in some areas of social welfare, as a way to promote active choice and autonomy (Mizrahi et al., 2009; Tower, 1994). As

Table 24.1   Client Participation Terminology, Modalities, and Benefits

	Definitions
Patient	Most commonly in medical and psychiatric settings and associated with a biomedical model of health services (McLaughlin, 2009), patients are often thought of as passive recipients of services, selected and provided by expert practitioners.
Client	Most commonly utilized term in social work literature and practice but critiqued as carrying connotations of passivity and powerlessness similar to *patient.* (Mizrahi, Humphreys, & Torres, 2009).
Consumer	Increasingly used in social services, particularly in the mental health field. Consumer is thought to convey active choice and autonomy in the selection of and participation in services (Mizrahi et al., 2009; Tower, 1994).
Service user	Primarily used in the United Kingdom, this term is thought to go even further than *consumer* in making explicit the right of those receiving services to have a voice in the planning, provision, and evaluation of services that they receive (McLaughlin, 2009).
	Benefits
Client empowerment	Empowerment can be understood as a process in which individuals or groups increase their ability to enact positive change in their lives and confront injustice. Clients may be empowered through the act of participating in decisions that impact the services they utilize as well as seeing tangible change that results from their efforts.
Increased responsiveness to client need	There has been significant empirical evidence that client participation is linked to the increased responsiveness of services to client need (LeRoux, 2009b). This benefits both clients and social service agencies, allowing for efficient and effective allocation of resources.
Improvement of service system	Above the level of individual service agencies, client participation in policy making, research, and social work education may allow for systemic change, creating an environment in which social work can be more effective in challenging social injustice.
Greater accountability to stakeholders	Participation of clients and community members can provide a way for public and private social service organizations to be held accountable to external stakeholders, including both clients and funders.
	Roles and Modalities
Client operated services	These are services that involve current or former clients at all levels of planning, management, and provision of services. Also known as consumer-operated services, consumer-delivered services (Salzer, 2002), or self-help agencies (Segal, Silverman, & Temkin, 2010), these organizations are most prevalent in the mental health field.
Clients on boards of directors	As members of boards of directors, clients are able to bring their understanding of the organization's constituency to programmatic and organization level decision making. This form of participation is not especially common, but it may be most frequent in mental health, disability, and aging services (LeRoux, 2009b; Tower, 1994).
Client advisory boards	Identified as the leading source of client involvement in mental health services, HIV/AIDS prevention and treatment, homelessness and housing, and child welfare (LeRoux, 2009b). Client advisory boards can be made up entirely of clients or can include a broader stakeholder base of community members (Bryan, Jones, Allen, & Collins-Camargo, 2007; LeRoux, 2009b).

(Continued)

Table 24.1   Continued

Task groups and planning committees	Social service organizations may seek client input in the planning of campaigns for public education or advocacy, fundraising events or time-limited projects (LeRoux, 2009b).
Client surveys	Client surveys are utilized by many social service organizations to capture satisfaction with services as well as client outcomes as a measure of program performance. This can be thought of as a form of research conducted internally within organizations, and it may or may not include client voice in the formation of survey questions.
Clients in social work education	Client input in social work education may take the form of leading and/or participating in training programs, designing course curricula, or participating in the evaluation of courses and students (Beresford & Croft, 2008).
Participants in research process	Clients may be involved in all phases of research, including identifying project objectives, selecting methodologies, adapting materials and consent procedures to fit the needs of the population, recruiting participants, collecting data, analyzing data, translating findings into educational materials, and disseminating findings and materials (Harris, 2005). In the United States, research practices that explicitly include clients or members of the community served are known as participatory action research (Taylor, Braverman, & Hammel, 2004) or community-based participatory research.

governments (United States and United Kingdom) increasingly seek to contract the provision of social services with the private sector, consumers may also be referred to as "customers," exercising choice within a "marketized" context and receiving services that are funded by out-of-pocket fees or government-subsidized benefits (McLaughlin, 2009; Tower, 1994). Finally, for many who use the term *consumer*, there is recognition that firsthand experience provides expertise that is more valuable than professional expertise in understanding the needs of those receiving services (Tower, 1994). Primarily used in the United Kingdom, *service user* is thought to go even further in making explicit the right of those receiving services to have a voice in the planning, provision, and evaluation of the services they receive (McLaughlin, 2009). The United Kingdom, as a welfare state, provides a different set of societal values related to the rights held by those receiving services.

Empowerment has been understood as "a process whereby persons who belong to a stigmatized social category throughout their lives can be assisted to develop and increase skills in the exercise of interpersonal influence and the performance of valued social roles" (Solomon, 1976, p. 6). The inclusion

of client voice, then, can be understood as essential to promoting empowerment among stigmatized client groups, allowing clients to influence the terms and dimensions of the services they receive. The benefits of client participation include (a) the empowerment of the individual client or client groups, (b) increased responsiveness of services to client needs, (c) improvement of the social service system at large, and (d) greater accountability in social service agencies to stakeholders including clients and funders (Hardina, 2004; LeRoux, 2009a; Rutter et al., 2004).

Client involvement can be facilitated through various modalities that incorporate client voice in social service agencies, social work training programs, and social work research processes. In Table 24.1, the first five modalities are listed in order of the degree of influence that clients can exercise in enacting the changes they wish to see. Clients hold the most power in client-operated services, where they are involved in decision making at all levels as well as the provision of services (Salzer, 2002). In these services, client empowerment is generally a stated goal, intrinsically linked to the ability of clients to shape the services they receive (Segal & Silverman, 2002; Segal et al., 2010). Further, where more traditional social service models may position clients and providers as mutually exclusive groups, client provided services pose an inherent challenge to this dichotomy and the power dynamics it supports.

When clients serve as members of boards of directors, their perspective can influence organization-level decisions. This level of participation is relatively uncommon but allows client participants to enact meaningful change. Client advisory boards can provide valuable input to an organization, but the degree of power and influence such boards have over organizational decisions varies. These advisory groups can be made up entirely of clients or can include a broader array of stakeholders that includes community members (Bryan et al., 2007; LeRoux, 2009b). Involvement of clients in time-limited projects (e.g., planning advocacy campaigns or fundraising events) is another modality for client participation. However, as this form limits the duration and scope of participation, clients do not have as much authority to direct or change services. Further, the temporary creation of a committee does little to disrupt the larger organizational structure (Rutter et al., 2004). Client input may also be captured through the use of client satisfaction and program performance surveys. Client surveys allow for the participation of a high volume of clients, capturing diverse arrays of client perspectives. However, unless survey participants see tangible changes that result from their input, surveys may not promote a feeling among clients that their perspective is truly valued, or, that they have real influence over the terms of the services they receive (Beresford et al., 2011).

The last two modalities of client participation involve social work research and education. It is difficult to determine the level of agency that clients may possess due to the delayed impact of research and education on services that will be provided in the future as opposed to an immediate impact on services experienced by participating clients. The level of involvement of clients in research can vary from consultation to collaboration, to complete control of the process by service users, or clients (McLaughlin, 2009). Known in the United States as participatory action research or community-based participatory research (CBPR), these research practices seek to

rebalance power dynamics between professional expertise and client or community expertise (Taylor et al., 2004). Including clients in social work education has been identified by clients themselves as an effective way to enact lasting change in the culture and practices of social work (Beresford & Croft, 2008; Stevens & Tanner, 2006). By creating an opportunity for students and practitioners to interact with service users outside of the workplace environment, an important power dynamic is shifted, where service users are positioned as knowledgeable experts rather than passive recipients, and social work students are able to gain insight into the types of services that clients prefer (Beresford & Croft, 2008). Based on the literature, this educational practice appears to be more common in the United Kingdom than in the United States.

RATIONALE FOR CLIENT INVOLVEMENT

As there are multiple practical approaches to the involvement of clients in research, policy, and practice, so there are differing ideological approaches to client participation, each with its own implications for how and why clients and service providers participate in these processes. This analysis focuses on two models, namely, the managerialist-consumerist approach and the democratic approach (Beresford, 2005; Beresford & Croft, 2008; McLaughlin, 2009).

Managerialist-Consumerist Approach

The primary goal of the managerialist-consumerist approach to client involvement is to collect input from service users to inform the system as a whole (Beresford, 2005). This is the dominant model of client involvement in social services (both in the United States and the United Kingdom) where clients and/or community members function as external stakeholders who provide data for discretionary use by the service system (Beresford & Croft, 2008). It has been termed *consumerist* based on the managerial emphasis on service efficiency and effectiveness and its tendency to equate the two. Though most social services are provided by nonprofit organizations, efficiency and effectiveness (particularly when conflated) are concepts derived from the for-profit sector; when the organizational goal is to maximize profitability, efficiency and efficacy may be synonymous. However, within the nonprofit human service context, practices to increase efficacy may not increase efficiency, and vice versa. Client participation is a salient example, as it requires additional time and resources, but it is utilized to ensure that services are effective. Client participation in the managerialist-consumerist model can be understood as playing the function of "market testing and feedback" where clients act as consultants, rather than partners, in organizational decision-making processes (Beresford & Croft, 2008).

The managerialist-consumerist philosophy of client participation is a "top-down" approach, originating from policy or organizational mandates as opposed to clients or advocacy groups (Beresford & Croft, 2008; Mizrahi et al., 2009). In top-down models, the social hierarchy that privileges professional expertise over client expertise remains intact, supporting what is known as a "power over" paradigm (Mizrahi et al., 2009). Within this paradigm,

> The response to the client voice is often subjected to a process of invasive labeling and hierarchical valuation derived from powerful social authorities who have assigned client culpability and client blame with reference to certain categories of service recipients. (Mizrahi et al., 2009, pp. 37–38)

Within such hierarchical models, it is apparent that clients have little if any control over how or whether their input is utilized.

Democratic Approach

In contrast to the managerialist-consumerist approach, the democratic approach focuses on increasing the agency of clients in the services they receive and in their lives as a whole. Developed by movements of clients and advocates, this approach has been described as explicitly political, calling for a redistribution of power and resources (Beresford & Croft, 2008). In this model, clients function as agents of social change, rather than as sources of data. The democratic model is a "bottom-up," or grassroots, approach designed to amplify the voices of those who traditionally hold the least power (Beresford & Croft, 2008). In bottom-up models of client participation, the driving motivation comes from clients or advocacy groups (Mizrahi et al., 2009). The democratic approach questions numerous aspects of social work practice, research, and education, by calling attention to the following issues identified by P. Beresford and S. Croft (2008).

1. *What is the nature of knowledge formation and knowledge claims in social work?* The democratic approach leads us to question the types of knowledge that inform social work practice. To what extent is it derived from or aligned with the knowledge of the populations and communities served?

2. *How should social workers be educated and trained for their roles, and by whom?* Traditionally, social workers are educated in professional degree programs as well as ongoing training provided in social service organizations. The democratic approach asks what types of knowledge inform course content and to what extent to they reflect client voice? What criteria are used to assess success in the completion of social work education, and who determines these criteria? To what degree do current or former service users hold teaching and training positions in academia and social service agencies or participate in educational or training programs?

3. *What and whose knowledge should social workers be informed by?* Again, this question examines the sources of information guiding social work interventions. According to EBP, social workers should incorporate evidence from research, their own professional expertise, and the expertise of the client in decision making. The democratic approach encourages social workers to examine their capacity to hear and incorporate client expertise.

4. *How are social work practices researched and evaluated and by whom?* Involving service users in all levels of research, including evaluation, may require significant investment of time and money as compared to more traditional approaches (Harris, 2005). As such, it is safe to assume that most service evaluation research processes are controlled by

professionals. However, involving former or current clients in research and evaluation practices may result in substantial and meaningful shifts in the research questions developed, the methodologies employed, and the interpretation of the findings.

5. *What is the purpose and nature of social work practice?* The democratic approach is explicitly concerned with the reallocation of power and resources. Thus, it pushes social workers to question both the means and the ends of social work practice to determine whether they are challenging the root causes of injustice experienced by clients, or, simply ameliorating the discomfort experienced in an unjust system.

6. *What is the nature of social work recruitment and employment policies?* The ways in which social service organizations recruit and hire social workers are clearly impacted by the degree to which service-user experience is valued in comparison with the possession of advanced degrees. Further, to what degree do organizations screen candidates for their understanding of client capacity, a key tenant of the democratic approach?

7. *Who shapes and controls social work education and social service institutions?* At a macro level, the democratic approach suggests a need to identify those who make decisions that impact social

work education and social service systems as a whole. Again, it is important to examine the representation of current or former service users among these ranks and question the extent to which these voices (or lack thereof) have an impact.

These questions raise significant issues for the social work profession and its capacity to be responsive and accountable to those whom it serves, by examining the degree to which client experience and voice shape the array of processes involved. Informed by the democratic approach, these questions examine all aspects of social work processes in order to reconfigure the control of power and resources and how these resources are dispersed: to whom, by whom, and who dictates the terms of this process.

EXAMPLES OF MANAGERIALIST-CONSUMERIST AND DEMOCRATIC APPROACHES

Within the various fields of practice addressed by human services, distinct discourses, policies, and practices have emerged to involve clients in the planning and delivery of services. For example, Table 24.2 illustrates participatory practices related to both democratic and managerialist-consumerist approaches to client participation in selected fields of practice.

Table 24.2   Client Participation in Fields of Social Welfare Practice

Social Work Subarea	Managerial-Consumerist (Top-Down) Approaches to Client Participation	Democratic (Bottom-Up) Approaches to Client Participation
Mental Health	**Mental Health Advisory Councils** • Established by mental health agencies in the 1970s in response to government mandate • Called for participation of mental health consumers and their family members in oversight of agency work • Participants provide input but do not have power to enforce changes • Main objective: improvement of services	**Self-Help Agencies (SHAs)** • Consumer-run organizations • Involve consumers at every level of organizational decision making • Participation linked to increased feelings of self-efficacy and understood as integral to recovery • Main objective: consumer empowerment

(Continued)

Table 24.2 Continued

Social Work Subarea	Managerial-Consumerist (Top-Down) Approaches to Client Participation	Democratic (Bottom-Up) Approaches to Client Participation
Physical and Developmental Disability	**Protection and Advocacy for Individuals With Developmental Disabilities (PADD)** • All states must have PADD program, mandated by federal government • Government employees act on behalf of clients (e.g., investigate reports of neglect or abuse) • Annual client and community review • Main objective: monitor and improve responsiveness of service system	**Independent Living Movement** • User-led movement within U.K.'s disabled people's movement • Formed in response to service user dissatisfaction with institutionalized care • Focus on supporting service users in achieving the level of autonomy they seek • Main objective: support and empower service users
Child Welfare*	**Citizen Review Panels (CRPs)** • Mandated by 1996 CAPTA Amendments • Meant to represent communities served by child welfare agencies, although rarely include birth parents • Evaluate welfare agencies and submit reports to federal government • Main objective: increased accountability	**Child Welfare Organizing Project** • Organizes birth parents around their rights within the child welfare system • Advocates for greater visibility and participation of birth parents in welfare agencies and their boards • Main objectives: empowering birth parents and creating systemic change
Poverty	**Community Action Projects (CAPs)** • Part of the 1960s War on Poverty, that promoted the "maximum feasible participation" of the poor • Participants provided input but often had little control over how or where it was used • Federal funding to CAPs was cut when recommendations threatened interests of political elites • Main objectives: alleviation of poverty through enhanced feelings of social inclusion	**Family Independence Initiative (FII)** • Organization that facilitates structured opportunities for families in poverty to generate solutions for themselves and their communities • Maintains that the families are the best experts. FII employees are not allowed to create action plans for clients, but they provide support • Main objectives: alleviation of poverty through collective empowerment of poor families

NOTE: *Discussions of client participation in child welfare have posited biological parents as "client," rather than the youth involved in the child welfare system. This may reflect the fact that age plays a further limiting role in the ability of young clients to participate in the design, delivery, and evaluation of services they receive.

CHALLENGES FACING CLIENT PARTICIPATION

Despite numerous benefits to clients, agencies, and the social welfare field, the implementation of client participation remains challenging in many ways. The barriers and tensions impacting the meaningful involvement of service users in organizational decision making range from ideological to pragmatic and threaten the efficacy and feasibility of client participation in social service organizations. These tensions include balancing stakeholder interests, meaningful involvement rather than tokenism, client heterogeneity, internal politics in advocacy groups, and the allocation of adequate time and funding.

Balancing Stakeholder Interests

It has been recognized in both the United Kingdom and the United States that an increasing proportion of social services is being provided through the nonprofit and for-profit sectors rather than public agencies, and funders have become increasingly powerful stakeholders. (Beresford & Croft, 2008; LeRoux, 2009a). The degree to which a funding source supports and/or requires client participation in organizational and programmatic decision making may play a significant role in the types of client involvement employed (LeRoux, 2009a).

In the United States, social services are typically funded through a combination of government and foundation grants, individual donors, and fees for services. As is the case in the United Kingdom, client participation is often tied to government funding as a mechanism for ensuring accountability (LeRoux, 2009b). Agencies operating on a fee-for-service basis are also likely to seek client input, reflecting a managerialist-consumerist approach (LeRoux, 2009a).

Meaningful Involvement Versus Tokenism

Client participation clearly holds the potential to provide great benefits to both clients and organizations. However, such participation may be seen as tokenizing when clients are consulted with regard to decisions that have already been made, when their input is not utilized, or when some are intentionally left out of the process (Woodford & Preston, 2011). Such limitations may be the result of a fear on the part of organizational leadership that greater power and involvement in the hands of clients could lead to greater scrutiny or risk for the organization or raise the expectations of clients (Woodford & Preston, 2011). Despite these potential risks, the primary benefit of client participation is the feedback that could lead to meaningful service improvements and increased responsiveness to client need. Similarly, increased expectations on the part of clients could reflect both individual and collective empowerment among clients as they gain greater access to resources.

Another aspect of meaningful involvement is the degree to which clients gain control over the terms of their involvement and the outcomes pursued. While the benefits of client participation may be apparent for human service organizations, participation does not always present immediate benefits to clients. For example, clients may complete surveys that allow a social service agency to demonstrate that they have met grant requirements, allowing for continued funding. However, client participation and input may or may not result in the implementation of changes called for by the clients. In most cases, organizations define the degree to which clients can participate, and organizational priorities may conflict with those of the clients themselves. When this is the case, there can be attrition among client participants who find that the process neglects or falls short of their needs (Beresford, 2005; Rutter et al., 2004).

Reflecting Heterogeneity in Client Groups

Despite efforts to promote client participation, some client voices may be more clearly and commonly heard than others. Outreach to promote client participation often garners more responses from those within client groups who hold positions of social privilege (Stevens & Tanner, 2006). The failure to elicit the same response from more marginalized members of client groups has been attributed to the practical challenges presented by the time commitments involved or scheduling and transportation issues, as well as a lack of trust related to discrimination against stigmatized client groups on the part of providers and clients' lack of identification with those in organizational leadership (Beresford & Croft, 2008; Hernandez, Robson, & Sampson, 2010; Stevens & Tanner, 2006). It is important to recognize that efforts to solicit client perspective show a need to take into account the vast diversity within client groups; positioning the voice of the most privileged clients as representative of all clients serves only to further marginalize those who may experience the greatest unmet needs.

Power Dynamics Within Advocacy Groups

Advocacy groups made up of clients, family members, social workers, and other concerned community members have been instrumental in securing client rights and increasing access to services for many vulnerable populations (Beresford & Croft, 2008;

Mizrahi et al., 2009). However, within such groups, there are differences of power and, at times, differing objectives. For example, the U.K. Independent People's Movement has been recognized as a service-user-led movement, advocating for the disabled. However, disabled individuals and their family members have historically disagreed on aspects of independent living, as family members feared for the safety of the disabled and/or had to take on greater support roles as disabled individuals moved out of institutionalized care (Beresford et al., 2011). The strengths-based nature of a client-centered approach can be undermined when advocates for vulnerable groups view the capacities of service users as limited.

Adequate Time and Funding

Studies of client participation initiatives have consistently noted that the meaningful involvement of clients requires additional time and resources (Beresford et al., 2011; Harris, 2005; Rutter et al., 2004; Stevens & Tanner, 2006; Woodford & Preston, 2011). While these expenditures may result in the more effective allocation of resources in the long run, the resources necessary to engage clients as partners may conflict with other service funder priorities (Hardina, 2005; LeRoux, 2009a, 2009b). User-led organizations often face particular challenges in securing adequate funding, despite their success in reaching and establishing trust with service users (Beresford & Croft, 2008).

PROMISING EMPOWERMENT PRACTICES

While there are many recognized benefits of client participation, the one that resonates most clearly with the priorities and principles identified in the *Code of Ethics* is that of client empowerment. Researchers have identified promising practices that contribute to the success of client involvement initiatives in facilitating client empowerment (Beresford et al., 2011; Hardina, 2005; Woodford & Preston, 2011). If clients are to influence not only the services they receive but also the ways in which they participate in planning and implementation, then it is important to recognize that there cannot be

a one-size-fits-all approach to client participation. Still, it is useful to highlight some approaches to client involvement that have been found to enhance impact, particularly in the collective and individual self-efficacy of clients. These include transparency, the involvement of clients at all levels of decision making, buy-in among clients and all levels of staff, and ongoing evaluation.

Clients' empowerment through participation stems both from articulating an understood need and seeing the implementation of their expressed ideas. For this to occur, it is necessary for researchers, agencies, and practitioners to communicate openly and honestly with clients about the influence they possess through participation. This transparency enables clients to make an informed decision about whether or not their participation is a beneficial use of their own personal resources (Beresford et al., 2011; Rutter et al., 2004).

The involvement of clients at all levels of organizational and programmatic decision making lends itself to client empowerment, as it affords former and current service users a greater opportunity to utilize input in tangible, meaningful ways. In addition, the ability of clients to identify with those in leadership positions may increase their willingness to engage in participatory processes, which in turn allows for a broader representation of client voice.

For client participation initiatives to be successful, both participating clients and service providers need to value the process and demonstrate a shared sense of its importance (Beresford et al., 2011; Hardina, 2004). Empowerment-focused client involvement is, by necessity, informed by a belief in the capacity of clients to contribute to positive change individually and collectively. This shared understanding motivates both clients and social workers to expend the additional resources needed to engage in the challenging task of shared decision making.

As client participation has been found to be most beneficial when clients participate in ongoing rather than time-limited ways, it follows that the regular and ongoing collection of feedback from clients can ensure that the practice of client involvement is serving its intended purposes. Further, the involvement of clients in formal evaluation of services can both empower clients and enlighten service providers who seek to prioritize and demonstrate responsiveness to client needs.

CONCLUSION

Social work literature and practice guidelines contain many references to the importance of client involvement and empowerment. The tensions and best practices in the implementation of client participation are often explicitly tied to differing service philosophies. The recognition of social work as a profession has historically been defined by the possession of a unique body of professionalized knowledge. However, the recognition of the lived experience of clients as "expertise" can challenge the wisdom of strict adherence to knowledge produced by professionals. It is clear that the ethics and efficacy of the social work profession are inherently linked to its practitioners' ability to listen and respond to client need, as most accurately expressed through the voices of clients themselves. This challenge raises questions for further research and discussion, several of which are noted below:

How can client voice be better operationalized for more meaningful inclusion in the Code of Ethics *and the promotion of evidence-based practice?* While both the *Code of Ethics* and models of EBP serve as guides for the profession and both reference the importance of client perspective, significant gaps remain in practitioner understanding of how to capture and utilize client voice.

What types of client participation practices are most beneficial to both clients and organizations? Social service organizations often engage in client participation practices that are linked to accountability to funders (LeRoux, 2009a), but attrition occurs among client participants when these practices do not also allow for empowerment. There is an ongoing need to identify practices that address the needs of clients and human service organizations in order to create more meaningful and sustained participation.

How do we bridge the gap between client and funder perspectives in defining effective *services?* There are often significant differences in the lived experiences of those who fund human service organizations and those who receive services, which may inform very different ideas about the nature of services needed. As funders hold increasing power over the way services are shaped, efforts to familiarize them with the articulated needs of clients become a vital way to amplify client voice.

How can representatives of client voice be solicited in ways that allow for a full range of representation, rather than selecting the most privileged of the group? If studies have found that client participation recruitment efforts receive the greatest response from those in client groups with the most social privilege, then it is clear that solicitation practices and opportunities for involvement need to be expanded in order to reach out to and engage more marginalized clients.

How do we address the "power-over paradigm" *in social work practice and education?* As the gatekeepers of communal and necessary resources, social workers hold power in their interactions with clients. However, social justice principles call for the need to challenge, rather than reinforce, existing power dynamics. For social workers to effectively address social injustice, their education must include awareness of the power they possess as well as strategies for using power *with*, rather than *over* clients.

How do we make sense of client "rights," *during a time of diminishing sense of social obligation to provide for those in need and a diminishing political support for social services as entitlements?* While this chapter did not focus on client rights as a policy issue, the ability of clients to shape the services they receive is clearly an issue of rights. In both the United States and the United Kingdom, there has been a move away from the welfare state model, accompanied by greater emphasis on individualism and the so-called free market (Beresford & Croft, 2008; Humphreys & Rappaport, 1993). In this context, public human service funding is repeatedly cut, resulting in increased dependence on client fees and private funding. This dependency may lead organizations to prioritize the interests of funders and paying clients over the voices of clients who do not have the resources to pay for the services that they need. Discussion of client participation has frequently been linked to literature on citizen participation and notions of citizen rights. If social services are not guaranteed as civic entitlements, how do social workers and the public conceptualize the rights of service users? While outside of the scope of the present analysis, this is a vital question for further research to contextualize client participation in the human service sector and address larger barriers it may face in working toward social justice.

REFERENCES

Beresford, P. (2005). Theory and practice of user involvement in research: Making the connection with public policy and practice. In L. Lowes & I. Hulatt, (Eds.), *Involving service users in health and social care research* (pp. 6–16), London, UK: Routledge.

Beresford, P., & Croft, S. (2008). Democratising social work—A key element of innovation: From "client" as object, to service user as producer. *Innovation Journal: The Public Sector Innovation Journal, 13*(1), 1–22.

Beresford, P., Fleming, J., Glynn, M., Bewley, C., Croft, S., Branfield, F., & Postle, K. (2011). *Supporting people: Towards a person-centered approach.* Bristol, UK: Policy Press.

Bryan, V., Jones, B., Allen, E., & Collins-Camargo, C. (2007). Civic engagement or token participation? Perceived impact of the citizen review panel initiative. *Children and Youth Services Review, 29,* 1286–1300.

Clark, J. (2000). *Beyond empathy: An ethnographic approach to cross-cultural social work practice* (Unpublished doctoral dissertation). University of Toronto, Ontario, Canada.

Gambrill, E. (2001). Social work: An authority-based profession. *Research on Social Work Practice, 11*(2), 166–175.

Gambrill, E. (2008). Providing more effective, ethical services: The philosophy and process of evidence-based (-informed) practice. In D. Lindsey & A. Shlonsky (Eds.), *Child welfare research: Advances for practice and policy* (pp. 51–65). New York, NY: Oxford University Press.

Hardina, D. (2004). Linking citizen participation to empowerment practice. *Journal of Community Practice, 11*(4), 11–38.

Hardina, D. (2005). Ten characteristics of empowerment-oriented social service organizations. *Administration in Social Work, 29*(3), 23–42.

Harris, M. (2005). Service user involvement at all stages of the research process. In L. Lowes & I. Hualatt (Eds.), *Involving service users in health and social care research* (pp. 190–198). London, UK: Routledge.

Hernandez, L., Robson, P., & Sampson, A. (2010). Towards integrated participation: Involving seldom heard users of social care services. *British Journal of Social Work, 40,* 714–736.

Humphreys, K., & Rappaport, J. (1993). From the community mental health movement to the War on Drugs: A study in the definition of social problems. *American Psychologist, 48* (8), 892–901.

LeRoux, K. (2009a). Managing stakeholder demands: Balancing responsiveness to clients and funding agents in nonprofit social service organizations. *Administration and Society, 41*(2), 158–184.

LeRoux, K. (2009b). Paternalistic or participatory governance? Examining opportunities for client participation in nonprofit social service organizations. *Public Administration Review, 69*(3), 504–517.

McLaughlin, H. (2009). *Service-user research in health and social care.* London, UK: Sage.

Mizrahi, T., Humphreys, M. L., & Torres, D. (2009). The social construction of client participation: The evolution and transformation of the role of service recipients in child welfare and mental disabilities. *Journal of Sociology and Social Welfare, 36*(2), 35–61.

National Association of Social Workers (NASW). (2009). *Code of ethics of the National Association of Social Workers.* Washington, DC: NASW.

Reamer, F. G. (1998). *The evolution of social work ethics* (Faculty Publications Paper No. 170). Retrieved from http://digitalcommons.ric.edu/facultypublications/170

Rutter, D., Manley, C., Weaver, T., Crawford, M. J., & Fulop, N. (2004). Patients or partners? Case studies of user involvement in the planning and delivery of adult mental health services in London. *Social Science and Medicine, 58,* 1973–1984.

Sackett, D. L., Straus, S. E., & Richardson, W. S. (1997). *Evidence-based medicine: How to practice and teach.* New York, NY: Churchill Livingston.

Salzer, M. A. (2002). Consumer-delivered services as a best practice in mental health care delivery and the development of practice guidelines. *Psychiatric Rehabilitation Skills, 6*(3), 355–382.

Segal, S. P., & Silverman, C. (2002). Determinants of client outcomes in self-help agencies. *Psychiatric Services, 53*(3), 304–309.

Segal, S. P., Silverman, C., & Temkin, T. L. (2010). Self-help and community mental health agency outcomes: A recovery-focused randomized controlled trial. *Psychiatric Services, 61*(9), 905–910.

Solomon, B. (1976). *Black empowerment: Social work in oppressed communities*. New York, NY: Columbia University Press.

Stevens, S., & Tanner, D. (2006). Involving service users in the teaching and learning of social work students: Reflections on experience. *Social Work Education, 25*(4), 360–371.

Taylor, R. R., Braverman, B., & Hammel, J. (2004). Developing and evaluating community-based services through participatory action research: Two case examples. *American Journal of Occupational Therapy, 58*(1), 73–82.

Tower, K. D. (1994). Consumer-centered social work practice: Restoring client self-determination. *Social Work, 39*(2), 191–196.

Woodford, M. R., & Preston, S. (2011). Developing a strategy to meaningfully engage stakeholders in program/policy planning: A guide for human services managers and practitioners. *Journal of Community Practice, 19*(2), 159–174.

25

SOCIAL JUSTICE AND THE ROLE OF NONPROFIT HUMAN SERVICE ORGANIZATIONS IN AMPLIFYING CLIENT VOICE

KELLY LEROUX

INTRODUCTION

It is a well-known fact that individuals with more education and money participate at higher rates in virtually every aspect of civic and political life (Brady, Verba, & Schlozman, 1995; Rosenstone & Hansen, 1993). Socioeconomic disparities in political participation rates perpetuate a class-based bias in public policy in which the voices of the poor and marginalized often go unheard in public discourse. As a result, the interests of marginalized groups remain underrepresented in policy outcomes and in the allocation of public resources. Macro-level social work practice emerged in the late 19th and early 20th centuries with an emphasis on organizational and community-level activities designed to address these disparities and to promote greater community and social justice (Schneider & Lester, 2001). Under the auspices of nonprofit human service organizations, macro-level social work activities seek to promote community change, organizing and

mobilizing marginalized groups, and, influencing public policy for the benefit of underrepresented segments of society.

Many in our society are plagued by economic injustice, racism, discrimination, and oppression. These social injustices result largely from deeply embedded inequalities in the American opportunity structure. From federal tax policies that benefit the wealthiest individuals to state budget cuts that drastically downsize Medicaid benefits, to local zoning ordinances that result in de facto racial segregation, injustices are visible throughout the policy system. Through their embrace of social justice as a core value of the profession, social workers can play an important role in challenging the public policies that result in and sustain these inequities.

Nonprofit organizations also have a special role to play in combating these inequities by serving as the voice for their client groups through advocacy. As Hoefer (2006) suggests, advocacy is the key to achieving social justice. While advocacy carried out by a social worker intervening on behalf of a client may produce positive change for that individual, broader social change is accomplished through class advocacy, which gives voice to entire groups affected by a particular social condition or public policy (Ezell, 2001). In representing the needs of their clients before lawmakers (legislative advocacy), nonprofits ensure that client voice gets expressed in the policy-making arena. Nonprofits also amplify client voice through education campaigns that raise public awareness of the cause they represent (cause advocacy). In either case, nonprofits can be particularly effective instruments of social change when they work together with mission-similar organizations to build advocacy coalitions that pursue social justice on behalf of their common clients. For example, Hale (2011) demonstrated how a national network of nonprofit organizations was influential in diffusing drug courts throughout the states in the late 1980s and, in the process, reframed drug use as a medical and psychosocial problem requiring treatment, shifting the emphasis away from it as a criminal issue.

This chapter examines the role of nonprofit human service organizations as vehicles for amplifying client voice where nonprofits serve as civic intermediaries by linking citizen-clients to governing systems and political processes. Nonprofit human service organizations can mobilize clients for political action related to specific issues and events by providing them with political education that can include participation in group decision-making processes (LeRoux, 2007). This chapter is focused primarily on the different ways that human service organizations give expression to client voice, including advocacy organizations and community organizing groups that promote social change.

While this chapter emphasizes organizational efforts to promote client voice, it is also important to acknowledge the "person-is-political" perspective which combines or integrates micro and macro social work roles (Netting, Kettner, McMurtry, & Thomas, 2012). The commitment to social justice and the belief in the dignity and worth of every person are commonly shared social work values, regardless of whether one's orientation is toward individuals or organizational and community practice. Indeed, the high rates of political participation demonstrated by social workers transcend micro and macro-level distinctions. In a national study of more than 500 hundred members of the social work

profession, Margaret Domanksi (1998) reports that over 90% voted in the most recent election, 81% had contacted an elected official at some point in their career regarding a national policy issue or problem, and 43% campaigned on their own personal time for a party and/or one or more political candidates. Thus, the activities that give greater expression to client voice in the macro arena are also carried out at the organization level where they depend on individual human service workers who practice, model, and inspire participatory behaviors among clients, as well as create opportunities within the organization to practice participation skills. The question to be examined in this chapter, then, is how this individual propensity for political activism might be translated into organizational and community level actions.

The next section identifies the civic intermediary roles of nonprofits and describes how each of these roles promotes the expression of client voice. It is followed by a discussion of the current and emerging influences that can threaten the ability of nonprofits to act as conduits for client voice. The chapter concludes with a look at some of the ways nonprofit human service organizations can use the power of collective action to strengthen and protect their roles as intermediaries of client voice.

NONPROFITS AS CIVIC INTERMEDIARIES

Nonprofit human service organizations act as civic intermediaries by giving expression to client voice in the policy arena and by empowering clients to participate in the political and policy-making system. The notion of nonprofits as civic intermediaries originates from the work on mediating structures, in which Peter Berger and Richard Neuhaus (1977) describe a number of community institutions through which mediation between citizens and the state might occur, including nonprofit social service organizations. While recipients of social service often harbor suspicions about government and political institutions (Soss, 1999), nonprofits are among the most highly trusted institutions by their clients (Allard, 2009). Based on extensive personal contact with marginalized groups, direct service staff in nonprofits can play an important role in encouraging, modeling, and affirming the expression of voice.

Moreover, nonprofit human service organizations have "built-in" mechanisms for teaching participation skills and the expression of voice in their day-to-day service delivery, ranging from the individual treatment planning process to opportunities for clients to serve on agency boards of directors and client advisory committees. Nonprofit human service organizations are also well suited to engage underrepresented groups in the political process based on their services to specialized populations and related interests. Reid (2001) suggests that "identity-based" nonprofits (e.g., race or ethnicity) often promote political activism that advances the groups' shared interest.

Mediating structures can empower people to act as citizens, especially restoring the voice of the poor in a democracy. Berger and Neuhaus (1977) also note that "the paradigm of mediating structures aims at empowering poor people to do the things the more affluent can already do; it aims to spread the power around a bit more" (p. 8). They argue that, for genuine democracy to exist, mediation "cannot be sporadic and occasional; it must be institutionalized in structures" (p. 4). The activities that are institutionalized reflect the roles, routines, norms, customs, values, and beliefs of an organization (March & Olson, 1995). Clarke (2000) further emphasized the importance of institutionalizing activities within nonprofits for shaping the political identities of individuals and groups. Drawing on the work of March and Olsen (1995) and Jones (1994), Clarke (2000) notes that nonprofits create "communities of interest" that promote political identities among clients and encourage them to act as democratic citizens.

Kramer (1981) expands the concept of nonprofits as mediating structures by observing that these organizations "mediate between groups of individuals and the larger society, integrating groups into that society, providing opportunities for value communication, development of community services, and the distribution of power" (p. 194). More recent empirical work by LeRoux (2009) identifies three conceptual categories for the civic intermediaries activities carried out by nonprofit human service organizations: political representation, political mobilization, and political education. Human service organizations perform a variety of activities within each of these conceptual categories,

all of which can amplify client voice in the political or policy-making arena. Each of these activities is examined in detail.

Political Representation

Nonprofit human service organizations function as civic intermediaries by representing the needs and interests of clients in the policy-making system. Pitkin (1967) defines *representation* as "to speak for, act for, look after the interests of respective groups" (p. 117). Attempts to influence policy on behalf of clients represents a form of substantive representation, or, what Guo and Musso (2007) describe as "an organization acting in the interest of its constituents, in a manner responsive to them" (p. 312). Political representation, or advocacy, reflects what Kramer (1981) describes as the "improver" role of nonprofits, in that human service organizations engage in advocacy not only for the direct benefit of their clientele groups but also in an effort to bring about broader social change.

Nonprofit human service organizations employ a wide range of strategies and tactics in their attempts to represent clients, and these efforts can be targeted at local, state, or federal levels, or any combination thereof. The pressure for change exerted by human service organizations may be directed toward lawmakers, administrative agencies, or both, depending on whether the organization is (a) taking a stand on a proposed or pending piece of legislation, (b) trying to influence administrative rules for a bill or ordinance that already exists, (c) trying to influence the budget process, or (d) simply trying to increase awareness of the organization's cause or needs of its service population. The most common advocacy activities carried out by nonprofits include testifying before legislative bodies, lobbying on behalf of or against proposed social welfare legislation, making a statement during the public comment portion of government meetings, informally talking and meeting with policymakers about their organizations and the needs of their service population, and participating in a government planning or advisory group (Berry & Arons, 2003; Ezell, 1991; LeRoux & Goerdel, 2009).

According to Kramer (1981), nonprofit advocacy has four goals: (a) influencing legislation or regulations, (b) improving governmental service programs, (c) securing government funds, and

(d) obtaining special benefits for clients. These goals are not mutually exclusive, as the pursuit of one may lead to the accomplishment of others. For example, nonprofit health centers may successfully lobby against proposed changes to state Medicaid rules that call for eliminating or reducing certain reimbursable services, thereby accomplishing the goals of influencing regulations and protecting benefits for clients. While there has been less research on the effectiveness of advocacy activities by nonprofits, the existing evidence suggests that advocacy efforts produce gains for both clients and their service organizations. For example, Pawlak and Flynn (1990) found that a majority of executive directors identified positive results for their agency and their clients as a consequence of their representational roles. The outcomes can include favorable funding decisions, the ability to defend against budget cuts, the adoption of legislation or ordinances that benefit their clients, and passage of favorable administrative rules that pertain to their client populations (Pawlak & Flynn, 1990). In a study of child and family service organizations, De Vita, Montilla, Reid, and Fatiregun (2004) interviewed agency leaders about their advocacy efforts and found that *successful advocacy* was defined as achieving one or more of the following outcomes: changing public policies and the political environment, achieving positive social outcomes for their service recipients, or achieving positive organizational outcomes.

Although advocacy is permissible under federal regulations, and further legitimized by the Filer Commission[1] as being an important role for nonprofit human service organizations, many leaders remain reluctant to embrace advocacy activities. Berry and Arons (2003) estimate that while approximately 2% of nonprofit organizations (defined by the Internal Revenue Service [IRS] as 501(c)(3) organizations) report any expenses associated with advocacy or

lobbying on their annual financial reports, those that report on advocacy activities without spending any money are closer to 30%. While there are many reasons for this lack of widespread engagement in advocacy, one key contributing factor is believed to be the lack of a clearly defined legal limit on nonprofit advocacy activities, causing confusion on the part of some nonprofit leaders and a desire to "play it safe" by avoiding advocacy altogether. As a result, it is not surprising that many human service organizations choose to engage in advocacy through coalitions or delegate their advocacy responsibilities to a state nonprofit association (De Vita et al., 2004; LeRoux & Goerdel, 2009). Resources and capacity are also key determinants of the propensity of nonprofits to advocate. Large nonprofits that rely on government to a greater extent for their funding have the capacity to conduct research and employ a government relations person to engage in advocacy, factors that have been linked to higher rates of advocacy (Berry & Arons, 2003).

The discussion thus far has focused on the advocacy activities carried out by service-providing organizations, but it is important to note that a great deal of representation is carried out by organizations whose sole purpose is to advocate on behalf of underrepresented groups. Although these nonprofits are relatively small in number compared to human service organizations, they are a powerful force in promoting social justice through research, public awareness, and direct lobbying. The Human Rights Campaign, for example, is a national nonpartisan organization with a mission to lobby lawmakers and educate the public to ensure the rights of lesbian, gay, bisexual, transgender, and queer (LGBTQ) individuals are protected. Human Rights Campaign is a national, nonpartisan, membership organization that effectively lobbies, provides grassroots and organizing support, and educates the public to ensure that LGBTQ individuals can be open, honest, and safe at

---

[1] The Commission on Private Philanthropy and Public Needs, more commonly known as "The Filer Commission" was formed in 1973 at the urging of John D. Rockefeller III and several other private philanthropists. Comprising foundation representatives, university academics, service agency executives, and congressional representatives and staff members, the commission was tasked with conducting a comprehensive investigation of giving, service, and voluntary organizations in the United States. The commission concluded its work in 1975, releasing several papers and reports that together offered the first systematic analysis of the U.S. nonprofit sector. The conclusions of the Filer Commission represent a major turning point in the history of the U.S. nonprofit sector, strengthening public support and legitimacy for nonprofits.

home, at work, and in the community. Many of these organizations are able to magnify their impact on public policy by functioning as advocacy "umbrellas" for service providers of a particular type. The Alliance for Children and Families, for example, is a national organization that provides advocacy on behalf of nearly 350 nonprofit child welfare providers throughout the United States. Given the advocacy mission, these and similar types of organizations do not face the dilemma of trying to balance service delivery with advocating for social change efforts.

While advocacy organizations are sometimes formed by professionals or persons with expertise in a particular social policy area, they often emerge from the self-organized efforts of individuals or groups affected by a particular issue. Originating at the community or state level and sometimes growing into mass-based movements, these self-organized initiatives often (but not always) evolve into large-scale, permanent organizations. One of the early examples of this type of self-organized initiative was The National Welfare Rights Organization (NWRO) which formed in the 1960s in response to the extreme poverty experienced by African Americans living in urban ghettos. Facing ubiquitous discrimination in the job market, the economic circumstances of urban African Americans grew dire, creating widespread demands for relief through the public welfare system. The urgency for survival among African Americans led to the formation of the NWRO, which succeeded in expanding the federal welfare system, extending relief from 745,000 individuals living in poverty in 1960 to more than 3 million in 1972 (Piven & Cloward, 1979). More contemporary examples of this type of self-organized advocacy movements include Mothers Against Drunk Driving (MADD), which emerged to advocate for stronger drunk-driving laws; the Association for Retarded Citizens (ARC), advocating for the passage of the federal Americans with Disabilities Act; and state chapters of the National Alliance for Mental Illness (NAMI), seeking to redefine mental health services through state legislation.

Through their advocacy activities, nonprofit organizations can play a critical role in expanding client voice in the policy system by representing their needs and interests before legislators and government decision makers. The act of representation is an important civic intermediary role for nonprofits, as they provide advocacy and voice for those who cannot speak for themselves in the policy system. For example, the representation role may be particularly important for nonprofit human service organizations that serve children, persons with severe disabilities, the frail elderly and critically ill, and immigrant and refugee populations who are often prevented from direct participation by citizenship status or language barriers. While advocacy can amplify client voice in the policy process by speaking *on behalf of* the needs and interests of persons served, other civic intermediary roles of human service organizations include promoting direct participation by clients in the political process.

Political Mobilization

Another way that nonprofits function as civic intermediaries for their clients is by encouraging their direct participation in the political process. Mobilization activities include (a) encouraging clients to attend public hearings or meetings to express their views, (b) encouraging or assisting them in writing, calling, or e-mailing legislators at local, state, or congressional levels, (c) registering them to vote and encouraging their participation in elections, and (d), in more rare instances, encouraging their participation in a demonstration or protest. Contacting elected officials to express opinions on policy issues, pending legislation, or budgetary matters is one of the oldest forms of political participation in the United States. However, the constituents from whom policymakers most often hear are not representative of the American electorate. As Brady et al. (1995) have shown, there is a direct relationship between income and contacting of elected officials, with those at the lowest ends of the income spectrum contacting elected officials the least often to express their views.

Yet nonprofit social service organizations are uniquely situated to facilitate contact between their clients and lawmakers offices. For example, Pagliaccio and Gummer (1988) found that nonprofit human service administrators play an important role in the casework function of congressional representatives and state legislators by mediating exchanges between clients and the local district offices of these representatives. In many instances, the casework function includes assisting clients in resolving problems with a government-funded benefit or service (e.g., social security, disability, or veterans' benefits) (Pagliaccio & Gummer, 1988). In other instances, the purpose of contact is to voice dissatisfaction or support of a proposed or pending piece of legislation, or, to oppose budgetary cuts for social service programs. Whatever the purpose, there is evidence that nonprofit human service agencies encourage client contacting of elected officials nearly as often as they advocate on their behalf (LeRoux & Goerdel, 2009).

The emergence of the Internet has clearly enhanced the mobilization function of nonprofits. As a result, many nonprofit human service organizations have expanded their mobilization activities through the use of e-mail listservs, sending out "action alerts," and providing links for clients to easily and quickly connect with their representatives. Despite the ease and efficiency associated with electronic mobilization methods, the persistence of a digital divide in which lower income groups continue to experience inconsistent Internet access suggests that nonprofits should not rely exclusively on electronic mobilization methods (Mossberger, Tolbert, & McNeal, 2008). For nonprofits to be effective in their mobilization activities, they need to employ a variety of strategies, including both Internet-based activities as well as personal, direct contacts with clients.

While research regarding the effectiveness of social service client-to-lawmaker contact is lacking, evidence from the electronic mobilization literature is encouraging and suggests that at least this form of contacting is effective. For example, policymakers report awareness of the Internet as a means of connecting with constituents and taking e-mail contacts seriously (Larsen & Rainie, 2002). Moreover, McNutt (2007) finds evidence that leaders of nonprofits that use these techniques consider them to be effective in getting the client's voice heard and in shaping policy outcomes.

Nonpartisan voter engagement activities represent another important facet of the mobilization function of human service organizations. Through their nonpartisan voter registration and get-out-the-vote (GOTV) efforts, human service organizations stand to play a critical role in promoting a fairer and more just democracy by engaging low-income citizens and marginalized populations in the voting process. With the goal of increasing voter registration among low-income and minority groups, Piven and Cloward began an initiative in 1983 called Human Service Employees Registration and Voter Education (Human SERVE) that had an objective of making voter registration possible in a wide range of public social service agencies, including health, housing, welfare, and unemployment agencies (Piven & Cloward, 1988). They called particular attention to the role that community-based nonprofits can play in achieving this objective, especially since publicly supported social services are delivered by nonprofit organizations acting as contract partners of the state (Allard, 2009; Salamon, 1995). Piven and Cloward's ideas were adopted by the Clinton administration and enacted into law by Congress in 1993 in the form of the National Voter Registration Act (NVRA), also known as the "Motor Voter" law. One of the goals of adding the nonprofit "agency-based" registration provisions to the law was to reduce historic disparities in voter turnout rates that fall along lines of race, income, age, and disability (Piven & Cloward, 1996).

The Motor Voter Act requires all offices of state-funded programs (including nonprofits) that provide services to persons with disabilities to offer voter registration forms to service recipients, assist them in completing the forms (if they wish to register), and send completed forms to the appropriate state official. While the law requires state-funded disability service providers to make voter registration available on-site for clients, the law is explicit in encouraging all other "nongovernmental entities" to offer nonpartisan voter registration opportunities as well.[2]

Even after voter registration opportunities were expanded through the 1993 National Voter Registration Act, registration rates remained disproportionately lower among low-income citizens and racial minorities. Throughout the United States, there are tens of millions of voting-age citizens not registered to vote, most of whom are urban residents (Chicago Board of Elections, 2011). Although all

---

[2] Although disability service providers are technically obligated by the NVRA to make voter registration available, evidence has shown they are no more likely to do so than other types of social service providers, with the main explanation that the law is not enforced (OMB Watch, 2007).

U.S. citizens have an equal opportunity to vote, there are many hurdles that keep voter participation rates lower among low-income groups, including (a) information barriers (related to voter registration deadlines, processes, polling locations, etc.), (b) language barriers, (c) frequent address changes and failure to update registration information, (d) new state laws requiring government-issued photo ID to register and vote, and (e) in more extreme cases, harassment and/or intimidation at the polls.

Given their close contact with lower voting populations, nonprofit human service organizations are uniquely suited to increase voter participation by low-income and marginalized groups. In addition to their frequent contact with low-income clients, nonprofits are often more highly trusted by clients than services provided by government voter registration offices. For example, one study of voter registration among minorities in Florida revealed that Black and Hispanic citizens (and citizens from Spanish speaking households) are over twice as likely to register to vote via third-party nonprofit groups as White citizens and those from English-speaking households (Donovan, 2011). In addition to providing on-site voter registration, nonprofits can also increase the likelihood of voting among their clients through various nonpartisan efforts designed to get-out-the-vote, including voting reminders in person, by phone, or mail, as well as providing rides to the polls on election day. Indeed, there is compelling evidence that voter registration and GOTV efforts by nonprofit human service organizations serve their intended purpose. Research suggests that personal contact with nonprofit agency staff is highly effective in increasing voter turnout among low-income persons, increasing the probability of voting by roughly 9.3 percentage points for each additional voting-related contact a client has with her or his nonprofit service agency staff (LeRoux, 2011b). Perhaps the most important actions that nonprofits can take in their voter mobilization work is to register nonvoters and help them become first-time voters; in essence, voting is habit forming where voting in one election substantially increases the likelihood of voting in future elections, by as much as 46% (Gerber, Green, & Shachar, 2003).

While increased rates of voting by nonprofit clients will not solve all of the problems of economic and social injustice in America, greater participation can, in fact, lead to numerous smaller gains in social justice. When nonprofit clients have the information they need to make informed choices about candidates, they can play an instrumental role in electing candidates who protect existing policies and programs (and support new ones) that benefit the poor and other marginalized groups, and the connection between voting and what it means for the individual may be especially apparent at the state and local levels. Politics becomes more personal to the individual when he or she benefits from a policy or program supported by a legislator he or she helped to elect. As a result of voting for and helping to elect candidates with a strong social welfare agenda, nonprofit clients may experience the daily benefit of increased job training opportunities, increased public assistance or unemployment benefits, better access to and coverage of medical care, improved child care or early childhood intervention programs, or increased transportation options. Racial minorities, who are disproportionately affected by poverty and social inequality, can be particularly influential in electing minority candidates, which has direct benefits for the represented racial group, particularly at the local level. For example, evidence has shown that the election of African American mayors and city council members increases the number of municipal jobs filled by African Americans, increases municipal contracts with minority-owned firms, leads to higher municipal spending on social welfare programs, and leads to municipal policies that produce more equitable distribution of economic development benefits (i.e., in exchange for municipal tax abatements, firms might be required to hire local residents, provide job training, provide low-income housing, etc.); see Elkins, 1995; Eisinger, 1982; Welch & Karnig, 1979.

Nonprofit human service organizations have the potential to foster a more representative democracy through implementation of the National Voter Registration Act and thereby advance the cause of social justice. Currently, fewer than one third of all nonprofit human service organizations in the United States engage in voter mobilization activities (LeRoux, 2011a). Yet if these activities are implemented on a more widespread basis as the NVRA sought to accomplish, then nonprofits and their clients have the potential to make a substantial impact on electoral outcomes.

Last, some nonprofit service organizations mobilize their clients for direct participation through demonstrations or protests. Often described as "unconventional" political participation (Patterson, 2004; Reeser & Epstein, 1990), such overt displays of opposition to existing or proposed policies are relatively rare among human service organizations. One study suggests that these are the least often employed forms of political participation by human service nonprofits and their clients, with fewer than 6% of agencies reporting that they have ever organized or participated in a rally, protest, or demonstration (LeRoux, 2004). This finding matches the evidence that social workers engage in protest activities least frequently among all political activities undertaken on their own personal time. Referring to protest activity as the "activist" role, Domanksi (1998) found that only 9% of social workers have participated in these types of activities.

Protest activities have the potential to politically empower marginalized groups and can be exceedingly effective, particularly when they are linked to broader social movements and social change efforts. As Piven and Cloward (1978) have demonstrated, acts of defiance and mass disruption are a true source of political power for the poor and the only forms of political participation that have ever produced large-scale, dramatic policy reforms. Yet it seems that these activities are destined to occur primarily outside the scope of nonprofits that focus more on conventional forms of political participation than unconventional social change activities. Given that leaders of human service organizations are often reluctant to engage in even the most conventional forms of participation (Berry & Arons, 2003), they may be particularly circumspect about engaging in, and encouraging protest activity among their clients, especially when the organization relies on the government for some portion of its funding. Social service agency leaders often have a fear of attracting negative attention from prospective donors, the local media, or elected officials, especially those that may hold power over the agency's resources (Bass, Arons, Guinane, & Carter, 2007). Therefore, the participation of clients in protest activities may be more client-initiated than organized through the service agency.

While this discussion has focused primarily on human service organizations, it is important to note that mobilization activities (encouraging citizen-clients to contact elected officials, vote, and engage in protest activities) are also commonly carried out through nonprofit community organizing groups. While community organizing groups may also press for legislative change and social reform, using some of the same approaches as advocacy organizations, community organizing groups differ in that they seek to empower community members and promote the general well-being of communities rather than specific interest groups. These objectives are typically accomplished by (a) identifying and training community leaders to become activists, (b) facilitating coalitions, (c) mobilizing community members to vote, (d) pressuring local lawmakers and government administrators for reforms that will benefit the community, (e) developing issue campaigns, and (f) organizing protest activities if conventional strategies fail to bring about the desired social change. For example, People Improving Communities through Organizing (PICO) is a federated system of faith-based community organizing efforts that works to create social change in low-income communities throughout the country. Typical of other community organizing groups, PICO uses the strategy of empowering community members through leadership training and civic capacity building so that they may pursue needed local reforms related to housing, health care, economic security, school improvement, youth development, and immigration reform.

Political Education

Low-income citizens are often disadvantaged by insufficient education and information needed to participate meaningfully in the political process (Brady et al., 1995). Nonprofits that function as civic intermediaries for their clients provide them with education about the legal apparatus of government, how it impacts them, and how to navigate it. Informational resources provided by nonprofit agencies may compensate for a client's lack of formal education or supplement existing knowledge of legal rules. Nonprofits educate their clients about the rights granted to them under state and federal laws. This may include education related to entitlement programs, due process rights, rights within a particular service system, or basic citizenship rights.

Moreover, nonprofits educate their clients about proposed laws and regulations that have the potential to affect them. For example, nonprofit mental health and health care providers often alert their clients about proposed changes to state Medicaid benefit packages (Mental Health Association of Michigan, 2005). Many nonprofit women's health and family planning clinics educate their clients, who are often low income, about proposed laws and judicial rulings that may threaten reproductive freedoms. These types of organizations may also provide clients with education on the positions taken by candidates running for office (including judicial candidates who are prospective appointees to the state and federal bench).

Some human service organizations that offer on-site voter registration choose to go a step further in assisting their clients with election participation by providing various forms of voter education (defined by the IRS established Rule 78-248, 1978-1, at http://www.irs.gov/pub/irs-drop/rr-07-41.pdf, p. 2). Authorized nonpartisan voter education activities by human service nonprofits include sharing information on (a) voter registration deadlines, (b) candidates, (c) ballot measures, (d) finding polling locations, (e) filling out a sample ballot, and (f) any other nonpartisan education intended to increase the likelihood of voting or making informed political choices. Providing voter education through forums (e.g., candidate debates, candidate positions on issues, and voting records) are clearly permissible so long as the organization's message is designed to encourage democratic participation rather than promote a candidate or specific political message (see IRS Revenue Rule 2007-41 for specific examples of nonpermissible activities and cases illustrating their application, at http://www.irs.gov/pub/irs-drop/rr-07-41.pdf, p. 1).

Nonprofit human service organizations also provide political education for their clients by structuring opportunities to learn about democratic deliberation and effective political participation. Nonprofits aid their clients in developing democratic participation skills by providing opportunities for them to serve on client advisory boards and committees, participate in program planning, and serve on ad hoc agency work groups or policy development committees within the organization. To the extent that nonprofits create these opportunities for clients to participate in organizational governance, they serve as models for their clients by exposing them to the process of deliberation, soliciting their input, and demonstrating responsiveness to their feedback. Evidence suggests these types of experiences can enhance the political efficacy of clients and help to transfer knowledge and skills to other settings. For example, Soss (1999) found in studying welfare bureaucracies that program designs that allow for client voices to be heard have the important effect of communicating information to clients about their status, about agency decision making, and about citizenship and government. By participating in the work of a service agency, clients can acquire the experience and skills required for participation in a democratic society.

Despite the importance of these voter education activities in the policy process, several internal and external organizational forces pose challenges in human service nonprofits that are described in the next section.

CHALLENGES TO THE CIVIC INTERMEDIARY ACTIVITIES OF NONPROFITS

Human service organizations encounter a variety of challenges in carrying out their civic intermediary roles that are impacted by forces within their own agencies as well as those of the surrounding environment. The greatest internal challenge for nonprofits seeking to operate as civic intermediaries is the view of agency leaders that advocacy and other political activities are not part of the organization's mission (Kimberlin, 2010). In their seminal study of advocacy, Berry and Arons (2003) discovered that many nonprofit leaders avoid advocacy because they are too consumed with day-to-day service delivery to think about it and believe that advocacy is outside the scope of the organization's mission. Bass et al. (2007) corroborate this finding among nonprofit executives who struggle to find the link between advocacy and the organization's mission. In addition, the civic intermediary activities of nonprofits may be thwarted by board members who view the organization's mission primarily as service delivery.

Another set of internal challenges relate to limited capacity and expertise (LeRoux & Goerdel, 2009; Berry & Arons, 2003). Organizations with smaller budgets, fewer staffers, and other capacity constraints simply may not have enough extra resources to devote to advocacy, helping clients contact officials, voter registration, and/or political education. A lack of relevant staff expertise is another capacity issue affecting the ability of nonprofits to act as civic intermediaries for their clients. Many of the civic intermediary roles (e.g., advocacy and voter mobilization) require knowledge of state and federal laws governing these activities and may prevent nonprofit human service organizations from participating in the political arena altogether. For example, LeRoux and Goerdel (2009) find that having legal expertise on the board or within the organization's staff substantially increases an organization's likelihood of political activity, while Berry and Arons (2003) find that having a government relations person on staff leads to higher rates of advocacy.

Although the expertise issue is primarily an internal challenge, it is compounded by the external challenge of ambiguous federal laws governing nonprofit human service organizations. Berry and Arons (2003) found that many nonprofit leaders do not fully understand the federal regulations governing advocacy activities or misinterpret references in the laws to the limitations of advocacy (Berry & Arons, 2003). For example, they find that roughly only half of nonprofit directors (54%) are aware that it is legally permissible to take a stand on legislation and only 32% are accurately informed that their organization can lobby while also operating as a recipient of federal funds (Berry & Arons, 2003). In addition to federal regulations, state laws often require nonprofits to register and annually report advocacy activities based on an understanding of these state laws.

State laws affect not only the advocacy work of nonprofits but also their voter engagement activities. Over the past decade, several states have adopted laws that discourage voter registration by nonprofit organizations and other states are considering such laws. These regulations often include (a) unrealistic deadlines for human service agencies to submit completed voter registration forms (24–48 hours), (b) heavy fines and/or criminal charges for failure to meet these deadlines, (c) arbitrary caps on the number of registrations that can be submitted by an organization, (d) fees for the voter registration forms, and (e) authorization required from the state elections board to register voters that can be denied without cause. The tension between these state and federal policies are being contested in the federal courts.

Finally, the political climate has been inhospitable over time for political advocacy, mobilization, and educational activities of nonprofits, and this represents another considerable external challenge for human service organizations. For example, a congressional coalition led by Ernest Istook (R) of Oklahoma organized a campaign in 1994 (following the passage of the 1993 NVRA reforms) to pass a bill that would prevent all lobbying by nonprofits that receive government funding. Although this issue was displaced from the congressional agenda by more pressing issues, the proposed Istook amendment cast a long shadow over the political activity of nonprofits and created a "climate of fear" with regard to advocacy among nonprofit leaders (Berry & Arons, 2003). Following the demise of the Istook amendment, several states initiated tighter regulations of nonprofit advocacy activities. These state laws, as well as those restricting the voter engagement work of nonprofits, contribute to a climate of fear.

The defunding and ultimate disbandment in 2010 of the national community-organizing, nonprofit-group Association of Community Organizers for Reform Now (ACORN) has further contributed to the climate of fear among nonprofit leaders. The organization emerged in the media, during the past several national elections, due to charges of voter fraud and developed a poor public image that led to its ultimate demise. While the actual incidence of voter fraud was significantly exaggerated by the media and conservative policy groups (Minnite, 2010), nonprofit leaders may find it especially difficult to undertake voter mobilization or other political activities in this post-ACORN climate due to a lack of support from their boards, fear of attracting negative attention from local media, and/or ideologically-opposed elected officials who may hold power over the agency's resources.

Many nonprofits have found a way to deal with these challenges through the use of coalitions and networks. There is clear evidence that the nonprofits that are most active in advocacy carry out this work through coalitions (De Vita et al., 2004; LeRoux & Goerdel, 2009). Nonprofits can organize themselves for social change and political action either through formal organizations (e.g., state or local nonprofit associations) or informal partnerships with human service organizations in their community or region. Coalitions and networks serve as vehicles for collective action and help human service organizations overcome the challenges to their political activities in two ways.

First, collaboration with other human service organizations on policy-related activities allows nonprofits to share the costs, both financial and political (e.g., sharing the costs of a lobbyist and/or a staff member to draft joint letters to elected officials, organize joint mobilization, or organize political education campaigns). Since collaboration provides a sense of "safety in numbers" and opportunities to spread the political risk across several organizations, nonprofits may be able to allay some of their fears about participating in the political process.

Second, the use of coalitions, partnerships, and networks provide nonprofit leaders with a venue to learn about the rules and best practices associated with political and social change activities. For example, state nonprofit associations disseminate information to their member organizations about laws and regulatory issues that affect nonprofits, including those related to advocacy, voter registration, and political education activities. Many state associations have "participation projects" that not only provide regulatory and technical information to its members on advocacy and election activities but also take an affirmative stance in encouraging member organizations to engage in advocacy, voter mobilization, and political education of clients. Moreover, Berry and Arons (2003) found that when

nonprofits are members of a state nonprofit association, not only do they engage in higher levels of political advocacy but their executive directors are also more likely to correctly comprehend the types of activities permitted under federal lobbying laws (when compared with leaders whose organizations were not a member of an association). Similar findings are reported by Bass et al. (2007), regarding the role of state nonprofit associations and the knowledge of permissible activities held by their members.

These partnerships may also alter the views of nonprofit leaders about engaging in the policy realm and help them to more fully appreciate the connection between policy-related activities and the mission of the organization. For example, Bass et al. (2007) profiled one organization that evolved from being "insulated" (focused on very specific services) to one that engaged in new efforts to network with state advisory panels and connect with various mental health policy initiatives as the executive director began to recognize the importance of these activities to "strengthening service delivery" (Bass et al., 2007, p. 39). For all of these reasons, nonprofits are in a better position to overcome the challenges to their status as civic intermediary roles when they are joined together for social change objectives that can be achieved through the use of coalitions, partnerships, and networks.

CONCLUSION

The voices of the poor and marginalized are dramatically underrepresented in the American policy process and in electoral outcomes, creating an elite bias in public policy that can perpetuate problems of underinvestment in public social welfare programs. Nonprofit human service organizations are uniquely equipped to help expand client voice in the political system given their responsibility for providing services to low-income and vulnerable populations and the high levels of respect and trust accorded to them by clients. Through their civic intermediary roles of political representation, mobilization, and education, nonprofit human service organizations act as conduits for client voice and as catalysts for direct participation by clients. To the extent that nonprofits embrace these roles, they are capable of giving greater expression to the needs and interests of marginalized groups and effecting social change in the process.

Schneider and Netting (1999) have stated that "in their commitment to working for the betterment of social living and social justice for all people, many social workers have steadfastly proposed and tried to influence social legislation, policies, and ordinances" (p. 349). Thompson (1994) has also argued that electoral participation "offers opportunities for social workers to enter in the political arena in a way that could both increase recognition of the profession and provide a conscience to the world of politics" (p. 457). When social workers draw on their personal strengths of political activism and commit to overcoming organizational challenges to political participation, they stand to significantly enhance client voice in the policy-making arena and thereby advance social justice as one of the core values of the profession.

REFERENCES

Allard, S. (2009). *Out of reach: Place, poverty, and the new American welfare state.* New Haven, CT: Yale University Press.

Bass, G. D., Arons, D. F., Guinane, K., & Carter, M. F. (2007). *Seen but not heard: Strengthening nonprofit advocacy.* Washington, DC: Aspen Institute.

Berger, Peter L., & Neuhaus, Richard J. (1977). *To empower people: The role of mediating structures in public policy.* Washington, DC: American Enterprise Institute for Public Policy Research.

Berry, J. M., & Arons, D. F. (2003). *A voice for nonprofits.* Washington, DC: Brookings Institution Press.

Brady, H. E., Verba, S., & Schlozman, K. L. (1995). Beyond SES: A resource model of political participation. *American Political Science Review, 89*(2), 271–294.

Chicago Board of Elections. (2011). Voter engagement 2012. Retrieved December 15, 2011, from http://www.chicagoelections.com/page.php?id=182

Clarke, S. E. (2000). Governance tasks and nonprofit organizations. In R. C. Hula & C. Jackson-Elmoore (Eds.), *Nonprofits in urban America* (pp. 199–221). Westport, CT: Quorum Books.

De Vita, C. J., Montilla, M., Reid, E., & Fatiregun, O. (2004). *Organizational factors influencing advocacy for children.* Washington, DC: Center on Nonprofits and Philanthropy, Urban Institute.

Domanksi, M. D. (1998). Prototypes of social work political participation: An empirical model. *Social Work, 43*(2), 156–167.

Donovan, M. K. (2011, October 27). *States move to restrict voting: What nonprofits can do to defend the right to vote* [Webinar]. Washington, DC: Fair Elections Legal Network.

Eisinger, P. K. (1982). Black employment in municipal jobs: The impact of Black political power. *American Political Science Review, 76*(2), 380–392.

Elkins, D. R. (1995). Testing competing explanations for the adoption of type II policies. *Urban Affairs Review, 30,* 809–839.

Ezell, M. (1991). Administrators as advocates. *Administration in Social Work, 15*(4), 1–18.

Ezell, M. (2001). *Advocacy in the human services.* Belmont, CA: Wadsworth/Thomson.

Gerber, A. S., Green, D. P., & Shachar, R. (2003). Voting may be habit-forming: Evidence from a randomized field experiment. *American Journal of Political Science, 47*(3), 540–550.

Guo, C., & Musso, J. A. (2007). Representation in nonprofit and voluntary organizations: A conceptual framework. *Nonprofit and Voluntary Sector Quarterly, 36*(2), 308–326.

Hale, K. (2011). *How information matters: Networks and public policy innovation.* Washington, DC: Georgetown University Press.

Hoefer, R. (2006). *Advocacy practice for social justice.* Chicago, IL: Lyceum Books.

Jones, B. D. (1994). *Reconceiving decision making in democratic politics.* Chicago, IL: University of Chicago Press.

Kimberlin, S. (2010). Advocacy by nonprofits: Roles and practices of core advocacy organizations and direct service agencies. *Journal of Policy Practice, 9*(3/4), 164–182.

Kramer, R. M. (1981). *Voluntary agencies and the welfare state.* Berkeley: University of California Press.

Larsen, E., & Rainie, L. (2002). *Digital town hall: How officials use the Internet and the civic benefits they cite from dealing with constituents on-line.* Washington, DC: Pew Internet and American Life Project.

LeRoux, K. (2004, September). *Empowering the disadvantaged: The role of nonprofits in promoting political participation.* Paper presented at the American Political Science Association Annual Meeting, Chicago, IL.

LeRoux, K. (2007). Nonprofits as civic intermediaries: The role of community-based organizations in promoting political participation. *Urban Affairs Review, 42*(3), 410–422.

LeRoux, K. (2009). The effects of descriptive representation on nonprofits civic intermediary roles: Testing the racial mismatch hypothesis in the social services sector. *Nonprofit and Voluntary Sector Quarterly, 38*(5), 741–760.

LeRoux, K. (2011a). Examining implementation of the National Voter Registration Act by nonprofit organizations: An institutional explanation. *Policy Studies Journal, 39*(4), 565–589.

LeRoux, K. (2011b). *Nonprofits strengthening democracy: Key findings from an agency-based nonpartisan voter mobilization experiment* (Policy Report). Retrieved from Nonprofit Vote website, http://www.nonprofitvote.org/nonprofit-voter-engagement-research.html

LeRoux, K., & Goerdel, H. (2009). Political advocacy by nonprofit organizations: A strategic management explanation. *Public Performance and Management Review, 32*(4), 514–536.

March, J. G., & Olsen, J. P. (1995). *Democratic governance*. New York, NY: Free Press.

McNutt, J. G. (2007). Adoption of new wave electronic advocacy techniques by nonprofit child advocacy organizations. In M. Cortes & K. Rafter (Eds.), *Information technology adoption in the nonprofit sector* (pp. 33–48). Chicago, IL: Lyceum Books.

Mental Health Association of Michigan. (2005). About us. Retrieved September 24, 2006, from http://www.mha-mi.org/

Minnite, L. C. (2010). *The myth of voter fraud*. Ithaca, NY: Cornell University Press.

Mossberger, K., Tolbert, C. J., & McNeal, R. (2008). *Digital citizenship: The Internet, society and participation*. Cambridge, MA: MIT Press.

Netting, F. E., Kettner, P. M., McMurtry, S. L., & Thomas, M. L. (2012). *Social work macro practice* (5th ed.). Upper Saddle River, NJ: Pearson Education.

OMB Watch. (2007). *States failing to implement National Voter Registration Act*. Retrieved July 10, 2007, from www.ombwatch.org/node/3354

Pagliaccio, E., & Gummer, B. (1988). Casework and Congress: A lobbying strategy. *Social Casework: Journal of Contemporary Social Work, 69*(3), 155–161.

Patterson, T. (2004). *We the people: A concise introduction to American politics*. New York, NY: McGraw-Hill.

Pawlak, E., & Flynn, J. (1990). Executive directors' political activities. *Social Work, 35*, 307–312.

Pitkin, H. F. (1967). *The concept of representation*. Berkeley: University of California Press.

Piven F., & Cloward, R. (1978). *Poor people's movements: Why they succeed, how they fail*. New York, NY: Vintage Books.

Piven, F. F., & Cloward, R. A. (1988). National Voter Registration reform: How it might be won. *P.S. Political Science and Politics, 21*(4), 868–875.

Piven, F. F., & Cloward, R. A. (1996). Northern Bourbons: A preliminary report on the National Voter Registration Act. *PS: Political Science and Politics, 29*(1), 39–42.

Reeser, L., & Epstein, I. (1990). *Professionalization and activism in social work: The sixties, the eighties, and the future*. New York, NY: Columbia University Press.

Reid, E. (2001). Nonprofit advocacy and political participation. In E. T. Boris & C. E. Steuerle (Eds.), *Nonprofits and government: Collaboration and conflict* (pp. 291–325). Washington, DC: Urban Institute Press.

Rosenstone, S. J., & Hansen, J. M. (1993). *Mobilization, participation, and democracy in America*. New York, NY: Macmillan.

Salamon, L. M. (1995). *Partners in public service: Government-nonprofit relations in the modern welfare state*. Baltimore, MD: John Hopkins University Press.

Schneider, R. L., & Lester, L. (2001). *Social work advocacy*. Belmont, CA: Brooks/Cole.

Schneider, R. L., & Netting, E. (1999). Influencing social policy in a time of devolution: Upholding social work's great tradition. *Social Work, 44*(4), 349–357.

Soss, J. (1999). Lessons of welfare: Policy design, political learning, and political action. *American Political Science Review, 93*(2), 363–380.

Thompson, J. (1994). Social workers and politics: Beyond the Hatch Act. *Social Work, 39*(4), 457–465.

Welch, S., & Karnig, A. K. (1979). The impact of Black elected officials on urban social expenditures. *Policy Studies Journal, 7*(4), 707–714.

26

Educating Social Work Students About Social Justice Practice

Beth Glover Reed and Amanda J. Lehning

Introduction

While social justice is a core value of the social work profession (National Association of Social Workers [NASW], 2009), integrating social justice content and skills into the social work curriculum has been a challenge for schools of social work. Few curricular models exist that address these issues, and little is known about how to initiate and implement these models. The profession as a whole needs examples of social workers engaged in practices that promote social justice principles and goals, as well as models for curricular, student, and faculty development that can facilitate these goals. This chapter provides a case study of a social justice curriculum change in the Masters in Social Work (MSW) program at the University of Michigan, School of Social Work (UM-SSW).

We first present the conceptual framework for the change, its foci, and location in the curriculum. We then describe the processes used to implement the change and learn from and inform each phase in its development over a 10-year period. This is followed by a description of five sets of knowledge and skill sets for social justice practice and then seven major areas of learning and development that informed the development of these skill sets and the efforts to increase the likelihood that students will learn them. We end with an overview of lessons learned, some next steps, and recurring issues.

The Social Justice Curriculum Initiative

The aims of the UM-SSW social justice curriculum are to

- educate professionals who can engage in socially just practice, using the knowledge, skills, attitudes, and actions necessary for identifying and achieving social justice goals and processes through their professional roles and within various institutional contexts;
- develop practitioners who are critically conscious change agents, that is, people with the capacity to identify and transform sources of inequality they encounter in their daily lives and not unintentionally collude with or perpetuate injustice (Freire, 1990); and
- create a transformative learning process necessary to teach future social workers to transform existing

oppressive or unjust systems into socially just alternatives (Van Soest & Garcia, 2003).

This social justice framework replaced earlier initiatives in place since the early 1970s. Earlier, each student had to complete at least one "minority-relevant" course to graduate. Every course also was to address multicultural, diversity, social justice, social change, and oppression issues, with each course description noting particular elements specific for the course. The goals emphasized the development of "culturally competent" practitioners, defined as professionals with the knowledge, skills, and awareness to work effectively with people from different cultural, ethnic, and racial groups (Arredondo, 1998; Sue & Sue, 1999) as well as understand and combat oppression and its effects.

Planners of the new social justice curriculum felt that these conceptualizations did not draw on most recent scholarship and relied too much on approaches critiqued by those concerned with social justice, that is, social workers are often educated to aid, treat, empathize, and give comfort but not respond to the larger social and economic inequalities creating illness and despair in the lives of the people they serve (Reisch & Andrews, 2001). The critiques further stress that not educating social workers to work for justice and challenge inequalities means that professional schools may be graduating practitioners who unknowingly and unconsciously perpetuate dynamics of cultural, social, and economic oppression despite good intentions (Freire, 1990). Even the term *minority-relevant* implies an unexamined "dominant" perspective by classifying those who differ from mainstream culture and higher status groups as "minorities." Curriculum evaluations also documented that the infusion of such diversity content was inconsistent and often included only what students called a "diversity day." Other concerns existed about accountability in designating and monitoring particular courses. For all these reasons, the UM-SSW embarked on a social justice curriculum initiative.

Conceptually, the revised curricular framework draws from scholarship and approaches originating from many sources, especially women's and cultural studies. The aim is to address multiple sources of power and difference simultaneously, recognizing that interlocking systems of privilege and oppression exist (Johnson, 2006; Mullaly, 2010). The motion explaining the rationales, elements, and proposed implementation steps for the change prepared for the governing faculty in 2001 was titled Intensive Focus on Privilege, Oppression, Diversity and Social Justice. The students coined an acronym for privilege, oppression, diversity, and social justice called PODS, which we use here as an easy referent, despite the centrality of other concepts reflected in the curricular change (e.g., *intersectionality, decentering, critical consciousness*, and *praxis*).

Social justice is defined as a core value of social work practice, requiring a vision of "just" practice, a "just" organization, a "just" community, a "just" policy, and a "just" society. Planners initially decided not to develop a common definition of social justice because definitions were likely to evolve and to vary depending on the issue, course, and context (to say nothing about the potential for contentiousness and delay in reaching faculty consensus). Nonetheless, faculty clearly rejected notions of justice that privileged particular groups of people over others due to citizenship, resources, or capabilities. For the planners, formulations included both desired outcomes and the processes and methods used to reach these goals, as well as the importance of human rights. They understood that structures, norms, and attitudes are continuously recreated through interpersonal, group and organizational dynamics that perpetuate power differences and exclusion and that they must be continuously monitored, revised, and challenged in order not to recreate inequities. As a result, social justice will never be fully reached because our sense of what is possible will evolve, and, because basic human and societal mechanisms will always re-create conditions for inequality that must continually be challenged. This understanding also influenced how the curriculum change was implemented.

The framework conceptualizes *privilege* and *oppression* as barriers to social justice that must be recognized and challenged when promoting social justice. The curriculum was intended to assist students with understanding how privilege and oppression occur within all diversity categories and simultaneously in multiple categories. Privilege refers not only to unearned advantage but also sometimes to the absence of disadvantage. Not recognizing privilege, especially one's own privilege, makes it difficult to see and understand oppression that others experience or to create potential alliances across social categories (Johnson, 2006). Oppression refers to all the mechanisms that create barriers to participation in society along with taking advantage of opportunities and exercising rights. The curriculum recognizes that multiple sources and types of oppression exist, including powerlessness, marginalization, exploitation, cultural hegemony, and violence (Young, 1990). Privilege and oppression frequently interact with one another, and the mechanisms that create them are often unrecognized and unchallenged.

The *diversity* dimension relates to human differences, especially those related to social locations associated with privilege and oppression. The curriculum assumes that attention to differences is *necessary but not sufficient* for socially just practice and marking progress toward social justice goals. Power and status issues need to be considered simultaneously because differences are especially important when associated with power inequalities.

The curriculum change is focused on how these dimensions work together, with the recognition that their importance and consequences will vary considerably, depending on multiple social and historical contexts. The concept of *intersectionality* acknowledges that everyone occupies multiple social locations (e.g., humans simultaneously experience gender, race, ethnicity, economic and social class, age, disability status, religious background, sexual orientation, and other categories). Most of us experience unearned advantage in relation to some categories and unearned disadvantage and exclusion in others. Multiple categories always interact with each other, influence experiences, and shape our worldviews. Their salience and impact are highly influenced by particular social contexts (e.g., Hulko, 2009; Mehrotra, 2010; Pastrana, 2010; Sakamoto & Pitner, 2005). The first use of the term *intersectionality* is usually attributed to Crenshaw (1991), although many other scholars and activists had raised related phenomena for

some years (e.g., Anzaldúa, 1987/1999; Collins, 1986, 1998, 2000; hooks, 1984; Lorde, 1984/2007; Smith, 1990). All assume that multiple sources of power and difference operate simultaneously through interlocking systems of privilege and oppression (Johnson, 2006).

These perspectives challenge categorical and "additive" models of oppression. Categorical approaches usually consider only one social location at a time and emphasize what defines this category in relation to others (e.g., characteristics of the Black family). Categorical models of oppression thus obscure important differences *within* categories and also the importance of contexts in making some elements more salient than others. Additive models of oppression assume that some types of oppression may be worse than others and/or that it is possible to rank them or quantify their effects. These notions of oppression are rooted in the either/or dichotomous thinking common within dominant paradigms (e.g., one must be either Black or White, male or female). Replacing categorical and additive models of oppression with interlocking ones creates possibilities for new approaches. For instance, with dichotomous thinking, privilege is usually defined in relation to "the other" (e.g., the opposite or the absence of the experience of oppression) and thus not studied or explored in its own right. One can also explore how everyone must negotiate multiple categories in different contexts simultaneously.

To recognize and navigate these sources of difference and power requires that instructors and practitioners are able to locate *themselves* in multiple social spaces, recognizing how power and perspectives are influenced by these locations. Working for justice requires the ability to recognize, challenge, or at least maneuver within the assumptions and processes that arise from dominant societal and status perspectives in order to recognize how unequal power differences are maintained and recreated through unrecognized assumptions and practices. Along with a commitment to social justice, Freire (1993) argued that demonstrating a capacity for *critical consciousness* is an important skill set in working for justice. The development of critical consciousness (what Freire [1993] calls "conscientization") is not only gaining knowledge about different social groups, which can be the primary focus of cultural competency approaches, but also it requires ongoing engagement in self-reflection, critical analysis, interaction, discourse, *and* action while paying special attention to power and privilege (Kumagai & Lypson, 2009). Freire (1993) called this iterative process *praxis*. Thus, critical consciousness is a key goal *and* method of social justice learning, and praxis represents processes used to acquire, sustain, and deepen critical consciousness. Educating for critical consciousness has been a cornerstone of social work education in Europe, Latin America, and elsewhere for decades but is less common in the United States (Finn & Jacobson, 2003; Freire, 1990).

Decentering is another important concept but was not discussed explicitly in the original curriculum change proposal. Decentering is a method for (a) analyzing and questioning initial conceptualizations and the privileged position typically granted to both the dominant culture and the expert researchers (Trinder, 1996) and (b) illuminating situations and our understanding of them from multiple perspectives and different cultural and status vantage points. The concept and skills for decentering have multiple origins. Decentering was a term used by Piaget in his theory of cognitive development as a process that emerges during the concrete operational stage (ages 7 to 12) when a child shows increased use of logic and ability to consider multiple aspects of a situation. Among critical theorists, Habermas (1984) critiques developmental theory and the possibility of objectivity by arguing that both are shaped by human interactions embedded in cultural and historical contexts. He proposed a process of systematically considering multiple perspectives and options as part of critical analyses in order to identify biases and alternative perspectives. This requires complex human communication since any individual's perspectives are limited by their experiences and social locations.

The authors and artists who developed concepts of intersectionality and interlocking notions of oppression stressed the value of explicitly considering marginal and multiple *standpoints* in the process of decentering. Since standpoints are positions and values from which one views and understands one's person and the social order, those in marginalized positions frequently have quite different standpoints from those with privilege closer to "the center." Those in marginalized positions describe the struggles of living on the margins and borderlands where they must consciously negotiate multiple categories and often possess different perceptions of and insights about the center. These concepts can also be expanded to inform global and indigenous analyses of various contexts (Denzin, Lincoln, & Tuhiwai Smith, 2008; Narayan & Harding, 2000; Sandoval, 2000; Tuhiwai Smith, 1999). *Intensive focus* refers to the centrality of these concepts in a course (see the next section).

Locating the Social Justice Elements in the Curriculum

To provide some sense of the organizational context for the curriculum change, the UM-SSW admits approximately 300 to 350 MSW students a year, with approximately 600 students enrolled in the program at any one time. Most students complete in four terms, but those with bachelor's degrees in social work stay three terms and extended degree students may complete in up to 6 years. Approximately 50 tenure-track faculty and another 50 adjunct faculty teach about 70 to 80 different courses a year, many offered in more than one term and several with many sections. Each student selects a double concentration, including one field of service (FOS) and one practice method (with the possibility of a minor method and several certificate options). The UM is located approximately an hour away from five major metropolitan areas and collaborates with some 600 community and governmental agencies to provide field instruction experiences for students concurrently with coursework and with some international and national placements.

The curricular change left in place the infusion of social justice issues within every course, but it designated all courses within the five FOS concentrations to "intensively focus" on PODS. The five FOS concentrations are children and youth, adults and aging, mental health, health, and communities and social systems. Each comprises a field placement and four types of courses: human behavior and social environment (HBSE), social welfare policies and services (SWPS), practice methods, and program evaluation. A total of 25 courses were reworked, since some concentrations offer alternative courses. Few students are exempted from any of these courses. They provide students with opportunities to address many types of social justice issues because of the multiple types of courses involved, and taken over three terms, they can facilitate the development of PODS-related knowledge and skills over time. Targeting courses across the curriculum required many faculty members to consider how to address PODS issues and skills intensively, since half of the faculty was assigned to teach at least one of these courses.

Intensive focus in these targeted courses refers to incorporating all these elements (privilege, oppression, diversity, social justice, intersectionality, decentering, critical consciousness, and praxis) into the basic framing of each course. Thus, social justice becomes the lens *through* which other key course goals (e.g., HBSE, SWPS, practice methods, and evaluation) are viewed and operationalized.

THE PROCESS OF THE CURRICULUM REVISION

Conceptual Frameworks for the Implementation Process

In addition to the knowledge that informed the content and foci of the curricular change, other conceptual frameworks helped planners think about the learning environment, the change process, planning and evaluation, mechanisms of change, and potential sources of resistance to change. The planners considered the entire system of the school and its environment and not just the context of the curriculum, particular courses, or methods of teaching. Specifically, structuration theory (Giddens, 1984) and cultural sociology (Bourdieu, 1990) provided ways to understand the dynamic interactions between social structures, individuals, groups, and organizations, and how these interactions shape assumptions and actions (Peet, 2005). These theories illuminate how people embody, create, and re-create social structures in their everyday consciousness and actions (Giddens, 1984; Ortner,

1996). Thus, individual action and social structure are not separate phenomenon but rather interconnected parts. Structuration theory includes the following elements:

- The activation of interpretive schemas (i.e., how individuals make meaning from experiences and perceptions, including feelings, mental habits, ideas, norms, resources, actions, interactions with others, and events [Giddens, 1984; Ortner, 1996])
- The integration of organizational structures (i.e., processes that shape organizational functioning, such as recruitment policies, curricular structure, and syllabi [Hays, 1994])
- The practice of organizational norms and group processes (i.e., assumptions and actions that guide, control, or regulate acceptable behavior and patterns of communication among members of a particular group, such as collaboration or conflict [Emirbayer & Misch, 1998])

Finn and Jacobson (2003) argue that this multidimensional framework for studying complex changes that are created by people and institutions should be integral to social work education.

Principles from action research and the learning organization literature also suggest that change emerges from the interactions of many constituents and components (Senge, 1990). In order to create change, organizations need to develop shared knowledge among constituencies and stakeholders, and change strategies need to take into account relevant subsystems, institutional structures, and larger contexts. Knowledge about the change process, including next steps, emerges from ongoing knowledge development and from identifying tensions and patterns within the change activities. Relationships and networks for dissemination and feedback are important. Leaders act as facilitators for change, generating opportunities for collective learning and meaning-making processes. Other models and theories that illuminated the complex and interactive dimensions of the change process include dissemination of innovation (Greenhalgh, Robert, MacFarlane, Bate, & Kyriakodou, 2004; Rogers, 1995); and complex adaptive systems (e.g., Hudson, 2000; Kiel & Elliott, 1997; Mace, 1997; Stewart & Ayres, 2001).

These frameworks were shared with all faculty and students throughout the implementation process, and each phase of the curricular change was informed by a multimethod evaluation process. Lessons learned in each phase were used to shape the goals and activities in the next. The whole process was guided by a leadership team of faculty, students, and field instructors working in conjunction with school administrators, several faculty-student committees, and committed groups of students and field instructors (see the Note and Acknowledgments section).

PHASES OF IMPLEMENTATION

Table 26.1 summarizes the five phases of planning and implementation over about a decade. At the end of every phase, faculty and students reviewed evaluation data and reports, identified lessons learned, and formulated next steps. Major tasks and activities for each phase are listed in the left hand column, evaluation and other knowledge development activities in the right.

Some important activities are not included in Table 26.1. Students developed their own initiatives related to PODS intensives, including town meetings and task groups. They planned and facilitated social justice sessions during new student orientation. A number of faculty retreats and school events occurred in different phases designed to influence overall skills, perspectives, and norms and the overall culture of the school. For instance, the school conducted an all-day event in phase II focused on the listen, affirm, reflect, add information (LARA) methods of dialogue (Alvarez, Fitch, & Reed, 2007). Field instructors were involved through focus groups and an all-day event on how to involve field education sites.

Research and evaluation methods throughout the phases included focus groups and surveys with

Table 26.1   Phases of Iterative Planning, Implementation, and Learning of PODS

Goals and Actions/Activities	Knowledge Development
Phase I: Conceptualize and Adopt PODS Curriculum (2 years, based on 25 years of previous work)	
• Faculty forums on social justice (6 sessions) • Student town hall meetings • Committees conceptualize curricular locations goals, components, implementation steps • Vote to adopt	• Review of history, current status • Examine literature on social justice learning • Identify principles, components, and vision for social justice
Phase II: Initial Implementation (2 years)	
• Develop initial resources and evaluation plan • Create initial frameworks • Assess and revise courses, one type at a time • Identify initial social justice knowledge and skills • Conduct faculty retreats, student sessions	• Assess initial school climate • Identify what works, barriers, challenges • Implement student focus groups, faculty interviews, and retreats • Review revised course descriptions/syllabi
Phase III: Address Gaps, Build on Successes, Create New Resources (2 years)	
• Develop resources for integrative, generative learning and portfolios • Revise competencies based on research • Begin assessment of field issues • Pilot integrative learning seminars • Conduct all school events • Prepare alternatives for accreditation	• Triangulate and decenter data on competencies • Conduct more student focus groups • Draft field resource guide based on data • Review course descriptions and syllabi for multisection courses • Evaluate events, faculty review of data
Phase IV: "Taking PODS to the Next Level"/Alternative Reaffirmation Project (two plus years)	
• Develop stronger links with field sites • Collaboratives with faculty, students, and field	• Process evaluation of all activities • Assessment of competencies

Table 26.1   Continued

Goals and Actions/Activities	Knowledge Development
• Incorporate integrative learning into field seminars • Develop resources for mentoring, dialogue • Conduct workshops for field instructors	• Collect many examples from field • Integrate competencies and mentoring into field educational agreements • Generate new components for resource guides
Phase V: Consolidate/Institutionalize Knowledge and Experience (3 years)	
• Pilot ongoing mechanisms for integrative, generative learning (paper and electronic) • Consider revisions needed in additional courses • Develop supervisory processes for field instruction	• Infuse PODS intensive into ongoing mechanisms for curricular evaluation • Build achievement of competencies into routine evaluations and portfolios • Complete evolving research materials and assist various constituencies to use them

students, interviews and focus groups with faculty and other constituencies, document analyses, and observation during and evaluation after PODS-related activities. Events with multiple constituencies were held periodically to review all data to identify lessons learned, formulate important principles and questions, and identify implications for the future.

Social Justice Knowledge and Skills

An important accomplishment from this curricular revision has been the identification and development of knowledge and skills important in working for justice. We first present and briefly describe these. Then, we discuss some of the activities and lessons learned that (a) helped the planners to formulate these definitions of knowledge and skills and (b) are helping the school to create learning opportunities more likely to help students to achieve them.

Soon after the school approved the PODS curricular change, planners constructed preliminary social justice competencies mostly from the literature on learning about social justice, clustered according to the major PODS dimensions of privilege, oppression, diversity, social justice, and praxis, all defined and operationalized intersectionally. Several types of research and evaluation were conducted to understand and continue to develop these constructs (e.g., student surveys, interviews, and self-reflective

essays; faculty experience in operationalizing the competencies in various course; and an analysis of assumptions underlying practice methods). New clusters emerged from these analyses.

Table 26.2 presents five sets of social justice knowledge and skills, clustered by the types of skills and knowledge required for implementing social justice practice, along with several crosscutting principles of considering multiple system levels simultaneously and working intersectionally. Issues of power, difference, working with diverse others within and across complex group boundaries (with both conflict and collaboration), critical thinking and analyses, and self-reflection and praxis permeate across the sets.

Note that praxis competencies are located at the center, overlapping with the other four sets that are placed in quadrants, indicating that each set of competencies informs all the others through praxis. The other four sets of competencies include (a) goals and processes for particular practice methods and steps (e.g., enacting vision and change by defining goals, assessment, planning, implementing, and evaluating actions), (b) working with others, (c) critical contextual thinking and analyses, and (d) use of self and regularly decentering and examining one's own social locations and motivations, as well as skills for maintaining resilience, agency, and joy. Students and practitioners may experience and need to enact these skills and knowledge quite differently depending on their social locations and goals.

Table 26.2 Core Knowledge and Skills for PODS Intensives

Set A: Social Justice Vision and Actions: Allow us to envision social justice possibilities and take action to move toward social justice goals (*enacting vision and change*)

Envision what social justice could look like in specific practice contexts.

Identify and implement steps toward social justice in specific practice contexts (practice methods and areas, including making linkages across practice levels and methods).

Use processes that promote social justice, including those that resist and reduce disempowering and marginalizing dynamics (e.g., use accessible language, attend to power and marginalizing dynamics in groups and organizations, value diverse leadership and participation styles).

Build on positive sources of power to envision and work toward social justice; work to reduce disempowerment.

Build on indigenous knowledge and experiences of individuals, groups, and communities in practice and evaluation.

Monitor actions to ensure they are promoting social justice and to identify and reduce unintended contributions to injustice.

Set C: Critical Contextual Thinking: Allow us to identify the sources, manifestations, consequences, and mechanisms of injustice and to recognize and develop more diverse and just theories and practices (*engaging in critical analyses*)

Analyze types, levels, and sources of power in practice contexts, theories, and actions.

Identify how inequities are manifested, maintained, and reinforced in social systems, theories, processes, and social work practice of different types and levels.

Recognize the impacts of privilege and inequities on various levels of social ecology (individuals, family, organizations, community, society).

Value and use multiple ways of knowing and constructing knowledge.

Understand how individual, family, group, community, organizational, nationality and citizenship history, culture, positionalities, sources of power (ascribed and earned), and multiple ways of knowing shape perceptions, attitudes, cognitive processes, actions, and consequences.

Analyze assumptions that underlie presumably universal practice methods (including evaluation and research [i.e., decenter dominant frameworks]).

Set B: Conflict, Dialogue, and Community: Allow us to recognize and honor differences and engage and work with others toward social justice goals (*working with others for justice*)

Demonstrate intersectional humility in communication and interactions with others.

Assess the advantages and disadvantages of working collaboratively within and/or across groups (defined by positionality and stigmatized status) and act accordingly.

Initiate and promote dialogue, alliances, and collaboration with others where and when appropriate within and across groups and boundaries.

Use conflict and negotiation skills toward social justice goals.

Incorporate insights from those with insider and outsider statuses into social justice planning and actions.

Foster environments and processes that are supportive and generative among those working for justice.

Set D: Critical Awareness, Use of Self, and Strengthening Strategies for Resilience and Generativity: Allow us to understand (locate and analyze) ourselves in social categories (positionalities), deepen critical consciousness, stay whole and engaged in social justice practice (*integrating social/political dimensions with individual experience*)

Recognize one's own positionalities on multiple dimensions, including nationality and citizenship (the relative power of the nation) and other insider/outsider statuses.

Recognize how these intersect with each other and change in interactions with others and in different contexts.

Learn from those with different voices, values, and experiences, including different ways of knowing.

Demonstrate knowledge and skills for intersectional humility (be able to suspend one's own assumptions and perspectives in order to understand and recognize alternative world views).

Use skills in (a) maintaining and strengthening one's own social support and self-care, (b) finding joy and meaning in one's practice. Cultivate and use a "critical third eye" (ability to observe and evaluate one's own actions and their consequences).

Set E: Praxis. Competencies for iterative integration and learning across domains A, B, C, D

NOTE: Consider multiple system levels simultaneously and use intersectionality.

COMPONENTS, ACCOMPLISHMENTS, AND LESSONS LEARNED

What Facilitated and Inhibited Social Justice Learning?

Based on 17 focus groups in the first year of implementation, participants identified many effective methods, including

- faculty modeling of the process of exploring privilege and critical consciousness related to multiple social categories;
- encouraging students to share their experiences and engage with each other;
- engaging with, recognizing, and normalizing conflicts as expected components of human interactions and progress toward social justice;
- using course assignments and activities to help students see how PODS concepts and skills were important in that course and could be used to work for justice and address the issues of privilege, oppression, and difference; and
- connecting course work with fieldwork, with case examples, activities, and assignments.

While many positive examples were given, students also identified many barriers to learning about social justice. One key area is when conflicts among students or between students and faculty were avoided, minimized, or allowed to continue without teacher facilitation to create a learning experience. Many reported examples of feeling suppressed by others, censoring themselves to avoid unpleasant interactions, or being uncertain about how to behave or what to say, fearing that they would be judged by other students. These examples suggest the kinds of power-related transactions that Foucault (1977) calls *surveillance*, in which people monitor and suppress themselves and each other to conform with internalized norms of what they believe to be "appropriate" or from fear of potential consequences. Students reported that they disengaged and stopped learning when there was conflict or tension in their classrooms that was not discussed or otherwise addressed.

Even though some students stated that classroom discussions keep "scratching the same surface" and complained about behaviors of other students, many did not recognize how their own ways of thinking, speaking, and making sense of things were contributors. The capacities to process current ideological and political discourse appear to be diminished, in part, by (a) a lack of dialogue with each other, (b) a limited understanding of political and cultural forces shaping assumptions, and/or (c) the absence of opportunities to explore their assumptions and generate meaningful alternatives. In fact, when students had opportunities to engage in meaningful dialogue, they often described these as "profound," "life changing," or "most memorable" (e.g., "we were able to get past all the labels and jargon and really hear different perspectives," "I discovered I had something in common with people I didn't even want to listen to before," "suddenly, all the theory I learned in my other courses made sense").

Students also reported many types of "disconnects." Some of these were related to the structure of the curriculum, but others were related to an absence of integrating and reflective mechanisms that allow students to identify, connect, and make sense of their experiences and learning. Especially important were gaps between the classroom and field placements and other sites of action and learning. Students reported greater knowledge about PODS as a result of coursework, but they did not believe they had the skills or opportunities to use this knowledge in their practice. Thus, they felt more awareness but not a greater sense of agency. Some felt more depressed and helpless about PODS issues than before they entered the SSW. Students felt that these disconnects impeded all learning but were especially problematic in the complex, emotional, and value-laden dimensions of PODS.

Unexpectedly, planners discovered that the process of participating in the focus groups altered many of these initial perceptions. Students often began the groups saying they did not think they had learned very much and were often angry about what they perceived they were not learning. After responding to questions about their experiences, however, students began to state that they had learned or accomplished more than they thought and had worked for justice in ways they had not recognized prior to the groups. In the groups, they could reflect and articulate knowledge and accomplishments that were "tacit" and "embodied," rather than conscious and explicit. The recognition that even simple opportunities to reflect on their experiences could help students identify what they were learning and feel more confident in their knowledge and skills led the planners to look for and develop additional ways to accomplish these goals and to address other disconnects in the curriculum between sites of learning.

Integration Mechanisms to Link Knowledge, Theorizing and Action at the Student Level

In phase three, the planners piloted a number of methods for building in reflective, integrative, and portfolio-based learning opportunities that also emphasized social justice in order to reduce some of the disconnects for students. The use of portfolios has been discussed in the social work literature in regard to three different purposes: professional development (Elliott, 2003), curricular assessment (Spicuzza, 2000), and integrating the classroom and field learning experiences (Risler, 1999; Schatz & Simon, 1999). Planners were interested in all of these purposes, with some focused on evaluation methods (e.g., Fitch, Peet, Reed, & Tolman, 2005a, 2005b, 2008) while others worked on developing methods and initial resources for integrative and reflective learning and mentoring (e.g., Alvarez et al., 2007; Zappella, Reed, & Peet, 2008). Later, portfolio elements were incorporated systematically into required field seminars. Existing materials and methods for portfolio-based learning were revised to be more aligned with course assignments, field assignments, and supervision. Extensive process notes, as well as feedback from students in evaluations, were reviewed when planning the next session and then summarized at the end of the term.

Students reported that the assignments and reflective activities helped them recognize and develop examples of their accomplishments, emphasizing social justice. Seminar activities encouraged students to develop their own definitions of social justice and articulate how they are especially relevant to their goals, practice methods, and practice areas. Each philosophy statement reflected the different ways that students understood and worked for justice. Students were encouraged to identify particular accomplishments and examples of how social justice

competencies are understood and implemented and to work with their field instructors to develop goals and agency assignments that continued this learning.

Integration Between Classroom and Field Education Sites

In phase four, collaboratives comprising faculty, field instructors, field liaisons, and students were developed in each FOS area to develop ways to strengthen school-field connections and to strengthen PODS elements in field education. These also considered how to promote integrative learning and portfolio development and employed skills in dialogue and working intersectionally. Many case and practice examples were developed, and collaboratives discussed how people's social locations influenced practice and supervision sessions, especially the different ways field instruction and practice reflected (or not) the values and components articulated in PODS knowledge and skills. The collaboratives also provided the opportunity for class and field instructors to share information and develop recommendations that were incorporated into ongoing field instruction practices in the form of educational agreements and supervision.

Reframing Instructional Strategies and Classroom Dynamics

In addition to addressing curricular and reflective disconnects, planners also began to reframe previous understandings of classroom dynamics originally perceived as barriers to social justice learning. This was precipitated by analyses of student focus groups conducted several years into the implementation process. Planners expected to find more positive examples and fewer barriers to PODS learning since there had been substantial transformation in teaching and many new elements. Despite the development of more positive examples of PODS implementation, all the negative classroom situations previously reported remained and students still viewed them as failures in instruction and their learning.

A closer examination of the data, however, revealed other interpretations. For example, research on the development of consciousness about one's social locations, and especially about privilege and oppression, suggests that an evolution in cognitive, affective, and skill development must occur (Goodman, 2001). Experiences and trajectories differ depending on whether people experience privilege or oppression related to a particular social location and how much they have previously engaged in analyses of power and privilege. Initially, some are unaware of the existence of privilege and oppression, while others have been conscious of these most of their lives. Some initially deny the existence of privilege or oppression while others may feel very angry, guilty, defensive, or blaming of others. A worldview framed in terms of absolutes can be common. With more positive exposure, many people develop more nuanced conceptual frameworks for understanding their own experiences and those of others, which results in recognizing more opportunities and options. Engaging in dialogue with others, learning more about all the topics in the social justice curricula, and exploring their own perceptions and experiences are important catalysts for this development. People, however, need to do this in quite different sequences and ways, depending on their backgrounds and experiences. Often, what some students need in order to learn may be experienced as hurtful by other students.

At the UM-SSW, students come from diverse and homogenous backgrounds with different levels of experience in exploring these issues. Many believe that some social locations (usually those on which they have experienced oppression) are most important and that too much attention is being paid to those that they perceive to be less important or serious. Some have been taught very negative attitudes about some social categories. Thus, a classroom can become a major site of struggle as students endeavor to get more attention paid to issues that concern them and less to those they consider to be less important or that threaten their equilibrium, and different students need quite different experiences to continue their learning.

Despite major work to increase skills in dialogue and conflict, managing these dynamics to promote learning is very challenging. In some ways, these dynamics have increased as the SSW focuses more explicitly on social justice since every new cohort of students must navigate them, and tensions and conflicts are now less suppressed. Reframing these as signs of, and opportunities for, social justice learning and not as instructional or personal failures has

been very helpful, and many faculty members now discuss this explicitly with students in their classes.

Important Elements of Courses That Intensively Focus on Social Justice

With all this work in mind, planners began to formulate some principles for constructing a course that intensively focused on social justice, based on the above and other analyses of course implementation. Early on, several assessment tools applied to course outlines (e.g., Reed & Peet, 2005) revealed that some PODS elements were not included at all or simply appeared in the readings or assignments rather than in class discussions, activities, linkages between classroom and field, or in course evaluation criteria. The review gave special attention to intersectionality and major dimensions of PODS, as well as language and how PODS elements were being understood and constructed within the course. Most courses were much stronger on the diversity and oppression elements (often applied categorically and not intersectionally) than on privilege, social justice, and praxis. Language used in some courses suggested considerable attention to intersectionality and connections across system levels for privilege, oppression, and social justice issues, but many did not.

A second review of courses compared sections that did intensively focus on PODS with those sections reflecting the older pattern of infusing curricular themes. Table 26.3 describes these comparisons. The third column describes the reasons why elements on each dimension are important for PODS learning.

All of the course descriptions and syllabi from PODS-intensive course sections included descriptions of teaching philosophy, ground rules for classroom climate and learning from diverse classmates, and often definitions of relevant social justice goals and processes. Note that these courses are explicit about the importance of constructing a climate and culture of the classroom conducive to social justice learning and the value of interactions with diverse classmates. Several PODS-intensive course descriptions explicitly normalized and presented conflict in student interactions as opportunities for social justice learning. The faculty members who included discussions of their teaching philosophy and why

Table 26.3   Comparison of PODS-Intensive Course and Course That Addresses Curricular Elements

Section Consistent With Curricular Themes	Section That Is PODS-Intensive	Rationales for Importance
Mostly, it uses the basic course template with no modification—cannot tell this is PODS-intensive course from description.	Course description has an extra paragraph describing how PODS elements are particularly relevant for the course.	PODS framing is important in the initial presentation of a course and its purposes. This should be tailored to fit the course.
Course description and syllabus are silent on how course will be conducted.	It includes a discussion of ground rules and the importance of dialogue and conflict.	Early attention to class climate and interaction norms is important.
• Initial session in the syllabi overviews goals and topics of the course, with no obvious reference to PODS • Second week begins a course topic	First two sessions emphasize PODS frameworks. The first defines social justice issues and goals relevant for this course. The second asks students to identify their values and positionalities in relation to course goals and topics. Students are asked to explore together what they bring to the course.	With early attention, PODS become the lens and framework for the course. Students develop initial criteria for viewing and critiquing all course topics. They identify relevant social justice goals and consider their critical consciousness in relation to this course. Students are encouraged to interact.
The text is strong on examples from diverse groups, with some examples of social justice issues (e.g., stigma, disability, age), but it pays little attention to multiple dimensions together and does not have a social justice framework.	It has at least one reading on every topic that is clearly PODS related. It covers most of the eight social location groups with some examples of how they interact. It includes readings about barriers to social justice and a critique. Unexamined privilege shapes the usual ways that disorders are conceptualized.	In addition to the initial framework, some PODS content and critiques are infused in readings for every week. It includes a regular critique on the sources of knowledge and how categories are constructed, which is important for critical consciousness and for recognizing underlying epistemologies.
One session includes values and ethics, and one session focuses on special populations, often toward the end of the course, with additional readings.	This section has a PODS-related issue and critique on each topic. Some weeks focus directly on relevant social justice goals with examples, such as on how unrecognized privilege is maintained and forms of oppression.	Students continually report the importance of facilitating dialogue, linking knowledge in the readings with a critique of their assumptions, and considering their application.
Students cannot tell about course processes from the course description.	This section includes a statement about the importance of sharing diverse experiences. In addition to ground rules, it states a philosophy of teaching and learning and strategies for implementation.	Students report the value of active discussion of their values, views, and experiences and regular analysis of social contexts. The literature discusses the importance of transparency regarding teaching methods and expectations.
The first assignment is a paper based on a book review with a list of potential books. The impact of	In the first assignment, students analyze a case from their practice by applying concepts from the course,	Students report the importance of linking their course and fieldwork and that the absence of these present

Table 26.3   Continued

Section Consistent With Curricular Themes	Section That Is PODS-Intensive	Rationales for Importance
cultural and age issues is mentioned but no other PODS elements. Another assignment is an exam at the end that covers basic course information with no mention of PODS.	and they share this with others in class. In another assignment, students take course concepts and use them to analyze how cases are conceptualized and understood in their placement. PODS-related evaluative criteria are clearly stated.	barriers to learning to apply PODS concepts. When the two sets of experiences are parallel and not linked, many students are unable to connect the theory and knowledge from the classroom to the field and vice versa.

they taught as they do were also those most frequently mentioned by students as directly modeling how they navigated their own multiple social locations by being transparent about their own struggles and successes in learning and practicing social work and social justice.

In terms of course structure and topics, social justice issues and frameworks were introduced in the first course sessions along with topics intended to develop a classroom climate that supports open interactions. Readings and issues related to justice were infused throughout most sessions, emphasizing multiple diversity categories, as well as a social justice critique of readings missing this emphasis. Assignments explicitly included elements and criteria related to social justice and frequently linked the classroom and field.

Courses with less focus on PODS usually included attention to groups representing different social categories, frequently just one at a time and not in every session. A common model was a special session on diversity later in the course that revisited previous topics in terms of how they could be applied to different groups. Most of them said little or nothing about teaching philosophy or classroom climate, and assignments were less likely to make explicit connections with fieldwork.

Using Decentering Approaches

Methods for decentering basic assumptions were used throughout the curriculum change process and were especially important in formulating the social justice knowledge and skill sets. In one method, very diverse students and analytic techniques were used to define and validate these. Special attention

was given to examining different lived experiences of oppression and culture (e.g., students of color and international students; and employing multiple categories of gender, age, and sexual orientation). In addition, once the revised knowledge and skill areas were defined, students and faculty from different social locations were asked to critique them, identify potential biases, and formulate new alternatives.

This review identified many ways in which the skill sets emphasized helping students from the dominant culture recognize their assumptions and experiences with those different from themselves. Language needed to be revised to capture the experiences and challenges faced by those occupying more marginal positions. These processes included managing multiple fluid identities and social contexts, boundary crossing (e.g., code-switching, double consciousness, culture brokering), working *within* one's own groups, or managing one's own reactions to oppression while working for justice. Less well-represented processes included emotional resilience, recognition and resistance to micro-inequities, an ability to survive because one has been tempered by difficult environments and experiences, and giving witness to experiences of oppression (e.g., educating others by sharing what it is like to experience oppression).

Decentering was also important in conducting the review of course descriptions and syllabi. Again, people with diverse perspectives and backgrounds were employed in the review, and techniques were used to highlight and understand differences in their approaches and perspectives, rather than look for commonalities. Different methods also illuminated different aspects. For instance, the analyses of the choice of words and how issues were stated led to different understandings than simply listing the topics covered. In collaboratives with field instructors, where facilitators probed for both similarities and differences, activities allowed the different constituencies to identify how their views might differ from others.

The Overall Endeavor

Focusing on social justice in the MSW curriculum also requires many other changes and considerable effort over time, including the creation of an organizational culture that supports dialogue and exploration of sources of conflict and connection. Many types of activities need to be repeated with every cohort of students as well as new faculty and field instructors. Faculty members need continuing opportunities to renew their commitment to this work, deepen skills, and broaden approaches. Not only do students begin in different places but so do faculty members and field instructors. Formal assessments and evaluation activities have been invaluable in facilitating ongoing learning.

In addition, both *what* and *how* of social justice curriculum redesign are important. *What* includes the definition of social justice, particular goals and processes for justice, components for particular courses, rationales, and different types of skills and approaches important for social justice learning. *How* focuses on skills and processes of instruction, the culture and climate of the school and the professional practice, interactions during implementation, and support and education for change among all constituencies.

The incremental implementation allowed each phase to be informed by earlier experiences and ongoing research and evaluation. Some faculty and students, however, were quite uncomfortable with this process, preferring a comprehensive plan, even though previous comprehensive plans frequently required considerable revision in practice. A great deal was learned about benefits, tensions, and methods for engaging in iterative evaluation and participatory research employing critical frames, consistent with previous work (e.g., Cahill, Cerecer, & Bradley, 2010; Gringeri, Wahab, & Anderson-Nathe, 2010; Mabry, 2010; Nygreen, 2009).

Faculty members also have different skills and styles in teaching, and the incorporation of social justice content into their classroom must be a good fit with their approach to their courses. In many ways, addressing PODS directly, especially by addressing privilege and multiple social locations simultaneously, can lead to much more awareness of classroom dynamics that are often suppressed or ignored. This can make teaching and learning much more rewarding, but also much more challenging and uncomfortable. Many professors in the school are concerned about engaging in potentially uncomfortable dialogues in the classroom if there are no mechanisms in place to manage them safely and comfortably. Others believe that these issues are never comfortable, but that discomfort can greatly facilitate many types of learning.

In addition, it is extremely useful to have mechanisms in place to identify and develop student leadership on social justice issues in each new cohort of students. These include students with a strong understanding of and commitment to social justice and/or who embrace engaging with diverse others and perceive these interactions as opportunities to learn more skills in several social justice domains (e.g., working with others, critical contextual analyses through decentering, raising one's own critical consciousness). Helping students to find like-minded collaborators can create initiatives within the larger student body that help to further ongoing development. In addition, making differences explicit and encouraging everyone to explore them openly can help to reduce the dynamics of surveillance and suppression (i.e., everyone not saying what they think and feel) that seriously limit dialogue and learning from others in the classroom and the hallways. Students committed to these principles can be powerful forces within classrooms.

SUMMARY AND NEXT STEPS

While implementing PODS continues to be a work in progress, the school is developing and refining many types of resource materials that (a) promote integrative and generative learning and portfolios, (b) support field instruction and mentoring and linkages between class and field-based learning sites, and (c) continue to conceptualize social justice elements. Efforts are underway, with the assistance of a new educational specialist, to help faculty incorporate more integrative learning and to develop or refine methods and assignments that can become examples of accomplishments in portfolios.

Faculty members are beginning to consider different phases of social justice learning in terms of what is useful for assignments, experiences, and mentoring as well as relevant content and experiences at the beginning, middle, and end of the MSW program (focused on reflecting, consolidating, and applying learning). Social justice elements are included in guidelines for supervision, assignments, and educational agreements for field instruction. Social justice skills and knowledge are infused through the overarching curricular competencies, and ways are being developed to routinely evaluate the achievement of these competencies.

The discourse and assumptions within the school have changed substantially, particularly in the emphasis on social justice and power rather than just diversity and the consequences of oppression. Implementation, however, is still uneven, depending on the instructor and the FOS. Less PODS-related instructor training is available for adjunct lecturers, not every field instructor has engaged in workshops on social justice, and incorporating social justice content into orientation sessions for new faculty, students, and field instructors is an ongoing challenge. Disagreements continue about the appropriate approaches to social justice education.

Some current students describe the PODS curriculum as "hit or miss" based on the extent of learning devoted to PODS and depending on the professor and the course topic. They continue to report that professors emphasizing experiential learning and a collaborative approach to assignments are more successfully integrating PODS. Students also have different perspectives regarding the extent to which PODS curriculum is integrated, depending on their own practice focus. For example, several current students who focus on macro practice observe that PODS elements seem better integrated into courses on interpersonal, micro-level practice than in macro-level policy and administration courses and practice. Alternatively, some interpersonal practice students

believe that the macro students engaging in policy, management, or community practice are being better equipped to address social justice and oppression within society.

Although much has been learned, much more is needed to create frameworks and skills for navigating the development of social justice skills and knowledge and negotiating all of the individual, group, classroom, agency, and school dynamics that emerge from different understandings of justice as well as the different levels of consciousness, knowledge, and skills. It is particularly important to develop and promote successful instructional strategies to reduce the norms of conflict-avoidance and the dynamics of surveillance and suppression that inhibit learning and dialogue in the classroom.

In some ways, the PODS focus has become so infused in the school that one professor remarked that many probably do not realize that it was approved for only specific courses. But with such an integrative approach, there is also a risk of paying less attention to PODS over time. The future of the PODS intensive as a work in progress continues to call for ongoing cycles of development, evaluation, and feedback to formulate and refine the PODS curriculum along with ongoing collaboration and dialogue among faculty, students, administrators, and field instructors.

NOTE AND ACKNOWLEDGMENTS

This chapter was written by an "insider" (one of the planners and implementers of the curricular change—Reed) and a relative "outsider" (a postdoctoral fellow who has been at UM-SSW for a year—Lehning). The interactions between us have helped us to clarify some important elements of this case. Many sections draw from evaluation reports and documents created as part of the change process, with contributions from many others. Some quotes included were drawn from early evaluation reports (authored primarily by Melissa R. Peet) and others from interviews conducted recently by the second author.

Many people were instrumental in planning, implementing, and evaluating this curriculum initiative. Robert Ortega and Mieko Yoshihama provided extensive leadership over the entire process, with Ortega focused on field instructor involvement and field instruction and Yoshihama focused on developing, revising, and validating the social justice competencies. Others who made significant contributions include Charles Garvin, Dale Fitch (who developed the initial electronic frameworks for portfolio-based learning and evaluation), David Burton, Larry M. Gant, Brett Seabury, Lorraine Gutierrez, and Edith Lewis. Peet was the evaluator through the beginning of Phase III, and her dissertation was based on this work (Peet, 2005). Her background in higher education was invaluable in assisting planners to place their work within the context of higher education, and she helped develop initial resource materials for integrative learning. Every associate dean has provided significant leadership in different phases, beginning with Siri Jaryatne, Richard Tolman (who led conceptualizing for the Alternative Reaffirmation Project [ARP]), Mary Ruffolo (who oversaw implementation of the ARP and institutionalized many elements), and currently Michael Spencer (who has been especially focused on creating opportunities and skills for dialogue). Elizabeth (Betsy) Voshel, director of the Office of Field Instruction, was an active planner from Phase III on and instrumental in infusing learnings into field instruction procedures and support materials. Multiple cadres of students contributed in many ways, by advocating strongly for moving more quickly, advocating for issues with faculty and others, participating in and helping to conduct evaluations, providing leadership within collaboratives, and drafting resource materials. Notable among these are Antonia Alvarez, Lara Law, Natalie Zappella, Amy Wineberger, Brooke deLeo, and Erin Maloney. Many field instructors also attended collaboratives and workshops and provided advice about next steps. Mary Ortega was especially helpful in conceptualizing approaches to supervision at difference phases. The school received the following financial and tangible support from many sources within the UM: the (then) dean of the School of Social Work Paula Allen-Meares, the Office of the Vice President for Research and the Office of the Associate Provost, the Center for Research and

Teaching (multiple minigrants plus active assistance), the Rackham School of Graduate Studies, and the Ginsberg Center for Service Learning.

The authors also wish to acknowledge current and past students and faculty who were interviewed recently about their experience with the change process and the current status of the implementation of social justice elements within the curriculum.

REFERENCES

Alvarez, A. R. M., Fitch, D., & Reed, B. G. (2007, October 29). *Integrative learning and portfolio development for social justice practice.* Paper presented at Council on Social Work Education Annual Program Meeting, San Francisco, CA.

Anzaldúa, G. (1999). *Borderlands/La Frontera: The new Mestiza.* San Francisco, CA: Aunt Lutes Books. (Original work published 1987)

Arredondo, P. (1998). Integrating multicultural counseling competencies and universal helping conditions in culture-specific contexts. *Counseling Psychologist, 26,* 592–692.

Bourdieu, P. (1990). *The logic of practice.* Stanford, CA: Stanford University Press.

Cahill, C., Cerecer, D. A. Q, & Bradley, M. (2010). "Dreaming of . . .": Reflections on participatory action research as a feminist praxis of critical hope. *Affilia, 25,* 406–416.

Collins, P. H. (1986). Learning from the outsider within: The sociological significance of Black feminist thought. *Social Problems, 33*(6), S14–S32.

Collins, P. H. (1998). The tie that binds: Race, gender, and US violence. *Ethnic and Racial Studies, 21*(5), 917–938.

Collins, P. H. (2000). Gender, Black feminism, and Black political economy. *Annals of the American Academy of Political and Social Science, 568,* 41–53.

Crenshaw, K. W. (1991). *Mapping the margins: Intersectionality, identity politics, and violence against women of color. Stanford Law Review, 43*(6), 1241–1299.

Denzin, N. K., Lincoln, N. K., & Tuhiwai Smith, L. (2008). *Handbook of critical and indigenous methodologies.* Thousand Oaks, CA: Sage.

Elliott, N. (2003). Portfolio creation, action research and the learning environment: A study from probation. *Qualitative Social Work, 2,* 327–345.

Emirbayer, M., & Misch, A. (1998). What is agency? *American Journal of Sociology, 103,* 962–1023.

Finn, J. L., & Jacobson, M. (2003). *Just practice: A social justice approach to social work*. Peosta, IA: Eddie Bowers.

Fitch, D., Peet, M., Reed, B. G., & R. Tolman, R. (2005a, February). *The use of ePortfolios in evaluating the curriculum and student learning*. Paper presented at Council on Social Work Education Annual Program Meeting, New York City, NY.

Fitch, D., Peet, M., Reed, B. G., & Tolman, R. (2005b, February). *Use of ePortfolios and XML in evaluating the curriculum and student learning*. Paper presented at Council on Social Work Education Annual Program Meeting, New York City, NY.

Fitch, D., Peet, M. R., Reed, B. G., & Tolman, R. (2008). The use of ePortfolios in evaluating the curriculum and student learning. *Journal of Social Work Education, 44*(3), 37–54.

Foucault, M. (1977). *Discipline and punish*. London, UK: Tavistock.

Freire, P. (1990). A critical understanding of social work. *Journal of Progressive Human Services, 1*, 3–9.

Freire, P. (1993). *Pedagogy of the oppressed: 20th anniversary edition*. New York, NY: Continuum.

Giddens, A. (1984). *The constitution of society: Outline of the theory of structuration*. Berkeley: University of California Press.

Goodman, D. J. (2001). *Promoting diversity and social justice: Educating people from privileged groups*. Thousand Oaks, CA: Sage.

Greenhalgh, T., Robert, G., MacFarlane, F., Bate, P., & Kyriakodou, O. (2004). Diffusion of innovations in service organizations: Systematic review and recommendations. *Milbank Quarterly, 82*, 581–629.

Gringeri, C. E., Wahab, S., & Anderson-Nathe, B. (2010). What makes it feminist? Mapping the landscape of feminist social work research, *Affilia, 25*, 390–405.

Habermas, J. (1984). *Theory of communicative action* (T. McCarthy, Trans.). Boston, MA: Beacon Press.

Hays, S. (1994). Structure and agency and the sticky problem of culture. *Sociological Theory, 21*, 57–72.

hooks, b. (1984). *Feminist theory: from margin to center.* Boston, MA: South End Books.

Hudson, C. G. (2000). At the edge of chaos: A new paradigm for social work? *Journal of Social Work Education, 36*, 215–230.

Hulko, W. (2009). The time and context-contingent nature of intersectionality and interlocking oppressions, *Affilia, 24*, 44–55.

Johnson, A. G. (2006). *Privilege, power, and difference* (2nd ed.). Oxford, UK: Mayfield Press.

Kiel, L. D., & Elliot, E. (Eds.). (1997). *Chaos theory in the social sciences: Foundations and applications*. Ann Arbor: University of Michigan Press.

Kumagai, A. K., & Lypson, M. L. (2009). Beyond cultural competence: Critical consciousness, social justice, and multicultural education. *Academic Medicine, 84*, 782–787.

Lorde, A. (2007). *Sister outsider: Essays and speeches*. Berkeley, CA: Crossing Press. (Original work published 1984)

Mabry, L. (2010). Critical social theory evaluation: Slaying the dragon. In M. Freeman (Ed.), *New Directions for Evaluation Series: Vol. 127. Critical social theory and evaluation practice*, pp. 83–98.

Mace, J. P. (1997). Introduction of chaos and complexity theory to social work. In D. J. Tucker, C. Garvin, & R. Sarri (Eds.), *Integrating knowledge and practice: The case of social work and social science* (pp. 149–158). Westport, CT: Praeger.

Mehrotra, G. (2010). Towards a continuum of intersectionality theorizing for feminist social work scholarship. *Affilia, 25*, 417–430.

Mullaly, R. (2010). *Challenging oppression and confronting privilege* (2nd ed.). Toronto, Ontario, Canada: Oxford University Press.

National Association of Social Workers (NASW). (2009). *Code of ethics of the National Association of Social Workers*. Washington, DC: NASW Press.

Narayan, U., & Harding, S. (Eds.). (2000). *Decentering the center: Philosophy for a multicultural, postcolonial, and feminist world*. Bloomington: Indiana University Press (Hypatia).

Nygreen, K. (2009). Critical dilemmas in PAR: Toward a new theory of engaged research for social change. *Social Justice, 36*(4), 14–35.

Ortner, S. B. (1996). *Making gender: The politics and erotics of culture*. Boston, MA: Beacon Press.

Pastrana, A. (2010). Privileging oppression: Contradictions in intersectional politics. *Western Journal of Black Studies, 24*, 53–63.

Peet, M. (2005). *We make it the road by walking it: Critical consciousness, structuration, and social change school* (Unpublished doctoral dissertation). University of Michigan, Ann Arbor, MI.

Reed, B. G., & Peet, M. R. (2005). Faculty development and organizational change: Moving from "minority relevant" to intersectionality and social justice. In M. Ouellett (Ed.). *Teaching inclusively: Essays on course, departmental, and institutional diversity initiatives* (pp. 473–491). Stillwater, OK: New Forums Press.

Reisch, M., & Andrews, J. (2001). *The road not taken: A history of radical social work in the United States.* Philadelphia, PA: Brunner-Routledge.

Risler, E. A. (1999). Student practice portfolios: Integrating diversity and learning in the field experience. *Arete, 23,* 89–96.

Rogers, E. M. (1995). *Diffusion of innovations* (4th ed.). New York, NY: Free Press.

Sakamoto, I., & Pitner, R. O. (2005). Use of critical consciousness in anti-oppressive social work practice: Disentangling power dynamics at personal and structural levels, *British Journal of Social Work, 35,* 435–452.

Sandoval, C. (2000). *Methodology of the oppressed.* Minneapolis: University of Minnesota Press.

Schatz, M. S., & Simon, S. (1999). The portfolio approach for generalist social work practice: A successful tool for students in field education. *Journal of Baccalaureate Social Work, 5,* 99–107.

Senge, P. M. (1990). *The fifth discipline: The art and practice of the learning organization.* New York, NY: Doubleday/Currency.

Smith, D. E. (1990). *The conceptual practices of power: A feminist sociology of knowledge.* Boston, MA: Northeastern Press.

Spicuzza, F. J. (2000). Portfolio assessment: Meeting the challenge of a self-study. *Journal of Baccalaureate Social Work, 5,* 113–126.

Stewart, J., & Ayres, R. (2001). Systems theory and policy practice: An exploration. *Policy Sciences, 34,* 79–92.

Sue, D. W., & Sue, D. (1999). *Counseling the culturally different: Theory and practice.* New York, NY: Wiley & Sons.

Trinder, L. (1996). Social work research: The state of the art (or science). *Child & Family Social Work, 1,* 233–242.

Tuhiwai Smith, L. (1999). *Decolonizing methodologies: Research and indigenous peoples.* London, UK: Zed Books.

Van Soest, D., & Garcia, B. (2003). *Diversity education for social justice: Master teaching skills.* Alexandria, VA: Council on Social Work Education.

Young, I. M. (1990). *Justice and the politics of difference.* Princeton, NJ: Princeton University Press.

Zappella, N., Reed, B. G., & Peet, M. (2008, July). *Educating for social innovation through eportfolios: Embodied knowledge, leadership & social change.* Paper presented at International Association of Schools of Social Work, Durban, South Africa.

27

Incorporating Social Justice Principles Into Social Work Practice

Jaclyn Grant and Michael J. Austin

The social work profession, through its work with individuals, communities, and societies, seeks to better the opportunities and outcomes of those who have been marginalized, oppressed, and isolated. While social work practice is based on the value of social justice, it has been difficult to operationalize social justice principles in daily practice. The human rights perspectives of humanistic social work and the human capabilities approach, emerging out of global efforts to promote social justice, provide a framework for implementing the goals and practices of social justice within the social work profession.

An explanation of humanistic social work, an emerging model of social work that incorporates both individual and community transformation, serves as an introduction to the inclusion of social justice principles into daily social work practice. Core principles of humanistic social work can be seen in current community practices, including restorative justice interventions. Restorative justice interventions provide tangible case examples of attempts to increase social justice in individual lives and society. The humanistic social work model offers one interpretation of what it means to incorporate social justice into practice: In the National Association of Social Workers' (NASW) *Code of Ethics* (2009), social workers are called upon to uphold social justice as a core value and to strive to expand social justice through collaboration with clients, advocacy, and policy and systems changes. An exploration of the human capabilities approach helps to provide direction for these pursuits. Understanding how specific human capabilities relate to social justice principles in the *Code of Ethics* can guide social workers toward action-oriented steps against social injustice.

Utilizing the core principles of humanistic social work and the human capabilities perspective, the chapter concludes with an assessment tool that can be used by social workers in their work with individuals and communities to assess their adherence to the *Code of Ethics'* call to stand against injustice and work to empower those who have been marginalized, oppressed, and isolated.

Defining Humanistic Social Work

At its core, social work is dedicated to promoting social justice in individual lives and communities. As noted elsewhere, social work draws upon the contributions of multiple social science and humanities disciplines. As a result, there are now multiple models of social work practice, including the growing field of humanistic social work practice that is defined as "a practice that seeks human and social well-being by developing human capacities; personal growth; and social relationships of equality, freedom and mutual relationship through shared social experience" (Payne, 2011, p. 31). Humanistic social work draws its core tenets from the philosophy of humanism, although it is also strongly influenced by transpersonal psychologies, microsociology, traditional social work practice, and human rights practices (Payne, 2011).

The philosophy of humanism focuses on the rational ability of individuals to enhance their personal development and to alter their life circumstances within a context of caring for one another through the betterment of society as a whole. While humanism is primarily considered to be a secular philosophy, there are individuals who incorporate humanist values into their religious faith and practices.

A key goal of humanistic psychology is client self-actualization. Humanistic psychologists utilize unconditional positive regard and the use of self as a way of capturing the interrelationship that occurs when a whole human (the worker) is assisting another whole human (the client) in order to promote self-actualization (Payne, 2011). The primary goals of humanistic social work are to improve the personal psychological efficacy of individuals and help create environments that are conducive to the fulfillment of personal development (Payne, 2011).

Psychological Efficacy

M. Payne (2011) defines personal efficacy as "the person's capacity to act to take their personal development forward" (p. 36). In this way, psychological efficacy is the goal of practitioners' work with individual clients. Humanistic social workers assist clients in order to increase their self-actualization and self-determination (Furman, Langer, & Anderson, 2006).

Humanistic social workers use a number of tools to achieve these goals, including the use of self in interactions with clients, informed consent, and participatory decision making (Payne, 2011). Humanistic social workers act "as whole beings in relationship with their clients, other whole human beings" (Payne, 2011, p. x). The practice involves helping clients to use their own knowledge, skills, and experience to increase their psychological efficacy. Humanistic social work utilizes informed consent because it promotes client responsibility, client control, and partnership in working toward goals; similarly, clients are encouraged and supported to be active participants in decision making as they demonstrate their equality in the relationship (Payne, 2011).

Environments Conducive to Social Justice

The dignity and humanity of all people is a central element in humanistic social work. Humanistic social workers focus on the achievement of social justice, diversity, and equality based on a belief in the inherent worth of all individuals. As noted by Payne (2011), "Equality is not a theoretical, high-level concern for social policy. Equality in society can be achieved only if every human interaction aims for equality" (p. 89). As a result, it is important for humanistic social workers to find ways to develop and maintain environments that are conducive to social justice in all of their work.

In addition to the equal access approach to services or opportunities, the equal outcomes approach to social justice focuses on the life outcomes of individuals and calls for additional supports for those who face inequalities, recognizing that the level of various resources needed to reach a given standard of living may vary among individuals and groups.

Included within the approach to equal outcomes is a focus on affective equalities. Affective equality includes "being an active part of society, being accepted by the people around us, being loved and supported, and having the opportunity to love and support others" (Payne, 2011, p. 70). Working toward affective equality can enable social workers to develop and promote culturally competent practices and policies.

In summary, humanistic social work focuses on the holistic well-being of individuals and communities. It seeks to honor the dignity of all humans through the promotion of psychological efficacy and the development of environments that are conducive to social justice. As an example of the principles of humanistic social work, restorative justice is an emerging practice in the field of criminal justice as described in the next section.

RESTORATIVE JUSTICE: A CASE EXAMPLE OF HUMANISTIC SOCIAL WORK

There are three common frameworks for responding to crime in communities: the retributive approach (the traditional criminal justice system), the rehabilitative approach, and the restorative approach. While there is some overlap between these approaches (Daly, 2002), the three frameworks contain unique principles.

Retributive approaches focus on determining the guilt and motivation of an offender, with a criminal justice system exacting punishment based on the severity of the crime. Rehabilitative approaches focus on helping individuals improve or restore the areas of their lives that led to crime in order to avoid future offenses. Restorative justice focuses on how crimes violate relationships and communities as a way to engage offenders and victims in determining how offenses can be addressed. As of 2008, there were over 300 restorative mediation projects operating in the United States alone and an additional 500 in Europe (Centre for Justice & Reconciliation, 2008).

Restorative Justice as Theory and Practice

Restorative justice includes both a set of values and a relatively nonprescriptive set of actions (Morrison & Ahmen, 2006; Pranis, 2004). Given the great variety of actions included within restorative justice work, the following definitions provide some of the key values and concepts (italics added):

- Restorative justice is a theory of justice that emphasizes *repairing the harm* caused by criminal behavior (Centre for Justice & Reconciliation, 2008, p. 1).
- Restorative justice is a *process* to involve, to the extent possible, those who have a stake in a specific offense and to collectively identify and address harms, needs, and obligations, *in order to heal* and put things as right as possible (Zehr, H., 2002, p. 37).
- Practices and programs reflecting restorative purposes will respond to crime by (1) identifying and taking steps to repair harm, (2) involving all stakeholders, and (3) *transforming the traditional relationship* between communities and their governments in responding to crime (Van Ness & Crocker, 2003, as cited in Van Ness, 2004, p. 96).

Restorative justice processes have shown promise in developing and delivering reparations for crimes and in reducing recidivism. The values and practices of restorative justice, including those of empowerment and restoring relationships and communities, align with social justice principles and the humanistic perspective of the social work profession.

Restorative Justice Interventions and Reparations

Restorative justice has been used both in conjunction with the criminal justice system and as an alternative to it, although interventions always take place after an offender has admitted guilt for a crime. Restorative justice interventions may be used in response to nonviolent offenses, such as vandalism and theft, (or after violent offenses, such as assault, rape, and murder), and involve victims, secondary victims, and community members. Involving community members helps offenders understand that "their actions not only impacted a real person but also negatively impacted the broader community in which they lived—that is, the community itself was also a victim" (Umbreit, Coates, & Vos, 2007, p. 28). Participation in restorative justice practices is intended to be voluntary for all involved parties.

There are multiple models of restorative justice intervention, and all restorative justice interventions involve a mediator or facilitator. The three most common models of intervention are (a) *victim-offender mediation* (victims of a crime are given the opportunity to meet with their offender[s] face-to-face to discuss the impact of the crime on their lives and to determine a mutually agreed-upon set of actions that the offender will take to make amends for the harm that was caused); (b) *family or community group conferencing* (brings together victims of a crime and their offenders to discuss the impact of an offense and to determine an agreed-upon plan for reparation by including family members of the victim[s] or offender[s], supporters of either party, criminal justice system representatives, as well as anyone else who was affected by the offense); and (c) *peacemaking or sentencing circles* (brings together victims, offenders, and any community members impacted by the offense to speak about the harm caused by the offense, the reparations to be made, and the process of being reintegrated into the community through a process that often involves passing an object that is symbolic of the offense, such as a talking stick with a symbol attached, around the circle to designate each member's turn to speak (Centre for Justice and Reconciliation, 2008; Ness, 2004; Umbreit et al., 2007).

The process of determining reparations for a harm that has been committed concludes with an agreed-upon contract that can include apologies, restitution for the crime, community service, and participation in rehabilitative support services (Baffour, 2006; Centre for Justice & Reconciliation, 2008). These contracts tend to focus on what actions the offender will take to restore the harm or relationship, rather than focusing primarily on punishing the offender (Richards, 2011).

Outcomes and Limitations of Restorative Justice Practice

In general, there is consensus among victims, offenders, and other involved parties that the restorative justice process is fair (Abrams, Umbreit, & Gordon, 2006; Latimer, Dowden, & Muise, 2005). Participants of restorative justice programs have been found to comply with their restitution agreements at higher rates than those who do not participate or those who do not qualify for restorative justice interventions (Latimer et al., 2005). In addition, offenders who participate in restorative justice programs are less likely, on average, to recidivate

than those who go through the traditional criminal justice system (Baffour, 2006; Latimer et al., 2005).

Despite these positive outcomes, some of the challenges in assessing the effectiveness of restorative justice interventions include (a) the voluntary nature of restorative justice interventions that can lead to self-selection bias (Bradshaw, Roseborough, & Umbreit, 2006); (b) a lack of recorded factors that may impact outcomes, such as prior histories of crime (Bradshaw et al., 2006); and (c) a lack of acknowledgment of other factors that may impact restitution compliance or recidivism, such as outside support systems (Bradshaw et al., 2006). Others note the importance of separating the idealism of restorative justice from the reality of victim, offender, and community experiences (Daly, 2002; Kenny & Clairmont, 2009; Richards, 2011).

In summary, restorative justice and social work share a common strengths-based and empowerment practice along with a need to balance empowerment with responsive regulation of behaviors (Burford & Adams, 2004; Van Wormer, 2004). The mutual decision-making process seen in the contract development process of peacemaking circles, victim-offender mediation, and family group conferences parallels the value of participatory decision making noted in the social justice ethics of the social work profession. With the focus of restorative justice on empowerment, restoring relationships, and healing communities, it is clear that these interventions reflect the social justice principles of the social work profession as well as the values of humanistic social work.

Restorative justice interventions demonstrate the primary attributes of humanistic social work practice in the following ways: adoption of a bifocal perspective, a human relationship approach, and the belief that individuals can and should be reintegrated into communities when they have been disenfranchised. The bifocal perspective of humanistic social work focuses on how to improve an individual's self-efficacy while also focusing on improving the community's conduciveness to social justice. Restorative justice interventions model this duality by striving to attain the rehabilitation of individual victims or offenders while also creating a supportive community conducive to healing relationships. Restorative justice interventions involve efforts to humanize victims and offenders in the retribution process, reflecting the humanistic social work value of human relations. Personal development is one of the goals of humanistic social work: This is seen in the creation of restitution contracts of victims and offenders in the restorative justice process.

The National Association of Social Workers' (NASW) *Code of Ethics* outlines a common core set of values and social justice principles. Although efforts such as restorative justice or humanistic approaches to social work align with the social work value of social justice, it is important to consider how these values and principles are incorporated into social work practice.

SOCIAL JUSTICE IN THE CODE OF ETHICS

With social justice as one of its core values, the NASW in its *Code of Ethics* (2009) makes reference to four principles related to social justice. Given the profession's focus on "service, social justice, dignity and worth of the person, importance of human relationships, integrity, and competence" (NASW, 2009, p. 5), it's no surprise that striving for and achieving social justice is based on principles that set forth ideals to which all social workers should aspire.

Striving toward social justice involves looking beyond the individual to the group, community, and societal factors that impact an individual's well-being. Recognizing the mutual impact of individuals and communities on one another is a distinguishing characteristic of social work practice. It is important that social workers not only consider how these external factors impact an individual or group but also take action to ensure that external environments are conducive to the well-being of individuals and groups.

The four social justice principles are described below.

Social Justice Principle 1: Partnership With and Advocacy on Behalf of Clients

The NASW's *Code of Ethics* highlights advocating *for* clients and collaborating *with* clients to advocate for social change as critical components of effective social work. The shared goal is to create environments in which individuals can reach their potential and exercise self-determination.

Over time, many social workers have focused primarily on the work of directly helping clients, while giving less attention to partnering with and advocating for clients to create social change. To fulfill this responsibility, social workers are called upon to listen to the needs and desires of their clients, to work with their clients to gain access to services they need, to advocate for new or increased services when there are gaps, and to empower clients and join with them in calling for more just social policies.

This aspect of the ethics code reflects the social work value of empowering clients. Encouraging and supporting clients in their pursuit of changes in the community or in social policies can empower clients as they seek to change systems or institutions that have been unjust, oppressive, or discriminatory. It is important for social workers to ensure that clients have the resources they need to engage in advocacy for social change and to anticipate resistance to social change. Although the contexts of advocacy may vary among social workers, all social workers can play a role in speaking up for and with their clients in unjust situations.

Social Justice Principle 2: Promotion of Cultural Competency and Equity

Cultural competency is a core social work value and calls for demonstrating "respect for difference, [and] support [for] the expansion of cultural knowledge and resources" (NASW, 2009, p. 27). By acknowledging the historical inequities in society, the NASW in its *Code of Ethics* links the promotion of cultural competency with advocating for equity for all people.

It is important to recognize that the *Code of Ethics* not only calls upon social workers to advocate for culturally affirmative policies in the broader society but also to ensure practices within the field of social work demonstrate cultural respect and affirmation. This involves engaging in self-reflective practice that analyzes and addresses one's own cultural biases, as well as internal and programmatic organizational assessments to fight against the perpetuation of discrimination, repression, and oppression within social work agencies.

Social Justice Principle 3: Opposition to Injustice and the Promotion of Empowerment and Equal Access

Social workers are called upon to advocate for a system where all people have equal opportunities and are empowered to utilize self-determination to make their own life choices. Given the significant inequalities currently present in society, how can social workers prioritize their efforts to stand up against injustices? As noted in the NASW *Code of Ethics* (2009), these efforts are carried out primarily on behalf of "vulnerable and oppressed individuals and groups of people (by focusing) primarily on issues of poverty, unemployment, discrimination, and other forms of social injustice" (p. 5).

Social Justice Principle 4: Advocacy for Environments Conducive to Social Justice

According to the NASW's *Code of Ethics*, there is an obligation to empower individuals to attain their basic needs as well as promote and sustain policies and environments that allow individuals and groups to exercise their rights and opportunities. Social policies and legislation significantly impact the environment in which people live and the types of services received.

While these four social justice principles compose a core social work value, little attention is given to their incorporation into social work practice. The *Code of Ethics* provides little elaboration as to what is meant by the term *social justice*, related either to its intellectual origins discussed elsewhere in this volume or its application in daily practice. Thus, it is important to note that interpretations of the term may vary significantly across fields of practice. For example, when the *Code of Ethics* authors speak of ensuring access to opportunities, what does it mean to ensure access, and what is meant by opportunities? For example, does ensuring access to educational opportunities mean simply that all children should have the opportunity to attend schools that meet baseline criteria, that all children should have access to postsecondary education, or

that all schools should provide an equitable enriching and adequate education? Who determines what is adequate? Should it include the opportunity to attend schools that expose youth to an array of extracurricular activities? If so, which activities? Should the focus be on ensuring access to equitable schools, or, on ensuring equitable academic outcomes? And if equal outcomes are to be ensured, what resources can or should be used to make sure this happens? Questions like these highlight the need for ongoing dialogue about the meaning and actualization of social justice.

These four principles provide guidance for taking action toward social justice; however, they do not identify a vision of what actualized social justice in communities would look like. Nussbaum's (1997) human capabilities approach provides a new way of operationalizing the social justice principles of the *Code of Ethics*.

THE HUMAN CAPABILITIES APPROACH

The "human capabilities approach" to human rights development, articulated by Amartya Sen and further developed by Martha Nussbaum (among others), provides a framework for conceptualizing how societies provide for their members. Nussbaum (1997, 1999) focused on assessing social well-being beyond the resources available to individuals by emphasizing the different human capabilities needed within a group or country to utilize various capacities to meet human needs.

In doing so, Nussbaum (1997, 1999) developed a list of 10 human capabilities (noted in Figure 27.1) "that can be convincingly argued to be of central importance in any human life, whatever else the person pursues or chooses" (Nussbaum, 1997, p. 286). While there is overlap between the capabilities, "all are of central importance and all are distinct in quality" (Nussbaum, 1997, p. 286). The capabilities approach is based on the realization that there may be an unequal distribution of services or resources in order to provide all people with the same capacity to meet their needs. Recognizing that the framework of the capabilities should be applied in a flexible manner based on local needs and culture, Nussbaum (1997) noted that the detailed descriptions of her list were not meant to be viewed as concrete. Nussbaum's human capabilities approach provides a framework for actualizing the four social justice principles within the context of daily practice.

- **Life.** Being able to live to the end of a human life of normal length; not dying prematurely or before one's life is so reduced as to be not worth living
- **Bodily health.** Being able to have good health, including reproductive health; to be adequately nourished; to have adequate shelter
- **Bodily integrity.** Being able to move freely from place to place; to be secure against violent assault, including sexual assault and domestic violence; having opportunities for sexual satisfaction and for choice in matters of reproduction
- **Senses, imagination, and thought.** Being able to use the senses, to imagine, think, and to reason—and to do these things in a "truly human" way, a way informed and cultivated by an adequate education, including, but by no means limited to, literacy and basic mathematical and scientific training; being able to use imagination and thought in connection with experiencing and producing works and events of one's own choice, religious, literary, musical, and so forth; being able to use one's mind in ways protected by guarantees of freedom of expression with respect to both political and artistic speech and freedom of religious exercise; being able to have pleasurable experiences and to avoid unnecessary pain
- **Emotions.** Being able to have attachments to things and people outside ourselves; to love those who love and care for us, to grieve at their absence; in general, to love, to grieve, to experience longing, gratitude, and justified anger; not having one's emotional development blighted by fear and anxiety (Supporting this capability means supporting forms of human association that can be shown to be crucial in their development.)
- **Practical reason.** Being able to form a conception of the good and to engage in critical reflection about the planning of one's life (which entails protection for the liberty of conscience)
- **Affiliation.**
  a. Being able to live with and toward others, to recognize and show concern for other human beings, to engage in various forms of social interaction; to be able to imagine the situation of another and to have compassion for that situation; to have the capability for both justice and friendship (Protecting this capability means protecting institutions that constitute and nourish such forms of affiliation and also protecting the freedoms of assembly and political speech.)
  b. Having the social bases of self-respect and nonhumiliation; being able to be treated as a dignified being whose worth is equal to that of others, which entails protections against discrimination on the basis of race, sex, sexual orientation, religion, caste, ethnicity, or national origin
- **Other species.** Being able to live with concern for and in relation to animals, plants, and the world of nature.
- **Play.** Being able to laugh, to play, to enjoy recreational activities
- **Control over one's environment.**
  a. Political. Being able to participate effectively in political choices that govern one's life; having the right of political participation and protections of free speech and association
  b. Material. Being able to handle property (both land and movable goods); having the right to seek employment on an equal basis with others; having freedom from unwarranted search and seizure; in work, being able to work as a human being, exercising practical reason and entering into meaningful relationships of mutual recognition with other workers

Source: Adapted from M. Nussbaum. (1999). Women and equality: The capabilities approach. *International Labour Review, 138*(3), 235.

Figure 27.1   Universal Human Capabilities

Life and Bodily Health

Social work is founded on a belief in the dignity and worth of all humans that includes the goal of assisting individuals in acquiring the ability to provide for their basic needs (e.g., food, shelter, clothing), safety, and good health. Providing for one's basic needs is intricately linked to the longevity of one's life. It is important to consider the impact of poverty, discrimination, and unequal opportunities on the ability of individuals "to live to the end of a human life of normal length" (Figure 27.1) and to exercise the capability for bodily health, described in Figure 27.1 as "being able to have good health, including reproductive health; to be adequately nourished; to have adequate shelter." Addressing these basic needs has been a core value throughout the history of the social work profession and occurs when social workers take action to ensure that clients have the necessary health care, housing, social supports, and other services needed to live a healthy life.

When there are barriers (structural or individual) to achieving these resources, it is important to work with clients to gain access to services or to change larger institutional systems. The human capability of meeting one's basic needs and utilizing affordable health care and nutrition are becoming out-of-reach for many people. The firsthand effects of economic distress are often reflected in health problems (e.g., individuals may suffer from malnutrition from a lack of healthy food, asthma from exposure to pollution, and risk of injury or illness from hazards in substandard housing), housing struggles, and the lack of provision for basic needs. Social workers can take action to inform policymakers about the impact of social policies on individual members of society as it affects their capabilities to attain their basic needs.

Bodily Integrity

In addition to securing the basic needs of individuals, the core principles of social work include the safety of individuals that is captured by Nussbaum's concept of bodily integrity, namely, the ability of an individual to be protected from assault, sexual violence, or forced decisions regarding reproduction. The bodily protection of one's self can be argued to be one of the most basic human rights.

The promotion of personal bodily security involves speaking up against intimate partner violence, sexual assault, and violence in the community. Social workers engage in preserving the bodily integrity of individuals by working in clinical or community advocacy programs related to domestic violence, community violence, reproductive rights, sexual assault and rape, and rehabilitation or restorative justice.

When people's safety is in danger, their ability to access services and opportunities may be hampered. For this reason, the tenet of bodily integrity in the capabilities approach is closely linked with advocacy for environments that are conducive to social justice. The ethics code (NASW, 2009) indicates that all people should "have equal access to the resources, employment, services, and opportunities they require to meet their basic human needs and to develop fully" (p. 27). Social policies can build protections for bodily integrity through the development of supports for people who have been victimized and through treatment or punishment for perpetrators. In a similar way, policy plays a significant role in matters of reproductive rights.

Senses, Imagination, and Thought

The capabilities of sensing, imagining, and thinking are essential for supporting the lives and cultures of others. They include the right of individuals "to use imagination and thought in connection with experiencing and producing works and events of one's own choice" (Figure 27.1). It is important to assess services or policies with respect to the degree to which they exclude or diminish the choices and rights of various groups. In addition to well-being and safety, social justice principles need to take into account the equality of education and intellectual and personal belief freedoms afforded to members of society.

The capacity for personal and creative expression is largely dependent upon the nature of a supportive environment. Freedom of expression, thought, and action that maximize one's sense of integrity depends upon policies that support such behavior. It is important to identify who is included and who is excluded in current policies (e.g., who does and does not have freedom of religious expression, freedom to voice dissension, etc.) as well as to promote policies that allow for equality of both access and opportunity.

Emotions

This capacity speaks to the social work value that individuals should be free to engage with their authentic emotions as well as develop relationships that allow them to connect with and express their emotions in a healthy manner. If environments are conducive to social justice (i.e., basic needs are provided for, safety is ensured, dignity and self-worth are affirmed), there may be greater freedom for demonstrating the capability of expressing and managing emotions. Thus, this capability demonstrates how social justice can be both a means and an end.

Practical Reason

Linked with the capability of utilizing one's mind and senses in a way that is protected by individual freedoms, the capability of practical reason features the ability of individuals to reflect on and make decisions about their own lives. This capability expands on the principle of client self-determination as a key element in achieving social justice. Social work practice often focuses on client empowerment and support by collaborating with clients to achieve their goals.

Affiliation

Nussbaum's affiliation capability has two primary components, namely, interpersonal relationships and the treatment of individuals. Both of these capabilities relate directly to the *Code of Ethics* with reference to providing "the social bases of self-respect and nonhumiliation; being able to be treated as a dignified being whose worth is equal to that of others . . . entails protections against discrimination on the basis of race, sex, sexual orientation, religion, caste, ethnicity, or national origin" (Figure 27.1; also see Nussbaum, 1999). This capability reminds social workers of the importance of addressing social policies that perpetuate discrimination as well as discriminatory interpersonal practices.

Social justice as a value guides social work practice to focus on engaging individuals and groups in interpersonal and societal interactions. Throughout the intervention process, it is important to identify and support the affiliations that clients have with others (e.g., social interactions, friendships, support networks) in order to develop, discover, and create environments that support their freedom and capacity to engage in healthy relationships. Through the promotion of social justice on an individual level, social workers can empower a client in a way that promotes self-respect and sense of dignity. As a result, clients are encouraged to advocate for their needs and the needs of their community. The nature of interpersonal relations impacts the existence of social justice in communities. The ability of communities to adopt practices and policies that support equality is often impacted by the affiliations of individuals within that community. It is necessary to promote affiliations that promote one's self-worth and ability to meaningfully engage with others in order to "ensure that all people have equal access to the resources, employment, services, and opportunities they require to meet their basic human needs and to develop fully" (NASW, 2009, p. 27).

In addition, it is important to note how societal structures impact the capability for affiliation among individuals and groups. The capability for affiliation includes caring for others, recognizing the equal worth of all people, and demonstrating compassion for others. Societal systems that perpetuate discrimination and inequality should be addressed in order to increase the potential of affiliation between individuals and groups. By standing up against discrimination and promoting the dignity of each human being, social workers and their clients can promote social justice and social change.

Other Species

When recognizing the intricate ties between the well-being of the world of nature (e.g., sources of food and companionship) and that of human beings, the ability to care for other species and nature is essential to the fulfillment of social justice. Environmental destruction often disproportionately impacts the lives of those who are marginalized by poverty, race, and social isolation. Social workers become involved in promoting the betterment of other species and, therefore, also the betterment of human beings, through involvement in environmental advocacy and educational movements and antipoverty movements.

Play

The capability to play is a key component of human well-being. This expands on the NASW's ethical notion of ensuring equal opportunities beyond the provision of basic needs to a level of provision and equality that allows individuals to move beyond living life filled with anxiety and fear to a life in which one has the capacity "to laugh, to play, to enjoy recreational activities" (Figure 27.1). For example, advocating for environments conducive to play could involve challenging unfair labor practices or addressing poverty and discrimination.

Control Over One's Environment

The capacity for control over one's environment relates to empowering individuals to exercise their political rights, ensuring equal access to goods, and creating environments in which individuals are treated with respect. In essence, promoting social justice involves influencing larger systems, including the promotion of policies and programs that enable individuals to gain control over their environment.

Social workers who are aware that particular groups of people are not exercising their right to vote or engage in the workforce can work with members of that group to increase public attention about the discrepancy and to advocate for change in social policy. When advocating in the political arena for equal access to services, employment, and resources, the goal is to create space for individuals to have the freedom to be able to engage in self-determination when it comes to making decisions about their self-sufficiency and affiliations. For example, Nussbaum includes in this capability the ability to possess a political voice, equal opportunities in employment, fair treatment as an employee, and the ability to own material goods.

Since policies directly impact political and material environments, it is important to ensure political participation, free speech, fairness in the workplace, and equal rights to property in order to create environments that promote social justice. As environments continuously change, it is important to assess the need for additional rights to promote social justice.

The process of applying the human capabilities approach has already been demonstrated in the field of education (as noted in Figure 27.2) and resulted in the development of four educational principles: "1) independent and critical thought, critical thinking, reasoning, reflection, learner agency, and responsibility for [one's] own learning; 2) knowledge for values, citizenship, [and] contribution to economic development; 3) bodily integrity and health, safety at school, no corporal punishment, freedom from sexual harassment and violence, choice in sexual relationships, [and] protection against HIV; and 4) respect for self, for others, for other cultures, [and for] being treated with dignity" (Walker, 2006, p. 170). As seen in this chapter, the application of the human capabilities approach can also inform the use of social justice principles and practices in the social work profession.

Education is a basic capability that affects the development and expansion of other capabilities, especially in the area of gender equity, and includes the following:

1. *Independent and critical thought:* critical thinking, reasoning, reflection, learner agency, and responsibility for (one's) own learning

   a. *Autonomy*—being able to have choices, having information on which to make choices, planning a life after school, reflection, independence, and empowerment
   b. *Aspiration*—motivation to learn and succeed, to have a better life, and to hope

---

Figure 27.2   Capability-Based Approach to Social Justice in Education

2. *Knowledge:* for values, citizenship, contribution to economic development

   a. Knowledge—of school subjects that are intrinsically interesting or instrumentally useful for post-school choices of study, paid work, and a career; girls' access to all school subjects; access to powerful analytical knowledge; knowledge of girls' and women's lives, of critical thinking, and for debating complex moral and social issues; knowledge from involvement in intrinsically interesting school societies; active inquiry, transformation of understanding, and fair assessment or examination of knowledge gained
   b. Voice—for participation in learning, speaking out, not being silenced through pedagogy or power relations or harassment, or excluded from the curriculum; being active in the acquisition of knowledge

3. *Bodily integrity and health:* safety at school, no corporal punishment, freedom from sexual harassment and violence, choice in sexual relationships, protection against HIV

   a. *Bodily integrity and bodily health*—not to be subjected to any harassment at school by peers or teachers, generally being safe at school; making own choices about sexual relationships; being able to be free from sexually transmitted diseases; being involved in sporting activities
   b. *Emotional integrity and emotions*—not being subject to fear, either from physical punishment or verbal attacks, which diminishes learning; developing emotions and imagination for understanding, empathy, awareness, and discernment

4. *Respect: for self, for others, for other cultures, and, being treated with dignity*

   a. *Social relations*—the capability to be a friend; the capability to participate in a group for friendship and learning, to be able to work with others to solve problems and tasks; being able to work with others to form effective, or good, groups for learning and organizing life in school; being able to respond to human need, and social belonging
   b. *Respect and recognition*—self-confidence and self-esteem; respect for and from others; being treated with dignity; not being diminished or devalued because of one's gender, social class, religion or race; valuing other languages, other religions and spiritual practices, and human diversity; showing imaginative empathy, compassion, fairness, and generosity; listening to and considering other persons' point of views in dialogue and debate in and out of class in school; being able to act inclusively

Source: Adapted from M. Walker. (2006). Towards a capability-based theory of social justice for education policy-making. *Journal of Education Policy.* 21(2), 170, 179–180.

Figure 27.2   Continued

CONCLUSION

Humanistic social work, restorative justice, and the NASW's *Code of Ethics* share common themes that guide efforts to promote social justice, namely, the belief in the worth and dignity of individuals, the engagement of individuals in planning and living their own lives, and creating environments that promote human rights and social justice. By understanding how the key tenets of social justice in the NASW's *Code of Ethics* align with specific human capabilities, it is possible to define specific social justice goals in

work with individuals and communities and to begin measuring the success of such interventions.

One approach to integrating social justice principles with human capabilities is to propose a tool or checklist that can accompany any agency intake form or service planning document, as noted in Figure 27.3. The questions in the tool are a reminder to consider a holistic and humanistic approach to client well-being. The use of this assessment involves an evaluation of the current needs of the client or group as well as an examination of the community context in which the client lives. By using information gathered from the client and community, responses to the questions can be used to help assess the impact of social injustice on the lives of clients. If answers to the assessment questions reveal adversity, social workers can implement the principles of humanistic social work to partner with clients to increase their access to services and resources while also engaging with the community to promote a more equitable and just environment. The assessment tool provides insight into focus areas for pursuing social justice in the community.

Principle 1: Collaborate with and advocate on behalf of clients for social change.

1. *Bodily integrity: Is community action taken to promote the bodily integrity and well-being of all individuals, and are there opportunities for being involved in these actions?*
2. *Affiliation: Does the client interact with individuals or groups that treat he or she with dignity and respect? Are there avenues available for addressing both subtle and overt discrimination?*
3. *Control over one's environment: Is the client able to participate in political processes? Does the client have access to basic necessities and employment or other income?*
4. *Practical reason: Does the client have opportunities to meaningfully participate in decisions that impact their life?*

Principle 2: Promote cultural competency and equity.

1. *Senses, imagination, and thought: Do legislative policies and programs that the client accesses support and promote cultural competency?*
2. *Affiliation: Does the client's environment (including programs accessed) promote freedom of expression? Do programs and institutions promote and take action to ensure equity for all people?*
3. *Control over one's environment: Do policies and programs ensure equity of opportunity, fair treatment under the law, and political participation for all?*
4. *Emotions: Does the client have supports with whom to express authentic emotion and connection?*

Principle 3: Oppose injustice and promote empowerment and equal access.

1. *Life: Does the client's access to resources and environment promote a natural lifespan?*
2. *Bodily health: Does the client have the information and resources needed to maintain good health?*
3. *Affiliation: Do the organizations and employment agencies with which the client interacts practice nondiscrimination?*
4. *Play: Do the demands on the client's life allow the capacity for some degree of play?*

Principle 4: Advocate for environments conducive to social justice.

1. *Bodily health: Are the housing, health care, and nutrition necessary for good health available and accessible in the client's community?*
2. *Bodily integrity: Are there resources and community support to address violence and assist victims? Does the client have access to information on reproductive choices?*
3. *Senses, imagination, and thought: Does the client have access to an adequate education? Does the client's environment support freedom of expression?*
4. *Affiliation: Does the client have a support network? Is the client's environment free from discrimination?*
5. *Control over one's environment: Is the client's environment free from barriers to political participation? Is the client able to exercise rights to employment and properties?*

Figure 27.3   Social Justice as a Core Social Work Value—Assessment Tool

6. Other species: Does the client have access to information about and resources for participating in the care for the natural environment? Does the client's exposure to her natural environment impact her health or well-being?

Figure 27.3   Continued

This tool is designed to complement existing agency assessment tools (e.g., a job skills assessment, a mental health assessment, child abuse or neglect assessment, etc.), and it can be easily adapted to fit local contexts. To effectively promote social justice, it is necessary to maintain an ongoing dialogue about specific goals and purposes in both social worker-client and social worker-community interactions. This framework and assessment tool provides another way to promote dialogue on the nature and practice of social justice.

REFERENCES

Abrams, L. S., Umbreit, M., & Gordon, A. (2006). Young offenders speak about meeting their victims: Implications for future programs. *Contemporary Justice Review, 9*(3), 243–256.

Baffour, T. D. (2006). Ethnic and gender differences in offending patterns: Examining family group conferencing interventions among at-risk adolescents. *Child and Adolescent Social Work Journal, 23*(5–6), 557–578.

Bradshaw, W., Roseborough, D., & Umbreit, M. S. (2006). The effect of victim offender mediation on juvenile offender recidivism: A meta-analysis. *Conflict Resolution Quarterly, 24*(1), 87–98.

Burford, G., & Adams, P. (2004). Restorative justice, responsive regulation and social work. *Journal of Sociology and Social Welfare, 31*(1), 7–26.

Centre for Justice & Reconciliation. (2008). *What is restorative justice?* Washington, DC: Prison Fellowship International.

Daly, K. (2002). Restorative justice: The real story. *Punishment & Society, 4*(1), 55–79.

Furman, R., Langer, C. L., & Anderson, D. K. (2006). The poet/practitioner: A paradigm for the profession. *Journal of Sociology and Social Welfare, 33*(3), 29–50.

Kenny, J. S., & Clairmont, D. (2009). Using the victim role as both sword and shield: The interactional dynamics of restorative justice sessions. *Journal of Contemporary Ethnography, 38*(3), 279–307.

Latimer, J., Dowden, C., & Muise, D. (2005). The effectiveness of restorative justice practices: A meta-analysis. *Prison Journal, 85*(2), 127–144.

Morrison, B., & Ahmen, E. (2006). Restorative justice and civil society: Emerging practice, theory, and evidence. *Journal of Social Issues, 62*(2), 209–215.

National Association of Social Workers (NASW). (2009). *Code of ethics of the National Association of Social Workers.* Washington, DC: NASW Press.

Nussbaum, M. (1997). Capabilities and human rights. *Fordham Law Review, 66*(2), 273–300.

Nussbaum, M. (1999). Women and equality: The capabilities approach. *International Labour Review, 138*(3), 227–245.

Payne, M. (2011). *Humanistic social work: Core principles in practice.* Chicago, IL: Lyceum Books.

Pranis, K. (2004). The practice and efficacy of restorative justice. *Journal of Religion & Spirituality in Social Work: Social Thought, 23*(1), 133–157.

Richards, K. (2011). Restorative justice and "empowerment": Producing and governing active subjects through "empowering" practices. *Critical Criminology, 19*, 91–105.

Umbreit, M. S., Coates, R. B., & Vos, B. (2007). Restorative justice dialogue: A multi-dimensional, evidence-based practice theory. *Contemporary Justice Review, 10*(1), 23–41.

Van Ness, D. W. (2004). Justice that restores: From impersonal to personal justice. *Journal of Religion & Spirituality in Social Work: Social Thought, 23*(1), 93–109.

Van Wormer, K. (2004). Restorative justice: A model for personal and societal empowerment. *Journal of Religion & Spirituality in Social Work, 23*(4), 103–120.

Walker, M. (2006). Towards a capability-based theory of social justice for education policy-making. *Journal of Education Policy, 21*(2), 170, 179–180.

Zehr, H. (2002). *The little book of restorative justice.* Intercourse, PA: Good Books.

28

FINDING THE COURAGE OF ONE'S CONVICTIONS

Reflections on a Lifetime of Social Work Practice

BRIAN CAHILL

with the assistance of Michael J. Austin

SETTING THE CONTEXT

Early in my career, I served in the Marine Corps Reserve and, upon discharge from active duty, went immediately to work in a Catholic group home for delinquent youth in a predominantly African American neighborhood. The agency sent me back to school for a graduate degree in social work, and I eventually became the agency's executive director. Later, I went to work for the Peace Corps and, with my family, spent 2 years in Africa. It was a temptation for me to change career tracks and look at overseas work, but we got caught up in violent government change, and it was time to come home and get back in the safe world that we knew.

Upon return, I worked in the state capitol for an advocacy organization, representing nonprofit children's service providers. Based on this experience, I was recruited to serve as executive director of one of these provider agencies in the southern part of the state that included a mix of residential and community-based mental health services and foster family

care and family preservation services. I loved the agency because it still gave me some contact with the kids. The agency provided me with a chance to return to running an organization where I had the opportunity to use my policy advocacy experience by participating in the city's planning council that included participants from universities, business, government, and nonprofits. It was an exciting time for me, and it helped me position the agency for a higher profile in a very large county and, at the same time, meet some of my own advocacy interests.

My next transition from the nonprofit sector to government came after a mayoral election in my hometown where a number of people who knew the new mayor and knew me recommended me for the position of director of the city's Department of Human Services. The move was a coming home, and it was to a community that I knew pretty well . . . and I was challenged by it. I left that politically appointed position after 4 years when the mayor was not reelected. I was recruited to work for a large national for-profit consulting firm that worked with state and local governments on human service programs. Within a few years, I was recruited back to the nonprofit sector to become director of a large Catholic youth organization that eventually merged with the large Catholic social service agency where I served as executive director until my retirement.

My boundary crossing experiences included all three sectors and reflected my keen interest in the politics associated with each position. My experiences in the Marine Corps, Peace Corps, city government, legislative branch of state government, child welfare services, and Catholic social services reflected my strong commitment to advocacy on behalf of others. In my position in the public sector, I was lobbied by advocacy organizations and provider groups in a city of activists where everybody has got something to say on every issue. I have never been in a job that had more of an incredible rush because of the interface of politics, policy, and service delivery where every day revealed different issues that were both challenging and fascinating.

TESTING MY SENSE OF SOCIAL JUSTICE IN THE PUBLIC SECTOR

The position of general manager in the San Francisco Department of Human Services is an extremely high-risk and stressful job due to the existence of strong advocacy and interest groups and an influential media. I experienced a number of politically volatile situations soon after taking charge. One of the first such experiences involved my decision to remove some children from a foster home who were perceived to be at risk. The case came to my attention since I was also serving at that time as the acting assistant director of California Children Services to cover the responsibility of a vacant senior management position. In view of the gravity of the situation, I approached the court to obtain permission to remove the children. The judge denied the request. In addition to receiving conflicting input from staff, I was in a fix because I was well aware of the danger that the children would be in over the weekend at the foster home. In what I considered the best interest of the children, I decided to have the children removed in spite of the judge's order. The judge held me in contempt of court and sentenced me to 6 weekends in the Sheriff's Work Alternative Program. There I spent time with those held on drug, driving under the influence (DUI), and domestic violence charges, and they found it hard to believe that the judge had sentenced a county agency director to do time. It turned out that the foster mother had been abusive, so the 6 weekends were worth it.

TESTING MY SENSE OF SOCIAL JUSTICE IN THE NONPROFIT SECTOR

As executive director of a Catholic nonprofit social service agency, I was always mindful of the fact that we staff members are the social service arm of the church. As the "face" of the organization, we represented the need to manage our religious identity as well as the people's perceptions of who we are because our name is Catholic Charities. In particular, we were constantly managing the tension between what our church teaches in the area of sexuality and how we carry out our mission in this pluralistic society, in the midst of never-ending battles related to domestic partners, abortion, contraception, gay marriage, and same-sex adoption. One approach that I adopted to help staff manage these tensions is captured in a session that I led on new employee orientation on Catholic identity.

I wanted new employees to know what they were getting into. What does it mean that we are a Catholic agency? And just as important, what does it not mean? It does not mean that you must be Catholic to work in this agency, and it does not mean you must be Catholic to receive services. However, it does mean that you need to understand our values, especially to care for those unable to care for themselves. In the Old Testament, there was the tradition of caring for widows, orphans, and sojourners. In the New Testament, there is Matthew 25: "What you did for the least of my brothers, you did for me." Today, our widows are single moms transitioning off public assistance, our orphans are the 82,000 children in the foster care system, and our sojourners are the people on the margins of society, whether it's from drugs or HIV or homelessness. If staff members can identify with this value of caring for others, it does not matter if they have a belief system or not. Somewhere in us is a calling that reminds us that we do have some responsibility in this world for our brothers and our sisters who are poor or vulnerable or marginalized. I also reminded the new staff that part of the vision of bringing together Catholic Charities and the Catholic Youth Organization was to provide opportunities for healthy growth and development for children and youth so that they do not become poor or vulnerable or marginalized.

In the staff orientation session, I focused on Catholic social teaching, especially charity and justice as noted in Figure 28.1. For all the flaws of the Catholic Church, Catholic social teaching has been a powerful and significant contribution to our society. Martin Luther King developed part of his philosophy based on these teachings. The American labor movement is based on these teachings. These are moral teachings applicable in all elements of our society and useful as a guide for how we should all relate to each other.

The Catholic approach to faithful citizenship begins with moral principles, not party platforms. The directions for our public witness are found in Scripture and Catholic social teaching. The following are key themes at the heart of our Catholic social tradition.

Life and Dignity of the Human Person

Every human person is created in the image and likeness of God. The conviction that human life is sacred and that each person has inherent dignity that must be respected in society lies at the heart of Catholic social teaching. Calls to advance human rights are illusions if the right to life itself is subject to attack. We believe every human life is sacred from conception to natural death, that people are more important than things, and that the measure of every institution is whether or not it enhances the life and dignity of the human person.

Call to Family, Community, and Participation

The human person is not only sacred but also inherently social. The God-given institutions of marriage and the family are central and serve as the foundations for social life. They must be supported and strengthened, not undermined. Beyond the family, every person has the right to participate in the wider society and a corresponding duty to work for the advancement of the common good and the well-being of all, especially the poor and weak.

Rights and Responsibilities

As social beings, our relationships are governed by a web of rights and corresponding duties. Every person has a fundamental right to life and a right to those things that allow them to live a decent life—faith and family, food and shelter, health care and housing, education and employment. In a society as a whole, those who exercise authority have a duty to respect the fundamental human rights of all persons. Likewise, all citizens have a duty to respect human rights and to fulfill their responsibilities to their families, to each other, and to the larger society.

Option for the Poor and Vulnerable

Scripture teaches that God has a special concern for the poor and vulnerable. The prophets denounced injustice toward the poor as a lack of fidelity to the God of Israel. Jesus, who identified himself with the least of these, came to preach the good news to the poor and told us, "Give to him who asks of you, do not refuse one who would borrow from you," Matthew 5:42. The church calls on all of us to embrace this preferential love of the poor and vulnerable, to embody it in our lives, and to work to have it shape public policies and priorities.

Dignity of Work and the Rights of Workers

The economy must serve people, not the other way around. Work is more than a way to make a living; it is a form of continuing participation in God's act of creation. Work is a way of fulfilling part of our human potential given to us by God. If the dignity of work is to be protected, then the basic rights of workers, owners, and managers must be respected—the right to productive work, to decent and fair wages, to organize and join unions, to economic initiative, and to ownership and private property.

Figure 28.1   Themes of Catholic Social Teaching

(Continued)

Solidarity

Because of the interdependence among all the members of the human family around the globe, we have a moral responsibility to commit ourselves to the common good at all levels: in local communities, in our nation, in the community of nations. We are our brothers' and sisters' keepers, wherever they may be. As Pope John Paul II has said, "We are all really responsible for all."

Care for God's Creation

The world that God created has been entrusted to us, yet our use of it must be directed by God's plan for creation, not simply by our own benefit. Our stewardship of Earth is a kind of participation in God's act of creating and sustaining the world. In our use of creation, we must be guided by our concern for the welfare of others, both around the world and for generations to come, and by a respect for the intrinsic worth and beauty of all God's creatures.

Figure 28.1   Continued

In the orientation sessions, I shared with staff our agency's positions on social justice issues; then, I got into the tricky issues of sexuality and how we manage the tension between what the Catholic Church teaches in terms of sexuality and how we are expected to carry out our mission in this very pluralistic society. In the area of domestic partners, the City of San Francisco mandated that all contractors must provide domestic partner benefits. The initial response of Catholic Charities was that this would be problematic in terms of church teaching as to who can be married. But creative heads came together on both sides, and Catholic Charities proposed that the city broaden its policy beyond gay and lesbian partner benefits to include any legally domiciled household member who is uninsured, including seniors and children. From the point of view of Catholic Church teaching, the criteria then became "need and household status" rather than sexual orientation. It also was a step toward universal health care. The city bought off on the compromise and this solution allowed us to be consistent with the teachings of the Catholic Church and the mandates of the city and county of San Francisco.

In another instance, the city mandated that our health plans provide direct abortion coverage. I explained that as a Catholic agency, that would never happen. On the other hand, because two thirds of our workforce members are women of childbearing age, I felt an equally strong obligation to respect their needs. The resulting compromise was that we agreed to add $50 a month ($600 a year) to each employee's flex credit benefit for any "uncovered medical expense," and to create a third-party, interest-free confidentially administered loan program to allow employees to borrow up to $600 a year for an "emergency uncovered medical expense."

When the issue of same-sex adoption emerged and the Vatican told us to stop doing same-sex adoptions, we found another creative solution. We transferred our workers to a neighboring adoption agency—not to work in their direct adoption program but to staff a statewide website, promoting the needs of hard-to-place children in the foster care system and responding to calls from potentially adoptive parents who expressed interest in those children. We significantly increased our impact in the adoption field by serving these vulnerable children without undermining church teaching. Unfortunately, this program ended as I left the agency.

Making Advocacy a Form of Daily Practice

While it is difficult to find time in the pressures of daily practice to write Op-Ed statements for publication in the local media, the first few years of my retirement finally gave me space to write. Even though I wrote many agency memos and statements throughout my years in practice, I did not give myself much credit for being a writer. As you see in the Op-Ed pieces in this chapter, I began to find my voice on the written page and discovered the therapeutic value of expressing my emotions and my concerns about the need to improve our society. I began to recognize that the "personal is political" and the "professional is political." In both cases, I began to find my "voice" by reflecting on the implications of personal experiences for professional practice and vice versa. The Op-Ed on police suicide in Figure 28.2 arose out of the loss of my son who was a police officer and took his life. It was very personal, but I also realized I wanted to use my professional experience as an advocate to educate the community.

Brian Cahill

Sunday, May 22, 2011

San Francisco Chronicle

My son John took his life in December 2008. He was a police officer for 19 years. He was a loving father. He was my first born. He was my rock.

When my son died, I learned about cops and suicide. I learned that the very characteristics that make a good cop can be lethal when that cop gets depressed. Good cops are highly functioning, are used to bringing control out of chaos and are willing to risk everything during a critical incident because they know the incident will come to closure.

My son had been through a painful divorce and did not feel he was functioning well in any aspect of his life. He did not feel he could control the chaos in his life. And he thought his problems, the multiple "critical incidents" he was encountering, would never come to an end. He was wrong on all three counts, but I know that is how he felt. I think that is when he decided to take control and bring things to an end. I think he felt that all of us who loved him and needed him would be better off if he were gone. He was wrong. He was so wrong.

Two years later, I am still grieving the loss of my son. I will be for the rest of my life. We were very close. We talked a lot about his situation and his depression. He was seeing a counselor, and he seemed to be doing all the right things to get through. Until the last year of his life, he was one of the most secure and vibrant human beings I knew. I realize now that my perception of who he was precluded me from seeing that he was capable of taking his life. I cannot say with certainty that, had I understood this "profile" of cops and depression and suicide, I could have stopped him. But I wish I had had the knowledge and the opportunity to try.

My son shot himself on a trail in the Santa Cruz Mountains. Whenever I sink into my own depression and horror triggered by that nightmare image, my wife reminds me that "his soul never touched the ground." I believe that.

My son was one of two San Jose police officers who committed suicide that year. The California Highway Patrol lost 13 officers to suicide between 2005 and 2007. The San Francisco Police Department has lost three officers in the last year. According to the National Police Suicide Foundation, more than 400 officers take their lives every year.

I do not know if SFPD and other police departments are doing everything they should to prevent suicides among their officers. And I am not qualified to tell them what their policy should be or how they should train. But I am qualified to tell every cop on the job to pay attention to this issue, for your own good and for that of your fellow officers. I am qualified to tell every father and mother of a cop, every wife and partner of a cop, every brother and sister of a cop, every close friend of a cop to pay close attention to this issue. I might not be completely objective, but I believe that if this could happen to my son, it could happen to any police officer.

The SFPD has begun to address this issue in its advanced officer training program. The department also has a strong peer support program. The Highway Patrol has developed a comprehensive approach to suicide

Figure 28.2   "Suicide Is Another Danger Faced by Cops," Op-Ed

(Continued)

awareness and prevention. San Jose Police Department has developed a suicide prevention policy and a department-wide, mandatory training program. Officers who are dealing with serious depression can come in and get help, have the situation treated confidentially, without the risk of losing their gun and their badge. A dozen cops have gotten help and have been able to stay on the job. I hope all police departments are or soon will be taking this approach. I hope the culture of "tough it out, don't show weakness" is changing.

Police work is incredibly challenging and stressful, not just physically dangerous but also fraught with conflict and controversy. Cops are not perfect. We know there can be errors in judgment, in some cases violations of the public trust or abuse. But the great majority of men and women who wear the uniform do their job extremely well and at times take great risks. Like many first responders, they constantly have to figure out how to achieve the necessary balance between the pressures and realities of their job and their responsibilities and needs when they are not on the job.

We who benefit from their protecting and serving us, especially those of us who know cops and whose loved ones are cops, have a clear moral obligation to do all we can to protect and serve them.

Brian Cahill is former executive director of Catholic Charities in San Francisco.

Figure 28.2   Continued

Growing up and living most of my life in San Francisco, it was clear to me that tolerance for diversity is what has made the city a world-class place to live and work. It was one of the first cities on this planet to openly address the issues of HIV/AIDS. I was bothered by the passage of Proposition 8 that prohibited gay marriage. I was even more bothered by the terrible language that my church uses to define its position against gay marriage and same-sex adoption. And I was outraged at the disrespect that some Catholic leaders show to gays and lesbians. Again, the personal is political as you can see in my second Op-Ed in Figure 28.3 related to my other son who is gay.

Brian Cahill

Sunday, March 13, 2011

San Francisco Chronicle

I am a Catholic who voted against Proposition 8 in 2008 and contributed $1,000 to the No on 8 Campaign, a Catholic who is sustained by regular Mass, scripture and prayer. I am also the father of a gay son, from whom I was slow to learn how painful, debilitating and denigrating are the constant legal and social reminders that he and those like him are not fully accepted members of the human community.

In their statement supporting Prop. 8, the California Catholic Bishops declared that marriage is "intrinsic to stable, flourishing and hospitable societies." Ironically, this is one of the compelling reasons gay and lesbian couples wish to be joined in civil marriages. They are seeking a structure and context for their love, commitment, fidelity and mutual support.

Many believe that the ideal for children is to be raised by a mother and a father, yet we know what the divorce rate is among heterosexual couples. We know there are 75,000 children in the California foster care system, a quarter of them waiting to be adopted. We know that these children have been victimized by the inability, neglect or abuse of their heterosexual parents. These mothers and fathers are living proof that sexual orientation is not a reliable indicator of good parenting.

Our bishops are clear that gays and lesbians must be respected and not disparaged, and I know they mean it. The archbishop of San Francisco, regardless of his position on Prop. 8, means it. His first response to specific issues regarding gays and lesbians is always pastoral.

Figure 28.3   "My Gay Son: The Face of Church's Lack of Respect," Op-Ed

But when gays and lesbians are referred to in a 2003 Vatican teaching as "objectively disordered," it is difficult for them to feel respected. When gay and lesbian couples are willing to assume full, loving parental responsibility for abused and neglected children who would otherwise languish in the foster care system, and church teaching characterizes them as "doing great violence to children" by raising them in same-sex households, it is difficult for those parents to feel respected. And if gays and lesbians were to read some of the bloggers on conservative Catholic websites, they might have difficulty distinguishing the comments of thoughtful conservative Catholics from those of irrational, homophobic extremists, and they would definitely not feel respected.

Prior to the passage of Prop. 8, the California Supreme Court ruled that as a matter of constitutional law, gays and lesbians have a right to form a family relationship. From the court's perspective, a family relationship is much more than a domestic partnership. It is about marriage.

In August 2010, the federal District Court ruled that laws defining marriage as heterosexual are unconstitutional and unjust. Even if the Ninth U.S. Circuit Court of Appeals allows the resumption of same sex-marriages, this issue will continue through the courts.

The issue of same-sex marriage will also be on the ballot again. The proponents of Prop. 8 have said that the voters' wishes should be respected. They should be careful what they wish for. In 2000, they won with 61 percent of the vote. In 2008, they won with 53 percent of the vote. In 2012, we will see how well they respect the voters' wishes.

I know that my son and his partner are made in the image and likeness of God. They are not perfect, but they are brilliant, creative, personable and moral. They are certainly not objectively disordered. I know, as do many fathers, mothers, grandparents, sisters, brothers, friends, neighbors, co-workers and fellow parishioners of gay and lesbian individuals and couples, that the relationship, the love, the friendship, the personal association, the proximity, put a human face on this issue and let us see that in the context of the human spirit, none of us are different and none of us should be anything less than fully accepted members of our human community.

Brian Cahill is the former executive director of Catholic Charities in San Francisco.

Figure 28.3   Continued

As I move from the personal is political to the professional is political, I also find my self drawing upon my social work values as related to social justice. As can be seen in Figure 28.4 in "Religious Liberty and Credibility," I focus on the efforts of the Obama Administration to find ways to improve our health care system. As you'll recall in my earlier example of health care benefits for the staff of Catholic Charities, I feel strongly about the access of all people to health care, not as a privilege connected to one's social status but as a human right related to treating people in need. I also felt that the American Catholic Bishops, in arguing for religious liberty, had little credibility on the issue of contraception, a church teaching that has been long dismissed by the great majority of Catholics.

Brian Cahill

Tuesday, February 21, 2012

San Francisco Chronicle

The recent compromise by the Obama administration on its proposed mandate of contraception was an appropriate response to legitimate and widespread Catholic concerns about religious liberty. Most Catholic

Figure 28.4   "Religious Liberty and Credibility," Op-Ed

(Continued)

organizations affected by the mandate found the compromise acceptable. The major holdout is the U.S. Conference of Catholic Bishops.

Even though the bishops have no credibility with their teachings on contraception, they were supported by the majority of Catholics in their initial response to the mandate. Now the conference is hanging out there all by itself with little Catholic support, not just because the great majority of Catholics have long rejected church teaching on contraception, not just because 95 percent of Catholic women of child-bearing age use contraception, but because American Catholics now know that 28 states, including California, have had similar mandates in place for some time.

And now American Catholics and the rest of the country know that the real agenda of the U.S. Conference of Catholic Bishops is to stop any government health care mandate. This is sad and ironic because the Catholic Church has historically been a strong advocate of health care access for those who need it. Worse, the conference is specifically demanding an exemption for any employer who would have a "conscience" problem with providing contraceptive coverage for employees. In other words, in the name of "religious liberty," these bishops want to force their religious belief on employees who do not share their belief. Not only is this effort turning religious liberty on its head, but it ignores the reality that affordable health care, including contraception, is the most effective way to significantly reduce abortion.

It has been clear for some time that the conference does not speak for the majority of American Catholics. There is no great evidence that the conference even speaks for all the bishops. The problem is that the bishops running the conference—with their overt political activism, with their inflammatory language and with their lack of pastoral sensitivity—have little credibility as true Catholic leaders. And it's not just in the area of contraception.

The conference freely jumps into the political arena on most sexuality issues, but has refused to issue a public statement condemning bullying of gay and lesbian youth.

Even after the contraception compromise was offered, Cardinal Francis George of Chicago described the Obama administration as making a "severe assault on religious liberty." This is the same bishop who only a few months ago expressed concern that a gay pride parade could result in anti-Catholic violence and compared the LGBT movement to the Ku Klux Klan. And Archbishop Charles Chaput of Philadelphia described the contraception mandate as the "embodiment of culture war." Four years ago, he told Catholics not to vote for Obama.

Cardinal Timothy Dolan of New York is the president of the U.S. Conference of Bishops. Last year, in an interview on "60 Minutes," he compared homosexuality to incest. And the other day, in attempting to defend his position against the contraception mandate, he assured us, "We bishops are pastors, we're not politicians," and later, "it's not that we hold fast, that we're stubborn ideologues, no."

There are many good bishops in this country who are pastors, who operate out of compassion, who are not ideologues and who understand that a necessary part of shepherding their flock, and a necessary part of serving those in need, is a willingness to manage the tension between Church teaching and how Catholic health and human service providers carry out their mission in a pluralistic society.

I am a Catholic. I go to Mass. I love my Church. I love its rich history of serving the poor, the vulnerable and the marginalized. I am not leaving.

But it seems to me that the Catholic bishops who have led the charge on this issue have succeeded only in showing how wide the gap is between the Catholic faithful and some of its bishops, have left the impression that the issue of conscience only seems to arise over matters of sexuality, have ended up intentionally or otherwise in bed with the likes of Newt Gingrich, have inadvertently become a potential obstacle to affordable health care for those most in need, and have further diminished the moral influence and teaching authority that many Catholics used to respect and desire from their bishops.

Brian Cahill is the former executive director of Catholic Charities of San Francisco.

Figure 28.4   Continued

My last example relates to those ignored and suffering alone in our prison system. As you can see in Figure 28.5, "Delayed Justice and Fiscal Prudence," I again tried to get those in power, including members of the legislature and judiciary, to pay attention to the way in which our prison system is so inefficient and flawed. I tried to put a human face on the men who are serving time far beyond their original sentence.

Brian Cahill

September 13th, 2011

Catholic San Francisco

Much attention has recently been given to the major flaws of the California prison system, including the inadequacy of the health care system, the various attempts to abolish the death penalty, the need for adjustments to the three strikes law, the wisdom of convicting 16-year-olds to life without possibility of parole, a U.S. Supreme Court order to reduce the overall prison population by 33,000, the impact of the current state budget crisis, and the recent policy shift of sending nonviolent drug offenders to county jail instead of state prison.

But there is one issue, if it can be addressed without hysteria and political grandstanding, which could result in a wonderful convergence of applied justice and sound fiscal policy.

For the last six years, I have had the privilege of serving as a volunteer at Our Lady of the Rosary Chapel in San Quentin Prison. I attend Mass and visit with the men on Sundays, and on Tuesday evenings I participate with two other volunteers and a dozen inmates in a spirituality group.

Almost all the men I spend time with are "lifers," but they have not received a sentence of life without the possibility of parole. On the contrary, their sentences specifically include the possibility of parole. Many of the men I know were convicted of second-degree murder in their teens or early 20s. Most of them were sentenced to 15 years to life. According to the sentencing guidelines, that meant that if they met all the criteria for rehabilitation they could be paroled in 12 to 15 years. There are 24,000 such term-to-lifers in the California prison system, and 8,000 of them have met all the criteria for rehabilitation, but have served time far beyond the criteria required for parole. Most of the men I know in this situation have served more than 20 years, and in some cases over 30 years. Each of these inmates cost the tax payers between $50,000 and $65,000 annually to house in our state prison system.

Ever since Willie Horton, a paroled Massachusetts inmate violently reoffended and, among other things, hurt the cause of presidential nominee Michael Dukakis, elected officials have been reluctant to take responsibility for paroled inmates. California Gov. Gray Davis, during his term, vetoed 98 percent of paroles granted. Gov. Arnold Schwarzenegger vetoed 70 percent. Also, during this time, the state parole board denied many paroles, not based on evidence showing lack of rehabilitation, but simply based on the nature of the original crime. However, in 2008, the California Supreme Court ruled that the parole board could not deny parole relying only on the nature of the original crime. The crime itself can still be a factor, but the court told the parole board to focus on whether the inmate would be a risk to public safety. Since Gov. Jerry Brown has taken office, he has only overruled parole board releases in 11percent of all cases.

The men I have come to know, these "lifers," are men of deep spirituality, full of insight and remorse for the crimes they have committed and the great harm and pain they brought to others. They are more than qualified and capable of returning to the free community, and in many cases, they will serve others in the free community. It should also be noted that while the recidivism rate for fixed term inmates is 70 percent, the recidivism rate for term-to-lifers is 1 percent.

Should they have been held accountable and punished for their crime? Yes! Should they be held beyond the term of their adjudicated sentence even though they have met all the rehabilitation criteria for release? No! They were sentenced with the possibility for parole. They have done their time and then

---

Figure 28.5 "Delayed Justice and Fiscal Prudence" (http://catholic-sf.org/news_select.php?newsid=7&id=58907)

(Continued)

some. They are not the same men they were when they did their crime. We need to see them and know them for who they are now, not who they were 20 or 25 years ago. We need to see them as living witnesses to the transforming power of faith. If we are followers of Jesus Christ, then we believe in forgiveness and redemption, and we need to live that belief.

It would appear that not all Christians are living that belief. Sen. Ted Gaines, a Republican from Placer County, has introduced SB 391, which would wipe out the Supreme Court ruling, and allow the parole board to revert to only considering the nature of the crime, and ignore issues of rehabilitation and safety of return to the free community. The bill was inspired by the parole of Phillip Garrido and his subsequent abduction of Jaycee Lee Duggard. The advocates of this bill, including the major victim support group, Crime Victims United, conveniently ignore that Garrido was paroled by federal and Nevada prison officials, and was never in the California system. This bill, were it to pass, would condemn most if not all of the 24,000 term-to-lifers to a lifetime behind bars, and give them no incentive to rehabilitate themselves. The legislation would drastically add to an already crowded prison system, and would radically increase the already overburdened state prison budget. Hopefully saner minds will prevail both from a justice and fiscal perspective, and kill this bill.

I do not know all 8,000 of the inmates who have met all the criteria for rehabilitation and are serving time beyond the sentencing guidelines, but the many men I have come to know over the last six years are remarkable human beings who amaze me and inspire me with their remarkable journeys of insight, remorse and spiritual growth. Many of them have a trust in God that is stronger than mine and stronger than most people I know on the outside.

I wish there was a system in place to conduct an expedited administrative review of the 8,000 inmates who have met all rehabilitation criteria and served time beyond the sentencing guidelines. I realize that may not be practical or politically feasible, but it is not unreasonable for our governor, as he appears to be doing, to allow the parole board to do their job consistent with the Supreme Court ruling, and consistent with the necessary goal of significantly reducing our overall state prison population. And it is not unreasonable for all of us to speak out against harsh, unjust and fiscally irresponsible measures such as SB 391.

We are obligated to show tangible compassion to crime victims and their families. But showing comparable compassion to those offenders who have made the difficult and challenging journey to insight and remorse and rehabilitation in no way diminishes the victims. In fact, I believe it honors the victims.

I have never been in a place where God's presence is more tangible, than the Catholic chapel at San Quentin. And I know that my fellow volunteers who serve in the Protestant chapel and in the areas that serve as temple and mosque, have the same experience.

These "lifers" are men who have caused a lot of pain and who have experienced a lot of pain. These are men who because they are so intimately familiar with pain and isolation and suffering, are close to God. Maybe some of that closeness will rub off on those of us who pay attention to them.

Brian Cahill is the former executive director of Catholic Charities CYO in the Archdiocese of San Francisco.

Reprinted with permission of Catholic San Francisco, newspaper of the Archdiocese of San Francisco.

Figure 28.5   Continued

CONCLUSION

I think I have always felt there was little space between the personal, the professional, and the political. In my last two highly visible jobs, I knew the only way to do the job well was to continuously take the everyday risk of being fired based on my values. Now that I am retired, it is definitely easier to speak out, particularly when new and unexpected personal experiences change my perspective or increase my sensitivity to an issue. In any event, the nature of the social work profession requires us to serve and to advocate and that requirement does not end with one's retirement.

INDEX

Note: f represents figures and t represents tables